This book is dedicated to the pioneers of subtle energy medicine, the men and women who persevered (and persevere) to create the visible out of the invisible. And to those who continue to live in the mystery of the unseen.

CONTENTS

ILLUSTRATIONS AND TABLES

ACKNOWLEDGMENTS

The true heroes of this book have been unsung through the ages. I'm speaking of the men and women who trusted their intuition and wisdom and, in a spirit of discovery, discovered and worked with subtle energy anatomy. Joining them have been scientists and researchers who have investigated proof of the subtle. These adventurers are responsible for helping the world accomplish a vitally important objective: the marriage of science and spirituality, of visible and invisible. They are working to create a world we all want to live in.

This book is the tangible result of a long-held dream of Sounds True founder Tami Simon. Its appearance here and now is testimony to her belief in that which is good, spiritual, and invisible—and continually transforms into physical reality with the guidance of leaders like her. Behind the project stood an entire staff of key players, including Jennifer Coffee, the project manager and in-house editor for this book. Jennifer coordinated the process of writing and illustrating and helped shape-shift the book into a usable document. Kelly Notaras, editorial director, applied keen insight to cull the mammoth first draft and usher it through its many stages of life. Sounds True Art Director Karen Polaski ran the extra mile in a long marathon to create the book's extraordinary design. And Richard Wehrman, illustrator, provided the most amazing and true renderings of the energy anatomy ever created.

The book took true form under the insightful eye and "red pencil" of Sheridan McCarthy, freelance editor, who undertook the impossible task of making sense of everything I wrote. I cannot say enough about her talents, wisdom, impeccable discretion, and wit—for it truly took a sense of humor to review this material with the perfectionism necessary. (How many editors have to ask questions such as, "How many invisible fields might actually emanate from a seeming infinite number of finite bodies?") Her work partner, Stanton Nelson, shared extensively in the "heavy lifting."

To Cathy Scofield, my friend and personal editor, a huge thanks. Her dedication to this project included sitting next to me on two (sleepless) twelve-hour flights between Minneapolis and Russia, reviewing my first attempts at writing this discourse, and, once home, staying up all night herself to pick away at my footnotes and thoughts. (I'm not sure she ever wants to see the word *chakra* again.) A thank-you also to the talented and uplifting Marcia Jedd, who contributed research for and assistance with the physical anatomy section.

To this group I add two incredible (and smart) human beings who catapulted me into the discovery stage by providing invaluable resources. The first is Steven Ross, Ph.D., who not only collected vast amounts of research for me through his organization, the World Research Foundation, but also encouraged me. I'll never forget one of his notes, in which he told me to trust myself, this project, and the higher guidance managing it. Dr. Ralph Wilson, naturopath, also came on the scene at the perfect time, directing me toward people and resources whose hidden knowledge has been illuminated in this book.

Anthony J.W. Benson, business manager, agent, and captain of the helm, deserves a thank-you bigger than words can contain. Ultimately, I owe this book to him, for he is the one who insisted not only that I should write it but that I could. He is the model of a person who merges the invisibility of integrity with the visibility of ethical action.

And finally, what mother could complete her acknowledgments without thanking her children? To my son Michael, blessings for being you and for deciding to also become a writer. I now don't feel quite as guilty about the twenty years he spent in a kitchen that has had papers rather than food in the cupboards, computers on the table, and books on the refrigerator. And to Gabe I offer an apology for the Christmas vacation at Disney World, during which your mother spent a good nine hours a day writing. Thank you for summing up the trip by stating, "Mom, you really need to get a life."

INTRODUCTION

*"The day will come when, after harnessing space,
the winds, the tides and gravitation, we shall harness for God
the energies of love. And on that day, for the second time in
the history of the world, we shall have discovered fire."*

— Pierre Teilhard de Chardin

How does a dedicated health care professional become the best healer possible? How might a patient become fully informed — and therefore receive optimum treatment? The answer doesn't entirely lie in following the established routes of a medically based education. We have only to look at the increasing rates of cancer, heart disease, mental illness, and stress-related conditions to know that the boundaries of healing have to stretch further. The well-worn path of Western allopathic medicine, which relies on measurable evidence of disease, and treatments that can be demonstrated in the lab — relying, in essence, on things that are readily apparent — does not hold all the answers we need. To achieve excellence, we must also consider and work with what is not apparent, with what cannot be seen. We must journey into the complex world of subtle energies.

This book is for anyone who seeks to positively engage with the health care profession. This group includes us all, for each of us will participate in the world of healing at some point in our lives, personally or professionally. The primary goal is to help healing professionals who wish to make the leap from being "good" healers to being "great" ones. Just as important, however, is the need of the contemporary "consumer," the person afflicted with or affected by dis-ease—a lack of ease in body, mind, or soul. The truth is that we *all* need to understand the information in this book, for it speaks to the self and reality behind the obvious, the stuff that composes the material world.

This book is an encyclopedia of subtle energy anatomy, the structures of the energies that underpin physical reality and our physical bodies. It is also a compendium of subtle energy tools and techniques: energy-based methods for making a difference. The goal of this work is to enable energetic shifts—those that affect change in the flow of energy—to create true healing.

All medicine is essentially energy medicine, for energy composes the world. And it is important to remember that all known and observable medical phenomena once dwelled in the subtle, or immeasurable, realms. X-rays, bacteria, and even the biochemical effects of aspirin were once unobservable. Many of the subtle energies you will encounter in this book have recently been measured, and we can fully expect that many of those yet to be measured will be one day. In the meantime, we must not let lack of scientific evidence constrain us from working with subtle systems; lack of "proof" has not impeded the effectiveness of the subtle energy practices that have been devised through the ages.

To save a patient's life, to calm the uneasy, or to put a smile back on a child's face, today's healers need to draw upon more than conventional wisdom. They need to learn to see into, through, and beyond the obvious to the true causes of health issues. The answers to questions about life and death lie in the unseen, and so all professional healers, no matter their professional affiliations, should strive to become subtle energy professionals as well.

What is subtle energy? Underlying physical reality are subtle, or indiscernible, energies that create and sustain all matter. The so-called real world—the one you can touch, smell, taste, hear, and see—is constructed entirely from these energies, which are imperceptible through the five senses. *In fact, all of reality is created from organized and changeable systems of subtle energy.* To most effectively help someone heal—to aid the sick, alleviate suffering, and bring hope where there is darkness—we must acknowledge and work with the subtle energies that create imbalances and disease. We must work causally, not just symptomatically. When we do, we expand the field of medicine to include the entire picture of the forces at work in illness and health.

Until a few years ago, modern medicine was divided into two main categories: Western and Eastern. Western health care, also called *allopathic medicine*, is mechanistic; Western practitioners seek to alleviate symptoms through scientifically documented methods. We must honor and revere this approach: where would we be without antibiotics or cardiac pacemakers? At the same time, Western medicine has been on the scene for a relatively short time. For thousands of years, what we now call *Eastern medicine* was dominant.

Eastern medicine is devoted to holistic care, which treats the total person—mind, body, and spirit—not just his or her symptoms. In the West, we use terms like *complementary* or *alternative* medicine to describe this approach. Elsewhere in the world, Eastern medicine is called *traditional* medicine. It is the medicine of the culture.

Western and Eastern methods seemed diametrically opposed, and the schism between them seemed unsurpassable, until practitioners and patients noticed that the two approaches enhance one another. With this discovery, a new health care process was born, termed *integrative care*: the marriage between West and East.

Western, Eastern, and integrative medicine are all vital paths to healing. But there is another component to truly full-spectrum health care. It is called *energy medicine*—specifically, *subtle energy medicine*. With knowledge of it, healing professionals can attain a new level of medical excellence. This is because all diseases are energetic, or related to the flow of energy. The optimum health care approach, therefore, encompasses energy issues.

Everything is made of energy: molecules, pathogens, prescription medicines, and even emotions. Each cell pulses electrically, and the body itself emanates electromagnetic fields. The human body is a complex energetic system, composed of hundreds of energetic subsystems. Disease is caused by energetic imbalances; therefore, health can be restored or established by balancing one's energies.

We can't see all the energies that keep the body healthy, however. Those we can see are called physical, or measurable, energies. Those that we can't yet perceive are called subtle energies. Subtle doesn't mean delicate. In fact, science is beginning to suggest that the subtle—the as yet immeasurable—actually directs the measurable and forms our physical framework.

The idea of subtle energies is not new, although the term itself is relatively recent. Its roots are embedded in human history. Thousands of years ago, our ancestors developed systems to work with these energies. Over time, they continued to codify and develop these systems, and the healing methods that were based on them, for a very important reason: *the systems worked*.

While subtle energy knowledge began intuitively, some of the most exciting work in the field today is happening in laboratories, clinics, institutes, and universities around the world, where *history* meets *research* to yield *proof*. Groundbreaking studies using leading-edge equipment, physics, and processes have developed a new set of subtle energy "mystics": scientists unveiling the mysteries of the energy system. For this reason, each section of this book emphasizes the scientific evidence substantiating the existence of subtle energy structures.

This book offers information on many different treatment methods based on subtle systems. At first glance, some of these methods might seem "nonmedical." What do color and sound have to do with healing? What might taste, gemstones, and numbers mean to the contemporary healer? The answer is—a lot. The treatments are doorways, modalities to help a healer gain access to the subtle energy realms and deliver healing. And they can serve as adjuncts to standard treatments.

Of course, all professional healers—Western, Eastern, or integrative—must follow a moral code to assure that they are of highest service. Conscious subtle energy healers, however, must address additional areas including boundaries, ethics, and intuition, a topic covered in Part I.

Part I also includes a lexicon of terms necessary to comprehend subtle anatomy and explanations of both traditional and cutting-edge energy concepts. Although subtle energy and physical energy operate in slightly different ways and under different rules, they are interconnected, and the subtle energy healer must have a good grasp of both.

Along these same lines, understanding subtle anatomy depends upon knowledge of physical anatomy, the topic of Part II. These anatomical lessons may remind you of your high school biology studies, but here we will emphasize the energetic aspects of the body's systems. The physical body, you will learn, is in fact an extension of the subtle energy system.

The remainder of the book is an exploration of subtle energy anatomy, beginning with the three main subtle energy structures: *fields*, *channels*, and *bodies*.

In Part III we investigate energy fields. Each cell, organ, and organism—including our planet—emanates hundreds of fields. Part III also introduces us to the concept of "geopathic stress," an emerging field of study emphasizing the adverse effects of certain natural and artificial fields on our well-being.

Part IV discusses the flowing systems of subtle energy: the channels. You will find an in-depth examination of meridian science and the various experiments that have recently validated and explained the existence of these subtle structures.

Part V features the subtle energy bodies such as the chakras, Kabbalah sephiroth, and a variety of other energetic units. We will spend the most time on the best-known chakric system, the Hindu, but we will also examine other systems of energy bodies, from Egyptian to African to South American traditions. We will also explore the "river" or subtle energy channels that connect the chakras to each other and the body, the nadis. (While the nadis can properly be categorized as channels, they are so inextricably linked to the chakra system that we will discuss them together.)

Finally, in Part VI, we will explore some of the hundreds of integrative healing systems that are in use today—those that employ at least two of the three main subtle structures (fields, channels, and bodies). Many of these, including Ayurveda and Reiki, may be familiar to you; others may not. This section also includes a representative list of additional subtle energy practices not covered in the book for your reference.

It is important to understand that these subtle systems have been shared between peoples and cultures for thousands of years. There are many, many theories about meridians, chakras, and energetic fields—and from expert to expert, they differ greatly. This book strives to offer the most traditional understanding of the energy structures, as well as a sampling of others. You are encouraged to do your own research and evolve your own understanding of the subtle energies and their healing traditions.

The information in this book has been culled from many sources: esoteric manuscripts, sacred texts, long-recognized medical authorities, active practitioners, scientific manuals, research laboratories, government agencies, associations, and information-specific journals. It draws from disciplines including quantum physics, bioenergetic science, sacred geometry, and books related to the specific healing areas covered. I have diligently recorded and cited these sources to help you in your own research.

You may discover, however, that some of this information has never before been cited in a contemporary book. In fact, various authorities over the centuries have actually repressed some of this research because it has presented such compelling evidence of the energy systems we are exploring; such information has been perceived as threatening to the established medical practice of the time.

How did I obtain this "hidden information"? Writing this book was its own odyssey. People appeared from out of nowhere to provide content or direction. The most vital contribution was made by one particular individual: Steven Ross, PhD, of the World Research Foundation Library (WRF). Dr. Ross has collected over thirty thousand volumes of research on health therapies and philosophies. Some of this work has not been available to the general public until now.

Regarding how to use this book, please understand that the information collected here cannot substitute for in-depth study or training. For example, you will be introduced to the meridians and a variety of meridian-based therapies, but not with the thoroughness necessary to prepare you for treating a patient. Instead, this material is intended to help you understand the meridians and the possibilities that in-depth learning can provide.

The book has been organized so that you do not have to learn the material in sequence—or even read all of it. You can concentrate on each section independently or on a stand-alone part of each section. I recommend that you use the index to cross-study the universality of certain topics. In fact, you will probably discover that the index is indispensable. To fully understand an idea, it is helpful to perceive it in different contexts, and many concepts—from mitochondria to geometry to spin theory—appear in nearly every section. Because you might choose to study only a particular topic or two, certain universal ideas are briefly redescribed in each section.

Above all, the book is organized to serve as a resource—a guidebook that verbally and visually presents information about the subtle energy systems. While there is a wealth of information between these two covers, there is much more knowledge available, and still to be discovered, about the subtle energy world. What is here can serve to guide you in further research, and in learning from the best source of all: you.

In the end, you must become your own "best authority" on subtle energies. You will sense and recognize the information that is pertinent to you and your practice, as well as which data may not apply to your goals. You will begin to recognize yourself—your own subtle energy systems—within these pages. That is because we all share the same energy systems. We share the gifts and abilities that enable us to draw upon the subtle—to work with the invisible—to help ourselves and others. And we share our place in the universe, our experience of being human on this planet. Each of us is poised to contribute to the growing knowledge of subtle body healing.

THE
SUBTLE BODY

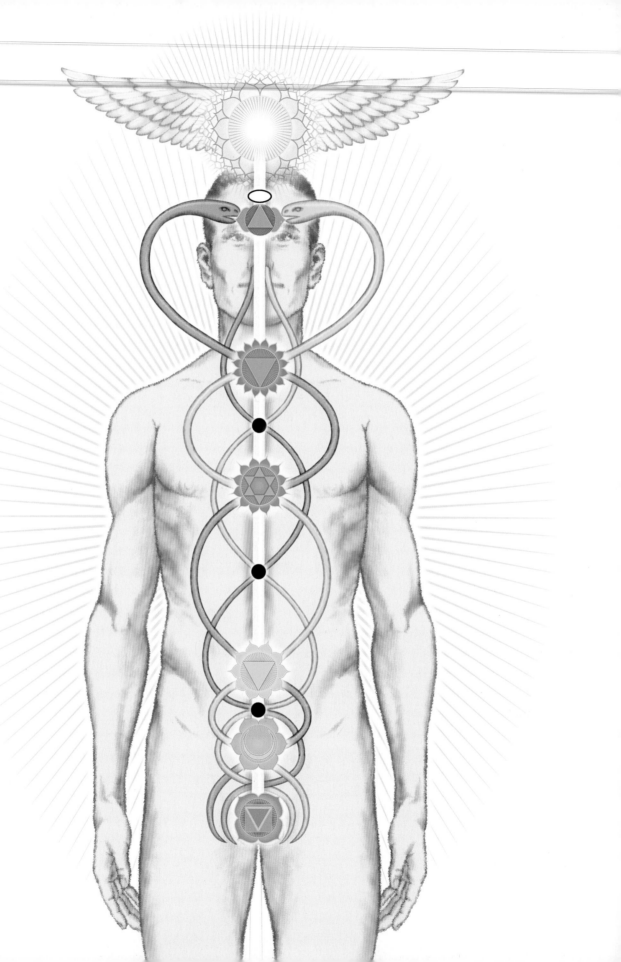

PART I

ENERGY AND ENERGY HEALING

What is "energy anatomy"? Look beneath the surface of the world—the world that includes your clothes, toaster ovens, philosophies, your skin—and you will discover a universe of swirling and subtle energies. While we do not know exactly what these energies are doing or how they are doing it, we do know that they are "here," forming the energies that underlie physical reality. They form *you*.

In this section we will examine the subtle energies that make up the world. We will define "subtle" versus "physical," walking the boundary lines between the two to distinguish the immeasurable from the measurable, the invisible from the visible. We will learn some of the basic principles of energy—what it is and how it works—and present the idea of an energetic anatomy, or system, constructed of subtle energy fields, channels, and bodies. We will briefly discuss each of these separate anatomical structures.

We will then take a look at doing healing work, whether it is associated with allopathic, complementary, integrative, or other healing philosophies. There are unique factors involved in being a subtle energy healer: someone who sees, senses, hears, and works with the subtle and less substantive energies. Special considerations involve questions about ethics, boundaries, training, and the use of intuition.

This section is an introduction to—and a portal into—the world of energy. It is a fascinating world, the point of contact for making the unknown, known—and for discovering what we still do not know.

ENERGY IS UNIVERSAL

Take a close look at your skin. If you really saw it as the ancients might have, you would perceive subtle lines and patterns—more subtle than wrinkles and pores. Dr. Giuseppe Calligaris, whom you will meet later in this book, illuminated these patterns. If you were ill, he would interpret their shapes to help you diagnose your disease.

Speak a few words. Did you know that through a special process called *cymatics*, your words, when vibrated onto a special sounding plate, can take geometric form? They might appear as mosaics or mandalas, triangles or pentagrams.

These are only two examples of the types of proofs and processes involved in the study of the human energy system. We are made of energy. Everything in the world is made of energy, which can be defined most simply as "information that vibrates." This energy—this manna of life—may express itself as patterns, sound, skin, thought, or even morning coffee, but it is all energy. We cannot see the subtler patterns of skin or the shape of our words, but they are there nonetheless. So it is with certain layers of the body and the world. Even though they are imperceptible to the five senses, they do exist.

This book offers insights into, research about, and explanations of the complex set of subtle fields, channels, and bodies that create the human being. These structures are made of subtle energy: energies that are too high or low in frequency to be easily measured. We can tell that they exist because they produce an effect.

We cannot talk about subtle energies without also examining *physical* or *gross energies*. The subtle cannot be separated from the physical any more than coffee can be pulled out of water and remain drinkable. Part of the proof that subtle energies exist, in fact, lies in the validation of physical energies.

Thousands of years ago, our ancestors saw energy in ways that have been dismissed in recent times. They did not use special microscopes, spectrometers, or other tools in their investigations, as we currently do. Instead, they employed their inner senses.

Subtle energy is simply energy that cannot be accurately measured using current scientific methods. It is not supernatural, paranormal, or scary—it is just energy. It obeys some—but not all—of the same laws as does physical matter, its counterpart. As the information presented in "A Model of Subtle Energy" on page 12 suggests, subtle energies operate on a different plane or continuum than do physical energies. Yet they can be at least somewhat defined in comparison to physical energy, as in this definition based upon ideas expressed in *The Science of Homeopathy*.[1]

Physical energy manifests in the positive timespace frame, is electrical in nature, and has positive mass. It travels slower than the speed of light and gives rise to gravity. This means that you can see it. Subtle energy, however, occupies the next timespace frame (or other timespace frames), manifests in the negative timespace frame and has negative mass. It is magnetic in nature and travels faster than the speed of light. It gives rise to what some call levitational force. This means that you can't see it—but can note its seemingly paranormal effects.

One reason that it is difficult to fully comprehend or explain subtle energies is that science still does not really understand energy—even in the classical sense.

TOWARD A DEFINITION OF ENERGY

In textbooks, *energy* is usually defined as the source of power that can be used to accomplish work or a goal, or to create an effect. In this book, we delve deeper to explain it as information that vibrates. Scientific research has proven that everything energetic contains information: data that tells an atom whether it should occupy a kidney or outer space.[2] Physical energy is structured by operating orders that instruct coffee, for example, to remain in the cup instead of flying through the cosmos.

Besides "being informed," energy also vibrates. Science—the classical textbook kind—has verified that everything in the universe vibrates. Furthermore, everything vibrates at its own unique speed. A brain cell moves differently than does a hair cell. Like-minded organisms vibrate in similar ways, but each individual unit differs slightly from its sibling group.

Vibration is produced in the form of *amplitude* and *frequency*: oscillations that generate more energy. These oscillations carry information that can be stored or applied. The information (as well as the vibrating oscillations) can also change depending on the nature of a particular interaction. All of life is made of information and vibration.

Energetics is the study of the components, principles, and applications of energy. Scientists are constantly changing their views about energetics, because the laws that apply macroscopically do not always work microscopically.

For example, according to classical physics, energy, which has mass (and therefore weight), cannot move faster than the speed of light. But as we will see in Part III, researchers have pulsed light *faster than the speed of light*. Perhaps we have not broken the classical laws here, but we have certainly stretched them.

In classical physics, a particle, which is a point of mass, can *only* exist in one place at a time. In quantum physics, a subatomic particle actually *has* to be in two places at once.[3] And some of these places might be other worlds. These kinds of rules, which are revealed through quantum physics, are closer to those that explain subtle energy. They imply that though subtle energies and their structures cannot be seen, they can be shown to exist.

The truth is that we know subtle energies exist because, as we will see throughout this book, we can perceive their effects. Historically, the forms of energy behind traditional science and medicine were subtle. We could not see microorganisms before the invention of the microscope—but they killed people anyway. Studying subtle energies has always led to important, and practical, discoveries. The pursuit might accomplish yet another goal: combining Western and Eastern philosophies.

MARRIAGE OF WEST AND EAST

Many books about energy anatomy emphasize the differences between Western and Eastern medicine. There are many terms for each protocol. Western medicine is also called *allopathic* or *traditional* care. It relies heavily on empirical scientific concepts, assessing symptoms for underlying causes, and alleviating these symptoms with tested and verifiable methods, such as prescription drugs, surgery, or devices.

Eastern medicine is often labeled *alternative, complementary,* or *natural* care. It is a holistic approach, treating body, mind, and soul, and addresses underlying causes rather than just symptoms. Toward this end, treatment might focus on physical healing, but also emotional, mental, and spiritual concerns. *Energetic medicine,* one of the labels for working with the subtle energy system, is often placed in this category.

Integrative medicine combines Western and Eastern modalities. A newly coined term for this unifying thought is *nonlocal medicine,* which asserts that the basis of physical reality does not lie within the physical universe, but rather, in the subtle planes and energies that run through everything. This philosophy universalizes medicine—and should, as all medical systems are actually energetic in nature.

There is not *and has never been* a true division between Western and Eastern thought. Asian and Hindu cultures (along with dozens of others around the world) performed brain surgery at least four thousand years ago.[4] A crude version of brain surgery, called trepanation, existed almost ten thousand years ago in areas now considered devoted to Eastern medicine.[5] Nearly three thousand years ago, the Egyptians, Chinese, and Central American Indians used mold as a progenitor to the antibiotics of today.[6]

Western medicine actually stems from the animism of shamanism. Shamans are "priest-healers." While they employ protocol now associated with Western medicine, such as the use of herbs and plants, they also use spiritual guides and ritual to journey through the cosmos for purposes of healing. The integrative ideas of shamanism buttress modern medicine, psychology, psychiatry, explorations into consciousness, and even some quantum physics theories.

Energy medicine, and the rigors of energy anatomy, do not "belong" to West or East. They cannot. Because everything is energy, all medicines are energetic. The only reason that energy work typically falls into the "Eastern" category is that we have not compared them correctly.

For example, Western anatomy relies on charts that say, "The liver is there." Cut into the body, and the liver *is* there. The East might track the liver through charts locating liver *energy* in a toe. Both are true: the physical liver *does* lie under the ribcage, and its subtle energies *do* flow into the toe.

These two modalities are actually one and the same. As energy expert and author James Oschman, PhD, writes, "any intervention in a living system involves energy in one form or another."[7] As Oschman defines it, energy medicine actually involves the study and applications of the body's relationship to electric, magnetic, and electromagnetic fields, as well as light, sound, and other forms of energy.[8] The body produces these energies and also responds to them in their natural and artificial (human-generated) states. The terms *energy medicine, energetic healing, biofield healing, bioenergetic healing, chakra healing, aura healing, energy work, meridian-based healing, energy anatomy, vibrational medicine, subtle energy healing,* and dozens of other similar labels simply refer to practices relating to a certain vibrational or frequency-based level of energy.

As Dr. Oschman points out, allopathic or traditional medical care *is* an energy-based practice, contrary to popular opinion. Most of us have experienced (or know someone who has experienced) the benefits of X-rays, MRIs, electrocardiograms, and other testing devices. These practices all employ energy and make energetic changes in the body.[9] Surgery can be seen as an energetic maneuver in that tearing tissue disturbs the body's vibrational field. Adding a device like a pacemaker provides new information to aid in heart function, assuring that it vibrates correctly instead of "skipping beats." Even prescription drugs work energetically, altering vibrations through chemical information that instructs cellular behavior.

The world might not be ready to completely link all medicines together under the umbrella of "energy"—yet. But in this book, we will attempt to do so, concentrating on the most unexplored area of energy medicine, that of subtle energies.

MEASURABLE AND SUBTLE ENERGIES: WORLDS KNOWN, WORLDS TO EXPLORE

Again, there are two basic types of energies: physical and subtle. The scientific terms for these are *veritable*, or measurable, and *putative*, or immeasurable. Many subtle structures are measurable, or at least observable, but the research demonstrating this has not penetrated mainstream newspapers (or medical schools) yet.

Throughout this book, you will find research documenting the existence of the various subtle energy structures. Some of this research was "lost" and is now "found," having been buried in the annals of time by accident or lack of public interest. More frequently, authorities who thought it challenging repressed the data. The core evidence for subtle energies in general includes the following:

- Use of various magnetic devices, such as the superconducting quantum interference device (SQUID), for perceiving electromagnetic energies beyond the bounds of the body. (This research is discussed in Part II.)
- A process that embeds a human intention onto a simple electrical device, thus showing the effects of thought on physicality.[10]
- Various experiments using inorganic, organic, and living materials that reveal a unique, secondary level of physical reality affected by human intention.[11]
- Measurement of the meridian and chakra systems, representative subtle channels, and energy bodies, revealing that they operate at higher levels of electromagnetism than the rest of the body.[12]
- Experimentation that shows that the human biofield operates at a unique level of physical reality.[13]
- The determination of L-fields and T-fields, or electrical life and thought fields, which organize subtle energies. (The research appears in Part III.)
- Research by scientists including Dr. Björn Nordenström that shows that where there is a flow of ions there are also electromagnetic fields at 90

degrees to this flow. Dr. Nordenström's research has determined a secondary electrical system in the body, which explains the in-body presence of the meridian channels and the complex nature of the human energy field. (This research is discussed in Part IV.)

Why are we unable to see these subtle fields? Human senses operate within a narrow range on the electromagnetic spectrum, the measurable band of energy that produces various types of light. Our eyes can only detect radiation, the term for the noticeable energy emitted by substances, in the range of 380 to 780 nanometers. That is visible light. Infrared light, which we cannot see, has a wavelength of 1,000 nanometers, and far-ultraviolet operates at 200 nanometers. We cannot see what we are not physically capable of seeing—nor trained to see. If subtle energies actually do occupy a negative time-space continuum, move faster than the speed of light, and have no mass, we can determine that we do not currently have the equipment needed to measure them. This does not mean that what is invisible does not exist.

THE STRUCTURE OF THE SUBTLE ANATOMY

The subtle energy anatomy is more than legend, a legacy from our ancestors. It is a workable system that is constantly being defined and redefined by its practitioners, who number millions worldwide.

There are three basic structures in energy anatomy. They all attract subtle energies from external sources and distribute them throughout the body. They transform subtle energies into physical energies and vice versa, before sending subtle energies back into the world. These subtle structures also create, underpin, and sustain their physical counterparts. In both worlds—subtle and physical—the three basic structures are *fields*, *channels*, and *bodies*.

Barbara Ann Brennan, an expert on the human energy field, states that the subtle energy structure sets up a matrix for cellular growth; it is therefore present before cells grow.[14] Dr. Kim Bonghan, a North Korean medical doctor and researcher, has concluded that one of the subtle energy structures, the meridian system, serves to link the etheric field (one of the subtle energy layers) to the developing physical body. (His work is further explored in Part IV.)[15]

Other researchers agree that the subtle energetic structures interface between the physical body and the subtle energies (and their domains). Subtle structures, however, differ in many ways from biological structures. For example, as husband-and-wife team of healers Lawrence and Phoebe Bendit explain, you cannot speak of a subtle energy structure such as the field as being located in only one place, such as out of the body. While physical bodies are restricted to place, the subtle field penetrates every particle of the body and extends beyond it. This is how it provides a template for the growing physical body.[16]

Subtle energies operate by different rules than do measurable energies. The subtle energy rules for the subtle structures are encoded with ideas from quantum physics, the study of energetic interactions on the micro level. These theories are described throughout the book. Subtle energies, rule breakers that they are, can stretch—and sometimes completely ignore—time and space, change form at will, and occupy many places at once.

Another unique characteristic of subtle energies is that within the subtle structures, they not only *adjust* the physical world, but also adjust *to* it. The most noteworthy sign of adaptation is the existence of the *polarity principle. Polarities* are interdependent opposites. The physical plane is dualistic in nature. While the subtle energies enter the physical realm "whole" or unified, they then split into contrasting natures.

Physical fields, for example, are electrical or magnetic. Opposing charges cause electricity, and magnets have two poles. Opposites create life as we know it. Subtle structures, like the meridians, are paired in polarities under a traditional Chinese concept called *yin-yang theory. Yin* represents the feminine qualities, and *yang*, the masculine. Both must be balanced to create the homeostasis necessary for health. The subtle meridians, however, also carry a form of energy called *chi* that is considered "heavenly," or unified.

Energy bodies often operate under the same dualistic principle. The Hindu chakra (subtle energy body) system describes a complex process called *kundalini*, in which feminine life energy rises to meet its complementary male energy. Upon merging these energies, the initiate achieves health and wisdom. This divine energy is conjoined, however, before entering the body and the physical universe.

THE KEY SUBTLE STRUCTURES

In this book, we will examine key subtle structures. The *subtle energy fields* are bands of energy that do not stop at the skin. These subtle (as well as physical) energy fields emanate from every living source, including human cells, organs, and bodies as well as plants and animals. There are also subtle fields in the earth and natural physical fields in the earth and skies that affect our subtle fields. In addition, there are artificially produced fields, such as those emitted from power lines and cell phones, that affect our subtle fields.

The main human subtle fields include the *auric field*, which surrounds the human body and links with the chakra energy bodies; the *morphogenetic fields*, which connect organisms within a group; the *Vivaxis*, which links the human body with the earth; and various other energy fields that link us to different planes and dimensions, such as the *etheric* and *astral* fields. There are also fields on the body and fields produced by sound, magnetism, electromagnetic radiation, geometry, and other means.

In addition to fields, the ancients perceived *subtle energy channels*, rivers of light that transport life energy in and around the body. In the ancient Chinese medical system, these channels are called *meridians* and the pulsing vital energy, *chi*. Other cultures besides the Chinese have recognized and dissected energy channels, developing their own glossaries and systems. Modern science is now using thermal, electromagnetic, and radioactive materials to prove the existence and explain the functions of these subtle channels. We might not see these channels when we cut into bodily tissue, but they assure its health. In Part IV, we will look at the meridian system and the theories behind it.

Our forebears also observed *subtle energy bodies*, organs that convert fast-moving energy into slow-moving energy. There are dozens of such energy bodies; the best-known are called *chakras*, which interface between the subtle energy structures and physical organs. Connected through a network of energy channels called *nadis*, the chakras appear in hundreds of cultures across the globe. The Mayan, Cherokee, and Incan systems join with that of the Hindu, the latter people usually being recognized as the creators of the energy body system. We will examine various chakra-based systems, traditional and contemporary, from several cultures, in addition to the ancient Jewish Kabbalah system, which poses distinct energy bodies. We will highlight the science of chakraology and examine the practices integral to these various subtle body systems, such as the rising of the kundalini, and a number of different healing systems dependent on energy bodywork.

WHY WORK WITH SUBTLE STRUCTURES?

Research cited throughout this book shows that subtle energies and structures actually create physical reality. By examining the fields, channels, and bodies of the subtle anatomy, you can potentially diagnose problems before they occur—or diagnose them accurately and holistically if symptoms are already present. Employing energetic diagnostics does not limit a practitioner or clinic to the subtle energy realm; modern medicine employs energetic protocol for both diagnosis and healing. Yet, detecting a problem in the subtle planes also invites holistic problem-solving. If you can fix a problem in the subtle structures, the subtle system can then share this solution throughout the entirety of the body—subtle and physical. Humankind throughout the ages has known these ideas; it is time to take advantage of them.

A PRIMER ON ENERGY

This section explains some of the basic concepts of energy in both the classical and quantum physics systems and provides a framework for discussions throughout the book.

THE FUNDAMENTALS: PARTICLES AND WAVES

Particle theory explains that all matter is made of many small particles that are always moving. There are particles in solids, liquids, and gases, and all of them continually vibrate, in varying directions, speeds, and intensities.[17] Particles can only interact with matter by transferring energy.

Waves are the counterpart to particles. There are three ways to regard waves:

- A disturbance in a medium through which energy is transferred from one particle within the medium to another, without making a change in the medium.
- A picture of this disturbance over time.
- A single cycle representing this disturbance.

Waves have a constructive influence on matter when they superimpose or interact by creating other waves. They have a destructive influence when reflected waves cancel each other out.

Scientists used to believe that particles were different from waves, but this is not always true, as you will see in the definition of wave-particle duality in this section.

Waves, or particles operating in wave mode, *oscillate*, or swing between two points in a rhythmic motion. These oscillations create fields, which can in turn create more fields. For instance, oscillating charged electrons form an *electrical field*, which generates a *magnetic field*, which in turn creates an *electrical field*.

Superposition in relation to waves means that a field can create effects in other objects, and in turn be affected itself. Imagine that a field stimulates oscillations in an atom. In turn, this atom makes its own waves and fields. This new movement can force a change in the wave that started it all. This principle allows us to combine waves; the result is the superposition. We can also subtract waves from each other. Energy healing often involves the conscious or inadvertent addition or subtraction of waves. In addition, this principle helps explain the influence of music, which often involves combining two or more frequencies to form a chord or another harmonic.

A *harmonic* is an important concept in healing, as each person operates at a unique harmonic or set of frequencies. A harmonic is defined as an integer multiple of a fundamental frequency. This means that a fundamental tone generates higher-frequency tones called overtones. These shorter, faster waves oscillate between two ends of a string or air column. As these reflected waves interact, the frequencies of wavelengths that do not divide into even proportions are suppressed, and the remaining vibrations are called the harmonics. Energy healing is often a matter of suppressing the "bad tones" and lifting the "good tones."

But *all* healing starts with oscillation, which is the basis of frequency. *Frequency* is the periodic speed at which something vibrates. It is measured in hertz (Hz), or cycles per second. *Vibration* occurs when something is moving back and

A MODEL OF SUBTLE ENERGY

STANFORD PROFESSOR Dr. William Tiller is a well-respected researcher, physicist, and expert on subtle energy. The model of subtle energy described here and its relationship to physical energies is based on several of his papers and books.[18]

Dr. Tiller says that we might not be able to measure subtle energies through physical means, but we can detect some of their signals. This is because, as they change one type of energy into another, they create a transducer signal at the magnetic vector. They also generate electric and magnetic signals that have observable effects.

Tiller's research has led him to state the following about subtle energies:

- They are manifested by people, as revealed in experiments that show subtle energies can increase electron sizes and numbers.
- A person can direct the flow of this energy through intention.
- This mind-electron interaction is effective even over great distances.

Subtle energies follow a different set of laws than do physical energies, and radiate their energy with unique characteristics. There is not just one type of subtle energy, however. Tiller postulates several subtle substances, each of which occupies a different time-space domain.

These domains are different levels of reality. Subtle energy flows downward from the highest, which Tiller calls "the Divine." Each level provides a template for the level below. As the subtle energy enters the next domain, it adapts—but also instructs. The laws differ on each of these levels because the energy gets denser.

Tiller's levels of subtle reality range from the most to the least dense:

- Physical
- Etheric (also called bioplasmic, prephysical, or energy body)
- Astral

forth. More formally, it is defined as a continuing period oscillation relative to a fixed point—or one full oscillation.

Everything in the universe vibrates, and everything that vibrates imparts or impacts information (the definition of energy). To broaden our discussion of particles and waves to include *health*, we can define health as the state of an organism with respect to its functioning at any given time. Good health occurs when an organism and its components (like cells and organs) vibrate at optimum functioning; bad health strikes when these components vibrate adversely, challenging the ability to function. External vibration or energy also affects all organisms, including people. If exposed to harmful vibrations or energy, the internal vibrations or energy in our bodies suffer, and we become unhealthy.

Vibrational medicine is the intentional use of a frequency to positively affect another frequency or to bring an organism into balance. It is one component of *energy healing*, which also uses information, and information and vibration together, to effect change. Energy healing encompasses all forms of allopathic

- Three levels of the mind:
  - Instinctive
  - Intellectual
  - Spiritual
- Spirit
- The Divine

The *etheric* level is just above the physical level. According to Tiller, etheric subtle energy penetrates all levels of material existence, and through the polarity principle forms atoms and molecules that make matter. Our mind interacts with the etheric energy (and above) to create patterns in the physical dimension. These patterns act like a force field that links us to the adjacent energy level.

Tiller's explanation of the physical level versus the etheric is similar to that proposed by the experts featured in "The Structure of the Subtle Anatomy" on page 8. He suggests that the physical realm occupies a positive time-space frame that is mainly electrical, in which opposites attract; over time, potential decreases, and entropy (chaos) increases. The etheric realm, conversely, is a negative time-space domain that is highly magnetic: like attracts like. As time passes in this realm, potential increases and entropy decreases; therefore, more order is established.

We might suggest that communication in the physical realm is accomplished through the five senses; to reach into the etheric level (and above), we must use our intuition—the sixth sense.

Within Tiller's model, the meridians and chakras operate like antennae that detect and send signals from the physical into the upper domains. These subtle structures interact between the physical body and the etheric (and other) realms, illuminating higher orders so that we can perceive them from the physical plane.

medicine—which only works with the relatively lower, or measurable, energy structures—as well as modalities that work with the subtle structures.

In terms of vibration, health depends on *resonance*, which occurs when one object vibrates at the same natural frequency as another object and forces the second into vibration. All medicine depends on achieving resonance. Surgical cutting disturbs bodily resonance but the stitches afterward hold the tissue in place so the body can reestablish harmony. Certain cells "resonate," or sense, vibrational discord and are able to reestablish it. White blood cells do this, sensing pathogens that disturb resonance. By eliminating these pathogens, white blood cells allow the body to regain harmony.

When an organism is healthy as a whole, its systems are *entrained*, or in rhythm with each other. Physicists define entrainment as the energetic interlocking of two rhythms that have similar frequencies; you can therefore only achieve entrainment through resonance between two similarly vibrating objects (or thoughts). With entrainment, a stronger external vibration does not only activate a response, it actually moves the second one out of its own resonant frequency. This is called *forced resonance. Coherency* describes a positive entrainment, and *dissonance* occurs when vibratory disturbances produce ill health.[19]

FORMS OF ENERGY

There are many forms of energy. Let's start with electrical and magnetic.

We are electrical beings: our bodies generate electricity and depend upon it for survival. *Electricity* is the flow of electrical power or charge. It can best be explained by opening up an atom.

Everything is made of atoms, and they are made of subatomic particles. The visible atomic units, or particles within or around the nucleus, are *protons, neutrons*, and *electrons*. Of these, the electrons are the smallest. They spin around the outside of the atom in shells, which look like layers of bubbles, and are therefore said to *orbit* the nucleus or center of an atom.

Electrons are held in place by an electrical force. They can shift from one shell to another. When they do so, they produce an effect: radiant energy. The word *valence* describes the power of an atom or a group of atoms that follow the movement of electrons. It can be pictured as a series of orbits in which the electrons travel.

Protons and electrons are attracted to each other, and so both carry electrical charges. A *charge* is a force inside a particle. Protons have positive charges and electrons have negative charges.

Charge is a critical concept in energy. Electric charge operates on an attraction principle and exists when a particle is attracted to an oppositely charged particle. Neutral particles lack charge and therefore do not attract other particles, at least electrically. Charge creates at least temporary unions in which different types of particles bond.

In the physical world, similar charges repel and opposite charges attract. Why do similar particles stay together inside the nucleus? A subatomic particle called a *gluon* (acts like glue) forces the togetherness. In the cosmos, gravity keeps things together.

The idea that opposites attract is similar to the yin-yang theory of traditional Chinese medicine, which is part of the polarity principle explained earlier in this chapter. Most medical and spiritual models are based on this search for completion.

When an atom is in balance, it has an equal number of positive and negative particles. (Neutrons are neutral.) When the numbers are uneven, the atom becomes unstable.

Electrons usually stay close to home in the shells. The shells closest to the nucleus hold fewer electrons than those farther away. The electrons in the closest shells have the strongest force of attraction to the protons. The ones farther out? These electrons can be pushed out of orbit and journey from one atom to another. Some of them can be found a football field away, relatively speaking.

While it is usually produced by electrons, electricity can also be generated by *positrons: antiparticles* that are the counterparts to electrons (defined in "The Quantum World" on page 18), and *ions*, which are atoms or groups of atoms that have changed their electric charge by losing or gaining an electron. The physical body depends upon ions to conduct messages across its various systems, including the nervous and cardiovascular systems. Usually made from chemicals such as potassium or calcium, ions convey the information held in electrical charges.

Ionization involves the movement of electrons from one atomic shell to another. As stated earlier, electrons tend to remain in their basic states, usually occupying the shells closest to the nucleus. If disturbed, an electron can be forced upward and out of the entire molecule. The original neutral molecule now becomes a *positive ion*. If the free electron connects to a neutral molecule, it changes it into a *negative ion*. If it instead attaches to a positive ion, it usually stays in one of the vacant energy shells and emits a *photon*, a unit of light explored in "Energy That Works" on page 16. Ionization plays a critical role in the transfer of energy throughout the body.

Again, electricity is the product of charged electrons. We only see an effect, however, when potential energy shifts to kinetic energy. *Potential energy* is stored energy. It is ready to be used, but is currently "sleeping." *Kinetic energy* is energy in motion. Electrons must flow to generate electricity, or kinetic and usable energy. Electrons can move many ways and in different mediums. They might run through circuits in computers, oscillate in antennae to transfer messages, or pulse through wires to make motors work. And they generate light and heat upon resistance.

ENERGY THAT WORKS

THERE ARE MANY types of energy used in our everyday lives. This is a list of a few recognized by science everywhere. Descriptions are only given here for those not described elsewhere.

Electricity. (see page 14)
Magnetics. (see page 17)
Electromagnetics. (see page 17)

Mechanical energy: Called *working energy*, in that movement occurs through a force acting on a mass, such as expanding gas firing a cannon ball. *Sound* is a form of mechanical energy.

Chemical energy: Uses energy stored in molecular bonds, the forces holding molecules together. An example is photosynthesis.

Thermal energy: The part of a system that increases with temperature. In thermodynamics, thermal energy is internal to a system and can also be called heat. *Heat* is defined as a flow of energy from one object to another caused by a difference in temperature between these two objects.

The *four fundamental forces* in the universe are *electromagnetics, strong nuclear force* (which holds together atomic nuclei), *weak nuclear force* (which causes certain types of radioactive decay), and *gravity* (an attraction between two objects). The major differences between the first three are these: electromagnetic interaction acts on charged particles; strong interaction acts on the subatomic quarks and gluons, binding them together to form protons, neutrons, and more; and weak interaction acts on subatomic quarks and leptons to transmute quarks, thus enabling a neutron to become a proton plus an electron and a neutrino. Yet another interaction called the Higgs interaction involves a *Higgs field*, which fills in space like a fluid. This process also provides mass to quarks and leptons.[20] (See Index for various types of particles.)

Light is oscillating disturbances, or an *electromagnetic wave*, in the electromagnetic field. It creates the *electromagnetic spectrum*, a continuum of different types of light that oscillate at different speeds and are described in Part III.

Photons are the basic units of light, as well as the fundamental particles responsible for the electromagnetic spectrum. A photon carries all electromagnetic radiations for every wavelength. Unlike many other elementary particles, it has no mass or weight, no electric charge, will not decay in empty space, and travels in a vacuum at the speed of light. Like all quanta, it is both a wave and a particle. Photons are created when a charge is accelerated and a molecule, atom, or nucleus shifts to a lower energy level (i.e., the electron moves between shells), or when a particle and its antiparticle are annihilated.

Electrons move because they are being pushed or forced into action by an electrical field. A *field* is a force moving through a medium that can transfer energy. This force exerts the same influence at every point. An *electric field* is created by a difference in electrical charge. The charged particles are actually pushed by the force, skipping from atom to atom, sometimes over great distances.

Electricity is also generated by magnets moving in a coil, through magnets and wire, by batteries, and through open circuits. It is measured in watts or kilowatt-hours (kWh). (See "Energy That Works," opposite, for further discussions about types of energy.) It is also produced by secondary sources such as coal, natural gas, solar, and thermal power.

Electrical flow produces a *magnetic field* caused by the spin of electrons around the nucleus of an atom. In fact, any current flowing through a conductor generates a magnetic field in the surrounding space.

This is an important fact in energy medicine. Electrons flowing through a wire or through living tissue create magnetic fields in the space around the wire or body. Your heart, muscles, organs, nerves, cells, molecules, and more create their own *biomagnetic field,* called *bio*magnetic because it is biologically based. *Bioelectrical fields* are those generated by biological entities.

More and more, the medical industry relies on devices that measure biomagnetic rather than bioelectrical fields, as bioelectrical fields are hard to analyze through the skin—even with the well-known electrocardiogram. Tissue is invisible to biomagnetic fields, however, which is why so many modern diagnostic devices, including magnetocardiograms, magnetoencephalograms, and magnetomyograms, are now used to assess the internal processes of the body. Whereas science has long used electricity to help heal the body, it is now turning to magnetism. *Magnetobiology* is the exploration of various ways to use magnetism for healing.

Not every object is magnetic, of course. The atoms in many objects are arranged so that the electrons spin in different or random directions, thereby canceling each other out. Magnets work differently in that they have two poles: north and south. These poles cause the electrons to spin in the same direction, establishing a current and therefore a magnetic field. The magnetic force flows from the north to the south pole. The north and south poles of two different magnets will attract each other; once again, opposites attract.

Electricity produces magnetism, but magnets can also make electricity: moving magnetic fields stimulate electrons, which then form electricity.

Electricity and magnetism together form the *electromagnetic field,* which is defined as a field that asserts a force on particles that have electrical charge. In turn, this field is affected by these stimulated particles, and is the foundation of light.

A *quantum* is the smallest unit that measures something physical. *Subatomic particles* are those that make up an atom. *Quantum mechanics* is the study and application of these small particles and *quantum theory* seeks to understand how they work. Quanta belong in the world of *quantum physics*: a discipline connected with, but also distinguished from, classical Newtonian-based physics.

Quantum mechanics was born when physicists discovered that matter, not just light, has wave properties. The strange actions of quanta suggested that the fundamental natural laws of classical physics were not really laws of certainty:

THE THREE LAWS OF THERMODYNAMICS THROUGH THE QUANTUM LENS

CLASSICAL PHYSICS RELIES upon the three laws of thermodynamics. These are laws about energy that tell us how energy functions and, therefore, what we can (and cannot) do with it. As practical as they might be for the Western medical practitioner, they are stretched by quantum occurrences.

The three laws are as follows:

First law: Energy likes to be *conserved;* therefore it cannot be created or destroyed, merely transformed.

Second law: Entropy (a measure of information) tends to increase. This means that the longer a system exists, the more disorder or unavailable information it contains.

Third law: As temperature approaches absolute zero, the entropy or chaos becomes more constant.

These laws govern the macrocosmos, but are not consistently true in the microuniverse of quanta. According to the second law, for instance, energy (or information that vibrates) gradually reduces in availability until it reaches absolute zero. Science cannot yet achieve absolute zero, but it can approach it. At this point, energy supposedly stands still. According to the first law, however, energy cannot be destroyed, which means the unavailable information has to go *somewhere*.

Atoms and mass can only store a limited amount of information, so this missing data is not hiding in a coffee cup. It is possible, however, that it *is* stored in anti- or parallel worlds, or perhaps in the subtle energy domains explored by Dr. Tiller in "A Model of Subtle Energy" on page 12.

MIT physicist Seth Lloyd supports the idea of other worldly portals in his book *Programming the Universe*. Quantum mechanics has proven that an electron is not only allowed to be in two places at once—it is required to be. Certain particles not only spin in two directions at the same time, but have to do so.[21] At really high speeds, atoms require more information to describe their movements, and therefore they have more entropy.[22]

However, an observer affects the outcome of whatever he or she is observing. As explained in the book *The Orb Project*, the effect of the observer they only explained probabilities. Quantum physics seeks to explain why quanta do not stay still in time and why they are not always located in just one space. A single electron or proton, for instance, can be here and somewhere else at the same time, and can even move two different ways simultaneously.

Here are further explorations of the basics of quantum physics.

More on Quanta

Currently, science works with twenty-four subatomic particles, including the electron, photon, and a half-dozen quarks. *Quarks* have an electrical charge equivalent to one-third to two-thirds of that found in an electron. *Leptons* are

on the quantum field causes reality to reorganize according to the observation. This means that a newly observed reality descends through the frequency levels below the quantum, becoming dense in material reality.[23] The nonobserved information becomes "lost" if it doesn't qualify as "real" or desirable to the observer. It is not eliminated; instead, the not-selected potential slips into a pocket of "elsewhere."

Conceivably, we can get it back. As Lloyd explains, we can access lost data by "flipping a qubit," a code phrase that means we can apply a magnetic field to force energy to shift from one state to another.[24] We have established that the subtle layer is atop the physical and that the etheric layer of subtle energies is magnetic in nature. Could it be that the information we cannot find—perhaps, the data that could make a sick person well—is lingering a plane above us?

We've one more law to face: the third law of thermodynamics. Experiments with absolute zero provide a new perspective on it, one that coaxes an understanding of subtle energy. Absolute zero is the point at which particles have minimum energy, called zero-point energy. Researchers including Dr. Hal Puthoff have identified this zero-point energy with zero-point field, a mesh of light that encompasses all of reality. (This field is further explained in Part III.) This field of light is a vacuum state, but it is not empty; rather, it is a sea of electromagnetic energy, and possibly, virtual particles—ideas that can become real.

Conceivably, energy should stand completely still at absolute zero, which would mean that information would become permanently imprisoned. Research on zero-point energy, however, reveals that nearing zero-point, atomic motion stops, but energy continues. This means that "lost information" is not really lost. Even when frozen, it continues to "vibrate" in the background. The pertinent questions are these: How do we "read" this background information? How do we apply it? These queries are similar to those we might ask about "hidden" information. How do we access suppressed but desirable data? The answers lie in learning about subtle structures, for these dwell at the interfaces between the concrete and the higher planes. Operate within the subtle structures, and you can shift a negative reality to a positive one, without losing energy in the process.

fundamental particles that are either neutrally charged or carry one-half unit of negative charge. They are involved in weak interaction. Quarks and leptons comprise and affect many other particles. *Tachyon* is the name given subatomic particles that are believed to move faster than the speed of light. *Force particles* are those that give rise to forces.

Wave-Particle Duality

Many subatomic particles operate like both waves and particles. They have on their "particle hats" when they are being created and annihilated. They wear their "wave hats" in between.

Antiparticles

Antiparticles are specific units of *antimatter*. Paul Dirac, an English physicist, introduced the concept in 1928, seeking to merge relativity and quantum mechanics. He theorized that every particle has its own companion particle that has the same mass and spin, but with an opposite charge. When an electron meets with its mate, the positron, they both disappear, leaving behind a pair of photons. Antimatter is also considered a source of energy.

Antiworlds

These are parallel realities that form when a path is *not* chosen. The "many worlds theory" and the "parallel universe theory" arose from this question: where are all the antiparticles? A related question is: where are all the choices "not observed" or not manifested in concrete reality? We know that antiparticles exist, for in 1932, Carl Anderson at the California Institute of Technology discovered a track of positrons—electrons' antiparticles—in a cloud chamber exposed to cosmic rays.[25]

Spin

Spin is the rotation of a particle around its axis. All particles spin, and can even spin around two different axes at the same time. But according to a theory called the *Heisenberg Uncertainty Principle*, you cannot be sure about the exact value of spin around those two axes. The spins around a vertical and horizontal axis are complementary—but if you know how one spins, you cannot know how the other does. Likewise, if you are certain about the spin of a particle, you will not be able to ascertain certainty about another one of its physical qualities, like speed. Measurement disturbs what is being measured.[26]

Entanglement

Through entanglement, two or more objects can interrelate and affect each other even when they are separated, perhaps by thousands of miles (or dimensions). This phenomenon is called *quantum entanglement*, and it relates to objects or particles that have once been connected.

As has been explored, the fundamentals of the energy world encompass both classic and quantum explanations. Add these two views together and what emerges but a layer of reality that connects and explains both: the subtle energy realm.

2

BEING AN ENERGY HEALER

What is a healer? All healers are energy workers, but are all energy workers "healers"? Does someone actually have to "heal people" to be considered a healer? Yes—if healing includes creating positive change, not only a cure.

Curing and healing are very different concepts. To *cure* is to erase symptoms. To *heal* is to assure a state of wholeness. A whole person is whole in spite of a missing leg, a flu bug, or a death sentence. A healer is essentially someone who helps another person realize his or her inherent wholeness, regardless of appearances or the outcome of treatment.

Being a healer involves following a code of honor, one that promotes healthy feelings, actions, thoughts, and beliefs in the patient—without compromising the same within the healer. Being a healer always involves being wise—and acting wisely. Being an *energy healer*, however, whether allopathic, complementary, Eastern, Western, spiritual, or any other sort, involves understanding energy and its effects. Being a *subtle energy healer* requires comprehending an even more unique set of issues.

In this chapter, we will briefly flesh out the basic beliefs and ethics required for being an energy healer (which all healers essentially are). This toolbox can be carried everywhere, much like the black bag used by doctors who make house calls. We will also examine a few of the special issues faced by a subtle energy healer, such as the appropriate use of intuition and insight, providing parameters that a subtle specialist can apply to his or her own practice.

REQUIREMENTS FOR WORKING ENERGETICALLY

A professional energy worker must decide how to operate in terms of techniques, beliefs, and ethics, diligently selecting training, behaviors, and boundaries that serve self and patients—even if the patients are children or friends. The most universal guidelines can be borrowed from the Hippocratic oath taken by many medical doctors upon graduation from medical school.

The succinct version of the oath is *to help and not harm*—but there is a lot of gray in between these two black and white edges. Let us consider an updated version of this oath, as applied to energy workers.

This outline of the oath is based on the classical version—the one sworn to the gods thousands of years ago. (The words of the oath are italicized, and comments about it are in standard text.)[27]

- *To benefit the sick according to one's ability.* Only treat the people you are qualified to treat.
- *Keep them from harm and injustice, or tell them if you think they are injuring themselves or someone else.* Report severe endangerments to authorities when necessary and do not overstep your own boundaries. If you are a hands-on healer, you are not trained to decide whether a cancer patient would benefit from chemotherapy.
- *To hold him who has taught me as equal to my parents.* Respect your teachers and seek out trainers, schools, and programs that are respectable.
- *Not give a deadly drug to anyone who has asked for it, or make a suggestion to this effect.* All energy is medicine—even subtle energy. Whether packaged as herbs, sound, light, words, or prescription medicine, medicine has an effect and is not to be used without full knowledge of its effects.
- *In purity and holiness I will guard my life and my art.* This means that *you* count. Your life and morals are important and are not to be sacrificed for your work.
- *Whatever houses I may visit, I will come for the benefit of the sick, remaining free of all intentional injustice, of all mischief, and in particular of sexual relations with both female and male persons, be they free or slaves.* Do not get involved with clients. Most professional and licensed medical professionals cannot date or see their patients outside of work unless treatment has ceased for two years.
- *What I may see or hear in the course of the treatment or even outside of the treatment in regard to the life of men, which on no account one must spread abroad, I will keep to myself, holding such things shameful to be spoken about.* Clients deserve privacy.

A contemporary version of the oath also recommends avoiding doing that which other specialists can do better. A professional sends clients to the correct referrals.

BEING A SUBTLE ENERGY TECHNICIAN: SPECIALIZED TRAINING

Being a subtle energy worker involves consciously learning techniques that could include, but also go beyond, the bounds of the allopathic medical discipline. A subtle energy professional has to address three technical areas to become a learned technician.

- *Expertise in at least one subtle energy practice.* There are great chiropractors who have also taken a few hours of acupuncture training. This does not make them specialists in acupuncture, nor outstanding energy workers. A qualified subtle energy professional must meet the following criteria:
  - Be knowledgeable about the subtle energies and the energy anatomy involved in the chosen area.
  - Understand the relationship between applicable subtle structures and the physical body.
  - Accept and have a working comprehension of the relationship between the energy area and the other components of the human self: mental, emotional, and spiritual.
  - If applicable, be attuned to and develop the intuitive aspect of the energy art.
  - If using intuitive faculties, also rely upon the intellect and common sense. Many Western medical doctors follow "hunches" to diagnose. That is superb—but they follow up with scientifically sound tests and procedures. Even an intuitive practitioner must do this. Consider how you can corroborate your intuition mechanically.
- *If one's practice is integrative, expertise in at least one other professional area.* Integrative medicine is exploding across America, joining a worldwide trend. In fact, some countries have never completely Westernized their medicine practice. Their traditional medicine *is* so-called complementary or integrative. An integrative Western practitioner in the Western world must have a degree that is academically and legally recognized, in addition to expertise in a subtle energy discipline. State law determines which degrees and training qualify.
- *Ongoing training.* Subtle energy medicine is one of the fastest-growing fields in the world, gaining recognition and validity, while also expanding in terms of the information that is available. Keep informed, read books, and take classes.

THE POWER OF BELIEF

An energy worker's effectiveness depends upon his or her beliefs (whether the person works subtly or not). A professional must ask these questions of him- or

RESEARCH SUPPORTS THE use of intuition in at least a limited capacity for subtle—and maybe even all—energy work. Norman Shealy, MD, for example, published a study referencing the work of eight psychics to diagnose seventeen patients. These diagnoses were 98 percent accurate in making personality diagnoses and 80 percent correct in determining physical conditions.[28]

Research by the HeartMath Research Center at the Institute of HeartMath in California is corroborating the existence of intuition and its accuracy. Most of its studies showcase the heart as a key intuitive center, responding even to information about the future. As an example, the heart decelerates when receiving futuristic, calming stimuli versus agitating emotional stimuli.[29]

A myriad of issues are involved in using intuition for energy work, including questions about boundaries; the importance or applicability of the information; accuracy of interpretation; the unpredictable and changeable nature of the future; the effects of the information on the recipient (i.e., to "prove" or "disprove" the data); and overriding all of these, the intuitive skills of the energy professional.

Regardless of the inexact nature of intuition, a professional should not be embarrassed to exercise intuition in his or her trade. Energy work is an art and has traditionally encompassed intuition.

herself: Do you believe in the effectiveness of your energy discipline? Do you believe in yourself? Do you believe in your client's ability to heal or grow? Answers to these and other belief-based questions impact professional success and safeguard personal well-being.

Your energy fields interact with your patients' fields. How you feel about yourself—what you hold near and dear in your heart-space—transfers into a client's heart-space, and from there, into his or her body. (There is more information about heart-centered healing below.) As mind-body practitioner Dr. Herbert Benson of Harvard puts it, "Our brains are wired for beliefs and expectancies. When activated, our body can respond as it would if the belief were a reality, producing deafness or thirst, health or illness."[30]

We know that what is believed can become because of two well-studied (but not completely understood) phenomena called the *placebo* and *nocebo* effects. The placebo effect occurs when administering a disguised but false drug or treatment. Subjects do not know they are receiving something medically ineffective. In fact, they are told it "will work."

Since 1955, researchers have been tracking the seemingly magical effect of the placebo, sometimes to their own dismay, as studies often reveal that not only do the placebos work, they sometimes work as well as (or better than) "real" medicine or treatments. For instance, many placebos have tested equal to children's cough medicines during recent studies.[31]

Studies also show that the placebo effect is not limited to drugs. It carries over into devices and physical techniques, such as the use of massage, naturopathic and chiropractic care, hydrotherapy, the use of heat and light, and more.[32] It also applies to healers and their effects on patients. As Michael Jospe, a professor at the California School of Professional Psychology states, "The placebo effect is part of the human potential to react positively to a healer."[33] A healer's attitude helps create patient outcomes.

What can heal can also harm. Consider the reverse of the placebo effect: the nocebo effect, which can be phrased this way: if you believe that something bad is going to happen, it probably will. Researchers have discovered that women who believed they were prone to heart disease were four times more likely to develop heart problems than women who had the same risk factors but lacked the negative attitude.[34] One study determined that nearly 100 percent of the people undergoing surgery who wanted to die (usually to reconnect with a deceased loved one), did.[35]

The placebo and nocebo effects reduce to *empathy*: the sharing of energy through energetic means. People empathize all the time, some better than others, as revealed in a study by Levenson and Gottman of the University of California at Berkeley. Researchers examined the physiological reactions in married couples when interacting empathetically and discovered that the heart rates of partners who excelled at empathizing mimicked each other. When one partner's heart rate went up, so did the other's, and vice versa.[36] These and other studies imply that an *ethical* and *effective* energy healer is a heart-centered energy healer.

THE HEART-CENTERED ENERGY HEALER

We intuitively know that the heart is the center of love and empathy, and studies are showing this to be true. In fact, empathy manifests in the electromagnetic field (EMF), which is generated by the heart in amounts greater than anywhere else in the body. The heart's EMF emits fifty thousand femtoteslas (a measure of EMF), in contrast to the ten generated by the brain.[37] Other research shows that when separated from the magnetic field, the heart's electrical field is sixty times greater in amplitude than the brain's field.[38] Through this field, a person's nervous system tunes in to and responds to the magnetic fields produced by the hearts of other people.[39] The heart's field is therefore one of the means by which a practitioner affects patients.

This effect leads to the question, What do you want to share? To generate positive outcomes for a patient, a practitioner must hold positive feelings in his or her own heart. Not only does good will profit the client, but it also benefits the practitioner as a person.

A set of studies by researcher Dr. Rollin McCraty of the HeartMath Institute in California, and described in his e-book, *The Energetic Heart,* helps explain the importance of positive energy.[40]

For decades, scientists have known that information is encoded in the nervous system in the time intervals between activities or in the pattern of electrical activity. Recent studies also reveal that information is captured in hormone pulses. Moreover, there is a hormone pulse that coincides with heart rhythms, which means that information is also shared in the interbeat intervals of the pressure and electromagnetic waves produced by the heart.

Negative emotions such as anger, frustration, or anxiety disturb the heart rhythm. Positive emotions such as appreciation, love, or compassion produce coherent or functional patterns. Feelings, distributed throughout the body, produce chemical changes within the entire system. Do you want to be a healthy person? Be sincerely positive as often as you can. You thus "increase the probability of maintaining coherence and reducing stress, even during challenging situations."[41]

What you as a practitioner believe will be shared—everywhere and with everyone you meet.

THE INTUITIVE HEALER

There are many forms of psychic abilities used in subtle energy-based healing. Everyone is born with various "psychic" abilities, as extensive studies have revealed.[42] These gifts can be developed and used to make intuitive assessments for physical and psychological problems. To date, over 150 controlled studies of healing have been published, with more than half revealing an effective application of intuition.[43] And the intuitive application of energy is one of the primary ways to deliver energetic healing.

As with the rest of life, you will not be good at every form of intuition or be able to use your gifts for every purpose. Practitioners often have expertise in certain areas and weaknesses in others. For example, one study described an intuitive diagnostician who could determine organ problems with a great deal of accuracy but was unable to identify fertility disorders.[44] One of the keys to using your intuition is to know which forms you are most gifted in. Following is a partial list of the various types of intuitive gifts that most frequently come into play with energy work. While some of them may seem far-fetched, there is ample literature describing all of these experiences.

Clairaudience (also called *channeling* and *transmediumship*): Gaining information from the spiritual realm, often involving the entrance of an entity in one's own body.

Clairsentience: Knowledge about the external world with no known source for the information.

Distant or absent healing: Ability to conduct diagnoses, perceive another's situation or needs, or send healing energy from a distance.

Divination: Obtaining psychic information by calling upon spirits or peering into the future.

Dowsing: The use of instruments, such as pendulums or dowsing rods, to transfer energy or obtain information.

Empathy: Sensing others' emotions, needs, or physical conditions. Includes *body-based empathy*, the ability to detect smells, feelings, sensations, bodily reactions, and the awareness of others' states in the self.

Hands-on healing: Use of the hands for diagnosis, interpretation, or energy shifting, either for present or distant subjects or groups.

Kinesiology: Sensing muscular change and reading the body's messages accordingly.

Mind-based techniques: The use of mind-altering substances or activities to activate intuition, such as hypnosis, sacred medicine, foods, music, sounds, and colors.

Precognition: Foresight of the future.

Projection: Ability to see into, sense, or visit other current realities.

Prophecy: Ability to see or sense what might happen, if all goes according to a divine plan.

Psychic surgery: The actual penetration of the body through psychic means. Can result in removal of tissue, bones, or other matter.

ONE OF THE most accessible ways to explore and increase psychic gifts is through a chakra-based approach. As I have proposed and described in other books, each of twelve major chakras houses a different type of psychic ability. Psychic talent is the raw ability to gather, decode, and send psychic information. Individual chakras operate on different vibratory bands; therefore each one works with a different type of psychic information. Psychic energy is simply a faster version of energy than sensory. What a person "picks up" or "gives off" can be translated into physical, emotional, mental, and spiritual energies of considerable impact—negative or positive.

We all have different innate gifts—and more-powerful versus less-powerful chakras. By evaluating which chakras are your strongest, you can also determine which psychic gifts are most available for your use.

This theory emphasizes that, while everyone is psychic, not everyone uses his or her innate gifts in an appropriate or healthy manner. Various issues, perhaps from childhood, culture, experiences, or religious upbringing, might create problems with psychic boundaries. Perhaps the fields around the body do not filter incoming psychic energy in a helpful fashion. Maybe internal programming is distorting the chakra's ability to correctly collect, interpret, or disseminate psychic data. Quite often, energy professionals are "too psychic," in that they absorb psychic information that is unhelpful or dangerous to themselves. This creates psychic boundary problems, which can be addressed by shifting from being *psychic* to being *intuitive*. This involves setting mindful, emotional, and energetic parameters to control the flow of energy in and out of the chakras and auric fields.

The following chart shows which psychic gifts are located within each chakra, how the gifts work when unfiltered, and how they shift when the operator develops intuitive boundaries.

FIGURE 1.1
CHAKRA-BASED PSYCHIC GIFTS: SHIFTING FROM PSYCHIC TO INTUITIVE

Chakra	Psychic Gift	Positive Psychic	Negative Psychic	Intuitive Gift
First	Physical sympathy (a factor in psycho-metry, dowsing, psychic surgery, kinesiology, telekinesis, and hands-on healing)	Senses others' physical problems and the reasons for them	Absorbs others' illnesses and physical conditions and cannot get rid of them	Physical empathy: registers others' physical conditions but releases them; can help heal them
Second	Feeling sympathy	Feels others' emotions and can decipher them	Absorbs others' feelings and holds them in own body	Feeling empathy: Reads others' emotions and can help heal them

FIGURE 1.1
CHAKRA-BASED PSYCHIC GIFTS: SHIFTING FROM PSYCHIC TO INTUITIVE

Chakra	Psychic Gift	Positive Psychic	Negative Psychic	Intuitive Gift
Third	Mental sympathy (often called clairsentience)	Knows what others are thinking or believe	Thinks that others' beliefs or thoughts are one's own	Mental empathy: determines belief-system causes of others' issues and provides clarification
Fourth	Relational sympathy (a factor in hands-on healing)	Can sense others' needs and desires; can channel energy for healing	Assumes responsibility for others' needs, unmet desires, and healing	Relational empathy: can determine others' needs and provide assistance, but invites divine help for the rest
Fifth	Verbal sympathy (also called channeling, transmediumship, telepathy, and clairaudience)	Can receive data from another person or spirit, as well as tones, music, or sounds	Cannot separate own thoughts from those outside of self; can be overtaken by spirits	Verbal empathy: controls opening and shutting for receiving communication
Sixth	Visual sympathy (also called clairvoyance, futuring, precognition, use of "The Sight," remote viewing, reading the aura)	Sees images, visions, pictures, colors with eyes or inner sight	No control over flow or type of images; often mainly negative; cannot interpret what is real	Visual empathy: receives revelation when needed, able to interpret; can heal others with visions
Seventh	Spiritual sympathy (also called prophecy and a factor in intentionality, prayer, meditation)	Can sense consciousness development, purpose, destiny, or spiritual guides of others	Vulnerable to spiritual attacks; overly affected by evil or negativity; sense of powerlessness	Spiritual empathy: manages access to higher guides to help self or others; uses prayer, meditation, intention toward healing
Eighth	Shamanic sympathy (a factor in soul journeying, remote viewing, retrocognition, projection, precognition, the exorcism or summoning of spirits, and work with restrictions)	Walks between worlds and dimensions; not bounded by time—past, present, or future	Vulnerable to entities and issues from other worlds, people, and own past lives	Shamanic empathy: can connect to or visit other worlds and dimensions to obtain information or healing energy or conduct energy and entity shifts

FIGURE 1.1

CHAKRA-BASED PSYCHIC GIFTS: SHIFTING FROM PSYCHIC TO INTUITIVE

Chakra	Psychic Gift	Positive Psychic	Negative Psychic	Intuitive Gift
Ninth	Soul sympathy	Can tell what is going on in others' souls	Takes on others' soul issues or global problems	Soul empathy: senses others' soul needs or global needs and determines how to create harmony
Tenth	Natural sympathy (a factor in natural-based healing)	Links with elements, beings, and energies of the natural world	Becomes a victim of natural elements, beings, and energies	Natural empathy: receives and can share information and healing energies from natural world
Eleventh	Force sympathy	Conduit for natural and energetic forces, such as wind or spiritual beings	Run by outside forces, leading to extreme negativity or out-of-control power	Force empathy: can pick and choose which forces to use, tap into, and direct for positive change
Twelfth	Personal aptitudes (special and unique abilities related to one's specific spiritual purpose—similar to the siddhi abilities discussed in Part V)	Differs person to person but always furthers directed use of the psychic for a higher purpose (Example: A teacher could decide to "receive" the psychic data to conduct a particular lesson; the intuitive process allows for control of subject matter, whereas the psychic does not)	Differs person to person but is an extension of personality traits (Example: If someone has a keen memory and is a teacher, this would involve psychic ability to "hear" data related to subject matter; this unfiltered process can expose the teacher to inaccurate or ineffective data)	Differs person to person but always helps others achieve their spiritual purpose (Example: A teacher would "receive" only the psychic information that would meet the highest ends of his or her students)

Retrocognition: Knowledge of the past.

Shamanic work: The art of energetic walking between worlds and dimensions with full access to all intuitive abilities, usually while in an altered state. Abilities might include *entity detection* and *exorcism*; dealing with *possession* (an attachment to an entity or a part of it) or *recession* (part of self is in something or someone else); *soul retrieval* and *healing* (the soul or part of it is absent from the body): delivering people from *energetic bindings*, such as *cords* (energetic contracts between two or more people or souls), or *life cords* (attachments between two or more parts of the self); *codependent bargains* (energy contracts where only one of the members gains); and *curses* (negative energy fields that hold one or more in bondage).

Spiritual techniques: The use of connection with a divine or nonlocal reality to induce change, including the use of religious prayer, intercessory prayer, nondirected prayer, nonlocal healing, meditation, and contemplation.

Telepathy: Mind-reading.

Visualization: *Clairvoyance* or perception of images, spirits, visions, or colors; reading the *aura* (energy field around the body); various types of perceiving (or creating) the future or the past, including *foretelling, precognition,* and *recognition;* and *remote viewing,* the ability to perceive what is going on outside of the self, sometimes at great distances.

One of the newest words in the lexicon of subtle energy healing is *intentionality.* This involves the projection of awareness toward a desired outcome or object. In many ways, it is the sum total of the psychic abilities. If you set a positive and noble intention, your intuitive abilities will naturally align to help achieve it.

As explored, all healers are energy healers. Following a code of ethics serves the healer as well as the patient. Subtle energy healers so commonly use intuition that it's important to add an additional level of ethics, one seeped in knowledge, practical application, and boundaries. Information such as that covered in this chapter can serve as a springboard for further exploration.

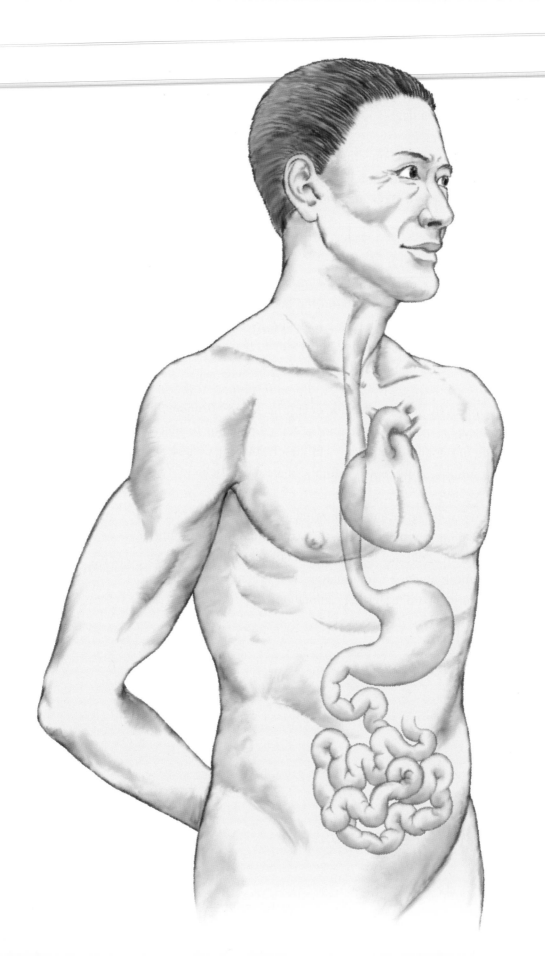

When we look in the mirror, we see ourselves, or at least our physical aspect. We imagine this form to be real; after all, it is flesh and blood. It is made of particles so slow moving that we can touch, see, hear, and sense them. And it is made of light that is invisible to the eyes. It is real, although it is not the only real body each of us has, for beneath (and around and within) is our subtle body.

Why explore the physical body in a book about energy anatomy? Moreover, why examine it in a book that highlights the subtle body?

Like the subtle body, the physical body is composed of energies. They are merely slower and of lesser intensity and vibration than are the subtle energies. While the rules governing the physical and subtle systems are different, these structures are intimately and intricately tied together. For this reason, it is important to understand them both.

So, as a prelude to our study of subtle body anatomy, this section explores the major physical systems of the human body. It is intended to provide a basic grounding in anatomical structures and processes, as well as to begin our investigation of the energetic nature of the body. This overview will be brief; it is not meant to be a substitute for a thorough medical anatomy course.

3

THE CELLS

The human body has more than one hundred million cells, the basic unit of life. Depending on function, cells vary in size, shape, and makeup and create energy for all of life's activities.

Cells divide and multiply, which is how the human body grows and changes. Cells with similar functions join together and form tissue. Tissues of similar functions form an organ. Groups of specialized cells perform various bodily functions. These include red blood cells, white blood cells, macrophages, neurons, muscle cells, and skin cells. A cell itself consists of protoplasm, a living substance that is 70 percent water, surrounded by a cell membrane, with a nucleus inside.

CELLS ARE THE BUILDING BLOCKS

Most cells have an outer membrane and within it, in a jellylike substance known as cytoplasm, are many tiny structures (organelles). The most important cellular substructures include:

Mitochondrion: Makes energy generation possible; site of aerobic respiration, where ATP (adenosine triphosphate) is made.

Nucleus: A tiny mass, usually in spherical or oval form, that is embedded in protoplasm and controls cell function. Contains genetic information in the form of DNA (deoxyribonucleic acid).

Nucleolus: Makes the necessary proteins for cell division; surrounded by the nuclear membrane and attaches to the endoplasmic reticulum.

Endoplasmic reticulum: A system of channels between the nucleus and cell membrane, also involved in the manufacture of protein.

Cell metabolism depends on a constant supply of raw materials and the removal of finished substances and waste via blood circulation. Cell activity is controlled by the nucleus and maintained by energy reserves. Each cell is like a factory with three stages of production: raw materials, manufacturing, and disposal.

Raw materials: Depending on the cell's function, only certain substances are allowed through its membrane. Each cell type requires different substances that are obtained from the body's circulatory system: carbohydrates, fats, amino acids, and various salts.

Manufacturing: This process takes place on the surface of the endoplasmic reticulum found throughout cytoplasm (the cellular wall). Examples of finished products are enzymes and hormones.

Disposal: Final product and waste substances are passed through the cell wall into interstitial fluid and then into the blood for circulation and disposal.

THE MITOCHONDRIA AND THE ELECTROMAGNETIC CELL[1]

Mitochondria make the physical energy for our cells. They are also implicated in the formation of subtle energies, as has been seen in research regarding the meridians, the subtle energy structures discussed in Part IV.

Only about 50 percent of cellular energy is provided for the body to use; the rest is required for cellular maintenance. Each cell is comparable to a battery, positively charged at the outer wall and negatively charged inside the wall. Thus every cell generates its own electrical activity and magnetic field. A healthy cell has an electrical charge of about seventy millivolts, volts serving as the measurement of electrical activity.

When the body is diseased or poorly nourished, a cell's membrane charge reduces to about thirty millivolts, which is insufficient for the transportation of nutrients into the cell. The physical metabolism slows, and cells die. The general electrical activity of the physical body is reduced as well.

Electricity occurs every time our muscles move, our blood pumps, our lymph flows, when we think and exercise. Reduced metabolism decreases activity on every level, decreasing the electrical and magnetic fields of the body. The body becomes more susceptible to disease, mood disorders, and aging. The dying cells multiply, but on a slower scale unless the mitochondria, the energy providers for the cell, are able to generate enough energy for cellular division and metabolic tasks—and electrical activity.

The body's electromagnetic activity depends in part upon ionic processes, which were discussed in Part I. Mitochondria participate in the life process by storing calcium, a contributor to the ionic exchanges of material and messages, as well as through other tasks.[2] Through their own electromagnetic activities, mitochondria initiate the release of neurotransmitters in the nerve cells and hormones in the endocrine glands.

MITOCHONDRIA AND MICROCURRENTS[3]

One way to look at mitochondria's actions is to see them as part of the body's microcircuitry. A microcurrent is a current of electricity measured in microamps, millionths of an ampere. As Kenneth Morgareidge, PhD, a physiology consultant writes, the application of microcurrents has enabled healing of connective tissue, including tendons and ligaments. The body itself can be viewed as a battery that creates its own microcurrents.

Microcurrents have been linked to sites of injury or "currents of injury." Dr. Robert Becker spent years tracking the electrical currents associated with animals' ability to regenerate limbs. The greater the current, the more complete the regeneration. These and other studies have led many researchers to view the body as a low-level, direct current generator—or a battery. Nerves carry these currents, but a more active conveyer is the glial cell (described later in this section). Research by Björn Nordenström, discussed in Part IV of this book, also reveals a secondary electrical system linking the connective tissue, the vascular system, and the meridians.

Dr. Morgareidge suggests that it is possible that the meridians actually establish the template for this microcircuitry while the embryo is developing. This implies that they continue to guide the body's electromagnetic process throughout life. In fact, the electromagnetic fields generated by the microcircuitry process might themselves form the map by which the body and its cells are organized. Ionization is a vital process for the conveyance of the electrical currents throughout the body and within the cells.

FIGURE 2.1
A HUMAN CELL

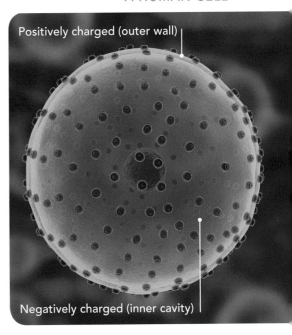

Positively charged (outer wall)

Negatively charged (inner cavity)

Dr. Morgareidge describes the role of mitochondria as vital to this templating process. Within the mitochondrion are cytochromes, special enzymes that move hydrogen ions across the mitochondrion membranes, powering the creation of ATP (see Chapter 15, "Metabolism"). The concentration of these ions and ATP power almost every cell process. Also involved with the ionization process of calcium, mitochondria provides critical assistance with moving electricity into action—and possibly with enabling the meridians to interface with the body via its microcircuitry.

4

DNA

Deoxyribonucleic acid, or DNA, is the code of life, as it houses our unique genetic information in the nucleus of every cell in the form of chromosomes, which are simply long strands of DNA molecules.[4] Each DNA molecule contains many genes, which direct the construction and maintenance of the human body.

While microscopic, the DNA molecule is one of the largest known molecules. It is arranged in a double helix, resembling a spiral ladder. DNA is a highly complex substance formed from a chain of chemical units called nucleotides. Each nucleotide unit contains sugar, phosphate, and one of four kinds of nitrogen-containing compounds called bases. The sugar and phosphate form the sides of the ladders and the bases link in the middle to form the rungs of the ladder in a double helix.

The four bases are adenine, cytosine, guanine, and thymine (A, C, G, and T). Two bases make up each rung. Compatibility of the bases limits the possible combinations to A-T, T-A, C-G, or G-C, with the bases forming different patterns along the length of the ladder. Combined, three bases form a codon, which encodes a single amino acid of a protein.

The particular order of the bases arranged along the sugar-phosphate backbone is called the DNA sequence. The sequence specifies the exact genetic instructions required to create a particular organism with its own unique traits.

BLUEPRINT OF THE BODY

DNA is like a fingerpint: it is unique to each person. Genes within each DNA molecule contain the information to make proteins, chemicals that enable the body to work and grow. By encoding a messenger ribonucleic acid (mRNA) with information for the ribosomes in the cell, DNA determines what proteins the cell makes. The sequence of amino acids produced correlates directly to a specific sequence of bases in the DNA.

MOTHER CELLS: THE GIFT THAT KEEPS GIVING

THERAPISTS SAY IT is hard to break the "mother bond" between mother and child, but research is suggesting that this bond goes deeper, lasts longer, and can be more dangerous or beneficial than previously thought. This is because the bond is not only biological, it is cellular. The cellular connection also suggests the presence of subtle energy bonds.

This connection begins at conception, with the mitochondria. The mitochondria, the intracellular energy generators within each cell, are inherited only from the mother's egg. The father's mitochondria, which are carried in the sperm, enter the egg, but do not contribute to the genetic information.[5]

Each person inherits thousands of generations of mitochondrial DNA through his or her mother's lineage.[6] This fact has led many anthropologists to suggest that we all descend from "Mitochondrial Eve" or "African Eve," an African woman believed to have been alive 140,000 years ago. According to this hypothesis, every human being shares the same mitochondria as this original mother. Y-chromosomes, which are carried by the sperm, are only inherited from the father; each of us also carries father-only genetics.[7]

For quite some time, scientists have known that cells from the mother, entering the child during the womb, may remain in the offspring's body for decades, if not an entire lifetime. Some of these cells are now being implicated in autoimmune dysfunctions, including lupus and rheumatoid arthritis, as well as in the body's ability to prevent or heal certain conditions.

J. Lee Nelson and other researchers at the University of Washington in Seattle have determined that some of these maternal cells might be the focus of antibody attacks, leading to autoimmune disorders. Normally the immune system only attacks foreign invaders, but in the case of autoimmune disorders, the body's antibodies attack its own healthy cells. This process is called *microchimerism*, and it applies to the presence of mother cells in progeny and the cells that linger from a fetus in the mother's body. Microchimerism has been found to affect dozens of tissues, including most of the major organs.[8]

Studies have also shown, however, that cells passed from mother to child during pregnancy can grow into functioning pancreatic cells that manufacture insulin within the child, suggesting a potential healing effect in some of these lingering maternal cells, perhaps preventing or alleviating the effects of diabetes.[9]

From the perspective of subtle energy, the ongoing presence of mother cells, as well as inherited mitochondrial maternal DNA, suggests further discussion about epigenetics (discussed in this section), morphogenetic fields, and miasms (both discussed later in the book). Epigenetics suggests that social and emotional events can be chemically programmed into non-DNA substances, which in turn influence DNA activity. These events are passed down intergenerationally.

Before a cell divides, the DNA duplicates so that the two new cells have identical DNA molecules. It takes a combination of approximately five hundred genes on each of the forty-six chromosomes to carry sufficient instructions for all the activities within the body, from body type to inherited instincts, from the color and size of our eyes to the speed of our reactions.

With the exception of the sperm and ova, which have only twenty-three chromosomes, the nucleus of every cell in the human body contains forty-six chromosomes, arranged as twenty-three pairs.

Each parent has a full set of forty-six chromosomes, but each only passes twenty-three chromosomes to their child. Siblings, for example, differ because each "inherits" a different set of twenty-three chromosomes from each parent. Only identical twins get exactly the same set of twenty-three chromosomes from each parent after a single fertilized egg splits into two identical eggs.

EPIGENETICS: BEYOND DNA[10]

For decades, scientists have assumed that DNA is the primal initiator of physical and even mental and emotional characteristics. Now it seems that there is "energy behind the energy" of DNA that turns the genes off and on, greatly affecting what each individual is —and will become.

Epigenetics is the study of *epigenomes*, certain chemicals and switches that instruct the genes. You have the same DNA in your toes that you do in your brain, but something tells genes in different locations how to operate, and when. Something also tells certain genes to kill cancers—or not—or cause plaque buildup—or not. That "something" just might be the epigenomes, consisting of substances including proteins and methyl molecules.

Epigenomes lie next to the double helix. They respond to alterations in the environment and then "toggle" the DNA. Epigenetic changes often occur during DNA transcription, when the DNA is being copied. One example involves *histones*, proteins that hold certain codes. DNA is wrapped around these epigenomes. Are you smoking and drinking too much? The histones know all your secrets. They "tattle" about your actions when the DNA duplicates. For instance, they might possibly tell your "cancer preventing" genes to keep quiet and your "cancer-causing genes" to speak up. Behaviors like smoking, eating, and drinking affect the epigenomes, but so do emotional factors, as has been shown in a study by researcher Michael Meaney.

Meaney, a biologist at McGill University, examined the brains of adults who were born with low birth weight. Those who had a poor relationship with their mothers had smaller hippocampi, one of the brain organs responsible for memory.

Those who had closer relationships had normal size hippocampi. In this and related studies, Meaney and others detected corresponding differences in the DNA methylation patterns (the methyl group is a set of atoms that interferes with chemical signals that put genes into action). In other words, lack of nurturing "turned off" the genes supportive of the hippocampi; love "turned on" these growth genes.[11]

It was once thought that each of us arrived in adulthood already formed, our DNA locked into place, but this is not true. Studies show that our environment continues to encode the epigenomes and therefore alter our DNA. Not only that, the evidence shows that the decisions encoded in the epigenomes can be passed down from one generation to the next—perhaps for several generations. What affected your grandmother might still be affecting you. What you do will be passed down to your great-grandchildren.

Unfortunately, what seems like a good thing for one generation might not yield the same fruit for the next. Marcus Pembrey, a clinical geneticist at the Institute of Child Health in London, presented data from two centuries of records from an isolated town in Sweden. Grandfathers who had ample food during their preteen years were more likely to have grandsons with diabetes—leaving a legacy that doubled the grandsons' risk of early death. These effects were gender specific. A grandmother's early experience was handed down to her female progeny.[12]

Just as we search for the energetic foundations of reality, so must we continue to explore the body for its energetic foundations. A subtle energy scientist would deepen the discussion of epigenetics, asserting that subtle energy fields, channels, and bodies provide information for the epigenomes. In the end, further research into the effects of energetics in both the DNA and epigenomes might construct the picture of reality we are all looking for.

DNA AS LIGHT

Studies by Fritz-Albert Popp and other researchers are dazzling the scientific community with a new understanding of DNA: DNA as light.

Popp has demonstrated that DNA operates not only chemically, the longstanding theory, but at a level beyond. It is essentially a storage unit for light and a source of biophoton emission.[13]

Photons compose the electromagnetic spectrum. They drive the body's processes. At different frequencies, photons produce different effects. Popp and others maintain that the body is actually surrounded by a field of light and that the DNA responds to (and interacts with) the various electromagnetic frequencies found in this field.[14] (We will return to this concept several times in this book, because each subtle energy structure interrelates with light, internally and externally.)

The physical body and its DNA rely upon light for health; certain types of light cause problems while others are beneficial—and even healing. Dr. Joan Smith-Sonneborn at the University of Wyoming exposed paramecia to far-ultraviolet radiation, which caused DNA damage and shortened the cells' lives. When these injured organisms were exposed to near-ultraviolet radiation (which is closer to visible light), the damage was repaired and the aging reversed.[15]

How does external light reach and affect us? Researchers David A. Jernigan, DC, and Samantha Joseph, DC, explored photons and discovered that they operate as waves and particles and enter the body primarily through the eyes.[16] The eye translates light into electrochemical impulses for the brain's interpretation; the light proceeds into the body's crystalline matrix or "fiber optic" network. By moving from the rods and cones into a different set of cells, called the *Muller cells*, the light accesses the crystal matrix of the body to reach every part of the body.

This crystal matrix is interrelated with quantum fields of photons that pulse throughout the body. These biophotons act upon the entire electromagnetic spectrum, transferring information through each of its layers. The movements are facilitated by the electromagnetic polarization of DNA, which acts as a guide to direct optical information. The electromagnetic and biophoton energies can either be coherent or incoherent.

This coherency is at least partly within our control. Studies have shown that holding positive thoughts in our heart creates coherency between electromagnetic and biophoton emissions, which then changes the DNA so that our bodies are healthier. In other words, DNA can at least partly be controlled by thoughts. Thought fields, T-fields, will be discussed in Part III.

FIGURE 2.2

THE DNA NEBULA
This 80-light-year-long nebula, discovered near the center of the Milky Way galaxy in 2006, is shaped like a DNA double helix.

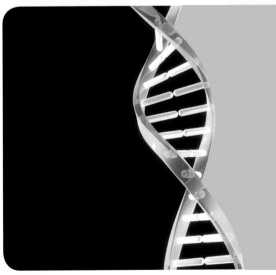

5

THE SKELETAL SYSTEM

The skeletal system of an adult consists of about two hundred and six bones. Bones provide support to the body, protect the internal organs, and create movement in conjunction with muscles. Bones also serve as a point of attachment for the muscles and produce red blood cells for the circulation system. Controlled by the endocrine system, bones also store the body's required calcium and phosphorus.

The skeleton has two main parts: the axial skeleton and the appendicular skeleton. The axial skeleton consists of the skull, spine, and ribcage. The appendicular skeleton houses the upper and lower limbs and the shoulder and pelvic girdles.

Bones are made up of water, minerals, and the cellular matrix that binds them together. They are surrounded by tough, fibrous periosteium into which muscles and ligaments are inserted. Bones are hard and rigid on the outside and lighter and softer on the inside. Bone hardness comes from mineral salts, primarily calcium phosphate, and bone strength derives from collagen, a fibrous protein, which also makes up the connective tissue.

BONE CREATION

Babies are born with over three hundred bones. The number reduces over the years through a process called ossification, a hardening of the cartilage in which the bones and cartilage fuse into larger units, creating fewer but larger bones.

When bones begin growing they are completely solid. They then develop hollow centers, which slightly reduce the bones' strength, while reducing their weight so as to facilitate muscle movement. The hollow centers of bone contain marrow, the material that manufactures blood cells.

Bones are formed from cartilage, a rubbery gristle that forms as vertebral discs and ligaments, with the exception of the clavicle and some parts of the skull, which ossify directly from membrane tissue. Bone-forming cells, called *osteo-blasts*, deposit a collagen-fiber matrix onto tendon, membrane, and cartilage. When the matrix is laid down, it is calcified by calcium carried in the blood. Hormones and diet govern this process.

BONES ARE AN ENDOCRINE GLAND[17]

The bones have a stronger connection to the endocrine system than had been previously known. A recent study published in the scientific journal *Cell* shows a distinct connection between osteocalcin, a vitamin K-dependent hormone, and the regulation of insulin. Using genetically altered mice, researchers found that osteocalcin, secreted by osteoblasts (bone-forming cells), is capable of stimulating insulin secretion and improving insulin sensitivity—one of the functions of certain endocrine glands.

The findings indicated that the skeleton helps regulate energy metabolism in a feedback-loop fashion. Apparently, the skeleton exerts an endocrine regulation of sugar homeostasis. Ultimately, the findings establish the skeleton as an endocrine organ that controls energy metabolism, which has important implications for the treatment of obesity and diabetes.

6

THE MUSCULAR SYSTEM

The human body contains about seven hundred muscles.[18] Muscles move bones. Behind body activities are complex mechanisms that make even the simplest action, such as pointing a finger, a complicated procedure involving the brain, nerves, and sense organs.

The muscular system consists of three types of muscle:

Skeletal muscle: Also called *striped muscle*, these muscles are moved voluntarily. They account for a sizeable amount of the body's mass, with most connected to the skeleton by tissues called *tendons*. They help move the various bones and cartilages of the skeleton, contour physique, and are responsible for reflex actions.

Smooth muscle: Found in organs such as the stomach, lungs, kidneys, and skin, these muscles work automatically. These involuntary muscles, controlled by the autonomic nervous system, assist in day-to-day functions like digestion, breathing, and removing waste from the body.

Cardiac muscle: This muscle, found only in the heart, never gets tired. It constantly works to pump blood in and out of the heart. Heart muscle is activated by electrical impulses from its own pacemaker, the sinoatrial node, which ripple throughout the heart. The heart also contains smooth muscles, but its functions are mostly performed by the cardiac muscle.

Muscles are made up of bundles of fibers known as fascicles. Each fiber is an elongated cell containing myofibrils, thread-like structures that contain thick myofilaments, which contain myosin, and thin myofilaments, which

RESEARCH IS REVEALING that the body is made of unique molecular liquid crystalline structures. These living structures can create, transmit, and receive biophotons to facilitate communication between tissues and molecules. This communication also relies upon a quantum field of biophotons. These two processes—the crystalline and the quantum—interact to spread information around the body.[19]

This crystal matrix is critical for health, as it interconnects a person's internal self with the environment. Light travels through the body's crystal matrix into the DNA, which then produces

"bio-holograms" that create the body.[20] The most conductive light-matrix is the connective tissue, the largest organ in the body. The connective tissue is crystalline in formation; the collagenous molecules that encase the organs are liquid crystals and the other, firmer tissues are considered solid crystals. The collagen molecules are also interesting in that they are semiconductors, able to convey electricity and information. The connective tissue can therefore process information just like the semiconductor chips in your computer.[21]

Many researchers suggest that the meridians operate through the connective tissue, as will be discussed thoroughly in Part IV. We will see that meridians have a lower electrical resistance compared to the surrounding skin. When stimulated, the meridian points cause the production of endorphins and cortisol. (Nonmeridian points do not create this effect.) The connective tissue is therefore considered one of the primary participants in the subtle energy anatomy, interlinking the biophoton and quantum, or subtle, with the physical.

FIGURE 2.3
FASCIAL CELLS
A fluorescent microscope image of fascial tissue cells, stained to show the nuclei (blue) and filamental structure (green).

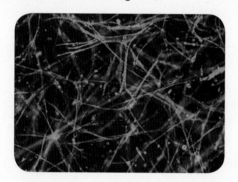

hold actin, troponin, and troposin. When triggered by impulses from the nervous system, the myofilaments glide along each other, chemically reacting as they meet and interlock. Ultimately, this chemical reaction produces a muscular contraction.

All our muscle cells are fully formed after the first year of life. When injured, muscles can repair themselves with care and proper nutrition. From about age thirty, a reduction in physical activity leads to muscle tissue being replaced by fat.

THE FASCIAL SYSTEM HOLDS IT TOGETHER

Connective tissues insulate the body and organs and transport nutrients and energy throughout the body. Tendons and ligaments are the body's strongest connective tissue and are considered part of the body's deep fascia. Fascia is the soft tissue component of the connective tissue system that extends from head to toe, surrounding muscles, bones, organs, nerves, blood vessels, and other structures. It is responsible for maintaining structural integrity and providing support and protection. It also acts as a shock absorber.

Most muscles are linked to bones by tendons, which transfer forces created by muscle to the connecting bone. In addition to attaching muscles to bone, tendons also attach muscles to structures, such as the eyeball. Where tendon meets bone, there is a gradual melding of the tendon fibers into the bone. Tendon sheaths, along with synovial fluid, aid in the smooth movement of the tendon, protecting the tendon from abrasive moving parts.

SOUND PATHWAYS[22]

SOUND, ONE OF the basic mechanical energies, is present everywhere and serves as a healing mechanism discussed throughout this book. This is because of its universality, both physically and subtly.

Every part of the body, from the cells to the toes, moves. Movement produces sound. The resulting sound waves and fields help regulate more than 50 percent of the body's biological processes. This is accomplished through the ligand/receptor interaction discussed in "The Biochemical Side of Emotions" on page 57. These interactions occur on every cell surface through sound frequencies between 20 and 20,000 Hz, the range of human hearing. There are special sound pathways in the body, however, that convey sound from site to site.

Sound enters through the cranial bones and hearing apparatus and travels through the body via the connective tissue. It uses water to speed vertically through the body at nearly five thousand feet per second. This transmission slows or stops when the connective tissue is too thick, inflexible, or dry—problems often created by incomplete emotional experiences. In a complete emotional experience, someone undergoes an event and has an emotional reaction, such as sadness and fear. The emotions initially cause a bodily disturbance such as tension or tightening. If allowed to fully sense and express the feelings, the person's body releases and returns to an equilibrium. If the person is unable to express the feelings or receive the needed comfort or validation, the body will remain tense and the tissue, especially connective tissue, will become blocked. Sound cannot flow through inflexible tissue as easily. Sound can, however, stimulate the blocked emotions and trigger the original memories or feelings.

Ligaments attach bone to bone and hold structures together, keeping them stable and allowing movement within normal limits. Without them, bones would become dislocated. Ligament connective tissue is primarily made up of white protein collagen and elastin, an elastic protein. Specialized cells called *fibroblasts* create new collagen fibers and repair damaged ones. Inside the fiber bundles is spongy tissue that carries blood and lymph vessels, providing space for nerves to pass through.

In addition to tendons and ligaments, fascia—the soft connective tissue within the body—is particularly conducive to manipulation and stretching because of its elasticity, a common technique in healing.

THE NERVOUS SYSTEM

A nerve is a bundle of motor and sensory fibers, often interlinked with connective tissue and blood vessels. The nervous system interprets information received from the outside world and internal organs, and initiates the appropriate responses. It is essential to sensory perception, including the control of movements and the regulation of body functions such as breathing. Arguably, the nervous system is the body's most important and complex network, vital for the development of language, thought, and memory.

As cell bodies, nerves pass chemical "batons"—neurotransmitters such as noradrenaline and serotonin—to each other at synapses (chasms that must be ionically crossed), which transmit messages and instructions around the body in an ongoing translation of chemical and electrical information. This relay occurs at intersections of nerves as their opposite ends link with each other. The need for translation enables the body to filter and access information rather than just react to stimuli. Nerves are especially important to understand in relation to the human energy anatomy; all parts of the subtle structure communicate physically through the nervous system. And the subtle system often relies on the electrical activity and magnetic fields generated by the nerves to operate in physical reality.

COMPLEX LAYERS

The vast nervous system is divided into two key areas: the central nervous system (CNS), with the brain and spinal cord, and the peripheral nervous system—all the rest of the nerves throughout the body.

The central nervous system: The brain and the spinal cord ultimately control the nervous tissue throughout the body, serving as its central processing unit. The spine communicates messages from the organs and tissues to the brain, which in turn encodes messages, sending them back via the spine.

The peripheral nervous system: Peripheral nerves initiate and perceive changes within and outside the body. This system serves the limbs and organs and connects the CNS to all other parts of the body and ganglia, groups of nerve cells sited at various points in the nervous system. The peripheral nervous system has two main divisions: the somatic nervous system, which is under conscious control, and the autonomic system, under unconscious control.

SOMATIC

The somatic system performs two roles. First, it collects information about the outside word from sensory organs, such as the nose. Signals from these receptors are then carried toward the CNS in sensory nerve fibers. Second, it transmits signals through motor fibers from the CNS to the skeletal muscles, initiating movement.

AUTONOMIC

The primary function of the autonomic system is to maintain various automatic functions of the body, like heart rhythm and the production of gastric juices. This system consists entirely of motor nerves that relay messages from the spinal cord to the various muscles. The autonomic system is controlled by the hypothalamus, an area of the brain that receives information about variations in the body's chemical makeup and adjusts the autonomic system to continue balance.

The autonomic system is also divided into two parts: the sympathetic and parasympathetic systems. Each uses a different chemical transmitter and operates differently. For instance, in the bronchial airways, the parasympathetic nerves cause constriction while the sympathetic nerves widen the passages.

THE BRAIN[23]

The brain is a 24/7 watchdog, running our lives. It constantly monitors and directs our body systems and functions, maintains maximum efficiency, preempts potential problems, and acknowledges and counters real dangers, damage, and injury.

The brain is the center of activity for the nervous system. Here, nerve signals from throughout the body are received, processed, and acted upon with appropriate responses. As the control center for sensory and motor activities, the brain controls thinking, memory, and emotion, as well as auditory and visual association. It also governs muscular actions, stimulating the body's movement.

The brain interprets information from the special sense organs related to sight, hearing, taste, smell, and balance. Together, the brain and spinal cord control many coordinated activities; simple reflexes and basic locomotion can be executed under spinal cord control alone.

The brain is divided into four major parts: the cerebrum, diencephalon, cerebellum, and brain stem.

Cerebrum: The area for much of our consciousness and processing power, the cerebrum also controls perception, action, reflecting, and creativity. It constitutes the largest part of the brain and consists of an inner core of white matter and an outer cortex of gray matter (cerebral cortex).

Diencephalon: This portion of the brain houses the interface of our electrical and chemical selves and serves as the control center of the endocrine system. It also includes the hypothalamus, which together with the pituitary and pineal glands choreographs an array of electrical and chemical signals that regulate our consciousness and physiology.

Cerebellum: Lying at the base of the cerebrum, the cerebellum is attached to the brain stem. It plays an important role in the control of movement, coordinating voluntary muscle activity and maintaining balance and equilibrium.

Brain stem: Housing the midbrain, pons, and medulla, the brain stem merges with the spinal cord below it. It regulates vital functions like breathing, heartbeat, and blood pressure.

THE CORTEX: THE BIG PICTURE

Much of our neural activity takes place in the gray matter found in the cerebral cortex. The cerebral cortex, the folded outer layer of the brain, accounts for about 40 percent of the brain mass and performs the highest level of neural processing, including language, hearing, sight, memory, and cognitive function (thought). The gray matter is composed of neurons, while the white matter of the cerebrum is made up of the processes of the nerve cells. The human brain is similar to the brains of other mammals, although our neural capacities are unique in their brain stem structures and the advanced neocortex, the most complex part of the cerebral cortex.

The folds of the cerebral cortex create a massive surface area for neural activity, with billions of neurons (nerve cells) and glial cells making up the substance of the brain. Neurons are electrically active brain cells that process information, whereas glial cells, which outnumber neurons by ten to one, perform supporting functions. In addition to being electrically active, neurons constantly synthesize neurotransmitters, chemicals that amplify and modulate signals between a neuron and another cell. Neurons have the ability to permanently change or deform—known as plasticity—which underlies basic learning and adaptation. Some unused neuron pathways, for example, may continue to exist long after memory is absent from consciousness, possibly developing the subconscious.

THE COMPLEX NEURAL WEB

The human brain houses a massive number of synaptic connections, allowing for a great deal of parallel processing. This processing is accomplished through the complex neural web, a net-like web of tissue that sifts through the mass of incoming information and decides what to pay attention to. The net fires signals around the brain, targeting the appropriate centers. If this driving force slows down or is prevented from occurring, the cerebral cortex becomes inactive and the person becomes unconscious.

BRAIN STATES

The brain undergoes transitions from wakefulness to sleep. These transitions are key for proper brain function. For instance, sleep is considered essential for knowledge consolidation, as the neurons organize the day's stimuli during deep sleep by randomly firing off the most recently used neuron pathways. Without sleep, it is possible to develop symptoms of mental illness and auditory hallucinations.

GLIAL CELLS

Science traditionally attributes nerve activity—and the effects of thinking—to neurons. New research is suggesting that the glial cells, the "support" cells of the central nervous system, actually modulate or govern the neuronal brain. Sensitive to electrical currents and magnetic fields, the glial cells are considered critical to the effects of electromagnetic activity in and on the body, affecting pineal gland functioning (and therefore our moods), the effects of the earth's magnetic field and solar activity, genetic and cellular activity and mutations, brain function, and other life functions.[24]

EMOTIONS AND THE BRAIN

There is truth in the adage, "It's all in your head." Since the early 1990s, researcher and author Daniel G. Amen, MD, has used a sophisticated brain scanning method called SPECT (Single Photon Emission Computed Tomography) to measure cerebral blood flow and metabolic activity patterns. His work has showed that certain brain patterns correlate with depression, distractibility, obsessiveness, violence, and other emotional issues.[25]

According to Amen, the deep limbic system of the brain governs our ability to bond, also operating as a mood control center. The size of a walnut, the limbic system includes the thalamic structures, hypothalamus, and the immediate surrounding structures. Amen has discovered that this portion of the brain manages emotional memories, emotional coloring, appetite and sleep cycles, and libido; it sets emotional tone, whether positive or negative. Amen has determined that the more active the system, the more negative someone's outlook. Conversely, the less active the deep limbic system, the more positive the person's attitude.[26]

THE BIOCHEMICAL SIDE OF EMOTIONS

On one level, emotions are not "feelings"; they are streams of biochemical properties that interact with the brain, *producing* feelings. Pioneering this theory is noted researcher Candace Pert, PhD, author of *Molecules of Emotion*, whose research demonstrates that internal chemicals—neuropeptides and their receptors—are the biological underpinnings of our awareness, manifesting as our emotions, beliefs, and expectations. These neuropeptides profoundly influence how we respond to and experience our world.[27]

Much of Dr. Pert's research involves receptor cells. Receptors are molecules made up of proteins that function as sensing molecules or scanners that hover in the membranes of cells. To operate, receptors need ligands, substances that bind to specific receptors on the surface of a cell.[28]

Ligands come in three chemical types. The first are neurotransmitters, small molecules of varying names such as histamine, serotonin, and norepinephrine. These transmit nerve impulses across a synapse or gap between nerve cells. Steroids are another form of ligands, and include the sex hormones testosterone, progesterone, and estrogen. Peptides are the third form, constituting most of the body's ligands. Peptides are essentially an informational substance. Like receptors, they are made up of strings of amino acids. Neuropeptides are smaller peptides that are active with neural tissue, while polypeptides are larger, typically containing between ten and one hundred amino acids. Pert uses the analogy of cells as the engine and receptors as buttons on the control panel. Ligands act as fingers that push the button to start the engine.[29]

BRAIN WAVES: ELECTRICAL MEASUREMENTS

THE BRAIN RECEIVES information like sound, touch, and temperature from all parts of the body and sends information to control breathing and heart rate and coordinate muscle activity. This information is sent by small electrical messages. Many of the brain's electrical messages also control thought and memory.

Every brain state is associated with characteristic brain waves. EEG (electroencephalograph) instruments are an accepted way to measure the electrical activity of the brain and thereby evaluate brain waves. Brain waves can indicate a state of health, consciousness, or activity. Some brain waves are optimum for daily life, others for meditation, and still others for achieving a healing state.[30]

Brain waves are measured in hertz, or cycles per second. Here are the four key bands of brain wave activity:

Beta: (13–26 hertz) Active, waking consciousness, eyes open. Highest in frequency and lowest in amplitude, these fast brain waves occur during concentration or mental work states.

Alpha: (8–13 hertz) Eyes closed, associated with states of relaxation, as well as daydreaming with eyes open. Average person can maintain awareness. Noted by slower brain waves, with an increase in amplitude and synchronicity.

Theta: (4–8 hertz) Quiet mind, body, and emotions. Deep relaxation, drowsiness, and light sleep stages. Average person cannot maintain awareness, while meditators can. Associated with stages one and two of sleep; slower in frequency and greater in amplitude than alpha waves.

Delta: (.5–4 hertz). Unconsciousness and deep sleep. Associated with stages three and four of sleep, delta waves are the slowest and highest amplitude brain waves. Delta sleep is our deepest sleep; its brain waves are least like waking brain waves. Sleepwalking and sleep talking commonly occur.[31]

At the border between states, brain waves typically show a mixture of patterns. For example, rapid eye movement (REM) sleep, the stage of sleep most associated with dreaming, is a combination of alpha, beta, and desynchronous waves.

According to research by the Virginia-based Monroe Institute, which studies consciousness, sound, and sleep learning, there is a fifth band of brain waves known as gamma waves, which run at approximately 28 hertz or greater. Their research has found this level marked by mystical and transcendent experiences.[32]

Dr. Pert found that our emotions are carried around the body by peptide ligands that change cells' chemical properties by binding to the receptor sites located on the cells. Because they also carry an electrical charge, they change the cells' electrical frequency. According to Pert, we constantly transmit and receive electrical signals in the form of vibrations. Our experience of feelings is the "vibrational dance" that occurs as peptides bind to their receptors; the brain interprets different vibrations as different feelings.

Certain cells become "addicted" to certain ligands. If we have been angry a long time, cellular receptors learn to accept only the "anger vibrations" and reject those that might cause happiness. Many holistic practitioners believe that the cells can actually begin to reject healthy nutrients or ligands, preferring instead the negative ones. This can lead to mood disorders, along with illness.[33]

THE ELECTROMAGNETIC PROPERTIES OF THE PINEAL AND PITUITARY GLANDS

It is well known that the body emits light, sound, heat, and electromagnetic fields, and that, like all other matter, it has a gravitational field. Studies of two important endocrine glands have demonstrated that the body is a source of electromagnetism, producing effects ranging from "tuning in" to the environment to "tuning in" to the paranormal. They also reveal the surprising importance of magnetism to the body.

MEASURING THE MAGNETIC BODY

The magnetic properties of the body are a relatively new discovery. During the late 1960s, the magnetic fields emitted by the heart were measured in numerous labs. Around this time, physicist David Cohen, using his own research and drawing from other research dating as far back as 1929, was able to measure the magnetic fields produced by electrical activities of the brain for the first time with the aid of an extremely sensitive magnetism detector known as superconducting quantum interference device (SQUID).[34]

By the early 1970s, researchers were starting to record the magnetic fields arising from other organs in the body as a result of their electrical activity. Today, the magnetoencephalogram (MEG) is considered a more accurate method of measuring brain electrical activity than the EEG, mostly because, unlike electrical signals, magnetic fields pass through the brain, cerebrospinal fluid, and skull undistorted. While the magnetic field around the heart is the strongest, the field around the head is also large and pulsing—and there seems to be a reason for this, as we will see in the following discussion on the pituitary and pineal glands.[35]

THE PITUITARY GLAND

The pituitary is a key endocrine gland. It stores hormones and works with the hypothalamus to fire off a host of physical actions. And it contains magnetite.

Scientists have known that magnetite, a magnetically sensitive compound of iron and oxygen, exists in animals ranging from bacteria to mammals. It apparently assists migrating birds in "finding north" and helps homing pigeons to find their way home.[36]

BIOFEEDBACK

BIOFEEDBACK USES INSTRUMENTS to provide feedback so a patient can learn how to monitor his or her own bodily functions. The most typical measurements include hand temperatures, sweat gland activity, breathing rates, heart rates, and brain-wave patterns.

You may already be familiar with the electroencephalogram (EEG), which measures brain waves. There are other biofeedback devices: the electromyograph (EMG) measures muscular tension; the electrocardiograph (EGF) records heart functions; and galvanic skin response (GSR) measures skin temperature. Typically, one process at a time is monitored, with feedback given immediately by tones, lights, digits, or needles moving on graphs.[37]

The principles behind biofeedback lie in understanding how the brain runs the body.[38] The cerebrum controls most conscious movements. The brain stem and spinal cord govern the less conscious relays of neurological input and output functions, like breathing. Many biofeedback techniques seek to increase conscious control over these regions, expanding the mind's ability to influence the body's consciousness and biochemistry. Biofeedback can thus be used to train the brain toward more relaxed or positive states, but it is also used for pain reduction, anxiety control, sleep disorders, and even critical illnesses.

Often, subjects are taught relaxation exercises with breathing and visualization. They then observe the changes in feedback, noting reduction in blood pressure or the achievement of an alpha-level consciousness. Over time, subjects no longer require instruments to achieve results. Biofeedback has been shown to help induce mystical states of awareness, similar to those found in Sufism, Zen, yoga, and other spiritual disciplines. It is also positively associated with altered states: an increase in alpha brain waves is matched by an increase in right-brain activities such as creativity and intuition, which encourages the development of psychic awareness, or extrasensory perception (ESP).[39]

Other forms of specialized biofeedback, such as thermal biofeedback, help with specific health problems such as peripheral arterial disease and chronic foot ulcers associated with diabetes. A public health researcher at the University of Minnesota has successfully used thermal biofeedback to relieve pain and improve healing, as reported in a recent clinical trial that shows patients with chronic foot ulcers healed completely within three months. This biofeedback method includes visualization techniques and guided breathing.[40]

In the 1990s, using high-resolution transmission electron microscopy, scientists discovered magnetite crystals in humans, within a cluster of nerves in front of the pituitary gland, behind the ethmoid sinus, a perforated bone in the skull forming parts of the nasal cavity and eye socket.

This cluster of magnetite crystals helps to explain the discovery of a complex magnetic field around the head, detected by the SQUID machine mentioned earlier. This may explain our sensitivity to magnetic fields, whether they emanate from the earth, skies, or other people.

THE PINEAL GLAND

The pineal gland serves as an electromagnetic sensor to regulate all kinds of states, from mood to ESP. It is the producer of melatonin, which regulates sleep.[41]

Researchers Iris Haimov and Peretz Lavie found that individuals who have a dysfunctional pineal gland have a difficult time sensing and relaying information through the electromagnetic fields. They then experience great difficulty falling asleep, as well as other health problems associated with a disturbed daily cycle.[42]

The pineal gland is associated with the seventh chakra, or plane of consciousness, representing an opening to divine energies. It is also the endocrine gland associated with the rising of the kundalini—a spiritualization process involved in chakra work. The pineal gland's role in enlightenment is tied to biochemical and electromagnetic interactions.[43]

FIGURE 2.4

PITUITARY GLAND

The pituitary gland generates a magnetic field due to magnetite crystals located near it.

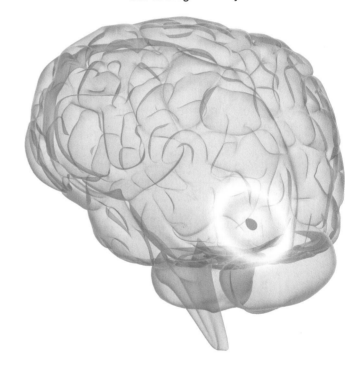

Biochemically, the pineal gland orchestrates an important "pecking order" of steps involving synthesis from the amino acid tryptophan interacting with various substances—and in some stages, the presence of light. Simplified, the sequence of production is tryptophan, serotonin, melatonin, pinoline, 5-methoxy-dimethyltryptamine (5-MeO-DMT), and dimethyltryptamine (DMT).[44]

Tryptophan is an essential amino acid found in most protein-based foods or dietary proteins. Melatonin, which is made at night, regulates circadian rhythm;

serotonin, made during the day, is a neurotransmitter that regulates sleep, body temperature, appetite, and emotions; pinoline is a neurochemical implicated in consciousness; 5-MeO-DMT, a psychedelic tryptamine, is found in certain toad venom, plants, seeds, and bark resin; and DMT is a naturally occurring tryptamine and neurotransmitter.

A portion of the scientific and spiritual community has linked these chemicals with mystical and psychic experiences. For example, Serena M. Roney-Dougal, PhD, of the Psi Research Centre in Glastonbury, England, has presented a large body of neurochemical and anthropological evidence suggesting that the pineal gland's production of pinoline may enhance a psychic-conducive state of consciousness.[45]

Pinoline is thought to act on serotonin to trigger dreaming. It also has hallucinogenic properties, and its chemical structure is similar to chemicals found in a psychotropic plant in the Amazon.[46] Studies suggest that the dream state is one in which we are most likely to have psychic experiences. Pinoline is believed to be the neurochemical that triggers this state of consciousness.[47]

DMT has also been called the "spirit molecule" because of its possible role in producing psychedelic states through the pineal gland. Research by Dr. Rick Strassman, among others, is suggesting that under specific conditions—such as near-death experiences, the use of shamanic psychedelics, and certain meditative states—the pineal gland might produce DMT, which then lifts us to different states of consciousness.[48] These and other studies of the pineal gland suggest that it truly might be the "spirit gland" it is considered to be in various mystical schools.

8

THE SKIN

The skin is the body's largest organ. In an adult, it covers approximately two square meters. It provides a protective waterproof layer, and as a sensory organ it regulates temperature. The skin absorbs and releases heat, keeping the body's temperature within operable limits.

Skin is one component of the external system that also includes hair and hair follicles, sebaceous and sweat glands, and the nails. It functions as part of the body's excretory system, removing water and small amounts of urea and salts through sweat. It also helps maintain the circulatory and nervous systems.

The skin is made up of two different layers of tissue: the dermis and the epidermis. The epidermis is the outer layer that is composed primarily of cells called *keratinocytes*, cells that are constantly dying, being shed, and then replaced by cells from layers beneath. New cells take between two and four weeks to form and reach the surface of the skin. Dead skin is transformed into a material called *keratin*, which is sloughed off as tiny, barely visible scales.

Underneath the epidermis is the dermis, a network of collagen and elastin tissue fibers interwoven with blood and lymph vessels, sweat and sebaceous glands, and hair follicles. Sweat glands are controlled by the nervous system and are stimulated to secrete, either as a result of emotion or the body's need to lose heat. Sebaceous glands lubricate the hair shaft and are controlled by sex hormones.

Both the epidermis and dermis layers contain nerve endings that adapt to detect pain, cold, pressure, and itching, which evoke protective reflexes or transmit pleasurable sensations like warmth and touch. Below the dermis is a variable layer of fat-storage cells that insulate the body against temperature extremes, as well as connective tissue and a small number of blood vessels.

Hair and nails are specialized forms of keratin. Finger- and toenails are produced by living skin cells, though the nail itself is dead and will not hurt or bleed if damaged. Cells in the hair follicles, which also contain a sebaceous gland, form hair and divide rapidly.

SKIN COLOR

Skin color derives from a dark biological pigment called melanin, also found in the hair and in the iris of the eye. The function of melanin is to protect the skin from harmful rays of the sun. All races have the same number of pigment cells— melanocytes—but genetic differences control the amount incorporated into the epidermal cells. The amount of melanin produced by these cells varies greatly. For example, in dark-skinned races, the melanocytes are larger and produce more pigment. Albinism is due to an absence of pigment-forming enzyme.

9

THE CIRCULATORY SYSTEM

Primarily consisting of the heart and blood vessels, this system distributes blood through a system of arteries, veins, and capillaries, among other components, to form a complete circuit.

Two forms of circulation work hand in hand in the body:

Systemic circulation: Carries nutrient-rich, oxygenated blood through-out the body. Oxygen and nutrients are deposited in body tissues. Waste products and gases are transferred to the blood. On completion of the circuit of the body, the blood returns to the heart with depleted oxygen levels and laden with carbon dioxide, a waste product of cell function.

Pulmonary circulation: Moves oxygen-depleted blood from the heart to the lungs, where gas exchange takes place. The blood is enriched with oxygen and returned to the heart to enter the systemic circulation again.

THE HEART

The heart pumps blood, supporting circulation. It starts the process by pumping blood into arteries via the aorta, the central artery. Blood is circulated through organs and tissues, delivering food and oxygen. The blood then returns to the heart through the veins, having finished its deliveries.

On its second circuit, the heart pumps the blood to the lungs, which re-place oxygen and remove waste. The blood is then returned to the heart with its oxygen refreshed.

Four heart chambers coordinate these functions, maintaining blood flow at a steady rate and optimizing blood oxygen levels. Each carries out a specific task aided by the valves of the heart, which control the flow of blood through the heart. These are the left and right atria, two thin-walled chambers of the heart that collect blood as it comes into the heart, and the left and right ventricles, two lower chambers of the heart that pump blood out of the heart to the lungs and other parts of the body.

THE HEART AS AN ELECTROMAGNETIC ORGAN

THE HEART IS the physical center of the circulatory system, managing over 75 trillion cells. It is also the electromagnetic center of the body, emanating thousands of times more electricity and magnetism than does the brain. Even more impressively, it is an organ of communication that can potentially manage the body's intuitive processes.

As we saw in Part I, the heart's electromagnetic field (EMF) is five thousand times stronger than that of the brain. Its electrical field is sixty times greater than that of the brain.[49] Not only is its electromagnetic capacity greater than that of the brain, but it is organically capable of performing certain brain-like functions. In fact, between 60 and 65 percent of its cells are neural, identical to those present in the brain. Energy—information that vibrates—flows constantly between the heart and the brain, assisting with emotional processing, sensory experience, memory and derivation of meaning from events, and reasoning.[50] In addition, the heart is one of the body's major endocrine glands, producing at least five major hormones, which impact the physiological functions of the brain and body.[51]

The heart has long been known as the center of the body, as well as the home of the soul. Under the correct conditions, such as when a person consciously "centers" or focuses in the heart, the heart begins to run the brain. (Most typically, the brain runs the body.) Entrainment or the management of the body through the heart rather than brain leads to higher functioning mental and emotional states, as well as a healthier body.[52] It also enables a person to screen the outer environment for "good messages" instead of "negative messages," enabling a more positive relationship with the external world.[53]

This "heart healing power" is possible because of the energetic nature of the body. All energy contains information and all cells are energetic. The closer a group of cells, the more likely they are to oscillate or vibrate in a coordinated rhythm, thereby producing a more powerful and intense signal. Heart cells are tightly organized, thus generating an extremely strong, shared signal, which is both electrical and magnetic. The heart's internal signal is stronger than any produced by other parts of the body because it is more intense. Thus can the heart dynamically move into the lead position in the body, its rhythms able to modulate or "take over" those of the other organs. What about its relationship with the external world? We are constantly receiving information—sometimes called "background noise"—from outside of ourselves. Not only can the heart override the

HOW DOES THE HEART BEAT?

With each heartbeat, the two atria contract and fill the ventricles with blood. Then the ventricles contract. This ordered series of contractions depends upon a complex electrical timing system.

The heartbeat is initiated by a tiny group of cells called the sinoatrial node, located in the right atrial muscle. The sinoatrial node sends an electrical signal around the heart just before every beat. Impulses pass from the sinoatrial node

incoming flow of communiqués, but it can also sort and filter information from the world outside of the body—even intuitive information.

As explained by researcher Stephen Harrod Buhner in his book *The Secret Teachings of Plants*, highly synchronized cells, such as those compactly organized in the heart, are able to use background noise to increase the amplitude of an incoming signal—if they are interested in perceiving it.[54] The heart will "hear" what it is programmed to "hear." If love resides in the heart, it will attune to love. If fear, greed, or envy resides within, the heart will access negativity.

Most people believe that the brain initiates the first response to incoming events and then orders our reactions. Analysis reveals, however, that incoming information first impacts the heart, and through the heart, the brain and then rest of the body.[55] Our hearts are so strong that they can actually formulate the most well known symbol of love: light. Research has shown that under certain conditions, a meditator can actually generate visible light from the heart. The meditation technique must be heart-centered, not transcendent. When this occurred during studies at the University of Kassel in Germany in 1997, the heart emanated a sustained light of one hundred thousand photons per second, whereas the background had a count of only twenty photons per

second. The meditations drew upon energetic understandings from several cultures, including the Hindu practice of kundalini.[56]

It has been said that the heart is the center of the body, but it might also be the core of a subtle universe—or perhaps a "subtle sun" generated by every individual.

FIGURE 2.5

THE ELECTROMAGNETIC
FIELD OF THE HEART

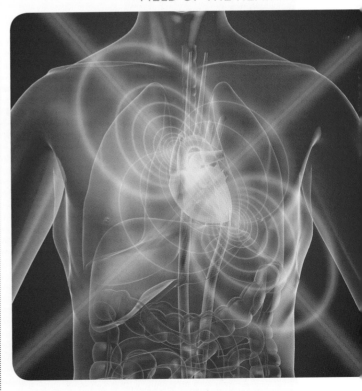

to both atria and make them contract. Another node, the atrioventricular, at the junction of the atria and ventricles, delays the impulse to contract. After the atria contract, an impulse is passed down through a specialized cardiac muscle called the *bundle of His* (named for Swiss cardiologist Wilhelm His), causing the ventricles to contract.

When the body is at rest, this cyclic routine occurs approximately seventy times per minute, and at a higher rate during stress or physical exertion. An electrocardiogram (EKG) machine can record these impulses.

THE BLOOD

Blood is carried in a network of vessels throughout the body. It leaves the heart for systemic circulation, is pumped through the aorta, and travels through the arterial system to supply the cells of body tissues and organs with oxygen and nutrients. Nutrient transfer takes place in tiny capillaries that connect the arteries and veins. Blood then travels through the veins to return to the heart.

Red blood cells play a big role in circulation as transporters, carrying oxygen from the lungs to the tissues through a protein called *hemoglobin*. These cells pick up carbon dioxide and take it back to the lungs, where it is eliminated with the breath.

White blood cells fight disease. There are several classifications of white blood cells, each of which play different roles. Plasma, along with other cells, clots wounds.

The life span of a red blood cell is around 120 days, while most white blood cells have a maximum life span of a few days.

10

THE RESPIRATORY SYSTEM

Respiration is the means of acquiring the necessary oxygen for cell and tissue maintenance, while disposing of unwanted carbon dioxide. A chief function of respiration is oxygen metabolism. The body's cells use oxygen much like a car burns fuel mixed with oxygen. In this case, the fuel is glucose (sugar). The waste products are primarily carbon dioxide and water. Oxygen is introduced into the body when we inhale and its by-products are released when we exhale.

Respiration involves the lungs and diaphragm and the upper respiratory tract: nose, mouth, larynx, pharynx, and trachea. Breathing involves the muscles between the ribs (the intercostal muscles) and the diaphragm, a dome of muscle that divides the chest and abdomen. When we breathe, air is inhaled through the nose, then moves down the trachea, and passes into the lungs. Oxygen and other substances pass from the air to the blood, and carbon dioxide passes from the blood to the air. The exchange of these gases occurs through the alveoli, tiny air sacs located at the end of bronchial tubes in the lungs. Here the blood in capillaries meets the air, picks up oxygen, and disposes of carbon dioxide.

Breathing can be consciously controlled, but is also a reflex movement. Our rate of breathing is controlled by the medulla oblongata, the respiratory center of the brain, and regulated according to the levels of carbon dioxide in the blood.

11

THE ENDOCRINE SYSTEM

Similar to the nervous system, the endocrine system is an information signal system. While the nervous system uses nerves to conduct information, the endocrine system mainly uses blood vessels as information channels. Endocrine literally means *direct secretion* into the bloodstream.

The endocrine system is an integrated system of small organs that control hormone production. It is responsible for slow, or long-term, changes in the body such as growth, and many of the gradual changes experienced during puberty or male and female menopause.

Endocrine glands are located throughout the body. They release hormones—specific chemical messengers, or mediators—into the bloodstream. These regulate growth, development, metabolism, and tissue function, as well as playing a role in mood.

Endrocine glands include the pituitary, pineal, thymus, thyroid, parathyroid, adrenals, pancreatic islets, ovaries, and testes. The placenta, which develops during pregnancy, also has an endocrine function. Typically, endocrine glands are ductless glands that secrete hormones directly into local blood vessels, which then circulate within the body via the bloodstream. These hormones travel to distant organs to regulate the target organ's function.

Hormones tend to be concerned with controlling or influencing the chemistry of the target cells. For instance, they determine the rate of food metabolism and the release of energy, as well as whether cells should produce milk, hair, or some other product of the body's metabolic processes.

Hormones made by the major endocrine glands, such as insulin and the sex hormones, are known as general hormones. The body makes many other hormones that act close to their point of production. For example, acetylcholine is made every time a nerve passes a message to a muscle cell, telling it to contract.

Diseases of the endocrine system include obesity, diabetes, mood problems, and sleep disorders. Endocrine diseases are often characterized by dysregulated hormone release (pituitary adenoma), inappropriate response to signaling (hypothyroidism), and lack of or destruction of a gland (type 1 diabetes).

ENDOCRINE GLANDS AND METABOLISM[57]

Metabolism is a series of chemical interactions that provide energy and nutrients to the cells and tissues. It is closely related to the endocrine system.

For example, the thyroid produces a hormone that directly regulates metabolism. Made of thyroxine (T4, or tetraiodothyronine) and triiodothyronine (T3), the thyroid hormone determines the body's general metabolic rate and energy production. Problems can make the metabolism too high, causing hyperthyroidism, or too low, resulting in hypothyroidism. The thyroid also produces calcitonin, which reduces and stabilizes the calcium content in the blood.

The pituitary gland also affects metabolism. Located at the base of the brain, this pea-sized gland produces its own hormones and influences the hormonal production of other glands. Together, the pituitary and the hypothalamus control many aspects of metabolism, working in harmony to provide the hormones required for the body's efficient operation.

The hormones leptin and ghrelin also help regulate metabolism in the body. Leptin, discovered in 1994, is actually produced by fat, essentially making fat an endocrine organ. Leptin tells the brain when to eat. While insulin instructs cells about burning or using fat or sugar, leptin actually controls energy storage and cell utilization. Leptin tells the brain what to do, not vice versa.

Ghrelin stimulates the appetite, increasing it prior to eating and decreasing it afterward. It is found in smaller amounts in the pituitary, hypothalamus, kidney, and placenta. It also encourages the secretion of growth hormones from the anterior pituitary gland.

12

THE DIGESTIVE SYSTEM

The body's digestive process breaks food into substances that can be absorbed and used for energy, growth, and repair. The digestive system,[58] sometimes called the *gastrointestinal system*, consists of the mouth, throat, esophagus, stomach, small intestine, large intestine, rectum, and anus. It is responsible for receiving food, breaking it into usable components (of fats, sugars, and proteins), absorbing the nutrients into the bloodstream, and eliminating the indigestible parts of food from the body as waste. Its organs also produce clotting factors and hormones unrelated to digestion, removing toxic substances from the blood and metabolizing drugs.

The abdominal cavity holds the main digestive organs. Its borders are the abdominal wall in front, the spinal column in back, the diaphragm above, and the pelvic organs below. Organs outside of the digestive tract—the pancreas, the liver, and the gallbladder—also play a critical role in digestion.

DIGESTION AND THE BRAIN[59]

The brain and the digestive system work together. Scientists have long known that the brain stimulates the digestive organs through parasympathetic activities such as sight, smell, and taste, which stimulate hunger. Psychological factors also impact hunger and digestion, influencing the movements of the intestine, secretion of digestive enzymes, and other digestive functions. Intense sadness or anger, for example, will set off a chain reaction that stimulates or reduces hunger, perhaps causing weight and digestive problems, and sometimes intestinal illnesses.

On the other hand, the digestive system also influences the brain. For example, long-standing or recurring diseases such as irritable bowel syndrome (IBS), ulcerative colitis, and other painful diseases affect emotions, behaviors, and daily functioning. This two-way association has been called the brain-gut axis.

Because of rich connections to the autonomic nervous system, the digestive organs are common sites of psychosomatic illnesses. Many IBS sufferers also have some type of psychiatric disorder; their IBS becomes more severe under stress. Crohn's disease has also been linked to emotional distress. Some panic attack sufferers also report bowel disorders, with intestinal triggers starting in the sympathetic nervous system. Other illnesses, too, such as cancer, adult-onset (type 2) diabetes, and rheumatoid arthritis are being studied for psychosomatic relationships.

Experts such as Michael Gershon, MD, propose that the stomach actually contains a second brain, rich with neurotransmitters of its own, which triggers IBS. Gershon says IBS is an example of the gut working in isolation, though he recognizes the brain-gut axis such as when "butterflies in the stomach" occur as a result of the brain sending a message of anxiety to the gut, which sends messages back to the brain that it's unhappy.[60]

13

THE EXCRETORY SYSTEM

The main role of the excretory system[61] is to filter out cellular wastes, toxins, and excess water or nutrients from the circulatory system. The body has many ways of ridding itself of waste products, products that must be removed so the body is not poisoned. These processes include the following systems and organs.

URINARY SYSTEM

The kidneys are the key part of the urinary system, the body's mechanism for elimination of waste extracted from the blood. They filter the blood, maintain the correct balance of water and electrolytes, and eliminate waste in the form of urine. Urine is sent from collecting ducts in the kidneys and ultimately moves into a tube called the urethra, which leads to the exterior of the body.

THE LIVER

The liver is multifunctional. Its main job is to process nutrient-rich blood from the gastrointestinal tract and adjust chemical levels for optimal metabolic function. The largest organ in the body, it is divided into two lobes and is supplied by the hepatic artery and portal vein.

To aid in digestion and excretion, the liver produces bile, a strong alkaline substance that breaks down fats. Bile is released through bile ducts in the liver, stored in the gallbladder, and secreted in the small intestine. Bile not only breaks down food to remove solid wastes, but also collects water from waste so it can be reused.

THE LARGE INTESTINE

The large intestine consists of the colon and the rectum. While the small intestine is primarily concerned with absorbing nutrients in the digestive process, the large intestine reabsorbs water and moves waste material toward the anus. The colon also removes salt and water from the material sent from the small intestine, releasing the rest as waste.

THE SKIN AND LUNGS

The skin and the lungs are considered excretory organs. The skin contains sweat glands that eliminate water, salts, and the urea (kidney waste) found in sweat. The lungs eliminate carbon dioxide and water.

14

THE REPRODUCTIVE SYSTEM

Sexual activity is a basic drive, one that humans share with all other animals. In humans, the reproductive organs and glands begin to develop and mature during puberty. They are involved in the creation of the next generation and, during fetal development, are linked with the urinary system.

Reproductive organs are divided into two parts: the external and internal genitals and the gonads. Male gonads are the testes and female gonads are the ovaries. During puberty the gonads begin to grow and become active under the influence of gonadotropic hormones produced in the pituitary gland. These hormones stimulate the production of the sex hormones: testosterone in males and estrogen and progesterone in females.[62]

THE MALE REPRODUCTIVE SYSTEM

The male contributes to reproduction by producing sperm. The sperm then fertilize the egg in the female body and the fertilized egg (zygote) gradually develops into a fetus.

Much of male reproductive anatomy is external. The male reproductive organs include the testicles, or testes, the epididymis (the housing area for sperm), the prostate gland, and the penis. The penis is the male urinary and reproductive organ, containing three cylinders of sponge-like vascular tissue that allow erection.

When the male is sexually aroused, the penis becomes erect and ready for intercourse. Erection is achieved when the blood sinuses within the erectile tissue of the penis become filled with blood.

During ejaculation, sperm leaves the penis in a fluid called *seminal fluid*, which is produced by three kinds of glands: the seminal vesicles, the prostate gland, and bulbourethral glands, also known as Cowper's glands. Each component of seminal fluid has a particular function. Sperm are more viable in a basic solution, so seminal fluid has a slightly alkaline pH. Seminal fluid also acts as an energy source for the sperm and contains chemicals that cause the uterus to contract.

The testes produce sperm and testosterone. They lie outside the abdominal cavity of the male within the scrotum sac. The testes begin development in the abdominal cavity but descend into the scrotal sacs during the last two months of fetal development. This is required for the production of sperm because internal body temperatures are too high to produce viable sperm.

SPERM

A mature sperm, or spermatozoa, contains twenty-three chromosomes that carry the genetic blueprint of the father and determine the paternally inherited characteristics of the child. The sperm also carries the genetic message that determines the sex of the child. A normal human male usually produces several hundred million sperm per day. Sperm are continually produced throughout a male's reproductive life, though production decreases with age.

THE FEMALE REPRODUCTIVE SYSTEM

Unlike the male, the human female has a reproductive system located almost entirely inside the pelvis. A finely tuned timing mechanism controls the major physical processes of female reproduction, through the stages of menstruation, conception, and pregnancy.

The vulva is the external part of the female reproductive organs. It covers the opening to the vagina or birth canal. The vulva also includes the labia, clitoris, and urethra. In addition to the vagina, the female reproductive organs are the ovaries, the fallopian (uterine) tubes, and the uterus.

During sexual arousal, there is slight engorgement of the breasts and congestion of the clitoris and labia, with increased vaginal secretions from the cervical canal and Bartholin's glands, small glands located on each side of the opening of the vagina that secrete mucus to provide lubrication. Vaginal secretions also increase during ovulation.

The ovaries produce ova (eggs) for fertilization. The uterus, or womb, nurtures the fertilized ovum, protecting it until pregnancy ends. The uterus is shaped like an upside-down pear, with a thick lining and muscular walls, and contains some of the strongest muscles in the female body. These muscles are able to expand and contract to accommodate a growing fetus and push the baby out during labor. When a woman is not pregnant, the uterus is only about seven and a half centimeters (three inches) long and five centimeters (two inches) wide.

The vagina is attached to the uterus through the cervix, while the uterus attaches to the ovaries via the fallopian tubes. The ovaries contain a set number of cells that lie dormant until puberty. At the onset of puberty, the ovaries are activated; some twenty ova enlarge and develop at the beginning of each menstrual cycle. At certain intervals, the ovaries release ova, which pass through the fallopian tube into the uterus. If sperm penetrates the uterus at this time, it merges with the egg to fertilize it. The nucleus of the ovum contains twenty-three chromosomes and, when joined with mature sperm, forms a cell of forty-six chromosomes to produce an embryo. A woman is fertile for about thirty-six hours in every menstrual cycle, around day fourteen of a hypothetical twenty-eight day menstrual cycle. Approximately every month, a process of oogenesis matures an ovum, which moves down the fallopian tube in anticipation of fertilization. If not fertilized, the egg is flushed out of the system through menstruation.

Fertilization usually occurs in the oviducts, but can happen in the uterus itself. The zygote, a fertilized egg, implants in the wall of the uterus, where it begins the process of forming an embryo, which becomes a fetus when further developed. When the fetus is able to survive outside the womb, the cervix dilates and the uterus contracts, propelling the fetus through the birth canal, or the vagina.

15

METABOLISM

Metabolism[63] is a process of energy exchange and production and is key to the body's survival. There are two types:

Anabolism: The build-up phase in which complex molecules and substances are created from simple molecules. Anabolism uses energy to construct components of cells such as proteins and nucleic acids.

Catabolism: The process of creating energy by breaking down complex molecules into simpler structures to help the body's cells work efficiently and correctly. Catabolism yields energy, such as the contraction of muscles that produces carbon dioxide and lactic acid, among other products, as well as the loss of heat.

THE THYROID AND METABOLISM

The thyroid gland secretes thyroid hormones, which control the speed of the body's chemical functions. It regulates basal metabolic rate (BMR), the rate of energy consumption recorded in relation to factors such as height, weight, age, and diet. BMR is measured in calories burned at rest. Calories are the energy expended by the body to maintain normal bodily functions. The BMR makes up about 60 to 70 percent of the calories we burn or expend and includes the beating of the heart, respiration, and maintenance of body temperature.

THE ROLE OF ATP, AN ELECTRON TRANSPORT CHAIN[64]

Adenosine triphosphate (ATP) is a multifunctional chemical compound that is vital to energizing the cells, which are powered by energy that it releases. Its role in metabolism is to transport chemical energy. The energy produced in the breakdown process (catabolism) is stored in ATP, ready for release when needed. The primary source of energy for constructing ATP is food. Once food is broken down into its various nutrients, energy sources can be used immediately to build new tissues or store energy for later use.

In the body, ATP is primarily produced in mitochondria, tiny cytoplasmic structures within cells. Mitochondria produce an electrical-chemical gradient, much as does a battery, by accumulating hydrogen ions in the space between their inner and outer membranes. The resulting energy comes from the estimated ten thousand enzyme chains in the membranous sacs on the mitochondrial walls. This electron transport chain produces most of our life energy.

ATP contains adenosine and a tail consisting of three phosphates. Energy is usually freed from the ATP molecule to do work in the cell by a reaction that removes one of the phosphate-oxygen groups, leaving adenosine diphosphate (ADP). When the ATP converts to ADP, the ATP is exhausted. Then the ADP is immediately recycled in the mitochondria, where it is recharged and comes out again as ATP.

16

THE IMMUNE SYSTEM

The immune system is the body's defense against illness and injury. Much of it is supported by the lymph-vascular system, a system of vessels that carry interstitial fluid around the body. This network works closely with the blood, particularly with white blood cells known as lymphocytes, essential to the body's defense against disease.

THE LYMPHATIC SYSTEM

The lymphatic system is in charge of cleansing and purifying the body's fluids. It is composed of several parts, including the lymph vessels, nodes, and organs, as well as the lymph itself, the fluid inside the lymphatic system.

Lymph vessels collect excess fluid, foreign particles, and other materials from the body's tissues and cells, filter them, and return the cleansed fluid to the bloodstream. These vessels are found in all parts of the body except the central nervous system, bone, cartilage, and teeth.

Lymph capillaries, the smallest vessels, run alongside the body's arteries and veins. The walls of these lymph capillaries are very thin and permeable, so large molecules and particles, including bacteria, enter the lymph rather than the blood capillaries. Some lymph vessels also contain an involuntary muscle that contracts in one direction, driving lymph forward.

Lymph nodes or glands lie along various points on the lymph pathways around the major arteries and close to the surface of the skin in the groin, armpits, and neck. A lymph node acts as a clearinghouse, filtering the lymph and destroying the foreign particles within it. As the lymph leaves a node, it also picks up lymphocytes and antibodies, protein substances that inactivate foreign particles.

The lymphatic system includes highly specialized lymphoid organs and tissues, including the thymus, spleen, and tonsils. The thymus serves as both a lymphatic organ and an endocrine gland, producing special lymphocytes. It secretes thymosin, which encourages the development of T lymphocytes. The spleen, with the highest concentration of lymphatic tissue in the body, filters blood and produces and stores lymphocytes. Tonsils are also specialized lymphatic tissues. They offer the first line of defense against bacteria invading the respiratory and digestive systems via the mouth and nose.

The composition of lymph depends on the location of the lymph vessel. For example, vessels draining the limbs contain protein, while lymph in the intestines is full of milky fat, called *chyle*, which has been absorbed from the intestines during digestion. Ultimately, lymph vessels drain into special veins near the heart via the right lymphatic duct and the thoracic duct, thus returning lymph into the bloodstream.

THE IMMUNE RESPONSE

The immune response is the body's reaction to invading organisms such as bacteria, viruses, fungi, and other types of pathogens. The body has several ways to fight foreign substances, depending on the nature and location of the invader. The two main types of response involve either the humoral immune system or the cell-mediated immune system.

Humoral response takes place in the body fluids (humors). Scavenging white blood cells (macrophages) engulf virus particles entering through cells at the surface of the skin. These macrophages break down the virus by distributing antigens to the circulating T lymphocytes. The attack has begun. Now antibodies targeted to the particular virus—and produced by plasma B cells—capture virus particles. Memory B cells are programmed to remember the virus in the event of future attack. Macrophages continue to break down the virus, protecting the body from further infection.

In the cell-mediated immune response, T cells or T lymphocytes, produced by the thymus, defend through a delayed action. The virus is first engulfed by circulated mast cells, which then present antigens to T cells. Various T cells,

FIGURE 2.6

"KILLER" CELLS ATTACKING A VIRUS

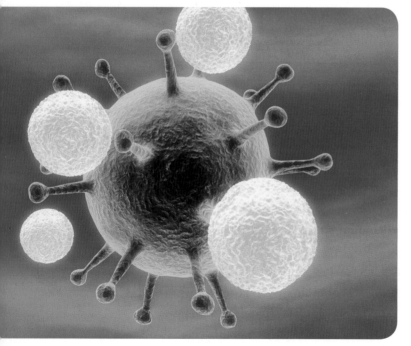

produced by the mast cells, now play their own roles. Memory T cells encode memory of the invading antigen for future attacks. Killer T cells destroy the antigen, and helper T cells recruit B and T cells to the site of the attack.

17

THE SENSES

There are five sense organs in the body. They are the ear, nose, eyes, skin, and tongue, which control hearing, smell, vision, touch, and taste respectively. Our senses are actually messages sent from these organs to the brain via the cranial nerves.

HEARING

The ear provides our sense of hearing and balance (equilibrium). It consists of three parts: the outer ear (receiver), middle ear (amplifier), and inner ear (transmitter). The outer ear gathers sound like a radar scanner. The middle ear is constructed of a gear-like assembly of bones that amplifies the sounds it receives. It then sends mechanical vibrations into the inner ear, which converts these vibrations into electrical impulses.

The organ of Corti lies inside the cochlea, a spiral structure in the inner ear, and allows us to hear even faint sounds. It is composed of rows of cells and hairs that are stimulated by movement of cochlear fluid. The organ of Corti sends impulses along the cochlear branch of the vestibulocochlear nerve, which transmits the signals to the auditory cortex in the brain's temporal lobe.

The ear also serves as our organ of balance. Its tiny vestibular organs monitor balance and alert the brain to changes in body position.

We hear sound waves, which are produced by vibrations of air molecules. The size and energy of these waves determine loudness, which is measured in decibels (dB). Total silence is 0 dB. Intensity is directly related to amplitude. One way to picture the amplitude of a wave is by seeing it as a wave that goes up and down through a baseline. This line is an "undisturbed space." The greater the distance between the line and the crest of the wave, the higher the intensity, the higher the decibels, and the more powerful the sound (although technically, amplitude is measured by its own formula, one that measures the amount of force over an area). Frequency refers to how many waves are made (or vibrate) per second. The more vibrations, the higher the pitch or tone of sound waves, expressed in terms of cycles per second, or hertz (Hz).

SMELL

Smell is probably the oldest and least understood of our five senses. As we have evolved, smell has retained its connection with parts of the emotional brain; odor has been intimately linked with emotion. Our sense of smell provides valuable information about the outside world, including danger signals. There is also a close connection between taste and smell, smell largely determining what we taste.

The sensory receptors for smell are found in the roof of the nasal cavity, just beneath the frontal lobes of the brain. This region is tightly packed with millions of small olfactory cells. Each has about a dozen cilia, or fine hairs, which project into a layer of mucus. Mucus keeps the cilia moist and traps odorous substances. The cilia bear chemoreceptors, specialized cells that detect the different chemicals causing odors and relay that information to the nervous system.

Varying types of chemoreceptors trigger the olfactory cells. Chemical substances dissolve in the mucous fluids, stick to the cilia, and cause the cells to fire electrical signals to the brain. The information is gathered, processed, and passed through a complicated circuitry of nerve endings in the cerebral cortex. The message is now identified and the smell becomes conscious.

VISION

The eye is our organ of sight. Each eye receives light rays reflected from an object, which are transferred to the retina in the back of the eye. The retina is the inner layer of the eye that receives images projected through the cornea and lens. Images are then converted into neural signals by the rod and cone cells of the retina. Millions of these cells make up the retinal surface, the rod cells being more sensitive to light and the cone cells more sensitive to color determination.

The optic nerve of each eye—a bundle of nerve fibers carrying tiny electrical impulses down tiny cables—is responsible for conducting neural signals from retinal cells to the brain's visual cortex for interpretation. This area of the brain receives and processes visual information, tracking the changing shapes and movements of incoming data. The parietal and temporal lobes of the brain enable us to recognize an image and make sense of it.

TASTE

The tongue is our organ of taste, or more formally, gustation. Our sense of taste is the crudest of our five senses, limited in range and versatility. Gustation is aided by our sense of smell. Like smell, taste is triggered by the chemical content of substances in food and drink and through contact with our taste buds as chemoreceptors.

The tongue is covered by thick epithelium containing about nine thousand papillae—taste buds—which are reformed and replaced within forty-eight hours when damaged, but become fewer with age. Taste buds are also found on the palate and throat. When food or drink is combined with saliva, the taste buds receive information through openings called *taste pores*. This triggers nerve activity in each taste bud, with the nerves sending impulses to the brain for interpretation.

Certain taste buds are receptive to specific flavors. For example, the front of the tongue is more sensitive to sweet. Taste buds on the throat and palate are more receptive to sour and bitter. While classical taste sensations are sweet, salty, sour, and bitter, more recently, psychophysicists and neuroscientists have suggested other taste categories: umami (savoriness, meaty) and fatty acid taste.[65]

TOUCH

This is also called the *tactile sense*. The levels of sensitivity in the body vary, depending on the concentration of nerve endings in each area. These endings lie in the surface of the skin and create the sensations of pain, pressure, and temperature. The concentration of nerve endings results in some areas of the body being more sensitive than others. The fingertips, lips, and tongue each have a large concentration of nerve endings and are particularly sensitive. The human body is inarguably physical, therefore measurable and mechanical. Examine any two individuals and you can predict the location of the brain, liver, and nervous system in both of them. Give each a hot chili and both will describe it as spicy rather than sweet. The body is more than simply a composite of physical parts, however. It is energetic. It is an electromagnetic system containing billions of oscillating cells and organs, each of which entrain or interlink to form a unified, if complex, electromagnetic field. It is simultaneously measurable *and* immeasurable; physical *and* subtle.

As we shall explore in the next section, "Energy Fields," each of us generates our own personal fields of energy. We also interconnect with others' fields as well as those emanating from organic and inorganic sources. Some of these fields are measurable. We know they affect us, and we them. Others are currently immeasurable. We know these seeming invisible fields exist, however, because of their effects. What are the various human, natural, and "otherworldly" fields that create our bodies, our planet—and life itself? The answers lie in Part III: Energy Fields.

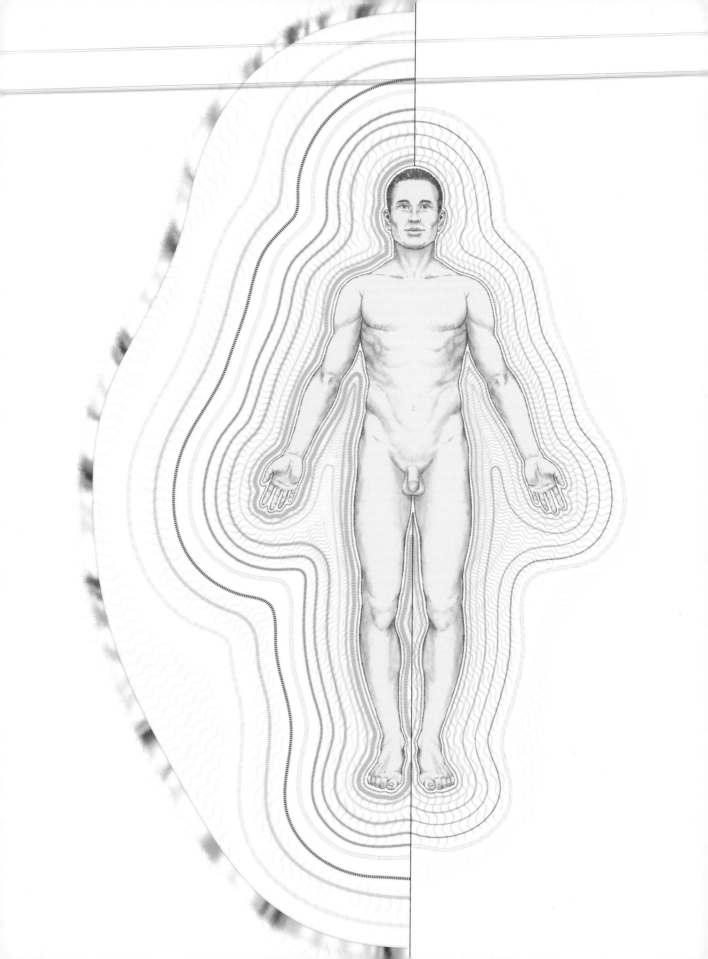

PART III
ENERGY FIELDS

Classically, a field is an area in which a force exerts an influence at every point. Like all energetic structures, a field involves a vibration of energy and can carry information. Fields operate on both physical and subtle planes, as do energy bodies and channels. But fields present mysterious phenomena. Albert Einstein believed that the universe is composed of interconnected force fields; recent physicists have pinpointed some of these fields (calling them spherical standing waves), viewing them as constructs of finite reality held within a greater infinity. Because of fields, reality is both local (or here and now) and nonlocal, which means that everything is interconnected. Therefore, some physicists suggest that all possible events exist simultaneously as wave patterns that are either becoming real—or disintegrating.[1]

In many ways, the future of healing and healing modalities that link allopathic methods and complementary practices lies in the area of fields, simply because they are found both inside and outside of the body. The ancients believed "as above, so below." A field can be deciphered, altered, molded, and analyzed outside of the body to alter the energies inside of the body—and vice versa.

Newtonian physics tells us that fields "send" information, transferring and delivering data like a mail carrier with letters. But what does the quantum physicist say? He or she will smile and suggest that in a field, information sometimes transfers more like Instant Messenger over the Internet—if not faster: your note is being read before you even send it.

The dynamics of fields is inviting a true change in medical practices, but also in our perspective of human beings. We are not isolated, closed circuits; we are interconnected, brilliant beams of energy. To truly understand this, it is important to grasp the nature of fields. To help accomplish this goal, this section will cover the basic types of fields:

- Measurable and subtle
- Universal
- Natural and artificially created
- Human

Notice that we will be examining the natural and physical world, in addition to the subtle universe. The measurable cannot be separated from the immeasurable.

ENERGY TERMS

YOU CAN USE this legend as a refresher. The full definitions were covered in Part I.

Amplitude: The extreme range of a fluctuating quality (strength). Fields have various strengths or amplitudes—are weak or strong.

Frequency: Number of vibrations per unit of time. Waves have frequency and waves produce fields.

Oscillation: Like a vibration. Fields are generated by oscillating frequencies.

Physical: That which is received with the physical body senses. Healers can often translate the psychic information carried by fields into physical knowledge or even tangible energy.

Psychic: That which is perceived with the subtle senses. Healers often perceive psychic information carried via others' fields (and geopathic fields as well).

Speed or Velocity: Distance covered by a field (or the information on it) in relation to a unit of time. Some fields move at the speed of light and can therefore transfer information at that speed; some physicists also suggest certain fields can transfer information (light pulses) faster than the speed of light, creating "psychic" information.

Spin or Rotation: A twirling or rotating movement. Fields can carry or be generated by spinning particles (or waves) that can create different forms.

Vibration: Rhythmic motion back and forth across a position of equilibrium by the particles of a fluid or an elastic area when its equilibrium has been disturbed, as in transmission of sound. Sound fields (generated by sound waves) vibrate differently than do electromagnetic fields. Different fields can carry information that runs at different vibrations.

Vibration = Frequency + Amplitude

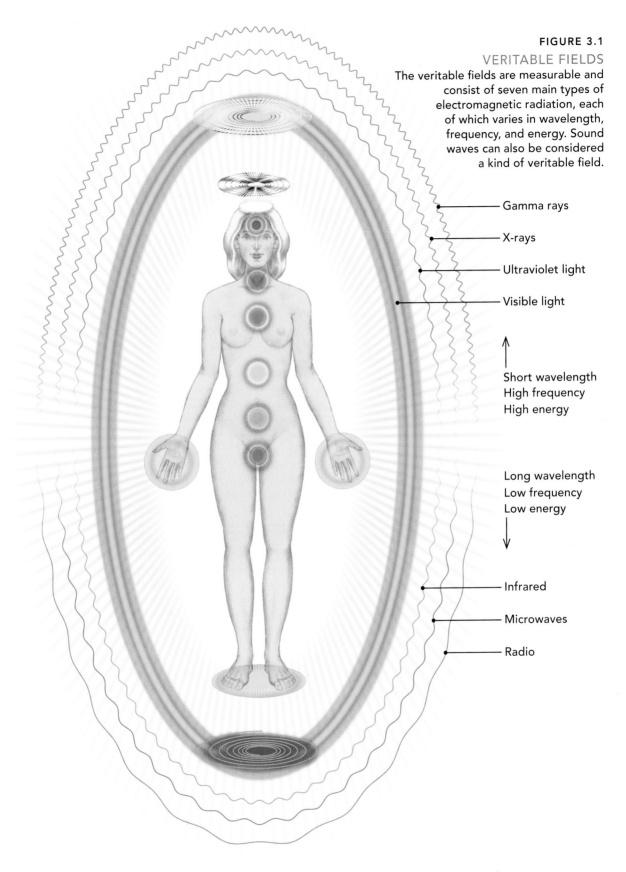

FIGURE 3.1

VERITABLE FIELDS

The veritable fields are measurable and consist of seven main types of electromagnetic radiation, each of which varies in wavelength, frequency, and energy. Sound waves can also be considered a kind of veritable field.

Gamma rays

X-rays

Ultraviolet light

Visible light

↑

Short wavelength
High frequency
High energy

Long wavelength
Low frequency
Low energy

↓

Infrared

Microwaves

Radio

Each of us (and the world) is made up of both measurable and subtle fields that create and sustain life. Fields obvious to the senses interact with those hidden from the senses; *all* fields interact to create beneficial and harmful effects on living organisms. The primary differences between physical and subtle fields are often simply the speed of the information and vibration involved. At some level, they can actually be perceived as the same fields—one flowing into another, one creating and sustaining the other.

Within the division of material and subtle energy lies yet another subdivision: that of form versus thought. Certain fields are managed by pure form, others by thought and the physical heart. To make use of these fields for health and wellness, it is vital to distinguish these functions.

18

A PRIMER ON ENERGY FIELDS

There are many different kinds of fields. In energy medicine, these are formally known by two terms: *veritable*, which can be measured; and *putative* or *subtle*, which cannot be measured.

The veritable or measurable energy fields are physical in nature and include sound and electromagnetic forces, such as visible light, magnetism, monochromatic radiation, and rays from the electromagnetic spectrum. Our body produces or is affected by all these energies.

Putative energy fields are also called *biofields* or *subtle fields*. Both of the latter terms will be used in this section. These fields explain the presence of vital life energy, such as the chi or prana of the Oriental and Hindu cultures. These energy fields are not separate from the mechanical or measurable fields; rather, they occupy a space and run at frequencies that cannot be perceived except through their effects. They are connected into the body by the meridians, the nadis, and the chakras, which are able to convert the fast-moving frequencies (chi and prana) into the slower and mechanical fields and forces (electricity, magnetism, and sound, among others). The energy channels and bodies are therefore "antennae" that receive and send information via the fields and transform this information so it can be used by the body.

The human body is affected by and creates both types of energy fields. The heart, for instance, serves as the human electrical center. Its electrical activity shapes the formation of the biofields that surround the body because it emits thousands of times more electricity and magnetism that do the other organs. But human and personal biofields also interconnect with greater fields that work in two directions; they receive and draw energy *from* us and also provide energy *to* us. Because we are actually composed of fields—as is the world—we have to see ourselves as interconnected rather than self-sustaining, constantly involved in the flux of becoming something new even as we shape and reshape the world.

Following are illustrations and descriptions of the major veritable (measurable) and putative (immeasurable, or subtle) fields.

THE VERITABLE FIELDS

The chief field that generates and perpetuates life is the *electromagnetic spectrum*. The other life-sustaining category is *sound fields*, also called *sound* or *sonic waves*. Let us examine these fields in relation to the illustration of energy fields.[2]

Each part of the electromagnetic spectrum manifests as radiation that vibrates at a specific rate and therefore is called *electromagnetic radiation*. Our body requires a specific amount of each part of this spectrum for optimal physical, emotional, and mental health. We can become ill or imbalanced if exposed to too much or too little of any particular stratum from the spectrum.

THE BASICS OF FIELDS

REMEMBER THE DISCUSSION of how atoms work in Part I? All matter, including the human cell, is created from atoms. Atoms are composed of protons and neutrons, which create the weight within an atom; electrons, which carry charge; and positrons, which represent the antielectrons and link the atom with its antiself. Each of these atomic units carries information and is constantly moving and vibrating, and is therefore "energized." The electrons move the most, usually in orbit around the cell's nucleus, the home of the proton and neutron. But electrons can also spin out and travel out of orbit. The tension between the electron and the rest of its world generates electricity; moving charges or currents then create magnetic fields. The combination of electrical and magnetic energies is an electromagnetic field.

Each of these atomic units moves at its own speed and, when combined with other units, creates a certain oscillation or vibration for the atom: a field. Motion produces pressure, and this creates waves. However, there are many waves—or fields—given off by a single atom, and the nature of these constantly changes, as the atom is continually moving.

Waves also create sound. Variations in pressure change the nature of the sound waves, and therefore the pitch. Though atoms tend to vibrate in a similar range, invading or greater waves can "throw them off," changing their function and sound.

In general, it is important to remember that every atom is unique, that atoms combine to form unique systems (such as lymph or blood fluids), and that they therefore produce unique wave structures. Waves produce fields, which move in a nonending flow in all directions. If you can work with the fields generated by a group of atoms (or even a single atom), you can determine the health or needs of those atomic structures, thus promoting healing. The various parts of electromagnetic fields and sound fields are always present; therefore, these fields are the easiest to work with.

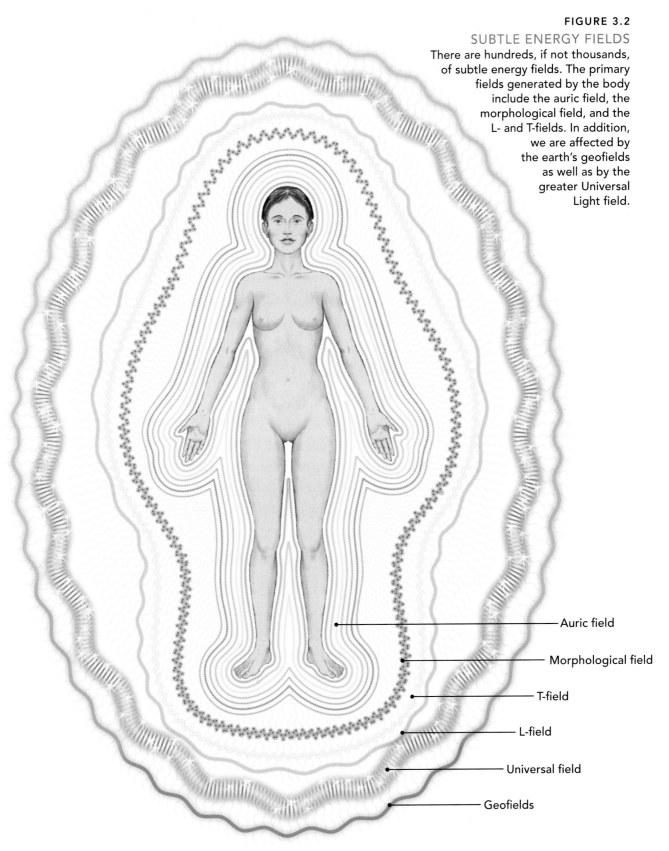

FIGURE 3.2

SUBTLE ENERGY FIELDS
There are hundreds, if not thousands, of subtle energy fields. The primary fields generated by the body include the auric field, the morphological field, and the L- and T-fields. In addition, we are affected by the earth's geofields as well as by the greater Universal Light field.

Auric field

Morphological field

T-field

L-field

Universal field

Geofields

Electromagnetic radiation is described as a stream of *photons*, wave-particles that are the basis of light. These are massless particles that travel at the speed of light. Each contains a bundle of energy, and therefore information. The only difference between the types of electromagnetic radiation is the amount of energy found in the photons. As figure 3.1 (see page 93) shows, radio waves have photons with the lowest measurable energies while gamma rays have the most energy. It is important to understand this flow of photons because photons actually compose the physical body, as demonstrated by the research of scientists including Fritz-Albert Popp (see Index). Photons also create a gigantic field, depicted as the "Field of Light" in this figure, which unifies all of creation. This field is described next in Chapter 19, "Two Unified Field Theories."

The electromagnetic spectrum is understood in terms of low and high energy, wavelength, and frequency. *Low* and *high energy* simply describe the information or energy of the photons. This is measured in electron volts. *Wavelength* is a way to measure the distance between two points on a wave. *Frequency* is the number of times that waves cycle per unit of time.

The basic premise of physical electromagnetism is this: *electricity generates magnetism.* We will explore electromagnetism in its many forms throughout this section, but most classical understandings depend on the fact that when electricity or charged electrons flow in a current, they create a magnetic field. These forces together comprise electromagnetism. However, according to *Faraday's law*, a changing magnetic field can create an electrical field. Magnetism can also operate in its own unique ways.

Sound waves are considered mechanical waves. They are an important set of waves that both affect us as human beings and emanate from us. They are defined as a disturbance that transports energy through a medium via the mechanism of particle interaction,[3] which means that sound waves are generated by some sort of interaction. They cannot "move" unless they are "moved." Sound waves run at specific vibrations and penetrate all of existence. Our own hearts create sound, as do the planets in the sky. We can hear some of these sounds and not others, but that does not mean that the inaudible sounds do not affect us. These and other mechanical waves affect us either positively or negatively.

THE PUTATIVE, OR SUBTLE, HUMAN ENERGY FIELDS

There are many types of subtle energy fields. Following is a brief overview of a few of them; the descriptions relate to figure 3.2. It is important to know that these fields, while seemingly surrounding the human body, also interpenetrate it. Fields do not stop at the skin. They are energies that move through mediums—including the skin and bodily tissue. In all likelihood, subtle fields determine the nature and health of their physically verifiable cousins, as is reflected by the research noted throughout this section and the rest of the book. As science keeps confirming, because illness and healing can be detected in the subtle fields before there is a physical response, they therefore have at least some "morphological," or initiating, effects on the body.

Know, also, that there is no way this book can list all the subtle fields—because they have not all been discovered. Every cell in the body and every thought generates a field. Every energy body, meridian, and chakra pulses its own field. In total, the field emanating from your body alone would occupy more space—or "antispace"—than your physical self. In many ways, you *are* your fields.

Each of the following subtle human energy fields will be discussed in length later in this section.

- The *human energy field* is primarily composed of the *aura*, a set of energy bands that graduate in frequency and color as they move outward from the body. Each of the auric fields opens to different energy planes and energy bodies and also partners with a chakra, thus exchanging information between the worlds outside and inside of the body.
- *Morphological fields* allow exchange between like-minded species and transfer information from one generation to another. These penetrate the aura as well as the electrical system of the body.
- *Geofields* act upon all living organisms, as do energies from outside the earth.
- The *universal light field*, called a "zero-point field," consists of photons or units of light that regulate every living thing. Our DNA is made of light, and we are surrounded in a field of light, thus the microcosm and macrocosm dance together.
- *L-fields and T-fields* are subtle electrical and thought fields, which are acted upon by electrical and magnetic energies. These fields compose the undetected aspects of the electromagnetic spectrum.

19

TWO UNIFIED FIELD THEORIES

There are two theories that seek to unify science and spirituality—to encompass all scientific knowledge and explain "reality." These are based on concepts related to fields and field dynamics.

THE UNIFIED FIELD THEORY

The unified field theory seeks to present a single field that marries fundamental forces and elementary particles according to quantum physics. As we saw in Part I, there are four fundamental forces: electromagnetic, strong and weak nuclear forces, and gravity. The elementary particles number in the thousands and include the subatomic particles. Albert Einstein conceived the term unified field theory in his attempt to unify his general theory of relativity and electromagnetism.

Elementary particles are the basic components of *quantum field theory* or *quantum mechanics*. This is a vast area of study that is revealing quirky facts of subatomic, or smaller-than-atom, reality, which include the following:[4]

- Mass can change to energy and energy can change to mass.
- The photon, the fundamental unit of light, has wave and particle capabilities.
- Matter, not just light, has wave capabilities.
- For every "here and now" particle, there is an antiparticle.
- An electron and its positron will destroy each other if they are in the same spot at the same time.
- There are virtual particles—those that do not exist or have a permanent existence except when they are observed or acted upon. Some physicists believe that they pop in and out of existence, and when "here," play a vital role in the functioning or creation of natural fundamemental forces, atomic shifts, and vacuum states.

- A single electron or proton can move in two or more directions at the same time.
- No two electrons can move with the same motion at the same time.
- Having once connected, two particles or wave-particles can continue to affect each other no matter where they are.
- The same particle can move or spin in two different directions at the same time.
- Entropy, previously defined as "lost energy," can also be defined as "hidden energy," which if concealed in an antiworld or "path not taken" in reality, could conceivably be rediscovered.
- Whereas Einstein asserted that mass cannot move faster than the speed of light, research has shown that pulsed light can move faster than the speed of light under certain conditions. Pulsed light has intervals between emissions, whereas continual or "regular" light operates as a steady beam of energy. The spaces between light flashes enable light to essentially slow down into matter.[5]

A unified field theory would have to explain how forces between objects are transmitted through the intermediary entities or fields. Part of the answer is this:

Strong nuclear force: Holds together quarks, which move slower than the speed of light to create neutrons and protons. The exchange particle is the gluon.

Electromagnetic force: Acts on electrically charged particles and uses the photon for exchanges.

Weak nuclear force: Responsible for radioactivity and acts on electrons, neutrinos, and quarks. Uses the W boson, an elementary particle.

Gravitational force: Acts on all particles that have mass via the graviton.

Scientists have not been able to incorporate gravity into their explanations, nor explain dark matter: a nonluminous matter that occupies about six times more mass than does luminous (light) matter. Therefore, this is not a truly unifying theory, though the following hypotheses might add to the understanding of energy:

Quantum foam: Roiling spacetime at the smallest levels, creating a foamy appearance that explains some inconsistencies in time and space.

String theory: Alters the definition of a particle from a point to oscillating strings or loops. The oscillations create mass and what finally looks like a particle. These loops might interconnect various dimensions. The closer you get to an electrical charge, the bigger a field grows, to the point of infinity.

Black holes and virtual particles: Black holes supposedly hold and never release energy. However, physicist Stephen Hawking showed that, theoretically, a black hole could release energy to the point of eventually disappearing. The only explanation is the existence of "virtual particles." If an electron and positron (an electron's antiparticle) come into existence, they annihilate each other. If born at the boundary between the inner and outer regions of the black hole, however, one of the particles is pulled into the hole and the other flies free.[6]

THE ZERO-POINT FIELD THEORY

The zero-point field theory also seeks to explain energy and the universe. The living being, a biophoton organism, is surrounded in a field of biophotonic light upon which it depends. This field is a near vacuum, although it is full of quantum particles and waves, including virtual, or transitory, particles. This sea of potential is susceptible to intention, responding first through the subtle fields of reality and finally in the physical realms.

Essentially, we are "frozen light," or biophoton machines. Through the zero-point field, we are interconnected in a "nonlocal reality" that permeates the cosmos. A *nonlocal reality* is one that is unmediated, unmitigated, and immediate. This means that events can occur through unknown forces, that the strength of an event is not dependent upon proximity, and that changes can occur instantly, despite distance. Many physicists have concluded that reality is indeed "nonlocal" in nature, as two particles, once in contact, can be separated and yet interact even at great distances.[7]

Studies of molecular and electrical systems, discussed throughout this section, show that our interactive capabilities extend way beyond our nervous system and that we are capable of processing intuitive, conscious, and subconscious information at every level.

The basic premise of the theory starts with the idea of zero point, the point at which atomic motion stops. We cannot quite get there—but we can come close, as was revealed in an experiment conducted by researchers including Lene Vestergaard Hau, who slowed light to a standstill at "zero" velocity or speed— meaning that the light vanished. Its imprint, however, did not. The "disappeared" light regenerated when stimulated by yet another light.[8]

Quantum theory explains why background radiation continued to emanate even when the light was standing still. The particles were not moving directionally, but they could flash in and out of existence. Where did they go? In and out of a zero-point field, which can store what is not here until we need it again.

The fact that we are made of light, that the body itself is a biophoton organism, has been well established by several researchers, including Fritz-Albert Popp, and is reported by Lynne McTaggart in her book *The Field*.[9] One of Popp's findings was that DNA itself is a storehouse of light, or biophoton emissions.

It seems that the more photons an organism's DNA emits, the higher it may stand on the evolutionary scale. The zero-point field plays a central role in originating and responding to this internal light. If a body of photons internalizes too much or too little light from the field, disease results. Popp concluded that organisms are the healthiest if they rely on a minimum of "free energy." This means that they each approach their own zero state, or nothingness.

20

THE NATURAL FIELDS

These are the fields related to the earth. They are all found in nature: in the earth, sun, or cosmos. Some are present in our bodies, and they all affect our health. These are subdivided according to "veritable" and "subtle." Veritable or physically measurable natural fields, however, may also run at subtle vibrations. Many of these natural fields are also called *geopathic fields*, in that they are generated by or affect the earth.

VERITABLE, OR MEASURABLE, NATURAL FIELDS

There are many natural fields. We have already described the electromagnetic field, consisting of electrical and magnetic fields, and introduced electromagnetic radiation.

In addition to the members of the electromagnetic group we have already discussed (radio waves, microwaves, infrared radiation, visible light, ultraviolet radiation, X-rays, and gamma rays), there is a band of electromagnetic radiation called *terahertz radiation*, which falls between microwaves and infrared radiation. Detected in the 1960s, T-rays, as they are called, are not yet fully understood, as in the natural state they are absorbed by the earth. Scientists have recently started creating these rays through high-temperature superconducting crystals that display a unique effect: when an external voltage is applied, a current flows back and forth between the stacks of this crystal at a frequency proportional to that of the voltage. T-rays are being analyzed for use in medical imaging, security, chemical research, astronomy, telecommunications, and quality control.

There are four additional kinds of bioenergetically active fields present in the earth's natural environment.

FIGURE 3.3

THE SCHUMANN RESONANCE

The Schumann Resonance is one of several natural earth-based magnetic fields. These affect the brain through the magnetite located near the pituitary gland, as well as through the pineal gland which, in turn, influences the perineural system and other parts of the body. The first waveform shown here is a Schumann oscillation. The second is an EEG image of the alpha brain state.

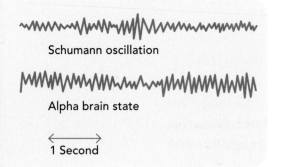

Schumann oscillation

Alpha brain state

1 Second

SCHUMANN WAVES

First identified by Professor W. O. Schumann in 1952, these are naturally occurring electromagnetic waves that oscillate between the earth and certain atmospheric layers. The waves are long with an extremely low frequency and are considered beneficial. NASA has performed extensive studies on these waves, which are part of the earth's natural electromagnetic radiation. They apparently run at the same frequency as the main control centers of the human brain, the hippocampus and hypothalamus. They also have the same frequencies as do our brain waves and follow a comparable daily pattern. Therefore, they help regulate the body's circadian rhythms, or internal clock. NASA astronauts, separated from these waves, felt distressed and disoriented, as the waves establish sleep patterns and endocrine functions. NASA now installs equipment aboard spaceships to mimic Schumann waves. Jet lag also seems linked to insufficient exposure to these waves. The farther from the earth's surface, the weaker the waves are.[10]

GEOMAGNETIC WAVES

There are sixty-four elements in the earth's crust. Each of these trace elements operates at an independent vibratory level and influences the earth's magnetic field. A geomagnetic wave is actually the sum of each of these elemental vibrations. Interestingly—and importantly—the red blood corpuscles contain nearly the same makeup as the earth's crust in relation to these vital minerals, and some researchers suggest that the overall wave influences our cardiovascular system.[11]

SOLAR WAVES

Solar waves emanate from the sun. Human health relies upon receiving the correct types of sunlight, in the right amounts. Sunlight affects the human endocrine system, metabolism, and human interactions with the geomagnetic frequencies. Lack of sunlight greatly affects the pineal gland, leading to depression, stress, and trouble sleeping, as well as disturbances in human circadian rhythms, our body's natural cycle.

SOUND WAVES

Sound is vibratory energy composed of timbre (tone or quality), silence, and noise, traveling at 770 miles per hour at sea level, depending on resistance factors, such as wind. Humans can only hear sound that vibrates at between 20 and 20,000 Hz, when it is perceived through the ears as electrochemical impulses that are sent to the brain. It can also be perceived through the skin and conducted through bone and other tissue.[12]

Sound is much slower than light, which travels at 186,000 miles per second. However, sound functions as a field, with particle and wave qualities, and also vibrates. In fact, all matter vibrates, and therefore, many researchers agree that all matter makes sound.

BETWEEN VERITABLE AND SUBTLE: WHAT ARE THESE WAVES?

There are waves that are hard to classify. They exist—we think—but they are not understood very well. Scalar waves fall into this category.[13]

SCALAR WAVES

Scalar waves were discovered by physicist Nikola Tesla around 1900 through experiments that revealed an unknown wave that runs at one and a half times the speed of light. They are considered longitudinal *standing waves* that are able to "tunnel" through matter. Essentially, a standing wave is not absorbed by its surroundings, while other waves are. Scalar standing waves are able to operate in such a way that their resonating frequencies do not absorb or link except through particular circumstances (such as through certain spins or vectoring frequencies). Some scientists consider them the basis of both the classical and quantum fields, and therefore the originating fields of the universe.

NATURAL SUBTLE FIELDS

There are many natural subtle fields related to the earth—besides electromagnetic fields and sounds that operate on the periphery of science. Here are just a few.

LEY LINES

Ley lines are energy lines on or in the earth that are electromagnetic in nature. They compare to the meridians or nadis in the body. There are ley lines in the earth, but also on other celestial bodies, such as the moon, planets, and stars. The earth is most affected by the gravitational energies of the ley lines on the heavenly bodies closest to earth.

Ley lines are dotted with points that are similar to the acupoints or the chakras. These might be electrical, magnetic, or electromagnetic. The magnetic nature of certain of these points might account for research that has shown that some

FIGURE 3.4
GLOBAL LEY LINES

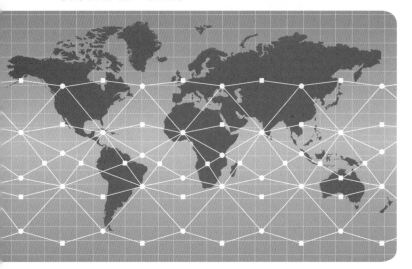

points along the ley lines possess higher magnetic energies than the average geomagnetic intensity.[14]

It is noteworthy that sacred centers, holy places, and worship sites are often located along the ley lines. These might be comparable to the earth lines described in cultures around the world, including the *songlines* of the Australian Aborigines: invisible lines they use to trek across the land.

THE HARTMANN GRID

Dr. Ernst Hartmann of Germany discovered this electromagnetic grid after World War II using a Geiger-Muller counter. It consists of a network of north-south and east-west lines that crisscross over the earth. He found that the grid lines showed higher counts of radiation than did the land in between. This count increased before an earthquake and was more concentrated around pyramids and famous cathedrals. The energy in the center of these famous buildings, however, was free from radioactivity.[15]

In comparison with ley lines, the Hartmann lines are closer together and aligned with more regularity. They are six to ten feet apart and each line is about twelve inches wide. The width of the lines broadens during a full moon, with sunspot activity, and drastic changes in the weather. They appear as structured radiation that arises vertically from the ground.

THE BENKER CUBICAL SYSTEM

Named after Austrian researcher Anton Benker, the Benker Cubical System is composed of energy lines about thirty-three feet apart. They look like square blocks stacked atop each other. They are magnetically aligned north-south and east-west. These blocks emanate radioactive walls of energy about one meter in diameter and are polarized alternatively as positive and negative. They are oriented toward the earth's pole. This system interpenetrates the Hartmann grid.

THE CURRY GRID

The Curry grid differs from the Hartmann grid and was ascertained by Drs. Whitman and Manfred Curry from Germany. It runs diagonal to the Hartmann grid and also carries electromagnetic energy. The lines are eleven and a half feet apart but do not widen during the moon cycles, as other grid systems do.[16]

BLACK LINES

Black lines appear to be naturally produced, localized lines similar to the *sha* or deadly energy lines in feng shui. In feng shui, the *sha* represents the inversion of chi or life energy and its presence reduces one's vital energy. In the Chinese system, sha is promoted by artificial energy sources including railroad and telephone lines and objects built with straight or rectangular lines, such as buildings.[17]

THE VIVAXIS: SUBTLE ENERGY BETWEEN THE HUMAN AND THE EARTH

There is a special energetic link between the human and the earth that connects the fields of both. Called the *Vivaxis*, it is described by Judy Jacka, ND, in her book *The Vivaxis Connection*.[18]

According to Jacka, the Vivaxis is actually a point or a sphere of energy, shaped like a fetus, located in the earth where the mother spent the last few weeks of pregnancy. This point links the developing being with the earth, no matter how far apart they are. It operates like an invisible, two-way umbilical cord throughout one's life and is formed from magnetic waves. Throughout our entire life, the incoming flow travels vertically to our current altitude and then horizontally to enter our left foot, before traveling vertically up our left leg. The outgoing energy flows out of our right hand, back to the Vivaxis. According to Jacka, disturbances in the geographic area of the Vivaxis can create chaos or problems within one's body.[19]

Vivaxis energies are considered subtle physical phenomena. They interconnect with the chakras and etheric energy bodies, but also all the physical and subtle grid lines and energies of the earth. Planetary and earth energies influence the body through the Vivaxis, even determining the flow of prana through the nadis.

21

THE RADIANT SHINE OF MOLECULES: LOST AND FOUND RESEARCH

The only way to really understand the importance of electromagnetism and fields is to examine molecular radiation, the ability of the molecule to emanate radiant energy.

Radiation is the name for the energy emitted by electromagnetic waves. It is considered an actual electromagnetic wave or a stream of photons. (Remember, electromagnetism is composed of photons in a quantum field.) In its many forms, as shown in figure 3.1, radiant energy is the foundation of molecular function and therefore holds primary keys for healing. Very little of the research relating to the healing potential of electromagnetism is taught in medical schools; in fact, it could be said that this knowledge has been "lost" and is ready to be "found."

Throughout history, physicians have been fascinated with one aspect of electromagnetism: *magnetism*, which involves working with just that part of the electromagnetic spectrum.[20] In AD 1000, a famous Persian physician relieved many disorders using magnets. In the early 1500s, the medical doctor Paracelsus wrote treatises on healing with magnetism. One of the most famous physicians, French surgeon Ambroise Paré, described in the early and mid-1500s how physicians could employ ground lodestone internally. (Lodestone is a magnetic element.) In the 1980s, healers in Israel mixed antibiotics with magnetic powder and then applied a magnet to the ill part of the body. The magnet drew the medication to the site of illness and kept it there long enough to exact a cure.[21]

Researchers have been analyzing the effects of electromagnetic therapies for a long time. One of the most important researchers in this area is Dr. Georges Lakhovsky, who in his book *The Secret of Life* demonstrates that all protoplasm emanates radiation. According to Lakhovsky, although atoms vibrate, the mechanisms of health and development are radiation waves, which oscillate throughout the body. Every cell emits its own frequencies or wavelengths of radiation, which interact with other cells' radiation to enable health. Disease occurs when these radioactive frequencies are disturbed, creating what he called an *oscillatory disequilibrium*.[22]

Writing in 1926, Dr. George Crile determined that cellular radiation actually produces the electrical current that supports the organism as a whole. He theorized that all issues in the body are governed by electrical charges generated by shortwave, or ionizing, radiation. Further, he asserted that all of life reduces to the bipolar nature of negative and positive charges.[23]

Crile's research into the nature of aberrant cells, including bacteria and cancer cells, supports this theory. He found, for example, that cancer is a bipolar mechanism, with the nucleus being positive and the cytoplasm negative. Bacteria act as positive poles while the lymph and tissues serve the negative role. Both bacteria and cancer cells must compete with the organism's cells for nutrition and attack the cells that have negative tissues (and a lower metabolism), which they can then defeat and "take over."[24]

Dr. Thomas Punck, a biophysicist at the University of Colorado Medical Center, studied the electrical aspects of a virus that attacks a specific type of bacteria, the *Escherichia coli*. He found that the virus "steals" electrical charges from charged metallic atoms, or ions, in the fluid surrounding cells. When it has "amped up" appropriately, it then attacks the bacteria. Yet another condition Dr. Punck explored revealed that healing was achieved when viruses were detached through application of ions.[25]

Over the years there have been many devices that healed illnesses, both minor and major, based on the simple theory of a bipolar reality. Many of these have been "lost" because medical science—or the business of medical science—has hidden the research and sometimes even outlawed the devices. One of the most notable is *radionics*, the use of a black box to heal someone through his or her field. (Radionics is fully discussed in "Radionics: Healing Through the Field" in Part VI.) Other important devices that utilize this bipolar reality include the Rife microscope and the Diapulse.

Dr. Royal Raymond Rife created "super" microscopes. He made his largest and most powerful, the Universal Microscope, in 1933. Consisting of 5,682 parts, it was composed of lenses, prisms, and illuminating units made of block-crystal quartz, quartz being transparent to ultraviolet radiation. The quartz could polarize light passing through the specimen, bending the light in order to perceive it from infrared to ultraviolet extremes. He was then able to characterize different pathogens and organisms by their colors and frequency. He also created a frequency generator to affect change in the studied specimens.

With his instruments, Rife showed that microbes gave off invisible ultraviolet light. He was then able to perform the following:[26]

- Disintegrate a microbe with a shortwave frequency of the correct value.
- Save the lives of animals given lethal doses of pathogens through exposure to the proper single-wavelength electrical energy.
- Convert friendly microbes into pathogenic microbes by altering the environment and food supply.

Rife also outlined ten different classes of microbes and showed that they could convert from one form to another simply through alterations in environment. Medical journals were not allowed to publish Rife's discoveries and doctors who used his tools were ostracized by medical societies.

The Diapulse machine received more notoriety. Developed by Abraham J. Ginsberg, MD, and Arthur Milinowski, a physicist, in the early 1930s, the Diapulse is an ultra-shortwave unit that uses radio waves for therapeutic purposes. Diapulse therapy works by pulsing the electromagnetic field in very short pulses. These high-frequency electromagnetic waves can be applied at high voltages without heating the patient's tissues. Animal studies at Columbia University conducted between 1940 and 1941 proved such treatments both effective and safe, and dozens of other studies have shown the same. Some of these studies have demonstrated the following results from the Diapulse machine:[27]

- In managing pelvic pain, it reduced the average hospital stay of patients to 7.4 days from 13.5 days.
- It enhanced wound healing considerably.
- It significantly reduced postoperative edema, as well as associated pain.
- It reduced pain, swelling, and discomfort in postsurgical dental patients.
- It accelerated the healing of bedsores beyond conventional methods.

Despite these results, the Diapulse was banned by the Food and Drug Administration (FDA) in 1972, and only permitted for sale again seventeen years later. It is currently used in several holistic areas of treatment including pain relief, bone problems, spinal issues, and dentistry.

Georges Lakhovsky, the author mentioned earlier, also invented an incredible healing device, a multiple wave oscillator, based on his theory that life is the "dynamic equilibrium of all cells, the harmony of multiple radiations, which react upon another."[28] His device used electromagnetic waves produced by a short-wave radio circuit, or short-wavelength oscillations, to neutralize disturbing rays, allowing diseased cells—those with abnormal oscillations—to return to normal. In one study, Lakhovsky inoculated plants with cancer, and was then able to cure them of it. He was able to heal many people of "incurable" cancers using his device.[29]

What else has been lost—that we must now "shine a light upon"?

22

L-FIELDS AND T-FIELDS:
THE PARTNERS COMPOSING REALITY?

Perhaps reality can be explained by one simple statement, maybe even this statement offered by Steven A. Ross, PhD, founder of the World Research Foundation and Library and an expert on bioenergy:

All of life reduces to electricity and magnetism acting on L- and T-fields. All matter is bipolar, held together by these unseen fields. All chanting, mantras, and meditation affect these polarities. All disease, illness, growth, decay, and emotions are regulated by them. You can fix your life by interacting with these underlying fields—and through them, create, act, and live closer to God.[30]

L-fields are subtle physical fields (measured electrically) and *T-fields* are thought fields. Each provides a blueprint and design for a different side of reality. Here are the two sides of the looking glass, the yin and yang of Oriental philosophy, the Shakti and Brahma of the Hindu religion. Also represented are electrical and magnetic frequencies, the two sides of matter that combine to create the electromagnetic radiation that constantly bathes and nurtures us.

This force—electromagnetism—underlies the entire universe, but it cannot be separated from the subtle fields that might determine its actions. Dr. Harold Saxton Burr, one of the most important theorists in the area of energy, stated it this way:

The Universe in which we find ourselves and from which we cannot be separated is a place of Law and Order. It is not an accident, nor chaos. It is organized and maintained by an Electromagnetic field capable of determining the position and movement of charged particles.[31]

Dr. Burr, who conducted his research at the University of Yale School of Medicine between 1916 and the 1950s, asserted that all of life is molded by electro-dynamic fields that can be measured with voltmeters. He called these "Life-fields" or "L-fields" and described them in many of his ninety-plus scientific papers, having determined that they comprise the architectural blueprint for life.[32]

Through a series of experiments on plants and animals, which have been repeated by other researchers, Burr showed that all living organisms are surrounded by these subtle energy fields. Changes in the electrical potential of these subtle fields led to alterations in electromagnetic fields. Some of these subtle changes concurred with alterations in sunspot activity or lunar phases; others were related to the specific organism. Regarding the latter, he spotted a specific L-field within a frog's egg, which later developed into the nervous system. With humans, he predicted women's ovulation cycles, found scar tissue, and diagnosed upcoming physical maladies—all by analyzing the person's L-field. These and other observations led to his belief that the L-field served as the developmental matrix for the body.[33]

In partnership with Dr. Leonard J. Ravitz, Jr., at the Department of Psychiatry at Yale, Burr discovered that certain electrometric techniques showed which patients would eventually be able to return to mainstream society and which would not. In summary, he proposed that these fields were morphological: that they revealed and perhaps created the future shape of an organism.[34] Ravitz later concluded that emotional activity and other stimulation mobilize the same electrical responses, and, therefore, that emotions are equated with energy. Ravitz also found that the L-fields disappeared entirely at death,[35] supporting the idea that they might originate life, not the other way around.

Burr's theory calls up latter-day hypotheses regarding the energy system. For example, as you will find in the discussion on the meridians, Dr. Bonghan of Korea determined that these energetic or subtle channels are morphological; they form and shape the organs and tissues. They work in and through the connective tissue and the secondary electrical system pinpointed by Dr. Björn Nordenström; therefore, the meridians might constitute one type or category of an L-field that acts upon the electrical frequencies of the body to affect and sustain parts of the physical body.

Dr. Burr diagnosed one-half of the dualistic nature of reality, but there is another field that complements the L-field. This is the T-field, which could also be called a *thought field*.

The term *T-field* comes from the observation that "thought has the properties of a field"—within the accepted definition of a field.[36] As we have seen, a field operates through a medium, has movement, and can transfer information. For centuries—even millennia—humans have observed that the mind manages matter. The classic exploration of this is packaged as the placebo and nocebo effects discussed earlier in the book: the power of belief to override physical realty, either positively or negatively. While Burr was forging his theory of the L-fields, several others were searching for the "cause behind thoughts." If the body has an originating field—one that sculpts it—does perhaps the mind have something that keeps it in shape? Another way to ask the question is this: *Is there thought transmission?*

Many researchers in Burr's era and later have shown that thought can leap from one person to another. Studies on twins who are separated showcase an uncanny ability for one to know the thoughts, actions, and feelings of the others.[37] Researchers at the Institute of HeartMath revealed that our heart attunes to future events far earlier than does our brain, especially in women.[38]

Earlier scientists, including Dr. J. B. Rhine of Duke University and Dr. S. G. Soal of the University of London, left a body of research testifying to the existence of ESP.[39] Another of these early researchers, Dr. Robert Rosenthal of Harvard, showed that an experimenter can influence the behavior of laboratory rats—a direct correlation to the scientific law that the observer affects what he or she is observing, and a conclusion that leads to the question: how?[40]

Other explorations that resulted in the theory of a T-field include a 1959 story that the U.S. Navy used ESP to communicate with submarines at sea.[41] About the same time, L. L. Vasiliev, professor of physiology at the University of Leningrad, published a work about experiments in mental suggestion. It represented forty years of scientific collaboration revealing that one person can and does influence another with no physical connection, reporting beyond a doubt that a "suggestion or thought in one mind can produce an effect across space in another—a classic demonstration that thought has field properties."[42] The name *T-field* then emerged as an explanation for this phenomenon.

Intuitive information—unuttered, mind-locked data—does pass from person to person. Energy medicine is largely dependent upon a practitioner getting an image, gut sense, or inner messages that provide diagnostic and treatment insight. Edgar Cayce, a well-known American psychic, was shown to be 43 percent accurate in his intuitive diagnoses in a posthumous analysis made from 150 randomly selected cases.[43] Medical doctor C. Norman Shealy tested now well-known intuitive Caroline Myss, who achieved 93 percent diagnostic accuracy when given only a patient's name and birth date.[44] Compare these statistics to those of modern Western medicine. A recent study published by Health Services Research found significant errors in diagnostics in reviewed cases in the 1970s to 1990s, ranging from 80 percent error rates to below 50 percent. Acknowledging that "diagnosis is an expression of probability," the paper's authors emphasized the importance of doctor-patient interaction in gathering data as a way to improve these rates.[45]

A field transfers information through a medium—even to the point that thought can produce a physical effect, thus suggesting that T-fields might even predate, or can at least be causative to, L-fields. One study, for example, showed that accomplished meditators were able to imprint their intentions on electrical devices. After they concentrated on the devices, which were then placed in a room for three months, these devices could create changes in the room, including affecting pH and temperature.[46]

Thought fields are most often compared to magnetic fields, for there must be an interconnection to generate a thought, such as two people who wish to connect. Following classical physics, the transfer of energy occurs between atoms or molecules in a higher (more excited) energy state and those in a lower energy state; and if both are equal, there can be an even exchange of information. If there really is thought transmission, however, it must be able to occur without any physical touch for it to be "thought" or magnetic in nature versus an aspect of electricity. Besides anecdotal evidence, there is scientific evidence of this possibility.

In studying semiconductors, solid materials that have electrical conduction between a conductor and an insulator, noteworthy scientist Albert Szent-Györgyi, who won the Nobel Prize in 1937, discovered that all molecules forming the living matrix are semiconductors. Even more important, he observed that energies can flow through the electromagnetic field without touching each other.[47] These ideas would support the theory that while L-fields provide the blueprints for the body, T-fields carry aspects of thought and potentially modify the L-fields, influencing or even overriding the L-field of the body.[48]

23

FIELD POLLUTION: GEOPATHIC STRESS

*G*eopathic stress refers to the harmful effects of natural and artificial fields and radiation from physical and subtle fields. The existence of geopathic stress is supported by scientific research, which has validated that constant or extreme exposure to geopathic stressors can result in mild to severe consequences in living beings exposed to them. These problems most typically include body pains, chronic fatigue, insomnia, cardiovascular disorders, irritability, learning challenges, infertility and miscarriage, behavior problems in children, and even cancer and auto-immune disorders.[49]

Examples of research into geopathic stress includes studies conducted by Dr. Hans Nieper, a world-renowned cancer and multiple sclerosis (MS) specialist, who showed that 92 percent of his cancer patients and 75 percent of his MS patients were geopathically stressed. Dr. Hager determined that geopathic stress was present in the 5,348 cancer patients he investigated, and German physicist Robert Endros, along with Professor K. E. Lotz of the School of Architecture in Biberach, analyzed 400 people who died of cancer to show that 383 had been exposed to geopathic faults or disturbances of the geomagnetic field.

POLLUTED NATURAL FIELDS: VERITABLE (MEASURABLE)

There are two types of measurable field stressors. The first is electromagnetic radiation. As we have seen, our bodies are composed of electromagnetic fields, both physical and subtle. Overexposure to strong electromagnetic forces can damage the fields and tissues inside the body and the fields surrounding the body. This section will detail some of the negative effects of electromagnetic pollution caused by natural as well as artificial (human-generated) means.

The other sources of measurable field pollution are the earth and sky. On earth, geopathic stress occurs primarily at the crossing points of the earth's natural energy lines, but also from radiation caused by subterranean running water, certain mineral concentrations, underground cavities, and fault lines. These are natural energies, but they are not beneficial to people or living beings over long periods of time. There are also fields of energy emanating from space, and these, too, can disturb our body's electromagnetic system. This section will also detail some of the problems stemming from planetary-based stressors.[50]

ELECTROMAGNETIC SPECTRUM POLLUTION

Overexposure to any of the basic types of electromagnetic radiation can be hazardous, if not life-threatening. The radiation can be natural, created by fields in the earth or the cosmos, or artificially produced. Here is a list of a few of the dangers of each and what kinds of damage they can cause.

Static electric fields: Electrical shock, which involves contact with a voltage high enough to cause a current flow through the muscles or into the hair. It can cause heart fibrillation, burns, neurological disorders, and death.

Magnetic fields: Under the wrong conditions, magnetic resonance imaging (MRI) can be dangerous or lethal: for example, if used when in the presence of certain defibrillators or implants. Other research is suggesting that magnetic pollution is a serious issue. (See Chapter 24, "The Power of Magnetism," for more information.)

Extremely low frequency (ELF) radiation: Some research has shown that exposure to elevated levels of ELF can result in a number of diseases or life-threatening problems. In fact, many people are so concerned about the constant exposure to power lines and electrical devices, to name a few ELF sources, that they have coined the term *electro-pollution*. Studies have shown that people living near power lines experience an increase in childhood and adult leukemia.[51] As well, certain power grid lines produce a magnetic field that might alter the flow of calcium ions, one of the ion conductors, in a way that is harmful to the body.[52] There is also concern about the ELF emanating from plugged-in appliances, which draw as much as 70 percent of their power while plugged in, not just when operating.

Radio frequency: There are many sources of radio waves, some natural (as from lightning storms) and some human-generated. Power lines emit low-frequency radio waves, and cell phones send radio waves in all directions. Radio waves in large doses are thought to cause cancer and other disorders.[53] Cell phones are the newest potential danger. When talking on the cell phone, your voice is transmitted at a frequency between 800 MHz and 1,990 MHz, in the range of microwave radiation. Between 20 and 60 percent of this radiation is transferred into your head, with some of the radiation penetrating an inch and a half into your brain.[54]

Visible light: Too much natural visible light can damage the retina. Problems from artificial sources result from inappropriate use of laser light and the use of light bulbs and fluorescent tubes that do not use the full light spectrum.[55]

Ultraviolet light: Ultraviolet light is just below the visible wavelength and has some of the same dangers as other ionizing radiation, including sunburn, skin cancer, and damage to the eyes.[56]

Gamma rays: Gamma rays can kill living cells. This enables them to serve as a valuable treatment for killing cancer cells, although the side effects include problems to the stomach lining, hair follicles, and a growing fetus. Gamma rays retard the cell division process.[57]

Infrared light: The most obvious danger to high exposure is burning of the eye or the skin.[58]

Microwave: In contrast to microwave energy from the sun, many researchers and consumers are concerned about the effects of using microwaves for cooking. Researcher Dr. Ing Hans Hertel, for example, discovered that microwaved food caused blood abnormalities similar to those leading to cancer. He was banned from discussing his findings by the Swiss Association of Dealers for Electroapparatuses for Households and Industry.[59]

X-Rays: Used to image bones and the internal body, X-rays can create a risk of DNA mutation and cancer.[60]

This outline provides examples of the different types of pollution caused by natural physical fields. Many of these fields were described earlier in this section.

Solar stress: Solar stress is caused by solar flares (sun spots) and magnetic storms and has been associated with increased cardiovascular failures.[61] It is thought that this occurs because the sun's activities affect the earth's geomagnetic field.

Geomagnetic fields: All living beings depend on the earth's geomagnetic field, but each of us must receive an appropriate amount or our health and welfare will be compromised. Researcher Dr. Wolfgang Ludwig discovered that an imbalance of Schumann and geomagnetic waves induces microstress in living creatures. From an Eastern perspective, the yang from the Schumann waves and the yin input from the geomagnetic waves must be in balance to support wellness.[62]

Geopathic stress and the Vivaxis: The Vivaxis, which is a subtle energy that connects living beings to the earth, can create disturbance or even illness in the body if it is exposed to abnormal or unhealthy energetic conditions, such as magnetic or electrical pollution. More information is available in Judy Jacka's book *The Vivaxis Connection.*

POLLUTION FROM NATURAL SUBTLE FIELDS

Natural subtle fields are not always harmless. Overexposure in any of the outlined areas can lead to problems. Most of the topics in this list were introduced earlier in this section.

Black streams: The radiation associated with these underground water veins often intensifies during sunspot activity and with lightning strikes. Other geological faults produce similar effects and also emanate high levels of radon gas, which creates toxicity and weakens the immune system.[63]

Hartmann lines: Alternate lines are positively or negatively charged, so the intersection is a "double positive" or a "double negative." The intersection points are challenging to the nervous system and can disturb our own personal electromagnetic fields.[64] The other stress caused can be explained in terms of yin and yang. The yin lines (north-south) are cold and correspond to winter ills, including cramps, humidity, and forms of rheumatism. The yang lines (east-west) are related to fire and can cause inflammation. Depending upon the seasonal cycles, these "double power" energies can create these symptomatic problems.[65] Dr. Hartmann also suggested that overexposure to the lines decreased the immune system's ability to defend itself against harmful bacteria. He determined an increased risk of cancer to people who lived or worked on these lines.[66]

The Benker cubical system: The intersection points of the cubical blocks are strong geopathic zones and are professed to be damaging to the immune system with extended exposure.[67]

Curry lines: Some experts believe that Curry lines are electrical, and that these lines create double positives, double negatives, or one of each at the intersections. Dr. Curry believed that the positively charged crossing points lead to accelerated cell division and possibly an increased chance for cancer growth, while the negative areas could lead to inflammation.[68]

A THEORY ABOUT OUR CURRENT CONDITION

What has led to our current level of geopathic stress? Why are we seeing so many illnesses as a result of field stress? There are a few reasons that stand out.

First, the earth's natural magnetic field has decreased in potency over time. About 4,000 years ago, it generated between two and three gauss and now has an intensity of about one-half gauss, signifying a reduction of nearly 80 percent.[69] On a microscopic level, the decline in the earth's magnetic field reduces the level of charge in subatomic particles, lessening the overall charge of atoms. Living bodies depend upon charged atoms and molecules to be superconductive, or to support the proper flow of nutrients and messages along the nervous system and through the fluid systems of the body. Not only does the human primary nervous system, including the brain and central nervous system, require this ionic balancing, but so does the secondary electrical system that Björn Nordenström discovered. This secondary nervous system likely interacts with the meridians and nadis. Insufficient magnetic input therefore adversely affects a human's subtle bodies and fields.

Second, artificially produced radiation can cause considerable harm to living organisms, and we are bombarding the planet with a plethora of human-generated electrical and magnetic fields, as well as oceanic amounts of radio waves, microwaves, and other radiations.

24

THE POWER OF MAGNETISM

agnetism has light and dark sides. Human bodies require external exposure to and generate their own magnetic fields. But too much of a good thing will negatively impact human physical and subtle systems, leading to physical illness and mental and emotional issues. This section explores the many roles magnetism plays in our lives.

THE BODY MAGNETIC

Much of our understanding about the effects of magnetism and magnetic fields is owed to Dr. Robert Becker, a pioneer in bioenergetic research. Becker used electricity and electromagnetic fields to stimulate the regrowth of broken bones; his findings have led to the invention of many electrical devices used in modern medicine. Through his research, he also determined the presence of a direct current (DC) electrical control system within the body.

Becker's discoveries were preceded by the research of Dr. Harold Burr, the originator of the theory of L-fields. Through his studies, Becker found a unique electrical control system—similar to that proposed by Burr—that is central to healing as well as the achievement of various states of consciousness.[70]

Becker determined that when a subject was in an altered state of consciousness (such as being anesthetized), his or her body exhibited electrical changes. This finding correlated consciousness states with a DC system that served as an alternative pathway for electrical messages between the brain and local tissue-healing systems. This electrical system, for example, would turn on when a body part was injured and turn off when the region was healing.

Becker discovered that this system transmitted information through the membranes of the *glial cells*. Glial cells are traditionally considered part of the support system for the nerves and the central nervous system. There are about ten to fifty times as many glial cells in the brain as there are neurons, which number approximately one hundred billion.

While traditional science asserts that the glial cells do not conduct electricity, Becker's work challenges this thinking. He found that the glial membranes actually fluctuate in electrical charge and voltage. In fact, Becker determined that the voltage change can be produced by an application of external energy fields, especially magnetic ones.[71]

FIGURE 3.5

THE MAGNETIC FIELD OF THE BODY

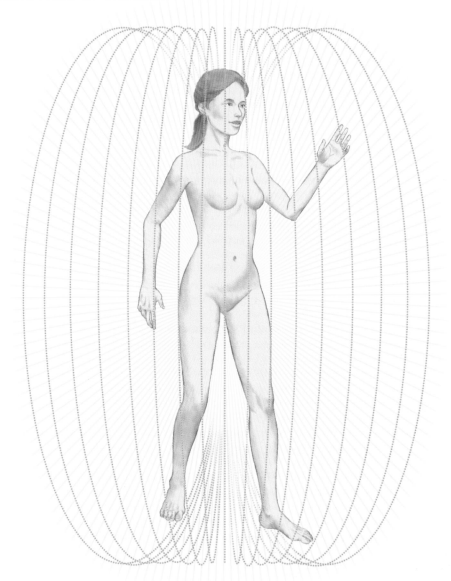

All living beings are bathed in a background magnetic field that resonates at 7.8 cycles per second, an oscillation comparable to the alpha-theta brain state. As we saw in Part II, we have magnetic-detecting materials in our brains. The human DC system, perhaps in relation to some of these magnetic-detecting materials, enables each of us to "pick up" on the geomagnetic frequencies of our surroundings, which in turn stimulates the alpha-theta brain waves.[72]

Becker's work dovetails with that of Dr. Björn Nordenström, who determined that humans have a secondary electrical system that works between the connective tissue and the cardiovascular system. Nordenström demonstrated that the flow of ions between damaged cells and blood vessel walls, especially in relation to the flow of current to or from an injured area, creates battery-like electrical effects that stimulate repair. Nordenström demonstrated that living organisms are systems of electromagnetic fields. Change the electrical properties of the body and you alter its health, positively or negatively. Becker's research showed that cells possess semiconductor properties—like those present in integrated electrical circuits. This finding means that our bodies are actually "mini-microcircuits," integrated circuits that work through semiconduction.

BEING A SEMICONDUCTOR: OUR MANY FIELDS

Modern engineers like using semiconductors because they respond to electrical fields; by controlling these electrical fields, engineers can control the effects of electricity as well as the magnetic fields produced by electrical fields. If living beings are semiconductors—or have these properties—the body's magnetic fields can also be controlled to create bioelectrical results.

This statement implies a simple scenario for healers: change our magnetic field, alter our health—except that we are each composed of millions if not billions of fields. As Dr. William Tiller, scientist and author, writes, every subtle level of substance creates a radioactive emission, just as every physical cell, organ, or system in the body generates a field. Our chakras, meridians, subtle energy bodies, and maybe even thoughts, generate a standing wave field or an auric field. Add up the billions of cells and there are quite a large number of magnetic fields. But follow Tiller, who insists that an auric sheath exists around the body for "every subtle body the human has," and the numbers of fields add up astronomically.[73] And the changes in the earth around us, as well as those we are creating in the earth, affect immeasurable biofields, each one necessary for our well-being.

One of our most important human magnetic fields is the aura, which is energetically connected to the chakras and discussed in this section. Many healing practices involve altering the magnetic field to create internal change.

Most distant healing practices, however, including prayer, probably involve manipulation of others' magnetic fields or auras. The use of magnets for healing also provides methods for altering the body's internal and external fields and therefore health.

THE POSITIVE—AND THE NEGATIVE

Certain magnetic fields or intensities are beneficial and others are not. Magnetic fields can alter nerve cells and the DC flow, resulting in an anesthesia-like decrease in pain. They can also alter the flow of calcium ions across tissue, such as muscle, thereby increasing local blood circulation and the delivery of oxygen to the tissues. Magnets have also been used in localizing cancer-fighting drugs.[74]

Each living being needs an appropriate amount of magnetism. *Magnetic-field deficiency syndrome*, or MFDS, is a term describing a limited exposure to the geomagnetic field. A Japanese research team led by Dr. Kyoichi Nakagawa showed that certain types of illness among Japanese city dwellers might be caused by the iron and steel girders used in large buildings. Apparently, these structures were shielding the inhabitants from the natural geomagnetic field.[75]

What can help can also hurt. For example, exposure to magnetic fields has been linked to the risk of miscarriage.[76] Evidence shows that exposure to 60 Hz magnetic fields with strengths of 3 mG or higher is associated with a significant increase in many types of malignant tumors, especially those relating to tissues with a quick rate of cellular replication, such as bone marrow and lymphatic tissue.[77] Research by Dr. Robert Becker also determined an increase in schizophrenic and psychotic behavior corresponding to peaks of abnormal geomagnetic activity.[78]

Our homes are equally susceptible to geomagnetic stressors, as research conducted by Ludger Meersman, a specialist in geobiology, revealed. There were zones of high- or low-intensity geomagnetic fields along the beds of sick individuals, while the magnetic fields were evenly distributed along the beds of most healthy individuals. The most abnormal readings correlated with the part of the patient's body that was afflicted. For instance, a high geomagnetic field would occur at the same bodily site as a cancer or arthritic condition.

HELPFUL OR HURTFUL?

One of the many reasons for these striking problems is that exposure to DC magnetic fields of several hundred gauss increases the number of glial cells, as was shown in a study conducted in 1966 by Drs. Y. A. Kholodov and M. M. Aleksandrovskaya at the Soviet Academy of Sciences in Moscow.[79] These and other studies suggest that magnetic intensities alter the glial cells, which then interface with the neurons. The body therefore responds to situations such as alterations in the geopathic field—those artificially produced in the environment—as well as, to quote Dr. Robert Becker, "fields produced by other organisms."[80]

Another reason that magnetic fields have both positive and negative effects is that a magnet has not only *one* but *two* effects on a living organism, each stimulated by the two forms of energy transmitted by the north and south poles. Research by Albert Roy Davis and Walter C. Rawls, Jr., as described in their books *Magnetism and Its Effects on the Living System* and *The Magnetic Effect*, reveals that these effects are physical but also related to consciousness or ESP. The earth produces the same effects, as it is itself a giant magnet.[81]

Basically, a magnet's south pole accelerates cellular growth rate and biological activity, making the tissues more acidic, while the north pole inhibits growth rate and biological activity and increases alkalinity. Davis and Rawls reduced tumors via north-magnetic applications and were able to increase the tumor size with south-magnetic applications. However, north-pole applications also reduced pain and inflammation and slowed the aging process in examined animals.[82]

In terms of ESP, Rawls and Davis discovered that the "third eye," or sixth chakra area of the brain, stimulates inner vision or awareness. Subjects experienced an increase in this ability, as well as peace and calm, by holding a magnet in the left palm or on the back of the right hand. In 1976, Davis and Rawls were nominated for a Nobel Prize in medical physics.

In summation, the electrical flow in the body is maintained by certain ions, such as sodium, potassium, calcium, and magnesium. Imbalances in these fundamental materials can cause disease—and can occur because of disease. These imbalances will alter the electrical activity of the body and therefore the actual appearance—shape and form—of the various magnetic or auric fields outside of the body. This might explain the ability of certain "auric readers" to use their psychic skills to perceive deep-seated problems in the body even before medical technology can detect them, as well as the reverse ability to heal the aura and therefore, heal the body. The link between the meridians and the electrical system of the body, as Nordenström proposed, also provides an explanation for healing through the meridians and acupoints. The glial cells act as yet another major player in the body's microcircuit system, receiving information from the magnetic spectrum inside and outside it, thus adding another dimension to Nordenström's discoveries.

Nordenström used his theories to cure cancer, sending electrical charges into a tumor to shrink it. What did Rawls and Davis discover but one of the primary concepts of healing? There is polarity to every aspect of life. Humans are electrical and magnetic, yin and yang, and health is dependent upon maintaining the appropriate balance of each. Humans are L-fields, acted upon by electricity. And humans are T-fields, acted upon by magnetism. Through the bipolarity that is "L," or electrical, humans generate life, movement, and activity. Through the bipolarity of our "T," or magnetic self, we attract what we need and what we can become. Humans are composed of the stuff of thought—and matter.

FIGURE 3.6
FORMS OF MAGNETISM

In his book *A Practical Guide to Vibrational Medicine,* Dr. Richard Gerber outlines many forms of magnetism.[83] Here is a brief description of each, along with a sample of its effects.

Magnetism	Effects
Ferromagnetism *(involving iron)*	May enhance north-pole effects
Electromagnetism *(produced by electron flow/currents)*	Positive and negative effects
Biomagnetism *(generated by ionic currents and cellular activity)*	Can reveal disease patterns
Animal magnetism *(from chi and prana)*	Life force is subtle magnetic; reveals etheric activity
Subtle magnetism *(from chakras, aura, and subtle bodies)*	Rules thought forms (T-fields)
Paramagnetism *(attraction to strong fields)*	Enhances plant growth
Diamagnetism *(repelling by strong field)*	Unknown
Geomagnetism *(from the earth)*	Necessary for life; can create geopathic stress
Solar magnetism *(from the sun; subtle and solar)*	Affects geomagnetic field; increases heart attacks and is necessary for life
Cosmic and stellar magnetism *(subtle magnetic currents from galaxy)*	Affects astral body and chakras

25

HANDS-ON AND DISTANT HEALING: PROVING SUBTLE FIELDS AND A NONLOCAL REALITY

Distant or absentee healing is a well-known concept and a reality among subtle energy healers, and even the religious, who use prayer and positive thinking to invite healing for people who are not geographically present. Considerable evidence underscores its effectiveness. It can be explained by energetic connectivity, which assumes the presence of fields that can generate these connections through what has been called a "nonlocal reality."

Studies on therapeutic touch professionals have demonstrated positive results in areas including pain relief.[84] In his paper reviewing sixty-one such studies, Dr. Daniel J. Benor, a respected medical doctor and author on bioenergy, states that "distance, even thousands of miles, does not appear to limit the effects of healing."[85]

Healing touch is another hands-on energy practice that works with the energy field to support the body's natural ability to heal. It is currently used in hospitals and clinics worldwide and is taught in universities, medical and nursing schools, and other settings. Research on its effectiveness in more than sixteen areas suggests that physical healing is possible through accessing the biofields.[86]

One particular study measured the effect of healing touch on the properties of pH, oxidation-reduction balance, and electric resistance in body fluids. These factors were linked to biological age. Before a treatment, the mathematically determined age of the touch-treated group was 62; after treatment it was 49.[87]

How do these and other such methods work? It is hard to know exactly, but one likely explanation is that energy fields can overlap and interconnect from one person to another. It is known that biofields exist because they have been imaged with newer technology, including Kirlian photography, aura imaging, and gas discharge visualization. Moreover, this equipment shows dramatic differences in the fields before and after energy treatments.[88] Other research establishes the ability of one person to affect another through these fields. For instance, studies at the Institute of HeartMath in California have shown that one person's electrocardio-graph (heart) signal can be registered in another person's electroencephalogram (EEG, measuring brain activity) and elsewhere on the other person's body. An individual's cardiac signal can also be registered in another's EEG recording when two people sit quietly opposite one another.[89]

This interconnectivity of fields and intention is a marriage of subtle energy theory and quantum physics. As Dr. Benor pointed out, Albert Einstein has already proven that matter and energy are interchangeable. For centuries, healers have been reporting the existence of interpenetrating, subtle energy fields around the physical body. Hierarchical in organization (and vibration), these fields affect every aspect of the human being.[90]

Studies show that healing states invoke at least the subtle biomagnetic fields. For example, one study employed a magnetometer to quantify biomagnetic fields coming from the hands of meditators and yoga and Qigong practitioners. These fields were a thousand times stronger than the strongest human biomagnetic field and were located in the same range as those being used in medical research labs for speeding the healing of biological tissues—even wounds that had not healed in forty years.[91] Yet another study involving a superconducting quantum interference device (SQUID) showcased large frequency-pulsing biomagnetic fields emanating from the hands of therapeutic touch professionals during treatments.[92]

While these fields extend far beyond the physical body, quantum physics explains how one person's field can interact with someone else's thousands of miles away. As we saw in Chapter 19, "Two Unified Field Theories," all living beings are interconnected in a nonlocal reality. Having touched, two particles can affect each other across time and space. Through intention, our personal field can interact with someone else's field and instantly transfer information. Research in resonance and sound shows that if living beings operate or resonate on similar vibrations, one can affect the other.

Yet another set of studies hints that there is sharing of energy and intention through the upper range of the electromagnetic spectrum. Replicated studies indicate a significant decrease in gamma rays from patients during alternative healing practices. This suggests that the body's gamma emitter, a form of potassium, regulates the surrounding electromagnetic field.[93]

Gamma rays materialize when matter (such as an electron) and its antimatter counterpart (a positron) annihilate on impact. As we have seen, antimatter has the opposite charge and spin of matter. When electrons and positrons collide, they release specific types of gamma rays. Years ago, Nikola Tesla suggested that the gamma rays found on earth emanate from the zero-point field.[94] Though it appears as a vacuum, this field is actually quite full, serving as a crossroads for virtual and subatomic particles and fields. When we perform healing, it is possible that we are actually tapping into this zero-point or universal field, shifting its power through intention.

Still another theory is that we are accessing *torsion fields*, fields that travel at 10^9 times the speed of light. These fields are hypothesized as conveying information without transmitting energy and with no time lapse.[95] Part of this suggested effect is based on the definition of time as a vector of the magnetic field. When torsion and gravitational fields function in opposing directions, the torsion field can conceivably alter the magnetic functions, and therefore the vector of time. When superimposed on a specific area in a gravitational field, it might also reduce the effect of gravity in that spot.[96]

These torsion fields have been researched by Peter Gariaev and Vladimir Poponin, Russian scientists who discovered that photons travel along the DNA molecule in spirals rather than along a linear pathway, which shows that DNA has the ability to bend light around itself. Some physicists believe that this twisting or "torsion-shaped" energy is an intelligent light, emanating from higher dimensions and different from electromagnetic radiation, giving rise to DNA. Many researchers now believe that these torsion waves *are* consciousness, composing the soul and serving as the precursor to DNA.[97]

26

SACRED GEOMETRY: FIELDS OF LIFE

I n comparison with "regular" geometry, sacred geometry asserts that by analyzing and working with geometric figures, one attunes to the mystical laws of creation. Geometry is an important part of energy healing because subtle energies often organize in shape and form. Because of this, healers throughout history have employed symbols by using psychic visioning and by constructing healing instruments in various shapes. Geometry is interrelated with sound.

Recent studies have indicated that geometry can be a matter of life—or death. According to one, the geometry of blood vessels is a factor that can lead to cardiovascular disease; the greater the angle between an artery and its branching blood vessels, the greater the potential for plaque buildup.[98] Another example: the geometry of the cervical spine correlates to cervical degenerative disease 70 percent of the time.[99]

Geometric theories began emerging thousands of years ago, most notably during the time of Plato and his predecessor, Pythagoras—although many of today's important principles were already in existence. The geometric proportions developed during this time period have been used by most civilizations since and applied to mathematics, art, architecture, cosmology, music, astronomy, and physics. Here are a few applications of sacred geometry—the mystical aspects of geometry, as applied to healing and energy.

BASIC GEOMETRY THEORIES

There are several geometry theories, proven mathematically, that apply to healing energies. These are:

Sine wave: A waveform with the shape of a sine curve: a single frequency indefinitely repeated in time. Used to depict frequency, waves, and vibrations, the underlying measurement of energy.

FIGURE 3.7
SINE WAVE

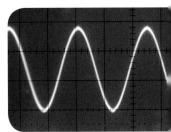

FIGURE 3.8
SPHERE

FIGURE 3.9
FIBONACCI
SEQUENCE

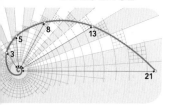

FIGURE 3.10
TORUS

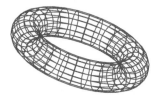

FIGURE 3.11
THE GOLDEN
SECTION

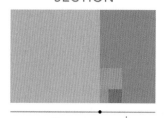

a   b

a + b is to a
as a is to b

Sphere: A three-dimensional closed circuit on which all points are a given distance from the center. Energetically, considered in many cultures to represent the void, relationship, origin of life, or perfect balance.

Fibonacci sequence: A repetitive numerical series in which each number except for the first two is the sum of the preceding two. Closely related to the golden section.

Torus: A donut-shaped geometric surface created by rotating a circle about a line in the same plane as the circle but not intersecting it. Part of the flower of life and a presence in physics and astronomy.

Golden section: A line segment sectioned into two according to the golden ratio, where "a + b" is to the longer segment as "a" is to the shorter segment "b." The ratio is approximately 1.6180 and often represented with the Greek letter *phi*. This ratio is linked to the golden spiral, a continually curved spiral found in nature, and the golden rectangle, in which the ratio of the longer side to the shorter is the golden ratio. Other related terms are *golden mean, golden number, divine proportion, divine section,* and *golden cut.* Considered an instrument of the divine in creation.

Merkaba: Two oppositely oriented and interpenetrating tetrahedrons. Often considered to be vehicles for soul travel or opening to higher consciousness.

Metatron's cube: Metaphysically recognized as the basis for the Platonic solids. It contains two tetrahedrons, two cubes, and an octahedron, icosahedron, and dodecahedron.

Flower of life: A figure composed of evenly-spaced, overlapping circles creating a flower-like pattern. Images of the Platonic solids and other sacred geometrical figures can be discerned within its pattern.

The Platonic solids: Five three-dimensional solid shapes, each containing all congruent angles and sides. If circumscribed with a sphere, all vertices would touch the edge of that sphere. Linked by Plato to the four primary elements and heaven. (See page 139.)

The applications of these shapes to music are important to sound healing theory. The ancients have always professed a belief in the "music of the spheres," a vibrational ordering to the universe. Pythagorus is famous for interconnecting geometry and math to music. He determined that stopping a string halfway along its length created an octave; a ratio of three to two resulted in a fifth; and a ratio of four to three produced a fourth. These ratios were seen as forming harmonics that could restore a disharmonic body—or heal. Hans Jenny furthered this work through the study of cymatics, discussed later in this chapter, and the contemporary sound healer and author Jonathan Goldman considers the proportions of the body to relate to the golden mean, with ratios in relation to the major sixth (3:5) and the minor sixth (5:8).[100]

Geometry also seems to serve as an "interdimensional glue," according to a relatively new theory called causal dynamical triangulation (CDT), which portrays the walls of time—and of the different dimensions—as triangulated. According to CDT, time-space is divided into tiny triangulated pieces, with the building block being a pentachoron. A pentachoron is made of five tetrahedral cells and a triangle combined with a tetrahedron. Each simple, triangulated piece is geometrically flat, but they are "glued together" to create curved time-spaces. This theory allows the transfer of energy from one dimension to another, but unlike many other time-space theories, this one makes certain that a cause precedes an event and also showcases the geometric nature of reality.[101]

The creation of geometry figures at macro- and microlevels can perhaps be explained by the notion called *spin*, first introduced in Chapter 1. Everything spins, the term *spin* describing the rotation of an object or particle around its own axis. *Orbital spin* references the spinning of an object around another object, such as the moon around the earth. Both types of spin are measured by *angular momentum*, a combination of mass, the distance from the center of travel, and speed. Spinning particles create forms where they "touch" in space. Many of these forms are geometrical in nature.

Cymatics studies reveal that different frequencies produce different patterning effects. The nature of these patterns at least partially depends on spin, the rotation around a central axis that determines the resulting movements. In his book *Mind, Body and Electromagnetism*, author John Evans shows that there are various patterns produced by frequency and spin in the human body; the pattern of a liver is different from that of a vertebra. He suggests that the cellular material of the body is patterned by electromagnetic waveforms with an ordering of frequency along the central axis.[102] Subtle energies might, through information, frequency, and spin, form the patterns that underlie the forms of our body—and what is this idea but still another description of geometry?

FIGURE 3.12
MERKABA

FIGURE 3.13
METATRON'S
CUBE

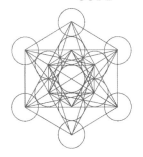

FIGURE 3.14
FLOWER
OF LIFE

FIGURE 3.15
PENTACHORON

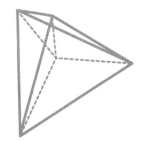

FIGURE 3.16

THE UNDERLYING GEOMETRY OF THE CHAKRAS

The underlying forms or geometric shapes that compose the chakras, as described by John Evans:

The lotus forms with large frequency-ratios.

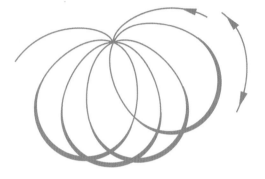

Petals emerge with opposite rotations with a frequency-ratio near unity.

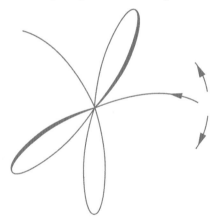

Vortices (or spirals) are created by similar rotations when the frequency-ratio is near unity.

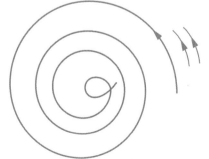

Quantum physics has also shown that two particles of different spin can be the same particle, and in a magnetic field, the photons generated by a spinning atom can have slightly different frequencies in the "up" versus "down" movement. A single object—or waveforms in relationship—can produce amazing shapes and forms, some in this reality, some in others. A simple change alters the vibrational qualities of the object and therefore its effects. And this is the basis of energy healing— changing frequency or spin through field dynamics.

Geometry plays a significant role in sound, as well as in applications of magnetism, as we shall discuss later in this section.

CALLAHAN AND GEOMETRY: FIELD RESEARCH ON SHAPES AND PARAMAGNETISM

Paramagnetism is the ability of a substance to resonate with magnetism. It helps explain the way that geometric energies influence the living.

Since time began, certain shapes have emerged over and over—and we must ask, for what reason? Why are the pyramids shaped like pyramids? How about obelisks; what properties do these "magnify"? It appears that different shapes literally attract magnetic energies and focus them in different ways. And the materials themselves influence the magnetic effects.

One of the main contributors to this field is Dr. Phillip Callahan, professor of etymology and a consultant to the U.S. Department of Agriculture. Callahan noticed that the different geometric shapes of the antennae and sensory apparatus in moths produced different effects, and so he turned his mind to studying human-made structures. How do different building shapes and materials affect life forms?

He centered one of his research projects on the round towers of Cashel, Ireland, which had a particularly lush plant growth around them.[103] Callahan believed that these towers may have been used as resonant systems for attracting and storing magnetic and electromagnetic energy from the

PLATO LIVED AROUND 400 BC and considered the triangle to be the building block of the universe. Based on this idea, he believed that the universe was created in a geometric progression. He presents this theory in his treatise, the *Timaeus,* in which he shows how triangles make up five solids—now called the *Platonic solids*—which form the four elements and heaven. Some of his ideas originated with Empedocles, who believed that everything in the world derives from combinations of the four elements through the interaction of opposing forces (similar to yin and yang of Chinese theory).

These solids were not new to the Greeks. Models of them were found among carved stone balls in Scotland from Neolithic times. However, Plato was the first to formalize the relationship between these unique solids and their representations, as shown below.

These solids are unique in that their sides and angles are all equal. Their faces form equal polygons and each possesses three concentric spheres. Plato envisioned these factors as signifying the Earth's basic structure, perceiving that these shapes formed a grid; as well, that their component structures enabled evolution.[104]

Mathematically, these are the only five shapes in the world whose vertices or points match the inside of a sphere; these are the Platonic solids. Many traditions envision the sphere as the symbol of the beginning of the universe, hence the importance of the three spheres identified with each of the shapes. From a healing perspective, one could imagine reducing an illness or issue down to its "symbolic state" to then achieve health by reconstructing the body or even thoughts to fit a more "solid" geometrical shape. This is the thinking behind healing methods including numerology and symbol healing, which are addressed in Part VI. As well, some healers believe that the Platonic solids form the underlying structure for various parts of the body, such as the cells themselves.[105]

FIGURE 3.17
THE PLATONIC SOLIDS

Tetrahedron
Four sides
Element: Fire

Cube
Six sides
Element: Earth

Octahedron
Eight Sides
Element: Air

Icosahedron
Twenty sides
Element: Water

Dodecahedron
Twelve Sides
**Element:
Cosmos (heaven)**

sun and earth. He analyzed the building materials and discovered that they were rich in paramagnetic properties. He also discovered that the arrangements of the towers throughout the countryside mirrored the position of the stars during the winter solstice. After his studies, Callahan concluded that the round towers produced frequencies that matched the meditative and electrical anesthesia portion of the electromagnetic spectrum.[106]

Other researchers have suggested that employing paramagnetic materials in house building, including wood and stone, can help neutralize the effects of electro- and geopathic stress.[107]

MAGNETIC FIELD INTERACTIONS WITH WATER: FORMATIONS OF GEOMETRY

The body, which is 70 percent water, has been compared to a crystal. Water itself has been analyzed at a crystal level through interaction with magnetism, and the results suggest that form is determined by thoughts and intention.

A water molecule has north and south poles, just as the earth does. These poles are separated by a dipole length, as in a magnet. This means that water has "memory": it can store information, as can a crystal.[108] Working from these fundamental principles, Japanese physicist Dr. Masura Emoto used a magnetic resonance analyzer (MRA) to photograph water samples from different sources. He then exposed these samples to prayer, sound, and words, taking before-and-after pictures.

One of the photos in his book *The Messages from Water* depicts water taken from the Fujiwara Dam in Japan. The just-sampled water molecules were dark and amorphous. Then Reverend Kato Hiki, chief priest of the Jyuhouin Temple, prayed over the dam for one hour, after which new samples were taken and photographed. The formless blobs had transformed into bright white hexagonal crystals-within-crystals.

Through his work, Emoto discovered that all substances have their own special magnetic resonance field. No two types of water look alike, in terms of their crystalline structures. But when exposed to a substance, the crystals in water change shape, eventually mirroring the substance. (For instance, water crystals might start to look like rock crystals when around a rock; algae when near algae.) Water crystals will also morph to duplicate thoughts and intentions, appearing beautiful if the thoughts are beautiful and ugly if the thoughts are ugly.[109]

He calls the principle behind this revelation *Hado*, or the source of energy behind everything. Hado represents the specific vibrating wave generated by electrons orbiting the nucleus of an atom. Wherever there is Hado, there is a field of magnetic resonance. Thus Hado—the source of all—is the magnetic resonance field itself.[110]

CYMATICS: SEEING SOUND, THE FIELDS OF LIFE

Cymatics, a term coined by Hans Jenny in his 1967 book of the same name, presents proof that vibration underlies all reality, and it reveals this truth through the study of sound waves in a medium. It is based on the observation that vibrating bodies produce patterns.

Cymatics means "matters pertaining to waves." Cymatic patterns are pictures of sound. The higher the frequency, the more complex the figures, with many shapes being comparable to *mandalas*, geometric designs used in meditation and ritual in many spiritual disciplines. Jenny's work suggests that the shapes and patterns of reality are created by the shapes of sound patterns interacting with vibration.

Jenny's work was in part based on that of Ernst Chladni, who in 1787 replicated the work of Robert Hooke from 1680 to show patterns produced by sand placed on metal plates and vibrated with a violin bow. The sand forms into what are now called *standing wave patterns*, such as simple concentric circles and even more complicated shapes. When a particular harmonic was sounded, it created a specific pattern. As one progressed along the harmonic series, the patterns also progressed in complexity.[111]

Using standing waves, piezoelectric amplifiers, and other materials, Jenny excited the plates with precisely measured vibrations and amplifications to produce demonstrations of the forms created from sound interacting with physical matter—everything in constant movement, for both sound and matter constantly fluctuate. He showed that even seemingly static geometric patterns are made of particles moving within those patterns.[112]

Jenny also discovered that upon being pronounced, the vowels of ancient Hebrew and Sanskrit took the shape of the written symbols for these vowels (our modern languages did not).

FIGURE 3.18

CYMAGLYPH OF THE HUMAN VOICE

Modern cymatics researchers John Reid and Erik Larson are continuing Jenny and Chladni's work with an instrument called the CymaScope. This image shows the physical harmonic structure of the vowel sound "oo."

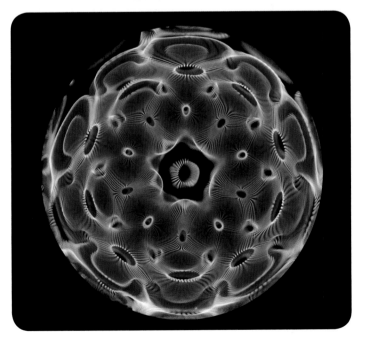

Jenny concluded his book by proposing that the generative power of reality is made up of three fields: vibration, which sustains physicality with two poles; form (or patterns); and motion.[113]

Together, these three fields create the entirety of the physical world. What seems solid is really a wave, and this wave is composed of quantum particles that are constantly moving. Even a still form is created by vibrations—moving patterns—or sound in visible form.

DOES IT ALL START WITH SOUND?

Like Hans Jenny, many shamans of yesteryear believed that sound was the origin of everything. They knew how to coalesce pictures of reality out of sound, even to effect genetic healing. This was done by many Amazonian shamans, who created three-dimensional images out of sound as part of their doctoring.

Sound has been considered so primordial that one of its scales, called the *solfeggio*, was kept secret for hundreds of years.[114] The solfeggio is a six-note scale and is also nicknamed "the creational scale." Traditional Indian music calls this scale the *saptak*, or seven steps, and relates each note to a chakra. These six frequencies, and their related effects, are as follows:

Do	396 Hz	Liberating guilt and fear
Re	417 Hz	Undoing situations and facilitating change
Mi	528 Hz	Transformation and miracles (DNA repair)
Fa	639 Hz	Connecting/relationships
Sol	741 Hz	Awakening intuition
La	852 Hz	Returning to spiritual order

Mi has actually been used by molecular biologists to repair genetic defects.[115]

Some researchers believe that sound governs the growth of the body. As Dr. Michael Isaacson and Scott Klimek teach in a sound healing class at Normandale College in Minneapolis, Dr. Alfred Tomatis believes that the ear's first *in utero* function is to establish the growth of the rest of the body. Sound apparently feeds the electrical impulses that charge the neocortex. High-frequency sounds energize the brain, creating what Tomatis calls "charging sounds."[116]

Low-frequency sounds drain energy and high-frequency sounds attract energy. Throughout all of life, sound regulates the sending and receiving of energy—even to the point of creating problems. People with attention deficit hyperactivity disorder listen too much with their bodies, processing sound through bone conduction rather than the ears. They are literally too "high in sound."[117]

Some scientists go a step further and suggest that sound not only affects the body but also the DNA, actually stimulating the DNA to create information signals that spread throughout the body. Harvard-trained Dr. Leonard Horowitz has actually demonstrated that DNA emits and receives phonons and photons, the electromagnetic waves of sound and light. As well, three Nobel laureates in medical research have asserted that the primary function of DNA is not to synthesize proteins, but to perform bioacoustic and bioelectrical signaling.[118]

While research such as that by Dr. Popp shows that DNA is a biophoton emitter, other research suggests that sound actually originates light. In a paper entitled "A Holographic Concept of Reality," which was featured in Stanley Krippner's book *Psychoenergetic Systems*, a team of researchers led by Richard Miller showed that superposed coherent waves in the cells interact and form patterns first through sound, and secondly through light.[119]

This idea dovetails with research by Russian scientists Peter Gariaev and Vladimir Poponin, whose work with torsion energies was covered in Chapter 25. They demonstrated that chromosomes work like holographic biocomputers, using the DNA's own electromagnetic radiation to generate and interpret spiraling waves of sound and light that run up and down the DNA ladder. Gariaev and his group used language frequencies such as words (which are sounds) to repair chromosomes damaged by X-rays. Gariaev thus concludes that life is electromagnetic rather than chemical and that DNA can be activated with linguistic expressions—or sounds—like an antenna. In turn, this activation modifies the human bioenergy fields, which transmit radio and light waves to bodily structures.[120]

FIGURE 3.19
CYMAGLYPH OF
THE RINGS OF URANUS

The pure sinusoidal tone of Uranus's rings, as picked up by the Voyager 2 spacecraft, produces this beautiful pattern when run through the CymaScope. The mathematical ratio of the golden section, inherent in the sine wave, is revealed in the pentagonal structure of this image.

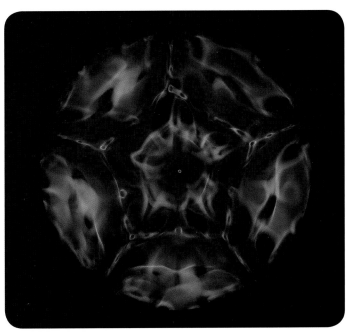

27

HUMAN ENERGY FIELDS

There are many human energy fields. These include the physically measurable electromagnetic and magnetic fields generated by all living cells, tissues, and organs, and the body as a whole. But there are also biofields—subtle or putative fields emanating from these pulsing units of life—as well as our subtle energy bodies, channels, and aspects of self. Here are brief descriptions of the most important human biofields.

MORPHOGENETIC FIELDS

In biology, a *morphogenetic field* is a group of cells that leads to specific body structures or organs. For example, a *cardiac field* becomes heart tissue. Scientist Rupert Sheldrake, in the early 1980s, was the first to label a learning field that instructs the scientifically recognized ones, calling them the *energetic* or *subtle morphogenetic* or *morphic fields*.[121]

Sheldrake suggested that there is a field within and around a morphic unit—the physical developmental unit of what later becomes a tissue or organ—that forms it. All living organisms—from cells to people—that belong to a certain group tune in to the morphic field and through morphic resonance develop according to the programs within that field. Resonance only occurs between forms that are similar, so a monkey would not take on the characteristics of a plant. According to Sheldrake, these fields serve as a database as well as a mental form.

Sheldrake's theory seeks to explain why members of a family pass down certain behaviors and even emotions and why species might share common characteristics and developmental patterns. Various studies have also shown that even when separated, members of certain species acquire similar traits or behaviors, a puzzle that can be explained by morphogenetic fields. Subtle in nature, they are not limited to time or space. This theory would portray DNA as the recipient of information from morphic fields, which instructs it to act in certain ways. Grandpa's musical gifts might be then carried on to grandson via morphic fields rather than DNA. Morphogenetic fields may instruct the epigenetic makeup, the chemical storage houses described in "Epigenetics: Beyond DNA" on page 43.

Sheldrake's philosophy also holds that past life memories could pass from lifetime to lifetime through a soul's morphic field. These memories would be nonlocal in nature and therefore not anchored in the brain or a particular life.

ETHERIC FIELDS

The word *etheric* is often used as a substitute for the terms *subtle* or *aura*. There are actually independent etheric fields around every vibrating unit of life, from a cell to a plant to a person, as well as a specific *etheric field* that is connected to the body, as described under "Special Fields" below.

The term *etheric* is a derivative from the word *ether*, which has been considered a medium that permeates space, transmitting transverse waves of energy. When associated with the entirety of the auric field, it surrounds the whole body. As a separate energy body, which is a more substantial and popular view, the etheric body links the physical body with other subtle bodies serving as a matrix for physical growth. As Barbara Brennan, a contemporary expert on the aura, suggests, it therefore exists before the cells grow.[122] Lawrence and Phoebe Bendit say the same of the auric field, asserting that it permeates every particle of the body and acts as a matrix for it.[123]

Dr. Kim Bonghan, whose research is outlined in "The Ductal Theory" on page 174, links the etheric body and the meridians, suggesting that the meridians are an interface between the etheric and the physical body. The etheric body creates the meridians, which in turn form the physical body.[124]

SPECIAL FIELDS

There are many different biofields that regulate various mental, emotional, spiritual, or physical functions. The following list of biofields is based on the work of Barbara Ann Brennan and others.

Physical field: Lowest in frequency. Regulates the human body.

Etheric field: Blueprint for the physical structure that it surrounds. There is also an etheric field for the soul.

Emotional field: Regulates the emotional state of the organism.

Mental field: Processes ideas, thoughts, and beliefs.

Astral field: A nexus between the physical and spiritual realms. Free of time and space.

Etheric template: Exists only on the spiritual plane and holds the highest ideals for existence.

Celestial field: Accesses universal energies and serves as a template for the etheric fields.

Causal field: Directs lower levels of existence.

THE AURA

Scientists have been investigating—and substantiating—the existence of the *aura*, the field that surrounds our entire body, for over a hundred years, adding to the knowledge our ancestors already possessed. This field consists of multiple bands of energy called *auric layers* or *auric fields*, that encompass the body, connecting us to the outside world.

The aura has been known by many names in many cultures.[125] The Quabalists called it an astral light. Christian artists depicted Jesus and other figures as surrounded by coronas of light. The Vedic scriptures and teachings of the Rosicrucians, Tibetan and Indian Buddhists, and many Native American tribes describe the field in detail. Even Pythagoras discussed the field, which was perceived as a luminous body. In fact, John White and Stanley Krippner, authors of *Future Science*, list ninety-seven different cultures that reference the human aura, each culture calling it by a different name.[126]

Science has been actively involved in penetrating the mystery of the aura since the early 1800s. During that time period, Belgian mystic and physician Jan Baptist van Helmont visualized it as a universal fluid that permeates everything.[127] The idea of the aura acting like a fluid—or flowing—as well as being permeable has remained consistent throughout history. Franz Mesmer, for whom the term "mesmerism" was coined, suggested that both animate and inanimate objects were charged with a fluid, which he perceived as magnetic, through which material bodies could exert influence over each other, even at a distance.[128] Baron Wilhelm von Reichenbach discovered several properties unique to this field, which he called the *odic force*.[129] He determined that it shared similar properties to the electromagnetic field, which had previously been investigated by James Clerk Maxwell, one of the fathers of electricity. The odic field was composed of polarities or opposites, as is the electromagnetic field. In electromagnetism, however, opposites attract. Not so in the odic field, where like attracts like.

Reichenbach also found that the field related to different colors and that it could not only carry a charge, but also flow around objects. He described the field on the left side of the body as a negative pole and the right side as a positive pole, similar to the ideas of Chinese medicine.

These and other theories have revealed the aura to have a fluid or flowing state; to be comprised of different colors, therefore frequencies; to be permeable and penetrable; and to be magnetic in nature, although it also has electromagnetic properties. Other research has underscored these theories and expanded one additional element of the auric field: its connection to the inner sanctum of the human being.

For example, in 1911 Dr. Walter Kilner examined the aura with colored filters and a special kind of coal tar. He discovered three zones: a dark layer next to the skin, a more ethereal layer flowing at a perpendicular angle to the body, and a delicate exterior with contours about six inches across. Most important, the conditions of this "aura," as he called it, shifted in reaction to a subject's state of mind and health.[130]

In the early part of the 1900s, Dr. Wilhelm Reich furthered our knowledge of the human field and its qualities through experiments studying a universal energy that he named "orgone." During his studies, he observed energy pulsing in the sky and surrounding all animate and inanimate objects and beings. Many metaphysicians believe that orgone is equivalent to chi or prana. He also noticed that areas of congestion could be cleared to release negative mental and emotional patterns and thus affect change. This emphasized the connections between the subtle and the physical energies as well as emotional and mental energies.[131]

Then in the 1930s, Dr. Lawrence Bendit and Phoebe Bendit observed the human energy field and linked it to soul development, showing that the subtle forces are the foundation of health.[132] Their observations are mirrored and expanded by those of Dr. Dora Kunz, a theosophist and intuitive, who saw that every organ has its own field—as does the overall body—which pulses with its own rhythm when healthy. When someone is ill, these rhythms alter, and problems can be intuitively seen in the field.[133]

When Dr. Zheng Rongliang of Lanzhou University in China measured the flow of chi from a human body with a unique biological detector, he showed that not only does the aura pulse, but that not everyone's field pulses at the same rate or intensity. This study was repeated by researchers at the Shanghai Atomic Nuclear Institute of Academia Sinica.[134]

Soviet scientists from the Bioinformation Institute, headed by A. S. Popow, actually measured the human field, or more specifically, the biocurrents manifested in the surrounding energy body. They discovered that living organisms emanate vibrations at a frequency between 300 and 2,000 nanometers. They called this field the "biofield" and discovered that people with a strong and widespread biofield can transfer energy more successfully. This research was later confirmed by the Medical Science Academy in Moscow.[135]

A special form of photography is actually able to take pictures of the auric field. In the 1930s, Russian scientist Semyon Kirlian and his wife, Valentina, invented a new photographic process that involves directing a high-frequency electrical field at an object. The object's pattern of luminescence—the auric field—can then be captured on film. Contemporary practitioners are using Kirlian photography to show how the aura responds to different emotional and mental states, and even to diagnose illness and other problems. Medical science is now using a heat aura, as well as other imaging processes, to show the different aspects of the body's electromagnetics.

One of the more compelling sets of studies in this area was conducted by Dr. Valerie Hunt. (Her research is covered in Chapter 38.) In *A Study of Structural Neuromuscular, Energy Field, and Emotional Approaches*, she recorded the frequency of low-millivoltage signals emanating from the body during Rolfing sessions.[136] She made these recordings using electrodes of silver and silver chloride on the skin. Scientists then analyzed the wave patterns recorded with a Fourier analysis and a sonogram frequency analysis. The field did, indeed, consist of a number of different color bands, which correlated to the chakras. The following results, taken from the February 1988 study, showed color-frequency correlations in hertz or cycles per second:

Blue	250–275 Hz plus 1,200 Hz
Green	250–475 Hz
Yellow	500–700 Hz
Orange	950–1050 Hz
Red	1,000–1,200 Hz
Violet	1,000–2,000, plus 300–400; 600–800 Hz
White	1,100–2,000 Hz

While mechanically measuring the subjects, healer and aura reader Reverend Rosalyn Bruyere provided her own input, separately recording the various colors she intuitively perceived. In all cases, her renderings were the same as those

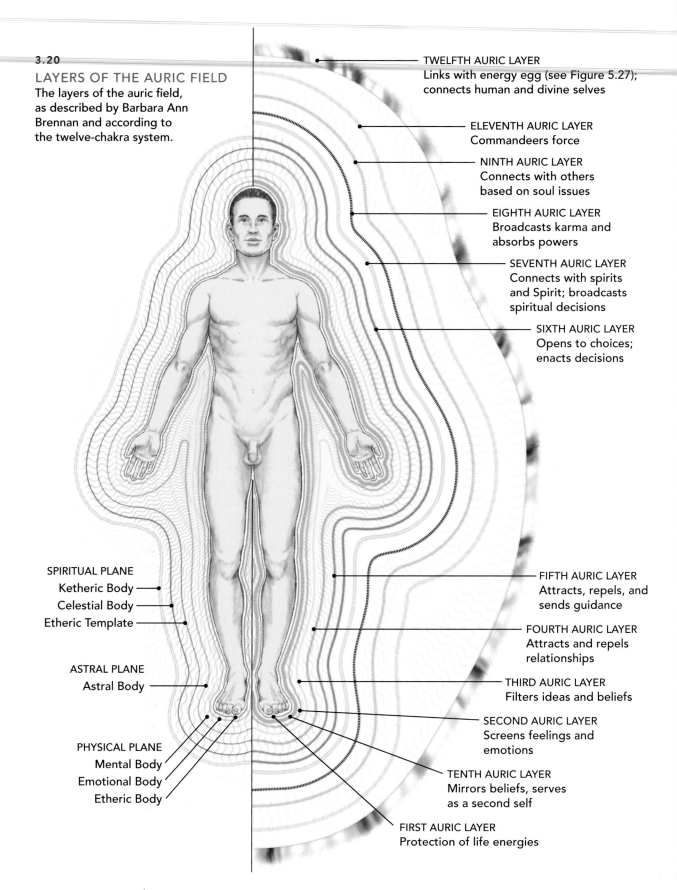

3.20

LAYERS OF THE AURIC FIELD
The layers of the auric field, as described by Barbara Ann Brennan and according to the twelve-chakra system.

TWELFTH AURIC LAYER
Links with energy egg (see Figure 5.27); connects human and divine selves

ELEVENTH AURIC LAYER
Commandeers force

NINTH AURIC LAYER
Connects with others based on soul issues

EIGHTH AURIC LAYER
Broadcasts karma and absorbs powers

SEVENTH AURIC LAYER
Connects with spirits and Spirit; broadcasts spiritual decisions

SIXTH AURIC LAYER
Opens to choices; enacts decisions

SPIRITUAL PLANE
Ketheric Body
Celestial Body
Etheric Template

ASTRAL PLANE
Astral Body

PHYSICAL PLANE
Mental Body
Emotional Body
Etheric Body

FIFTH AURIC LAYER
Attracts, repels, and sends guidance

FOURTH AURIC LAYER
Attracts and repels relationships

THIRD AURIC LAYER
Filters ideas and beliefs

SECOND AURIC LAYER
Screens feelings and emotions

TENTH AURIC LAYER
Mirrors beliefs, serves as a second self

FIRST AURIC LAYER
Protection of life energies

demonstrated mechanically. Hunt repeated this experiment with other psychics with the same results.

BUT WHAT *IS* THE AURIC FIELD?

We know it exists—but what *is* the auric field? Scientists including James Oschman, author of *Energy Medicine*, consider it a biomagnetic field that surrounds the body.[137] As Dr. Oschman says, "It is a fact of physics that energy fields are unbounded."[138] This means that our biomagnetic fields extend indefinitely. Modern equipment can now measure the heart's fields—the strongest of those originating from an organ—up to fifteen feet away. As for the aura's job, science has determined that this magnetic field conveys information about events taking place inside the body, rather than on the skin.[139] Its purpose is therefore vitally linked to our internal health.

The biomagnetic field is composed of information from each organ and every bodily tissue. The heart's currents determine its shape, as the heart is the body's strongest electrical producer. The primary electrical flow is therefore established by the circulatory system. As well, the nervous system interacts with the circulatory system and creates distinct flows, seen as whirling patterns, within the field.

We cannot fully understand the function of the aura without knowing what it is made of—and we're still working on that. Barbara Ann Brennan summarizes scientific research to suggest that it is made of "plasma," tiny—perhaps subatomic—particles that move in clouds. Scientists propose that plasmas exist in a state between energy and matter. Brennan says that this "bioplasma" is a fifth state of matter.[140] Rudolf Steiner, a brilliant author and philosopher, suggested that the human energy field is made of ether, an element comparable to a negative mass, or a hollowed-out space.[141] We can only surmise, but perhaps the field is actually made of both electromagnetic radiation (specifically magnetism) and an antimatter that allows a shift of energy between this world and others. Thus the propensity of healers to deliver healing energy based on intention is a matter of creating enough intensity in the "here and now" energies to access an equivalency in the antiworlds. What we accomplish within our own

LAYERS OF THE AURIC FIELD

BARBARA ANN BRENNAN proposes seven basic layers of the auric field. These graduate from the body, linked with each of the seven basic chakras. The chakras also attune to different subtle bodies, which combine to compose three basic planes. These planes are accessible through the auric fields.[142]

Brennan is also able to intuitively perceive two levels beyond the ketheric, which she calls the *cosmic plane*. She associates these with the eighth and ninth chakras. The eighth appears fluid to her, while the ninth is composed of a crystalline template.[143]

FIGURE 3.21

THE ASSEMBLAGE POINT

The Assemblage Point is a cluster of energy lines that connect to the body and surround it.

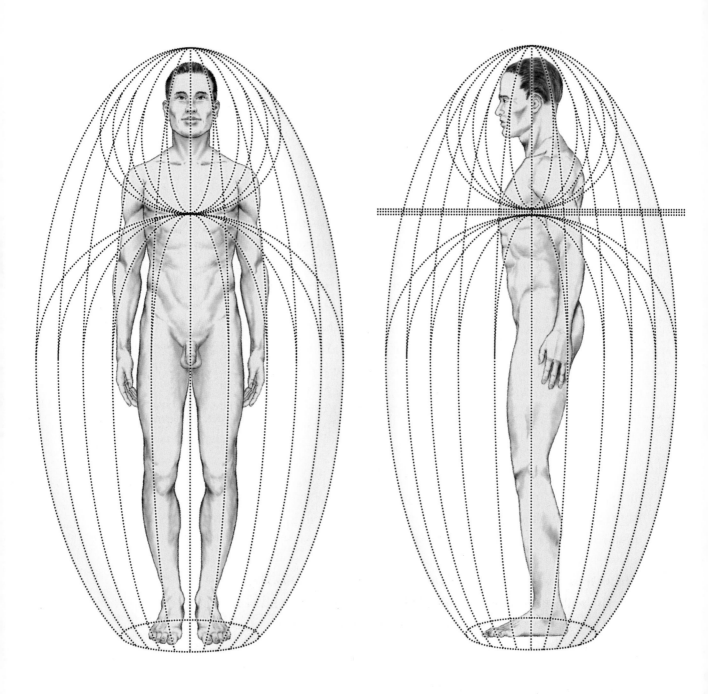

MIASMS: INTERGENERATIONAL DISORDERS PASSED THROUGH THE FIELD

THE TERM *MIASM* is owed to Samuel Hahnemann, the originator of homeopathic medicine. By 1816, Hahnemann was stumped by patients who had incurable diseases. He therefore deduced the presence of miasms, or "peculiar morbid derangement of our vital force":[144] basically, deep-seated or inherited tendencies. He treated these tendencies with homeopathy. Modern practitioners often do the same, also testing for miasms and their solutions with methods including electrodermal screening.

Hahnemann originally proposed three miasms, which are:

Psora: Creates underfunctioning; relates to the itching diseases of the skin but underlies most diseases.

Sycotic: Causes overfunctioning.

Leutic: Causes self-destruction.

Since Hahnemann's time, other miasms have been added. The key ones are:

Tubercular: Creates restriction.

Cancer: Causes suppression.[145]

There are many ways to explain miasms. One is that they are passed down through the morphogenetic fields discussed earlier in this section. Another is that they relate to epigenetics, which explains the effects of social and emotional phenomenon on the genes. Dr. Richard Gerber proposed yet another idea in *A Practical Guide to Vibrational Medicine*, which asserts that human physical and subtle bodies can develop layers of energetic armors composed of unhealed issues. For example, we can carry the energy imprint of a severe viral infection as a vibrational pattern. While we do not have the "disease," we have the predisposition for it—and for similar sorts of conditions. And these vibrational patterns can be passed down from one generation to the next.[146] This theory would embrace both the presence of the morphogenetic fields and the epigenetic inheritances.

field can be delivered like an instant message on the Internet to another individual's energy field.

THE TWELVE-CHAKRA SYSTEM AND THE AURIC FIELD

Figure 3.20 illustrates how the auric fields relate to the twelve-chakra system covered in chapter 40. The twelve-chakra system furthers Brennan's ideas about an eighth and ninth chakra, as well as higher fields.[147]

Auric fields are graduating layers of light that manage the energy outside of the body. Auric fields connect to the chakras, creating a symbiosis between what happens inside and outside of a person.

The Seven Rays are the seven attributes of God. As a system, the Seven Rays explains that our subtle energies act as transformers to convert high vibrational energies into form—the physical body. Every body contains the energies of all the rays, just as every physical body has chakras, but our particular soul and personality rays determine our potentials for strengths and weaknesses. This also means that energies affecting an individual's subtle energy bodies can result in mental, emotional, or physical illness to the physical body.

The concept of the rays originated in Vedic literature, where they are associated with the seven *rishis*, advanced masters who acted as agents of the absolute. Each ray has a different color, symbol, chakra entry and exit point, occult energy, and symbology specific to its role. Radionic practitioners frequently use the Seven Rays to augment their diagnosis and treatment of patients following a spiritual path.

THE ASSEMBLAGE POINT: CLUSTERED ENERGY LINES[149]

The *assemblage point* modality describes a cluster of energy lines or strings that penetrate the body at a particular point. While they are not part of the physical body, they immediately surround it, passing through the chest and out of the back. Each string is about one centimeter in circumference or less. The strings closest to the body are strongest and most intense; those farther away diverge and their energetic power diffuses.[150]

Practitioners report that the entry point is quite tender and between one-half and one centimeter in width. Research using infrared digital thermometers and image scanners shows that this point is about 0.2 degree centigrade lower than the surrounding skin.

There are several theories supporting the existence of the assemblage point. Paraphrased, these center on the understanding that we are composed of an oscillating energy field with an epicenter: the assemblage point. The form of this human energy field is dependent upon the location and entry angle of this point, and in turn regulates someone's biological and emotional state. However, the position of this point is determined by the biological activity inside the body. By working with this point, we can positively affect our health and lives.

Highly negative situations, such as rape or financial ruin, can shift the assemblage point into a detrimental position, thereby causing physical and emotional upheaval. Childhood trauma and drama can prevent the assemblage point from even settling in a healthy position; it seems the point settles into a specific point at about seven years of age. The various shifted positions—too far up or down, to the right or the left—adversely affect the entire system, especially the brain. Practitioners often use stone crystals or electronic gem therapy to shift and shape the Assemblage Point.

Our exploration of fields has included the measurable and the subtle, as well as the universal. The excursion has incorporated natural and artificially created fields, as well as various human varieties. We've discovered that every living organism, from small to great, emanates and is affected by fields of energy that, in large part, create the foundation for life itself. Channels are yet another structure underlying physical reality, and serve as the focus of the next section, Part IV: Channels of Energy.

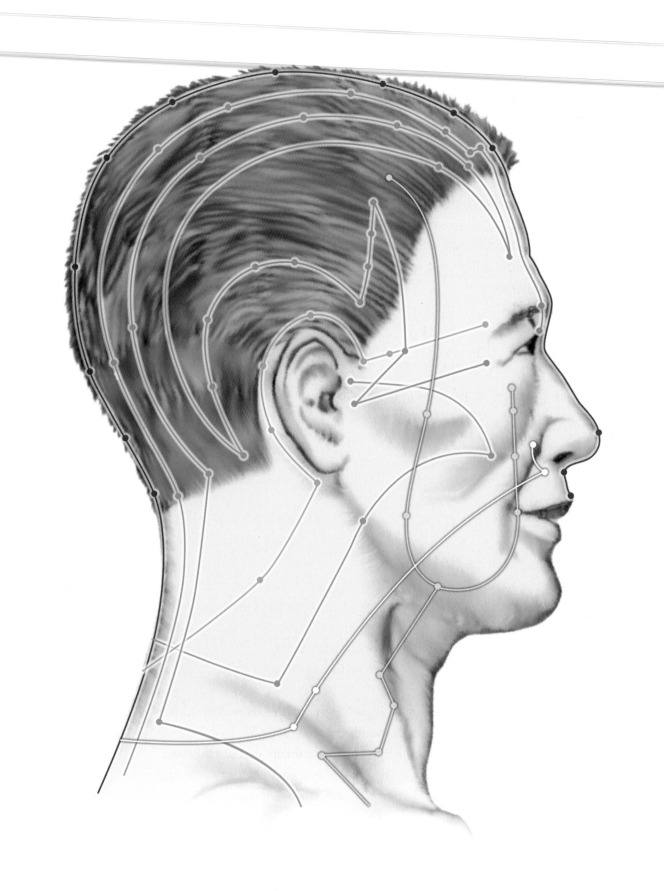

PART IV

CHANNELS OF ENERGY: CHANNELS OF LIGHT

The human body is an energetic system with channels that serve as rivers of energy—or rivers of light—to provide structure for the body. These channels interconnect the physical universe with the pulsing, living tissues inside of us.

Over five thousand years ago, the Chinese discovered a set of subtle energy channels that look like rivers flowing through the body. These channels are called *meridians*. This perception led to one of the oldest forms of medicine, traditional Chinese medicine, which represents the basis of Eastern medicine. The treatment modalities based upon them are *meridian-based therapies*, which assist in the delivery of chi, the subtle energy required for life.

Knowledge of these meridians gave rise to a complex and highly evolved medical system, based less on anatomy than on *holism*, the perception that a person is a whole being, not a collection of parts. The basic tenet of meridian therapy is that you must treat the root cause of a presenting problem—body, mind, spirit, and emotions—rather than only the symptoms. The ancient Chinese pictured a person as a circle rather than an assemblage of units. But this circle does not encompass only the individual. Each person—each living organism—is interconnected within a universal matrix. What is "in here" is essentially connected to everything "out there."

Traditional meridian therapy draws upon the *five-phase theory*. This idea is complex, a cumulative explanation of meridian-based therapies. In contrast to the ideas behind allopathic medicine, the five-phase theory describes the *relationship* between all things, rather than outlining independent factors. Besides expressing that everything reduces to five basic elements, it asserts four other major ideas: yin and yang, or polar opposites; the internal and external sources of disease; the cyclical order of life, as revealed in the cycles of the seasons;

and the existence of channels of energy that distribute the chi—the meridians. The five-phase theory explains the exact nature of "beingness"—the self as an energy being.

What began as an esoteric theory is now emerging as verifiable science, as research explains the meridians as transporters of chemical, electrical, and etheric energies. Mapping meridians thermographically (measuring heat), electronically, and radioactively with modern technology, studies and applications of these amazing streams of energy are closing the gap between Eastern and Western thought. Just as the meridians are energetic in nature, so are they physical in nature—and influence. Just as *we* are physical, so are we energetic.

Throughout our explorations of energy channels, we will continually return to the core theme of this book—and the underlying philosophy of the ancient Chinese: it is all about energy. Illness is an energetic disturbance or imbalance. Conversely, healing is a process of restoring or asserting energetic balance. By looking past the obvious—by seeing *underneath* and ultimately *through* the sinew, tissue, and skin—the Chinese discovered that disharmony in the subtle channels precedes illness. What if you, too, could "see in the dark," as did our Chinese friends? In fact, what if you could actually learn how to *see the dark—and light it?* You, too, would become the healer—and healthy person—that you could be.

28

THE HISTORY OF
MERIDIAN-BASED THERAPY

Most scholars track meridian-based therapies back to the classic text, the *Huangdi neijing*, or the *Yellow Emperor's Inner Classic*, dated to approximately 2698 BC, as well as the *Shennong bencao*, translated as the *Materia Medica of the Divine Husbandry*. The *Huangdi* outlines Chinese medicine as a healing art, while the *Shennong* is devoted to pharmacology. Huangdi was the Yellow Emperor, and the book records dialogues between him and his physicians on medical issues.[1]

Another important classic is the *Nanjing*, or the *Classic of Difficult Issues*, which is also called the *Huangdi bashiyi nanjing*, or the *Yellow Emperor's Classic of the Eighty-one Difficult Issues*. Scholars disagree on the exact author and date of this book. Some consider it the work of Bien Que, a physician who lived sometime between the sixth and third centuries BC. Others track it to the Yellow Emperor. Still others date it to the first to third century AD and a different author. Whatever its origins, the *Nanjing* presents a highly systematic and detailed outline of what has become traditional Chinese medicine.

In 1973, excavators discovered yet another text, now called the *Mawangdui corpus*, named after the tomb in which it was discovered at Changsha, Hunan. The burial is dated to 168 BC. This piece is famous for what it does not include, as well as what it does. It describes eleven instead of twelve meridians—seemingly "missing" a meridian. While it offers an archaic yin and yang philosophy, it describes acupuncture points and other basic five-theory "necessities." Interesting, however, is its inclusion of fifty-two "magical recipes," such as those to be used against demonic forces, which provides evidence of a shamanistic heritage to meridian therapy.[2]

Even today, meridians cannot be "seen." Researchers are proving their existence and offering explanations for how they work, but the naked eye—that of a surgeon cutting into the skin or an X-ray tech examining a film—cannot perceive these streams of energy. Modern equipment and techniques, however, are showing the existence of chi and enabling us to evaluate its makeup. Previous to these recent scientific validations, however, the system flourished because it was successful.

The Chinese system did not stay in China. Buddhist priests spread the knowledge of these channels and the five-phase theory to Japan, while practitioners dispersed the knowledge in other directions. Westerners were the last to catch on, primarily through the words of French Jesuits, who went to China in the sixteenth and seventeenth centuries to perform missionary work. They introduced anatomy and other Western ideas and then brought the knowledge of traditional Chinese medicine back to the West with them.[3]

Now meridian-based therapies have "caught fire" in the West. They can be found in hospitals and clinics and are being utilized by many kinds of professional healers. There are many contemporary applications, but perhaps one of the most marked and scientifically viable is that of acupuncture as an analgesic. One of the best-known researchers in the area of pain relief is Dr. Bruce Pomeranz at the University of Toronto. He discovered that stimulated acupuncture points activated myelinated nerve fibers, which in turn sent impulses to the spinal cord, midbrain, and hypothalamus-pituitary region in the diencephalon. The diencephalon is made up of the thalamus and the hypothalamus, which regulate many of our sensory and motor systems and many parts of our autonomic nervous functions as well.[4]

Acupuncture elevates the level of endorphins, pain-reducing chemicals that occur naturally within the body. Endorphins bind to the opiate receptors throughout the nervous system and stop pain by eliminating the pain messages to the brain and increasing the "feel-good" messages. Once stimulated, the hypothalamus-pituitary region releases beta-endorphins, which enter the bloodstream and spinal fluid. This process has also been successfully used with both acupuncture needles and electrical stimulation. The greatest pain relief occurs long term, with low-frequency, high-intensity applications done in repeated treatments.[5]

The Chinese and other Oriental meridian therapists have used acupuncture as an analgesic for centuries, not only for people but also for animals. In fact, the majority of acupuncture studies are about pain relief. As an analgesic, acupuncture works 70 to 80 percent of the time, as compared to 30 percent for a placebo.[6]

The evidence for the meridians will make more sense if you can first picture the basics of the meridian system. Every element of meridian-based thought—from yin and yang to the flow of chi during certain times of the day and its influence on the emotions—is now being substantiated by science.

AN OVERVIEW OF
THE MERIDIAN SYSTEM

he term *meridian* is the most common translation of the Chinese word *ching-lo*, often written as *jing-luo*. But it is not an exact rendering. *Ching* means "to pass through" and *lo*, "to connect." The original meaning was closer to the word *channel*; hence many systems call the meridians "channels" and their secondary support conduits the "collaterals." On the meridians lie *xue*, or "holes": entryways into the meridians. Contemporary practitioners usually call these *acupuncture points* or *acupoints*.

The meridians[7] are energy pathways for chi, the true foundation of the traditional Chinese system. Chi is vital energy and is analogous to the *prana, mana, maya,* and *orgone* of other systems, as well as the *ki* of the Japanese healing world. It is also spelled "qi" in many traditional systems. Chi is the force that animates and informs everything.

There are two basic vibrations or levels of chi (although there are technically three types, which are discussed in "The Basics of Chi" later in this chapter and in "The Three Vital Treasures" on page 218). On one level, chi is inanimate and perceived as a simple life force or energy. It flows from the air into our lungs, from our excretory system into nature. On another level, it is conscious intelligence, or information.

In locating chi, the early Chinese theorized what we are only now beginning to discover scientifically. In contemporary terms, we would say that everything is energy. Matter vibrates at a relatively slow frequency, and so it is referred to as physical matter. Energy that vibrates at a velocity exceeding light is subtle matter. Chi is the subtle energy that creates all physical matter.

There are twelve major meridians, which are also called the *major trunks*. These twelve meridians form a network of energy channels throughout the body for the distribution of chi, thereby controlling all bodily functions and connecting all parts of the body to each other. Each of these pathways is linked to a specific organ or organ system, therefore revealing the body as a circle of interdependent parts, not a collection of separate pieces. The chi passes through the body in a regular, twenty-four-hour pattern; therefore, these twelve major meridians participate in every facet of life's daily metabolic and physiological processes.

The *twelve standard meridians* run on the surface of the body, either on the chest, back, arms, or legs. They are: Lung, Large Intestine, Stomach, Spleen, Heart (sometimes called the Pericardium or Heart Protector), Small Intestine, Urinary Bladder, Kidney, Pericardium, Triple Warmer (sometimes called the Triple Heater or Three Heater), Gallbladder, and Liver. These terms refer to biological functions and not structural organs; however, all but the Triple Warmer and Heart meridians are connected to a specific organ system. The Triple Warmer is thought to govern the chi level of the entire body, as it controls the distribution of all types of chi. The Heart meridian works with the Triple Warmer to control the body's overall energy level, but is also vital to the functioning of the heart.

In addition to the major meridians there are *eight extraordinary channels*, also called *vessels*. They are: the Du, the Ren, the Dai, the Chong, the Yin Chiao, the Yang Chiao, the Yin Wei, and the Yang Wei meridians.

The eight vessels are first formed *in utero* and represent a deep level of energetic structure. They store and drain chi, also serving as reservoirs that ferry chi and blood along the twelve regular channels. These secondary meridians are not associated with specific organs or meridians; rather, they connect the main meridians, serving as the means through which the main meridians connect with the organs and other parts of the body. The most important of these extra meridians are the Governor vessel, which runs along the middle of the back, and the Conception vessel, which courses along the front of the body. Some modern practitioners consider these two vessels as equal to the main twelve, and so count fourteen main meridians.

In all, there are three meridian groups associated with the regular meridians, each with twelve meridians. The *divergent meridians* rise from one of the twelve main meridians and pass through the thorax or abdomen to connect with an organ before surfacing at the neck or head. The *muscle network meridians* allocate chi from the twelve major meridians to the muscles, tendons, and joints. This distribution is considered superficial because these meridians do not contact any organs. The *cutaneous network meridians* run alongside the regular meridians in the cutaneous skin layer; these, too, are considered superficial. Some systems present these as part of the sensory nervous system.

Along the twelve major meridians are more than 400 acupuncture points, as classified by the World Health Organization. (Some systems enumerate between

500 and 2,000 points.) These are labeled according to name, number, and their corresponding meridian.[8] Every meridian contains 25 to 150 acupuncture points (acupoints) particular to it, and terminates at the end of a finger or toe. Each meridian has specific points that most accurately describe its current condition. There is an "alarm point" in the frontal midline of the torso that reacts whenever chi is imbalanced in a specific meridian. This alarm point has a corresponding "associated point" along the spine that echoes the problems in that meridian. These points are shown on the meridian illustrations (see pages 185–201).

Each organ system carries its own brand of chi, which allows it to perform certain unique physical as well as energetic functions. Western medicine specializes in analyzing the physical functions of an organ, such as the production of enzymes by the liver. Eastern medicine adds an understanding of the energetic functions of an organ and the system of that organ—the particular and holistic roles it plays within the complete self.

Chi is perhaps best visualized as a continuum of energy rather than something that can be defined microscopically. It is at once inanimate and animate. It is free flowing and unconscious as well as delineated and conscious. It is also made up of two opposite sets of information: female and male, or yin and yang.

Yin is the earth energy that signifies the feminine qualities on this planet and is cool in nature. *Yang* is the heavenly energy that represents the masculine side and is hot in nature. Chi is a combination of these two divergent spectrums of energy, as well as many other specific expressions of nature. It is also described in terms of the five elements: fundamental, living forces of energy that are constantly in motion. These elements are the foundation of the five-phase theory of diagnosis and treatment, which is outlined later in this section. Each of these elements corresponds to one of the five major organ systems, which in turn can be classified by its relationship to a season of the year, a time of the day, a color, a sound, a smell, an emotion, a food . . . and so much more. Together, the yin-yang theory and the five-element theory reflect a universal law; everything relates in a complex set of interdependent relationships that underlies the physical level of reality.

The yin-yang theory is crucial to understanding the meridians. Everything within the body—and the meridian system—is dualistic. Each meridian, for example, consists of two parts. The outer part operates at the surface of the skin to collect energy. This is considered a yang function. The inner part serves the internal organs by transporting energy to an organ or body system site. This is a yin process.

The major meridians are subdivided into yin and yang groups. The yin meridians of the arm are Lung, Heart, and Pericardium. The yang meridians of the arm are Large Intestine, Small Intestine, and Triple Warmer. The yin meridians of the leg are Spleen,

Kidney, and Liver. The yang meridians of the leg are Stomach, Bladder, and Gallbladder. Yang energy governs the Governor vessel and yin the Conception vessel.

Meridians are also classified as excitatory (yang) or inhibitory (yin) according to the polarity of the chi they manage. The organs connected to yin meridians are also considered yin, or inhibitory, and the organs connected to yang meridians are considered yang, or excitatory. Because the yin and yang aspects of a meridian interconnect, you can treat a yang-related condition in an organ and produce an effect in the yin side of the meridian.

All meridians are paired, or have a polar opposite (see "The Cycles of Chi: The Body Clock" on page 228). Polar meridians are twelve hours apart in the twenty-four-hour cycle. These paired meridians are similar in some ways, but contrast in others. For example, the Spleen and Triple Warmer are polar meridians. Both affect the immune system and are radiant circuits, yet they can also negatively react to each other. If the Triple Warmer is too excited, the Spleen meridian is inhibited, and vice versa. The Triple Warmer is at its energetic peak between 9 p.m. and 11 p.m.; the Spleen meridian is at its peak between 9 a.m. and 11 a.m.

YIN AND YANG: MEETING OF THE OPPOSITES

YIN-YANG THEORY PROPOSES that there are two basic types of forces. These are opposing and yet mutually interdependent. When combined, yin and yang energies create a unified, supreme energy—the one that originated the universe and continues to flow throughout it.

Yang is the male, excitatory energy. It is dynamic, stimulating, and logical. It creates height and represents the sky and heavens. In the Chinese model, it is considered hot, or able to produce heat. Yin is the female, inhibitory energy. It is static, calming, and intuitive. It is represented by the low points in land or nature and is signified by earth and the underground. It is considered cool, or able to produce coolness.

Yin and yang characterize two different types of chi. There are also yin versus yang meridians and organs. If these become out of balance,

serious health issues can arise. Too much heat, for example, underlies pain and inflammation. Too much cold causes stagnation and blockage. Each is needed to balance the other; for example, heat can drive out cold, while cold can reduce heat. Because yin and yang are relative to each other, there is always a relationship fostering the "other" condition. For example, we can only understand heat if there is cold.

Yin can lead to yang and yang can lead to yin. One flows into the other—and then returns. For instance, ice (yin) when warmed by yang becomes water, which when heated by further yang, becomes vapor. The body's activity (yang) is supported by its material form (yin), and the physical form is sustained by the body's activity.

This balance is achieved by a check and balance of control and inhibition. Sometimes, yin must increase to benefit our system: we might

According to five-phase theory, each meridian is associated with an element. This relationship, including the related yin-yang properties, can be shown in this chart:

FIGURE 4.1
YIN AND YANG MERIDIANS

Yin-Yang Meridian	Element
Lung (arm-yin) and Large Intestine (arm-yang)	Metal
Stomach (leg-yang) and Spleen (leg-yin)	Earth
Heart (arm-yin) and Small Intestine (arm-yang)	Fire
Bladder (leg-yang) and Kidney (leg-yin)	Water
Pericardium (arm-yin) and Triple Warmer (arm-yang)	Fire
Gallbladder (leg-yang) and Liver (leg-yin)	Wood

Every part of the body is mirrored by something else in—or outside—the body. This viewpoint has generated an amazingly profound—and complicated—medical system. Underneath this brilliance, however, is simplicity. All traditional Chinese modalities essentially reduce to a single process: assessment of the chi through the meridians.

be tired and in need of rest. Yin takes over to relax us. Yang, or movement, must decrease to allow this shift. (We are not able to take a nap when we are jogging.) The opposite must occur when it is time to get busy. There is a reason that people are sometimes referred to as "couch potatoes." Sitting around watching television while snacking on chips is a yin practice, but is not good for our girths or minds. We have to give up some yin to make way for yang's healthy contributions. Likewise, all yang is not healthy; we must rest and not continually run marathons, either of the mind or the body.

In the Chinese system, all of life is a cycling of yin and yang, including the seasons, which continually exchange yin (winter) for yang (summer), with the seasons in between for balance. At its peak, one extreme often gives rise to the other. For example, the solstices occur when the sun is at its northern or southern extreme, and therefore mark a change in light. December 21 is a low point for light; June 21 is a high point. Winter solstice is yin or dark and gives rise to yang or light; summer solstice is the opposite. This mirrors the way our bodies flow from one extreme to the other, in a constant ebb and flow of yin and yang.

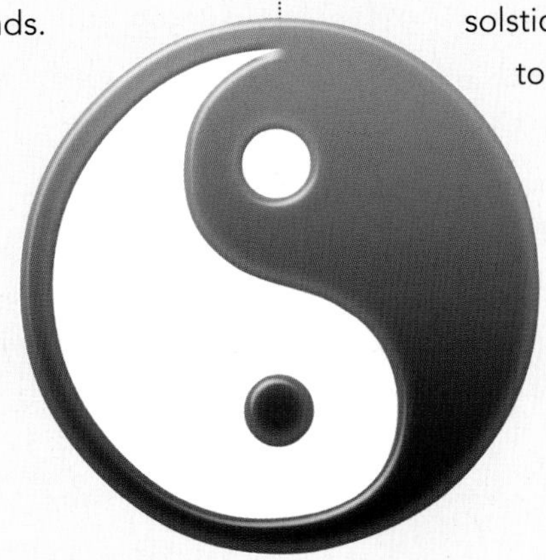

Chi has many translations, as nearly every culture has its own version, but in general, it is the vital energy of the universe. Chi is the pure and free-flowing energy that activates and nurtures life and connects the small and the great.

The ancient Chinese thought of chi in a continuum. *Material chi* is unconscious and creates the physical universe; it is measurable, in that it forms the measurable universe. *Subtle chi* is immeasurable, in that it formulates the as yet immaterial universe and consciousness. When flowing through the meridians, the channels for chi distribution, chi is both free flowing (or unconscious) and informed (or conscious). In this latter guise, chi conveys information from one bodily site and system to the other, as well as to and from the universe.

Chi reduces and disperses in alternating cycles of negative and positive energies, or yin and yang. In the process, it can appear in many shapes and forms. As with all energy, it cannot be destroyed; it merely transforms from one state to another. Everything is a temporary manifestation of chi—especially the physical universe.

Chi is considered the source of all movement in the body as well as the universe. In its intelligent state, it actually links the mundane with the spiritual, or our own bodies with our spirits. As such, it is often connected with the breath, is seen as the source of vitality, is considered the measurement of our energy, and creates and sustains the personality.

In Japan, it is called *ki*. To East Indians, it is *prana*. The ancient Picts of northern England called it *maucht*, and the Christians have long considered it a gift from the *Holy Spirit*. The Greeks and the Egyptians called it the *Art of Mysteries* while the Haitian Voodoo called it *The Power*. To those in the Appalachian Mountains, it is *The Shining*. More recent researchers might call it *bioenergy, biomagnetism, electrochemical energy, electromagnetic energy, subtle energy,* or just plain *energy*.

There are different ways of looking at chi, according to different theoretical systems. A popular version in Qigong, a movement-based healing process discussed on page 385, is as follows:

Heaven chi: Involves the energies of the universe, such as sunlight, gravity, and magnetism.

Earth chi: Involves everything on earth, such as land, seas, wind, plants, and animals.

Human chi: Energy as related to humans.[9]

These three forms of energy are interdependent. Heaven chi influences earth chi, and both of these influence human chi. In the Chinese system, all three types of chi flow through the Triple Warmer meridian, which controls their distribution. From there, it travels through the twelve meridians on a twenty-four-hour cycle, its flow varying according to the seasons of the year. In addition, it moves through the two main vessels: one in the center of the front of the body (the Conception vessel) and one that rises up the center of the back (the Governor vessel).

One way of perceiving these interdependent forms of vital energy is through a discussion of Tai Chi, which is both a way of life and a "soft" or "energetic" version of martial art. *Tai chi* means "the ultimate," and involves progressing toward the ultimate existence, partially through a series of movements that move chi through the body. In Tai Chi, the three levels of energy can be accessed along three stages of development. The basic level is *life energy* and is inherent in every organism. The next stage is *chi*, a higher-than-normal manifestation of life energy. The third level, *heavenly chi*, is a higher form of energy than chi. According to Tai Chi, chi generates a form of energy called *jing*, also called *nei jing*, or the internal power. One practices Tai Chi not only to produce more chi but to transform it into the more elevated jing. Another purpose for practicing Tai Chi is to produce *li*, a physical force.

In the five-phase theory, chi is often presented in these three forms, called the three vital treasures:

- Basic essence or *jing*
- Energy or life force or *chi*
- Spirit and mind or *shen*[10]

In turn, these three types of vital energy subdivide according to organ systems, as you will find in "The Three Vital Treasures" on page 218 and in Chapter 34, "Five-Phase and Related Diagnostic Theories."

Another system presents six other versions of chi. These are:

Clean chi: In the clean air we inhale.

Waste chi: Takes wastes out when we exhale.

Material chi: A combination of clean and waste chi and food nutrients.

Nourishing chi: Derived from digested food; the chi that then circulates through our body and nourishes the entirety.

NEW WAYS TO LOOK AT OLD CHI

THE NEWEST THEORY in chi is *mechanical chi*. Dr. Yury Khronis, a Russian-born physicist, created a complex chi generator machine a few years ago. Working with an Eastern-trained chi master named Dong Chen, he has been able to produce chi energy electronically. For example, he has a chi pattern called "quiet mind" that shifts the brain into low-frequency theta waves and another that produces patterns for each chakra point.[11]

One theory of how the machine works is that, though chi is a subtle energy, it can be carried on electromagnetic energies. This idea echoes William Tiller's model of energy discussed in Part I, which asserts that there is a polarity between subtle and material energies. Electromagnetic patterns of energy can therefore contain subtle imprints that can be perceived through the normal five senses.[12]

PHYSICAL CHI

Studies by researchers including Professor Kim Bonghan are suggesting that chi, in addition to being an etheric substance, might also be made of physical material. As is explored in "The Marriage of Subtle Energies and Matter in the Meridians" on page 174, Dr. Bonghan determined that chi is a fluid composed of several chemicals and electricity. Many bioenergetic professionals propose that what is subtle is also physical.

Protective chi: Chi formed from food; the chi that provides defensive maneuvers as it circulates through the superficial tissues of the body and the skin.

Functional chi: The types of chi associated with a particular organ system or meridian.

Nourishing chi is considered yin and protective chi is labeled as yang.[13]

There are also more than seven hundred cavities that are commonly used in acupuncture, acupressure, and Qigong. These are the body's natural cavities, such as the sinus, gastric, nasal, and joint cavities, many of which hold organs or are filled with fluid. Because of variances of energy, you must increase or decrease your energy so that none of the chi cavities or meridians becomes blocked.

THEORIES OF THE EXISTENCE, PURPOSE, AND FUNCTIONING OF THE MERIDIANS

Meridians are pathways for many different types of physical and subtle energies. While invisible to the naked eye, they are circuits of positive and negative energies, as well as bodily fluids, and have been measured using various methods. As well, the 400 to 500 assorted meridian points (numbers vary according to the system) used in acupuncture, a process involving needling the meridians through energetic gateways, display unique and scientifically viable electrical characteristics that distinguish them from the surrounding skin. Electromagnetic in nature, acupuncture points can be found by hand, through testing with microelectrical voltage meters, and through the use of applied kinesiology or "muscle testing," which tests the body's reactions to concepts or substances. (Kinesiology is discussed in Part VI.) Scientific research supports five different but interrelated theories about meridians.

BIOMECHANICAL THEORY

The biomechanical explanation centers on research that seeks to validate the existence of the meridians. Some research, such as that conducted by Drs. Claude Darras and Pierre De Vernejoul, involves tracking the meridian system with radioactive tracers. Further research by Dr. Liu YK identified the location of acupoints on the motor nerves.[14] These and other studies show that the meridians are part of the body's mechanical framework and interact with the anatomical system.

BIOELECTROMAGNETIC THEORY

There is no mystery here; the human body is an electrical-magnetic phenomenon. For decades, scientists have probed the marvel called the "current of injury." Whenever the skin is injured, the wound area emits electrically charged ions into the surrounding tissue, creating a weak electrical charge, comparable to the charges produced by batteries. This electric current serves a vital function: it excites a healing response in the nearby cells. Considerable research has applied this physiological reality to explain the effectiveness of acupoint stimulation.

STANDING WAVE THEORY

In 1986, two researchers, Fritz-Albert Popp and Chang-Lin Zhang, teamed up to create a model called the *standing wave superposition hypothesis*. In short, they portrayed the overall meridian system as a holographic image of the body represented in the ears and the feet. It also sought to explain the interconnectivity of the points.

MICROCIRCUITS: A SECONDARY ELECTRICAL SYSTEM

EVER-INCREASING NUMBERS OF scientists are proposing that the meridian system is part of a secondary electrical system—one that might include but is also different from the established circulatory and central nervous systems.

Through his research, Dr. Björn Nordenström discovered that electricity, as well as blood, flows through the bloodstream, but seems to "feed" two different (but interrelated) systems.[15] A well-respected Swedish radiologist, Nordenström discovered that the body has the equivalent of electric circuits that run throughout it, which he describes in his book *Biologically Closed Electric Circuits: Experimental and Theoretical Evidence for an Additional Circulatory System*.[16] Nordenström has determined that these circuits are switched on by an injury, infection, tumor, or even the normal activity of an organ. According to him, these voltages build and fluctuate, coursing through the arteries and veins and across capillary walls.

The biological circuits operate by accumulated charges, which oscillate between the twin polarities of positive and negative. Larger vessels serve as cables, with blood plasma conducting the charges. In permeable tissue, such as connective tissue, the intra-cellular fluid conducts the ions. These ions move through the cells via cellular openings and pores. Electrons cross through the walls using enzymes. However, when subjected to an electrical field, such as one generated by an injured muscle, the arterial walls close. This forces the ions to move through the bloodstream and along the capillary walls. In effect, there is a "secondary electrical circuit" in the body.

The implications of this work are staggering. By shifting the ionic flow—and moving between circuits—we can potentially cure diseases including cancer and autoimmune disorders, as Nordenström has demonstrated by apparently curing more than eighty people of cancer.

Previous to Nordenström's discoveries, scientists believed that every human action involves the conduction of electrical signals along the fibers of the nervous system. Now it appears that all bodily processes also involve the ebb and flow of biologically closed electrical circuits.[17] His research also at least partially explains how meridians and acupuncture points function. The process is anchored in electromagnetism. In his book, Nordenström makes several conjectures in this area, including:

Also called the Zhang-Popp theory, the standing wave theory of meridians includes a scientific principle called *superposing*. Superposing involves the interaction of waves, a topic explored in "The Fundamentals: Particles and Waves" on page 11. Standing waves were introduced in "Scalar Waves" on page 107. We will review some of this information to show its application to meridians.

Superposing occurs when two or more similar waves combine to form a third and more complex one. These waves create something new—but also continue as they were before. Some interact a little differently, however. *Interference* happens when two waves start at the same point but approach each other from different directions. When these two waves are in rhythm with each other, the result is a *constructive interference*, or reinforcement. The resulting wave is twice as

- Acupuncture points serve as receivers of subtle energy signals from the outside world, much like a sophisticated radar system.
- These sites receive all types of energies, not only physical, as reflected in research that shows Qigong masters being able to affect the body's electrical properties with mental processes and force fields.
- This process might explain the placebo and nocebo effects, and spontaneous remission of cancer, to name a few mind-body phenomena. In other words, messages of faith or belief can themselves filter into the acupoints and create a shift in the secondary electrical system, which promotes healing.[18]

Nordenström concludes that the forces flowing in the secondary system can be thought of as chi and the positive and negative charges, the yin and the yang. The secondary system "is" the meridian system, at least in part. The bioelectromagnetic forces influence the life and death of the cells and the body as a whole, revealing the cycles of the five elements and their associated organs.[19]

Nordenström's experimentation led to a cancer curative. By inserting stainless-steel needle electrodes directly into lung tumors and applying ten volts of positive electricity with a negative electrode applied to the skin of the chest, Nordenström succeeded in destroying cancerous tissue.[20]

Robert O. Becker, a lead researcher in the effects of electricity in the body, asserts that both positive and negative electricity will increase cancer. Degeneration from electrical applications occurs through the alterations in ionization produced by electrical charges: for example, when the electricity shifts the local pH.[21] Becker has performed his own experiments, some of which led to the conclusion that cancer cells exposed to certain electrical factors grew at least 300 percent faster than the controls (again, whether the electricity was positive or negative). Research by investigators including Dr. Abraham Liboff, a professor of physics, revealed that the critical factor in reducing or increasing cancerous growths didn't lie in the charge of electricity, but rather in the application of magnetic fields.[22] Research discussed throughout this book shows that north- versus south-pole magnetic fields create opposite effects in regard to tissue growth or decrease.

amplified as the original ones. *Destructive interference* occurs when the waves are out of synch, and now they cancel each other out. *Standing or stationary waves* are waves that do not move. They form when two progressive waves come from opposite directions and meet—and then create a harmonically pleasing vertical wave. According to the Zhang-Popp theory, the waves from the acupuncture points and the meridians work through constructive interference.

The skin is high in electrical conductivity, partially because it is composed of sodium, potassium, and other electrically charged ions, including proteins and DNA, which give off electromagnetic radiation when accelerated or stimulated. This conductivity depends on the internal electrical field, which is determined by the interference pattern from the superposition of the numerous waves. The skin's highest conductivity is at the acupoints.[23]

Needling creates a disturbance in the standard wave pattern and activates the current of injury response. At this point, there is a transformation in the electromagnetic field, which in turn changes the physiological responses.[24] The field changes are not only local, but occur within the entirety of the body's fields: hence the "holographic nature" of this theory.

CONNECTIVE TISSUE THEORY

This theory is based on the existence of cytoskeletal structures in every cell in the body. These structures, in effect, form connective tissue. Nuclear magnetic resonance has shown that the muscles are organized in "liquid-crystalline-like" structures that change drastically when exposed to electromagnetic fields.[25] This alteration occurs because connective tissue carries static electric charges and is influenced by pH, salt concentration, and the dielectric constant of the solvent. Many scientists now believe that the meridians lie within this "liquid network," or at least, stimulate its responsiveness. In other words, this liquid network carries the electromagnetic responses elicited from acupuncture.

CONNECTIVE TISSUE, ENERGY, AND THE ACUPOINTS

Dr. William Tiller has conceived a theory that explains how meridians interface the etheric, or subtle, energies within the physical body. His ideas are primarily based on research about the role of the connective tissue and meridian science.

Research has shown that there is an electrical resistance of about 50,000 ohms between any two acupoints, and over the same length of normal skin, a resistance of twenty times less. The resistance changes depending upon what we do; for example, it increases during sleep and even more when we are emotionally excited.

These and other experiments have led some researchers, as Tiller notes, to conclude that acupoints are located in shallow depressions in the planes between two or more muscles. They are contained within vertical columns of connective tissue and surrounded by even thicker and more dense skin tissue. This external tissue is not a good electrical conductor, which indicates that the acupoint is indeed a relatively independent conductor.[26]

As Tiller explains in his book *Science and Human Transformation*, the "connection" between the connective tissue and the meridian system can be explained this way. Acupoints are situated in surface depressions along the cleavage planes between two or more muscles. They are surrounded by loose connective tissue, which in turn is surrounded by thick and dense connective tissue of the skin—which is not a good conductor of electricity. When a serious imbalance exists in the meridian, there are differences in the resistance patterns that do not exist when there is a balance.[27]

When there is a serious imbalance (such as from disease), a suction-like force holds the acupuncture needle in place, letting it go when there is temporary balance. This works for all acupuncture-type treatments, including acupressure, moxabustion, needles, electric current, and laser light. This stimulation generates endorphins in the bloodstream, which in turn generate enkaphalines in the brain—all natural opiates of the body. Serotonin has also been found to serve as a mediator for acupuncture analgesic in both the brain and the spinal cord.

This theory does not completely explain some of the histological or tissue changes that occur during acupuncture, which, Tiller says, shows that meridians must process subtle as well as physical energies. Tiller postulates the existence of particles that he calls "deltrons" that connect these two energies.[28] These deltrons allow Tiller to make the following claims:

- The meridians, which lie in the connective tissue, are antennae for subtle energies.
- The acupuncture antennae are primarily at the etheric rather than the physical level, which explains the lack of histological differences between the acupoints and the surrounding tissue.
- Subtle energy waves flow along the etheric meridians, yielding a flow of magnetic vector potential along the meridian channels.
- This flow creates an electric field along the channel, which pumps ions along the channel to increase the ionic conduction of it, and then increases the electrical conductivity of the acupoints at the skin surface.[29]

This model suggests that the external electromagnetic field and the subtle energy systems of the body can communicate through the internal physical and subtle substances of the body—including through the meridians. He also suggests that this transformational communication between the etheric body and the physical body is one reason that magnets can influence the acupuncture points.

HYALURONIC ACID: A MISSING LINK?

What might join the connective tissue with our microcircuit system? One possibility might be hyaluronic acid (HA).

HA is a component of connective tissue. Its job is to lubricate and buffer. Involved with wound healing, it links with fibrin, which assists in clotting, to form a three-dimensional matrix that enables tissue reconstruction.[30] As we will explore in "The Marriage of Subtle Energies and Matter in the Meridians" below, researcher Dr. Kim Bonghan deduced that on the physical level, chi is made up of electricity and high-energy chemical substances, including hyaluronic acid, which compose the fluids flowing through meridians.[31] Hyaluronic acid is present in the umbilical cord and so exists in the human physical body starting at birth.

As we have seen, Dr. Nordenström determined that there is a secondary electrical system in the body generated by blood vessel "cables" surrounded by an electromagnetic field. Dr. Ralph Wilson, a naturopathic doctor, proposed that these fields are held in place by hyaluronic acid molecules that create function tubules, or zones, which serve as conduits for the ions, and that these ions are the chi.[32] Current research suggests that HA plays at least an offstage role in conducting chi.

THE DUCTAL THEORY

Research by Professor Kim Bonghan suggests that the meridians are a series of ducts, or tubes, that carry chi. He discovered that the meridians are formed after the initial marriage of the sperm and ova, develop *in utero*, and are then released throughout the body.

THE MARRIAGE OF SUBTLE ENERGIES AND MATTER IN THE MERIDIANS

One of the most important figures in the science of bioenergy is Dr. Harold Burr, whose work was discussed in Part III. Through his research, Burr discovered that an electrical axis developed in the unfertilized egg that corresponded with the future orientation of the brain and central nervous system in the adult.[33] This electrical axis serves as a guide for a directional energy field that provides spatial orientation to the cells in the developing embryo. It was also discovered that the contour of the electrical field of the embryo followed the shape of the adult electrical field.

Dr. Burr theorized that an electrodynamic field establishes the organization of a biological system. This field is partially constructed by its physical and chemical components and is electrical in nature. Dr. Randolph Stone, the inventor of polarity therapy, said it even more succinctly:

Energy waves build the human body by radiation in intra-uterine life, as a pattern of energy currents, and continue to maintain it by this energy flow as wireless currents.[34]

Through Nordenström's work, we have seen that there is a secondary (or perhaps primary) electrical system in the body. Furthermore, the meridians are electromagnetic in nature as well as effect, and so are able to link us with other internal and external electromagnetic fields. Research on connective tissue locates the meridians at least partially within the connective tissue. Darras and de Vernejoul's work in tracking the meridian system interplays with that of other researchers, including Becker and Motoyama, in substantiating the ancients' view of the meridian lines. Tiller's theory that the meridians are subtle as well as physical systems seems to offer them as "all-inclusive": physical-chemical, electrical, and etheric in nature. Electrographic researchers have found that changes in the acupuncture points "may precede the changes of physical illness in the body by hours, days, or even weeks," which furthers the case that the meridians somehow "program" the physical body.[35]

And all of this reduces to this question: Where do the meridians "come from"?

Professor Kim Bonghan at least partially answered this question. Publishing his research in 1965, he used a high-powered electron microscope to test fluid flowing from the meridian localities. In this way, he determined that the fluid was comprised of several life-forming substances, including DNA, adrenaline, estrogen, and hyaluronic acid. The proportions of these substances in the fluid far exceeded that found in other bodily fluids, including the blood and lymph. He therefore concluded that this fluid was the material aspect of chi, a blend of high-energy chemical substances and electricity.

Bonghan then experimented with the embryos of several species and discovered that a chicken began to develop its meridian system within fifteen hours of birth. Through further analysis, he determined that the ectoderm, endoderm, and mesoderm, and all the organs, are organized by the embryonic energies (subtle energies), which in turn serve as a template for the material energies. Furthermore, he defined the meridians as a tubular system that is divided into superficial and deep systems, which in turn is further subdivided. Here are some of his findings:

Internal duct system: This consists of free-floating tubes within the vascular and lymphatic vessels. These tubules penetrate the vessel walls at two points, entry and exit sites. The fluids in these ducts usually flow in the same direction. Bonghan theorizes that these ducts were formed differently and maybe earlier than the blood and lymph systems, and might serve as spatial guides for the development of these bodily systems. In other words, the vessels grew around the meridians, not the other way around.

Intra-external duct system: Found along the tops of the internal organs, these form a network separate from the blood, lymph, and nervous systems.

External duct system: This travels along the outer surface of the walls of the blood and lymph vessels and is also found in the skin, where it is known as the superficial duct system.

Superficial duct system: This is the one known to most meridian-based therapists.

Neural duct system: This runs within the central and peripheral nervous systems.

The beauty of these ductules is that they interweave all parts of the body, deep and superficial. These ducts are linked through what Bonghan called the "terminal ductules" of various systems, which stretch into the nuclei of the tissues' cells. And interspersed along the meridians are very small corpuscles that correspond with, but also lie underneath, the acupoints.

The sum of this research is that the meridians (along with other subtle energies) might in fact organize our physical bodies. Etheric in nature, they are also physical, composed of a complex interweaving of chemicals, electricity, and electromagnetic forces that carry chi—a physical and etheric energy—that feeds our bodies, minds, and souls.[36]

31

THE HISTORY OF
MERIDIAN SCIENCE

Research leading to the scientific validation of the meridians began in 1937, when a prestigious British medical journal featured an article by Sir Thomas Lewis describing an unknown network of what he believed to be cutaneous nerves connected to the autonomic nervous system. Lewis postulated that this network was not made of nerve fibers, but was instead a network of thin lines.[37] This was one of the first Western confirmations of a system suggesting the existence of meridians.

In 1950, Yoshio Nakatani showed that when someone was ill, the acupuncture points along the affected meridian tested significantly lower in electrical resistance in comparison with the surrounding skin. The resistance values also changed with the time of day, ambient temperature, and use of acupuncture, as well as the physical activity and emotional state of the subject. He named the points *ryodurako points*, which have become the basis for some electroacupuncture therapies, including electrodermal screening.[38]

Nakatani's work has been duplicated many times, with researchers consistently revealing a difference in electrical conductivity between acupuncture and nonacupuncture points.[39] Research also shows that the resistance of acupoints ranges from 100 to 200 kV, while nonpoints have higher resistance reaching up to 1 mV; it also shows that acupoints are about 50 percent more conductive than the surrounding points.[40]

Perhaps Dr. Ioan Dumitrescu, a Romanian physician, conducted the most sophisticated research in this particular area. Dumitrescu used electrographic imaging to scan the body, noting where electrically radiant points appeared. Most of these points, which he called *electrodermal points*, correlated with traditional acupoints. Through his research, Dr. Dumitrescu reached a few foundational conclusions:

- The points only appeared where there was current or imminent pathology.
- These points exactly mirrored the classic Chinese meridian theories; the diseased organs were related to the standard corresponding meridians.
- The larger the electrodermal points, the more active the disease.

In conclusion, he determined that these points are "electric pores" that exchange energy between the body and the electric medium. Working energetically, they link the body and the surrounding energy fields. Therefore, the meridian system is an interface between subtle and physical energies.[41]

We now enter the laboratory of Dr. Robert Becker and associates in the late 1970s. Their research identified lower resistance values for over 50 percent of the acupoints along the Large Intestine meridian. Becker theorized that the acupoints are amplifiers of a semiconducting direct current (DC) that travels along the perineural cells, which are conductors wrapped around the nerves in the body. This DC system becomes negative in the extremities, such as at the ends of the fingers and toes, and positive when it enters the trunk and head.

We already know that the body emanates—and is—a gigantic electromagnetic field and that the body's circuitry, which is electrical, generates the magnetic portion of the field. Electromagnetism depends upon the polarities of positive and negative charges—the yang and the yin—of the system. The skin acts like a viscous liquid mixture. Outside of it, the charges are negative, and inside they are positive. Becker found that the acupuncture points were more positive than the surrounding skin and that an inserted needle would "short circuit" the mixture for several days. His theory was that electrical activity happened because of the ionic reaction between the metal needle and the body's fluids, and the low-frequency pulses of electricity generated by the twirling needle.

According to Becker, the generated electrical energy would flow through the meridians, which operate like wires in a DC battery system, to the brain. In this we see the flow of chi within the meridians. More important, Becker saw the meridians operating with a greater field, an inhomogeneous one that is determined by the underlying structures in the body, including the tissue, muscles, bones, and skin. This field is influenced by the relationships between these physical structures in terms of resistance, polarities, interference, and resonance. Acupuncture acts by interconnecting these structures through the field via the meridians, which can be seen as lines of force in the body.[42]

In 1978, R. J. Luciani produced Kirlian photographs of a light emission diode (LED) effect of acupoints along the Small Intestine and Large Intestine meridians, which further substantiated the existence of the meridians as depicted in classical Chinese medicine.[43] But the biggest leap forward in acupuncture revelations occurred in 1985, when Pierre de Vernejoul at the University of Paris injected a radioactive marker, technetium 99, into subjects at the classical acupuncture points. He found that the isotope would travel thirty centimeters in four to six minutes along the classic meridian lines.[44] De Vernejoul, along with other researchers including Jean-Claude Darras, then made numerous and random injections into the skin, but not at acupuncture points, and also injected the substance into the veins and lymph channels. But the tracer migrated only from the acupuncture points.[45]

The study involved morphological research (studying structure and form), differential analysis, and sequential and simulated studies.[46] It also applied postinjection stimulation using mechanical, electrical, and thermal means, including a needle and a laser beam. The fact that the tracer did not correlate with typical body parts showed that the pathways are not part of the vascular (blood) or lymphatic systems. Rather, researchers suggested that the pathways are related to the connective tissue. There is, therefore, a neurochemical mechanism involved in spreading information along the meridians.

The researchers also found that the tracer migrated faster in healthy patients than in sick ones, supporting the traditional Chinese theory that you can detect an illness by examining for the flow of chi (vital energy) through the meridians—and perhaps underscoring the idea that by treating the chi, you can assist the person in resuming health.

The French study was supportive of earlier work done by Dr. Liu YK in 1975. Dr. Liu studied the location of acupoints at the motor nerves and discovered that these points related to the regions where the motor nerves entered the skeletal muscles. There was also a cluster of encapsulated autonomic nerve mechanoreceptor sites at these points.[47] Carrying Dr. Liu's work forward, Dr. N. Watari of Beijing performed further research and published his results in 1987. He discovered that the volume density of acupoints corresponding to blood vessels was higher than surrounding tissues by fourfold; density of acupoints corresponding to nerves was nearly one and a half times that of surrounding tissues.[48] The French studies, along with Dr. Liu's and Dr. Watari's, support a biochemical view of the meridian system.

Yet another researcher has created valid scientific evidence for the meridians. Dr. Hiroshi Motoyama, a physician, electrical engineer, and expert on the energy of ancient systems, designed six experiments to corroborate the existence of the meridians.[49] His first test concentrated on the Triple Warmer meridian because it does not correspond to anything in Western medicine's concept of anatomy. Motoyama used electrodes at several points along the Triple Warmer meridian to measure alterations in the galvanized skin potential (the electricity in the skin) and then inserted an acupuncture needle into the point of the meridian on the left wrist. After leaving it there for two minutes, he applied a slight electrical stimulus.

Six out of nine subjects showed a galvanized skin potential reaction at all measuring points along the Triple Warmer (although these had not been needled), and many reacted to several other points. The greatest changes were in the points located farthest away from the inserted needle, probably because these two points (called the *alarm* and *associated points*) are known as the strongest points within each meridian. There are no neurological connections between the stimulated point and those that reacted, which indicates a different physiological communication. Motoyama's other five experiments, done in similar fashion, showed similar results.[50]

Still another researcher happened upon a patient whose condition suggests the presence of the meridian system. Dr. Yoshio Nagahama, a physician with Chiba University in Chiba, Japan, discovered that one of his patients, who had been struck by lightning, could now feel the "echo," or movement, of the chi when needled. Dr. Nagahama inserted a needle at the source of each meridian and had the patient use his finger to track the course of the echo while Dr. Nagahama timed the flow. The patient, who did not know about the meridian system, traced each meridian precisely, and at a rate much slower than that represented by neurological transmissions.[51]

And then—there was light. A group of scientists working under Professor Kaznachejew at the Institute for Clinical and Experimental Medicine in Novosibirsk, Russia, focused a light beam onto different parts of the body.[52]

Their goal was to measure the skin's reaction to radiation in the visible light spectrum. Imagine their surprise at seeing a speck of light ten centimeters away from the illuminated surface. They then watched as this light spread under the skin—along the meridian pathway and most obviously emanating from the acupuncture points.

GENDER DIFFERENCES IN THE MERIDIAN SYSTEM

ARE THERE SEX-RELATED differences between the meridian systems of men and women? A study at the California Institute for Human Science revealed one major distinction. The chi in the meridian systems of men moves faster and with greater intensity than in women during hot and cold seasons. Conversely, the chi in women's meridians moves faster and with greater intensity during mild seasons. Both men and women show the same types and levels of activity within their meridians, however, which suggests that they share the same energy anatomy.[53]

The pathway traveled was dependent on the color of light. White traveled the farthest, followed by red and then blue. Green was the slowest and journeyed the least distance. This study suggests the meridians as a "light distribution system."

This work was later verified and furthered by other researchers. One, Dr. Gregory Raiport at the National Research Institute of Physical Culture in Moscow, used laser acupuncture to treat physical problems as well as addictions, depression, and anxiety. Dr. A. L. Pankratov of the Institute for Clinical and Experimental Medicine in Moscow verified that the acupuncture-meridian system conducts light, especially in the white and red spectral range, when a light source is held against, or within one to two millimeters of, the acupoint.[54]

32

THE MAJOR MERIDIANS

MERIDIAN NUMBERING AND ABBREVIATIONS

The main meridians are numbered from 1 to 12, with two secondary meridians numbered 13 and 14. There are several different abbreviation systems that represent the meridians in "shorthand." This is one commonly used system:

1. Lung (LU)
2. Large Intestine (LI)
3. Stomach (ST)
4. Spleen (SP)
5. Heart (HE)
6. Small intestine (SI)
7. Bladder (BL)
8. Kidney (KI)
9. Pericardium (PC)
10. Triple Warmer (TB)
11. Gallbladder (GB)
12. Liver (LR)
13. Conception Vessel or Ren (CV)
14. Governor Vessel (GV)[55]

PRIMARY AND SECONDARY MERIDIANS

There are twelve major meridians and several secondary ones. Here we will explore the specifics of the twelve major meridians and the two most important vessels, or secondary meridians. In addition to descriptions of how energy flows within each meridian, there is a brief summary of its function as well as a few of the basic symptoms associated with disharmony.

The twelve basic meridians flow down both arms or legs, depending on the meridian. These descriptions therefore apply to both limbs. (There are many ways to depict the pathways and the physical ailments associated with each meridian. The following are summaries with examples, and not meant to be substituted for professional sources.)

The twelve major meridians are all subdivided as yin or yang and named according to their associated organs. The Triple Warmer and Pericardium are not directly connected to specific organs, but they play important roles in the body.

The detailed charts on the following pages illustrate the twelve major meridians as well as the two main secondary meridians. They also indicate the meridian's yin or yang status and depict each meridian's divergent or "deep" path, which branches off the main meridian to connect the meridians at a deep level.[56] The charts for the individual meridians indicate the transporting, alarm, and associated points, with their elemental associations. A brief written description of each meridian follows (it starts below).

1. THE LUNG MERIDIAN

This meridian begins at the Triple Warmer near the navel, runs inside the chest, and surfaces in front of the shoulder. Here it branches out from the armpits to run down the medial aspect of the upper arms and crosses at the crease of the elbows. It continues until it splits into two more branches, one flowing to the tips of the thumbs and the other to the ends of the index fingers. One branch runs from the chest to the large intestine.

The lung regulates chi throughout the body as well as breathing and many water channels, such as the kidney and bladder. Symptoms of disharmony include distension of or a full sensation in the chest, asthma, allergies, coughing, panting, belching, restlessness, cold limbs and hot palms, shortness of breath, skin issues, and overall fatigue.

2. THE LARGE INTESTINE MERIDIAN

The Large Intestine meridian starts in the tip of each index finger and rises along the lateral side of the forearm and the anterior side of the upper arm to reach the highest points in the shoulder. Here it diverges into two branches. One travels internally into the lungs, diaphragm, and large intestine. The other flows externally, passing the neck and cheek to enter the lower teeth and gums, and then on to the end of the nose.

The Large Intestine meridian rules elimination and communicates with the lungs to regulate the transportation functions of the body. This meridian primarily underlies diseases that affect the head, face, and throat. Disharmony is indicated by toothaches, runny noses, nosebleeds, swelling

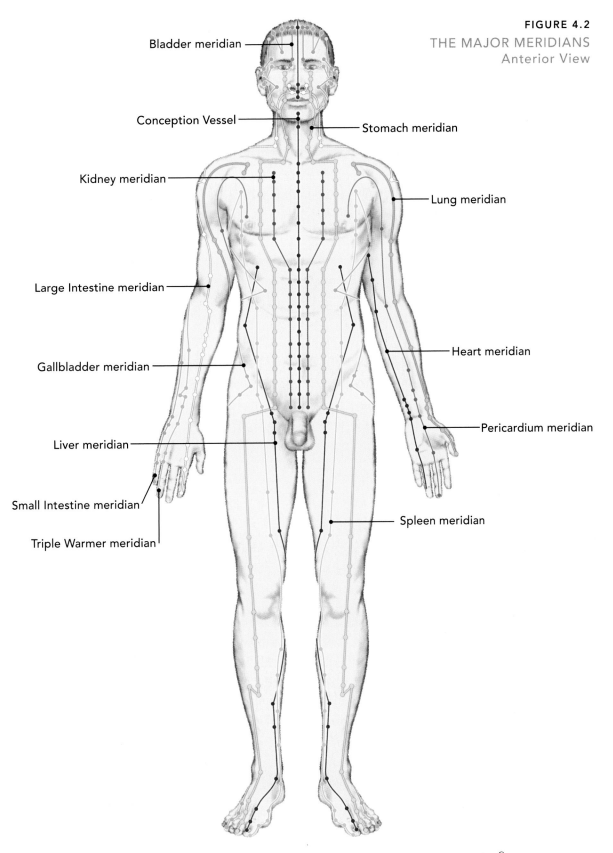

FIGURE 4.2
THE MAJOR MERIDIANS
Anterior View

Bladder meridian

Conception Vessel

Stomach meridian

Kidney meridian

Lung meridian

Large Intestine meridian

Heart meridian

Gallbladder meridian

Liver meridian

Pericardium meridian

Small Intestine meridian

Triple Warmer meridian

Spleen meridian

FIGURE 4.3
THE MAJOR MERIDIANS
Posterior View

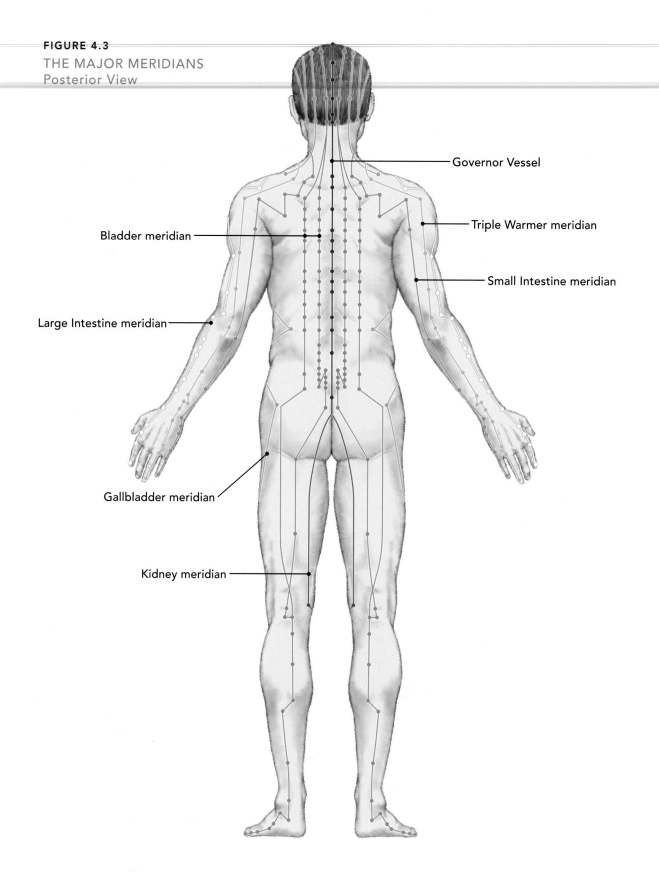

Governor Vessel

Triple Warmer meridian

Small Intestine meridian

Bladder meridian

Large Intestine meridian

Gallbladder meridian

Kidney meridian

FIGURE 4.4
LUNG MERIDIAN
Tai Yin

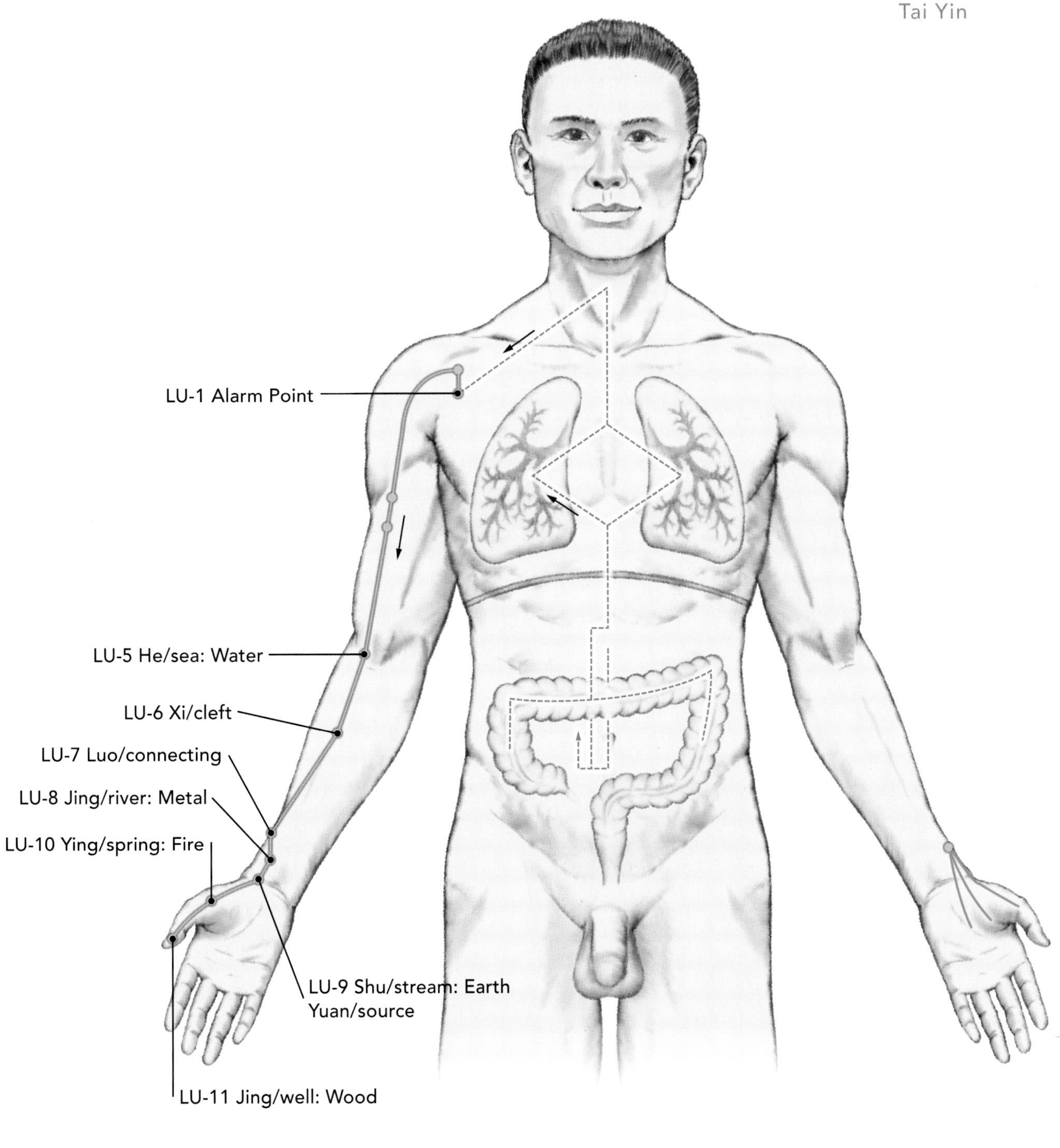

LU-1 Alarm Point

LU-5 He/sea: Water

LU-6 Xi/cleft

LU-7 Luo/connecting

LU-8 Jing/river: Metal

LU-10 Ying/spring: Fire

LU-9 Shu/stream: Earth
Yuan/source

LU-11 Jing/well: Wood

FIGURE 4.5
LARGE INTESTINE MERIDIAN
Yang Ming

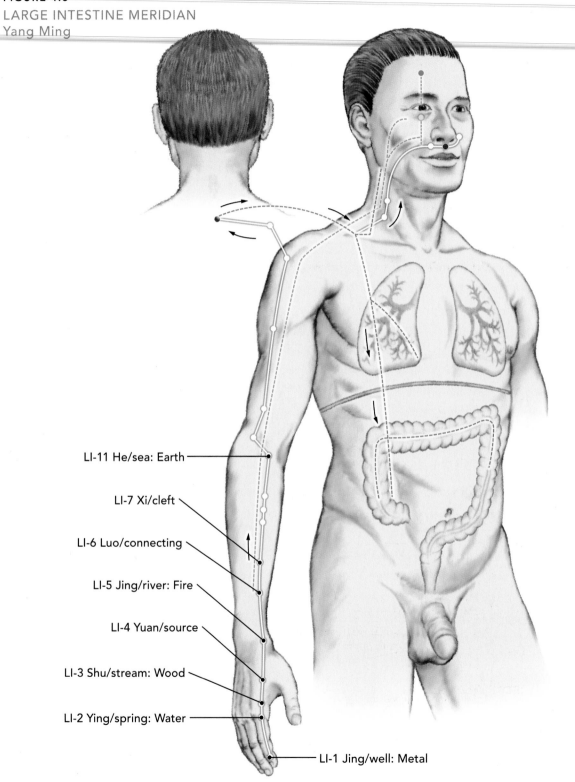

LI-11 He/sea: Earth

LI-7 Xi/cleft

LI-6 Luo/connecting

LI-5 Jing/river: Fire

LI-4 Yuan/source

LI-3 Shu/stream: Wood

LI-2 Ying/spring: Water

LI-1 Jing/well: Metal

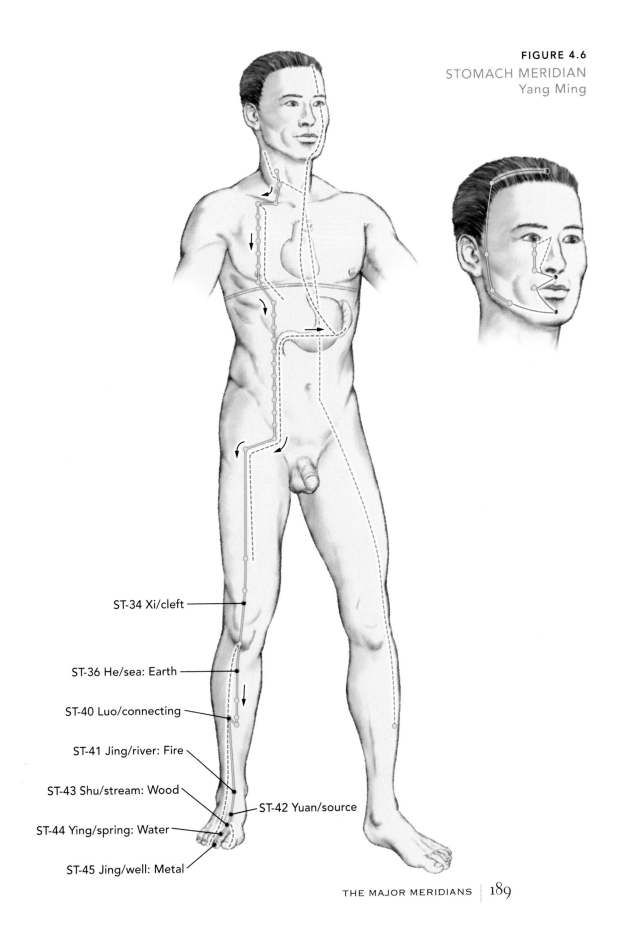

FIGURE 4.6
STOMACH MERIDIAN
Yang Ming

ST-34 Xi/cleft

ST-36 He/sea: Earth

ST-40 Luo/connecting

ST-41 Jing/river: Fire

ST-43 Shu/stream: Wood

ST-42 Yuan/source

ST-44 Ying/spring: Water

ST-45 Jing/well: Metal

FIGURE 4.7
SPLEEN MERIDIAN
Tai Yin

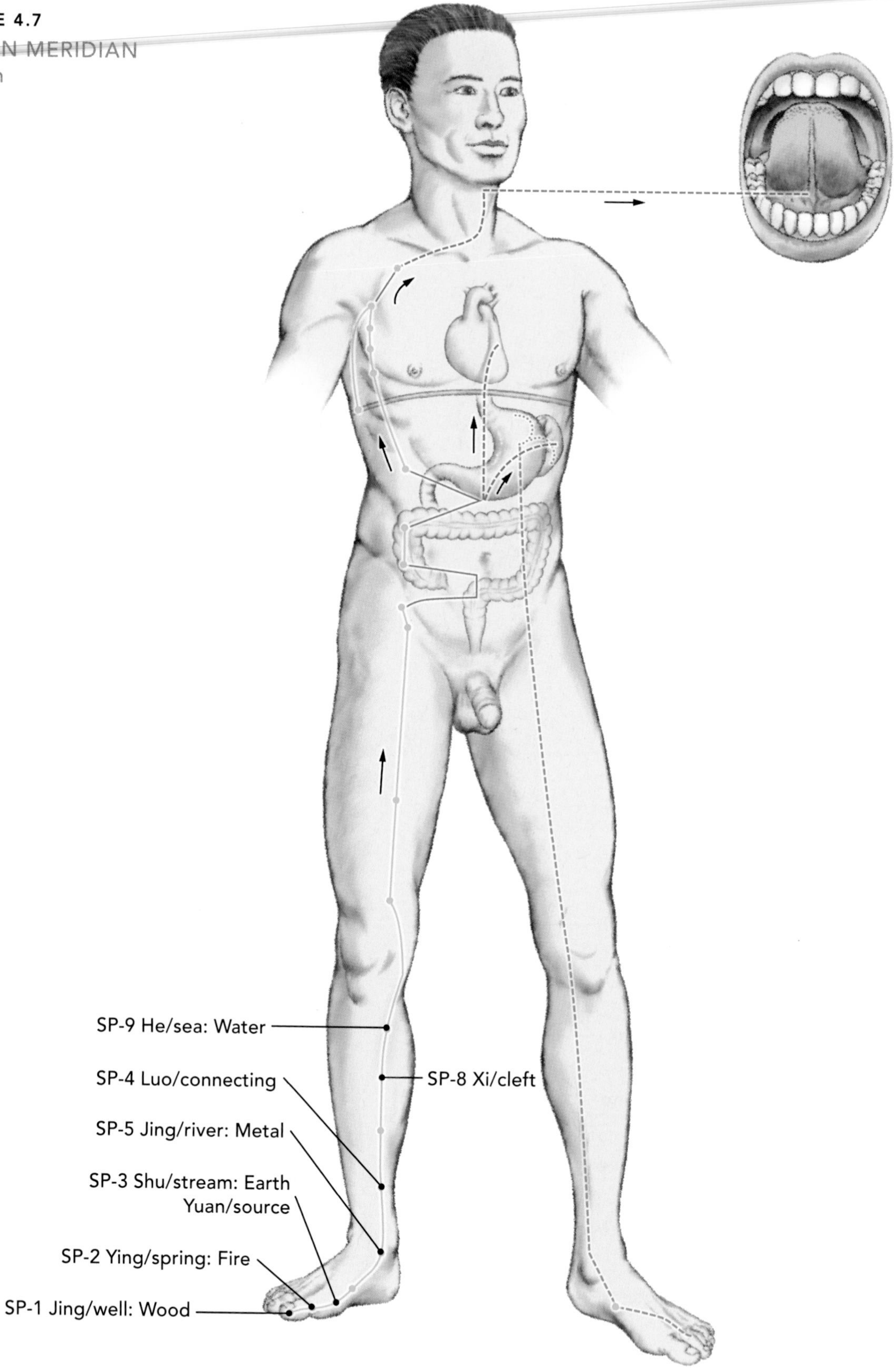

SP-9 He/sea: Water

SP-4 Luo/connecting

SP-8 Xi/cleft

SP-5 Jing/river: Metal

SP-3 Shu/stream: Earth
Yuan/source

SP-2 Ying/spring: Fire

SP-1 Jing/well: Wood

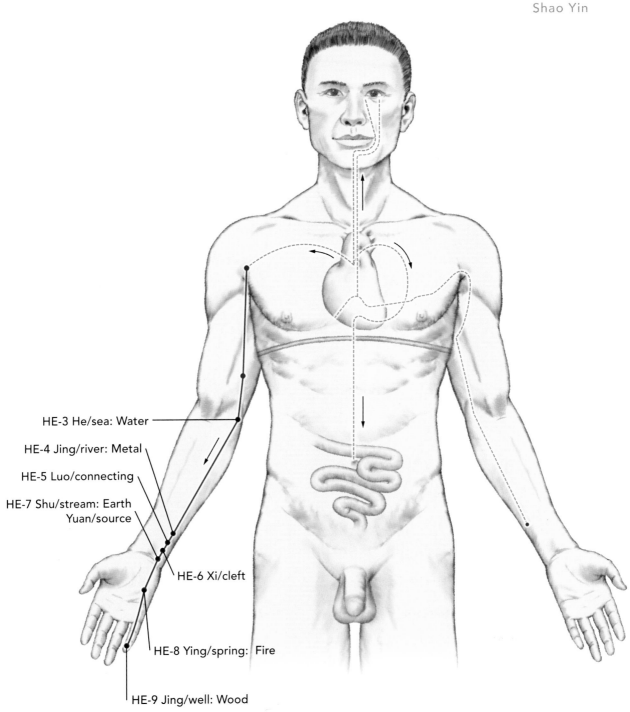

FIGURE 4.8
HEART MERIDIAN
Shao Yin

HE-3 He/sea: Water

HE-4 Jing/river: Metal

HE-5 Luo/connecting

HE-7 Shu/stream: Earth
Yuan/source

HE-6 Xi/cleft

HE-8 Ying/spring: Fire

HE-9 Jing/well: Wood

FIGURE 4.9
SMALL INTESTINE MERIDIAN
Tai Yang

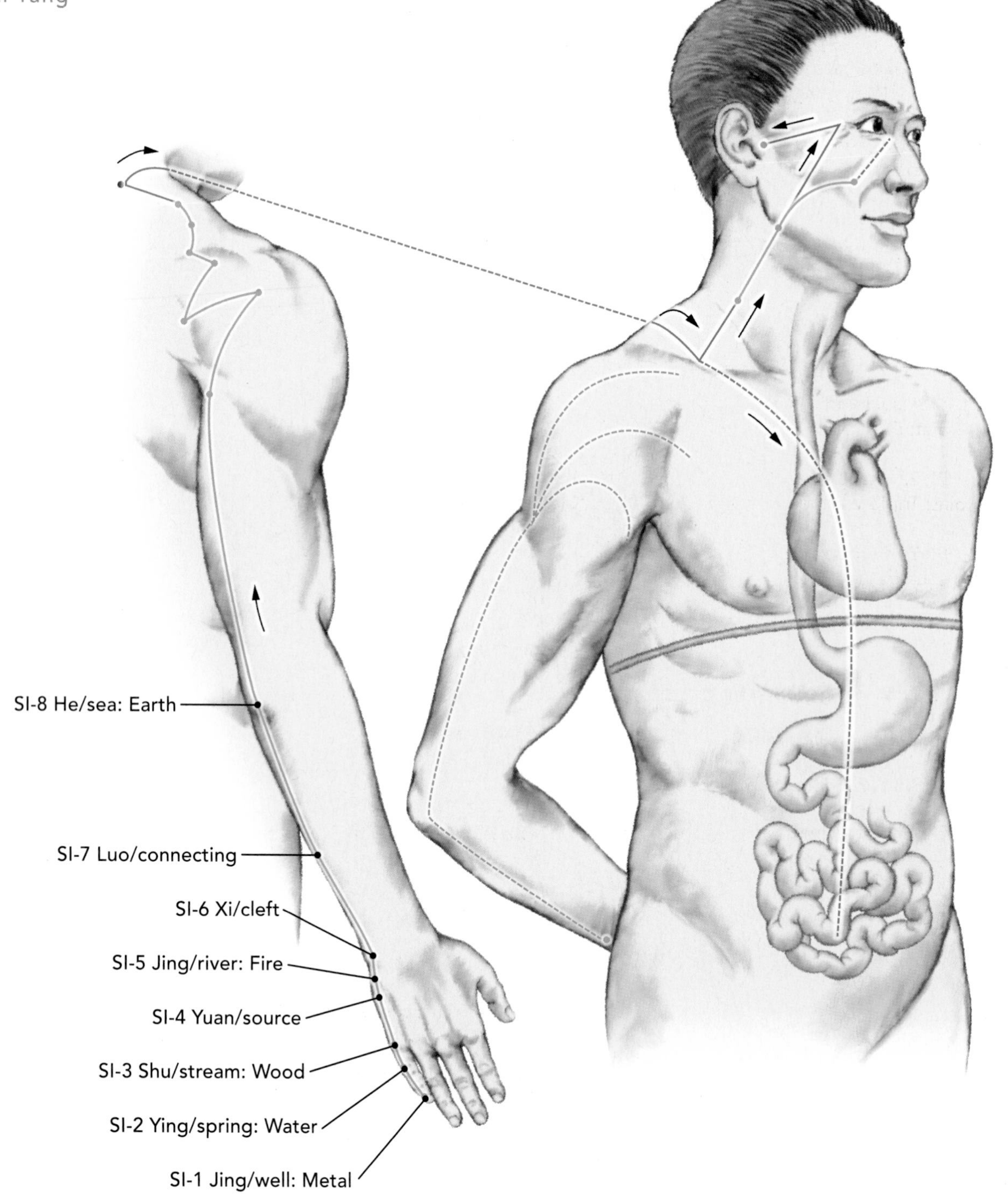

SI-8 He/sea: Earth

SI-7 Luo/connecting

SI-6 Xi/cleft

SI-5 Jing/river: Fire

SI-4 Yuan/source

SI-3 Shu/stream: Wood

SI-2 Ying/spring: Water

SI-1 Jing/well: Metal

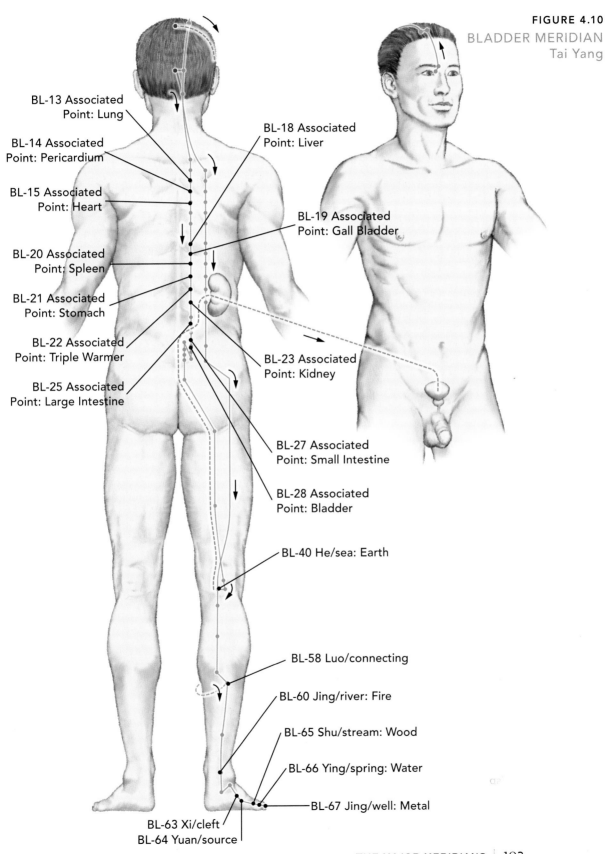

FIGURE 4.10

BLADDER MERIDIAN
Tai Yang

BL-13 Associated
Point: Lung

BL-14 Associated
Point: Pericardium

BL-15 Associated
Point: Heart

BL-20 Associated
Point: Spleen

BL-21 Associated
Point: Stomach

BL-22 Associated
Point: Triple Warmer

BL-25 Associated
Point: Large Intestine

BL-18 Associated
Point: Liver

BL-19 Associated
Point: Gall Bladder

BL-23 Associated
Point: Kidney

BL-27 Associated
Point: Small Intestine

BL-28 Associated
Point: Bladder

BL-40 He/sea: Earth

BL-58 Luo/connecting

BL-60 Jing/river: Fire

BL-65 Shu/stream: Wood

BL-66 Ying/spring: Water

BL-67 Jing/well: Metal

BL-63 Xi/cleft
BL-64 Yuan/source

THE MAJOR MERIDIANS | 193

FIGURE 4.11

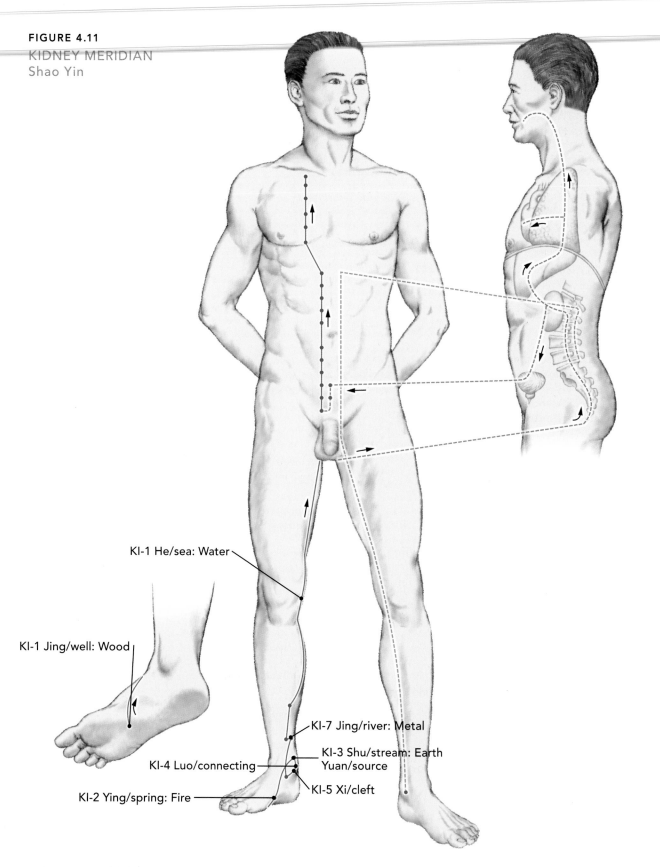

KIDNEY MERIDIAN
Shao Yin

KI-1 He/sea: Water

KI-1 Jing/well: Wood

KI-7 Jing/river: Metal

KI-3 Shu/stream: Earth
Yuan/source

KI-4 Luo/connecting

KI-5 Xi/cleft

KI-2 Ying/spring: Fire

FIGURE 4.12

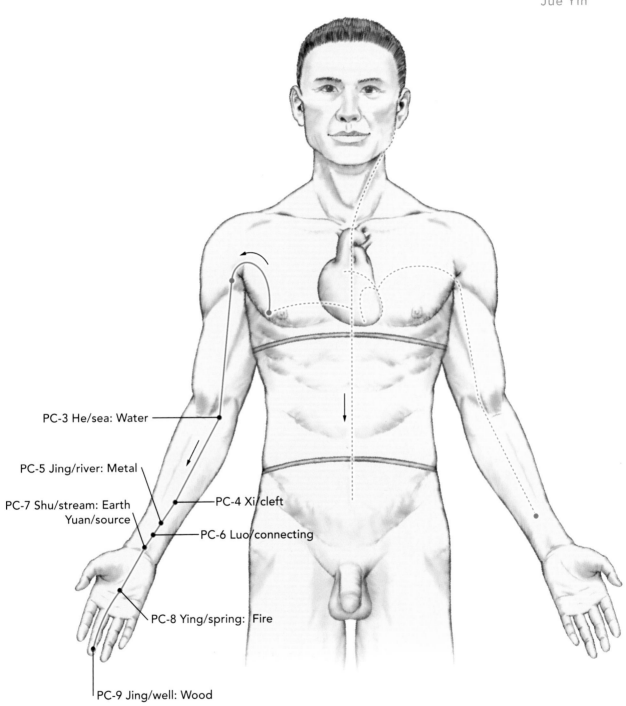

PC-3 He/sea: Water

PC-5 Jing/river: Metal

PC-7 Shu/stream: Earth
Yuan/source

PC-4 Xi/cleft

PC-6 Luo/connecting

PC-8 Ying/spring: Fire

PC-9 Jing/well: Wood

FIGURE 4.13

TRIPLE WARMER MERIDIAN
Shao Yang

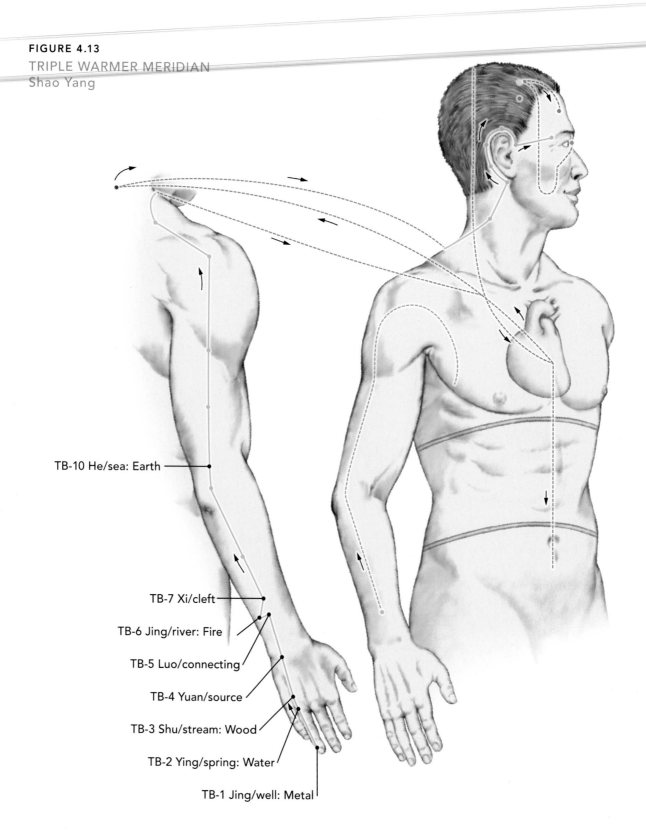

TB-10 He/sea: Earth

TB-7 Xi/cleft

TB-6 Jing/river: Fire

TB-5 Luo/connecting

TB-4 Yuan/source

TB-3 Shu/stream: Wood

TB-2 Ying/spring: Water

TB-1 Jing/well: Metal

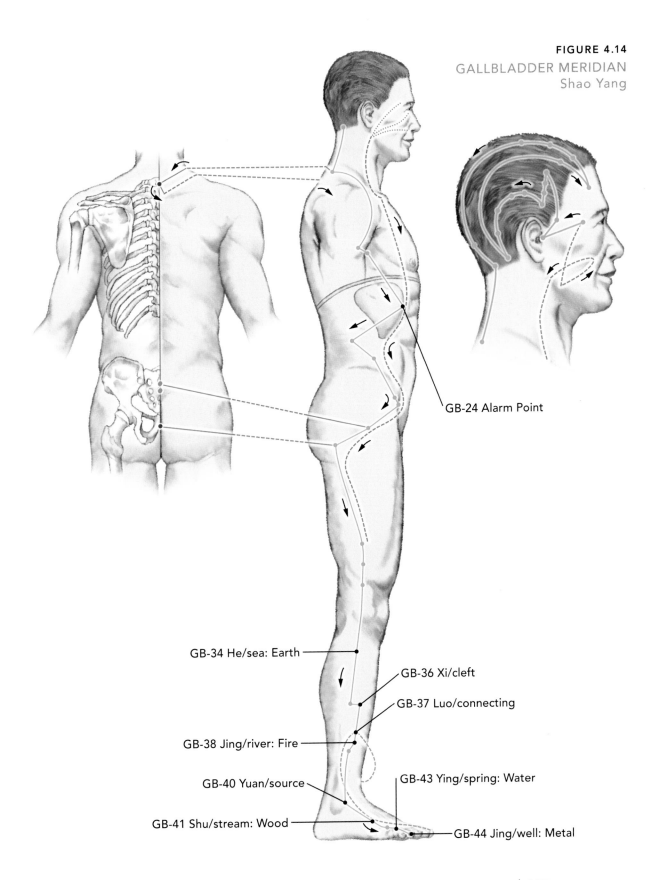

FIGURE 4.14
GALLBLADDER MERIDIAN
Shao Yang

GB-24 Alarm Point

GB-34 He/sea: Earth

GB-36 Xi/cleft

GB-37 Luo/connecting

GB-38 Jing/river: Fire

GB-40 Yuan/source

GB-43 Ying/spring: Water

GB-41 Shu/stream: Wood

GB-44 Jing/well: Metal

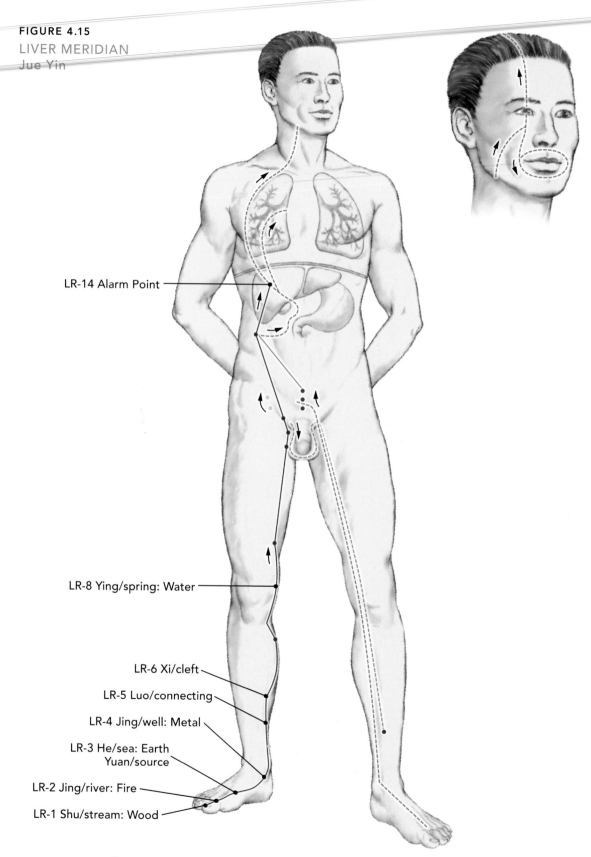

FIGURE 4.15
LIVER MERIDIAN
Jue Yin

LR-14 Alarm Point

LR-8 Ying/spring: Water

LR-6 Xi/cleft

LR-5 Luo/connecting

LR-4 Jing/well: Metal

LR-3 He/sea: Earth
Yuan/source

LR-2 Jing/river: Fire

LR-1 Shu/stream: Wood

FIGURE 4.16

CONCEPTION VESSEL

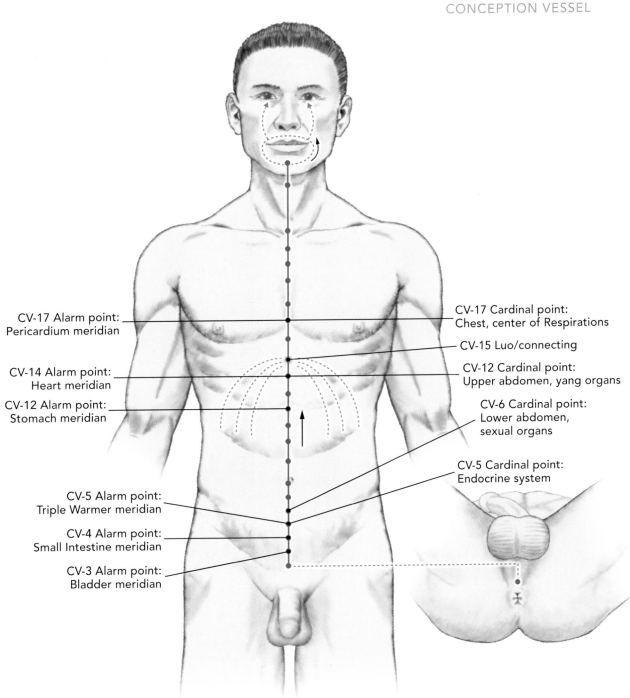

CV-17 Alarm point:
Pericardium meridian

CV-14 Alarm point:
Heart meridian

CV-12 Alarm point:
Stomach meridian

CV-5 Alarm point:
Triple Warmer meridian

CV-4 Alarm point:
Small Intestine meridian

CV-3 Alarm point:
Bladder meridian

CV-17 Cardinal point:
Chest, center of Respirations

CV-15 Luo/connecting

CV-12 Cardinal point:
Upper abdomen, yang organs

CV-6 Cardinal point:
Lower abdomen,
sexual organs

CV-5 Cardinal point:
Endocrine system

FIGURE 4.17

GOVERNOR VESSEL

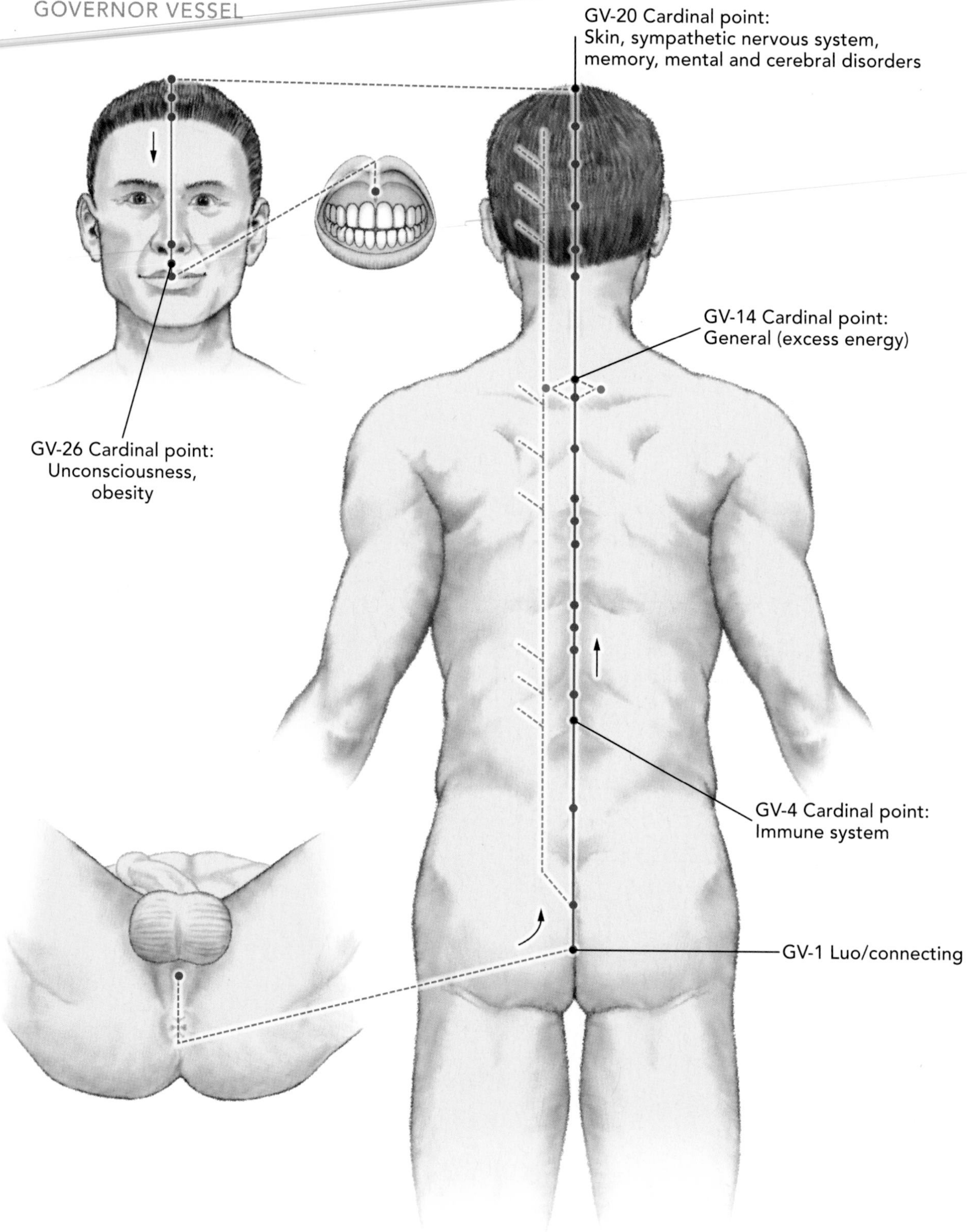

GV-20 Cardinal point:
Skin, sympathetic nervous system,
memory, mental and cerebral disorders

GV-26 Cardinal point:
Unconsciousness,
obesity

GV-14 Cardinal point:
General (excess energy)

GV-4 Cardinal point:
Immune system

GV-1 Luo/connecting

FIGURE 4.18
HEAD MERIDIANS

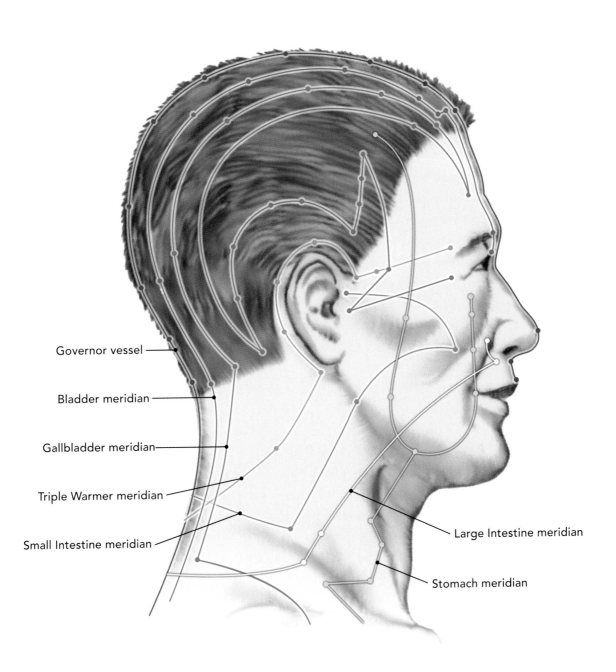

Governor vessel

Bladder meridian

Gallbladder meridian

Triple Warmer meridian

Small Intestine meridian

Large Intestine meridian

Stomach meridian

of the neck, yellow eyes, dry mouth, excessive thirst, sore throat, pain in the shoulders, arms, and index fingers, as well as intestinal cramping, diarrhea, constipation, and dysentery.

3. THE STOMACH MERIDIAN

The Stomach meridian emerges from the end of the Large Intestine meridian just under the eyes. It then goes around the nose to encircle the bridge of the nose, simultaneously going down around the mouth and up each cheek to the forehead. It then travels from the lower jaw through the neck to the sternum, where it divides into two branches. One branch passes down the chest, belly, and groin, and continues down each leg, ending at the tip of the second toe.

The Stomach meridian works closely with the Spleen meridian to perform digestion and absorption. Together, the two meridians are called the *acquired foundation*, in that they lay the foundation of digestive health for the body. The Stomach meridian assures that the chi descends or is passed into the internal system. Diseases involving the Stomach meridian typically produce gastric disturbances, toothaches, and mental issues (such as obsessively "going over" the same issues), as well as problems associated with the meridian's path. Irregularities can appear as stomachaches, mouth sores, digestive disturbances, fluid in the abdomen, hunger, nausea, vomiting, thirst, a distorted mouth, edema, swollen neck, sore throat, shuddering, yawning, and a gray forehead. Mental dysfunctions include antisocial and phobic behavior.

4. THE SPLEEN MERIDIAN

The Spleen meridian starts at the big toe and moves along the inside of the foot, crossing at the inner ankle. It then continues to climb until it ends at the armpit. One branch leaves the abdomen and runs inside the body to the spleen, linking with the stomach and the heart.

The spleen is a vital immune organ and essential for transforming food into chi and blood. It is also considered to house thoughts, governing the quality of thought available to the mind. Symptoms of related diseases include a distended abdomen, loss of appetite, hepatitis, bleeding disorders, menstrual disorders, loose stools, diarrhea, flatulence, anorexia, stiffness, swollen or stiff knees or thighs, and pain at the root of the tongue.

5. THE HEART MERIDIAN

The Heart meridian starts in the heart and consists of three branches. One goes to the small intestine. Another runs upward past the tongue toward the eyes. The third branch crosses the chest to travel down the arm, ending at the inside top of the little finger, where it connects with the Small Intestine meridian.

The heart governs the blood and the pulse, as well as the mind and spirit. As might be expected, problems with the Heart meridian usually result in heart problems. Problems are indicated by dry throat, heart pain, palpitations, and thirst. Other symptoms include pain in the chest or along the inner side of the forearm, heat in the palm, yellow eyes, insomnia, and pain or cold along the meridian pathway.

6. THE SMALL INTESTINE MERIDIAN

The Small Intestine meridian begins in the outside tip of the little finger and goes up the arm to the back of the shoulder. At the intersection of the Bladder meridian, it diverges into two branches. One branch moves internally through the heart and stomach to settle in the small intestine. The other branch travels externally around the checks on the face, passing through the eye and ear. A short branch off the cheek links the meridian to the inner corner of the eye, where it connects with the Bladder meridian.

The Small Intestine meridian separates the pure from the impure, including foods, fluids, thoughts, and beliefs. Problems in the Small Intestine meridian usually create diseases of the neck, ears, eyes, throat, head, and small intestine, as well as certain mental illnesses. Symptoms can include fevers, sore throats, swollen chin or lower cheek, stiff neck, fixed head stance, hearing problems or deafness, yellow eyes, and severe pain of the shoulder, lower jaw, upper arm, elbow, and forearm, and disorders including irritable bowel syndrome.

7. THE BLADDER MERIDIAN

The Bladder meridian begins its journey at the inside edge of each eye and travels over the top of the head (where it visits the brain) to the back of the neck. Here it splits in two parts. One (the inner branch) travels into the base of the neck and moves down, parallel with the spine. At the bottom, it reaches into the bladder. The other moves across the back of the shoulder and then runs downward alongside the inner branch. The two branches move through the buttocks and join at the knees. Each meridian now continues down the back of the lower leg, circles the outer ankle, and finally ends at the tip of the little toe, where it connects with (but is not the start of) the Kidney meridian.

The Bladder meridian is in charge of storing and eliminating fluid waste. It receives chi from the Kidney meridian and uses it to transform fluids for eliminating. Dysfunction of the Bladder meridian leads to bladder problems and symptoms including urinary disorders, incontinence, and problems in the head including headaches, protruding eyeballs, runny nose, nasal congestion, neck tension, yellow eyes, tearing, and nosebleeds. Lower-body issues include pain along the spine, buttocks, and calf muscles, lumbar pain, unbendable hip joints, groin issues, and tight muscles around the knee and in the calves.

8. THE KIDNEY MERIDIAN

The Kidney meridian initiates between the long bones of the second and third toes, near the sole of the foot. It travels the inside of the leg, entering the body near the base of the spine. At the kidneys, it splits into two branches. These pass through the chest and intersect at the Pericardium meridian and from there, journey to the base of the tongue. (A small branch divides at the lungs to link with the heart and the pericardium.)

According to classical sources, kidneys "grasp the chi." They are the "residence" of yin and yang. They also rule the bones, teeth, and adrenal glands. Lack of nourishment results in kidney-based problems such as swelling, diarrhea, and constipation. Other symptoms include backaches, ear problems, anorexia, restlessness, insomnia, weak vision, lack of energy, constant fear, dry tongue and hot mouth, spinal and thigh pain, immovable lower limbs, cold, drowsiness, and painful and hot soles of the feet.

9. THE PERICARDIUM MERIDIAN

The Pericardium meridian starts near the heart, where it divides into two branches. One emerges from the lower chest area to reach the armpit before reversing down the arm to end at the tip of the middle finger. The other branch takes the same path but stops at the ring finger, where it meets the Triple Warmer.

The Pericardium meridian works closely with the Heart meridian; in fact, the pericardium is a bag that contains the heart, protecting it from foreign invasions. This meridian governs the blood and the mind (along with the Heart meridian), thus affecting blood and circulation as well as personal relationships. Disharmony in the Pericardium meridian is caused by heart and blood dysfunctions. The most common problems manifest as chest, heart, and breast problems, with symptoms including chest discomfort, tachycardia or other arrhythmias, swelling in the armpit, red face, spasms of the elbow and arm, and mania.

Note: The heart stores *shen,* or mental energy. Many mental or emotional problems relate to an imbalance in shen. The Pericardium is an important meridian for any symptoms related to mental illness. There are specific shen points listed in classical and other acupuncture manuals.

10. THE TRIPLE WARMER MERIDIAN

The Triple Warmer is not represented by a physical organ. Rather, it is important because of its job, which is to circulate liquid energy throughout the organs. It begins at the tip of the ring finger and flows over the shoulder to the chest cavity. Atop it, it splits into two branches. One branch travels through the middle and lower parts of the body, uniting the upper, middle, and lower burners (hence the name, Triple Warmer or Burner). The other runs externally up the side of the neck, circling the face to finally meet the Gallbladder Meridian at the outer ends of the eyebrow.

The Triple Warmer distributes a special chi called *source chi*, which is produced by the kidneys. It governs the relationship between all the various organs, allocating chi between them.

Upper Warmer or Burner: Distributes chi from the diaphragm upward; most commonly associated with lungs and heart (respiration).

Middle Warmer or Burner: Delivers chi to bodily areas between the diaphragm and navel; associated with stomach, spleen, liver, and gallbladder (digestion and assimilation).

Lower Warmer or Burner: Transports chi below the navel; associated with reproduction and elimination.

Problems with the Triple Warmer typically manifest as water retention, stiff neck, and ailments with the ears, eyes, chest, and throat. Symptoms include those related to water imbalance, such as swelling, urinary incontinence and difficulties, and tinnitus (ringing in the ear).

11. THE GALLBLADDER MERIDIAN

The Gallbladder meridian starts as two branches emerging from the outer corner of the eye. An external branch weaves around the face and ear before traveling to the hip. The other branch crosses the cheek and descends to the gallbladder to meet up with the other branch. This rejoined branch now runs down the lateral side of the thigh and lower leg and makes its way to the tip of the fourth toe. Another small branch separates from the meridian at this point and ends at the big toe, where it connects with the Liver meridian.

The Gallbladder meridian runs the gallbladder, which makes and stores bile. On an energetic basis, it governs decision making. It is closely connected to the liver; therefore, many symptoms display as liver issues, including bitterness in the mouth, jaundice, and nausea. Other symptoms include frequent sighing, headaches, pain in the jaw and outer corner of the eyes, swelling in the glands, mental illness, indecisiveness, fever, and pain along the meridian.

12. THE LIVER MERIDIAN

The Liver meridian starts at the top of the big toe and travels up the leg to the pubic bone. It then circles the sexual organs, enters the lower abdomen, and travels upward to connect with the liver and gallbladder. It moves up to the lungs to connect with the Lung meridian before curving around the mouth. It then splits and one branch goes up to each eye. The two disjointed branches finally meet at the forehead and travel over the top of the head.

To some Chinese practitioners, the liver is considered the "second heart" of the body, thus indicating its importance. This meridian assures the flow of emotions, chi, and blood, controls the body's immune response as well as sinews (tendons, ligaments, and skeletal muscles), absorbs what is indigestible, and is associated with the eyes. Liver meridian issues most frequently appear as problems in the liver and genital systems. Symptoms can include dizziness, high blood pressure, hernias, distended lower abdomens in women, nausea, watery stools with undigested food, allergies, incontinence, muscle spasms, retention of urine, eye problems, and moodiness or anger.

13. THE CONCEPTION VESSEL (REN MAI)

As does the Governor vessel, the Conception vessel distributes chi to the major organs and maintains the proper balance of chi and blood. The Conception vessel runs down the front of the body, starting just below the eyes. It circles around the mouth to the chest and abdomen before landing at the perineum. Problems with this vessel include uneasiness, hernias, and abdominal issues.

14. THE GOVERNOR VESSEL (DU MAI)

As does the Conception vessel, the Governor vessel transports chi to the major organs and balances the chi and blood in the body. The Governor vessel starts at the perineum and travels to the coccyx before making its way to the back of the head. Flowing over the head, it then travels down the front of the face to stop at the canines in the upper jaw. Disharmony in this vessel can cause symptoms including stiffness and scoliosis.

HEAD MERIDIANS

The head is a complicated map of acupuncture points, as shown in figure 4.18. The yang meridians initiate in the head and flow downward, but all meridians are represented by head points.

33

THE BASIC ACUPUNCTURE POINTS

The points are the entryways to the meridians. They are called *acupuncture points*, *meridian points*, or *acupoints*.

Each of the points has a particular effect on the different currents and organs in the body. Their names and purposes differ slightly from system to system, but there are some commonly accepted points. Here are a few.

THE FIVE TRANSPORTING POINTS

In five-phase theory, there are five "transporting points" that are described using a river analogy. Chi moves along the rivers or channels of the meridian as does water in a river, lake, or other body of water. For instance, chi might "bubble up" from a spring before "gliding" into a channel.

The five major transporting points are located on each channel, starting at the fingers or toes and stopping at the elbows or knees. At each point, the flow of chi appears as it is described by name: Well, Spring, Stream, River, and Sea.[57]

More formal names are:

Jing (well): Where the chi "bubbles up." These are the first on the yang channels or last on the yin channels, with the exception of certain points on the tips of the fingers and toes.

Ying (spring): Where the chi "glides" down the channel. Two types, the nan jing and nei jing, describe ying-spring points for heat in the body and changes in complexion.

Shu (stream): Where the chi "pours" down the channel. Shu-stream points are indicated for treating heaviness in the body and pain in the joints, and for intermittent diseases.

Jing (river): Where the chi "flows" down the channel.

He (sea): Where the chi collects and then travels deeper into the body.[58]

THE FIVE-ELEMENT POINTS

Each major meridian has points that represent the five elements. These points, called the five-element points (or sometimes the five-phase points), initiate at the fingers and toes but can also be found in the limbs. See figures 4.1 to 4.17.

THE CARDINAL POINTS

The cardinal points are specific to a condition, function, or area of the body. The Conception vessel (Figure 4.16) and the Governor vessel (Figure 4.17) each have four cardinal points.

OTHER IMPORTANT POINTS

Many traditional Chinese practitioners employ additional points in their work:

Yuan—source points: There is one yuan/source point on each meridian. Its job is to release source chi when needled.

Xi—cleft points: Chi accumulates in these points and must sometimes be needled or stimulated to flow properly.

POINT STIMULATION AND THE BRAIN

DO POINTS REGISTER in the brain? According to researchers from the University of Southampton, United Kingdom, and the Purpan Hospital of Toulouse, France, the answer is yes.

Studies using magnetic resonance imaging (MRI) and positron emission tomography (PET) showed that stimulation of acupuncture points has distinct effects on cortical brain activity.

The research revealed a considerable amount of brain activation and deactivation in response to the stimulation of traditional Chinese acupuncture points. For example, the points associated with hearing and vision resonated the parts of the brain related to these functions. Pain is controlled by a complex matrix of bodily interactions, and even there, stimulated points were associated with the effects of pain relief. Acupuncture, it seems, can "get to the point."[59]

Luo—connecting points: Each of the twelve meridians has a luo point, which diverges from the main meridian to form a luo meridian.

Mu—front alarm points: Located on the front of the body, these are situated next to particular organs. They have an effect on the organ but not the associated meridian. They are called *alarm points* because they react strongly when pressed upon, and are therefore useful in diagnostics.

Shu—back points: These lie on muscles on either side of the spine. Organ chi is transported to and from these points, making them very helpful for diagnostics.

Hui—meeting points: These have a unique effect on certain tissues and organs. There are several meeting points for them.

Window to the sky points: Located on the upper third of the body, these points must be open to restore the connection between earth (the lower two-thirds) and heaven (the upper third). In one model, these points enable access to spiritual energies, particularly one's own spirit.[60]

FIVE-PHASE AND RELATED
DIAGNOSTIC THEORIES

Traditional Chinese medicine is based on the five-phase or five-element theory (*wu-hsing*). It is closely related to several other theories and philosophies that present diagnostic approaches for healing.

In a sentence, one could paraphrase the five-phase theory in this way:

Chi flows through the meridians in perfect balance, unless disturbed by internal or external forces that disrupt the elemental units of life.

Let us examine this theory, which is rooted in the five elements but is also interwoven with philosophies including ideas about the organs, seasons, and directions; zang-fu theory; an understanding of chi as three vital treasures; six divisions; eight principles; seven emotions; and the three phases of the Triple Warmer. All disease is seen as an imbalance between these interacting energies.

The basic premise of the five-phase theory is that there are five elements in nature: earth, metal, water, wood, and fire. These elements cycle in phases through the seasons and the organs and each is represented by a certain color. The human body is made of these natural materials, and proper treatment of the body involves working with the correct element and its cyclical timing.

The five elements represent energies that succeed each other in a continuous cycle. The Chinese did not emphasize the elements themselves—rather, the movement between them. Together these movements make up chi, the vital force.

Each element is associated with a particular bodily system as well as an internal organ. Each organ is either yin or yang. Zang-fu theory describes the organs' functions and interactions. *Zang* refers to the yin organs—Heart, Liver, Spleen, Lung, Kidney, and Pericardium. *Fu* stands for the yang organs—Small Intestine, Large Intestine, Gallbladder, Bladder, Stomach, and

FIGURE 4.19
FIVE-PHASE CHART

KEY
1. **Viscera**
2. **Bowels**
3. **Element**
4. Sense organ
5. Tissue
6. Emotional activity
7. Season
8. Atmospheric state
9. Sound
10. Color
11. Taste
12. Direction
13. Time of day
14. Odor

1. **Liver**
2. **Gallbladder**
3. **Wood**
4. Eye
5. Tendon
6. Anger
7. Spring
8. Wind
9. Shout or calling sound
10. Green
11. Sour
12. East
13. 11 p.m. to 3 a.m.
14. Rancid

1. **Heart**
2. **Small intestine**
3. **Fire**
4. Tongue
5. Blood vessel
6. Joy
7. Summer
8. Heat
9. Laughing
10. Red
11. Bitter
12. South
13. 11 a.m. to 3 p.m.
14. Scorched

1. **Kidney**
2. **Urinary/bladder**
3. **Water**
4. Ear
5. Bone
6. Fear
7. Winter
8. Cold
9. Groaning or deep sighing
10. Black
11. Salty
12. North
13. 3 p.m. to 7 p.m.
14. Putrid

1. **Spleen**
2. **Stomach**
3. **Earth**
4. Mouth
5. Muscle
6. Overthinking
7. Late summer
8. Wetness
9. Singing
10. Yellow
11. Sweet
12. Middle
13. 7 a.m. to 11 a.m.
14. Fragrant

1. **Lung**
2. **Large intestine**
3. **Metal**
4. Nose
5. Skin and hair
6. Grief
7. Autumn
8. Dryness
9. Weeping or crying
10. White
11. Spicy
12. West
13. 3 a.m. to 7 a.m.
14. Rotten

Triple Warmer. Each zang is partnered with a fu, and each pair is assigned one of the five elements, as shown in figure 4.20.

The organs and elements either generate or destroy each other in a particular pattern. This idea is a reflection of the Chinese principle of restoring equilibrium through balancing opposites (yin-yang) or of *wuxing*, which refers to the interlocking nature of the five elements. The idea of wuxing explains that each element exerts a generative and subjugative influence on one another. Wood will generate (or feed) fire and fire will generate new earth. Elements also subjugate or destroy each other. A practitioner diagnoses which elements might need to be generated or decreased and will figure treatment accordingly. Understanding this cycle is the key to creating balance within the system.

GENERATIVE INTERACTIONS

wood	*feeds*	fire
fire	*creates*	earth
earth	*bears*	metal
metal	*collects*	water
water	*nourishes*	wood

DESTRUCTIVE INTERACTIONS

These are often called "overcoming" interactions, as they involve one element being destroyed or changed by another:

wood	*parts*	earth
earth	*takes in*	water
water	*quenches*	fire
fire	*melts*	metal
metal	*chops*	wood

The ancient Chinese had a different idea of anatomy than Western physicians. Instead of being characterized by their position in the body, the organs were understood by the role they played within the overall system. They were therefore described by their interdependent relationships and connection to the skin via the blood (*xue*), fluids, meridians, and the three vital treasures described below.

Just as organs flow in five phases, so do the seasons and points on the compass. There are four directions, with China representing the fifth (at the center).

Unlike the Western compass, the Chinese compass emphasizes the south. This is summer, the hottest time of the year. It is appropriately linked to fire. West

FIGURE 4.20

THE FIVE CHINESE ELEMENTS

Element	Wood	Fire
Color	Green	Red
Season	Spring	Summer
Organs	Liver and Gallbladder	Heart and Small Intestines, Triple Warmer, and Pericardium
Direction	East	South
Quality	Lesser Yang	Yang
Flavor	Sour (acid)	Bitter (herb)
Sense Organ	Eyes	Tongue and Speech
Secretions	Tears	Perspiration
Emotion	Anger	Joy
Nature	Warm	Hot
Adverse Conditions	Wind/Heat/Dampness	Heat/Dryness
Depleted or Congested	Qi Blood	Blood Moisture
Voice	Shouting	Laughing
Body Part	Muscles/Tendons	Blood Vessels
Smell	Rancid	Scorched
Climate	Wind	Heat
Grain	Wheat	Millet
Fruit	Peach	Plum
Meat	Fowl	Lamb
Vegetable	Mallow	Coarse Greens
Development	Birth	Growth
Emotions—Balance	Self-respect and Decisiveness	Joy, Calm, and Love
Emotions—Excess	Anger and Irritability	Nervousness or Euphoria
Emotions—Deficiency	Guilt and Depression	Depression
Physical Symptoms	Stiff Neck and Headache	Indigestion and Insomnia
Planets	Jupiter	Mars
Nourished by	Water	Wood
Nourishes	Fire	Earth
Restrained by	Metal	Water
Restrains	Earth	Metal

Earth	Metal	Water
Yellow	White	Black/Blue
Late Summer/DoYo (the nine days before and after equinoxes and solstices)	Fall	Winter
Spleen and Stomach	Lung and Large Intestine	Bladder and Kidney
Center	West	North
Neutral/Balance	Lesser Yin	Yin
Sweet	Spicy	Salty
Mouth and Taste	Nose and Smell	Ears and Hearing
Saliva (Lips)	Mucous	Saliva (tongue and teeth)
Sympathy	Grief	Fear
Neutral	Cool	Cold
Dampness/Cold/Heat	Dryness/Heat/Cold/Phlegm	Cold/Dampness/Dryness/Heat
Qi Moisture	Moisture Qi	Essence Moisture
Singing	Weeping	Groaning
Flesh	Skin/Body Hair	Bones and Marrow, Hair (head)
Fragrant	Rotten	Putrid
Humid	Dry	Cold
Rye	Rice	Peas
Apricot	Chestnut	Date
Beef	Horse	Pork
Scallions	Onions	Leeks
Transformation	Decline	Stagnation/Death
Sympathy and Concentration	Release of Grief	Courage with Caution
Worry and Compulsiveness	Depression and Self-pity	Fear and Panic
Distraction and Need for People	Inability to Grieve	Foolhardiness
Obesity and Indigestion	Sweat or Cough	Cold Feet or Low Back Pain
Saturn	Venus	Mercury
Fire	Earth	Metal
Metal	Water	Wood
Wood	Fire	Earth
Water	Wood	Fire

is the setting of the sun and is associated with autumn and metal, while north is winter and water (the opposite of the south). East, the rising sun, is linked with spring and wood. Earth is related to the center of the compass and late summer. If any of these phases are out of balance, the entire system is unbalanced. Blocks or stagnation anywhere can result in problems, as can excess or lack. A proper diagnosis will integrate all of these factors.

THE THREE VITAL TREASURES

The Three Treasures, sometimes called the Three Jewels, are keystones in traditional Chinese medicine. From the Taoist perspective, these three treasures constitute the essential forces of life, which are considered to be three forms of the same substance. These three treasures are:

- *Jing*, basic or nutritive essence, seen as represented in sperm, among other substances.
- *Chi*, life force connected with air, vapor, breath, and spirit.
- *Shen*, spiritual essence linked with the soul and supernaturalism.

Most often, jing is related to body energy, chi to mind energy, and shen to spiritual energy. These three energies cycle, with jing serving as the foundation for life and procreation, chi animating the body's performance, and shen mirroring the state of the soul.

THE SIX ATMOSPHERIC STATES

Many versions of traditional Chinese medicine describe six different atmospheric states that the elements might occupy. Each organ system prefers a particular state, which is shown on the "Five-Phase Chart" (figure 4.19). The states are:

- Dryness
- Wetness
- Heat/fire
- Summer/heat
- Cold
- Wind

THE FOUR LEVELS (OR STAGES)

There are four levels to healing. These first appear in *Discussion of Warm Diseases* by Ye Tian Shi, written in the late 1600s and early 1700s. These levels or stages evolve in order from the surface to deeply internal; and from a light sickness to death.[61] These stages are, in this order:

- The *wei level* is defensive. It is named after *wei chi*, which guards the body in the skin. It is usually the initial stage of most infections and diseases, caused by the attack of different winds, or atmospheres. A common example problem is *warm wind*, which is *warm evil* combined with the *wind* that attacks the skin. Symptoms on this level often involve the lungs and skin and call for releasing the problematic atmospheres.
- The *chi level* is internal. It describes the battle between the vital chi (or *zheng chi*) of the body and the warm evil. The warm evil has attacked the zang-fu, producing excessive symptoms, usually *internal excess heat*. Symptoms arise based on the particular organ systems involved.
- The *ying level* is nutritive. The warm evil (a pathogenic mild heat) has dominated the chi level and is confronting the ying, the chi or precursor of the blood. Ying travels through the blood vessels and the heart, which houses *shen*, the energy of the mind.
- The *xue level* is the blood. Once the warm evil has entered the blood, the Liver and Kidney systems are involved and bleeding starts. Death can soon follow.

THE SIX STAGES (ALSO CALLED THE SIX CHANNELS)

Traditional Chinese medicine also refers to the *six stages*, a system similar to the four levels theory, but which reduces all disease to six evolutionary states and deals with the attack of wind or cold. These six stages were first presented by Zhang Zhongjing in the *Shang Han Lun* around AD 220.

The six stages are described in relation to their hand- and foot-related meridians. They progress a person from exposure to an invading illness to death, often through an attack by wind or cold evil. (The "Five Chinese Elements" chart on page 216 relates them to additional factors.)

TAI YANG OR GREATER YANG

Hand tai yang: Relates to Small Intestine. Clarifies information for the heart, runs digestion and absorption, sorts ideas.

Foot tai yang: Relates to Bladder. Associated with fluids; balances body; protects; regulates excretory functions; monitors adaptation.

Tai yang invasion: There are many different types of tai yang invasion, but all describe the initial invasion of an external cold evil through the skin. A disease might originate with a wind or external deficiency; cold or external excess; jing or blood syndromes; fu or zang syndromes; or yin or yang syndromes.

YANG MING OR BRIGHT YANG

Hand yang ming: Relates to Large Intestine. Transports, drains, manages excretory functions; reflects negativity.

Foot yang ming: Relates to Stomach. Sea of nourishment; regulates senses; affected by emotional stress.

Yang ming invasion: As the illness invades the body's interior, the "upright chi" and "evil chi" turn the pathogen into heat. Yang ming might impact the affected meridian or the related zang-fu organs.

SHAO YANG OR LESSER YANG

Hand shao yang: Relates to Triple Warmer. Thermoregulator; monitors three warmers.

Foot shao yang: Relates to Gallbladder. Breaks down fats; associated with toxicity; regulates judgment and decision-making.

Shao yang invasion: This stage involves the need to release the evil pathogens (cold and wind) of the exterior and the heat in the interior. In this stage, we recognize that the pathogen is internal *and* external.

TAI YIN OR GREATER YIN

Hand tai yin: Relates to Lung. Governs chi, respiration, skin, bodily hair, and water passages.

Foot tai yin: Relates to Spleen. Manages transportation and major changes, the blood, muscles, and limbs.

Tai yin invasion: This stage involves an invasion into the Spleen and Stomach zang-fu, with internal cold and dampness.

SHAO YIN OR LESSER YIN

Hand shao yin: Relates to Heart. Dominates cardiovascular vessels and the heart and holds the mind.

Foot shao yin: Relates to Kidney. Stores essence; governs reproduction and development, water metabolism, bone, and brain marrow; receives chi.

Shao yin invasion: There are two types of shao yin syndrome: deficiency of the yang chi and cold, and a deficiency of yin and heat.

JUE YIN OR ABSOLUTE YIN

Hand jue yin: Relates to Pericardium. Associated with Triple Warmer; protects and attaches to the heart.

Foot jue yin: Relates to Liver. Distributes chi; cleanses; relates to authority issues.

Jue yin invasion: This is the last stage of illness caused by cold evil. It is a weakness of chi.

THE EIGHT GUIDING PRINCIPLES

The eight guiding principles reveal how to detect and work with the energetic imbalances in the body. In fact, the principles consist of four polar opposites, which are as follows.

INTERNAL/EXTERNAL

Internal/external determines the location but not the cause of the problem. Internal organs are often affected by an emotional issue, and less frequently by an unknown cause or an external factor. External disorders are either caused by an outside-of-the-body pathogen that attacks suddenly or an acute or chronic invasion in the channel. External symptoms might involve the hair, muscles, and peripheral nerves and blood vessels, while internal systems involve the organs, deep vessels and nerves, brain, and spinal cord.

HOT/COLD

Hot/cold indicates the nature of the imbalance and the overall energy of the patient. *Full heat* or hot is excess heat in the interior. *Excess heat* is too much yang. *Empty heat* is deficient yin in the interior (usually caused by Kidney yin deficiency.) *Full cold* is excess cold in the interior. *Excess cold* comes from too much yin. *Empty or deficient cold* is a deficiency of yang. Hot and cold can co-exist within the system. Cold symptoms might involve chills and pale skin, while hot symptoms could involve a raging fever and high metabolism.

FULL/EMPTY

Full/empty describes *excess* versus *deficiency*. It indicates the presence of a pathogen as well as the condition of the bodily chi. *Full* describes the presence of an internal or external pathogen or stagnated chi, blood, or food. *Empty* indicates no pathogen but weak chi, yin, yang, or blood. *Mixed* portrays the presence of a pathogen and weak chi, blood, yin, or yang. Full or excess symptoms often accompany a condition that is acute or sudden-onset, while empty or deficiency syndromes are more chronic and slow-moving.

CHI, BLOOD, AND FLUIDS: THE THREE UNIFYING INGREDIENTS

THE FOUR LEVELS, six stages, and eight principles all revolve around the same three bodily ingredients: chi, blood, and non-blood bodily fluids. While a serious illness involves all three, many problems revolve around issues with one or another. These are the main conditions involving blood, chi, or the fluids.

CHI CONDITIONS

Deficient chi: Not enough chi to perform the necessary functions.

Sinking or collapsed chi: The Spleen chi cannot perform its supportive functions.

Stagnated chi: The chi flow is impaired. If congested or stuck in an organ, there can be pain, sluggishness, or stiffness.

Rebellious chi: The chi flows in the wrong direction.

CORE BLOOD PATTERNS

Blood deficiency: Because of Spleen chi deficiency (in providing necessary support materials), the Heart and Liver are negatively affected. The Heart governs blood and the Liver stores it. Lacking chi, the heart cannot effectively pump the blood and the liver cannot properly cleanse it.

Blood stagnation: The blood is not flowing normally because of an obstruction.

FLUID (*JIN YE*) ISSUES

Fluid deficiency: Too much heat or dryness or deficient blood can create dryness.

Stagnation of fluids: If the yang cannot transport the fluids, they can accumulate to cause dampness (such as edema or phlegm).

YIN/YANG

Yin/yang is a synthesis of the other categories. Yin equals interior, empty, and cold. Yang equals exterior, full, and hot. It can also describe two kinds of emptiness: deficiency (not enough yin or yang) and collapse (critical "collapse" or recession of yin or yang).

THE TRIPLE WARMER (*SAN JIAO*, TRIPLE HEATER, TRIPLE BURNER, OR THREE BURNERS)

The Triple Warmer system is another helpful diagnostic modality, specifically for determining problems caused by wind-heat or, in some systems, damp-heat. This system was developed by Wu Ju Tong in the late 1700s and described in his book *A Systematic Identification of Febrile Disease*.

The system tracks wind-heat according to its position in the Triple Warmer. It is usually used in conjunction with herbal medicine rather than acupuncture. The three stages are:

The above problems can combine to create chi and blood deficiency and stagnation. A scenario might involve the stagnation of chi over time, which creates stagnation in the blood. Conversely, blood deficiency can also lead to chi deficiency. If the chi cannot move the blood, the result might be stagnated blood.

For example, a disorder might be described as an invasion of "wind-cold" or "wind-heat." As you might imagine, wind-cold might produce chills or dampness whereas wind-heat could result in fevers and sweating.

General traditional theory asserts that when under stress, the body's meridian system becomes imbalanced. Many factors cause stress, including physical, emotional, mental, or spiritual challenges, psychological issues, biochemical problems, and even electromagnetic difficulties such as geopathicstress. Even natural environmental factors such as excess cold, damp, wind, dryness, or heat can create imbalance. Under duress, the blood, chi, and fluid cannot flow normally, usually leading to congestion (excess or blockage) or depletion (deficiency or weakness). Symptoms of these imbalances can be found through the meridians even before they manifest physically. Once these problems appear physically, these underlying causes can impede the body's healing ability.

The meridian therapist essentially stimulates the acupuncture points to restore balance. Stagnant chi calls for stimulation. Cold chi needs warmth. As we will see in the section on meridian treatment modalities, diagnosis, and treatment, there are many paths open to a meridian specialist, including needling and non-needling techniques, massage, energy work, diet, herbs, and more.

Upper jiao: Upper part of the body, covering the Heart, Lungs, and Pericardium. Invasion of the lungs and skin; can also affect Stomach and Spleen.

Middle jiao: Midsection of the body, including the Spleen, Stomach, Gallbladder, and Liver systems. If the Spleen becomes injured by dampness, it cannot transport raw materials, which in turn affects the Stomach and muscles.

Lower jiao: Lower section of the body including the Small and Large Intestines, Kidneys, and Bladder.

THE SEVEN EMOTIONS AND THE CORRESPONDING ORGANS

raditional Chinese practitioners understand that emotions affect physiology. Therefore they typically assess and treat the emotions, especially in relation to the organs that they impact.

There are seven basic emotions in the Chinese system: joy, anger, worry, thought (pensiveness), sadness, fear, and shock. Each emotion influences a specific organ. Under normal conditions, this relationship helps someone respond to life events, but when the emotions are excessive or underdeveloped, the body will eventually become sick.

Excessive anger, for example, is dangerous to the liver and other parts of the body. The liver is where anger dwells. Extreme irritation or rage will amplify the liver energy, which will then rush to the head, potentially causing high blood pressure or headaches, or in the worst-case scenario, stroke.

While emotions *affect* the organs, it is important to remember that they are also created *in* specific organs. An organ "gives rise" to an emotion. Here is a list of these correlations:

The heart	*gives rise to*	joy
The liver	*gives rise to*	anger
The lungs	*give rise to*	worry and sadness
The spleen	*gives rise to*	thought
The kidneys	*give rise to*	fear and shock

THREE BASIC EMOTIONAL PATTERNS

Complicating matters is the fact that there are three basic emotional patterns. These involve:

An emotion giving rise to another emotion, which can cause a roller coaster of reactivity:

Anger	*gives rise to*	joy
Joy	*gives rise to*	thought
Thought	*gives rise to*	worry and sadness
Worry and sadness	*give rise to*	fear and shock
Fear and shock	*give rise to*	anger

One emotion overcoming another emotion, creating an imbalance:

Anger	*overcomes*	thought
Thought	*overcomes*	fear and shock
Fear and shock	*overcome*	joy
Joy	*overcomes*	worry and sadness
Worry and sadness	*overcome*	anger

One emotion reducing another emotion, creating balance:

Worry and sadness	*reduce*	joy
Thought	*reduces*	anger
Anger	*reduces*	worry and sadness
Fear and shock	*reduce*	thought
Joy	*reduces*	fear and shock

The key in healing the body emotionally is to use an emotion that can overcome or transform. For example, anger overcomes thought, but when thought is transformed into fire, the anger reduces, and the body achieves balance.[62]

THE SEVEN EMOTIONS AND THE ORGANS

This chart describes the seven emotions and how excessive emotions damage the correlated organs.

FIGURE 4.21
THE SEVEN EMOTIONS AND THE ORGANS

Emotion	Damage to Corresponding Organ
Joy	Excessive joy consumes Heart energy, leading to deficient Heart energy. It also relaxes the heart, so it cannot function effectively.
Anger	Excessive anger consumes Liver energy, leading to deficient Liver energy. It also rises to the head, creating headaches, high blood pressure, and potentially strokes.
Worry and sadness	Excessive worry and sadness burn up Lung energy, leading to deficient Lung energy, and also cause abdominal pain and swelling.

FIGURE 4.21
THE SEVEN EMOTIONS AND THE ORGANS

Emotion	Damage to Corresponding Organ
Thought	Excessive thought consumes Spleen energy, leading to deficient Spleen energy, and causes congestion in the spleen.
Fear and shock	Excessive fear and shock consume Kidney energy, leading to deficient Kidney energy. Fear also forces Kidney energy downward, causing lower-body problems and kidney conditions. Shock creates chaos in the kidneys, which impairs their efficiency.

QUALITIES OF FOODS THAT HEAL THE EMOTIONS

The five basic flavors in foods are often used to transform an emotion into fire and recalibrate the body. Foods can also be used to boost important emotions as well as reduce overstimulated emotions.

FIGURE 4.22
FOODS AND EMOTIONS

Healing Foods	Organs Enhanced	Emotions Enhanced	Emotions Reduced
Sour	Liver and gallbladder	Anger	Thought
Bitter	Heart and small intestine	Joy	Sadness and worry
Sweet	Spleen and stomach	Thought	Fear and shock
Pungent	Lungs and large intestine	Worry and sadness	Anger
Salty	Kidneys and bladder	Fear and shock	Joy

SIMILARITIES: MERIDIANS AND OTHER ENERGY CHANNELS

Many professionals perceive commonalities between the meridians and their corollaries and the nadis of Hindu literature, which are also related to the energy bodies called the *chakras*. While the nadis are technically considered channels, they are only referenced in this section and are more fully described in Part V on energy bodies. This choice of placement is due to the interchangeable relationship between the nadis and the chakras: one fuels the other.

Vedic literature is the traditional source of chakra-based information. It originated in India and Southeast Asia, although other cultures, including the Mayan, profess authorship. Chinese medicine started in China and spread to Korea,

THE CYCLES OF CHI: THE BODY CLOCK

IN TRADITIONAL CHINESE medicine, working with the *body clock* provides important feedback for diagnosing and treating chi imbalances. You can also support a particular organ if you know when it is at its most or least active state through a myriad of techniques including traditional treatments, proper foods, exercises, breathing, emotional focus, and practices including Qigong, which features organ-specific movements.

All organ functions ebb and flow as the chi circulates within the body every twenty-four hours. This concept of *chi cycles* is based in the observation that the twelve meridians are symmetrical on the left and right sides of the body; they also interconnect. The chi flows through each organ, and therefore the meridian system, like a serpent winding around the same river, providing the opportunity for the release of stagnation and inviting the organ to operate at its optimal level.

Chi begins its daily flow in the Lungs and traverses to the Large Intestine before continuing to its next destination. It finally stops at the Liver, before it begins again. If the chi is blocked in a certain organ, it will not be able to completely activate that organ or continue its journey with enough intensity to fully benefit the next organ systems. Practitioners often encourage patients to relay the timing of a symptom of a specific problem, or of chronic issues, as they can then figure out which organ might be blocked. By properly diagnosing the point of a blockage, a practitioner can treat the underlying problem and also the entire person.

THE BODY CLOCK

Lungs	3 a.m. to 5 a.m.
Large Intestine	5 a.m. to 7 a.m.
Stomach	7 a.m. to 9 a.m.
Spleen	9 a.m. to 11 a.m.
Heart	11 a.m. to 1 p.m.
Small Intestine	1 p.m. to 3 p.m.
Bladder	3 p.m. to 5 p.m.
Kidneys	5 p.m. to 7 p.m.
Pericardium	7 p.m. to 9 p.m.
Triple Warmer	9 p.m. to 11 p.m.
Gallbladder	11 p.m. to 1 a.m.
Liver	1 a.m. to 3 a.m.[63]

FIGURE 4.23

THE CYCLES OF CHI: THE BODY CLOCK

Chi moves through each meridian in a two-hour cycle, as shown on this Body Clock. For two hours of the day, each meridian achieves its optimum performance. Polar meridians are twelve hours apart. These brother-sister meridians are similar yet contrasting. For example, the Spleen and Triple Warmer meridians, while opposing one another, both regulate the immune system and are radiant currents. One, however, is yin and the other is yang. If one is undercharged, the other becomes overcharged; therefore, one affects the other. You will also notice that they are exactly opposite at their peak times. The Spleen meridian is at its most active between 9 a.m. and 11 a.m.; the Triple Warmer, its opposite, is at its most active between 9 p.m. and 11 p.m.

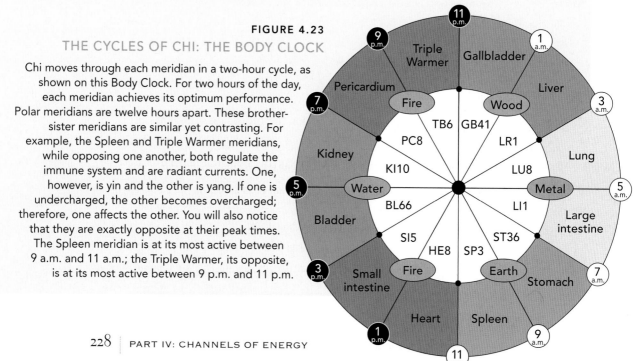

Japan, and Vietnam. Buddhist knowledge crossed between both, but not until 700 AD or so. So we can see that the two systems developed independently of each other; however, they correlate in a number of ways.

VITAL ENERGY

The Chinese call it *chi*; the Hindu name is *prana*. Both energies are seen as the vital, subtle energy that sustains all of life. Some systems of Chinese medicine postulate five types of chi (original or prenatal; chi from the organs; chi from the organs and bowels; defensive or external and constructive or internal chi; and evil chi, or pathogens that invade from the exterior). Still others name chi according to the elements. In feng shui, there are five elements: wood, water, fire, metal, and earth. (Different systems have different numbers and types of chi.) As well, many Hindu systems profess five types of prana that are also related to the organs: *prana*, *apana*, *ayan*, *udana*, and *samana*.

ENERGY CHANNELS AND BODIES

In the Vedic system, prana flows through the nadis to feed the chakras, while in the traditional Chinese world, chi flows through the meridians to serve the organs. As Dr. William Tiller proposed in his book *Science and Human Transformation*, the meridian, which exchanges information within the electromagnetic spectrum and at an etheric level, "probably represents the 'subtle nadi' of the ancient Hindu teachings."[64]

In Tiller's model, meridians serve as "antennae" for subtle and physical information. The chakras are similar antennae points, which, in contrast to the meridians, function at more etheric and subtle levels.[65] If the chi becomes partially or fully blocked etherically in the meridians (and therefore, in the nadi), it also does so in the physical body. Restore the flow through acupuncture, or another means of increasing the ionic flow, and the problem clears up physically as well as etherically.

Some esoteric scientists, however, compare the secondary chakras with the acupuncture points, considering both as "nodal positions of vibrational energy."[66] How might these two systems interconnect? Most energy scientists consider the chakras to be transducers of subtle energy. Meridians seem to begin *in utero* as subtle energies and then become conveyers of physical energies. Chakras have their root in both the nervous system and the endocrine glands, anchoring them in the physical body, just as the meridians are firmly grounded within the connective tissue and serve as a secondary electrical system. The interplay could be based in the three basic energy bodies that surround and penetrate the human body. These, according to Dr. Hiroshi Motoyama, are the physical, causal, and astral bodies, which operate at different vibrational rates.[67]

Seen as three concentric circles, they link to each other through the chakras, which in turn supply energy through the thousands of nadis that run through the system (and are also fed by the nadis). Dr. Motoyama asserts that the gross, or most physical, of the nadis (versus the subtle nadis) correspond to the meridian system. Both the nadis and the meridians, according to classical literature, are filled with body liquid, an energy that serves as a layer between the physical and subtle parts of our being, and both are situated in the connective tissue.[68]

THE ROLE OF EMOTIONS

In both the secondary chakra system and the acupuncture points, emotions play a vital role in creating the internal situations that can lead to health or disease.

THE ROLE OF FEMININE AND MASCULINE

In the Hindu system, male and female are represented by the kundalini (life energy) flow of the feminine serpent energy, which rises to join with the male energy available in the crown energy center. In Chinese medicine, yin and yang are polarity energies, reflecting magnetic and electrical, feminine and male, and all other dualistic qualities.

ELECTROMAGNETISM

Classical thought and research suggest that both the meridians and the chakras are linked through electromagnetic channels or bodies, and therefore relate through positive and negative charges.

THE SYSTEM AS LIGHT

As Dr. Alberto Villoldo, an expert on indigenous shamanism, asserts, master healers do not work on the physical body but rather through a luminous field of light that serves as a template for all aspects of our being. Chakras and meridians are part of the luminous energy field that creates and sustains physical reality.[69] Specifically, the meridians resemble the flux lines, or *cekes*, known to the descendants of the Inca as *rios de luz*, or "rivers of light."[70] (See "The Incan Energy Model" on page 296.)

WIND CHANNELS

In the Mayan healing system, some practitioners compare the meridians to "wind channels," stating that most of the key points in the Chinese system correlate with those in the Mayan.[71]

As seen, Asian cultures have used subtle energy-based medicine for thousands of years, their theories supported by practical application and real-life results. Their dedication is being saluted by empirical research, which is slowly transforming the subtle nature of the system into a more measurable science—although the mystery and art of channel-based practices still remain. The study of energy channels opens the door to yet another area of study, that of energy bodies. We now turn to Part V, Energy Bodies: Chakras and Other "Light Switches," to complete the voyage through the subtle anatomy.

I magine that you are handed a pair of glasses. Through them, you can perceive the actions of the atoms, the movement of the quanta, and the stream of your own consciousness. You can see the entirety of the universe—within yourself.

Ancient cultures—including the Indian Vedic, Egyptian, Tibetan, Hebrew, Chinese, and Mayan—understood that each of us is a reflection, a microcosm, of the wider universe. As it says in *The Emerald Tablet*, an ancient book about alchemy:

That which is Below corresponds to that which is Above, and that which is Above corresponds to that which is Below.[1]

This can also be said about our individual energy systems. Our subtle system mimics the external universe. Our physical self copies the subtle. These two selves unify us with the greater universe.

In Part V, we will examine the primary energy organs within our subtle energy system, starting with the chakras. These are the power centers that run the "you inside of you." Each of these chakras is paired with a particular layer in the auric field (see Part III), concentrations of light that regulate the "you outside of you." While chakras interface with the energy meridians of the body, chakras are even more involved with the *nadis*: conduits that disperse life energy (called *prana*) throughout the body. Because there is a vital relationship between the chakras, other energy bodies, and the nadis, we will explore the nadis in depth.

We will also venture into the chakric systems of different peoples, lands, and time periods, exploring ancient and modern ways to better understand our energetic selves with chakra knowledge. Part of the journey involves visiting other energy bodies—such as the *etheric*, *astral*, and *causal bodies* and the Jewish *sephiroth*—as well as various planes of existence and processes of activity, including the mystical

Hindu practice of *kundalini*. We'll explore several chakra systems, mainly to make a point: there is no "right" or "wrong" system of energy bodies. The Hindu alone postulated anywhere between four and twelve chakras—sometimes even more. You are encouraged to research further any or all of the systems presented here to come to your own conclusions and create your own protocol.

As we investigate this topic, we will not only define and examine the "self within the self," the energy bodies that construct our physical reality, but also the cosmos within the self. Chakra knowledge is as old as humankind—and perhaps, even older than that. Perhaps, it is even as old as the "Ein Sof" of the Jewish Kabbalah, the light that began it all.

36

ENERGY BODIES

There are countless energy bodies within a living organism. In some respects, every cell and organ within the body is an energy body. Each receives energy. Each breaks down, metabolizes, and disseminates energy. Each is operated and managed by a complex set of frequencies, and performs an equivalent service to other energy bodies. The major difference between *physical organs* and *subtle energy organs* is just what their names imply. Physical organs process only physical energy, while subtle energy organs process subtle energy *as well as* gross or physical energy.

Hindu tradition, usually considered the taproot of energy body knowledge, maintains that there are two types of energies. These are:

Gross energy: Material energy, also called the *saguna*, or energy "with attributes."

Subtle energy: "Extramaterial" energy, also called *nirguna*, or energy "without attributes."

Gross energy is unconscious energy, while subtle energy is conscious. Subtle energy bodies are able to transmute one type of energy into the other, with each energy center performing its own unique function within the anatomical structure of the body's energy system. As such, these centers tie together different parts of the body, the body with the cosmos, and all aspects of being with one another—physical, emotional, mental, and spiritual.

THE KEY ENERGY CENTERS: CHAKRAS

Chakras are the crux of the system. Also called *energy centers* or *energy organs*, they negotiate both physical and subtle energies, transforming one into the other and back again. There are dozens (if not hundreds) of centers and processes in attendance, but most agree that chakras are the dominant aspect.

The Hindu system alone, featured strongly in this section, has dozens of variations within it, including the Tantric and the yogic. Each variation offers "the" truth. In one tradition, there are four chakras; in another practice, there are eleven. The coloration, sounds, placement, and exact roles of the chakras differ, even though they are entirely within the same cultural tradition. We'll look at the most commonly accepted versions, along with the most typical (Western) spellings and definitions, as well as systems from around the world. Know that each culture has established a unique stamp on its chakra tradition. Few energetic systems are identical; the word *chakra* and its associated concepts might mean something slightly different to an African shaman than to a traditional Chinese medical doctor.

See figure 5.8 for the seven-chakra system, which is most typically used by esoteric physicians.

AN OVERVIEW: WHAT IS A CHAKRA?

What are chakras and what do they do for us? Ancient traditions have been careful to pass "chakraology" from generation to generation. Let us explore the most commonly accepted ideas about the chakras, from both a historical and a scientific perspective, before presenting a few variations of the chakra system.

There are many definitions of *chakra*, but they all evolve from the Sanskrit meaning of the word: "wheel of light." Most authorities agree that chakras are subtle energy centers that are located at the main branchings of the nervous system. They serve as collection and transmission centers for both subtle, or metaphysical, energy and concrete, or biophysical, energy.

Chakras are envisioned as either circular, or when emerging from the body, vortices that are conical in shape. According to various Sanskrit sources, a circle holds many meanings. For example, it describes a rotation of *shakti*, or feminine life energy, denotes *yantras* (mystical symbols) that direct reality, and references the different nerve centers in the body.[2] These and other analyses of the word reduce to a simple definition of the word *chakra*:

FIGURE 5.1

ANATOMY OF A CHAKRA

Each chakra can be seen as a pair of conical vortices emanating from the front and the back of the body. Together, these vortices regulate our conscious and unconscious realities, the psychic and sensory energies, and our subtle and physical selves.

A chakra is a circular-shaped energy body that directs life energy for physical and spiritual well-being.

Chakra systems differ with regard to location of the chakras, physical function, numbering, and other details. Some commonly accepted systems are as follows.

THE HINDU CHAKRA MODEL

To the Hindus, the chakras are part of the esoteric anatomy. They are interconnected with the nadis, which are meridian-like channels that carry energy around the body. Some ancient texts defined four chakras plus a metaphysical one. Still other venerable texts report five, six, seven, or more chakras. The basis of this system proposes that the chakras interface with other energy bodies to assist in the rising of kundalini, a type of life energy that invites union with the Divine.

THE TANTRIC CHAKRA MODEL

In this system, chakras (often numbering eight) are emanations of consciousness from Brahman, the Divine. This higher energy descends from the spiritual realms through gradually lower frequency levels, until finally coming to rest in the base of the spine as kundalini, a sleeping serpent. Along the way, the different types of consciousness are preserved in various chakras: energy bodies that lie along the spine. Each chakra represents a separate level of consciousness. Through yoga, one reawakens the kundalini energy so it can rise through the higher chakras and eventually transform one back into the highest state. In other words, the chakras provide the path of returning to enlightenment.

THE TRADITIONAL CHINESE CHAKRA MODEL

The Chinese model presents the circulation of chi, or life energy, through the meridians rather than the nadis, but there are many similarities between this and the Hindu system. As with the basic Hindu model, the chakras are located in the cerebrospinal areas. They are part of the process of evolving into union with the deity. Depending on the system, there are six to eight chakras involved.

A WESTERN VIEW OF CHAKRAS

Arthur Avalon is a widely accepted Western authority on the Tantric yoga (or kundalini yoga) version of the chakras. Avalon perceives them as seats of consciousness, numbering seven (or six with an "extra one"). He also calls them *lotuses* or *padma* of the body. Avalon considers them subtle rather than physical centers, as he places them within the central nadi, the nadis serving as a subtle energy conduit system. Unlike other Westerners, Avalon does not consider the chakras part of the nervous system itself, because layers of the spinal cord separate the chakra from the body. The goal is to awaken the kundalini or serpent power, which sleeps in feminine form at the base of the chakra system, so it rises and "pierces" the upper chakras. Once the kundalini reaches the top center, an aspirant is freed from the continual cycle of death and rebirth; he or she is "enlightened."[3]

Modern derivative chakra systems usually outline seven chakras, which ascend along the spine from the coccyx area to the top of the head. They are often affiliated with: an aspect of consciousness or a major theme; a color; an element; a sound; a lotus (with differing numbers of petals); and interactions with the physical, emotional, mental, and spiritual aspects of being human. Each chakra is also frequently associated with a gland of the endocrine system and a nervous system nexus (*plexus* or *ganglia*). Nearly every cultural chakra system considers the chakras a vital part of an enlightenment or spiritualization process.

Most systems place the chakras at the same basic locations:

First chakra	Groin
Second chakra	Abdomen
Third chakra	Solar plexus
Fourth chakra	Heart
Fifth chakra	Throat
Sixth chakra	Forehead
Seventh chakra	In the top of the head

A few chakra systems place the seventh chakra atop the head, instead of above the head. C. W. Leadbeater, who wrote about the chakras in the 1930s, established the second chakra near the spleen, slightly higher than the third chakra, which he located at the navel. He also pulled the heart chakra slightly to the subject's left.

My own examination indicates the seven basic chakras as well as five additional chakras located within the overall body energy system—but these further five chakras are not within the physical body. Other esoteric professionals, including Barbara Ann Brennan, author of *Hands of Light*, postulate chakras above the typical seven, describing an eighth and ninth chakra above the head.[4] Katrina Raphaell, author of *The Crystalline Transmission*, describes a twelve-chakra system, with another chakra at the top of the head, two out-of-body chakras above the head, another in-body chakra below the heart and above the solar plexus, and yet another out-of-body chakra beneath the feet.[5] In general, however, most sources agree on the first seven chakras.

Researchers in subtle energy technologies, as well as those in the medical community, are evolving our understanding of the chakras. A synthesized definition of chakras from a scientific point of view might be this:

> *Chakras are energy transformers, capable of shifting energy from a higher to a lower vibration and vice versa.*

As such, chakras interact with the flow of subtle energies through specific energy channels to affect the body at the cellular level, as reflected by hormonal and physiological levels in the physical body.

What are these amazing "wheels of light"? How did they become so popular across time and culture? Let us briefly examine the history of the human chakra system before discussing the scientific theories behind it.

THE HISTORY OF CHAKRA KNOWLEDGE

Throughout the ages, diverse and widespread cultures understood that people are not solely composed of mundane matter. We are made of vibrations: frequencies that interact with, and sometimes react to, the world outside of ourselves. Our ancestors knew what Einstein asserted only recently: energy cannot be destroyed; it can only change form. We might therefore picture our ancestors as wearing "possibility glasses." Through the optical glass of intuition, they were able to describe and work with the energy bodies that could turn gross (physical) matter into subtle energy, and subtle energy into gross matter. The chakras were clearly central to this conversion process.

Most researchers believe that the chakra system began in India more than four thousand years ago, a classification of *esoteric anatomy*, an outline of the various subtle energy bodies and channels that affect the human body. The knowledge descends from the Vedanta philosophy, which was written down in the Upanishads around 800 BC. *Vedanta* means "the end of the Vedas," and refers to the name of four sacred Hindu texts originating in 1500 BC. These texts are called *Tantras*. In general, the chakra system branched into two sections: the Vedic and the Tantric (now alive within Ayurvedic medicine and Tantric yoga, for example).

The term *tantra* comes from two words: *tanoti*, or to expand; and *trayati*, or to liberate. Tantra therefore means "to extend knowledge that liberates." Tantra is a life practice based on teachings about the chakras, kundalini, hatha yoga, astronomy, astrology, and the worship of many Hindu gods and goddesses. Tantric yoga originates in pre-Aryan India, around 3000 to 2500 BC. Many other varieties of Tantric yoga or spirituality have arisen from it, including Tantric Buddhism. Each system derived from Tantric yoga has a unique view on the chakras and their related gods, cosmology, and symbols.

The history of chakras, as complex as it sounds so far, is even more complicated. The chakra system is intertwined with—and maybe even created by—several different cultures. Although usually associated with India, Tantric yoga was also practiced by the Dravidians, who originated from Ethiopia, as is revealed in the many similarities between predynastic Egyptian and African practices and ancient Indian Tantric beliefs.[6]

For example, numerous Hindu deities are rooted in "India's black civilizations, which is why they are often depicted as black."[7] Some historians point out that early Egyptians were greatly affected by African beliefs,[8] and in turn influenced Greek, Jewish, and, later, Islamic and Christian thought, in addition to the Indian Hindu.[9]

Other cultures also exchanged chakra ideas. Many practices of the early Essenes, a religio-spiritual community dwelling in Palestine in the second century BC through the second century AD, mirrored those of early India.[10] The Sufis—Islamic mystics—also employed a system of energy centers, although it involved four centers.[11] The Sufis also borrowed the kundalini process from Tantric yoga, as did certain Asian Indian and American Indian groups.[12]

As we shall see, the Maya Indians of Mexico, the Inca Indians of Peru, and the Cherokee Indians of North America each have their own chakra method. The Maya believe that they actually taught the Hindu the chakra system.

The chakra system was brought to the West in yet another roundabout way. It was first thoroughly outlined in the text *Sat-Chakra-Nirupana*, written by an Indian yogi in the sixteenth century. Arthur Avalon then delivered chakra knowledge to Western culture in his book *The Serpent Power*, first published in 1919. Avalon drew heavily upon the *Sat-Chakra-Nirupana* as well as another text, *Pakaka-Pancaka*. His presentation was preceded by *Theosophic Practica*, a book written in 1696 by Johann Georg Gichtel, a student of Jakob Bohme, who refers to inner force centers that align with Eastern chakra doctrines.[13]

Today, many esoteric professionals rely on Anodea Judith's interpretation of Avalon's work, to which she has added additional information about the psychological aspects of the chakras.[14]

Steeped in history, embedded in the spiritual traditions of the world, chakras are now quickly moving to the forefront of yet another discipline: science.

37

KUNDALINI, THE UNIFYING FORCE

There are numerous energy bodies and channels in the Hindu system. You will be introduced to many of them as you explore this section. There are the chakras and the nadis; the three bodies of incarnation; and the five *koshas*, or subtle bodies. Furthermore, there is a power, a force—a consciousness—that unifies these independent subjects.

The narrative of the kundalini is a story of the gods—the gods within each of us. It tells of the merging of our internal female and male energies and of the transcendence beyond both. It is a four-thousand-year-old Hindu tale.

Once there was a single consciousness that unified everything. Within this consciousness were two beings: Shiva, the *infinite* supreme consciousness, and Shakti, the *eternal* supreme consciousness. Shiva represents time, and Shakti, space. Here is the yang of Oriental medicine, cloaked in the Shiva figure, and the yin shown within the Shakti.

These two beings separated, creating a distinction between matter and consciousness within the universe—and within the children of the universe, including people. Shakti lies within us all, coiled within our root chakra in the guise of a serpent. In this form, she is the *Kundalini Shakti*, the "power at rest."[15] She only becomes manifest, however, when she moves—and that is her ultimate goal, to rise through the denseness of the body until she can rejoin her great love, Shiva, who resides in the seventh chakra. When unified, the two create through supreme consciousness.

Shakti is not just an ethereal being. She is seen as the cause of prana, or life force. She has sound and form; she is composed of alphabet characters, or *mantras*. When Shiva and Shakti join, they create *nada* (pure cosmic sound) and *maha bindu* (the supreme truth that underlies all manifestation). What does this mean for the initiate who fuses these two beings—these two parts of him- or herself? The graduate is freed from the confines of the physical body. Innate powers—mystical, magical abilities—awaken. Moreover, the soul is freed from the wheel of life that forces reincarnation.

Science tells a similar story, using different words. According to recent studies, the entire world can be reduced to frequency and vibration. As we saw in Part III, we are all composed of the L-fields and T-fields that form unified frequencies. We are all made of the "male" and the "female," the electrical and the magnetic. If we can achieve the balance and blending of each, then there is harmony, and within that harmony, healing. To follow the path of kundalini is not "only" to achieve an enlightened state of mind. It is to heal the mind, soul, spirit—and body.

How does the kundalini work? It involves the energies you will study in this section:

The chakras: The circular energies of light that regulate the physical body and await spiritual activation.

The nadis: Subtle energy streams or conduits that interact with the chakras and the physical body. These convey prana, or subtle energy, to cleanse the physical body and invite the kundalini upward through the chakras. In scientific terms, these could be seen as force-motion lines. (See "Nadis: Channels of Energy" on page 272.) The primary nadis involved in the kundalini rising are the *Sushumna*, or nadi central, in the spine; the *Ida*, which is on the left side of the spine and represents feminine energy; and the *Pingala*, which is on the right side of the spine and signifies male energy. As the kundalini arises through the Sushumna, the Ida and Pingala—coiled around the nucleic seven chakras—activate the chakras and result in a continual rising of the kundalini.

The koshas: Veils of energy that confine the spirit or essential self. These five sheaths lift as an initiate evolves physically, mentally, spiritually, and energetically.

The subtle energy bodies: The three basic energy bodies that contain the human and spiritual dimensions.

THE KUNDALINI PROCESS

What follows is an abridged version of the kundalini process:

Prerising: The initiate experiences all the vicissitudes of life, including lack of control over his or her everyday physical existence. Picture the Shakti kundalini serpent coiled in the base of the spine, awaiting activation and the Shiva energy in the seventh chakra awaiting his lost mate.

Development: By moving from one kosha level to another, the initiate encourages activation of the nadis, opening of the chakras, and an eventual activation of the Shakti kundalini in the first chakra. This evolution involves cleansing of the body, learning, and healing of the body, mind, and soul.

Rising of the kundalini: As the kundalini rises through the Sushumna, the chakras are activated, one at a time, by the three main nadis: the central Sushumna and the surrounding Ida and Pingala. This leads to increased understanding and health in the areas governed by each chakra.

Transformation: The seventh chakra receives the arising kundalini, and Shakti and Shiva—male and female—are unified. Many systems say that the energy now resides in the sixth chakra, where it can be further focused.

Activation of powers: Some energetic systems relate that during and because of this process, the *siddhi*, or powers, become active, leading to seemingly magical abilities including invisibility, levitation, the ability to heal, and more (see "The Siddhi: Powers from the Subtle Bodies" on page 285). Through the transformation process, the material energy of the body is altered by the nature of the prana, freeing the initiate from the confines of the physical laws.

38

SCIENTIFIC PRINCIPLES MEET CHAKRA THEORY

Each chakra influences the body in unique physical, emotional, mental, and spiritual ways. This is because each energy organ vibrates at its own frequency and spins at its own particular velocity.

Remember the definition of energy we have been working with: information that moves. Therefore, information has speed and frequency. Varying speeds and frequencies change the information in each tiny piece of energy.

Information with a speed faster than light is received as subtle energy, and can be interpreted via the chakra. Information that moves at the speed of light or slower is received by the chakra as sensory, and will impact physical reality. A chakra can accept and transform both types of energy, turning them back into information useful to the individual.

A chakra vibrates from inside the physical body to the outside, radiating the information through the skin. It also pulls information from outside into the body, transforming it for reception. Even out-of-body chakras connect into the physical body. This in-and-out streaming of energy means that the chakras actually look more like bands of nonending energy, rather than the conical vortices they are often depicted as.

Not only does chakra energy flow like a never-ending river, this energy flow attracts other energies in the universe. Some of these interact to form a mini-universe of the self, including the auric field—layers of energy that surround the human body—and other energy channels, bodies, and fields that flow within and outside the self (these include the nadis as well as secondary energy bodies, such as the causal and emotional bodies).

Each chakra vibrates at a different frequency. The lower in the body it is, the slower the vibration; the higher in the body, the faster the vibration. People who are attuned to these frequencies see them as light and color. The in-body chakras occupy visible light, with the lowest touching into the infrared portion of the color spectrum and the higher body chakras, the ultraviolet portion.

The lower a chakra is within, or in relation to, the body, the closer it is to the infrared spectrum of light. The higher the chakra is within, or in relation to, the body, the more it stretches into the ultraviolet frequencies of light. Red is the first visible color we see after we pass the infrared and nonvisible band of light. It is associated with the first chakra, in the groin. Violet is the last color that we can see before we shift into ultraviolet frequencies, and is the color we associate with the sixth chakra in the forehead.

This illustration of the chakra color spectrum (figure 5.3) poses questions about the visibility of the chakras. One of the foremost questions is this: If the chakras are there, and vibrating in these color frequencies, why are we unable to perceive the colors with our physical eyes? Our brain waves usually oscillate between 0 and 100 cycles per second (or Hz). (See Valerie Hunt's study in "Scientific Research" below.) Chakras vibrate in a band between 100 and 1,600 Hz. This means that our brains are simply not trained to perceive oscillations or frequencies as high as those that the chakras regulate.

Intuitive people through the ages, however, have recurrently discerned six, if not seven, chakras. The primary six (the first through sixth chakras) have frequencies associated with the physically visible spectrum (red, orange, yellow, green, blue, and violet). Intuition often discerns only that which the brain allows it to discern. If the brain says, "I cannot see infrared or ultraviolet," our intuition will not distinguish colors—or chakras—in the lower or higher spectrums. This might account for the reason that so many esoteric practitioners locate the seventh chakra, which has the frequency of white light, above, rather than within, the human body. It is "otherworldly," or outside of the norm. It might also explain why some psychic individuals identify chakras lower and higher than the body. They might simply be able to distinguish "shades of gray" that others do not know how to look for.

FIGURE 5.2

CHAKRAS AS WAVES

Chakras have traditionally been described as "wheels of light": vortices of spinning energy that emanate from the spine. From a psychic's point of view, they are more often seen as bands of loosely interconnecting waves that carry information into and out of the body.

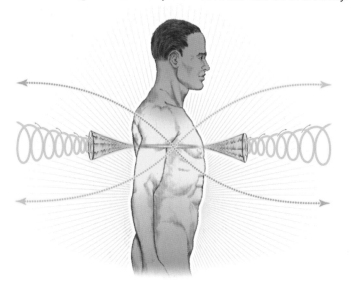

SCIENTIFIC RESEARCH

Considerable research is validating the existence of the chakras, with Dr. Valerie Hunt serving as a pioneer. For the past twenty years, Hunt, a professor of kinesiology (the study of human movement) at the University of California in Los Angeles, has measured human electromagnetic output under different conditions. Using an electromyograph, an instrument that measures the electrical activity of the muscles, Hunt discovered that the physical body emanated radiation at sites typically associated with the chakras. In addition, she discovered that certain levels of consciousness were linked to specific frequencies.[16]

When people in her studies were thinking of daily situations, their energy fields measured frequencies in the range of 250 Hz. This is the same frequency as the heart. When psychic individuals had their energy fields tested on the electromyograph, their frequency ranged in a band from 400 to 800 Hz. Trance specialists and channelers fell into the 800 to 900 Hz range, and mystics, connected continually to their higher self, had a energy field, or etheric body, above 900 Hz.

Hunt's findings correlate with traditional chakra lore: the chakras can be stepping-stones to enlightenment, each inviting a different spiritual awareness and increasing the frequency of the subtle body. In fact, the manufacturer of the equipment adapted the machine to measure higher frequencies, and it was found that a mystic had an average subtle energy field frequency of 200,000 Hz.[17]

Hunt also found changes in coloration emanating from the chakra points when subjects were being rolfed, as she discusses in an abstract cowritten by Dr. Wayne Massey and others.[18] Rolfing is a form of massage that achieves structural integration by means of manipulating the myofascia.

FIGURE 5.3

CHAKRAS ON THE ELECTROMAGNETIC SPECTRUM

While a subject was being rolfed, measurement was conducted with Fourier analysis and a sonogram frequency analysis. As subjects were monitored with equipment, noted healer Reverend Rosalyn Bruyere recorded the colors she saw through psychic vision.

The registered frequencies were measurable by color but also sound. Both Bruyere's psychic vision and the frequency recording equipment reported the same changes in coloration, chakra to chakra. The colors were observed to be the same as in metaphysical literature: root, or first chakra, was red; "hypogastric," or second chakra, was orange; spleen, or third, was yellow; heart, or fourth, was

FIGURE 5.4

CHAKRAS AND THE ENDOCRINE SYSTEM

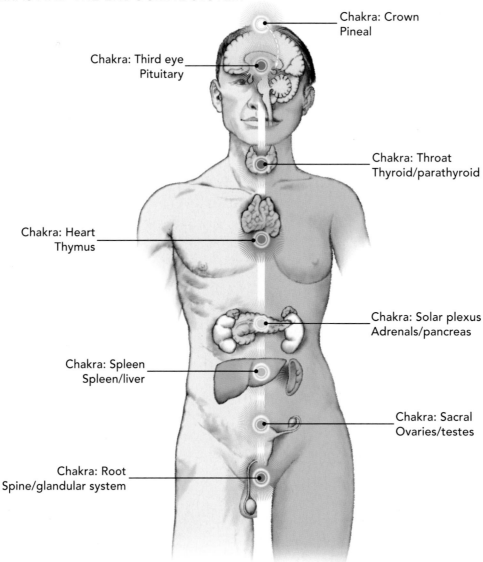

Chakra: Crown
Pineal

Chakra: Third eye
Pituitary

Chakra: Throat
Thyroid/parathyroid

Chakra: Heart
Thymus

Chakra: Solar plexus
Adrenals/pancreas

Chakra: Spleen
Spleen/liver

Chakra: Sacral
Ovaries/testes

Chakra: Root
Spine/glandular system

green; the throat, or fifth, was blue; the third eye, or sixth chakra, was violet; and the crown, or seventh chakra, white.

One of Hunt's concepts is that, from a quantum perspective, the body is more than a conglomerate of systems (such as endocrine, neuromuscular, or cardiovascular). Instead, all systems and tissues are organized by energy: specifically, bioenergy. The study suggests the existence of the chakras and recognizes them as involved with the physical, emotional, and energetic natures of our being.

Yet another study, conducted on an extremely clairvoyant individual, Dora van Gelder Kunz, suggests the existence of the chakras. Mrs. Kunz was asked to observe two hundred people with various diseases and to describe their illnesses in terms of alterations in the nonphysical bodies and the chakras.[19] Dr. Shafica Karagulla, researcher and author of the book *The Chakras and Human Energy Fields*, compared Mrs. Kunz's reports with standard medical diagnosis. Researchers in this study discovered that diseases do alter the behavior of chakras and nonphysical bodies in terms of color, luminosity, rhythm, rate, size, form, elasticity, and texture.

One exciting outcome of this research was a detailed correlation between the chakras and the endocrine glands. The researchers discovered that a problem with a particular gland would show up in the chakra. If the pineal gland was disturbed, for example, the crown chakra would be as well. The correlation found between chakras and endocrine glands is as shown in figure 5.4.

As is apparent from this illustration, the researchers found eight main chakras (adding the spleen), rather than the more traditional seven chakras. They also noticed the existence of minor chakras in the palms of the hands and the soles of the feet.

Dr. Hiroshi Motoyama, a scientist and a Shinto priest, also investigated the science of the chakras. He has conducted numerous studies to verify the energy system, many of which have become the basis of his more than twenty books. Dr. Motoyama has created a device to detect minute electrical, magnetic, and optical changes in the vicinity of a subject. It is called the apparatus for measuring the functioning of the meridians and corresponding internal organs, or AMI. During one test, Motoyama found that increased activity of the heart chakra area actually produced a weak but measurable physical light. Subjects were asked to press a button whenever they thought they were experiencing psi-energy, or psychic sensations such as inexplicable feelings, pictures, or sounds. These internal feelings correlated to objectively measured periods of heart activity. Experiments similar to this one led Motoyama to conclude that mental concentration on a chakra is the key to activating it.[20]

These and other studies led Dr. Motoyama to deduce that certain individuals can project their energy through the chakras, a statement supported by Itzhak Bentov, a researcher of physiological changes associated with meditation. Bentov has duplicated Motoyama's findings regarding electrostatic energy emission from the chakras.[21]

Dr. Motoyama suggests that the chakras are represented in the central nervous system by the brain and nerve plexuses, as well as in the meridian acupuncture points. Though chakras are separate from the central nervous system and the meridians, Motoyama considers the chakras as superimposed upon these other two systems, rather than occupying the same physical space.[22]

As Dr. Motoyama explains, the chakras supply the physical body with outside energy through the nadi system, a circuitry that spreads subtle energy throughout the body. Motoyama states that the "gross nadi" equate with the meridian system, and together they represent a "physical but invisible system of physiological control" located within connective tissue.[23]

These are some of the ways that science is closing in on ancient knowledge. We are beginning to see that all cosmologies—the mundane, the physical, and the mystical—might very well be the same.

39

CHAKRA SYSTEMS
FROM AROUND THE WORLD

Western tradition frequently attributes the chakra system to the Hindus. The truth is that chakra systems have endured in all corners of the globe. Some are of Hindu origin, others appear to have grown organically, and yet others, including the Mayan, profess to be "the" source for even the Hindu chakra system.

THE SEVEN HINDU CHAKRAS

Hindu means "of the Indus," the river that stretches from the Tibetan Himalayas along modern Pakistan into the Arabian Sea. Here, several ancient cultures have mixed the ideas and ideals that form the current Hindu chakra system.

According to Hindu philosophy, the chakras are considered subtle energy bodies located within the spinal cord, housed within the innermost core of the *Sushumna nadi*. This is called the *Brahma nadi*, the carrier of spiritual energy. The nadis carry subtle energy throughout the body and are critical allies in the rising of the kundalini, the activation of life energy in the lowest chakra. When awakened, this kundalini energy ascends the spine, the chakra column, and spreads throughout the body to invite enlightenment.

The core of the Sushumna nadi is considered a spiritual energy body, not a material energy body; therefore, the chakras are most often referred to as subtle in nature. Some Hindu systems, however, connect the chakras with the gross nerve plexuses, which are outside of the spine. In these systems, the chakras are considered physical as well as subtle and are considered the foundation of all existence, psychologically and physically.

MULADHARA, OR ADHARA: THE FIRST, BASE, OR ROOT CHAKRA

The Muladhara or Adhara chakra is the foundation of the Vedic chakra pantheon. It is the first of the in-body chakras lying at the base of the spine. From here arise the nadis, the subtle energy channels that carry life energy throughout the body. As such, the first chakra is considered the subtle energy center of the coccygeal nerve plexus but is also of vital importance in forming a physical and psychological foundation for our lives.

The Muladhara is associated with the elephant, which carries the seed-sound of the chakra. The energy of Muladhara helps us persevere; if anything, elephants are solid, dependable, and persevering. This being helps us harness and direct the energy needed to endure—and thrive—in life.

The Muladhara is geometrically represented as a square that contains a circle. Within the circle is a downward-pointed triangle: the image of a female

HINDU CHAKRA LEGEND

THERE ARE SEVEN basic Hindu chakras, although some Tantric versions add several others in the forehead. Three additional forehead chakras will be described in this book. The many Hindu texts vary slightly; therefore, this outline will present the most popular concepts, definitions, and word spellings. Here is a condensed template of the many traditional aspects of the chakras.

First we will give the Sanskrit title for the chakra and its secondary names, then an overview of the chakra. Additional aspects covered are:

Other names: Other Hindu names, if applicable.

Meaning of name: Meaning of the Sanskrit term for the chakra.

Main aspect: Generic description of chakra main function.

Location: The physical location of the chakra as related to the spine, nearby organs, or its associated nerve plexus (also called *sthula sarira*).

Related organs: A partial list of the organs regulated by or associated with this chakra.

Symbol: Also called the *yantra*, the symbol relates to the shape of the chakra. Typically, a chakra is associated with a geometric shape and a lotus with different numbers of petals and colors.

Color of chakra: The overall color of the chakra.

Components: Each chakra is associated with elements, and there are colors, sounds, and lotus petals associated with each:

GROSS ELEMENT
Elements are called *tattwas*. For the five physical elements, or *bhutas*, see figure 5.8.

SUBTLE ELEMENT
The *tanmatra*, or more spiritual element.

COLOR OF ELEMENT
As per Tantric yoga, the color of the gross element.

sexual organ. The lotus associated with Muladhara has four red petals; red is the most typical color associated with the first chakra. The lotus is contained within a yellow square, which signifies the earth element. Thus the passion and life-evoking red of the first chakra can be considered as bounded and grounded by earth energies. The mantra is *lam*, which stops our energy from descending beyond our foundation, our first chakra. Some sources perceive a lingum, or concentration point, in the middle of the triangle, a reflection of the male and female

FIGURE 5.5
FIRST CHAKRA: MULADHARA

SOUND OF ELEMENT

Called the *seed sound* or *bija-mantra* of the element; the sound generated by the element in this chakra.

CARRIER OF SOUND

Every chakra is represented by an animal, or *vahana*, that carries the seed sound. Each animal reflects a certain quality available through the chakra.

PETALS

Every chakra is illustrated by a lotus, or *padma*, with a specific number of petals. The petals themselves are associated with certain sounds, deitites, and meanings.

Predominant sense: The specific sense associated with this chakra.

Sense organ: The *jnanendriya*, or organ managing the related sense.

Action organ: The *karmendriya*, or organ that generates the primary physical activity of this chakra.

Vital breath: The type of breath managed by this chakra, if present.

Cosmic realm or plane: Most chakras connect to a *loka*, or cosmic realm, or a distinct plane; when applicable, either or both are listed.

Ruling goddess: Each chakra is supervised by a specific female goddess, the feminine divine.

Ruling god: Each chakra is overseen by a particular male god, the masculine divine.

Ruling planet: Planet considered aligned with this chakra.

The lingum: Some chakras host linga, also called *granthi* or *knots*, that must be unwoven for the kundalini to rise.

energies present in all living form. The god overseeing this chakra is Brahma, the creator lord. Traditionally shown with four heads, four faces, and four arms, he is able to see and rule in all directions. His consort, Dakini, serves as the doorkeeper to the physical realm. In each of her four hands, she holds a symbol of life—and of death—and of the path of life in between.

Psychologically, the Muladhara chakra regulates our primal needs and physical existence. It is the chakra most closely associated with our physical survival. Here we decide to live or die, and how it is that we shall survive—or thrive. It is seen as fashioned from the element earth, therefore providing a foundation in the physical world.

THE FIRST CHAKRA: MULADHARA

Other names	Adhara, Patala
Meaning of name	Muladhara combines *mul*, or base, and *adhara*, or support The name reflects its ultimate purpose, which is to serve as our basis in physical life; it is often called the *root chakra*
Main aspect	Security
Location	In the physical body, at the base of the spine, between the anus and genitals
Related organs	Bones, skeletal structure, coccygeal nerve plexus, adrenal glands
Symbol	Four red petals, containing a square with a downward triangle
Color of chakra	Red
Components	
Gross element	Earth
Subtle element	Attraction/smell
Color of element	Yellow
Sound of element	*Lam*
Carrier of seed sound	The elephant, *airavata*, which represents the ability to direct our life force for meeting goals
Petals of the lotus	Four blood-red petals
Predominant sense	Smell
Sense organ	Nose
Action organ	Feet
Vital breath	*Apana*
Cosmic realm or plane	The natural earth, *Bhu Loka*
Ruling goddess	Dakini, gatekeeper of physical reality
Ruling god	Brahma, creator of physical reality Ganesh, the elephant-headed god who bestows protection and removes obstacles, is also frequently affiliated with this chakra

Ruling planet	Saturn
Lingum	Here is the knot of Brahma, which we must disintegrate if we are to throw off the veils of illusion that make us perceive earth as a prison

SVADHISTHANA: SECOND CHAKRA

This chakra initiates the expansion of one's individuality. Its location at the sexual organs reflects the instinctual need to develop a specific personality, but also to reach out to others. The watery element of this chakra encourages us to enjoy the rhythms and cycles of life. The animal most frequently associated with this chakra is the crocodile, which lies in the water awaiting the opportunity to express itself—whether to sunbathe or to kill.

Our psyche seeks to express itself through the second chakra. Muladhara, the first chakra, represents the ground of existence; the second chakra, Svadisthana, creativity. How are we to live and share our passions? Our dreams? Our desires? Can we do this with integrity? The presiding god energy of this chakra, Vishnu, balances the creation of Brahma and the destructive powers of Shiva. We all have generative and degenerative forces within ourselves; when do we apply these, and for what reasons? The presiding goddess of the second chakra, Rakini Shakti, drinks from the nectar of the seventh chakra—the ambrosia of the gods. She asks the question: Are we willing to fill ourselves with the sweetness of life—and love?

The symbol of the second chakra is a crescent moon within a circle. Outside this is a lotus with six orange-red petals (some systems see these as white). The mantra is *vam*, which nourishes our body's fluids. The symbolism of this chakra centers on the moon, which is laden with sexual symbolism. It is said that the moon god, when new, travels through the world to fertilize the waters. In turn, the water nourishes the plants, which sustain the animals and finally, people.

FIGURE 5.6

SECOND CHAKRA: SVADHISTHANA

Psychologically, the second chakra encourages the development of our unique personalities, our ability to create and nurture, and our need for love and sweetness.

SECOND CHAKRA: SVADHISTHANA

Other names	Adhishthan, Shaddala
Meaning of name	Dwelling place of the self, from *sva*, self or prana, and *adhisthana*, or dwelling place Also means "six-petaled"
Main aspect	Sweetness
Location	In the physical body, lower abdomen, between navel and genitals
Related organs	Sexual organs, bladder, prostate, womb, sacral nerve plexus, kidneys
Symbol	Six orange-red petals Inside lies a lotus flower and a crescent moon that contains the *makara*, the crocodile
Color of chakra	Orange
Components **Gross element** **Subtle element** **Color of element** **Sound of element** **Carrier of seed sound** **Petals of the lotus**	 Water Attraction/taste Color or water transparent, white, light blue *Vam* Crocodile (*makara*), the unseen (as in our desires) that lies underwater Six vermilion-red petals
Predominant sense	Taste
Sense organ	Tongue
Action organ	Hands
Vital breath	*Apana*
Cosmic realm or plane	Astral or the sky, *Bhuvar Loka*
Ruling goddess	Rakini Shakti, who drinks nectar from the seventh chakra
Ruling god	Vishnu, who combines creation and destruction
Ruling planet	Pluto

MANIPURA: THIRD OR SOLAR PLEXUS CHAKRA

The Manipura chakra presents itself as a brilliant, luminescent jewel. Elementally associated with fire, it is like a bright sun in the middle of the body.

This center, which manages the digestive process and organs, also influences the nervous system and the immune process. Digestion is a reflection of the ability to digest and assimilate everything—including thoughts. Thus, this center determines the health of both our bodies and minds.

This chakra is co-ruled by Rudra and Lakini Shakti. Rudra is the lord of Manipura. An aspect of Shiva, he appears as a chariot rider of the sun, whose arrows cause destruction and disease. He demands that we organize our minds and experience, deciding what needs to be "burned away" or retained. Lakini Shakti is a benevolent form of the goddess of destruction, Kali. She encourages us to set goals and concentrate on what we need to do—and think—to achieve our aspirations.

The third chakra is represented by a downward-pointing triangle within a circle. The triangle has "Ts" that act as doorways into the swastika shapes that they attach to. The swastika, a Sanskrit symbol for well-being, whether the legs bend clockwise or counterclockwise—in this case the legs are angled to the left—is a symbol of fire, the gross element of this chakra. The ten petals of the lotus are blue—as blue as the center of a hot flame; therefore, this chakra is both constructive and destructive. The fire element relates to the Hindu theory that digestion is accomplished through heat; therefore, food is burned to create our vital energy. Within this chakra, we hear the sound *ram*, a fitting tone, as the ram is also the carrier of the sound mantra. Rams provide courage and support for moving into the world.

Psychologically, Manipura is the center of our personal power. For some, this translates as a consuming need for information; in others, for authority. Within this chakra are the keys to finding balance and deciding how we are going to achieve our dharma, our life purpose, rather than just live out our karma, or past experiences.

FIGURE 5.7
THIRD CHAKRA: MANIPURA

HINDU CHAKRA DEVELOPMENT

THERE ARE MANY theories about chakra development: the natural, progressive order of the opening of the chakras. The most well-known Tantric outline is this:

Chakra	Age of Development
Muladhara	1 to 8
Svadhisthana	8 to 14
Manipura	14 to 21
Anahata	21 to 28
Vishuddha	28 to 35

There are no ages formally associated with the Ajna and Sahasrara chakras.

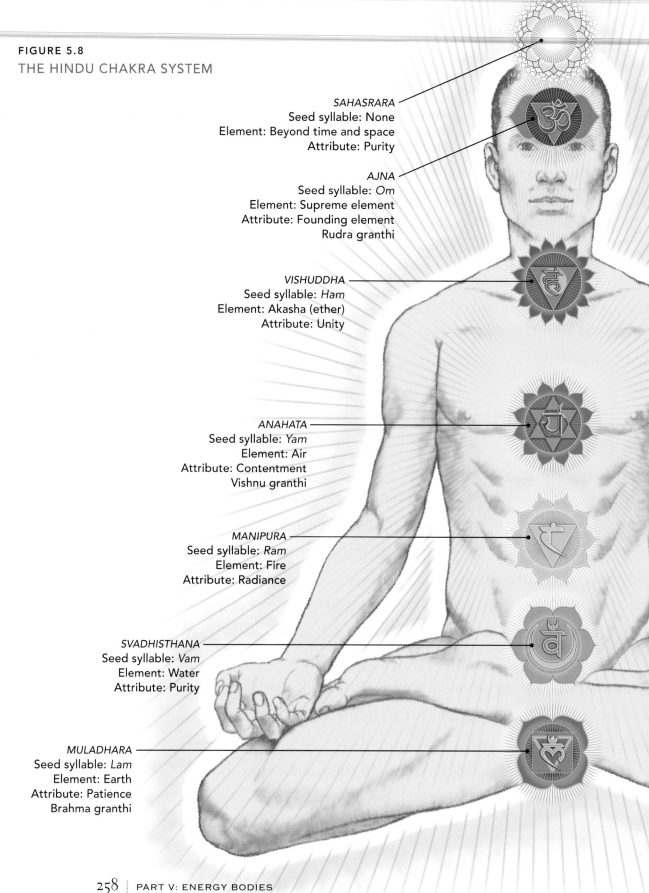

FIGURE 5.8
THE HINDU CHAKRA SYSTEM

SAHASRARA
Seed syllable: None
Element: Beyond time and space
Attribute: Purity

AJNA
Seed syllable: *Om*
Element: Supreme element
Attribute: Founding element
Rudra granthi

VISHUDDHA
Seed syllable: *Ham*
Element: Akasha (ether)
Attribute: Unity

ANAHATA
Seed syllable: *Yam*
Element: Air
Attribute: Contentment
Vishnu granthi

MANIPURA
Seed syllable: *Ram*
Element: Fire
Attribute: Radiance

SVADHISTHANA
Seed syllable: *Vam*
Element: Water
Attribute: Purity

MULADHARA
Seed syllable: *Lam*
Element: Earth
Attribute: Patience
Brahma granthi

THE ELEMENTS

Each of the five basic Hindu elements serves the lower chakras. The elements both sustain and provide a service to the chakra and can be represented in many forms, including shapes. The higher two chakras work with higher elements or with a synthesis of the lower ones. Ajna carries *mahat,* or the "supreme element," which includes three aspects: mind, intellect, and I-consciousness—awareness of self. The gross elements of the other chakras evolve from the Supreme Element. Sahasrara is pure consciousness; its element is therefore beyond time and space.

THE LOTUS

What could be a more beautiful representation of a chakra than the lotus? Each is represented by a lotus of a different color and with a specific number of petals.

The petals are configurations made by the position of the nadis, or channels, at a particular center and are manifested by the prana in the living body. When the *vayu* (breath) departs, the lotuses cease to manifest. They are also considered manifestations of the kundalini, and, in total, they create the physical aspect of the Shakti kundalini, or the "mantra body." In short, the petals represent the physical aspect of the kundalini's subtle energy.

There is a seed sound at the center of every lotus, with the exception of the 1,000-petaled Sahasrara lotus. This is the subtle sound made by the vibration of forces in the center of the lotus. In general, the lotus figure contains all the special and unique configurations of a chakra and its meaning.

THE LINGA, OR GRANTHI: UNLOCKING THE KNOTS

The linga, or granthi, are locks within the body that bind energy. We must unlock these if we are to free the energies stored within them and achieve our full divinity.

These locks lie within the Muladhara, Anahata, and Ajna chakras, or the root, heart, and third eye chakras. These locks often dissolve as the kundalini rises.

The linga are usually associated with two basic symbols, each of which represents a different form of divinity. The lingum is formed like a penis, modeled as a rounded pillar. The *trikona,* or yoni, is vagina-shaped and represented by a downward-pointing triangle. The lock found in the Muladhara chakra has its own lingum, which is also wrapped in the "serpent," or kundalini Shakti. The Shakti kundalini must uncoil and begin her ascent through the Sushumna before the lingum can release.

THIRD CHAKRA: MANIPURA

Other names	Manipurak, Nabhi
Meaning of name	City of gems *Mani* means jewel or gem; *pura* means dwelling place; and *nabhi* means navel
Main aspect	Lustrous gem
Location	Between the navel and the base of the sternum
Related organs	Central or solar plexus–based nerve plexus, digestive organs and system; some authorities say muscles and immune and nervous systems
Symbol	A ten-petaled lotus Within is a downward-pointing triangle surrounded by three T-shaped swastikas
Color of chakra	Yellow
Components **Gross element**	Fire
Subtle element	Form/sight
Color of element	Fire red
Sound of element	*Ram*
Carrier of seed sound	The ram, promoting spiritual warriorism (strength, wisdom, and bravery)
Petals of the lotus	Ten blue petals
Predominant sense	Sight, vision
Sense organ	Eyes
Action organ	Anus
Vital breath	*Saman* or *Samana*, helpful in digestion
Cosmic realm or plane	Celestial plane or heaven; *Svarloka*
Ruling goddess	Lakini Shakti, who provides inspiration and concentration with compassion
Ruling god	Rudra, an elder destructive force
Ruling planet	Sun

ANAHATA: FOURTH OR HEART CHAKRA

It is said that the enlightened can hear the sound of the universe within the Anahata chakra. Indeed, the heart is the center of the human body, the most vital human organ. As we have seen, the heart emanates thousands of times more electricity and magnetism than the brain does. Anahata's central organ, the heart, beats our existence with each pulse, revealing that, indeed, all of life is about sound and rhythm.

The heart holds the second of the *granthis*, or locks, the knotted energies we must untangle if we are to free our divinity. The heart is the domain of several

Hindu deities. Krishna is one of the incarnations of Vishnu, and is affiliated with higher love and heart-love. Under him, we find the lord god Isvara, an aspect of Shiva, who is known for his mystical approach to love and life. Isvara is often connected to the siddhi powers. (See "The Siddhi: Powers from the Subtle Bodies" on page 285.) Isvara also helps break down the barriers between the self and the world. Kakini Shakti rules with him, helping the devotee coordinate his or her heartbeat with the rhythm of the universe. The antelope also leaps within this chakra, illustrating the mastery of air.

FIGURE 5.9
FOURTH CHAKRA: ANAHATA

The heart's symbol is two superimposed triangles within a circle, one pointing upward and the other pointing down. These form a six-pointed star. The lotus has twelve petals, often seen as red, although the element, air, is considered gray in color. The emanating sound is *yam*.

The heart chakra has many complicated symbols. Two triangles portray the complete union of the male and female energies, unlike the lingum in the first chakra, which is concerned with merging sexually. The air element, however, is not considered the "vital breath," but a conveyer of sound and energy. The mystical nature of this air suggests that the sound is actually outside of time and space, that it encourages an understanding of matters beyond everyday concerns.

Psychologically, the heart chakra is devoted to love and compassion, as well as other ingredients needed to become truly loving within and outside of the self.

FOURTH CHAKRA: ANAHATA

Other names	Hritpankaja, Dvadashadala
Meaning of name	Heart lotus *Hrit* means heart and *pankaja*, lotus Also twelve-petaled; *dvadash* is twelve and *dala* means petals
Main aspect	Love and relationships
Location	In the physical body, the center of the chest, the heart

FOURTH CHAKRA: ANAHATA

Related organs	Cardiac nerve plexus, respiratory and cardiac systems, thymus gland
Symbol	A twelve-petaled lotus Inside are two intersecting triangles that create a six-pointed star
Color of chakra	Green
Components	
Gross element	Air
Subtle element	Impact/touch
Color of element	Colorless, gray, or tepid green
Sound of element	*Yam*
Carrier of seed sound	Antelope, which reflects the passion and joy of being alive
Petals of the lotus	Twelve deep red petals
Predominant sense	Touch
Sense organ	Skin
Action organ	Sexual organ
Vital breath	*Prana*
Cosmic realm or plane	Balance, or home of the siddhi and saints; the *Maharloka* realm
Ruling goddess	Kakini Shakti, who synchronizes our heartbeat with the universe
Ruling god	Isvara, who assists us in bonding with the world
Ruling planet	Venus
Lingum	Here is the Bana lingum, or granthi of Vishnu, which must be dissolved to eliminate the perception of separation

VISHUDDHA: FIFTH OR THROAT CHAKRA

Vishuddha is the center for communicating our truth to the world. It is about giving voice—or music or sound—to our inner heart, and in turn hearing what the world has to reply.

This is the last of the chakras that processes the gross or physical elements. Within its location, we prepare to ascend the ladder of consciousness, to shift into the chakras devoted to spirituality. It is time to ask what needs to be said to make this transcendence possible.

This chakra is supported by Airavata, a white elephant with six trunks. He is the god of elephants, the ruler of the clouds. In contrast to the elephant of the first chakra, Airavata is not restricted in any way. He moves freely within the plane of ether and space, opening to the rays of the cosmos. The gods

Ardhvanarisvara and Sakini Shakti provide additional mentorship. The feminine Sakini instructs each of us on mastering the five elements, as well as psychic communication. She bestows higher knowledge and helps to activate the siddhi, or life powers. Ardhvanarisvara is androgynous. He encourages us to blend the feminine and masculine traits of ourselves.

FIGURE 5.10
FIFTH CHAKRA: VISHUDDHA

Symbolically, the fifth chakra looks like a downward-pointing triangle within a circle, which in turn encompasses a smaller circle. The lotus wears sixteen petals, which most systems present as violet blue. It is governed by ether, the most subtle of elements. The mantra *ham* energizes and harmonizes the throat.

Psychologically, the fifth chakra opens us to higher wisdom, our guides, and our own souls. Many sources consider it to be the center of dreams. At the fifth chakra, if we can determine what truths we really want to represent, we can reach our inner dreams and achieve meaningful lives.

FIFTH CHAKRA: VISHUDDHA

Other names	Kanth Padma, Shodash Dala
Meaning of name	Pure or throat lotus *Kanth* means throat, while *padma* means lotus Also sixteen-petaled; *shodash* equates to sixteen, and *dala* means petals
Main aspect	Communication and self-expression
Location	Throat
Related organs	Laryngeal nerve plexus, vocal cords, mouth, throat, ears, thyroid and parathyroid glands
Symbol	Lotus with sixteen petals that contains a downward-pointing triangle Inside the triangle is a circle symbolizing the full moon
Color of chakra	Blue

FIFTH CHAKRA: VISHUDDHA

Components	
Gross element	Ether
Subtle element	Vibration/sound
Color of element	Smoky purple
Sound of element	*Ham*
Carrier of seed sound	White elephant, which delivers harmony and grace
Petals of the lotus	Sixteen smoky purple petals
Predominant sense	Hearing
Sense organ	Ears
Action organ	Mouth
Vital breath	*Updana*
Cosmic realm or plane	Human plane; *Janaloka*, the ending of darkness
Ruling goddess	Sakini Shakti, with five heads for mastering the elements and psychic realm
Ruling god	Ardhvanarisvara, a god with five heads that represents mastery over the five elements
Ruling planet	Jupiter

AJNA: SIXTH CHAKRA OR THIRD EYE CHAKRA

FIGURE 5.11

SIXTH CHAKRA: AJNA

Solar and lunar energies meet and mix in the sixth chakra, combining the following principles: earthliness, liquidity, conscience, neutrality, austerity, violence, and spiritual devotion. The Ajna dissolves duality, allowing us to stop seeing "good" and "bad," to cease differentiating between "I" and "you," until we can accept the greater unity within the cosmos. Here we might draw upon our "third eye," or inner sight, to peer through "reality" into the truth underneath.

Herein lies the third granthi, or knot. It is the Rudra knot of the Itara *lingum*, illustrated as luminescent white lightning. Through its energy, we are provided the opportunity to see everything as sacred and holy.

Shiva, the lord of destruction, governs the sixth chakra. He controls the subtle mind, thereby teaching us how to control our desires and compulsions. Hakini Shakti rules with him as the gatekeeper of the third eye. An aspect of the kundalini Shakti, she has six heads, which represent enlightenment, thought control, concentration, meditation, superconscious concentration, and undivided attention. She gives the drink of nectar (*soma*), the liquid of immortality, to those she favors. (See "Three Additional Chakra Bodies" on page 266 for more on the Soma chakra.)

Ajna is represented by a downward-pointing triangle within a circle. There are only two petals to its lotus. It is transparent and made of light, for its purpose is to help us see clearly. Its mantra is the divine *aum*, which connects the beginnings and endings of all things. This chakra is not associated with a specific element or animal representative, although some connect it with the black antelope, a carrier of light. Sometimes the Ajna is called the center of the supreme element—the light that generates all other elements. As such, it is usually considered to hold the seed syllable, OM, as depicted in figure 5.11, although some sources describe it with a different syllable.

Mentally, the Ajna relates to our cognitive and sensory faculties. It is here that we move beyond concrete and mundane information to formulate abstractions and higher thoughts. Therefore, one of the primary roles of this chakra is to bridge the subtle realms, governing the *koshas*, or two sheaths, that form the entirety of the subtle body (*suksma sarira*). (See "Beyond the Chakras" on page 281.) We can now discover the true self and set out upon a journey that creates a desirable future.

SIXTH CHAKRA: AJNA

Other names	Bhru Madhya, Dvidala Padma
Meaning of name	Command; and point between the eyebrows *Bhuru* means eyebrows, while *madhya* means in between Also called two-petaled lotus
Main aspect	Perception and self-realization
Location	Above and between the eyebrows
Related organs	Medulla plexus, pituitary gland, eyes
Symbol	Lotus with two large petals, one on each side, around a circle that contains a downward-pointing triangle
Color of chakra	Purple/indigo
Components	
Gross element	Light
Subtle element	Supreme element; all other elements are present
Color of element	Transparent
Sound of element	*Om*
Carrier of seed sound	Some say none; others a black antelope, a vehicle for the god of the winds
Petals of the lotus	Two petals

SIXTH CHAKRA: AJNA

Predominant sense	Neutral
Sense organ	Mind
Action organ	Mind
Vital breath	No vital breath but a harmonic convergence
Cosmic realm or plane	*Tapasloka*, plane of austerity; home of the blessed
Ruling goddess	Hakini Shakti, with six heads, who represents perfected meditation
Ruling god	Shiva, the god of destruction and the divine dance; Shiva is partnered with the feminine
Ruling planet	Pisces
Lingum	The Itara lingum is the granthi of Rudra. When unlocked, it maintains the changes made by the kundalini

Ajna is considered to be beyond the gross, concrete elements, carrying instead a "supreme element" that serves as the foundation for the elements processed in the lower chakras.

THREE ADDITIONAL CHAKRA BODIES: CONNECTIONS FOR THE AJNA

There are three additional chakra bodies that play a vital role in the ascension of the kundalini through the Ajna chakra. Grouped under the title "Soma chakra," they are the Soma, Kameshvara, and the Kamadhenu.

The Soma chakra is located within the Sahasrara and found just above the Ajna. There are many perceptions of this chakra. Some systems perceive it as a collection of three independent chakras, others as two chakras with a sub-chakra, and still others as chakra-like bodies functioning through the Ajna. We will look at the Soma chakra as two sub-chakras with a chakra-like bridge. The two sub-chakras are the Soma and the Kameshvara; the bridge is the Kamadhenu.

The general Soma chakra is illuminated as a light blue-white lotus with twelve petals (sometimes sixteen), with a crescent of silver. This moon is the source of the nectar (*soma*) for the body, which is said to flow from *Kamadhenu*, the white cow-faced goddess.

She is a "wish-giving" cow, available to the initiate who has pierced through the Rudra granthi. At this level, one has surrendered his or her personal neediness, and asks for only for that which will bless the world. She functions as a connection between the two sub-chakras (and in some disciplines is considered to occupy her own chakra).

The Kameshvara chakra is just above the spot where Kamadhenu resides. Here the kundalini in one of her many forms, the Kameshvari, is united with lord Param Shiva. Inside this chakra is a triangle surrounding Kameshvara and Kameshvari. In Tantric yoga, it is called the *A-KA-THA-Triangle* and is formed by three of the nadis: the *vama*, *jyeshtha*, and *raudri* nadis. The same nadis form a triangle in the Muladhara chakra and enfold a version of Shakti and Shiva.

When Shakti rises to the Kameshvara, knowing, feeling, and doing evolve into truth, beauty, and goodness. This is due to the combining of three *gunas* and three *bindus*. (See "The Bindu Forces" on page 269.)

Kameshvara is a strikingly handsome male god. Seated like a yogi, he embraces the Kameshvari, the most beautiful of women. Their union is known as *tantra* or expanded consciousness, as it combines enjoyment (*bhoga*) and detachment (*yoga*).

SAHASRARA: SEVENTH OR CROWN CHAKRA

The Shiva and Shakti—the masculine and feminine—join within Sahasrara to create *brahma-ranhdra*, the transcendence of both. Within this chakra, the individual personality dissolves into the essence of the all.

This is the chakra of one thousand petals. These petals represent the fifty letters of the Sanskrit alphabet along with their twenty permutations. The magnitude of these vibrations enhances the seventh chakra's role in governing and coordinating the other chakras.

FIGURE 5.12
SEVENTH CHAKRA: SAHASRARA

This chakra is unique in many ways. All other chakras feature upward-pointing lotuses. In the Sahasrara, the lotuses point downward, symbolizing freedom from the mundane, and divine rain from its petals. Some yogis actually report that having achieved this chakra, the fontanel (soft spot) atop the head dampens with the "dew of divinity."

The Sahasrara chakra was not considered an in-body chakra in the classical Hindu system. Traditionally, it is pictured as lying *atop* the head. More contemporary systems establish it *in* the top of the head. No matter which location you prefer, the idea is the same: it represents a space unto itself.

Sahasrara creates the fifth *kosha*, the *anandamaya sheath* that doubles as the *causal body*. After ascending to the Sahasrara, we shift this sheath and become free from the constraints of the physical realm as well as the "wheel of life," the vehicle that initiates reincarnation. Once released from the causal body, we enter one of the three higher planes, or *koshas*, beyond the body, the *Satyaloka*, or "abode of truth." We also achieve *samadhi*, or the state of bliss and being-ness associated with transcendence. This state is associated with the teachings of Krishna in the Bhagavad-Gita and the eighth branch of Patanjali's classification of yoga. (See "Patanjali's Eight-Step Method of Yoga" on page 271.) There are many layers of samadhi, the highest involving an identification with the highest states of consciousness, and finally, the individual is absorbed into the all.

The Sahasrara is considered beyond most symbolic representations, although the chakra is usually perceived as white.

The Sahasrara is considered beyond senses, sense organs, and vital breath. As such, it is often described without a seed syllable, as shown in figure 5.12, although some sources depict it with an OM.

SEVENTH CHAKRA: SAHASRARA

Other names	Bhru Madhya, Dvidala Padma
Meaning of name	Void, dwelling place without support, thousand-petaled
Main aspect	Spirituality
Location	Top of or just atop the head
Related organs	Upper skull, cerebral cortex, pineal gland
Symbol	The thousand-petaled lotus
Color of chakra	White; also seen as violet or gold
Components **Gross element** **Subtle element** **Color of element**	There is no associated gross element, subtle element, or color in Sahasrara
Sound of element	*Visarga* (a breathing sound)
Carrier of seed sound	The motion of *bindu*, a dot above a crescent
Petals of the lotus	1,000 petals, rainbow hues
Action organ	Pineal gland
Cosmic realm or plane	Truth or *Satyaloka*
Ruling goddess	Shakti joins here with Shiva

SEVENTH CHAKRA: SAHASRARA

Ruling god	Shiva joins here with Shakti
Ruling planet	Ketu

HINDU CHAKRA TYPES

Individuals tend to draw energy from one chakra more than the others. We also tend to "reside" in specific chakras while climbing the ladder of kundalini. The following character descriptions are based on reflections by Harish Johari, a well-respected expert on Eastern spirituality and the author of several books on Indian and Tantric chakras.[24]

THE BINDU FORCES

BEFORE MANIFESTATION, THE *param bindu* (supreme consciousness) assumes a threefold character that appears as a triangle. Each point of the triangle is represented by a *bindu*, or force, that interacts with the other bindus to lead to enlightenment. These three bindus are red (*rakta*), which represents *Brahmi*, the energy of Brahma the creator (also called *bindu*); white (*shvait*), which represents *Vaishnavi*, the energy of Vishnu the preserver (*bija*); and a mixed color, which stands for *Maheshvari*, the energy of Maheshvara the destroyer, or Shiva himself (*nada*).

The param bindu (which creates the three triangular bindu forces) forms *kamkala*, the principle of actualizing energized consciousness (Shakti), in the form of subtle sound frequencies. The param bindu, now seen as three separate Shaktis, flows through three different nadis to represent three types of consciousness. The *Vama nadi* transforms into *knowing*; the *Jyeshtha nadi* into *feeling*; and the *Raudri nadi* into *doing*. When the kundalini rises to unite with the supreme consciousness in the Kameshvara chakra, the three bindus mix with three *gunas* (*sattva*, *ragas*, and *tamas*), which are qualities of energy. These newly merged energies now form *supreme bindu* and three qualities necessary for enlightenment: truth (*satyam*), beauty (*sundaram*), and goodness (*shivam*).

The following chart illustrates the aspects of consciousness involved in this process.

FIGURE 5.13
ASPECTS OF CONSCIOUSNESS

Nadi	Description of Consciousness	Appearance of Consciousness	Created sound	Attribute	God Form
Vama	Volition (*iccha*)	Feeling	Subtle sound, *pashyanti*	Creation	Brahmi
Jyeshtha	Knowledge (*jnana*)	Knowing	Intermediary sound, *madhyama*	Preservation	Vaishnavi
Raudri	Action (*kriya*)	Doing	Articulated sound, *vaikhari*	Dissolution	Maheshvari

THE MULADHARA PERSONALITY

Someone ruled by the Muladhara chakra is often confronted with life lessons about security—or rather, the desire to be physically and financially secure. The behavior of these people is often compared to that of ants, which ardently work for their queen. Their sense of self is often based on gaining approval or following the laws. Thus, for these people, their lessons are often about confronting and freeing themselves from greed, lust, sensuality, and anger. Like the earth element, Muladhara personalities are physically strong and productive. They often win competitively because of their drive and strength.

THE SVADHISTHANA PERSONALITY

A Svadhisthana individual is most likely devoted to the higher things in life—art, music, poetry, and the jewels of creativity. While beautiful, this lushness also presents temptation away from the spiritual path, with the major diversions involving sexuality, sensuality, and indulgence.

A second-chakra person is likely to experience mood swings or emotional inconsistency. Desire is rooted in the second chakra, and can lead to love and the enjoyment of pleasures, but also to frivolity or just plain selfishness. The Svadhisthana path is often called the way of the butterfly, for life is full of so many joys, it can be hard to remain in one place for long. It is important to develop discipline to balance the compulsion to experience.

THE MANIPURA PERSONALITY

This chakra embraces the planes of karma (the past), dharma (one's purpose), and the celestial plane. Its focus is to atone for one's past errors. Manipura is the fire chakra, and people who dwell here tend to be fiery; the key to joy lies in the application of the heat. Is it used to avoid the past—or to work toward a positive future?

Third-chakra people tend to be temperamental but are also able to commit to their goals. They are often driven by the need to be recognized and to succeed.

The chief issue to confront is ego. By confronting issues of pride and control, the Manipura person is able to embrace the best features of its major animal, the ram. The ram can walk nimbly into the highest of mountaintops; so can the third-chakra individual.

THE ANAHATA PERSONALITY

When the lotus unfolds, the twelve petals invite the movement of energy in twelve directions. This activates twelve mental capabilities: hope, anxiety, endeavor, possessiveness, arrogance, incompetence, discrimination, egoism, lustfulness, fraudulence, indecision, and repentance (as described in the *Mahanirvana*

Tantra, a detailing of Tantric rituals and practices, edited for Western audiences by Arthur Avalon (pen name of Sir John Woodroffe) in 1913).[25] Twelve divinities in the form of sound assist with the process involved in confronting, dealing with, and healing one's way through these twelve qualities.

A heart-based person might find him- or herself greatly challenged by the so-called negative qualities that stir in the heart. However, these people have dealt with the challenges of the lower chakras and can now evolve to feelings of devotion, compassion, selflessness, and love. In the end, they can become as the antelope, able to move as does light in the world: swiftly, gently, and firmly.

THE VISHUDDHA PERSONALITY

The Vishuddha chakra invites rebirth. As we climb through the lower chakras, we embrace—and learn how to master—each of the grosser elements. We now enter the plane of ether.

Those who live at this level are often perceived as dreamy, musical, inspired, and learned. What flows through the fifth chakra is sound, in all its varieties. There are two ways to live in this space. We can either become distracted and irresponsible—secretive and alone within our knowledge—or we can seek and share truth.

THE AJNA PERSONALITY

The Ajna personality has bridged light and dark, matter and spirit, masculine and feminine, and is now able to share light with the world. The Ida and Pingala nadis end at the Ajna, for those who have completed the course of the kundalini. This

PATANJALI'S EIGHT-STEP METHOD OF YOGA

MANY DEVOTEES WORK their way upward through the *koshas*, healing the three bodies of incarnation (*sariras*) described in "Beyond the Chakras: The Hindu Line-up of Energy Bodies" on page 281 by following Patanjali's eight-step path to yoga. In the Yoga Sutras, the famous yogi Patanjali recommended the following process:

- Learning restraint (*yama*)
- Developing spiritual discipline (*niyama*)
- Using postures (*asanas*)
- Gaining breath control (*pranayama*)
- Achieving withdrawal of the senses (*pratyahara*)
- Developing mental concentration (*dharana*)
- Performing deep meditation (*dhyana*)
- Attaining higher consciousness (*samadhi*)

Of these, the first six correlate to working with the body and the last two relate to accessing the spirit. These stages correlate to the movement through the *koshas*, or levels of development, and prepare the way for the rising of the kundalini.

person is now able to live beyond time: to know the past, present, and future and yet not be defined by these parameters.

This capability must be carefully managed, for to skip any part of the development process is to end up "spacey" or "checked out," disassociated from daily life and the concrete world. Ideally, the Ajna individual is able to maintain a state of nondualistic consciousness. In practical reality—there is practical reality, like shopping for groceries and paying bills—the Ajna person must bridge the spiritual reality with the physical. If they can do this, Ajna people can become true "lights" unto the world.

THE SAHASRARA PERSONALITY

The Sahasrara is the highest extension point for the rising kundalini. Here, the individual "I" dissolves into the greater spirit, paradoxically creating an opportunity to be one's true self. Someone who lives at this level exists in constant revelry, being "self" and "all" simultaneously. Ideally, this union invites detachment from the physical body, and with that, freedom from pains, troubles, and humiliations of the world. But this separateness can also lead to impassiveness, aloofness, and a sense of being alone in a group.

The Sahasrara personality is usually able to manifest through his or her siddhi, or powers. This presents amazing opportunities to help others. Many achieve guru or near-guru status because of their awakened and amplified gifts. Some Sahasrara individuals confuse being gifted with being special, however, becoming egoists. In other words, some Sahasraras are addicted to the fame and fortune that follow the higher gifts.

NADIS: CHANNELS OF ENERGY

While nadis are technically channels of energy, and could have been included in Part IV, they are so closely associated with chakras and the kundalini process that they can really only be understood in relationship to them. For this reason we will explore the nadis in detail here.

The word *nadi* comes from the Sanskrit root *nad* and means "movement." According to the most ancient Hindu scripture, the Rigveda, *nadi* means "stream," an appropriate term since the nadis transport various subtle energies throughout the body. In this role, they operate like channels, or a delivery system, for the chakras, to help clear and manage the physical system and to play a vital role in the rising of kundalini.

The first mention of the nadis was in the earliest Upanishads written in the seventh to eighth centuries BC. The ideas were developed in the later Upanishads and the yoga and Tantra schools.

Nadis are often compared to the traditional Chinese meridian system. Both distribute energies and interact with the chakras. There are several differences, however. Most traditional Chinese medical systems work with twelve major meridian pathways. There are many more nadis than this. The first Upanishads suggested 72,000 nadis,[26] and others indicate that there are anywhere from 1,000 to 350,000 nadis—the ancient text, the Shiva Samhita, asserts the higher amount.[27] Most systems, however, including Ayurveda and the Tibetan tradition, agree on about 72,000 different nadis. One of the ancient texts describes the nadis this way:

> *Now in the heart abides the self, junction of hundred nerves [nadis] and one. Of these hundred each sends forth another hundred and then the latter send forth offshoots, seventy-two, each a thousand times. In these pervades and flows Vyana.*[28]

Some experts state that while meridians have a physical counterpart in the meridian duct systems, the nadis interact with the physical nervous system. Apparently, the nadis not only conduct prana throughout the body, but also convert it into different types of energy for organs, glands, and tissues.

Not all experts correlate the nadis to the nervous system, however. Dr. Hiroshi Motoyama, author of over twenty books on Oriental medicine, does not correlate the nadis with the nerves. He deduces that since the main nadi, the Sushumna, lies in the middle of the spinal column and the nerves are outside of this center (they run within the spinal canal, which encases the spinal cord), it cannot be physically associated with the physical nerves. He also points out that spinal and nervous system cells originate from different progenitors.[29]

As we saw in Chapter 38, "Scientific Principles Meet Chakra Theory," Motoyama believes that the nadis and meridians might be identical. For instance, he perceives a close correspondence between the Governor vessel meridian and the main nadi, the Sushumna, as they are anatomically linked and serve similar functions. He theorizes close associations between other meridians and some of the other major nadis. This establishes support for the idea that no matter the exact role of the nadis, there is a strong interconnection among the chakras, meridians, and the nerves.[30]

According to the Tantric yoga system, which is derived from the Hindu tradition, there are two types of nadis:

Yoga nadis: These are immaterial, invisible channels of subtle energy. Within this grouping are two types of nadis:

- *manas*, channels for the mind (sometimes called *manovahini* or *manovahi* nadis)
- *chitta*, channels of the feeling self (also called *chittavahii* nadis)

Gross nadis: These are material, visible channels of subtle energy. This set includes nerves, muscles, vessels of the cardiovascular and lymphatic systems, and the acupuncture meridians.[31]

Both gross and subtle nadis can carry prana. Those that fulfill this mission are called *pranavahi* or *pranavahini* nadis.

Nearly everyone seems to agree that there are three key nadis: the Sushumna, or main nadi; the Ida, on the left side of the body; and the Pingala, on the right side of the body. The major chakras are fed by the Sushumna, which runs inside the vertebral column from the base of the spine to the center of the brain.

For their part, the Ida and the Pingala nadis cross like a double helix and relate to the sympathetic nervous trunks on the sides of the spinal cord. Together, these three nadis interact to cleanse the physical body and to stimulate the rising of the kundalini through the Sushumna. If done appropriately, this process also unfolds the siddhi, or seemingly magical gifts.

In all, there are fourteen major nadis. Just as the Sushumna is equated with the Governor vessel in the meridian system, so is each nadi associated with a different meridian.[32]

SUSHUMNA NADI

Flow: This is the central nadi that passes through the spinal column. The flow starts in the base, or Muladhara, chakra and stops in the Sahasrara chakra at the crown, where it splits into two streams. The anterior passes through the Ajna, or brow chakra, before reaching the *Brahma Randhra*, the seat of supreme consciousness that lies between the two hemispheres of the brain and the Sahasrara chakra. The posterior travels behind the skull before reaching the Brahma Randhra. The Sushumna is made of three yoga nadis, which are arranged in layers. These are:

- **Outer layer:** The Sushumna. Difficult to perceive, this brilliant red layer is considered to exist outside of time.
- **Middle layer:** The *Vajrini*, or *Vajra nadi*. Shimmering in nature, this nadi exhibits two contrary natures: the sun and toxicity.
- **Inner layer:** The *Chitrini*, or *Chitra nadi*, pale and illuminated in coloring.

BREATH AND THE THREE MAIN NADIS

A YOGI SEEKS enlightenment by working with the three main nadis. The most common illustration of them shows the Sushumna depicted as straight wand with two snakes (the Ida and the Pingala) coiled around it. This is familiar to us as the caduceus, symbol of medical practice.[33] The Ida and Pingala converge at nose level, the Ida from the left and the Pingala from the right. Four times, the Ida and the Pingala cross the Sushumna, intersecting with and surrounding the chakras, thus arranging an upward path for an activated kundalini.

How does one activate the sleeping snake? The basic process involves using prana (breath) to guide energy through the Ida and Pingala to the base of the spine. An initiate breathes through one nostril at a time, activating either the Ida or the Pingala and the other nadis simultaneously. The Sushumna is only active when the breath comes through both nostrils, which only occurs about ten times per hour if one is using the correct procedure. At this point, inhalation and exhalation cease; the other nadis stop operating; and the kundalini (specifically, the Shakti kundalini) is able to rise through the Brahma nadi. As it ascends, it harmonizes with the Ida and Pingala and the chakras they encircle, stimulating the chakric energy. In the upward path, the Ida and Pingala alternate at each chakra until they reach the Ajna, where they rejoin the Sushumna. This upward force is created from the fusion of the negative ions of the prana and the positive ions of the apana, one form of the breath.

It is said that when the breathing ceases through this process, called *pranayama*, the physical body stops aging. In addition, the siddhi, or gifts of power, are stimulated through this process.

An initiate must prepare his or her body for this kundalini process. Common preparation practices including using *asanas* or postures, meditation, fasting, nadi cleansing, and other methods to purify the body. If the body is not completely ready, the kundalini will fall back down, causing a negative experience.

Reflects the nature of the moon and goodness from the heavens. Connected to dreams and visions and important to poets and painters. This nadi ends in the *Brahma Dvara*, the door of Brahma, the Creator. It is here that the kundalini travels to its final resting place within the Soma chakra.

Centered within the Sushumna (or the three nadis composing it) is the Brahma nadi, a stream of purity. This nadi connects to the Brahma Randhra.

Roles: The Sushumna serves as the main distributor of prana to the subtle energy organs and the chakras. It is usually inactive when other nadis are active and operational when they are quiet. It also works with the flow of the Ida and the Pingala to regulate breath (prana) and activate the rising of the kundalini.

FIGURE 5.14

THE SUSHUMNA

The Sushumna is the central nadi. It is composed of three separate nadis and, within these, the Brahma nadi or stream of purity. Various schools of thought depict the Sushumna in different ways, usually red, clear, or yellow. This particular depiction reflects Harish Johari's view.

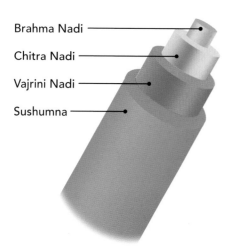

Brahma Nadi ——————

Chitra Nadi ——————

Vajrini Nadi ——————

Sushumna ——————

IDA NADI

Flow: Starts below the Muladhara chakra, but is also associated with the left testicle in men. Ends in the left nostril. It is also stimulated through this nostril. Some schools of thought reverse this flow, in terms of origination and termination, especially during the first stage of kundalini activation.

Some esoteric systems associate this nadi with the sympathetic nervous system, as it is on the left side of the spine. Yet others consider it a mental rather than a nerve channel.

Roles: Part of the left channel of the nadi system. Relays pranic and mental energy. Associated with the moon. Is considered a feminine symbol that exhibits correlated functions, such as conserving energy, increasing serenity, calming the mind, and accentuating maternal urgings. Magnetic in nature. Restores energy to the brain. Through its lunar associations, relates to the psyche or soul. Some yoga systems (such as that of Svara yoga) recommend keeping the Ida (and the left nostril) open during the day, so as to balance the sun's energy. It is dominant from the new moon to the full moon.

PINGALA NADI

Flow: Starts below the Muladhara chakra and ends in the right nostril. It is also activated through this nostril. Some schools of thought reverse this flow.

Roles: Part of the right channel of the nadi system. Conveys pranic and mental energy, primarily those considered solar. Associated with the sun, a masculine symbol, it provides energy for physical movement and activities. Also associated with vitality and power, it is electrical in nature and enables mental quickness and supports constructive actions. Some yoga systems recommend breathing through the right nostril at night to add balance to the lunar energy of night. It is dominant from the full moon to the new moon.

True enlightenment is also contingent upon the appropriate merging of the male and female energies. The Ida nadi is primarily feminine and the Pingala nadi is considered masculine. They are each represented by a specific color, heavenly body, and river to indicate their properties. The Sushumna is a combination of male and female and yet more than either. It is therefore considered to be a pure, diamond-like energy, functioning with its own fire.

The table below depicts the descriptive energies of these three nadis, also listing a river connected to each. The corresponding river tells a story that relates to Hindu geography. The Ida is associated with the Ganges River; the Pingala, the Yamuna River; and the Sushumna, the Sarasvati River. The Hindu believe that these three intermingle and form a sacred site—even though the Sarasvati does not technically mingle with the other two rivers. Because of its ability to join the union invisibly, they believe that the Sarasvati is the holiest of all rivers in the world.[34] The geographic marriage of the streams is seen as the key to self-unity.

FIGURE 5.15
THE MAIN NADIS AND THEIR REPRESENTATIVE ENERGIES

Name	Location	River	Color	Heavenly Body	Symbolism
Ida	Left	Ganges	Yellow	Moon	Female
Pingala	Right	Yamuna	Red	Sun	Male
Sushumna	Center	Sarasvati	Diamond	Fire	Transcendent

THE LESSER NADIS

Following is a list of the lesser nadis and how they assist each of the three main nadis.

Gandhari

Flow: Starts in the corner of the left eye and ends at the big toe of the left foot.

Roles: With the Hastajihva nadi, the Gandhari nadi assists the Ida nadi and forms the left channel. Brings psychic energies from the lower body to the Ajna chakra.

Hastajihva

Flow: Starts at the corner of the right eye and stops at the big toe of the left foot.

Roles: With the Gandhari nadi, the Hastajihiva nadi supports the Ida nadi and creates the left channel. Carries psychic energy from the lower body to the Ajna chakra.

Yashasvini

Flow: Runs from the left ear to the big toe of the left foot.

Roles: Along with the Pusha nadi, the Yashasvinj nadi complements the Pingala nadi. These three form the right channel.

FIGURE 5.16

KUNDALINI CADUCEUS

The caduceus, often used as a symbol of medical practice, is modeled after the coiling of the Sushumna, Ida, and Pingala nadis. The serpent kundalini lies asleep at the bottom of the spine, the base of the Sushumna nadi. The Ida and Pingala converge at nose level, the Ida from the left and the Pingala from the right. These two nadis cross the Sushumna four times, intersecting it and also surrounding the chakras, thus arranging an upward path for the activated kundalini. The breath provides vital support for this process.

Pusha

Flow: Flows between the right ear and the big toe of the left foot.

Roles: With the Yashasvini nadi, the Pusha nadi assists the Pingala nadi and creates the right channel.

Alambusha

Flow: Originates at the anus and ends in the mouth.

Roles: Provides prana for the assimilation and elimination of food. Also helps assimilate ideas and thoughts.

Kuhu

Flow: Starts in the throat and ends in the genitals.

Roles: Assists the Chitrini nadi to carry bindu (bindu as semen, differentiated from bindu forces) and enable ejaculation. Certain spiritual exercises can help one retain sexual secretions and so realize samadhi, or a state of nonduality.

Shankhini

Flows: Initiates in the throat and then travels between the Sarasvati and Gandhari before ending in the anus.

Roles: Activated through cleansing of the colon and anus.

Sarasvati

Flow: Starts in the Muladhara chakra and ends in the tongue; some sources say it begins in the tongue and ends in the vocal cords.

Roles: Through purifying disciplines, this nadi helps with manifestation: what you say becomes true. Responsible for the sharing of knowledge. Is considered by some a companion to the Sushumna.

Payasvini

Flow: Moves between the Pusha and the Sarasvati nadis and stops in the right ear. Physically, flows between the lobe of the right ear and the cranial nerves.

Roles: Yogis activate this nadi by wearing pierced earrings that activate the part of the earlobe connected with the cranial nerves. It seems the resulting access to environmental energies amplifies the link to the higher self.

Varuni

Flow: Between the Yashasvini and the Kuhu nadi, starts at the throat and terminates at the anus.

Roles: As a Pranavahi nadi, it purifies toxins in the lower trunk and with the apana, a particular breath, and assists with excretion. When disturbed, causes an increase in wind, air, or inertia in the lower area of the body.

Vishvodara

Flow: Between the Kuhu and Hastajihva nadis, residing in the navel or umbilical area.

Roles: Assists with digestion. Stimulates the pancreas and adrenal glands and, with the Varuni, distributes prana throughout the body, especially through the Sushumna.

PRANAYAMA: THE VITAL BREATH

There are many forms and types of energy in the traditional Hindu system. The most basic is *prana*, meaning energy, breath, or life force. It also stands for air, spirit, subtle energy, or the upward-moving currents in the body.

The root word of *prana* is *pra*, which means "to fill." Prana is therefore the energy that fills the entire universe. It is often associated with the life force of breath, which fills everything. Prana is present in all things, animate or not. This is the root of the Hindu energy system—and also of its most important development process, *pranayama*.

Pranayama is the science of the breath. While *prana* represents the infinite life force, *ayama* means to increase, stretch, or control. *Pranayama* therefore indicates the practice of filling with breath, or life, with control. In practice, pranayama is a set of breathing exercises designed to bring more oxygen to the brain, activate the subtle energy system, and control the life energy in the body.

Breathing is both a neurological and a motor activity that supports all bodily systems. Oxygenation is critical for the health of the body, but also the mind. As well, the exhalation part of the breath releases wastes and toxins.

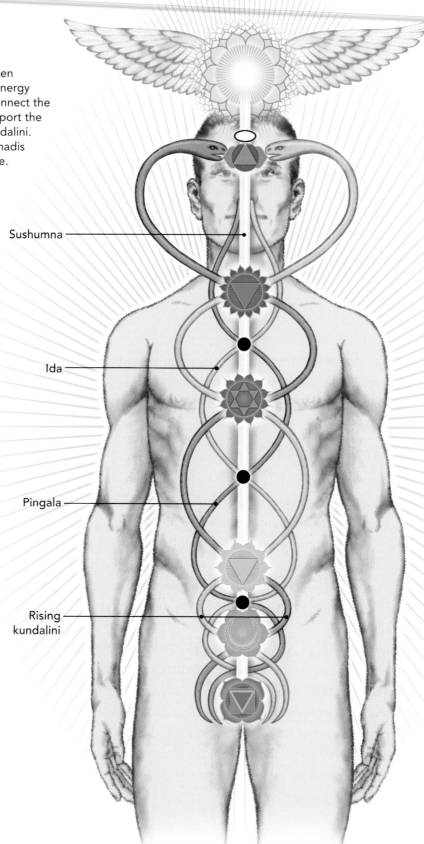

FIGURE 5.17

THE THREE MAIN NADIS

There are fourteen major nadis or energy channels that connect the chakras and support the rising of the kundalini. The three main nadis are pictured here.

Sushumna

Ida

Pingala

Rising kundalini

During everyday life, we take between ten and sixteen breaths a minute; at rest, between six and eight. We cycle our nostril breathing, using one nostril or the other. During these cycles, different elements dominate. Every chakra is vitalized when the element it needs is dominant.

When evaluating at the lower-end everyday rate (ten breaths per minute or six hundred an hour), the following occurs. While one nostril overrides the other, the air element prevails for eight minutes; then fire for twelve minutes; then earth for twenty minutes; then water for sixteen minutes; then ether for four minutes. The chakras also switch in governance during these times, shifting from fourth to third, first, second, and then finally the fifth. The nadis are active during these times, except the Sushumna, which activates during the last minute, or ten breaths, of the hour, when both nostrils work together. This time period is not connected to the rising of the kundalini.

A Hindu or Tantric yogi spends considerable time learning how to regulate the breath, for it is the main process for activating the kundalini. Regulation is achieved through changing and holding bodily positions, timing the rhythm and number of breaths, and working with various types of breath. For instance, a practitioner wishing to achieve kundalini might breathe through one nostril at a time or both, breathe through the mouth, or alternate the pace of inhalations and exhalations. When combined with the asanas, or postures, pranayama builds internal heat, the heat necessary to awaken the sleeping serpent.

BEYOND THE CHAKRAS: THE HINDU LINE-UP OF ENERGY BODIES

Every energy system includes energy bodies beyond the chakras, some so numerous it is hard to count them all. In the classical Hindu system, there are three basic energy bodies, which interface with five sheaths, or *koshas*, that relate to the different levels of reality. Let's look at these dimensions and see how they relate to the overall Hindu system.

The Taittiriya Upanishad describes five bodies or sheaths called *koshas* that "cover" or contain our higher consciousness. The koshas are contained within three bodies of incarnation: subtle energy bodies that govern different levels of development and the koshas.

The koshas constitute layers, or veils, that originate with the material body and transcend to the ethereal realms. You could picture them as circles that shift ever outward. Evolution from one kosha to another occurs as the kundalini rises through the chakras—which itself happens as one evolves from being primarily physical to becoming spiritual. This progression to enlightenment occurs with concentration on the most ordinary of matters, such as eating, breathing, movement, and mindfulness, as well as emphasizing your higher wisdom.

There are three bodies of incarnation (*sariras*) that correlate with the koshas. These are:

- The gross body (*sthula sarira*), or physical body, which is composed of the five elements.
- The subtle body (*suksma sarira*) that holds the chakras and the nadis.
- The causal body (*karana sarira*), the vehicle for our soul.

The following description of the koshas is subdivided according to these three bodies of incarnation. Some systems, however, call the subtle body the "astral body" and teach that the gross body holds the first kosha; the astral contains the second, third, and fourth; and the causal, the fifth. In this view, the astral body connects to the physical body by a thin thread, which some traditions call the silver cord. When this is severed, the body dies.

This is a description of the koshas and their placement within the three bodies; their progression as introduced earlier in this section; and the key

THE FIVE PRANAS

THERE ARE FIVE types of prana, air or breath, also termed *vayus* or *prana-vayus*.[35]

Prana: Fills the head, heart, lungs, and throat. This is the primary life breath and is present in the air moving in and out of our nasal passages. Governs inhalation, sneezing, spitting, belching, and swallowing. Our personal prana is our portion of the cosmic life force with which we manage our energetic processes, especially what we take in from food and water, our five senses, the breath, and ideas we absorb through our minds.

Udana: Located in the head and throat. Udana governs exhalation and speech. When we are dying, udana pulls our consciousness upward and out of the body.

Vyana: Located in the entire body. Initiates movement in the circulatory, lymphatic, and nervous systems. Moves energy to the periphery of the body through the nadis.

Samana: Located in the navel and small intestine. Samana digests, assimilates, and heats foods and incoming energies. Performs the same job for our impressions, thoughts, and ideas.

Apana: Located in the colon. Apana governs downward impulses, including exhalation, urination, excretion, elimination, menstruation, birth, and sexual activities. Plays a vital role in the opening of the Brahma nadi and movement of the kundalini.

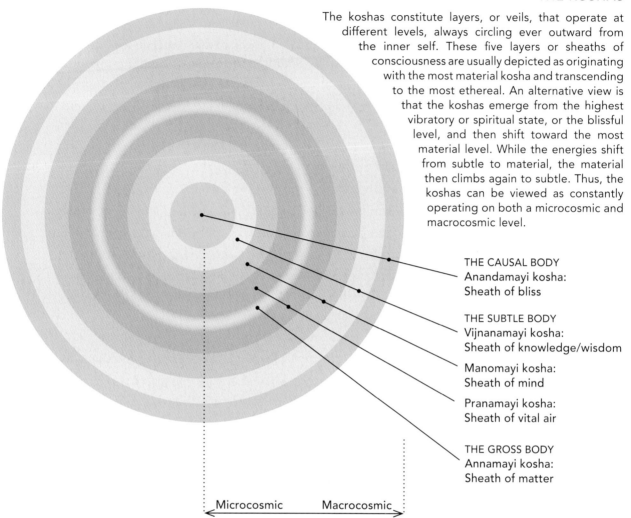

FIGURE 5.18

THE KOSHAS

The koshas constitute layers, or veils, that operate at different levels, always circling ever outward from the inner self. These five layers or sheaths of consciousness are usually depicted as originating with the most material kosha and transcending to the most ethereal. An alternative view is that the koshas emerge from the highest vibratory or spiritual state, or the blissful level, and then shift toward the most material level. While the energies shift from subtle to material, the material then climbs again to subtle. Thus, the koshas can be viewed as constantly operating on both a microcosmic and macrocosmic level.

THE CAUSAL BODY
Anandamayi kosha:
Sheath of bliss

THE SUBTLE BODY
Vijnanamayi kosha:
Sheath of knowledge/wisdom

Manomayi kosha:
Sheath of mind

Pranamayi kosha:
Sheath of vital air

THE GROSS BODY
Annamayi kosha:
Sheath of matter

Microcosmic   Macrocosmic

traditional methods and contemporary measures used to evolve through each kosha.

THE GROSS BODY

Anandamayi Kosha: Sheath of Matter

Basic description: The cellular body. As we become aware of our physical body, we establish our foundation in the *sthula sarira*, or tangible body, which is sustained by food. Therefore, proper fueling—from food—is the chief medicine for the body's ailments: all koshas are sustained by the Hindu traditional elements.

Traditional tools: The asanas, or physical movements, including hand gestures known as *mudras*, and diet. This kosha is the impetus for the emphasis on diet in Ayurveda, the yogic system of medicine.

Contemporary methods: In addition to exercise, methods include eating healthfully, using air and water as cleaners or filters, and exploring the energetic and physical healing practices found throughout this book.

THE SUBTLE BODY

Pranamayi Kosha: Sheath of Vital Air (or Prana)

Basic description: The mental body. This sheath supports mental and psychic activity and personal consciousness. Sometimes considered the location of the nadis. Many systems place the chakras in this kosha. In Ayurveda, this kosha is associated with air and the *dosha* called *vata*. (Doshas are further described in "Ayurveda" in Part VI.) After focusing on the body, we focus on the breath.

Traditional tools: Usually involve a breathing discipline and tools such as outlined in "Patanjali's Eight-Step Method of Yoga" on page 271. The goal is to activate the five forms of *vata* or *vayu*—air. Common nadi development techniques include the asana, meditation, breath work, visualization, mantras or chanting, and bodily cleansing.

Contemporary methods: All of the above, including the practical use of air-purifying machines in office and home and the use of any rhythmic tool (sound, music, and so on) to assist in establishing rhythmic breath.

Manomayi Kosha: Sheath of Mind

Basic description: Centered on mental functioning, the dramas in our minds, and the nervous system. Focuses on understanding and getting control of the nine different moods or *rasas*—in other words, our tendencies toward depression, worry, anxiety, distraction, mental chatter, and the like. In Ayurveda, this kosha is affiliated with the dosha *pitta* and its element, fire. It shuts downs during sleep.

Traditional tools: Breath work, meditation, use of mantras or chants, visualization, sensory withdrawal.

THE SIDDHI: POWERS FROM THE SUBTLE BODIES

AS WE DEVELOP the five subtle bodies, we invite the awakening of the siddhi, or "miraculous powers." These incredible abilities, said to be exhibited by yogis and gurus, include levitation, performing healing, psychic abilities, and becoming invisible.

One can open the siddhi by focusing on the sites of the subtle bodies, in addition to the element, shape, syllable, and deity connected to them. This chart reveals the connections between the subtle bodies, their associations, and specific siddhi.[36]

The transformation process involves several of the following steps, which are done for each subtle body. To achieve the awakening of the siddhi, a student will do the following:

1. Focus on the physical bodily location of the subtle body.
2. Attune to the element within him- or herself.
3. Suspend breathing. During this time (about three minutes), connect the breath to an element outside of the self. If it is the earth, connect to the ground; if it is the air, connect to the sky.
4. Gain an intuitive sense of that element.
5. See within the self the mandala or symbol, along with its syllable, associated with this element.
6. Sound the syllable.
7. Receive a revelation from the deity associated with that element.
8. Meditate on that deity until the practitioner completely releases fear of perishing from this element.[37]

Some spiritual groups believe it is dangerous to open the siddhi, as they will pull a student away from a spiritual path, lead to arrogance, or challenge the gods. Many, however, assert that these supernatural powers are not available to only a chosen few: they are latent within us all.

FIGURE 5.19
SIDDHI POWERS

Location of Subtle Body	Element	Shape	Syllable	Deity	Benefit
Between feet and knees	Earth	Yellow square	*Lam*	Brahma	Victory over earthly death
Between knees and anus	Water	White crescent	*Vam*	Vishnu	No risk of death by water
Between anus and heart	Fire	Red triangle	*Ram*	Rudra	No risk of death by fire
Between heart and eyebrows	Air	Black hexagon	*Yam*	Isvara	Power to move like the wind through the air
Between eyebrows and top of the head	Ether	Blue circle	*Ham*	Shiva	Power to journey through cosmic space

Contemporary methods: All the traditional tools as well as the use of mental health therapy, energy-release tools like emotional freedom technique (EFT), or other healing processes as described in Part VI.

Vijnanamayi Kosha: Sheath of Knowledge (or Wisdom)

Basic description: Wisdom is knowledge beyond sensory perception. Here sits the intellect *(buddhi)* and the sense of self *(ahamkara)*. In this sheath, we make the leap from ego understanding, which involves being stuck in time and space, to pure consciousness.

Traditional tools: Cultivation of detachment, which is available only after we have harmonized the first three bodies. This takes observation without emotion.

Contemporary methods: Study of the zero-point and other universal fields to assess one's place in the universe. Also, understanding of the observer-phenomenon: the observer affecting the outcome, as covered in Part I.

THE CAUSAL BODY

Anandamayi Kosha: Sheath of Bliss

Basic description: This is more a state than a place, in which we realize the non-dualistic consciousness—the meeting of Shakti and Shiva in the seventh chakra and ascent to enlightenment. At this point, many Hindu believe that one can arrest bodily aging and activate the siddhi powers. This sheath is related to the causal body, which is also called the seed body. Think of an acorn. It contains the codes and blueprints for the oak tree. In the same way, we have always held the secrets to our own self-realization, but have not fully grown into the true self. The causal body holds these seeds, including karmic issues—those we need to work through to grow and change.

Traditional tools: Can be achieved through yogic development and raising the kundalini, as well as selfless service, focus on the divine, and intensely focused meditation.

Contemporary methods: The above, as well as learning how to set—and live—one's intention.

ENERGY BODIES FROM OTHER CULTURES

There are hundreds, maybe thousands, of energetic systems functioning in the world, many of which include, or allude to, the chakras and other energy bodies. The following handful of systems represents some of the different ways of looking at the subtle energy cosmos within ourselves.

THE HIMALAYAN BONPO CHAKRA MODEL: A TIBETAN ENERGY SYSTEM

In this model, advocated by modern teacher Tenzin Wangyal Rinpoche, the chakras are considered *pranic*, or life energy, centers. There are six major centers, each linked to one of six realms of existence or *lokas*. An individual performs yoga to tap into the positive qualities latent within these chakras, often using sound and visualization in the form of a "seed syllables" (mantras) and symbolic gestures and practices to open these dormant chakric powers.[38]

Bön is the second most popular religion in Tibet; oral tradition asserts it began over seventeen thousand years ago, although modern scholars set the date as much later. Over the centuries, the original teachings have evolved through three main developmental time periods. Given that it started in the Tibetan Himalayas, it is sometimes referred to as the Himalayan Bonpo system (or a similar set of terms) or call the Tibetan system. It is also connected to many yoga practices and is considered a Tantric or body-based discipline. Tantra is a process for achieving enlightenment through spiritual practices.

The Bön professes nine categories of teachings, also called the Nine Ways or Nine Vehicles. Each category is unique in characteristics, practices, and outcomes. The lower levels include medicine and astrology and the highest is referred to as the "Great Perfection," the vehicle for enlightenment. The ultimate achievement of the Bön practices is attainment of a "rainbow body" at death, at which time the adept releases the five gross elements, transforming them into pure light. The body now displays multicolored light, or the rainbow body. The qualified are no longer bound by dualism, such as life and death.[39]

A central focus of Tibetan healing is the five elements, which are similar to those found in many other spiritually based healing systems. Perceived as measurable or substantial in relation to the body, they originate with the Great Mother (the Creator) as subtle energies. In their primordial state, they are called the five pure lights and each is represented by a color. The elements and their colors are:

- space, white or colorless
- air, green

CHAKRA: THROAT

Primordial syllable: A
Antidote: Peace

Loka seed syllable: SU
Loka: Jealous god realm
Negative emotion: Pride

Element seed syllable: DRUM
Element: All five elements

FIGURE 5.20

THE TIBETAN SIX-CHAKRA SYSTEM

The Tibetan tradition describes six chakras, each representing an element and a *loka*, or realm of existence. Each chakra is associated with a particular negative emotion, and each is associated with a buddha whose positive qualities can purify or counteract the negativity of that loka. In order to purify the lokas, the practitioner visualizes the element and loka syllables for each chakra, as well as the primordial syllable "A" (pronounced "Ah") as a representation of all possible buddhas, while simultaneously chanting a mantra containing the syllables of the buddhas of the six realms. In practice, many more detailed images accompany this visualization.

CHAKRA: NAVEL

Primordial syllable: A
Antidote: Wisdom

Loka seed syllable: TRI
Loka: Animal realm
Negative emotion: Ignorance

Element seed syllable: MAM
Element: Water

CHAKRA: LEFT FOOT

Primordial syllable: A
Antidote: Love

Loka seed syllable: DU
Loka: Hell realm
Negative emotion: Hatred

Element seed syllable: YAM
Element: Air

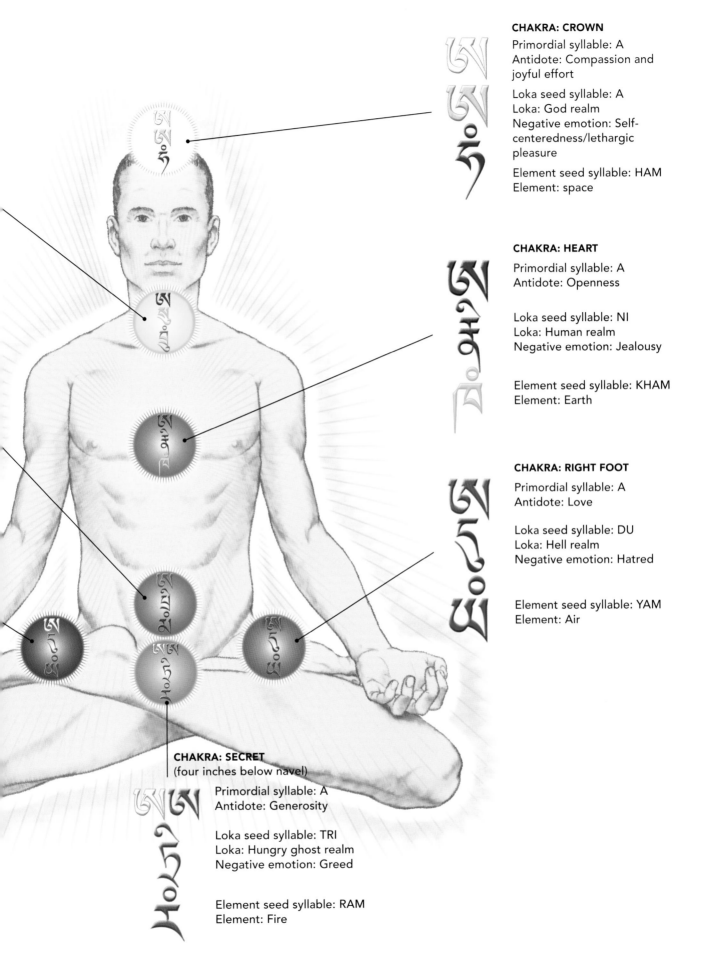

CHAKRA: CROWN

Primordial syllable: A
Antidote: Compassion and joyful effort

Loka seed syllable: A
Loka: God realm
Negative emotion: Self-centeredness/lethargic pleasure

Element seed syllable: HAM
Element: space

CHAKRA: HEART

Primordial syllable: A
Antidote: Openness

Loka seed syllable: NI
Loka: Human realm
Negative emotion: Jealousy

Element seed syllable: KHAM
Element: Earth

CHAKRA: RIGHT FOOT

Primordial syllable: A
Antidote: Love

Loka seed syllable: DU
Loka: Hell realm
Negative emotion: Hatred

Element seed syllable: YAM
Element: Air

CHAKRA: SECRET
(four inches below navel)

Primordial syllable: A
Antidote: Generosity

Loka seed syllable: TRI
Loka: Hungry ghost realm
Negative emotion: Greed

Element seed syllable: RAM
Element: Fire

- fire, red
- water, blue
- earth, yellow

Healing is accomplished by achieving balance within and between the elements, wich become unbalanced for many reasons, creating disease. According to Tenzin Wangyal Rinpoche, a primary cause of elemental blockage and disease is negative emotions. By transforming the perception of an experience from negative to positive, one improves quality of health and also promotes spiritual growth. The Tibetan method for altering perceptions involves conducting spiritual practices on the six realms (or levels) or existence, the *lokas*, which are dimensions or planes as well as classed of sentient beings.

Each of these six realms exists within us and is connected to a specific chakra. Under certain circumstances, such as karmic or destined, a loka "opens" within a person, who then experiences the emotions and perceptions of the beings that exist within this realm. The loka then confers a negative experience, which can be countermanded and even transformed by working with the related chakra. In the Tibetan system, chakras are energetic crossroads of gross, subtle, or very subtle channels, which number anywhere from 84,000 to 360,000, depending upon the approach. There are three main channels: the central and the two side channels, and all carry prana or life energy. Health is determined by the flow of this energy.

THE TIBETAN SIX-CHAKRA SYSTEM

The Tibetan chakra system has six chakras, each of which is associated with a different loka or plane of existence as well as one of the five elements in the Tibetan energetic tradition. Each loka and each element is associated with a specific color. The chakras are located at the bottom of the feet, four inches below the navel, the navel, the heart, the throat, and the top of the head.

One way to clear a chakra and improve pranic flow is to work with seed syllables, both by sounding them and visualizing them. In the Hindu system, all chakras except the seventh, the Sahasrara, have seed syllables, although sometimes the seventh chakra is said to resonate with OM. In the Tibetan Bön system, as taught by Tenzin Wangyal Rinpoche, each chakra has one seed syllable representing one of the five elements, another representing the realm or loka of that chakra, and yet another representing the particular buddha whose positive qualities can purify the negativity of that realm.[40] This is just one of many energetic practices in both the Buddhist and Bön Tibetan traditions. See figure 5.20 for a depiction of the seed syllables for each chakra and their respective associations. It is recommended that anyone wishing to practice this method receive a transmission of the teaching from an authentic source.

A TANTRIC APPROACH TO ENLIGHTENMENT: LADY YESHE TSOGYAL

As its own practice, Tantra was originally developed in India between 500 and 1300 AD. In Sanskrit, the word means "web" and signifies the web-like connection between opposites, such as body and spirit and masculine and feminine. Tantra is essentially a collection of purification rituals and as such, has been integrated into several spiritual disciplines over the years, including many Hindu and Buddhist systems.[41]

Systems adopting Tantric processes are often more similar than dissimilar. The Tibetan Bön (Himalayan Bonpo) system is Tantric in approach and shares many common features with several processes, among them those described in the book *Lady of the Lotus-Born*.[42] The book, a translation of a Buddhist text over a thousand years old, features the true story of Lady Yeshe Tsogyal, noted as the first Tibetan to most fully achieve enlightenment. Following a Buddhist path, Yeshe Tsogyal becomes a guru of substantial power. Her purification process mirrors that described in the Tibetan Bön system and involves undertaking a twelve-step progression up the spine involving the *twelve nidanas*.

The twelve nidanas are a chain of causal phenomenon leading to future rebirths and suffering. One can analyze and release these interdependent issues (or links) through various means; Yeshe Tsogyal accomplished this by moving the energy of *bodhichitta*, or thoughts of awakening, up the spine, stopping at each of the twelve "grounding spots" or energy centers in the spine. The method released the "wind" or subtle energies via a process of Tantric union with Guru Padmasam-bhava, who brought the practice to Tibet in the eighth century AD.

THE MAYAN ENERGY SYSTEM

The early Mayan religion was really a "spiritual science," connecting diverse areas of study including math, geometry, astronomy, medicine, philosophy, and cosmology. More often than not, its energetic principles and systems mirrored the ancient Hindu; in fact, they might even predate it.[43]

At their cultural peak, the Maya professed an energetic anatomy hinting of chakras, forces, deities, and similar symbology to the Hindu energy system. An early Vedic writer, Valmiki, author of two of the most sacred Hindu books (the

Ramayana and the Mahabharata) stated that the Naga Maya brought their culture to India.[44] In his book *Secrets of Mayan Science/Religion,* Mayan author Hunbatz Men adds that the Naga Maya delivered their culture to other parts of Asia and to Africa as well, where they were called *Mayax,* according to an Egyptian priest-historian.[45]

Similar to people of the Jewish and early Christian faiths, the Maya identified with a living tree. The Jewish Kabbalah is based on the "Tree of Life," which emanates energy bodies that encourage the attainment of higher consciousness. The Maya followed a similar path of enlightenment to gain the cosmic faculties of Kukulcan, a serpent-god comparable to the Hindu serpent kundalini and predecessor to the Aztec Quetzalcoatl.

Mayan initiates were taught when young how to manage their physical and mental energy. They referred to their spirit as *k'inan,* or "of solar origin." They could achieve Kukulcan status upon learning how to transform sacred energy in body and mind, which they did by developing the seven powers housed in the body.

The seven powers were represented across the 21,000 sacred sites of their land in pictures, sculpture, carvings, and stories. Seven was a powerful number to the early Maya, reminiscent of their self-proclaimed galactic origins. As did the Cherokee (see "The Tsalagi [Cherokee] Energy System" below), many Maya believed that they came from the stars and settled on earth.

The seven powers or forces were sometimes called the *chacla,* a similar word to the Hindu "chakra." To the early Maya, the chakras related to the Milky Way and its movement. One ascends as a light through one's seven centers, starting from the primary center. *Chacla* also means "this my red," which references the color of the primary center. Like the Hindu, the Maya placed the first chakra in the coccygeal area.

The Hindu describe the chakras with flowers (lotuses), and the Maya use the word *lol,* which means "flower." *Lil* refers to vibration and the *o* references consciousness with spirit. We return to the idea that everything in the universe is vibratory. As did the ancient Hindu, the Maya used words, tones, geometry, breathing, and other measures to help awaken the dormant powers.

THE TSALAGI (CHEROKEE) ENERGY SYSTEM

Many indigenous cultures carry knowledge of the subtle energies; among them are the traditional Tsalagi, the native term for the Cherokee people of North America. Author Dhyani Ywahoo shares this sacred knowledge in her book, *Voices of Our Ancestors.* Ywahoo received this tribal knowledge from her grandparents, Nellie Ywahoo and Eo-nah Fisher; it has been passed down for twenty-seven generations.[46]

The Tsalagi track their roots back to the Pleiades. Their otherworldly knowledge is called the "Fire of Wisdom." It is a complex interplay of spiritual ideals, naturalism, mystical associations, and what today would be called quantum and mechanical physics. They attribute many of their teachings to the instruction of the "Pale One," who came to the Smoky Mountains in 837 BC. He was born of a "woman who knew no man," whose grandmother

THE TSALAGI NUMEROLOGY

NUMBER SYMBOLS ARE important to the sacred way of the Tsalagi (Cherokee) people. They are also associated with color, a particular spiritual goal, and a stone. The number one, for instance, is represented by a circle and is considered the primary source of life. Depicted as a white light turning blue, a number one encourages personal will and can help clarify and heal issues related to individuality. Its power is reflected within a quartz crystal. The number nine is symbolized by a nine-pointed star and signifies the structure of universal consciousness. Inviting enlightenment, nine is opalescent in coloring and accessible through a fire opal.[49] The zero represents the "Great Mystery," the unmanifested potential within us all.[50]

had dreamed of such miracles. The child was known as the "seed of the stars," coming again to bring people into right relationship with self and others.

As does the Hindu, the Tsalagi story begins with the earth. The earth is a network of meridians, grids, and connections; the physical body mirrors these. The Tsalagi also attach great significance to trees, seeing them as communicators of vibrations in ongoing conversations between all living beings and the stars. The White Pine is seen as a symbol of life and of the transmutation of aggression to peace, its roots penetrating deep into the ground, where it gathers wave pulses that are then transmitted into the atmosphere, entraining the human brain to the earth's frequencies.[47]

The Tsalagi believe that there is a flow to manifestation from spirit to matter. The material world was spun from a realm of light called Galunlati, through the grace of Star Woman, daughter of the father of all.[48] The primary belief is that there are five principles, five tones, and five rivers of color and sound that pass through the navel. These energies flow, one to the other, in this way from emptiness to sound (also called intention), from intention to wisdom, and from wisdom to love.

These three ideas (intention, wisdom, and love) are mirrors of the Hindu bindus, or points of the sacred triangle, the shape that gives birth to form.

For the Tsalagi, there were five sounds that arose from the nothingness. These tones connect the left and right hemispheres of our brain and can assist with healing. Each organ in the body resonates to one of these overtones, which move in a cycle or pentatonic scale—a commonality among native cultures. (*Penta*

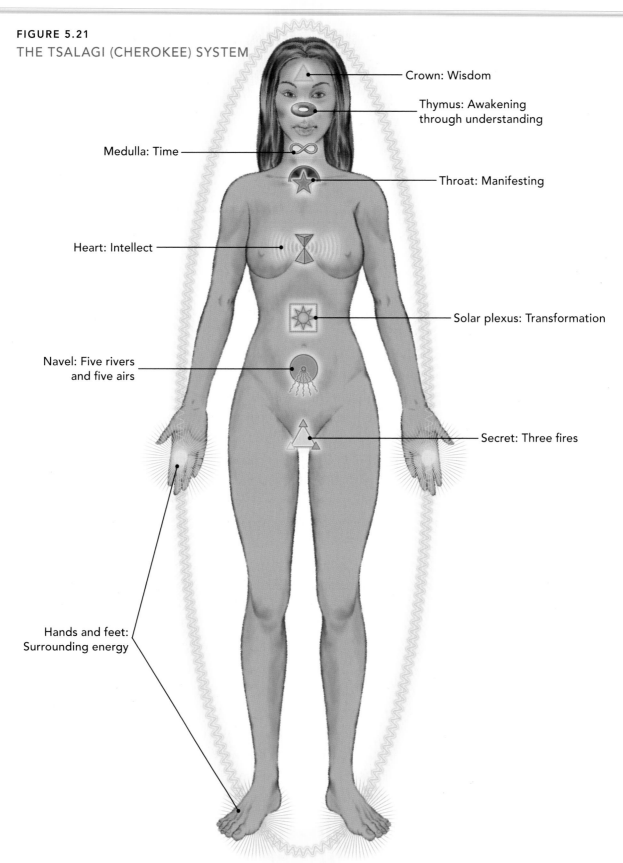

FIGURE 5.21
THE TSALAGI (CHEROKEE) SYSTEM

Crown: Wisdom

Thymus: Awakening through understanding

Medulla: Time

Throat: Manifesting

Heart: Intellect

Solar plexus: Transformation

Navel: Five rivers and five airs

Secret: Three fires

Hands and feet: Surrounding energy

means "five.") The movement of these sounds and harmonies—these songs—are received through the top of the head and the base of the spine. When blended in and expanded through the heart, these harmonies invite higher consciousness; it is an alchemical process that encourages an energetic transformation.[51]

Bioresonance

According to Tsalagi wisdom, there are two shells around the earth. The outer is solar; the inner is lunar. "Wind-shields," or energetic forces, move within these shells in relation to the tectonic plates and tides, creating changes in the earth's magnetic field. The lunar currents respond to the lunar shield around the earth, while the solar currents of the spine reflect the external solar wind-shield shifts. As well, other layers of energy surround the earth, including an electromagnetic field and a "lightning gridwork" that conveys energies within it and between layers. In the Tsalagi system, our bodies are set up in much the same way. Lunar and solar energies shift in and through our spines in spiraling circles, while our nervous system transmits energies much like the lightning grid. The counterclockwise swastika portrays these movements. The human and the earth systems both function in "bioresonance," or through a biological harmonizing. In practice, the human responsibility in this energetic exchange is fulfilled by conscious appreciation of the elements that make up all of life.

For the Tsalagi, we live in a field of mind; this field interconnects with the earth and the stars. To develop into our highest potential, we must send "fire" up the spine to animate the entire self. The spine is considered a ladder to heaven. There are three fires that burn in the spine, each fulfilling a different purpose:

Blue fire of will	Clear intention to act
Compassion fire	Understands and manifests purpose
Fire of active intelligence	Acts in harmony

These three fires must penetrate the five doorways in the body where energy can become blocked. These doorways are reflective of the basic chakras:

Solar plexus: Here, one transforms feelings, such as anger, and negative thoughts, in order to achieve higher action.

Heart: The heart holds the intellect. Around it are two electrical fields. One moves clockwise, the other counterclockwise. These generate purpose, the manifestation of dream in physical reality. To heal the heart is to become a balancing point between heaven and earth. This healing usually involves dealing with issues of compassion, grief, and fear.

Throat: Here is the power of the voice, the ability to say it and make it so. The key is to use this power wisely.

Medulla: The medulla rests at the base of the skull. It is a receptacle of past issues and problems, even those carried over from other lifetimes. This doorway invites the opportunity to live in the present.

Crown: Located in the fontanel, this gateway emits fluid once an aspirant has completed lessons, all of which center on nonattachment. This doorway formulates a full connection to the higher field of consciousness and the opportunity to fully embody the wisdom of the three burning fires.

In addition to these five energy centers, there are four more: one in the "secret" region of the reproductive organs; one at the navel, which receives the five subtle airs and the five rivers that feed the five bodily organ systems; one at the thymus; and one at the hands and feet, considered to be connected by a single energy that ascends one side of the body and descends the other.

Interestingly, the Tsalagi perceive the universe as a great crystalline plate, suspended by four spiraling cords. The plate is in a constant state of vibration, as are all things upon it. Other plates, other universes, exist as well, but can't actually touch each other. This cosmology bears some resemblance to the string theory of quantum physics, and brings to mind the relationship between sound and form demonstrated by the burgeoning science of Cymatics (see page 141).

THE INCAN ENERGY MODEL

Alberto Villoldo, author of *Shaman, Healer, Sage*, shares information about the body's subtle energy system that he received from his Incan mentor, Don Manuel Quispe. Within this cosmology, each of us has a luminous energy field, called a *popo*, which surrounds our physical body. Composed of light, it transfers information in and out of the body. It has four layers: the causal, the psychic (or soul), the mental-emotional (or mind), and the physical. Our personal and inherited memories and traumas are stored in the luminous energy field, with each layer holding its part of events. It therefore serves as a template for our life and how we live it.

The luminous energy field is shaped like a bagel, which mirrors the magnetic field of the earth. Energy flows out the top of our head to follow the luminous

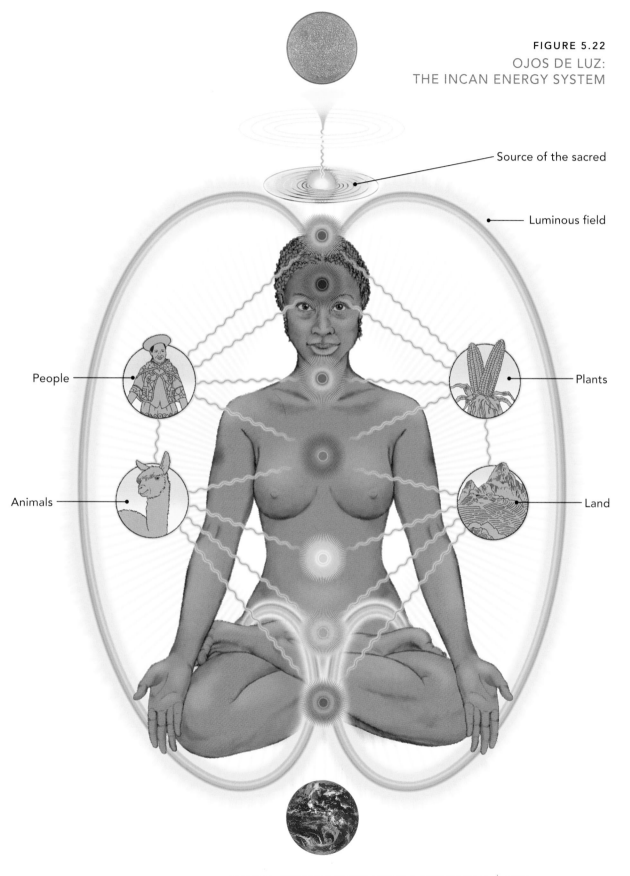

FIGURE 5.22

OJOS DE LUZ:
THE INCAN ENERGY SYSTEM

Source of the sacred

Luminous field

People

Plants

Animals

Land

FIGURE 5.23
THE INCAN PUKIOS

Aspect	First Chakra	Second Chakra	Third Chakra	Fouth Chakra
Element	Earth	Water	Fire	Air
Color	Red	Orange	Yellow	Green
Instinct	Survival, procreation	Sexuality	Power	Love
Body correspondences	Elimination of wastes, rectum, legs, feet	Digestion, kidneys, adrenals, urinary tract, menstrual pain, loss of appetite	Stomach, liver, pancreas, spleen, storing and releasing energy	Circulatory system, lungs, breast, heart, asthma, immune deficiencies
Psychological correspondences	Food, shelter, safety	Power, money, sex, control, fear, passion, self-esteem, incest	Courage, power	Love, hope, compassion, intimacy
Glands	Ovaries, testes	Adrenals	Pancreas	Thymus
Seeds	Kundalini, abundance	Creativity, compassion	Autonomy, individuation, fulfillment of dreams, longevity	Selfless love, forgiveness
Negative aspects	Hoarding, chronic fatigue, predatory behavior, abandonment issues	Fear, fighting	Gastrointestinal disorders, anorexia, sorrow, pride, ego, low energy, victim mentality, shame	Resentment, betrayal, grief, loneliness, abandonment

energy field, at which point it penetrates the earth for about twelve inches and re-enters the body through our feet. The chakras are organs of this field.

Chakras are known in South America as *ojos de luz*, "eyes of light." Don Manuel also referred to them as *pukios*, "light wells." The chakras extend threads of light, *huaskas*, that reach beyond the body, connecting the body to the natural world. These threads also reach back and forward through time, from birth and personal history to our destination.

Like the Hindu, the Inca perceive seven chakras; however, they also describe two additional chakras. The eighth chakra is located above the physical body, but still within the luminous energy field. It is called the source of the sacred: *wiracocha*, our connection to the Creator. The ninth chakra, known as the *causay*, is outside the body, and at one with all creation, the Creator's connection to each of us. The lower five chakras receive sustenance from the earth, and the upper four receive their nourishment from the sun.

Fifth Chakra	Sixth Chakra	Seventh Chakra	Eighth Chakra	Ninth Chakra
Light	Pure light	Pure energy	Soul	Spirit
Blue	Indigo	Violet	Gold	Translucent white light
Psychic expression	Truth	Universal ethics	Transcendence	Liberation
Throat, mouth, neck, esophagus	Brain, eyes, nervous system	Skin, brain, hormonal balances	Architect of the body	None
Manifesting dreams, creativity, communication	Reason, logic, intelligence, empathy, depression	Selflessness, integrity, wisdom	None	None
Thyroid, parathyroid	Pituitary	Pineal	None	None
Personal power, faith, will	Enlightenment, self-realization	Transcendence, illumination	Timelessness	Infinity
Betrayal, addictions, sleep disorders, fear of speaking out, toxicity	Delusion, inadequacy	Psychoses, regression, cynicism	Templates of disease	None

THE INCAN CHAKRA ANATOMY

As explained in *Shaman, Healer, Sage*, chakras in the Incan tradition are seen as direct pipelines to the neural network. In a child, they display their true colors, which fade over time due to trauma and toxic residue. The resulting decrease in frequency accelerates physical aging. Clearing the chakras reactivates their purity and enables a "rainbow body," thus called because the chakras reflect the colors of the rainbow.

Chakras extend luminous threads that reach beyond the body and connect with the external environment, including trees, plants, mountains, and other people. At death, the soul leaves the body and rejoins the eighth chakra, before returning to the grid pattern formed by the luminous energy field. The ninth chakra is inviolate of life events, as it never entered the river of time (or time-space) and therefore remains our sacred connection to the Creator.

While alive, all energy comes from five sources:[52]

- Plants and animals
- Water
- Air
- Sunlight
- Biomagnetic energy (*causay* in Incan)

Plants, animal nutrients, and water are processed through the digestive tract, while air is processed through the lungs. Sunlight is processed through the skin, and causay through the chakras.

The chakras therefore serve as connectors to the world outside of the self, vessels for purification, and tools for transitioning to higher spiritual realities.

The Great Secret

According to the Incan cosmology, the Immense Force we know as God manifested from the unmanifested void 12 billion years ago. This Force was omnipresent

INCAN BANDS OF POWER RITUAL[53]

ALBERTO VILLOLDO INSTRUCTS students in the Bands of Power ritual in order to enable energetic protection. This process links six of the chakras to the five elements so that they may be nourished directly. It involves establishing five bands at various places in the body.

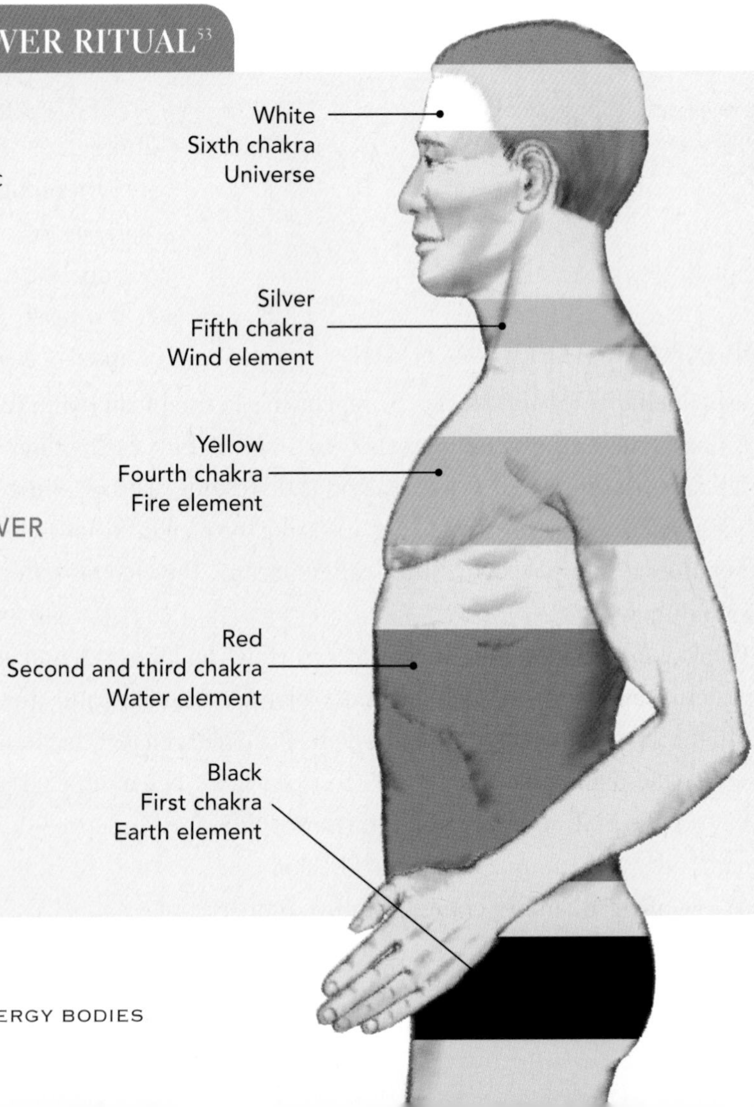

FIGURE 5.24
THE INCAN BANDS OF POWER

White
Sixth chakra
Universe

Silver
Fifth chakra
Wind element

Yellow
Fourth chakra
Fire element

Red
Second and third chakra
Water element

Black
First chakra
Earth element

and omniscient, but it separated into all forms of life in order to experience Itself. Each form has all features of the All. It keeps its own nature a secret from itself, however, in order to gain experience. The energy system of the body is set up to enable a return to this knowing.

The Incan Pukios or Chakras

The eighth chakra hovers a few inches overhead like a spinning sun, our connection to Great Spirit, where God dwells within us. It then expands into a luminous globe.

The ninth chakra is the source of the eighth chakra, Spirit. It lies outside the luminous energy field and extends through the cosmos. Outside of time and space, it connects to the eighth chakra by a luminous cord.

AN OCCULT CHRISTIAN ENERGY SYSTEM
BASED ON THE REVELATION OF ST. JOHN

There are many occult energy practices that have sprung from Christianity. Zachary Lansdowne presents one such system in his book *The Revelation of Saint John*. Through a comparative analysis of the Christian Bible's last book Lansdowne outlines an energetic system for soul evolution. His theory is that the book of Revelation is a veiled description of esoteric Christian beliefs and a map to enlightenment. He presents the following energetic system in his book.[54]

According to Lansdowne, there are four parts to the personality: the physical, vital, emotional, and mental bodies. The causal body is the heart of God and holds one's most noble thoughts. The soul serves as an intermediary between "the living stream" that flows "from the heart of God to the physical cells,"[55] while divine will expresses from God's heart in seven rays of color and is transformed by seven archangels during meditation. Lansdowne also outlines seven chakras (similar in location and function to those in the traditional Hindu system), which are awakened during a kundalini rising that begins when we act and think consciously. After being transformed by the kundalini, a chakra is awakened to the following gifts:

Crown chakra: Insight that brings freedom.

Brow chakra: Wisdom.

Throat chakra: Penetrating insight and deep understanding.

Heart chakra: Intuition that discerns between truth and illusion.

Solar plexus chakra: Observation of emotion with detachment.

Sacral chakra: Cultivation of higher motives, such as charity, love, and mercy, and the ability to act on higher principles.

Base chakra: Mental silence and spiritual will.

EGYPTIAN AND AFRICAN ENERGY BODIES

The ancient Egyptians enjoyed an orderly energy cosmology, which was also the basis of the spiritual practices of the African Zulus. The Zulus belonged to a secret society called the Bonaabakulu Absekhumu.

Both systems professed a Tree of Life similar to that of the Jewish Kabbalah. They also had a set of energy bodies including the chakras and several others that are analogous to those of the Hindu. The earlier Egyptian system can be traced back to the reign of Pharaoh Khufu and the third dynasty in 3900 BC. Here are examples of these similar systems.[56]

Egyptian Energy Bodies

The ancient Egyptians envisioned several different energy bodies. Though they were separate, each energy body also interacted with the others. There were between five and nine. This list describes the most commonly appearing energy bodies:

- The *physical body*. The body was referred to as the *ht* or *jrw*, meaning "form" or "appearance," during life. At death, the body was called the *khat*, which means "the corruptible."
- The *ka*. Ka roughly translates as the "double" or "vital force." It is the part of a person that exists beyond death.
- The *khabit*. The shadow. The lower nature, ruled by the senses.
- The *shekem*. The area of divine powers and life energy.
- The *ba*. Similar to the contemporary idea of the soul, the ba represents all the nonphysical qualities that compose a person.
- The *akh* (also called the *khu*). The term means "transfigured spirit," the "shining one," or the "luminous one." It is equivalent to one's higher self, denoting the form one takes in the hereafter.

- The *khaibit* (also *shwt*). This is the shadow, or hidden self, most often connected to the dead or the other worlds.
- The *ren*. Meaning "name," the ren is the part of the self that makes things real. Naming is considered an important manifestation process across many cultures. To name something is to manifest it.
- The *sahu*. The glorious spiritual body, used to transport the *ka* to the heavens after death.

African Energy Bodies

According to the Zulu tradition as described to Patrick Bowen, a Caucasian who was taught by the Zulus in the early 1900s, the basic energy bodies identified by the Zulus are:

- The physical body (*umzimba*)
- The etheric body (*isltunzi*); etheric counterpart to the physical body
- Lower mind (*amandhla*); holds life force and energy
- The animal mind (*utiwesilo*); passions, emotions, and instincts
- Human mind (*utiwomuntu*); consciousness, intellect, higher feelings
- Spiritual mind (*utiwetongo*); higher planes that create spiritual awareness
- The ray (*itongo*) or spark of universal spirit[57]

The Tree of Life and the Egyptian (and African) Chakras

The ancient Egyptians and the African Zulu connected the different aspects of the human with their own version of the Tree of Life, called the *Kamitic*, as well as with the chakras. The spheres are similar to those described in the Kabbalah in Chapter 40. The following chart is one version of these connections.

FIGURE 5.25
THE EGYPTIAN AND AFRICAN CHAKRAS AND THE TREE OF LIFE[58]

Division of Spirit	Chakra	Sphere	Governs
Khab	Root (first)	Lower half of tenth	Physical body
Khaibit	Navel (second)	Upper half of tenth	Animal nature
Sahu	Solar plexus (third)	Seventh, eighth, ninth	Lower self
Ab	Heart (fourth)	Fourth, fifth, sixth	Spirit above and mundane below
Shekem	Throat (fifth)	Third	Creative words
Khu	Brow (sixth)	Second	Oracular powers
Ba	Crown (seventh)	First	*Itango* or source of creation

THE QOLLAHUAYAS: ENERGY BODIES IN THE LAND

The Hindu energy system reflects the geography of India; the Egyptians show-cased the Nile. High in the Andes are a people who embrace the land to an even greater degree: to them, the mountain and their own bodies are anatomically the same.

Since early times, various Andean cultures have compared their environment and villages to anatomical paradigms of animals and people. The Peruvian peoples planned their cities in relation to birds or animals. The Inca designed Cuzco to look like a puma. The villagers of Jesus de Machacha in Bolivia refer to their land with descriptions of the cougar.

One particular culture, the Qollahuayas, live in separate areas of their Bolivian mountain home, Mount Kaata, but consider themselves united because each of the three distinct regions represents a part of a human body. There is Apacheta, the mountainous highland, which signifies the head. Here the grasses and wool symbolize hair and lakes form the eyes. Kaata is the trunk and the middle region of the mountain. Her crops mirror the viscera and trunk of the metaphorical body. Diviners circulate blood and fat to the other parts of the mountain through ritual and ceremony. Then there are the lowlands of Ninokorin, where rows of corn, vegetables, and orchards represent legs and toenails.

The Qollahuayas not only make this analogy—they live it. A washed-away riverbed can create illness; health is restored when the mountain is fed. But humans also create their own disorders, namely through social and environmental disrespect. Problems between people will create a disturbance in the human body but also the land, and must be resolved through a ritual involving the sick person's social group as well as a healing for the land. The major causes of illness are considered social disturbances and land disputes, for which a diviner works with earth shrines to restore balance.

One might frown at this idea except for the profound effectiveness of the Qollahuaya healing system. Qollahuaya medicine men, or *curanderos*, gather herbs, animal products, and minerals to use for medicinal purposes. Their medicine bags include over a thousand remedies, some equivalent to aspirin, penicillin, and quinine. For hundreds of years, they have also conducted surgery, including brain surgery. Many well-known individuals of the area have been cured from seemingly incurable diseases by these medicine men.[59] The diviners apply supernatural methods, "arranging tables" to feed the earth. These tables consist of animal and plant products that give the land what it requires to flourish.

THE TWELVE-CHAKRA SYSTEM

One contemporary chakra system is the Twelve-Chakra System, which I developed and describe in detail in two other books.[60] It is based on the classical Hindu chakra system, but includes an additional five chakras that are outside of the physical body. While these additional chakras have yet to be measured or recorded, I discovered them through my work as an energy healer. Having developed an understanding of these additional energy centers, I now make frequent use of them.

The additional chakras are found above the head, below the feet, and around the body. Many other chakra systems include chakras beyond the seven that have been reviewed so far in this book. The *Narayana* system, a yoga derivative, works with nine chakras, as does the chakra system expounded upon in the Yogaranjopanishad; while the *Waidika* system, a Layayoga method, outlines eleven major chakras.[61] Some schools add an eighth chakra, the Bindu or the Soma, to the typical seven.[62]

Many esoteric practitioners locate chakras beyond the physical body, as do some of the more traditional systems. In yogic tradition, it is important to remember that the seventh chakra is located "above the top of the head," not "at the top of the head."[63] Other traditions place a chakra underneath the feet, as David Furlong describes in his book *Working with Earth Energies*,[64] as does Katrina Raphaell.[65] Nearly all systems recognize secondary or minor chakras. One researcher outlines twenty-one minor and forty-nine minute chakras, in addition to the basic seven.[66] Most systems reference chakras in the hands and feet, the basis of the twelve-chakra system's eleventh chakra, which surrounds the body but is strongest around the hands and feet.[67]

The twelve-chakra system features the traditional seven, plus these additional chakras. What makes the twelve-chakra system different? The extra five chakras.

Eighth chakra: Just above the head. This chakra is seen as housing several additional energy bodies, including the *Akashic Records*, which is everything ever seen and done; the *Shadow Records*, that which was unseen as pertaining to the Akashic Records; and the Book of Life, which reflects the positive aspect of all events. The eighth chakra is the place of karma through which individuals can connect with all planes, dimensions, and time periods, including alternative or parallel realities.

Ninth chakra: One and a half feet above the head. This chakra contains the "seat of the soul," the spiritual genetics that generate physical reality, such as the physical genes. It also carries the soul purpose and the symbols that sustain the uniqueness of a soul. Through it, a practitioner can:

- Customize energetic healing so as to exactly fit the individual
- Obtain information explaining someone's life path—and upcoming decisions
- Conduct energy healing to make genetic repair by using symbology

Tenth chakra: A foot and a half under the feet. This is the "grounding chakra," which opens to elemental energy and passes it into the body through the feet. It holds personal soul history as well as stories and energies from one's heritage. It connects a person thoroughly into nature and the natural world. This chakra is extraordinarily useful for anchoring individuals into everyday reality, addressing and healing legacy issues (including genetic disease), and opening to the elemental energies necessary for health.

Eleventh chakra: Surrounding the body and concentrated around the hands and the feet. This energy center helps individuals command and transmute physical and supernatural forces. Through it, one can seize command of external energies and direct them for good. It is extraordinary for producing instant change inside and outside of the body.

Twelfth chakra: Surrounding the eleventh chakra and the entirety of the body, this energy center represents the outer bounds of the human self. It connects to the body through thirty secondary chakras, described in *New Chakra Healing*. It channels spiritual energies found outside of the total auric field. Just outside of the twelfth chakra is the "energy egg" (see figure 5.27), a three-layer film that regulates the linkage between the spiritual realms and the physical body.

THE TWELVE-CHAKRA SYSTEM AND THE SPIRITUAL POINTS

The twelve-chakra system accesses prisms of energy that are similar to the chakras but lie outside of the human field. They mesh spiritual energy with physical matter. There are twenty spiritual points, which are in addition to the twelve chakras. Here are these twenty points with a description of where they link into the spine. They are labeled as points 13 to 32. As well, there is an additional "point" that serves as an overriding spiritual principle.[68]

FIGURE 5.26
THE SPIRITUAL POINTS AND THE SPINE

Point	Spinal Area	Vertebra
Point 13: Yin	Lumbar	Second
Point 14: Yang		First

FIGURE 5.26
THE SPIRITUAL POINTS AND THE SPINE

Point	Spinal Area	Vertebra
Point 15: Balance of polarities	Thoracic	Twelfth
Point 16: Balance of similarities		Eleventh
Point 17: Harmony		Tenth
Point 18: Free will and freedom		Ninth
Point 19: Kundalini		Eighth
Point 20: Mastery		Seventh
Point 21: Abundance		Sixth
Point 22: Clarity		Fifth
Point 23: Knowledge of good and bad		Fourth
Point 24: Creation		Third
Point 25: Manifestation		Second
Point 26: Alignment		First
Point 27: Peace	Cervical	Seventh
Point 28: Wisdom		Sixth
Point 29: Enjoyment		Fifth
Point 30: Forgiveness		Fourth
Point 31: Faith		Third
Point 32: Grace and divine source consciousness		Second
Principle of Love		First

CHAKRAS AND THE ENDOCRINE GLANDS

Each of the twelve chakras operates through an in-body endocrine gland. This assures that the out-of-body chakras can interact with the physical body and create change within it.

Traditionally, the heart, diaphragm, bones, and connective tissue have not been considered endocrine glands, or hormone producers. But the heart is now medically considered an endocrine gland—in fact, one of the major hormone producers or regulators in the body. The bones have also been demonstrated to be hormone producers and other tissues and organs have been shown to have effects on the hormones. (See Part II.) The diaphragm, for instance, regulates the flow of breath, oxygenation being key to the distribution of hormones. And the relationship works both ways. As Dr. Dave Harris, a specialist in spinal cord injury, reports, one of the modern treatments for connective tissue problems, such as osteoarthritis involving bone and cartilage pain and

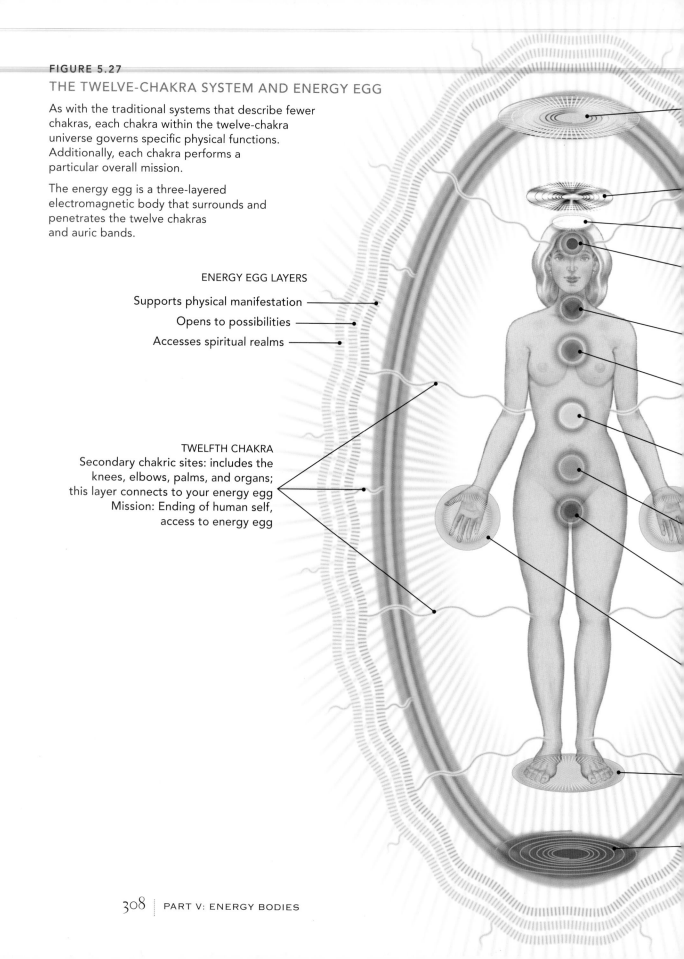

FIGURE 5.27

THE TWELVE-CHAKRA SYSTEM AND ENERGY EGG

As with the traditional systems that describe fewer chakras, each chakra within the twelve-chakra universe governs specific physical functions. Additionally, each chakra performs a particular overall mission.

The energy egg is a three-layered electromagnetic body that surrounds and penetrates the twelve chakras and auric bands.

ENERGY EGG LAYERS

Supports physical manifestation ——

Opens to possibilities ——

Accesses spiritual realms ——

TWELFTH CHAKRA

Secondary chakric sites: includes the knees, elbows, palms, and organs; this layer connects to your energy egg Mission: Ending of human self, access to energy egg

NINTH CHAKRA
Diaphragm; pineal gland; corpus callosum and other
higher learning centers including the cortex and neocortex
Mission: Soul programs and plans

EIGHTH CHAKRA
Thymus (immune system); memory retrieval functions;
aspects of central nervous system; thalamus; right eye
Mission: Karma and universal linkages

SEVENTH CHAKRA
Pineal gland; parts of hypothalamus; higher learning and
cognitive brain systems; parts of immune system
Mission: Purpose and spirituality

SIXTH CHAKRA
Pituitary gland; parts of hypothalamus; visual and olfactory systems;
memory storage; some problems with ears and sinus; left eye
Mission: Vision and strategy

FIFTH CHAKRA
Thyroid gland; larynx; mouth and auditory systems;
lymph system; thoracic vertebrae
Mission: Communication and guidance

FOURTH CHAKRA
Heart and lungs; circulatory and oxygenation
systems; breasts; lumbar and thoracic vertebrae
Mission: Relationships and healing

THIRD CHAKRA
Pancreatic system; all digestive organs in stomach area,
including liver, spleen, gallbladder, stomach, pancreas,
and parts of kidney system; lumbar vertebrae
Mission: Mentality and structure

SECOND CHAKRA
Affects part of adrenal system; intestines; parts of kidney function;
some aspects of reproductive system; sacral vertebrae and the
neurotransmitters determining emotional responses to stimuli
Mission: Feelings and creativity

FIRST CHAKRA
Genital organs and adrenals; coccygeal vertebrae;
affects some kidney, bladder, and excretory functions; skin
Mission: Security and survival

ELEVENTH CHAKRA
Parts of skin, muscles, and connective tissue
Mission: Forces and energy conversion

TENTH CHAKRA
Feet, legs, and bones
Mission: Legacies and nature

loss, is androgenic hormone treatment (using testosterone, growth hormone, progesterone, or DHEA).[69]

The endocrine glands that correlate to the twelve chakras are illustrated in figure 5.27.

CHAKRA DEVELOPMENT AND AGE

The chakras are fully developed by the time an infant is born, but they activate at different times during our lives. It is thought that before conception, the ninth and tenth chakras actively interface with the soul and spiritual guidance to select the proper genes.

By birth, the first chakra is already active and for a short time after birth, so is the seventh chakra, which connects to the fontanel. The fontanel closes sometime during the first few months of life, establishing a thorough reliance on the first and most physically based chakra again. The other chakras activate one at a time until a person is fully mature, with chakras one to six opening individually between *in utero* and fourteen years of age (chakra seven activates at age fourteen). At this point, the body continues to open the additional chakras, but now in seven-year spans.

First Chakra:	Womb to 6 months
Second Chakra:	6 months to 2.5 years
Third Chakra:	2.5 to 4.5 years
Fourth Chakra:	4.5 to 6.5 years
Fifth Chakra:	6.5 to 8.5 years
Sixth Chakra:	8.5 to 14 years
Seventh Chakra:	14 to 21 years
Eighth Chakra:	21 to 28 years
Ninth Chakra:	28 to 35 years
Tenth Chakra:	35 to 42 years
Eleventh Chakra:	42 to 49 years
Twelfth Chakra:	49 to 57 years

At age fifty-six, the chakras remain in the twelfth-chakra development stage, which was entered at age forty-nine. But for the first time during life, two chakras become simultaneously active. A person also reengages the first chakra (and at the next juncture at age sixty-three, remains in the twelfth-chakra and reenters the second chakra).

The issues laid down during childhood (*in utero* to age fourteen) become operating programs and determine thought, emotion, and behavior. However, during each year beginning at age fourteen, the body sequentially reprocesses the lower-chakra issues so that new decisions can be made. (This also means that at age fifty-six one is in two fully mature chakras and also sequentially recyling the lower seven chakras.) The following list shows the first seven-year reactivation cycle:

Age 14   Recycles first chakra
Age 15   Recycles second chakra
Age 16   Recycles third chakra
Age 17   Recycles fourth chakra
Age 18   Recycles fifth chakra
Age 19   Recycles sixth chakra
Age 20   Recycles seventh chakra

CHAKRA STRUCTURE

Chakras have their own configuration and can be reduced to three different parts or sections. These three aspects are present in all chakras, not only through the lens of the twelve-chakra system. Each chakra has a left and right side from the frontal view of the body; a front and back side (the front side of a chakra is on the front side of the body; the back side is on the back side); and an inner and outer wheel. The inner wheel of a chakra is literally inside of an outer wheel; both rotate in relationship with each other.

Chakras can be analyzed structurally, but also informationally. All chakras carry messages that are emotional, mental, physical, and spiritual. In this section we will be considering the mental ideas encoded within the chakras that determine our overall well-being, self-concept, and behaviors.

In general, the left side of the body, and therefore the left side of the chakra, represents feminine, or yin, energy, and the right side masculine, or yang, energy. Each body half is ruled by the opposite brain hemisphere; the right side of the body is governed by the left hemisphere of the brain, and vice versa.

Masculine energy is physical, active, dominating, and linear, and will reflect one's internal male as well as one's relationship with men and patriarchy. Female energy is spiritual, reflective, passive, and intuitive, and will reflect one's inner female as well as relationship with women and matriarchy. An injury on the left side of the body could therefore be considered as an issue within or with the feminine side of reality. A distortion in the energetic flow on the left side of a chakra could also indicate a feminine-based issue while a deformation in the flow on the right side of a chakra could signify a masculine-natured issue. (The sides of a chakra are determined through the eyes of the person being examined.)

A chakra has a back side and front side. In general, the back side regulates unconscious, primal programs, and spiritual matters, while the front side oversees conscious and day-to-day needs. Inside the chakra is an inner wheel, which should harmonize with the outer wheel. The inner wheel links to the subconscious but also, potentially, the higher self one's personal spirit. The outer wheel's programming tends to reflect issues that force conformity with the world. These are often dysfunctional and are based in at least one of these negative misperceptions:

I am unlovable.
I am unworthy.
I am powerless.
I have no value.
I am bad.
I do not deserve.

These negative perceptions regulate the subconscious, which in turn runs our unconscious and our conscious selves. They create disharmony within the body's subtle energy system and prevent the rising of the kundalini. Negative perceptions also cause problems in the auric field and attract negative situations into our lives.

The inner wheel usually reflects our spirit's knowing or truths. These truths link to the supraconscious, the highest aspect of the mind. The beliefs within the inner wheel counteract the dysfunctional beliefs, and will include:

I am lovable.
I am worthy.
I am powerful.
I have value.
I am good.
I deserve.

This inside wheel processes with particles and waves that move faster than the speed of light, whereas the outer wheel works with sensory energy. Because of this, the inner wheel can transform the body, mind, and soul through zero-point energy (see Index) and enable near-instantaneous healing and problem resolution.

The following table describes the functions of and issues addressed by the four chakra parts: back, front, inner sphere, and outer sphere.

FIGURE 5.28
CHAKRA INFRASTRUCTURES

Chakra	Back	Front	Inner Sphere	Outer Sphere
First Chakra	Unconscious security issues; how others' security issues affect you.	Interface with everyday life; how you carry yourself in the world.	Is regulated by your soul's relationship with the Divine.	Your movement in the world. Over-functioning causes harried and hyper-active behavior. Underfunctioning creates sloth and laziness.
Second Chakra	The feelings you unconsciously carry; your unconscious response to the feelings of those around you; decisions about which feelings of others you will pick up and hold onto and which you will not.	How you express your feelings into the world; your ability to translate your feelings into creative responses.	Do you believe the Divine has feelings? Your response sets the rhythm of this wheel. If you disregard the spirituality of feelings, you will be judgmental, closed, and unsympathetic to others. If you fail to translate the spiritual messages behind the feelings, you will be emotional, hypersensitive, and codependent.	Establishes the ways you act as a feeling person in the world. Repressed feelings will attract people who exhibit these feelings to you or cause illness. If you hold feelings that are not yours, you will feel crazy and out of control.
Third Chakra	Your unconscious beliefs about power, success, and your deserving of both.	Your ability to succeed in the world.	Frequency is established by your internalized beliefs about your place in the world. Do you believe the Divine has special work for you and that you have unique gifts? If you do, you will feel healthy and balanced. If you do not, you will feel strained and continually disappointed in yourself.	Maintains your boundaries with the world. If you believe your work is divinely guided, you will perform well and command respect.
Fourth Chakra	Your unconscious beliefs about relationships; keeps you connected to people you have not let go of.	Your major and minor relationships; your ability to give and receive.	The relationships within: self to self; Divine to self; self and Divine to all aspects of the self.	Balance: relationships between self and all aspects of self with the world and others in it.

FIGURE 5.28
CHAKRA INFRASTRUCTURES

Chakra	Back	Front	Inner Sphere	Outer Sphere
Fifth Chakra	The type of guidance you are willing to receive, which can be from lower or higher planes.	Determines which tapes or messages regulate your communication—those that are healthy or those that are not.	What you are willing or unwilling to say or express. How others will perceive your communication. If the frequency is too fast, you are not listening to the Divine. If it is too slow, you are listening to lower-ordered beings.	Responds to your intention
Sixth Chakra	Potential futures. All choices enter through the back side of the chakra. Your inner ability to see these choices is dependent on your self-image.	The path chosen. If you train yourself, you can look ahead from this place in time and see what choices you still face.	Place of your spirit's image of you and of your life.	Projects your self-image, which tells others how to respond to you.
Seventh Chakra	The types of spirits and spiritual beliefs programming your belief system; sometimes these hold you hostage.	How you project your image of the Divine and spiritual self into the world; the religion you follow and the values you live.	If healthy, your spiritual beliefs and discipline will match your purpose and the Divine's desires for you. If not, there will be discord.	Reflects how you carry out your spiritual beliefs.
Eighth Chakra	Patterns or parts of your past guiding your decisions.	How you express these patterns through life choices—decisions about a mate, friends, work, use of your spiritual gifts, and more.	Reflects ability to forgive yourself for past mistakes; you can release all karma and have a clear inner sphere if you are able to forgive.	If unforgiving of self or of others, every aspect of your life will reflect prior decisions.
Ninth Chakra	Beliefs held in your own and others' souls about universal love, global needs, and care for others.	Ways you express care for others in everyday life.	Can serve as portal for spiritual truths that, if entering, assist your spirit in integrating in your body.	Shows how you have carried spiritual truths into action.

FIGURE 5.28
CHAKRA INFRASTRUCTURES

Chakra	Back	Front	Inner Sphere	Outer Sphere
Tenth Chakra	What aspects of the natural world you draw upon or bring into your life.	How you interact with nature and the things of nature. Will even show whether herbs or natural healing will work.	Place in nature that can hold the seed of your spirit if you allow yourself to be grounded in physical reality.	Reflects how well you live as a physical being, a product of nature, the world, and your ancestry—not just of divinity.
Eleventh Chakra	Beliefs aiding or impairing your ability to alter and transmute energy.	How you influence the physical and energetic worlds around you; which beings of energy and spirit you draw into you, as aid or foe.	Place of contact through which your spirit can draw upon energetic powers and forces.	Reflects proper or improper use of supernatural power.
Twelfth Chakra	This chakra does not have a front side or back side. The inner sphere concerns your divinity; the outer sphere relates to how well this divinity is reflected in your everyday human existence.			

ENERGY BODIES IN THE TWELVE-CHAKRA SYSTEM

There are dozens if not hundreds of energy bodies in the twelve-chakra pantheon. Here are a few that can be helpful for energy practitioners.

THE MAIN BODIES OF THE SELF

There are seven main energy bodies in the twelve-chakra system.[70] These are:

The spirit: The immortal and eternal essence that carries one's spiritual truths, which also formulate the spiritual purpose and gifts (related to psychic abilities and the Hindu siddhi). From an Eastern perspective, the spirit carries the dharma or mission.

The soul: The aspect of self that moves through time and space to garner experiences. Typically, the soul carries at least one major misperception that underlies all negative karma, or harmful repetitive patterns.

The mind: The aspect of self that carries beliefs and thoughts. The mind is a "nonlocal entity" interconnecting with other minds through a thought-field. There are many parts to the mind. The "higher mind" links with the spirit and the supraconscious; the "middle mind" connects with the brain (or physical body) and the unconscious; the "lower mind" represents the soul and the subconscious.

The physical body: The carrier of the mind, soul, and spirit and the holder of the chakras. The other aspects of self plug into the chakras through the planes of light, levels of awareness that bridge life and death and assist in soul evolution.[71]

The chakras: Regulate all aspects of human existence, both physically and through the subtle energies as twelve vortices that link with the endocrine system. The "you inside of you."

The auric field: Manages the relationship of the self with the world through twelve bands or layers that protect, filter, and emit information. The "you outside of you."

The energy egg: The energy egg, illustrated in figure 5.27, is an electromagnetic body that penetrates and surrounds your twelve chakras and auric bands. It creates the outer rim of your human energy system, psychically appearing as a pulsating, three-layer field of incandescent energies. Working with the energy egg for healing helps achieve several goals. Through the energy egg, you can clear negative programs, connect your higher consciousness to your everyday consciousness, diagnose and release negative energies, and attract the spiritual energies or "waves" that create lasting change.

THE THREE LAYERS

First layer: Physical, this layer is located right next to the twelfth auric field and the body. It relays information-energy between the body and inner psyche and the world at large. Through it, you deflect or attract energies to support physical manifestation based on internal programming (often subconscious or soul-based). This layer can be contacted through the pineal gland, but also through the twelfth auric field and chakra, which connects into thirty-two secondary spots in the body.

Second layer: Imaginative, this layer is in between the first and third energy egg layers. It looks like a thin line of energy that intersperses black energies and white energies. This layer attracts that which you imagine within your unconscious. You could call it the layer of wish-making and dreaming. If your programming is warped, you will access energies that deter you from destiny, or form fantasies that are unrealistic. If your use of the second layer is healthy, your twelfth chakra and auric field enable the manifestation of desires into your everyday life.

Third layer: Spiritual, the aura farthest from the body. This layer is an incandescent, shimmering body of energy that interconnects the outer rim of the twelfth chakra and auric field and the spiritual realms that lie beyond the human self. It attracts only that which fits your highest spiritual needs and purposes; it is therefore connected to what you could call your highest consciousness. It can actually call energies into your life that do not yet exist on this planet, but which will benefit you and other people. The possibility for producing physical and emotional miracles lies in working with this layer.

SECONDARY ENERGY BODIES

Following are a few of the secondary energy bodies within the twelve-chakra system.

- The *causal body* regulates the physical body.
- The *mental body* processes thoughts and feelings.
- The *emotional* or *blue body* holds feelings.
- The *pain body* records your relationship with pain and holds the energy of pain itself.
- The *gray body* connects you with beings from this dimension and others.
- The *tar body* holds the codes of your spiritual purpose and spiritual destiny.
- The *silver body* attaches to the Akashic Records, the memory of everything you have ever done, said, or thought—or might in the future.
- The *silver cord* connects the soul to the body while you are alive.
- The *physical etheric body*, next to your physical body, holds all the energetic programs affecting your health and well-being. It is the same as the tenth auric layer, which lies outside of the skin and associates with the tenth chakra. This etheric body can psychically journey separately from the body, as when one is dreaming.
- The *soul etheric body* covers the soul and holds its energetic memories, imprints, and needs. It can travel separately from the soul through the various planes of existence.
- The *etheric mirror* reflects your essence as human and divine and is a template for physical health and function. It is located in the etheric realms and mirrors your optimum human state to you, generating the correct and

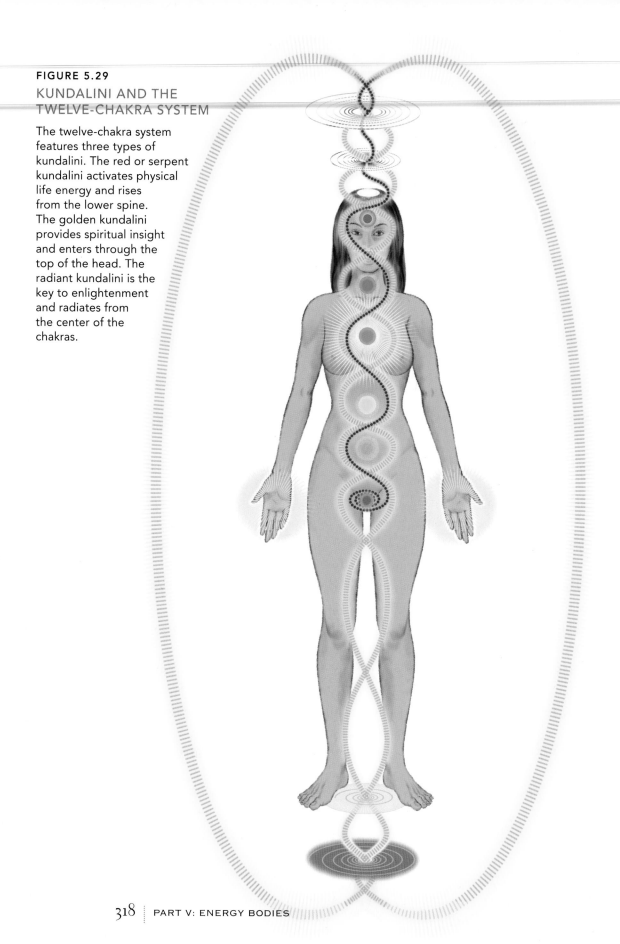

FIGURE 5.29

KUNDALINI AND THE TWELVE-CHAKRA SYSTEM

The twelve-chakra system features three types of kundalini. The red or serpent kundalini activates physical life energy and rises from the lower spine. The golden kundalini provides spiritual insight and enters through the top of the head. The radiant kundalini is the key to enlightenment and radiates from the center of the chakras.

perfect codes for your physical and energetic body. Through it you access accurate DNA patterns and use intention, vibrational methods, or various techniques to translate healing directly into the body.

- The *light body* is a series of vibratory energy bands that emanate from the central core of the body. When opened, these surround the body and allow it to tap into the various planes of existence that surround the body.

KUNDALINI AND THE TWELVE-CHAKRA SYSTEM

THE TWELVE-CHAKRA SYSTEM features the traditional serpent or red kundalini—the undulating, rising snake that awakens—but also two other kundalini processes. *Radiant kundalini* is comparable to the actual enlightened state, the shimmering of one's spirit throughout each chakra and therefore, the entire body. This kundalini can only be activated when someone is willing to fully serve others and the divine. Its appearance is also contingent on the fulfillment of yet another kundalini: the *golden kundalini*, which descends from on high rather than rising from below.

The golden kundalini is personalized spiritual energy. It carries the wisdom of one's individual soul into the body along a "river" of divine white light. The process begins when even a tiny amount of serpent, or red, kundalini has ascended to the crown chakra. At this point, the ninth chakra, which lies about a foot and a half above the head, opens to the cosmic energy that continually swirls above it. This white energy reflects the merged union of the feminine and masculine divine, the energy of "God" and the "Goddess." Upon entering the ninth chakra, this celestial energy turns golden, colored by the golden hue of the ninth chakra.

The ninth chakra contains an individual's soul "genes," the codes that make a soul unique. The stream of divinity absorbs the personal traits, patterns, gifts, and purpose of the soul and then flows into the body, first passing through the eighth chakra, which is also atop the head, before entering the physical body through the seventh chakra at the crown. From here, the now golden kundalini travels through the chakra system, depositing the soul's wisdom and also activating the spiritual energies present within the center of each chakra. The golden kundalini also conjoins with the red serpent kundalini, paradoxically merging and remaining separate. It also softens the sometimes harsh effects of the red kundalini and eventually, interlaced with it, runs up and down the spine and around the auric field to serve as a protective membrane.

The radiant kundalini can only be activated after the red and golden kundalinis have both been awakened and are working in concert. This kundalini literally radiates from the center of each chakra, which contains the spiritual essence of a person, and marks him or her as an in-body avatar.

Perhaps the best illustration of the golden kundalini was Sri Caitanya Mahuprabhu, or the "Golden Avatar." Caitanya lived in the early 1500s in Bengal, and was well known for his supernatural powers and compassionate nature.[72]

Chakras function on bands of frequency. If these are disturbed by any number of factors, such as childhood issues, soul misperceptions, disease or trauma, abuse, religious or cultural negativity, prejudice, or other problems, these vibrational bands go "off pitch." To cope, the body reaches into the world to attempt to fill in or subtract energy to rebalance itself. Unfortunately, most of the seeming solutions are addictive or dangerous substances or behaviors, each of which operate on and emit a set frequency.[73]

One primary addiction area is food. Over 60 percent of Americans are now overweight and about 30 percent of these are considered obese.[74] One of the reasons for food addictions is malnutrition, which is a global problem, even among nations that have affluence and a cornucopia of foods. The soil has been stripped of nutrients; our water sources are polluted; and chemicals, hormones, and additives are altering the makeup of the food as well as of our bodies. Lack leads to cravings. In addition to psychological factors, such as addictions to looking young and thin, as well as to fast foods, the Western world in particular is a replete with food issues.

Each chakra has a different relationship with physical substances including food. Following is an outline of addictive issues that arise through the various chakras.

FIGURE 5.30
CHAKRAS AND ADDICTIONS

Chakra	Addictions: Substances/Behaviors
First	Hard drugs, alcohol, work, sex, being ill or sick, getting in accidents, exercise, cutting, sadistic or masochistic behaviors, spending, debt, milk, fat, and meat
Second	Gluten, wheat, starchy carbohydrates, grain-based alcohol, chocolate, certain or all emotions (as in emotionalism)
Third	Work, perfectionism, marijuana, caffeine, carbonated beverages, corn-based alcohol, beer, and corn-processed sugar
Fourth	Ecstasy (the drug); love (as in having to be in love all the time); specific relationships (persons you can't "let go of"); smoking; wine, sugar, sweets, and false sugars, such as saccharin or aspartame
Fifth	Compulsive talking or reading; compulsive overeating; smoking or chewing of tobacco
Sixth	Self-hatred (as in poor body image); appearances (as in compulsively worrying about); chocolate; and all mood-altering substances and behaviors, including hand-washing, criticalness, and more
Seventh	"Uppers" or "downers"; fanatical religion; prayer or meditation to avoid reality; depression or anxiety

FIGURE 5.30
CHAKRAS AND ADDICTIONS

Chakra	Addictions: Substances/Behaviors
Eighth	Substances that can be used in healing, such as tobacco, nicotine, coffee, and alcohol; the shamanic personality uses these to attempt to process others' issues, which he or she absorbs
Ninth	Poverty, scarcity, doing good for others—to the point of hurting the self; the ninth-chakra personality is an idealist and can sometimes hurt the self to help the world
Tenth	Psilocybin mushrooms; exercise that involves the outdoors if used for escapism (such as hiking); concentration on animals or nature if used to avoid people; root vegetables or foods, nuts, chemicals
Eleventh	Negativity, power (as in having to be in control)
Twelfth	Immature behaviors and relationships of any sort

THE JEWISH MYSTICAL ENERGY SYSTEM: THE ANCIENT KABBALAH

NOTE: There are many spellings for Kabbalah: Kaballah, Quaballah, Qabalah, and Kabala, among others. There are also other ways to spell *sephiroth*—the major consciousness centers of the Kabbalah—including *sefirot* or *sephirot*, as well as the names of the different sephiroth. The spellings chosen are not meant to select a "right" over a "wrong" way. They will be used consistently, however, for ease of reading.

THE ROOTS OF THE KABBALAH

The Kabbalah is a mystical energetic system originating with the ancient Hebrews. It is perhaps the most universal and fundamental energy system, explaining the origin of the world, the Creator, a complex set of energy bodies, and the connecting between the human and the divine. While labeled as "Jewish," components of the Kabbalah are widely dispersed among dozens of cultures and across thousands of years. The system presented here is considered a mixture of the Jewish Kabbalah and ideas from the Egyptian, Chaldean, and African Kabbalah, as well as contemporary applications as presented by authors including Ted Andrews and Rabbi Laibl Wolf.[75]

The word *Qabalah* comes from *qibel*, "to receive." One legend asserts that the knowledge of the Kabbalah was first given to Moses on Mount Sinai during the burning of the bush. Another story relays that God taught it to the angels, who then passed it on to the children of earth so that we may overcome the earth plane and ascend again to the heavens. Whatever the true origin of the Kabbalah, the story leaps forward to Rabbi Joseph ben Akiva, who lived between AD 50 and 132. In a trance state, Rabbi Akiva wrote a number of papers called "The Way of the Chariot" (*Maaseh Merkava)*, reflections on sacred Jewish knowledge. He conducted this illuminating soul journey with three other colleagues, all of whom received a vision of God made of infinite light. Only ben Akiva survived the experience.

His work was expanded and eventually called the Kabbalah, centuries later, by the mystic Solomon ibn Gabirol. The Kabbalists formed a secret society, looking for the mysterious connections between the teachings of the Torah and other subjects, including numbers and the Hebrew alphabet. Yet another formulation, called the Zohar, became the backbone of the Kabbalistic world.

The Kabbalah starts with the idea that we are each a mini-universe. All forces of the universe are available to us, but to manifest them we require a map. The Tree of Life is such a map, revealing the keys to accessing the energies, powers, forces, and life forms of the universe in our lives.

The Tree of Life symbolizes the microcosmic and macrocosmic view of the universe. In reference to the Tree, we are rooted in the earth and stretching toward the heavens. This Tree evolved from the beginning of time—when there was only nothingness (called *Daath*). Everything existed within this nothingness, but nothing had begun—until the Divine evolved through nine stages of manifestation to end with a tenth, physical embodiment. This way the Divine laid a "return path" for our own evolution and attainment of enlightenment. Each stage can be seen as its own branch. These branches are the Ten Holy Sephiroth, or spheres of consciousness. There are twenty-two lines, called paths, connecting these different sephiroth. Together, the sephiroth and the paths form the Twenty-two Paths of Wisdom, gateways of experience to greater spiritual attunement.

These sephiroth are equivalent to energy bodies, and the paths analogous to energy channels. Together, they compose an energy system equivalent to the Hindu chakra/nadi system that encourages soul evolution through the serpentine flow of kundalini. Unlike the Hindu centers, however, the sephiroth are not considered true physiologic centers. Rather, they are symbolic centers, and the body is metaphor.

THE TEN SEPHIROTH

The sephiroth can be described in many ways. Typically a sephira is related to a specific title, which reflects its primary principle or energy: a God name, revealing one particular nature of the one true God; an archangel or order of angels serving as gatekeepers or guides for that sphere; a placement in relation to the body; a vice, or the potential imbalance that occurs if we do not fully realize the sphere's lessons; a virtue, or the quality necessary to fully embody this sphere; a learning, which represents the wisdom we can achieve through this sphere; a celestial body; and a color.

FIGURE 5.31
THE TREE OF LIFE: THE TEN SEPHIROTH

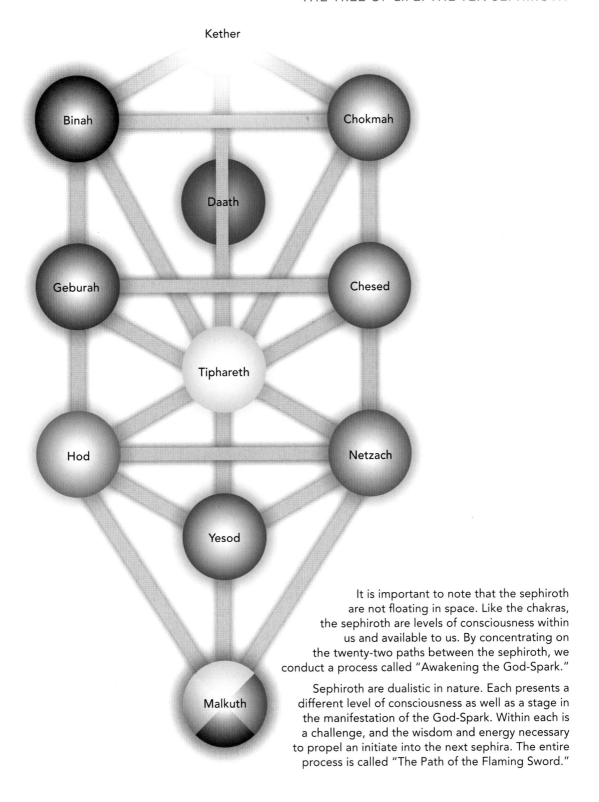

Kether

Binah

Chokmah

Daath

Geburah

Chesed

Tiphareth

Hod

Netzach

Yesod

Malkuth

It is important to note that the sephiroth are not floating in space. Like the chakras, the sephiroth are levels of consciousness within us and available to us. By concentrating on the twenty-two paths between the sephiroth, we conduct a process called "Awakening the God-Spark."

Sephiroth are dualistic in nature. Each presents a different level of consciousness as well as a stage in the manifestation of the God-Spark. Within each is a challenge, and the wisdom and energy necessary to propel an initiate into the next sephira. The entire process is called "The Path of the Flaming Sword."

Malkuth, for example, is the tenth sphere and provides a connection with the elemental world. Its God name is Adonai HaAretz, the God that works within the physical world. This sephira is attended by the archangel Sandalphon and the angelic order of the Ashim or the Flames of Fire, essentially the saints from earth. Located near the feet, it rules the body and senses, brings forth the vices of inertia and greed, and calls forth the virtue of discernment. Earthen in coloration, it rules the celestial body of the earth.

Following is an overview of each of the ten sephiroth in addition to a space called *Daath*, which is technically not a sphere or sephira. Rather it reflects the empty space that holds everything that could be created.

THE SEPHIROTH AND CHAKRIC ASSOCIATIONS

THERE ARE MANY ways to work with the Tree of Life, including through its association to the chakra system—and through it, to the physical body and the different bodily systems. The following is an outline of these relationships, according to Will Parfitt in his book, *The Elements of the Qabalah*.[76]

FIGURE 5.32
SEPHIROTH AND CHAKRIC ASSOCIATIONS

Bodily System	Sephira, Chakra, or Path	Human Attribute or Body Part
Central Nervous System	Kether	Life energy and consciousness
	Chokmah	Left hemisphere of brain
	Binah	Right hemisphere of brain
	Sixth and seventh chakras	Head and back
	Path 1–2	Left eye, ear, pituitary
	Path 1–3	Right eye, ear, pineal
	Path 2–3	Nose, mouth
	Path 1–6	Spinal cord
	Paths 6–9	Spinal cord, solar plexus
Cardiovascular and Respiratory Systems	Tiphareth	Heart, thymus
	Fourth chakra	Heart, thorax
	Path 2–6	Arteries, oxygenated blood
	Path 3–6	Veins, deoxygenated blood
	Path 4–5	Spleen, lymph
	Path 4–6	Left lung
	Path 5–6	Right lung

MALKUTH, THE TENTH SPHERE: CONNECTING WITH THE ELEMENTAL WORLD

Malkuth is the closest to our daily consciousness and most directly affects our physical life. It receives energies from each of the other sephiroth, as it was the last to incarnate the Divine Spark. It allows us to access the Divine within the physical realm.

YESOD, THE NINTH SPHERE: ESTABLISHING YOUR FOUNDATION

Yesod is the sphere in which everything is possible. It presents the deepest images and motives of our mind and personality. From it, we form the ideas and beliefs that will manifest in the physical world.

Within Yesod, we notice the rhythms and cycles of life and our own desires. Here lie the subconscious and the biological and psychic functions of our lives. Working with Yesod allows you to create visualizations, templates for accessing energy from the other levels.

FIGURE 5.32
SEPHIROTH AND CHAKRIC ASSOCIATIONS

Bodily System	Sephira, Chakra, or Path	Human Attribute or Body Part
Digestive and Excretory Systems	Netzach	Left kidney
	Hod	Right kidney
	Third chakra	Solar plexus/abdomen
	Path 4–7	Large intestine (descending), rectum
	Path 6–7	Stomach
	Path 5–8	Large intestine (ascending and transverse)
	Path 6–8	Liver, gallbladder, pancreas
	Path 7–8	Small intestine
	Path 9–10	Bladder, skin
Reproductive System	Yesod	Sexual organs
	Second chakra	Inner and outer sexual organs
	Path 7–9	Male: left seminal vesicle, vas deferens Female: left uterine tube, ovaries
	Path 8–9	Male: right seminal vesicle, vas deferens Female: right uterine tube, ovaries
Locomotor System	Malkuth	Body as a whole, feet
	First chakra	Legs, feet, skeletal and muscular systems
	Path 7–10	Left skeleton, bones, muscles
	Path 8–10	Right skeleton, bones, muscles

HOD, THE EIGHTH SPHERE: ACHIEVING EMPATHETIC THOUGHT

Hod is often called *Glory*, which describes the types of thoughts and ideas we want governing our minds. This sphere is primarily devoted to communication; on it we are encouraged to work with higher ideas, words, and teachings, often those related to alchemy and the mysteries. Hod also governs travel, movement, and thinking.

NETZACH, THE SEVENTH SPHERE: EMBRACING MEANING THROUGH FEELINGS

Look around—the world is full of beauty, and on Netzach we are presented the insight to see it. Here, we are asked to become aware of the profound exquisiteness of creation, and to triumph over the emotions that prevent us from being grateful.

We all know that emotions can lead into bliss or despair. Netzach represents feeling, and on the Tree of Life it is counterbalanced with Hod, or thought. True mastery over—and with—our emotions, including our sexual drives, is possible if we balance these two seeming polarities by reaching for love. It is little wonder that Netzach is represented by a lightning bolt—the inspiration we need to create with our passions.

TIPHARETH, THE SIXTH SPHERE: OPENING THE WISE HEART

This is the place of sheer wonder, where we find the sun of truth within ourselves. Tiphareth is located at the center of the Tree of Life, revealing its importance. Here we are asked if we are willing to give of ourselves—even to the point of sacrificing ourselves—for the love of others.

GEBURAH, THE FIFTH SPHERE: SUMMONING INNER STRENGTH

Are we ready to own and reveal our inner strength and power? Geburah governs change and decisions, inviting us to leap forward with courage—intelligently. On this level, expect to uncover the upside and downside of power, for we cannot achieve our will without learning about the two-edged sword of force. Ultimately, this sphere raises our conscious awareness of the ethical use of power and force.

CHESED, THE FOURTH SPHERE: OPENING THE FLOW OF LOVE

Chesed is at the core of humanity's aspirations for compassion and grace. The energy on this sphere is often compared to the fluidity of water. Here we must allow the stream of higher feelings to quench the needs of others.

DAATH, THE NON-SPHERE THAT IS THE VOID

Each of us has the potential for greatness—great good, or great evil. We make the choice in Daath, the void from which everything has—and will—emerge. Here, in our upper heart area, we find the gateway through which we can "pull creative energy" and manifest what we truly desire, if we can confront our fears of the unknown.

BINAH, THE THIRD SPHERE: SHIFTING TO HIGHER THINKING

Herein lies understanding, the achievement of shifting from mundane and critical thinking to higher thoughts. Within Binah, we are encouraged to see through our struggles and perceive what we are gaining through them.

CHOKMAH, THE SECOND SPHERE: SEEING THROUGH ILLUSION

In Chokmah, we are invited to peel away deception and cloudy thinking, revealing the pure wonder of the universe. This sphere often calls forth our inner gifts and extraordinary abilities.

KETHER, THE FIRST SPHERE: ACCEPTING THE CROWNING GLORY

Kether lies at the crown, the top of the Tree, where we are closest to the unified energy of Ein Sof. This is our source—the place we descended *from* and are now ascending *to*. It was the first manifestation of creation and represents purity.

HEALING WITH BODIES OF LIGHT

As we've seen, the human body is really a universe composed of energy bodies—swirling vortices of light that literally transform sensory energy to spiritual, and vice versa. By employing the knowledge of these bodies of light in healing, one is able to convert what is possible and make it probable—and potentially, quite real.

What are some of the processes that help practitioners and patients make use of chakra knowledge, as well as that of the other subtle structures? Turn to Part VI to find out.

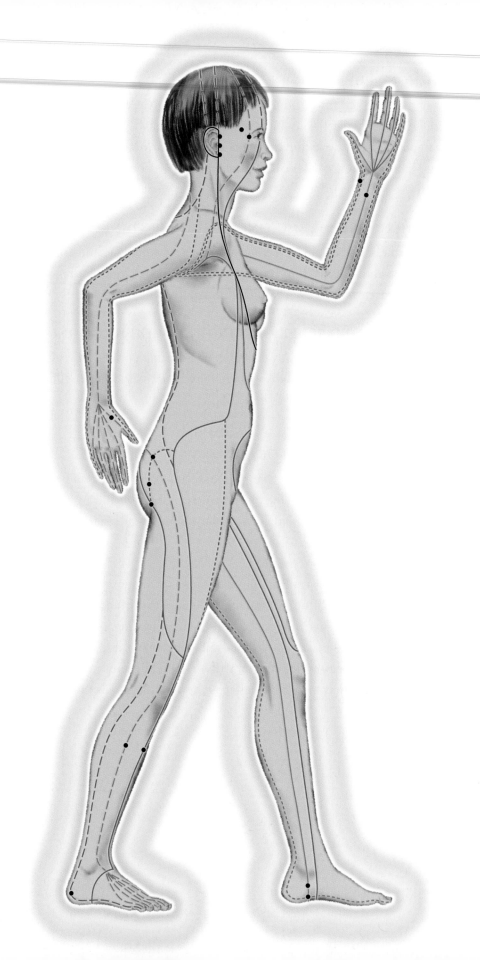

PART VI

ENERGY PRACTICES

This section describes a variety of vibrationally based healing systems that affect the subtle anatomy. Many of them are based in the physical body but also work with or through the subtle energies.

The healing systems featured here incorporate subtle energy work and at least two of the three main energetic structures: the fields, channels, or bodies. This section also includes brief descriptions of dozens of other energy healing practices that have not been described in the book so far. There are hundreds of energy-based practices; these are simply representative of those that are available.

ACUPUNCTURE

Acupuncture is the practice of placing needles along the acupoints of the meridian system in order to restore balance in the body.

Acupoints are located just below the epidermis. Specially designed needles are inserted into these points, usually about a quarter of an inch into the skin, to help correct the flow of energy within the body. The practitioner might leave the needles following the puncture or twist or twirl them for up to ten minutes. They might be left in from a few minutes to about half an hour.

Traditional practitioners often employ moxibustion, which is described below, as an adjunct to acupuncture.

Some of the more contemporary treatment techniques include stimulating the acupoints with color, tuning forks, an electric current, or magnets, as discussed in the sections below. Other leading-edge techniques include use of a *tae shin*, a small springlike device that substitutes for a needle; a

FIGURE 6.1
ACUPUNCTURE

Acupuncture involves the placement of needles along the points of the meridian system in order to balance the body.

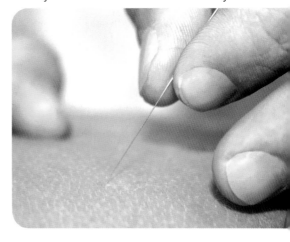

piezoelectric stimulator, best known for assisting with pain relief; and the HeNe or helium-neon laser.[1]

ACUPUNCTURE ANALGESIA

Acupuncture has been used for centuries as a pain reliever; some people use it instead of anesthesia for surgery. This form of acupuncture, called *acupuncture analgesia*, has its basis in body chemistry. Researchers have long understood that certain sites in the body can produce endorphins, which raise people's spirits as well as their resistance to pain. Scientists have also discovered that morphine exists within the body, which might account for some of the pain-dulling responses of acupuncture. A French research team has described a new pain pathway called the *spino-ponto-amygdaloid pathway*, which seems to facilitate pain relief. Other theories concentrate on the existence of serotonin receptor sites throughout the body, which might also be accessible through acupuncture.[2]

MOXIBUSTION

Moxibustion involves the use of dried mugwort leaves that, upon being lit, are placed close to an acupuncture point to create warmth. The mugwort comes in a cigar-like stick or in a paste. Moxibustion is most frequently used for chronic diseases such as arthritis, PMS, abdominal and stomach problems, indigestion, chronic diarrhea, and other similar conditions. It should not be used with force or to treat hot conditions; nor is it to be applied to the womb area of a pregnant woman. Moxibustion can also be used in conjunction with the needles during acupuncture.

FIGURE 6.2
MOXIBUSTION

Moxibustion is the practice of placing burning dried mugwort leaves near an acupuncture point. The leaves help pull toxins out of the body.

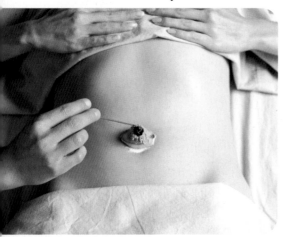

CUPPING

Cupping involves creating a vacuum with a cup to release stagnation in the body, usually using an earthenware, glass, or bamboo cup. Varying size cups are applied depending on the body part being worked on. A cotton ball is burned in the cup to create a vacuum and, after safely discarding the ball, the cup is placed over the acupuncture points that require attention. The cup is kept in this position for five to ten minutes to encourage the drawing forth of the chi. The patient is often left with bruising, which disappears in a few days. Because of the bruising, care should be taken to be certain the patient does not have a blood or skin condition that could worsen with this treatment.

ELECTROACUPUNCTURE AND ELECTRODERMAL SCREENING

FIGURE 6.3

CUPPING

Electroacupuncture is a form of electrotherapy that directs an electric current through the acupuncture points. It begins with tracking the electromagnetics of the patient's body and continues by delivering a treatment electrically.

With cupping, a practitioner uses a cup to create a vacuum along a meridian line or acupoint to stimulate chi.

Electroacupuncture is an extension of acupuncture needling. One of the first forms of it was invented in China in 1934.[3] Treatment involved sending electrical currents between two needles. The system has since been modernized. In its fundamental form, a practitioner first conducts a diagnosis and then inserts needles. Next, the needles are attached to an electrical device, which delivers a continual flow of electrical pulses, the frequency and intensity of which can be adjusted. Several pairs of needles can be used at the same time.[4] The benefits of electroacupuncture, as opposed to manipulating the needles by hand, is that the stimulation is more consistent, controlled, and of stronger intensity.

This fundamental type of electroacupuncture is most frequently used for pain relief and to treat physical trauma. Versions of it are called *percutaneous electrical nerve stimulation* or PENS. According to traditional Chinese medicine theory, pain is caused by congestion or stagnation. The additional stimulation is thought to "jolt" the stagnation and therefore, reduce inflammation.

How does electroacupuncture work? Probably the same way that acupuncture does. The theory is that the electrical current stimulates the acupuncture points, exciting the nerve pathways in the deep tissue and spine. This activates the body's ability to stop pain signals from reaching the brain and produces analgesia in the form of endorphins and enkephalins.

A new wave of electroacupuncture devices has flooded the market. Some of these are based on the Ryodoraku system, developed by Dr. Yoshio Nakatani, who presented his research in 1951. He found a series of highly conductive points running up and down the body, closely matching the meridians. He called them the *Ryodoraku*—good (*ryo*), electro (*do*), and line (*radu*)— and called the points *Ryodoten*.[5] Nakatani theorized that many of the points he used occurred along tracts of the autonomic nervous system and represented internal dysfunctions. Needling renders the points electrically benign and results in symptomatic relief.

The majority of Western devices are based on the work of Reinhold Voll of Germany. In 1958, Voll combined acupuncture with a galvanometer to diagnose and treat energy imbalances. His method is called Electroacupuncture According to Voll (EAV), as well as *electrodermal screening* (EDS), bioelectric functions diagnosis (BFD), bioresonance therapy (BRT), meridian stress assessment (MSA), and bioenergy regulatory technique (BER). Voll expands upon traditional acupuncture in three ways. He discovered previously unknown meridians, which he called "systems," as well as unknown points on the classic meridians, and unknown functions of existing points. His understanding of meridians incorporated traditional Chinese thinking and covered concepts involving the tissues, joints, skin, lymphatic drainage, and allergic reactions.[6]

THE KUBOTA ZONE ACUPUNCTURE SYSTEM[7]

Dr. Naoki Kubota, who holds several degrees in acupuncture, created a highly effective acupuncture system after more than thirty years of practice and study. The Kubota system uses single-needle acupuncture techniques to deliver pain control, healing, cleansing, and balancing. It is included in this book because his chart demonstrates a thorough treatment program that combines Western and Eastern thought. It also highlights techniques from both traditional Chinese and Japanese acupuncture.

Kubota's system blends the science, theories, and techniques of both Oriental and Western medicine. He has studied Japanese and Chinese acupuncture and worked with Western medical doctors in their practices. His Oriental training is in the centuries-old form of Japanese acupuncture called *Ishizaka Ryu* and the ancient Chinese acupuncture system of *Hua Tuo Jiaji*.

Based on his work with these Oriental systems, Kubota believes that the spine and spinal areas are the most important ones in the body; in terms of meridians, he emphasizes the Governor vessel and the Bladder meridians. He also works with more than three hundred acupuncture points on the spinal area, including the meridian points, Hua Tuo Jiaji points, and newfound points. Other traditions, including yoga and Taoism, also believe that the spine is the center of the body and the site of the main energy flow. Many Westerners would not argue with this, as anatomically the nerves start in the brain and travel down the spinal cord, thereby regulating the entire body.

As do most Eastern practitioners, Dr. Kubota understands that the energy flow of the body, blood, and bodily fluids must be in constant, unobstructed motion, or disease and pain will set in. He works mainly with the crossing points of the gravity line and the spine. These are: cranio-atlas, cervical-thoracic, thoracic-lumbar, and lumbar-sacrum.

It is common to have indurations, or signs of inflammation, midway between each of these areas. These indurations receive the primary concentration of treatments.

The application of Kubota Zone Acupuncture is different from other acupuncture procedures. In traditional Oriental acupuncture, multiple needles are inserted at specific points on the body and left in place for a duration of time while the patient lies still. Kubota Zone Acupuncture uses one needle that is applied through a tube to many specific points on the body. The needle is repeatedly inserted and removed in a continuing motion. At no time is it inserted and left in place. This procedure is painless and does not require the patient to remain still. Pain relief usually occurs within a short period of time, and healing begins. Dr. Kubota provides training in the four main needling processes used in his program.

AURA-SOMA THERAPY[8]

Aura-Soma therapy is a relatively new phenomenon on the color healing scene. Developed by Vicky Wall, this healing method combines the vibrational powers of color, crystals, aromas, and lights to harmonize all aspects of the self. Many of Wall's ideas originated in early studies among the Hassidim, as her father was a Kabbalah scholar and a follower of Zohar; these are mystical traditions that employ knowledge of philosophy, energy, and medicinal herbal therapies.

In the early 1980s, Vicky became blind, but was able to "feel" a voice that enabled her to create "magical bottles" of various colors, each of which represents a different property. Her system is based on the idea that every color is a wavelength of light that can influence the emotions through the chakras. A patient selects his or her own bottles or colors, thereby self-diagnosing and self-healing.

MEANING OF THE AURA-SOMA COLORS

Red: Energy, grounding, survival issues.
Coral: Unrequited love.
Orange: Independence/dependency; shock and trauma; insight and bliss.
Gold: Wisdom and intense fear.
Yellow: Acquired knowledge.
Olive: Clarity and wisdom.
Green: Space; search for truth.
Turquoise: Communication, especially related to mass media or creativity.
Blue: Peace and communication.
Royal blue: Knowing why one is here.
Violet: Spirituality, healing, service.
Magenta: Love for the little things.

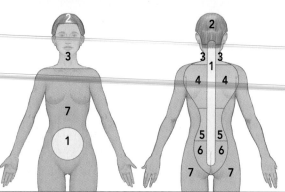

FIGURE 6.4
KUBOTA ACUPUNCTURE ZONES[9]

Zones	Left Side of the Body						
1 Primary Zone	Primary Treatment for the Whole Body, Abdomen Front, Paraspinal Back						
2 Cranial Zone	Brain, Pituitary, Hair, Scalp, Head						
3 Face and Cervical Zone	Other Relationships	Organs		Endocrine Glands	Joints	Musculature	Sense Organs
		Yang	Yin				
	Schizophrenic Mental Diseases Migraine Arterial Concentration of All Organs	Gallbladder C5–C7 Stomach C5–C7 Duodenum C5–C7	Left Lung C5–C7 Heart, Liver C3, C5–C7 Pancreas C5–C7	Pituitary Posterior Lobe C5–C7 Anterior Lobe C8 Thyroid C5–C7 Pineal C5–C7	Shoulder, Elbow, Radial Hand, Foot, Big Toe, Sacroiliac Joint, Inner Knees C5–C7 Ulnar Hand, Plantar Foot, Toes, Sacroiliac Joint C8	Trunk, Lower and Upper Extremities Musculature C5–C7	Frontal Sinus C2, C3 Maxillary Sinus C5–C8 Eye C5–C8 Inner Ear C8 Mouth C3, C5–8
4 Thoracic Zone	Lack of Concentration Stagnation / Anger Depression Moodiness / Fear Instability Blood Density Stagnation Connective Tissue Diseases Kidney Stones Mammary Glands Crystallization of Body Fluid	Gallbladder T2–T4, . T8–T10 Stomach T2–T4, T11, T12 Duodenum T2–T5 Small Intestine T3, T4 Large Intestine T2–T4	Left Lung T2–T4, T8–T10 Heart T1, T5–T7 Liver T2–T5 Pancreas T2–T5 Spleen T11, T12 Left Kidney T2, T3, T11, T12	Parotid T1, T2 Pituitary Posterior Lobe T2–T4, T8, T9–T12 Pituitary Anterior Lobe T5–T7 Thyroid T2–T4, T6, T7 Parathyroid T11, T12 Appendix T2, T3, T9 Adrenals T11, T12 Gonads T8–T10 Pineal T2, T3, T6, T7, T11, T12	Shoulder, Elbow, Radial Hand, Big Toe, Sacroiliac Joint, Inner Knees T3–T6 Shoulder Elbow, Ulnar Hand, Plantar Foot, Toes, Sacroiliac Joint T1, T5, T6, T7 Foot Hips, Knee (posterior) T8–T12 Mandibular Joint, Knee (anterior) T11, T12	Lower and Upper Extremities Musculature T2–T12 Trunk Musculature T2–T5, T8–T12	Eye T1, T2, T3, T4, T5, T6, T8, T9, T10 Maxillary Sinus T1–T7, T11, T12 Ear T1, T5, T6, T7 Mouth T1–T12
5 Lumbar Zone	Lymph Sexual Organs Vascular Tone Blood Count Defensive Mechanism Crystallization of Body Fluid	Stomach L1, L4, L5 Bladder Urogenital L2, L3 Small Intestine L4, L5 Large Intestine L4, L5	Spleen, Left Kidney L1–L3 Pancreas L1, L4, L5 Left Lung L4, L5	Pituitary Anterior Lobe L4, L5 Thyroid L1, L4, L5 Appendix L4, L5 Pineal, Gonads L1–L5	Mandibular Joint, Knee (anterior) Hip, Left Foot L1 Foot, Sacrum, Coccyx, Knee (posterior) L2, L3 Shoulder, Elbow, Radial Hand, Foot, Big Toe, Sacroiliac Joint, Inner Knee L4, L5	Trunk L1–L5 Upper Extremities L2, L3 Lower and Upper Extremities Musculature L2–L5	Maxillary Sinus L1 Frontal Sinus L2, L3 Sinus L4, L5 Mouth L1–L5
6 Sacrum Coccyx Zone	Mental Behavior Hormone Metabolism Kidney Stones Sciatica	Small Intestine S1–S3 Bladder Urogenital S3–S5	Heart S1–S3 Liver S1–S3 Left Kidney S3–S5	Pituitary Anterior Lobe S1–S3 Adrenal, Pineal, Epididymis S3– S5	Shoulder Elbow, Ulnar Hand, Plantar Foot, Toes, Sacroiliac Joint S1–S3 Foot, Sacrum, Coccyx Knee (posterior) S3–S5	Trunk, Upper Extremities Musculature S1–S3 Lower Extremities S3–S5	Inner Ear S1–S3 Maxillary Sinus S1, S2 Eye, Ear S1, S2 Mouth S1–S5
		Bladder Urogenital	Left Kidney	Adrenals, Pineal, Epididymis	Foot, Sacrum, Coccyx, Knee	Lower Extremities	Frontal Sinus, Mouth
7 Symptomatic Zone	Upper and Lower Extremities, Trunk						

Center of the Body	Right Side of the Body							Zones
Area of Primary Concentration of Treatments	Primary Treatment for the Whole Body, Abdomen Front, Paraspinal Back							1 Primary Zone
	Brain, Pituitary, Hair, Scalp, Head							2 Cranial Zone
Spinal Chord Segments	Sense Organs	Musculature	Joints	Endocrine Glands	Organs		Other Relationships	3 Face and Cervical Zone
C1–C8	Eye C5–C8 Ear C8 Inner Ear C8 Maxillary Sinus C8 Mouth C5–C8	Trunk, Lower and Upper Extremities Musculature C5–8	Shoulder, Elbow, Radial Hand, Foot, Big Toe, Sacroiliac Joint, Inner Knees C5–C7 Ulnar Hand, Plantar Foot, Toes, Sacroiliac Joint C3	Pituitary C5–C7 Pituitary Anterior Lobe C8 Thyroid, Thymus C5–C7 Pineal, Appendages C5–C7	**Yin** Lung, Liver, Pancreas C5–C7 Heart C8	**Yang** Stomach, Small and Large Intestines C5–C7 Duodenum, Ileum C8	Schizophrenic Mental Diseases Migraine Arterial Concentration of All Organs	
T1–T12	Eye T1, T3–T10 Maxillary Sinus T5–T7, T11, T12 Ear T1, T5–T7 Mouth T1–T12	Trunk, Lower and Upper Extremities Musculature T1–T12	Shoulder Elbow, Ulnar Hand, Plantar Foot, Toes, Sacroiliac Joint T1 Foot, Hip, Knee (posterior) Foot, Hip, Knee (anterior), Mandible, Shoulder T3, T11–T12	Parotid T1, T2 Pituitary T2–T4, T11, T12 Pituitary Posterior Lobe T8–T10 Pituitary Anterior Lobe T1, T5, T7 Thyroid T2–T4, T11, T12 Parathyroid T11, T12 Adrenals T11, T12 Gonads T3, T9–T12 Pineal T11, T12	Right Lung T2–T4, T9 Heart T1, T5–T10 Liver T2–T4, T8–T12 Pancreas T3, T9–T12 Kidney T11, T12	Duodenum T1–T7 Stomach T3, T4, T11, T12 Gallbladder T2, T3, T8–T10 Large Intestine T2, T4 Small Intestine T3, T4 Pylorus T11, T12 Bladder T11, T12	Lack of Concentration Stagnation Anger Depression Moodiness Fear / Instability Blood Density Stagnation Connective Tissue Diseases Kidney Stones Mammary Glands Crystallization of Body Fluid	4 Thoracic Zone
L1–L5	Frontal Sinus L2, L3 Sinus L4, L5 Eye L4, L5 Mouth L1–L5	Trunk Musculature L1, L4, L5 Lower Extremities L2, L3	Foot, Hip, Knee (posterior) L2, L3 Knee (anterior) L1 Foot, Sacrum, Coccyx L2 Shoulder, Elbow, Radial Hand, Foot, Big Toe, Sacroiliac Joint, Inner Knee L4, L5	Pituitary L4, L5 Thyroid L1, L4, L5 Parathyroid L1 Adrenals L2, L3 Pineal, Appendages L1–L5 Gonads L1 Pineal L2, L3	Right Lung L4, L5 Liver, Pancreas L1, L4, L5 Right Kidney L1–L5	Stomach L4, L5 Gallbladder L4 Urogenital L2, L3 Small and Large Intestines L4, L5	Lymph Sexual Organs Vascular Tone Blood Count Defensive Mechanism Crystallization of Body Fluid	5 Lumbar Zone
S1–S5	Inner Ear S1–S3 Maxillary Sinus S1–S3 Eye, Ear S1–S3 Mouth S1–S5	Trunk, Upper Extremities Musculature S1–S3 Lower Extremities S3–S5	Shoulder Elbow, Ulnar Hand, Plantar Foot, Toes, Sacroiliac Joint S1–S3 Foot, Sacrum, Coccyx, Knee (posterior) S3–S5	Pituitary Anterior Lobe S1–S3 Adrenals, Pineal, Epididymis S3– S5	Heart S1–S3 Kidney S3–S5	Duodenum, Ileum S1–S3 Bladder, Urogenital S3–S5	Mental Behavior Hormone Metabolism Kidney Stones Sciatica	6 Sacrum Coccyx Zone
Coccyx	Frontal Sinus, Mouth	Lower Extremities	Foot, Sacrum, Coccyx, Knee	Adrenals, Pineal, Epididymis	Right Kidney	Bladder Urogenital		
	Use as Symptomatic Treatments							7 Symptomatic Zone

Pink: Unconditional love and caring.

Clear (white): Suffering and the understanding of suffering.

Ayurveda is an ancient health system from India, at least three thousand years old, that considers disease a matter of improper balance, or lack of moderation. Meaning "knowledge of long life," Ayurveda works closely with the chakra system as well as knowledge of various energetic fields, and is as complex and thorough as the traditional Chinese medical system. Legend states that it was received in divine revelation from the Lord God Brahma.

There are eight areas of Ayurveda practice, which include internal medicine; surgery; ear, eyes, nose, and throat; pediatrics; toxicology; purification of the organs; health and longevity; and spiritual healing.

The core philosophy is that disease is science-based and usually begins with *purana indigestion,* the "parent of all diseases." This means that most diseases start in the gastrointestinal tract, where undigested food, called *ama,* congests. When we eat improper food or are upset when eating, we begin to progress down five stages of disease:

1. *Chaya.* The initial stage. The imbalance is situated in the gastrointestinal tract and is best treated with diet.
2. *Prakopa.* The buildup stage. Ama collects, liquefies, and causes symptoms including thirst, burning sensations, flatulence, and the spread of toxicity into the circulatory system.
3. *Prasava.* The spreading stage. The toxins journey through the main circulatory systems of the body and settle at a weak spot.
4. *Sthana-sanskriya.* Toxins accumulate at the weak spot, creating an improper balance of one of the three *doshas* (see "Three Constitutions, or Doshas" below). The disease emerges fully. At this point, a patient begins to take medicine.
5. *Dosha-kara.* Administering of medicine to treat the symptoms. Seen as changing the disease environment.

THE MENTAL ASPECT OF DISEASE

Shad-vritta means "mental culture." Ayurveda embraces the philosophy that disease has a psychic foundation. Illness starts in the mental field, and so it is important to maintain high ethical standards and integrity in one's life in order to prevent disease.

Two chief emotional traps are anxiety and anger, which are considered mental pollutants. Shad-vritta principles are grounded in the teachings of the Bhagavad-Gita, a sacred writing, and include being noble, compassionate, speaking the truth, controlling negative thoughts, avoiding self-consciousness, doing one's duty, maintaining mental equilibrium, and cultivating learning and forgiveness.

THREE CONSTITUTIONS, OR DOSHAS

Eating correctly, as well as tending to emotions, depends upon the patient's body type or constitution, which is called a *dosha*. Doshas are determined by elements as well as physical attributes. These are the three principles behind the doshas:

- *Vayu-dosha* is an impulse principle that manages the nervous system and is made of air and ether.
- *Pitta-dosha* is an energy principle that runs the bile, or metabolic, system and is composed of fire and water.
- *Kapha-dosha* is a body fluid principle that regulates the mucus-phlegm, or excretory, system and is made up of water and earth.

A brief description of the body types, based on these doshas, is as follows:

Vayu-ja persons: Tall and lean, hairy, talkative, shifting mind, earthy skin, prefer hot and oily dishes, tend to be constipated, love to travel, enjoy life, unsteady sleep.

Pitta-ja persons: Medium build, sweat a lot, pink skin, early baldness, impatient, fairly talkative, love to eat and drink, brave and ambitious, average sleep.

Kapha-ja persons: Short and stout, sweat a lot, white skin, steady mind, can be silent, normal appetite and thirst, rest a lot, and sleep deeply.

EIGHT PILLARS OF DISEASE PREVENTION

The Ayurveda system seeks not only to heal, but to prevent disease. It does this through an eight-part regimen for health.

- *Dina-charya*—following a healthy daily routine
- *Ritu-charya*—adapting to the seasons (described below)
- *Shad-vritta*—the proper mental culture

- Timely attention to nature's calls
- Inherent qualities of liquids and solids
- Rules for eating
- Proper sleep
- Environment

RITU-CHARYA: FOR EVERYTHING, A SEASON

These are the six Ayurveda seasons. Each is accompanied by recommended actions to assure health.

- March–April—*Vasanta-ritu*, spring. Light diet and light sleep.
- May–June—*Grishma-ritu*, summer. Eat light and drink cold fluids.
- July–August—*Varsha-ritu*, monsoon. Reinforce the appetite and eat hot foods.
- September–October—*Sharad-ritu*, short summer. Eat cool, sweet, and astringent foods.
- November–December—*Hemanta-ritu*, winter. Time to eat and exercise a lot.
- January–February—*Shishira-ritu*, cold winter. As with Hemanta-ritu, eat and exercise, and also spend time in reflection.

SIX RASAS: THE TASTE OF HEALTH

Diet, one of the most important factors in Ayurveda, reduces in part to properly combining, avoiding, or increasing foods and spices of different natures. These are the six basic *rasas*, or tastes.

Sweet: Adds earth and water; nourishes, cools, and moistens; includes rice, wheat, and sugar.

Sour: Adds earth and fire; warms and oils; includes acidic fruits.

Salty: Adds water and fire; dissolves, softens, and stimulates; in all salts.

Bitter: Adds air and ether; cools, dries, and purifies; in green vegetables and spices such as turmeric.

Pungent: Adds air and fire; warms, dries, and stimulates; in ginger.

Astringent: Adds air and earth; cools and dries; in honey, buttermilk, and mixed foods.

THE CALLIGARIS SYSTEM—WHERE L-FIELDS AND T-FIELDS FIELDS MEET: SECRETS OF THE SKIN

Dr. Giuseppe Calligaris discovered that certain lines and points on the skin operate just like meridians, except that they form geometrical patterns. Calligaris determined that these "linear-chains of the body mind," as he called them, related to conscious and unconscious parts of the mind and can be stimulated to enhance our paranormal abilities.[11]

Calligaris tested these coordinates and points, which are organized longitudinally and latitudinally, and found that they have less electrical resistance than the skin around them. (The meridian points also test as less electrical than the skin around them.) He determined that their intersections act like mirrors and accumulators of cosmic energy and that by applying a force against the point, one could active a higher intelligence—an "echo of vital vibrations of the universe."[12]

Calligaris believed that the human brain was a concave mirror for the universal consciousness. His ideas were rejected by the academic community of his time, and he died lonely and poor in 1944. His books are very rare, but he was mentioned in the *Autobiography of a Yogi* for his work with the paranormal. As Calligaris pointed out, if certain areas of the skin are agitated, one can see objects at a distance.[13]

This is an overview of Calligaris's system, as described in a lecture by Hubert M. Schweizer and distributed by the World Research Foundation.[14]

Calligaris's system reflects physical ailments, but also the effects of thoughts, emotions, and conditions related to the auric field. His underlying philosophy is simple: biological systems emit radiation. This radiation provides information about the harmony and disharmony of an organic system. There are thousands of spots on the skin that can be stimulated mechanically, but also with a thought-form. Calligaris's system therefore merges L-fields and T-fields within the human skin. And these skin lines form geometric patterns, thus underscoring the spiritual and scientific research on the importance of shape in creating form.

Calligaris found that sick radiation, such as that of a person with cancer, can

FIGURE 6.5
THE CALLIGARIS SYSTEM: HAND AND ORGANS

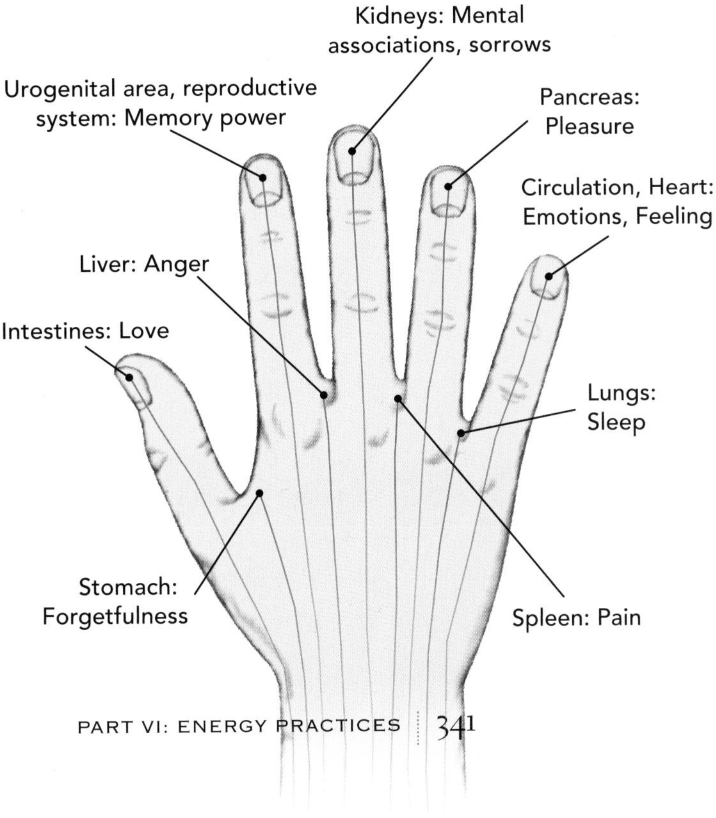
Kidneys: Mental associations, sorrows
Urogenital area, reproductive system: Memory power
Pancreas: Pleasure
Circulation, Heart: Emotions, Feeling
Liver: Anger
Intestines: Love
Lungs: Sleep
Stomach: Forgetfulness
Spleen: Pain

be detected up to twenty meters away.[15] This might explain some of the reason that energy healers often intuitively perceive (and can work on) illness such as cancer in others, even lacking conscious knowledge. His techniques are therefore helpful for both healing and diagnosing.

These lines and points represent the spots of the greatest electrical conductivity. There are many ways to find them through mechanical means. Manually, you can press the head of your thumb or middle finger to stimulate the lateral and middle lines of the arm. Continue stimulation and the vertical lines and transversal lines sensitize and begin to "crawl" kinesthetically, generating physical feelings including warmth, cold, tickling, and itching, as well as emotions. These sensations indicate that one has isolated one of the lines or points.

Thought forms also engage the points and lines, so one can concentrate on a certain idea and stimulate the corresponding skin area. Other methods are provided in the materials available from the World Research Foundation.[16]

CHAKRA EVALUATION: SHAPE, SPIN, AND SPEED

Some people can readily see chakras, while others can detect them through other means, such as use of a pendulum. Most chakra authorities agree: a healthy chakra spins clockwise in both spheres; is shaped as a uniform, round circle; and is rhythmic. It should emanate, front and back, about a foot away from the body. Its circular shapes should be about one foot in circumference.[17]

CHAKRA SHAPE

The ideal shape of a chakra is round and full. Misshapen or distorted shapes indicate physical, emotional, mental, or spiritual problems. In general, a shift of shape toward the right side of a chakra (from the subject's perspective) indicates issues of a masculine nature, such as domination and power, action and behavior, logic and rationality. If the shape shifts toward the left side of the chakra, the person may be dealing with feminine issues: receiving and responding, learning or healing, creating or feeling.

Here are some basic meanings of the general chakra shapes that people perceive:

Round: Healthy and balanced.

Lacking substance on right: Oriented toward unconscious programming, emotions, and right-brain creativity, but lacking action and follow-through.

Lacking substance on left: Geared toward conscious behavior and actions, left-brain analysis, but lacking creativity and intuition.

Lacking substance on bottom: More spiritual than practical.

Lacking substance on top: More practical than spiritual.

CHAKRA SPIN

Ideally, a chakra should hold a solid, even spin. Both the front side and the back side should be coordinated and moving in the same direction. Clockwise usually indicates health, and counterclockwise, a blockage or a misperception. A healthy spin (in the outer sphere) should appear round, even, and about one foot in diameter.

However, the outer spheres of the chakras spin counterclockwise when one is clearing or detoxifying. For women, this commonly occurs just before, during, and after menstruation. It is also common during long periods of puberty and menopause and, for both sexes, during times of crisis, such as after an accident, death in the family, job loss, medical surgery, major illness, or during post-traumatic stress recovery. Certain prescribed medicines and natural drugs or herbs will force the outer wheels to spin backward.

In some individuals, the outer sphere of the eighth chakra always flows backward. This way, the eighth chakra continually cleanses the subtle energy bodies of waste products. Some individuals are *heyoke*, or "counterclockwise," personalities. All of their chakras' outer wheels spin backward all the time. These are shamanic personalities who represent the opposing points of view for the world. In these cases, the outer wheel of the eighth chakra usually spins clockwise.

It is difficult to physically evaluate the inner wheel of a chakra. It is easiest to work with it using your intuition, such as pointed out in Part I, chapter 2. In general, you want to establish the spin of the outer wheel in concert with the inner wheel, not the other way around. Nearly always, the inner wheel is healthy if the outer wheel is moving clockwise; the inner wheel is nearly always healthy in any case, as it reflects the spirit's nature.

Here are ways to evaluate for spin:

Round, uniform, and even swing, clockwise: Healthy and functioning.

Round, uniform, and even swing, counterclockwise: Attempting to create health or balance by processing or clearing negative energy.

Nonuniform or uneven swing, counterclockwise: Chakra is blocked and unable to clear itself.

Elliptical or straight line in a vertical direction: Developed but impractical spiritual views, closed to real-life perspective or unwilling to take action.

Elliptical or straight line in a horizontal direction: Practical but lacking spiritual perspective, closed to the big picture or divine assistance.

Elliptical or straight line, swinging to the right (of the subject): Oriented toward action and the day-to-day, known as the masculine perspective, but lacking the emotional or spiritual, known as the feminine perspective.

Elliptical or straight line, swinging to the left (of the subject): Geared toward inspirational, feminine, or intuitive influences but lacking practical, grounding action.

Not moving or nearly still: Indicates a closed chakra. Function is shut down. This is a good place to look for a block or a cause of a presenting issue.

Large swing: Usually means very open, healthy, and functioning. If too large and imbalanced in comparison to other chakras, it means the chakra is overstrained and overfunctioning. Determine which chakra this one is compensating for.

Small swing: Underfunctioning; must be cleared and opened.

EVALUATING SPEED

Ideally, a chakra should hold a solid, even spin, and the inner wheel should move about twice as fast but in rhythm with the outer wheel. The lower the chakra, the slower both wheels should be moving. Both the front side and back side ought to move in the same direction, usually clockwise from the point of view of the tested subject. Too fast indicates an anxiety-producing situation. Too slow involves a depression situation. Anxiety is a physical as well as psychological state. It reflects the fear of the future and establishes a too-quick rhythm in the physical and subtle systems. Depression reflects an attachment to the past and creates a too-slow rhythm in the physical and subtle systems.

Here are other diagnostic tips:

Wheel too slow: Indicates damage from previous overuse, exhaustion, fatigue, blocks, strongholds (unhealthy attachments between beliefs, or between beliefs and feelings), and probably repressed memories or feelings.

Wheel too fast: Indicates current overuse; overstrain; acting to compensate for a weaker chakra or chakra wheel; or a desire to escape certain life events, people, feelings, or issues. Could be an attempt to release negative energy.

Outer wheel fast, inner wheel slow: Lack of spiritual, emotional, intuitive, or creative drive or perspective; underdeveloped beliefs, feelings, or spiritual sense; overconcern with the physical, or appearance.

Outer wheel slow, inner wheel fast: Lacking action, commitment to follow through, physical drive, or energy; overconcern with spiritual or psychic matters; fear of moving into the world; exhaustion in the physical.

Wheels out of synch: Inner beliefs and needs do not match with outer reality or action.

USING A PENDULUM FOR EVALUATION

The easiest way to evaluate for general chakra shape, spin, and speed is to use a pendulum, an object on a chain or a string. When held and allowed to swing freely, a pendulum will respond to the electromagnetic frequency from a chakra, back side or front side. When holding a pendulum over the chakra area, you are primarily evaluating the outer wheel of the chakra. If the outer wheel is moving counterclockwise, the inner wheel is probably doing the same. The inner wheel nearly always runs clockwise, unless there is an extreme crisis, including at birth and at death. The inner wheel is best analyzed using your intuition, as noted in Chapter 2, "Being an Energy Healer."

You can make a pendulum assessment of the chakras by having a partner stand over you, holding the pendulum six inches to a foot over the center of a chakra. Record information about shape, direction, movement, and apparent speed of the circling pendulum. No movement could indicate mistrust of the other person or the process, in either person, or a completely blocked chakra. Test to see if the other side of the chakra, or a chakra just above or below the problem area, is too open as compensation. To test the chakras below and above the head, as well as around the body, have the subject lie down and hold the pendulum above the appropriate sites.

Healing of imbalances can be done with colors, shape, tone, sound, light, and numbers.

In addition to being associated with physical processes in the body, chakras are connected to mental, emotional, and spiritual dimensions of human life. A chart of the issues that affect the chakra infrastructures can be found in the section "The Twelve-Chakra System" in Part V.

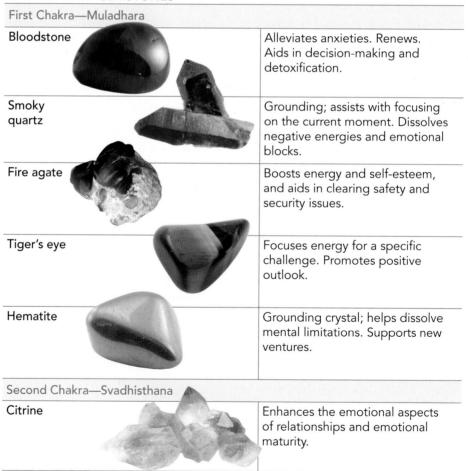

CHAKRAS AND GEMSTONES

Gemstones have been used to help clear, infuse, and balance the chakras for thousands of years. Every gemstone operates at a certain frequency, as do the chakras. Using intention, a practitioner working to balance the chakras can "program" a gemstone for many purposes, including healing, purifying, and adding energy to the physical body.

There are many ways to work with gemstones. In general, it is important to remember that energy follows intention. You can simply hold a stone in your hands and meditate or pray over it, visualizing or sensing the task you want it to perform. Then you can clear a gemstone the same way, or set it in the sun so nature can purify it for you.

Following is a list of gemstones that relate to the specific chakras as presented by Liz Simpson in *The Book of Chakra Healing*.[18]

FIGURE 6.6
CHAKRAS AND GEMSTONES

First Chakra—Muladhara		
Bloodstone		Alleviates anxieties. Renews. Aids in decision-making and detoxification.
Smoky quartz		Grounding; assists with focusing on the current moment. Dissolves negative energies and emotional blocks.
Fire agate		Boosts energy and self-esteem, and aids in clearing safety and security issues.
Tiger's eye		Focuses energy for a specific challenge. Promotes positive outlook.
Hematite		Grounding crystal; helps dissolve mental limitations. Supports new ventures.
Second Chakra—Svadhisthana		
Citrine		Enhances the emotional aspects of relationships and emotional maturity.

FIGURE 6.6

CHAKRAS AND GEMSTONES

Carnelian		Dispels boredom, apathy, and passivity. Bolsters energy toward taking action in emotionally difficult situations. Also dispels sorrow.
Moonstone		Enhances the feminine, alleviates oversensitivity, and soothes emotions.
Golden topaz		Stimulates the first three chakras. Provides clarity for new perspectives, enhances inner serenity, and creates a lightness of spirit. Reenergizes.
Rutilated quartz		Beneficial for meditation, healing, and increasing spiritual consciousness and awareness. Draws out negativity. Stabilizes relationships.

Third Chakra—Manipura

Yellow citrine		Accesses personal power and bolsters self-esteem. Helps overcome addictions to substances and is beneficial for digestive issues.
Sunstone		Brings good fortune and relieves tension.
Calcite		Cleanses blockages and boosts natural energy. Aids with problems in the pancreas, kidneys, and spleen.
Malachite		Connects the solar plexus with the heart chakra. Helps with dreams.

Fourth Chakra—Anahata

Rose quartz		Known as the "love crystal," heals heart, relationship, and bonding issues. Promotes self-love and healing of "inner child" issues, or problems from youth.

FIGURE 6.6
CHAKRAS AND GEMSTONES

Watermelon tourmaline		Activates the heart chakra and invites a connection to the higher self. Soothes emotional dysfunctions and promotes interconnectivity.

Fifth Chakra—Vishuddha

Turquoise		Strives for honest and full communication. Aids with articulation of inner feelings or needs; clears blocks to self-expression or perceptive listening.
Sodalite		Bolsters objectivity and forges a link between the unconscious and conscious mind. Invites new perspectives. Lightens the heart.
Lapis lazuli		Encourages self-expression and access to the "muses," creative gifts and drives. Enhances clear communication with others.
Celestite		Aids in receiving, synthesizing, and interpreting challenging ideas and spiritual principles. Provides a doorway to other dimensions.
Aquamarine		Reduces stress and promotes tranquility. Aids in the presentation of ideas, especially to the larger world. Helps one assimilate self-knowledge.

Sixth Chakra—Ajna

Calcite		Amplifies the powers of the third eye, including intuitive visioning.
Purple fluorite		Called the "stone of discernment," integrates the left and right hemispheres of the brain. Eliminates impurities and falsities.

FIGURE 6.6

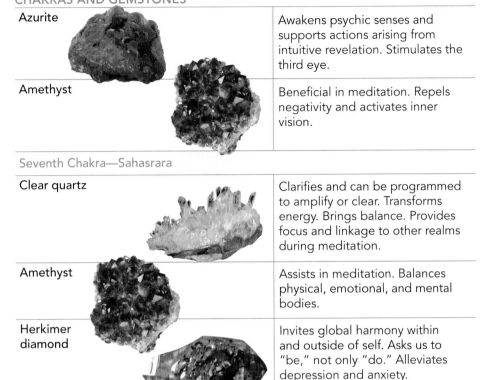

Azurite	Awakens psychic senses and supports actions arising from intuitive revelation. Stimulates the third eye.
Amethyst	Beneficial in meditation. Repels negativity and activates inner vision.

Seventh Chakra—Sahasrara

Clear quartz	Clarifies and can be programmed to amplify or clear. Transforms energy. Brings balance. Provides focus and linkage to other realms during meditation.
Amethyst	Assists in meditation. Balances physical, emotional, and mental bodies.
Herkimer diamond	Invites global harmony within and outside of self. Asks us to "be," not only "do." Alleviates depression and anxiety.
Diamond	The name means "lover of god." Activates spiritual awareness and connections. Moves us toward our highest potential.

CHAKRAS AND THE ELEMENTS

The twelve-chakra system works with ten elements. The primary four elements are similar to those found in most other systems: water, earth, air, and fire. From these, six other elements are formed: metal, wood, stone, ether, light, and star. Imbalances of any of these elements can create the vibrational disturbances that cause or support disease and all other issues; conversely, using or balancing these elements can correct subtle and physical conditions.[19]

There are many ways to work energetically but also concretely with the elements. The visual intuitive can picture an element working within the body, a chakra, or an auric layer, setting an intention to create change. The verbal intuitive might "order" that an element perform a task through internal commands or by literally speaking into the body, a chakra, or an auric layer. A more sensory-based intuitive can assume the presence of an element and work with it through hands-on techniques or by imagining that it is producing the necessary change.

Energy healers can also use stones, substances, liquids, or other pertinent materials representing the desired element. These might be placed on or near a client's acupoints or chakras, or in the auric field. Elements can also be mentally or intuitively programmed into water through intention or prayer to produce a particular goal. By drinking this water, one imbibes its effects. People seeking change or healing can also carry objects representing the needed element. This object can serve as a focal point for guided visualization, meditation, and self-healing.

Here are the basic properties of the ten elements and a few suggestions on how to work with each element:

Fire: Eliminates, purges, and burns away. Adds energy, excitement, and new life. Is the basis of the kundalini process and is important in healing. For instance, it can purify the blood or lymph of toxins. Field-based practitioners can imagine fire cleansing the auric field, paying special attention to the first auric field, which is red and primal-based. Meridian-based practitioners might use moxibustion during acupuncture or energetically imagine fire burning through the appropriate meridian channel. Chakra-based practitioners apply fire in the center of the chakra nearest the problematic area, using intuitive or hands-on techniques. Stones involving the fire element are usually red and relate to the first chakra. Do not use fire intuitively on the heart or a critically inflamed area, as fire can enhance anger and inflammation.

Air: Transmits ideas and ideals. Allows the spread of energies from place to place or person to person. Active when moving and directed; inactive, yet ripe with potential, when still. Use it to "blow away" bad beliefs or initiate helpful ones. Field-based work can include using feathers, breath, or sound. Meridian-based practices might involve clearing negative beliefs by "speaking truth" intuitively or verbally into the appropriate acupoint. Chakra-based methods include using sound, intuition, and stones at the third chakra.

Water: Transmits psychic and feeling energies, soothes and heals, washes and cleanses. Use to cleanse your lymph system or intestines of toxins, both psychic and physical; to purify the body from old and repressed feelings (self or others); and to calm tissue after surgery. For stroke in the brain, imagine washing the crusted site with water before repairing the ruptured tissues with an earthen or stone wall. Consider "programming" your drinking water with prayer and intention for specific purposes. Field, meridian, and chakra-based practitioners might all program water with intention to assist clients and prescribe stones for the second chakra. It's also helpful to use fountains or running water in practice rooms to promote a cleansing atmosphere.

Earth: Builds, solidifies, and protects. Earth can rebuild tissue after surgery, soothe any inflamed area, and repair tissues. Ideal for holding malleable structures, such as cell walls. Field-based practitioners can review the earth-based energies in a client's environment, checking for and alleviating geopathic stress conditions. Channel-based practitioners employing herbs, foods, or substances can analyze a client's use of these materials (which are earth-based in that they create tissue). All practitioners can use tenth chakra stones in healing work.

Metal: Protects, defends, and deflects. Use it in the auric field to deflect harmful energies. Visualize a metal armor around the liver or kidneys if you are taking medication (this will also draw heavy metal toxicity out of these organs). This armoring technique can be used on any organ to stop or prevent attacks from external energies or entities—such as forces that create cancer. Use it as a mirror to reflect or deflect negative energies. Purge it from your system if you have heavy metal toxicity, chronic fatigue, or cancers. Many autoimmune diseases often involve a harmful overabundance of metal. Silver-colored metals and stones might be used to enable metal-based effects.

Wood: Adds buoyancy, adaptability, and a positive attitude. Insert it in areas of depressed or counterclockwise spin to help set spin clockwise. If depressed emotionally, add wood to the mind by picturing trees or plants. Use it to integrate new tissue or ideas into the body, such as after an organ replacement. Will bring good cheer to a depressed state. If an individual has high blood pressure, add wood for relaxation. All practitioners might employ actual wood products or substances on or near their clients.

Stone: Strengthens, holds, and toughens. Use stone in the tenth chakra to keep the soul grounded in the body. Imagine putting all soul or subconscious issues or emotions, such as shame, into a stone and then throwing the stone into the ocean. Add stone to a weak blood vessel or around a stroke site. Stone will hold other elements in place; if you need to keep new beliefs or tissues anchored so they can root, build a stone retaining wall to do so. Practitioners can employ "real" stones to clear or program the energy fields or chakras; meridian-based healers can surround a client with the appropriate stones during treatment to increase effectiveness.

Ether: Holds spiritual truths; can be used to infuse any system, energy body, mind, or soul with such spiritual truths. Ether is liquid gas. It is actually the "fifth element," the spiritual energy that scientists and metaphysicians have attempted to define for millennia. Through prayer and meditation, any type of practitioner can program the ether for healing and specific purposes.

Light: Can be directed, spun, fashioned, summoned, or eliminated to produce almost any desired effect. Light is electromagnetic radiation of various wavelengths. "Dark" light, which constitutes frequencies closer to infrared and below, is composed mainly of electrons that carry intelligence about power; "light" light, composed of frequencies near or above the ultraviolet range, is fashioned chiefly from protons that hold intelligence about love. Bring balance to any problem with the correct light. If you are depressed, you could add "light" light to uplift—or "dark" light to gain the energy necessary to make behavioral changes. For more ideas on using light, see "Color Healing" and the various chakra systems in Part V, which often use color for diagnosis and healing.

Star: Uses spiritual truths to form and purify physical matter. Release negative misperceptions by formulating the truth. Imagine this truth enfolded into a star, and insert the star into the appropriate auric field, energy channel, or chakra. This technique can even be used to alter DNA. Star will also force the release of a misperception or harmful pattern in the body. Use it when burning away an inaccurate perception in any consciousness level, then stimulate correct beliefs with ether. (Star is made of fire and ether.) Star stones relate to the seventh or twelfth chakras.

COLOR HEALING (SEE ALSO COLORPUNCTURE)

Color therapy is an aspect of light therapy. Light was used for healing among the ancient Babylonians, Egyptians, and Assyrians, as well as among the later

Greeks and Romans. Dr. Harry Riley Spitler was the first to apply colored light phototherapy through the eyes, publishing a book called *The Syntonic Principle* in 1941. Also in the 1940s, researcher Dinshah Ghadiali founded Spectrochrome, a method of using colored lights directly on the body. His research showed that the body could be healed by systematically exposing it to colored lights. (For instance, premature babies with Bilirubin Syndrome can be medically treated with blue light.) Ghadiali's work was attacked by groups including the American Medical Association, although he was staunchly defended by medical practitioners, including Dr. Kate Baldwin, senior surgeon at the Women's Hospital of Philadelphia. Dr. Baldwin asserted that Spectrochrome had cured gonorrhea, syphilis, cancer, ulcers, and other conditions. Despite the support of Dr. Baldwin and other professionals, the government destroyed his books and papers in 1947 and the FDA obtained a permanent injunction against his institute in 1958.[20]

In the 1980s, Dr. Norman Rosenthal at the National Institute of Mental Health recognized the existence of seasonal affective disorder (SAD): deprivation of full-spectrum light and the resulting depression.

Recent research is substantiating the amazing powers of light for healing. Sunlight stimulates the pineal gland to produce melatonin, which is necessary for sleep, ease, and happiness.[21] High-intensity lights are being used to cure cancer and viral conditions and even alleviate the symptoms of Alzheimer's disease.[22]

Nobel Prize winner Albert Szent-Györgyi has concluded, through studies and research, that light striking the body alters the basic biological functions involved in digestive processing, as well as enzymatic and hormonal interactions. Some colors can actually cause bodily enzymes to be five hundred times more effective.[23] Color affects more than our bodies; it also influences our mind. According to Dr. Jacob Liberman, a pioneer in the therapeutic use of color and light, the colors present in the body indicate our state of consciousness, which also means that our state of consciousness reflects how well we use color.[24]

The key to achieving a therapeutic effect is using the right color, or wavelength. Infrared light reduces the severity of a heart attack by up to 50 percent, reverses blindness in animals, and heals oral sores. Red light helps wounds heal more quickly and reverses skin aging. Blue light (as well as red light) can kill bacteria. Blue light can also reset the biological clock, treat seasonal affective disorder, and help people with Alzheimer's disease sleep better at night. Ultraviolet light keeps bacteria and viruses from reproducing and can sterilize air and water.[25]

Light apparently transfers energy to the mitochondria within the cell and assists the body in healing itself. It also alters the speed of various chemical processes.

"We are living photocells," says Liberman. The body gives off light of all colors, takes it in through our physical structures, and emits and receives light through our subtle bodies.[26]

Liberman emphasizes the findings of a scientist named Cabal, who in the 1800s linked light with the hypothalamus.[27] The hypothalamus is the brain's center, regulating our autonomic nervous system and the master endocrine gland, the pituitary. The pineal serves as the body's light meter, taking in information through the eyes but also from the earth's electromagnetic field. The correct light used at the appropriate intensity, speed, and color can shift imbalances in the autonomic nervous and endocrine systems.

These explanations underscore the discoveries of researchers Dr. Fritz-Albert Popp and Dr. Hal Puthoff, who have determined that we are bathed in a field of light—inside and out. While our bodies are surrounded in the "zero-point field," our DNA also acts as a biophoton machine.[28] (See Index for other references to zero point and DNA.)

There are dozens if not hundreds of color- and light-based healing modalities. Here are just a few.

THE CHAKRA SYSTEM—PLAYING WITH LIGHT AND COLOR

You can do healing work with the chakras by applying colored light or stones on the chakric locations of the body. Each chakra governs a different part of the nervous and hormone systems, relates to a different age of development, and signifies different gender issues. By knowing which chakric area relates to these three concerns, a practitioner can work to achieve healing through color.

Steven Vazquez, PhD, an expert in phototherapy, proposed that the bottom chakras govern the sympathetic nervous system, which is active during stress or danger and regulates the pulse and blood pressure. The top chakras manage the parasympathetic nervous system, which controls involuntary and unconscious body functions (such as the autonomic nervous system). In general, the sympathetic nervous system is the stress-producer and the parasympathetic nervous system maintains and restores the body.[29]

Regarding issues relating to time, the lower a person works in the chakras, the more frequently they talk about the past. The middle chakras govern the present day and the higher chakras tap into thoughts about the future or beyond time.[30]

The body also subdivides according to gender. As in figure 6.14, there are four quadrants. The masculine chakras are on the bottom of the body and the entire right side, and the feminine chakras are located on the lower region of the body and the left side.[31]

We know, as the arrow shows, that the infrared spectrum runs under the lower chakras and the ultraviolet spectrum is available over the higher chakras. When working with colors yellow and downward, a practitioner is able to access issues from the past and activate the sympathetic nervous system. Working the green upward activates the parasympathetic nervous system. Blue-green to blue and into indigo triggers present-day concerns, while violet and upward relates to issues in the future or beyond time. Masculine issues are most accessible from green up to violet, while feminine issues pertain to the colors yellow and downward. The left side of the body governs all feminine functions and the right side, the masculine.[32]

A practitioner using the twelve-chakra system featured in Part V would work with the infrared spectrum to deal with the tenth chakra, which lies under the feet and reflects genealogical foundations. The chakras above the head, including the eighth and ninth, transcend time, as do the eleventh and twelfth chakras around the body. These operate in the ultraviolet wavelength or higher. These additional five chakras can be accessed through intention, as well as with the colors stated for each of the chakras in the twelve-chakra system chart, figure 5.27.

Dr. Vasquez also states that the front sides of the chakras regulate our conscious reality and the back sides, our unconscious, as depicted in figure 6.9.

ADDITIONAL COLOR TECHNIQUES USING THE TWELVE-CHAKRA SYSTEM

There are many ways to use colors for healing. This information draws upon research from several esoteric systems and scientific research, reflecting a broad base of knowledge.[33]

Color and Diagnosing

The color of a chakra determines an individual's current state of health and spiritual development. A clear-colored or appropriately colored chakra is aligned with the Divine and is probably fairly healthy. Discoloration, markings, muddy, black colors, or intuitive perception of sounds that are off-key indicate imbalance or disease. Very black or thick areas might reveal interference or penetration by external energies or entities.

The color and shape of a chakra pinpoint balance issues. If all the coloration is on one side of the chakra, you are missing half the picture, which indicates stuck beliefs and emotions.

Empty spaces usually indicate a fragmentation: a part of the self is held or in bondage elsewhere. "Elsewhere" can be another lifetime, a different dimension or plane, or even a place within the self. It might also indicate recession, the sublimation of a part of the self in something or someone else.

You can use the following color charts for chakra healing. The first chart, "Color Energies," indicates which colors could be used to fill in missing or tinted areas. The second chart, "Harmful Colorations," aids in deciphering the presence of problems.

You can use the coloration system with symbology, geometry, and number symbols. These techniques are all vibrational healing methods and can be integrated.

Coloring Your Healing

Each color represents a different type of energy. Following is a simplified understanding of the energies of the main colors.

These colors can be applied with phototherapy or mechanical devices (by a skilled practitioner), through psychicism, by wearing them, placing colored objects in the environment, applying stones, or via intention.

FIGURE 6.7
COLOR ENERGIES

Color	Meaning of Energy
Red	Life energy
Orange	Creativity and feelings
Yellow	Intellect
Green	Healing
Pink/rose	Love
Blue	Communication
Purple	Vision, clarification of choices, and results of decisions
White	Divine will, spiritual destiny
Black	Power for movement; force behind change
Gold	Harmony
Silver	Transference of energy from one place to another
Brown	Practicality and grounding

FIGURE 6.8
HARMFUL COLORATIONS

Condition	Problem
Too many or distorted red tones	Overstimulates passion, anger, ego, or survival fears

FIGURE 6.8

HARMFUL COLORATIONS

Condition	Problem
Too many or distorted orange tones	Creates emotionalism or hyperactivity
Too many or distorted yellow tones	Overemphasizes certain mental ideas or beliefs to create falsehoods or judgments
Too many or distorted green tones	Overstimulates the drive for relationships, codependency, and the perceived need to heal what does not need healing
Too many or distorted pink tones	Can create a sense of love where it does not exist
Too many or distorted blue tones	Causes the perceived need to obtain more and more guidance or to overexplain oneself
Too many or distorted purple tones	Causes compulsive planning or difficulties in seeing or sorting out choices
Too many or distorted white tones	Overstimulates the sense of spirituality and deemphasizes the need for power and action
Too many or distorted black tones	Unbalances spiritual energies with an emphasis on power; can cause powerlessness, emotionalism, or greed
Too many or distorted gold tones	Causes excessive idealism and a resulting loss of hope
Too many or distorted silver tones	Creates susceptibility to psychic sources
Too many or distorted brown tones	Muddies the waters and results in confusion, hyperpracticality, and mundane obsessions
Too many or distorted gray tones	Shadows or covers an issue, causing lack of clarity
Neutralizing	Erasing intensity creates emptiness and powerlessness; voodoo and mind control use these methods
Imposition of a different color	Forcing a color over someone else's, thus achieving control over the other person; this is also called creating an "overlay"
Blotching	Creates inconsistency, making it hard for a victim to rely on him- or herself

FIGURE 6.9

COLOR THERAPY: CHAKRA AND BODY REGION ASSOCIATIONS

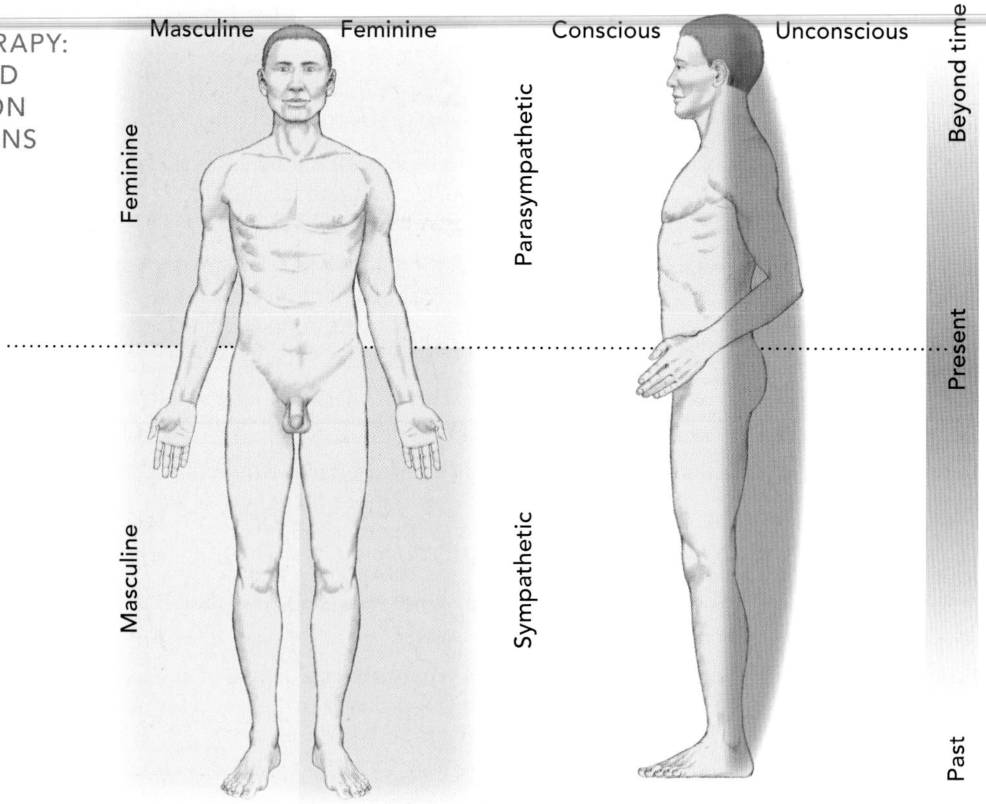

Masculine
Feminine
Conscious
Unconscious
Feminine
Masculine
Parasympathetic
Sympathetic
Beyond time
Present
Past

COLORPUNCTURE

Peter Mandel, a German researcher and healer, developed colorpuncture over thirty years ago. It uses light with pure color on acupuncture points and other gateways on the skin for healing and relaxation purposes. It has become widely accepted in Germany and across Europe as a substitute for or adjunct to acupuncture, and is quickly becoming popular as a treatment elsewhere.

Mandel based his work on research by scientists including Dr. Fritz-Albert Popp, who discovered that the body's cells communicate with each other through a steady stream of photons, or wave-particles of light. Using Kirlian photography, Mandel determined that the acupuncture meridians absorb and disseminate colored light within the body. He then compared energetic conditions, as perceived through the Kirlian method, with the physical symptoms of his subjects, finally experimenting to determine which colored lights would positively affect these conditions.

Mandel named his system Esogetics, which combines the words *esoteric* with *energetic*. He divides treatments into body, soul, and spirit levels, using a pen torch (flashlight) with ten color-coded crystals to infuse the color gateways with light. (There are no needles; the pen torch applies color only.) The light is delivered to acupuncture points, meridians, body zones, and sacred geometric grids in the form of seven basic colors, which add or decrease energy to the meridian system.

MANDEL'S COLORPUNCTURE SYSTEM

Peter Mandel's colorpuncture system is based on his "Esogetic Model," which showcases six factors that affect health. The fundamental principle is that illness and pain occur when an individual has strayed off his or her life path. Colorpuncture relays the information contained in light into the unconscious so people can access their own inner knowledge for healing—and regain direction. For example, a treatment might release an emotional blockage and thus heal a nervous system condition. With less neurological stress, patients can now devote themselves to their individual spiritual purpose.[34]

Mandel's model is a holographic representation of how energy is produced in the body. Three of the six factors (called molecules) represent the subtle energies. These are the chakras, formative field, and converter model. The other three factors describe the physical reality. These are the body systems, the coordination system, and the transmitter relays.

Esogetics employs seven basic colors. In general, the warm colors—red, orange, and yellow—add energy, while the cool colors—green, blue, and violet—decrease energy. A practitioner adds energy to stimulate and tonify and decreases energy to sedate and soothe.

Mandel also combined colors in complementary pairs and used them simultaneously to treat the same acupuncture meridian. He discovered that warm and cool colors, when used together, balance yin and yang energy flows.

Primary Colors and Their Effects

Here is an outline of Mandel's uses of various colors:

Red: Most yang, warm, and stimulating. Produces heat. Stimulates vital energy and circulation of the blood. Stimulates sensory nervous systems and energizes the five basic senses. Stimulates the healing of wounds without pus. Used in treatment of chronic infections. Too much red leads to anger and hyperactivity.

Orange: Gentle yang, tonifies. Stimulates appetite, relieves cramps and spasms, increases blood pressure, induces vomiting, relieves gas, builds bones. When used with blue, regulates the endocrine system. Stimulates joy, optimism, and enthusiasm.

Yellow: Yang, and the brightest of all colors. Strengthens motor nervous system and metabolism, and aids conditions of the glandular, lymphatic, and digestive systems. Stimulates intellectual functions; boosts cheerfulness and confidence.

Green: Neutral yin. Slightly cooling. Treats conditions of the lungs, eyes, diabetes, musculoskeletal and inflammatory joint problems, and ulcers. Is antibacterial and aids in detoxification. Calms, soothes, and balances.

Blue: Yin or cool. Relaxes body and mind, reduces fever, congestion, itching, irritation, and pain. Treats high blood pressure, burns, inflammations with pus and diseases involving heat. Contracts tissues and muscles. Calms and tranquilizes when used on the pituitary and pineal acupoints. Helpful for insomnia, phobias, and endocrine imbalances. Not indicated for depression as it is a melancholy color.

Violet: Most yin color. Aids the spleen, reduces irritability, and balances the right brain. When combined with yellow, increases lymph production, controls hunger, and balances the nervous system. Acts on the unconscious.[35]

Complementary Colors

The complementary color pairs are: red-green, orange-blue, and yellow-violet. Together, these colors balance yin and yang. For example, red might stimulate the blood and improve circulation while green calms conditions creating stress. Blue might assuage pain while orange lifts fear or depression causing tension. Yellow will strengthen the nervous system while violet calms it with a meditative state.

DIET AND TRADITIONAL CHINESE MEDICINE

One of the most widely used traditional treatments is altering the diet. Dietary intervention is personalized according to an individual's pattern of disharmony.

Foods bring warmth or coolness, which in turn balances the yin and yang. If someone is too warm or has too much heat (or yang), cool foods are prescribed. If someone is too cool or has too much cold (or yin), then warm foods are prescribed. A practitioner frequently determines the thermal reactions of a patient by his or her reaction after eating.

Each food has yin (cool) and yang (warm) qualities, but one is often dominant. In general, the following statements are true: Bitter and salty flavors are yin. Pungent and sweet flavors are yang.

An excess of yin can lead to sluggishness, laziness, depression, weight gain, hypo-conditions, and emotionalism, while an excess of yang is revealed by hyper-activity, tenseness, nervousness, anxiety, and aggressiveness.

Here are some common foods and their thermal qualities:

Cooling foods: Celery, lettuce, broccoli, spinach, tomatoes, bananas, watermelon, barley, millet, wheat, pork, eggs, crab, ice cream, and soy sauce.

Neutral foods: Beets, turnips, carrots, lemons, apples, rice, corn, rye, potatoes, yams, beef, and rabbit.

Warming foods: Scallions, squash, cabbage, kale, oats, tuna, turkey, salmon, lamb, chicken, shrimp, ginger, sugar, garlic, and pepper.

EMOTIONAL FREEDOM TECHNIQUE (EFT)

Emotional freedom technique (EFT) is a simple-to-use healing method similar to acupressure, best known for providing relief from pain, disease, and emotional issues. It is based on a new discovery that involves tapping the traditional meridian points on your body with your fingertips.

Its two basic premises are as follows: "The cause of all negative emotions is a disruption in the body's energy system. . . . And because our physical pains and diseases are so obviously connected with our emotions. . . . Our unresolved negative emotions are major contributors to most physical pains and diseases."[36]

Gary Craig created EFT in the mid-1990s, and it has grown in popularity since. It is not meant to replace qualified medical advice, nor does his organization promise that it works in all cases, but it is a helpful technique that has produced stellar results. EFT is supported by considerable anecdotal evidence and endorsements from several well-known healers.

EFT has been applied to psychological and physical conditions, including performance issues, serious diseases, depression, anxiety, post-traumatic stress disorder, pain relief, allergies, blood pressure problems, relationship issues, general stress, addictions, phobias—basically, anything from colds to cancer.

EFT's effectiveness follows the proposition that negative emotions are built in these stages:

1. a negative experience occurs, resulting in
2. a negative emotion, which leads to

3. an inappropriate programming in the body, which

4. disturbs the body's energy system.[37]

In theory, you cannot remove a negative emotion unless you simultaneously rebalance the energy system; therefore, you must utilize a protocol that does both at the same time. The basic EFT technique involves focusing on a disturbing memory, emotion, pain, or malady. Simultaneously, the practitioner uses his or her fingers to tap on a series of twelve points that correlate to the Chinese meridians. The procedure completes by tapping while focusing on a positive affirmation.

EFT can be learned as an adjunct to a current therapeutic practice or as a stand-alone therapy. Practitioners are encouraged to exercise common sense before using this technique on anyone with a serious emotional disability. The entire procedure is available at www.emofree.com.

THE FOUR PATHWAYS APPROACH TO HEALING

The Four Pathways is a healing system I developed based on my research that integrates Eastern, Western, and indigenous healing practices. It suggests that there are four levels of awareness that add up to a greater reality: the space in which we know heaven and earth as the same. Because we exist on all four levels simultaneously, any shift of position on any one of the pathways results in significant changes on the others. Illness is caused by an imbalance in the energies on any one or several of these pathways. The chakras serve as portals allowing movement between these levels of awareness.

Usually, only a crisis will force people to see beyond the physicality of life: the basis of the elemental pathway, the material plane. The power pathway showcases supernatural energies and forces, and changes that are greater than those possible on the elemental pathway. The imagination pathway involves using creative magic and intention to shift energies from the quantum universe to the physical, while the divine pathway invokes the highest "medicine" of all: the miracles available through acceptance of our own divinity.[38]

THE FOUR PATHWAYS AND THE QUANTUM DIAMOND

The Four Pathways approach employs a geometric design for healing and manifesting, based on knowledge of the Platonic solids, Pythagorean ideas, hermetic alchemy, quantum mechanics, the Kabbalah, and spin theory. It is called the *quantum diamond* (developed in collaboration with Carolyn Vinup, sound healer).

The quantum diamond is a diamond-shaped, interdimensional object with five cords connecting the two sides of the diamond and an empty space in the middle. These five cords, when halved, can be seen as ten cords, forming twelve important points in time-space, if one also adds the two opposing points.

A diamond is basically two triangles with their bases connected. The triangle plays a vital role in Platonic philosophy, which suggests it as the fundamental shape of creation—as does causal dynamical triangulation theory (CDT), which proposes the triangle as the basic shape of the interdimensional walls. Five is a creative number among mystical mathematicians and physicians. Both symbols, the triangle and the number five, are seen as underlying creation. The top of the triangle inhabits material reality and "here and now" time-space, while the bottom of the triangle dwells in antimatter. The inner region of the diamond is occupied by "zero point," the vacuum that is rich with potential. (See the Index for these concepts.)

The model is similar to that of the Kabbalah, which has ten sephiroth and is occupied by Daath, or the void in the center. The sephiroth are considered stepped-down manifestations of Ein Sof, or God, which can be pictured as a point of light that emanates through all the planes of the sephiroth. (See Chapter 40.) This model is identical, except that it also suggests that the creation energy streams simultaneously from both "above" and "below"; in essence, God manifests through the lowest of vibrations, which are closer to material reality and the lower end of the electromagnetic spectrum, as well as the higher vibrations, which are closer to the spiritual realms and the higher end of the electromagnetic spectrum. The entire unit, when spinning, revolves like the double helix of DNA. Anyone can program intentions for healing or manifesting along the cords, thus actualizing the energetics of the body, mind, and soul. The shape of the quantum diamond then energetically transfers these intentions into the genes and the body's electromagnetic system.

GEOMETRY AND SOUND IN HEALING

In the book of John in the New Testament of the Bible, we are told that the beginning of the world started with "the Word." What is a word but a tone—a sound—and perhaps, a shape?

All of space exists in a state of readiness; 90 percent is made of dark matter, waiting to be shaped by word—or vibration. Recently, by projecting thought into water, Dr. Masaru Emoto showed us that we could form our reality, down to the most basic of molecules. (See "Magnetic Field Interactions with Water" on page 140.) Throughout the 1900s, Swiss researcher Hans Jenny projected pure tones onto fine grains of matter or liquid and watched as distinct geometric shapes took form and life. He called this cymatics. (See "Cymatics" on page 141.) Tone transforms matter into patterns of nature.

Sound and shape are both forms of energy, and they often intersect. Just as tones create certain effects in the subtle body, so do shapes, and either can be used for healing.

At least in part, this phenomenon is explained by spin theory, one of quantum physics' favorite theories. Spin theory, as we have seen, describes the angular momentum carried by a particle. When several particles are spinning at the same time, the effect is the same as a group of toddlers running wild without a babysitter in the room. Watch closely, however, and the random movement reveals an elegant grace. For "composite particles," or the group of toddlers, spin is the *combination* of spins of each particle (or kid) plus the angular momentum of their motion around each other. It is chaos, but somewhere in there is a kind of order.

All vibrating particles or waves—or wave-particles, such as photons, the units of light—have spin. That means that every sound has a particular spin. And so does a collection of sounds. A song creates a unique "spin," just as does the note B. If you were able to draw a line from one note to another—from one end of a spin to the next—geometrical configurations would emerge.

In this way, sound and geometry are intertwined.

GEOMETRIC MEANINGS[39]

Different geometric patterns hold different meanings. Whole or complete symbols, usually perceived intuitively, signify health or can be psychically or energetically imprinted to create health. Altered symbols, those which appear broken or distorted, cause energetic and therefore physical disturbance. Here is a sampling of the meanings of geometric symbols, based on research in Pythagorean and sacred geometry.

FIGURE 6.10
GEOMETRIC SYMBOLS: HELPFUL AND HARMFUL

Symbol		Whole	Altered
Circle		Wholeness	Causes hurt, injury, damage, or separation
Square		Foundation	Used to overthrow or topple systems
Rectangle		Production	Imprisons or exposes to danger
Triangle 		Preservation and immortality	Creates illness, disease, imbalance, and death

FIGURE 6.10

GEOMETRIC SYMBOLS: HELPFUL AND HARMFUL

Symbol		Whole	Altered
Spiral		Creation and cycles	Forces abrupt endings, cessation of cycles or rhythms
Five-pointed star		Alchemy and movement	Stifles, contains, suffocates, lowers vibrations
Six-pointed star		Resurrection	Causes stuckness, despair, and depression
Cross		Human-Divine connection and spiritual protection	Accentuates ego or causes extreme dejection

In addition, an "X" marking represents the presence of evil or anticonsciousness.

HERBS AND TRADITIONAL CHINESE MEDICINE

Many traditional Chinese doctors are proficient herbalists. In traditional Chinese medicine, an herb and its uses are evaluated in several ways, including nature, taste, affinity, and primary (and secondary) actions:

Nature: Either cooling or heating, as well as relaxing, energizing, moistening, or drying. Cooling herbs such as peppermint or spearmint, for instance, would awaken the system and alleviate lung congestion.

Taste: There are five tastes: sour, bitter, sweet, spicy, and salty. Bitter herbs, for example, are drying. As with cooling herbs, these are good for lung congestion or colds.

Affinity: Certain herbs work best with particular organ systems; this is the herb's affinity.

Primary action: How does the herb affect the system? They might dispel or move; purge or expel; tonify or strengthen; or restrain and serve as an astringent. Many herbs create a primary and also a secondary effect.

There are hundreds of herbs stocked in the Chinese apothecary, which are combined in thousands of different ways. A few of the "must haves" include:

Astragalus: Immune booster.

Dong Quai (or Tang Kuei): Improves circulation and builds blood; balances the female endocrine system.

Fo Ti (Ho Shou Wu): Blood cleanser, increases energy, boosts sexual ability.

Garlic: For high blood pressure and cholesterol; antiseptic and antifungal.

Ginger: Warms; stimulates digestion; decreases nausea.

Ginseng: Restores sexual and digestive energies.

Ginseng (Siberian): Increases energy and assists the immune system.

Green tea: Boosts heart health, lowers cholesterol, and has shown documented anticancer effects.

HOMEOPATHY

Homeopathy is a vibrational, or energetic-based, system of medicine developed by Dr. Samuel Hahneman. It operates under "the law of similars": the idea that the same substance that produces symptoms in a healthy person can cure them in a sick person. Hahneman created a systematic procedure for testing substances that called forth problematic symptoms on all levels: physical, emotional, mental, and spiritual. He then matched these symptoms with illnesses to learn which substance to give for which illness.

Hahneman also experimented with dilutions for these homeopathic—or "similar to the pathology"—remedies. He discovered a process called *potentizing:* when he mixed a remedy with water and shook it appropriately, its effectiveness increased. He eventually reduced the solution until no molecules remained from the original substance. Yet it still worked. Currently, hundreds of solutions created from minerals, plants, and diseased tissues have been studied and proven beneficial—and thousands more have been at least partially proven.[40]

Homeopathy works with *constructive resonance*, as Dr. Richard Gerber explains in his book *A Practical Guide to Vibrational Medicine*.[41] Gerber paints the portrait of someone whose healthy body usually vibrates at 300 cycles per second. When sick, the body might leap to 350 cycles per second, the higher vibration stimulating the production of white blood cells as an immune response to the bacteria. As Gerber points out, the resulting fever or symptom is actually a good, not a bad, response. Now, we could put energy "in" that vibrates at only 300 cycles per second, and the body will absorb it. But will this lower vibration do what needs to be done—the marshalling of the body's defenses? No. We need to bolster the body's healing mechanisms with medicine that vibrates at 350 cycles a second—the job of a homeopathic remedy. By adding *to* a symptom, you support the body in responding to the reason there *is* a symptom.

There are many ways to potentize a solution. One striking radionic procedure was developed by Malcolm Rae. A vial of alcohol, water, or a mix of both is set on a static device and potentized with a radionic process for a short time period. (Radionics is related to radiesthesia, the physical or etheric use of radiation toward a certain end. See "Radionics: Healing Through the Field" on page 387.) All the solutions are charged for the same amount of time with a charging disc coded with varying concentric circles and radial lines. The spacing between these lines is changed to serve as a code for a desired homeopathic remedy.[42] Homeopathic remedies can also be produced in certain electrodermal screening processes and tested for accuracy with kinesiology.

Some individuals make their own homeopathic preparations by holding a vial of water and simply praying or meditating "into" the water. If strong enough, this intention can alter the crystal structure of the water molecules and deliver a homeopathic remedy. Scientific evidence of this approach has been published using the research on water done by Dr. Masaru Emoto of Japan.[43]

CONSTITUTIONAL PRESCRIBING

In this approach, a practitioner is trained to select homeopathic remedies based on the entire life history of the patient. A meridian therapist might decide that one of the five basic constitutions fits a particular client and use this information as part of a decision about treatment.

HOMEOPATHIC REMEDIES AND MERIDIAN THERAPY

There are several meridian therapies that employ homeopathic remedies. Here is a brief description of a few of these.

Neural Meridian Therapy

Neural therapy involves the injection of homeopathic remedies into the body's acupuncture points. Through this process, remedies are mainstreamed into the autonomic nervous system, which governs involuntary body functions. The remedies integrate easily and smoothly into the system through sensors in the skin, which deliver the vibration to organs and tissues via the nerves.

Qualified practitioners often mix a mild anesthetic in the injection, as well as one or more homeopathic ingredients or other natural remedies. The injection points are acupoints that run on the imbalanced meridian.

Electropuncture/Electrodermal Screening

A solution is created based on the patient's electronic-resonance reaction to the remedy. In other words, the patient's reaction to a remedy is tested after the diagnosis. The possible curative is placed in the electrical circuit and the practitioner checks if its vibration shifts the meridian from under- or overfunctioning to normal. Some devices can actually "create" the homeopathic remedy with electrical or magnetic vibrations that "program" water or alcohol.

Kinesiology

The practitioner uses "muscle testing" to determine if a homeopathic remedy corrects a meridian imbalance.

KINESIOLOGY, OR "MUSCLE TESTING"[44]

Kinesiology is a diagnostic process that has been popular in chiropractic for some time, and is now making inroads in meridian therapy.

The word kinesiology comes from the Greek word *kinesis,* which means "motion." It is the study of muscles and the movement of the body and is considered a form of biofeedback. Through it, a practitioner concentrates on a subject and then tests the muscular strength of a client, usually using his or her arm. Depending upon the system, muscular weakness signifies an imbalance concerning the subject, and muscular strength indicates a balance in regard to the subject. For

MANUALS OR "REPERTORY BOOKS" FOR PRESCRIPTIONS

BASED ON THE diagnosis, a trained practitioner can use either of the two main guidebooks for determining an appropriate homeopathic solution. These are:

Materia Medica: This guide catalogues the symptom indications for the different homeopathic remedies. It also lists the organs associated with each remedy. Using this source, a meridian therapist looks up symptoms and then correlates remedies with organs. (There are several versions of the *Materia Medica;* Samuel Hahnemann himself is the author of the classic one.)

The Kent Repertory: This guide outlines the symptoms of organ systems and lists the homeopathic remedies that might relate to these organs. With this manual, a meridian therapist can look up an organ and then choose between remedies.[45]

example, if the practitioner is thinking about sugar and the patient's arm lowers with slight pressure, the patient might have an adverse reaction to sugar. This use of the muscles is the reason that kinesiology is often called "muscle testing."

Applied kinesiology analyzes the chemical, structural, and mental aspects of the body's current state. It takes into account the following key functions of the body:

- Nervous system health (N)
- Neurolymphatic system (NL)
- Neurovascular system (NV)
- Cerebral-spinal fluid (CSF)
- Acupuncture meridians (AMC)

Kinesiology was developed in the early 1960s in the form of applied kinesiology (AK) by Dr. George Goodheart, a chiropractor from Detroit. AK was originally used to analyze biomechanical and neurological functions including posture, gait, ranges of motion, and physiological responses to physical, chemical, or mental stimuli. Over the years, these examinations have broadened to include testing of the entire nervous system, as well as vascular and lymphatic systems, nutrition, fluid functions, and environmental factors. Goodheart added meridian therapy in the late 1960s.

In Dr. Goodheart's system, AK evaluates the flow of energy in the meridians. Imbalances can be corrected using needles, lasers, electrical stimulation, small tape patches with metal balls, or by stimulating certain spots. Yet another version of kinesiology, Touch for Health (TFH), integrates acupuncture theory with the Western approach to kinesiology. (Kinesiology is meant to serve as an adjunct to, not substitute for, standard diagnosis.)

MAGNETS AND MERIDIAN THERAPY

In light of research revealing the acupoints as electrical in nature, we can understand the efficacy of electrical-based therapies. But magnetics?

Electric currents produce magnetic fields. We can alter an electric current or charge and affect its magnetic counterpart—and vice versa. The meridian system produces magnetic fields that are measurable using the superconducting quantum interference device (SQUID) mentioned earlier.

For example, the SQUID has revealed a magnetic corona around the head.[46] The field magnified by the SQUID apparently outlines the Governor vessel, which divides the scalp into two symmetrical parts. The area reflecting one particular acupoint (GV20) appears to sink into the surface of the corona to mirror the meridian system but not the anatomical mappings of the body.[47] Working these or other related points can theoretically affect the electrical conductivity of a meridian or the field as a whole.

We know that magnetism can have a healing effect. Certain fast-growing tissues, particularly tumors, are electrically negative. Their growth is significantly slowed or even regressed upon application of currents from a positive pole.[48] Magnetism has been known to reduce pain and inflammation, improve circulation, stimulate the immune system, assist with sleep, accelerate healing, and alleviate nervous system disorders. The proper use of magnets helps the body align its own electromagnetic field and connect correctly with the earth's field.

Physically, pain is caused by the transmission of electric signals along a pathway of nerves. The signal starts at the injury site and travels the central nervous system to reach the brain. Damaged tissue emits a positive electrical charge, which depolarizes the nerve cells and throws them out of balance. Bioenergetically, electrical charges are active and positive and magnetic charges are considered negative and receptive. The receptive quality of magnets balances the meridian points that are overstimulated, thereby relieving pain, reducing swelling, and soothing the nervous system.[49]

Recently, magnetism has been added to the repertoire of healing techniques for meridian-based therapies. Therapeutic magnetic devices are licensed in a number of countries, especially Japan, as they claim to be effective in the treatment of bone and muscular conditions, migraines, and especially pain-related problems.

A growing body of research is showing that the body responds with analgesic effects when a magnetic field is used on appropriate acupoints. In one study, a DC magnetic field with less than five hundred gauss produced local pain relief, while a mild magnetic field (twenty gauss) applied continually produced an effect along the entire meridian.[50] This result has been duplicated in numerous scientific studies and in anecdotal evidence of patients around the world—and is one of the reasons that meridian therapists are turning to magnets as an assist in their healing practices.

A number of well-respected doctors use magnetic therapy and acupuncture in their practices, including Dr. William Pawluk, a medical doctor licensed both in the United States and Canada, and assistant professor at Johns Hopkins University School of Medicine. Gary Null, PhD, who has conducted extensive research on magnet therapy, recommends using magnets in combination with other healing modalities, including acupressure, therapeutic touch, and deep tissue massage.[51]

MASSAGE

The field of massage encompasses many specialties, far too many to list and describe in this section. Here we explore two types.

SHIATSU

Shiatsu is a hands-on therapy that uses the palms, thumbs, and fingers to deliver healing through pressure, a process effectively described by its name; *shi* means "finger" and *atsu* means "pressure." Shiatsu focuses on particular sections of the body to correct bodily imbalances and promote health. It is also considered a viable way to heal specific illnesses.

Shiatsu is similar to traditional Chinese medicine (TCM) in that it focuses on specific bodily locations. Unlike TCM, however, the most strategic of these points are based at anatomically functional sites, rather than energetically based areas. They are called *Tsubo points*, *tsubo* meaning "vital point" or "important place." Many of these points, however, do interface with the traditional meridian points.

The Practice of Shiatsu

Shiatsu is usually conducted with the patient fully clothed and lying down, but sometimes sitting up. The practitioner diagnoses and immediately begins treatment through his or her thumbs, adding palm- and hand-based pressures in the process. Shiatsu combines many techniques, including shaking, rotating, pressing, hooking, vibrating, patting, plucking, lifting, pinching, brushing, and more. One school employs walking on a person's back, legs, and feet. A session usually concentrates on the basic Shiatsu points (BSP), and secondarily on the Keiketsu Shiatsu points (KSP).

In general, Shiatsu is based on the same anatomical and physiological principles as chiropractic and many types of Western massage. Unlike these modalities, however, Shiatsu uses only the thumbs, palms, and fingers.

In traditional Eastern care, including acupuncture and herbal medicine, practitioners first diagnose and then conduct therapy. Instead of first performing a diagnosis, a Shiatsu practitioner uses his or her thumbs to gather salient information about the patient, such as general condition, specifics about the skin, muscles, and organs, and body temperature. The practitioner then immediately adjusts his or her actions in order to deliver treatment through the Tsubo points. The idea is to call forth the body's natural healing powers by adjusting biofunctions.

The basis of Shiatsu lies in knowing which Tsubo points to employ, how much pressure to use, and what type of pressure is beneficial. There are many different types of pressure, each of which can be used to identify problems and deliver healing.

The Shiatsu Points

There are two types of Tsubo points, which are:

FIGURE 6.11

BASIC SHIATSU POINTS

The Shiatsu points effect change
throughout the body, and are unnamed.

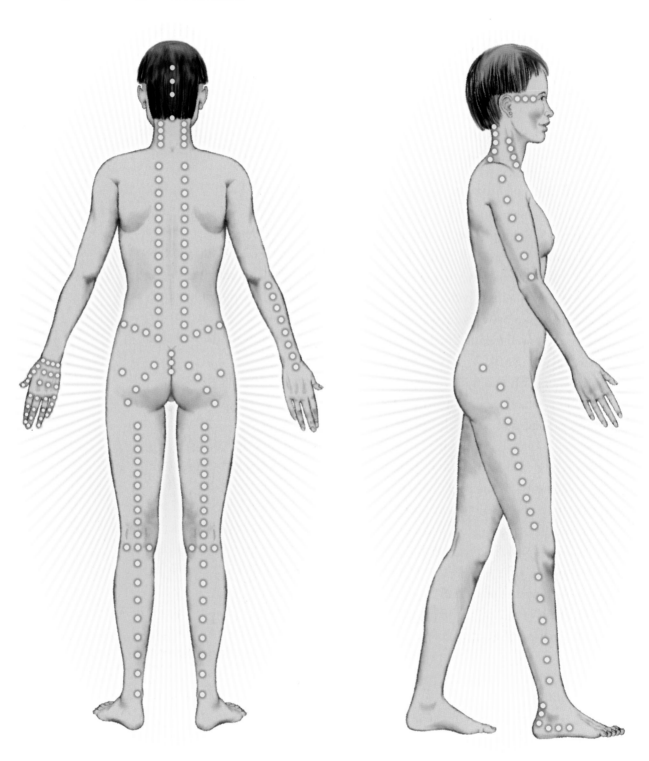

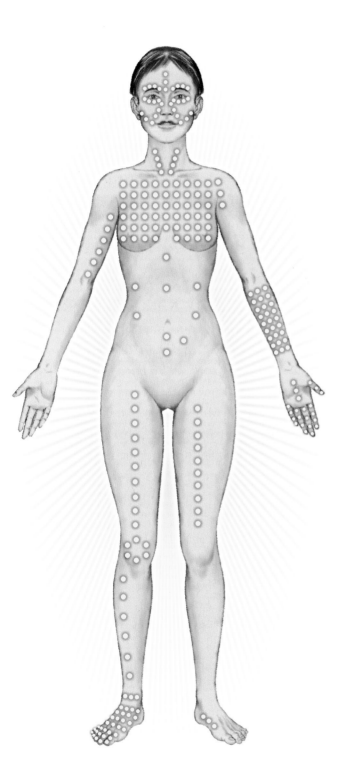

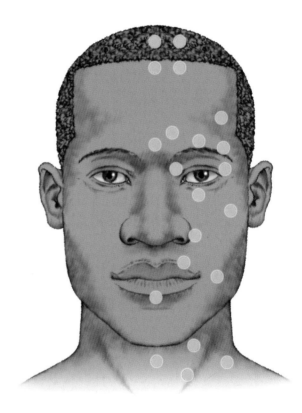

FIGURE 6.12

KEIKETSU SHIATSU POINTS

These points relate to specific concerns or imbalances and are related to the meridian points in traditional Chinese medicine. This is a sampling from the Keiketsu Shiatsu point system (anterior head and neck), provided as an example for the entire system.

Basic Shiatsu points (BSP): These 660 points cover the entire body. These do not have names, and a practitioner often works with many or all of them to restore balance to the body.

Keiketsu Shiatsu points (KSP): These points are also referred to as pathological reflex points and are connected to the cutaneovisceral reflexes of the sensory nerves. The KSP are located in the same places as are the meridian points; they therefore have names derived from their Chinese parent points. These points are worked on for specific symptoms and problems. Some KSP interface with the BSP.

Practitioners usually spend about 80 percent of their time on the BSP and 20 percent on the KSP.[52] In addition to the Tsubo points, a Shiatsu practitioner also refers to *dermatomes*, subsections of the body controlled by specific spinal nerves, the dorsal roots.

The History of Shiatsu

Shiatsu was invented by a young Japanese boy, Tokujiro Namikoshi, in 1912. When he was seven years old, he cured his mother of rheumatism using only his thumbs, fingers, palms, and the application of pressure. As he matured, he discovered the 660 basic points, which he linked to bodily parts and functions through his studies in anatomy and physiology. In 1957, Shiatsu was accepted as a healing modality by the Japanese medical department of the Ministry of Welfare.[53]

There are also several versions of Shiatsu collectively called *Derivative Shiatsu*. One popular style, Meridian Shiatsu, incorporates the meridian therapy of traditional Chinese medicine. Zen Shiatsu encompasses Zen philosophies in its practice. Tao Shiatsu involves mental concentration and supplications to the Buddha.

This discussion highlights the work of Kiyoshi Ikenaga, who focuses on the anatomical and physiological aspects of the Tsubo points.

How Shiatsu Works

The basis of Shiatsu is to prevent and heal illnesses or imbalances by stimulating the immune system and accessing the patient's natural healing powers. Shiatsu practitioners usually treat the entire body. As the "whole" heals, independent bodily systems are then restored. Shiatsu professionals are knowledgeable about the effects of stimulating Tsubo points on such physical systems as the circulatory or nervous systems.

Because it works systemically, a treatment provides the following benefits:

- Invigorates the skin
- Flexes the muscles
- Circulates bodily fluids
- Entrains (or coordinates) the nervous system with other bodily systems
- Regulates the operation of the ductless endocrine glands
- Balances the skeletal system
- Soothes the digestive system[54]

Why does Shiatsu emphasize the thumb, which "reads" the body to diagnose and also deliver healing? The thumb is replete with Meissner's corpuscles (light touch receptors), Pacinian corpuscles (deep pressure receptors), Krause's end bulbs and Ruffini's endings (crude touch receptors), and thermareceptors that detect warmth and cold. It is a highly sensitive organ and an ending point for certain meridians (as well as brain receptors).[55]

The hands themselves are effective diagnostic and healing instruments because the palms contain a high concentration of negative ions, which partner with the blood's positive ions. The most positively charged element in blood is calcium. The negative ions from the practitioner's hands increase the calcium level in the blood, decreasing the compounds that lead to illness.[56]

Shiatsu is also considered an effective way to achieve pain relief, as is explained by the "gate control theory," which can be illustrated this way:

1. An area is injured.
2. Messages about the injury are transferred through "thin fibers" to a "pain center" in the central nervous system. This pain center is located at the dorsal vertebra, which is fed by thin and thick nervous fibers. This site serves as a "gateway" to the brain.
3. The thin fibers open the gateway, telling the brain there is an injury. When the brain "hears" there is an injury, it produces pain.
4. The thick fibers close the gateway, so the brain does not "hear" about the injury—or respond with messages that create pain.
5. Shiatsu, done accurately, stimulates the thick fibers, thus closing the gateway and alleviating pain.

Shiatsu also reduces pain through its effect on the ductless endocrine glands, stimulating endorphins.

Thai massage is an ancient technique based on energy lines as well as the chakras. Thai massage channels differ somewhat in locality from those employed by Shiatsu and Chinese therapists, although they are all described as working energetically and physically in much the same ways.

Most Thai massage scholars state that there are ten main lines, called *sen*, but they do not agree upon their locations. There are three major types of lines: main, extension, and branch. These compare to the Hindu nadis and the meridians in the following ways:

Sen Sumana: Identical to the Hindu Sushumna nadi and a combination of the Ren Mai and Du Mai channels of the Chinese tradition.

Sen Ittha and Sen Pingkhala: Related to the Hindu Ida and Pingala nadis and the Bladder meridian of the Chinese system.

Sen Sahatsarangsi and Sen Thawari: Combine to form the Chinese Stomach meridian.

The sen are comparable to rivers of energy, and the chakras to whirlpools in the rivers. The seven major chakras are positioned along the centerline, or Sen Sumana, and several minor chakras are peppered around the body.

Thai massage uses pressure points, which are not formally labeled, but rather relate to the areas they affect and the disorders they address.

MERIDIAN DENTISTRY

Many dentists and oral practitioners are expanding their practices to include meridian theory. Figure 6.13 shows the link between the teeth and various meridian lines.[58]

Meridian dentistry is most often part of a new type of medicine called *biological medicine*. Biological medicine takes a holistic view of the human body. Rather than reducing it to separate systems, it assesses the function of each system. Tests may include analysis of blood, urine, and saliva; dental and skin examinations; hearing and vision tests; cardiovascular tests; kinesthetic evaluation, and more. A biological dentist understands that the mouth and teeth are critically connected to the other parts of the body because of the meridian system. Conventional doctors and dentists, on the other hand, usually separate dentistry from the rest of the medical system.

FIGURE 6.13
MERIDIAN DENTISTRY

7 & 8: Kidney, Bladder
Fear, Shame, Guilt, Broken will, Shyness, Helplessness, Deep exhaustion

6: Liver, Gallbladder
Anger, Resentment, Frustration, Blaming, Cannot take action, Manipulation

4 & 5: Lung, Large Intestine
Chronic Grief, Overcritical, Sadness, Controlling, Feeling trapped, Dogmatic, Compulsive, Uptight

2 & 3: Pancreas, Stomach
Anxiety, Self-Punishment, Broken Power, Hatred, Low self-worth, Obsession

1: Heart, Small Intestine, Circulation/Sex, Endocrine
Loneliness, Acute Grief, Humiliation, Feeling Trapped, Inhibition, Lack of Joy, Greed, Feeling Unlovable

9 & 10: Kidney, Bladder
Fear, Shame, Guilt, Broken will, Shyness, Helplessness, Deep exhaustion

11: Liver, Gallbladder
Anger, Resentment, Frustration, Blaming, Cannot take action, Manipulation

12 & 13: Lung, Large Intestine
Chronic Grief, Overcritical, Sadness, Controlling, Feeling trapped, Dogmatic, Compulsive, Uptight

14 & 15: Stomach, Spleen
Anxiety, Self-Punishment, Broken Power, Hatred, Low self-worth, Obsession

16: Heart, Small Intestine, Circulation/Sex, Endocrine
Loneliness, Acute Grief, Humiliation, Feeling Trapped, Inhibition, Lack of Joy, Greed, Feeling Unlovable

32: Heart, Small Intestine, Circulation/Sex, Endocrine
Loneliness, Acute Grief, Humiliation, Feeling Trapped, Inhibition, Lack of Joy, Greed, Feeling Unlovable

30 & 31: Lung, Large Intestine
Chronic Grief, Overcritical, Sadness, Controlling, Feeling trapped, Dogmatic, Compulsive, Uptight

28 & 29: Pancreas, Stomach
Anxiety, Self-Punishment, Broken Power, Hatred, Low self-worth, Obsession

27: Liver, Gallbladder
Anger, Resentment, Frustration, Blaming, Cannot take action, Manipulation

25 & 26: Kidney, Bladder
Fear, Shame, Guilt, Broken will, Shyness, Helplessness, Deep exhaustion

17: Heart, Small Intestine, Circulation/Sex, Endocrine
Loneliness, Acute Grief, Humiliation, Feeling Trapped, Inhibition, Lack of Joy, Greed, Feeling Unlovable

18 & 19: Lung, Large Intestine
Chronic Grief, Overcritical, Sadness, Controlling, Feeling trapped, Dogmatic, Compulsive, Uptight

20 & 21: Stomach, Spleen
Anxiety, Self-Punishment, Broken Power, Hatred, Low self-worth, Obsession

22: Liver, Gallbladder
Anger, Resentment, Frustration, Blaming, Cannot take action, Manipulation

23 & 24: Kidney, Bladder
Fear, Shame, Guilt, Broken will, Shyness, Helplessness, Deep exhaustion

FIGURE 6.14

THE THAI ENERGY SYSTEM

These are the ten main *sen* lines used in Thai massage, according to the system developed by the authors of *The Art of Traditional Thai Massage Energy Line Charts*. This illustration shows the main lines and the chakras, and briefly lists a few of the ailments pertaining to each sen line.

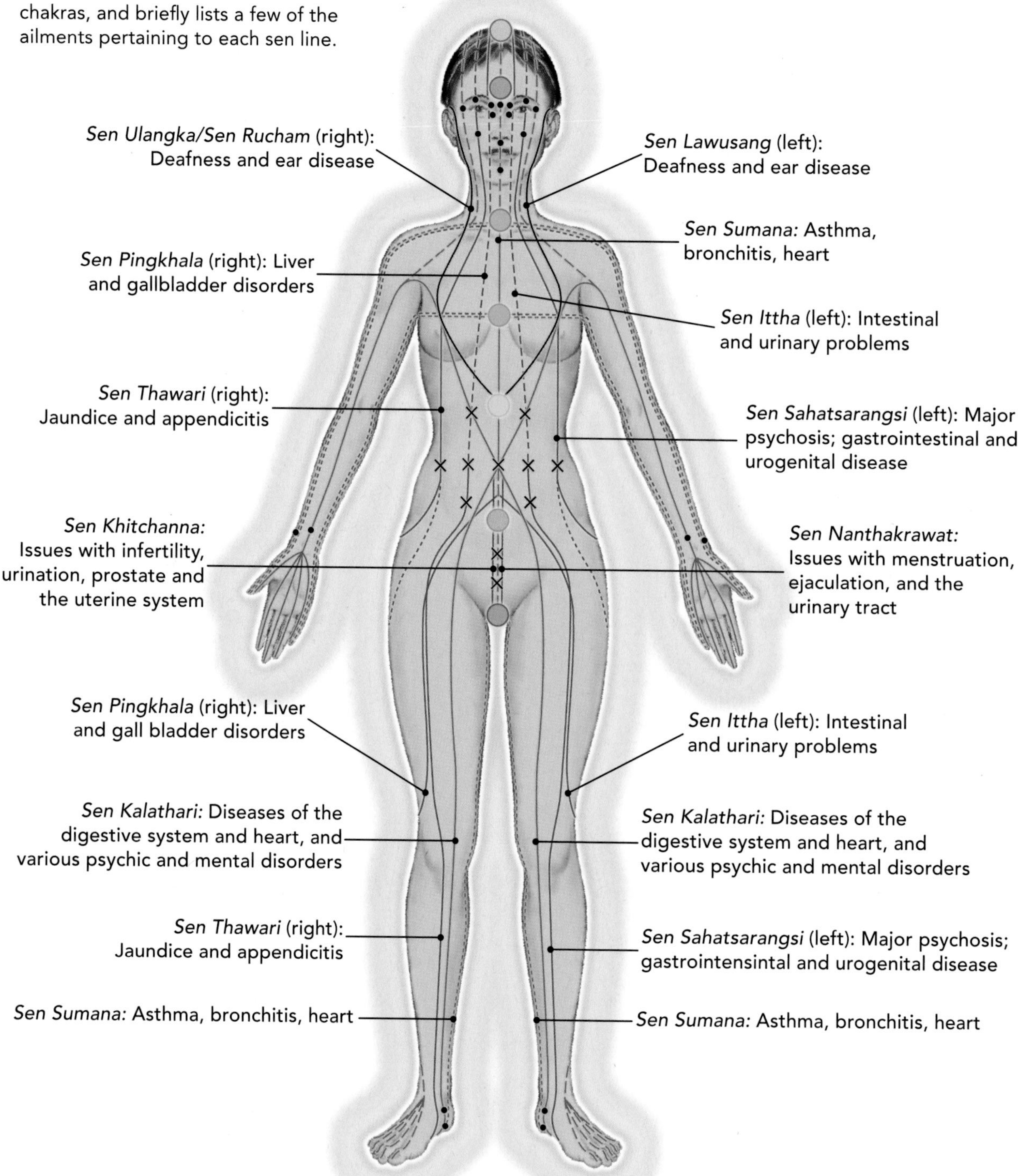

Sen Ulangka/Sen Rucham (right): Deafness and ear disease

Sen Lawusang (left): Deafness and ear disease

Sen Sumana: Asthma, bronchitis, heart

Sen Pingkhala (right): Liver and gallbladder disorders

Sen Ittha (left): Intestinal and urinary problems

Sen Thawari (right): Jaundice and appendicitis

Sen Sahatsarangsi (left): Major psychosis; gastrointestinal and urogenital disease

Sen Khitchanna: Issues with infertility, urination, prostate and the uterine system

Sen Nanthakrawat: Issues with menstruation, ejaculation, and the urinary tract

Sen Pingkhala (right): Liver and gall bladder disorders

Sen Ittha (left): Intestinal and urinary problems

Sen Kalathari: Diseases of the digestive system and heart, and various psychic and mental disorders

Sen Kalathari: Diseases of the digestive system and heart, and various psychic and mental disorders

Sen Thawari (right): Jaundice and appendicitis

Sen Sahatsarangsi (left): Major psychosis; gastrointensintal and urogenital disease

Sen Sumana: Asthma, bronchitis, heart

Sen Sumana: Asthma, bronchitis, heart

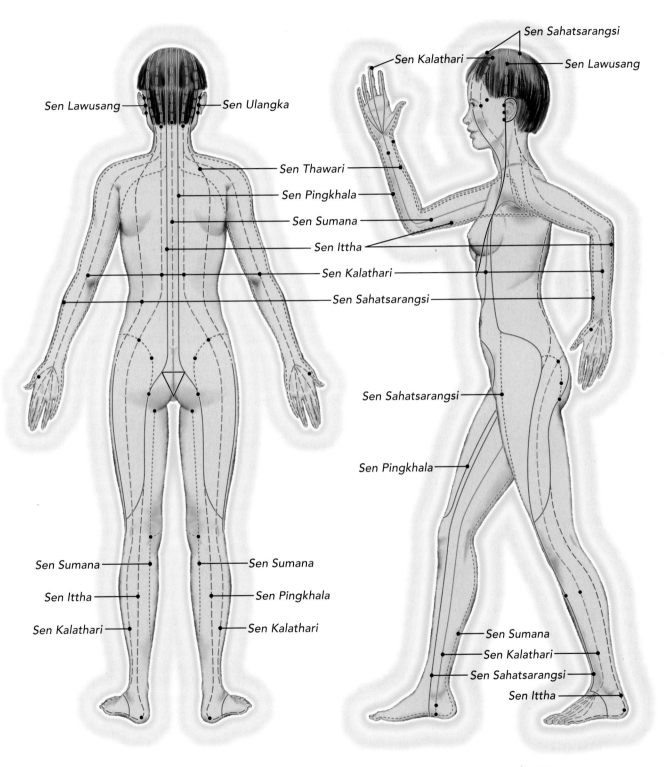

Sen Sahatsarangsi

Sen Kalathari

Sen Lawusang

Sen Lawusang

Sen Ulangka

Sen Thawari

Sen Pingkhala

Sen Sumana

Sen Ittha

Sen Kalathari

Sen Sahatsarangsi

Sen Sahatsarangsi

Sen Pingkhala

Sen Sumana

Sen Sumana

Sen Ittha

Sen Pingkhala

Sen Kalathari

Sen Kalathari

Sen Sumana

Sen Kalathari

Sen Sahatsarangsi

Sen Ittha

FIGURE 6.15
BUDDHIST
MUDRAS

Dhyani Mudra
(gesture of
meditation)

Vitarka Mudra
(teaching gesture)

Dharmachakra
Mudra (gesture of
turning the wheel
of the teaching)

Bhumisparsha
Mudra (gesture of
touching the earth)

Abhaya Mudra
(gesture of
fearlessness
and granting
protection)

Through the meridian system, each tooth connects to an organ or bodily system. An unhealthy tooth can therefore contribute to an organic disorder. Conversely, a problem within another part of the body can create problems with the teeth.

Most biological dentists recommend the removal of mercury amalgams, due to the negative effects of mercury on the body. Mercury is a poison that can cause chronic fatigue, depression, joint pain, and other maladies. Root canals are also suspect, as they can hide a low-grade infection that weakens corresponding meridian organs. Of the many breast cancer patients treated by biological practitioner Dr. Thomas Rau at the Paracelsus Klinik in Switzerland, almost all have had a root canal–treated tooth in a premolar or molar tooth. These teeth are on the same meridian pathway as are the breasts. It is not believed that the cancer originates in the teeth; rather, cancer-causing microbes migrate from the breasts to hide in the teeth and constantly infect the woman.[59]

Biological practitioners might participate in an overall patient health program or independently prescribe oral supplements, homeopathy, and other care, based on meridian testing.

MUDRAS: ENERGY SYMBOLS

Cultures around the world have assigned meaning to movement. *Mudras* are one of the primary movements used in the Hindu spirituality for shifting energy.

A *mudra* is an esoteric hand gesture that activates specific powers or energies. From the Sanskrit word for "seal," these symbolic poses are a vital part of ritual worship, dance, and yoga in many countries and cultures. They have been imbued with many different meanings according to culture or practice. For some practitioners, mudras are magical formulas, invoking powers including fearlessness, teaching, protection, and healing. For others, they provide a link to a specific deity or to the divine in general. Still other individuals use mudras to activate specific psychic abilities, or the channels of chi or prana between the body and the mind.

Mudras always involve specific movements of the hands and fingers, although some expressions also involve the elbows and shoulders. Each pattern represents a different energy and is often used in concert with a mantra (chant), asanas (posture), liturgy, or visualization.

MUDRA GESTURES

There are over five hundred different mudras and meanings, across cultures. However, they are all based on four basic hand positions: the open palm, the hollowed palm, the closed fist, and the hand with fingertips together.

THE FIVE BUDDHA FAMILIES

THE "FIVE BUDDHA FAMILIES" is a Buddhist path for working with the mind that can be applied to healing.[60] This ancient Buddhist understanding of universal energies was translated into modern psychological relevance by Chögyam Trungpa Rinpoche in the 1970s. It refers to five methods of categorizing personality and spiritual nature. Each of the five families can be explained in terms of several aspects, which can be enacted positively or negatively. Knowing one's own personal make-up is equivalent to understanding a style of enlightenment, or neurosis. This knowledge also imparts particularly helpful ways to meditate, relate socially, better oneself psychologically, and evaluate appropriate health care approaches.

The key to evaluating others as well as the self is to adopt an attitude of *Maitri*, or unconditional friendliness. This enables productive assessments of behavior, intellect, and temperament.

The five families are typically depicted as the mandala of the *tathagatas*, or buddhas. Each represents a different aspect of enlightenment but also a neurosis, buddha, location on the mandala, element, season, and color, as is shown by the chart.

FIGURE 6.16
THE FIVE BUDDHA FAMILIES

Family	Attribute	Neurosis	Buddha	Location	Element	Season	Color
Vajra	Mirror-like wisdom; clarity	Aggression	Akshobya	East	Water	Winter	Blue
Ratna	Equanimity; richness	Pride	Ratnasambhava	South	Earth	Autumn	Yellow
Padma	Discriminating awareness; passion	Grasping passion	Amitabha	West	Fire	Spring	Red
Karma	Accomplishing; activity	Jealousy	Amogasiddhi	North	Wind	Summer	Green
Buddha	All-encompassing space; spaciousness	Ignorance of cyclical existence	Vairochana	Center	Space	No affiliation	White

THE BUDDHIST MUDRAS

In the Buddhist system, most poses invoke a certain force or encourage a spiritual attribute. At left, and on page 382, are ten important Buddhist mudras.[61]

A TIBETAN MUDRA SYSTEM: THE FIVE FINGERS

In certain Tibetan sects, each of the five fingers represents one of the five main elements, the hand itself being a synthesis of all five.[62] Each mudra presents a

FIGURE 6.15

Varada Mudra (gesture of granting wishes)

Uttarabodhi Mudra (gesture of supreme enlightenment)

Mudra of Supreme Wisdom

Anjali Mudra (gesture of greeting and veneration)

Vajrapradama Mudra (gesture of unshakable confidence)[63]

unique combination of elements that establishes the conditions for the presence of a certain deity.

MUDRAS AND SPIN THEORY

Physics might provide an explanation of—or a doorway into—the effectiveness of the mudra. Spin theory is associated with the rotation of a particle or body around an axis. In quantum physics, we look at this spin in relation to angular momentum and wave-particles, not just rotation and particles. The spin carried by the tiniest of particles—subatomic ones—can be graphed as geometric shapes or lines drawn from one point to another. One might even imagine that some of these points—the spaces penetrated by up-and-down, sideways, or other movements—connect to subtle energy fields and even other dimensions.

Is it possible that a focused practitioner, a master of mudras, can actually create connections between different energy fields, worlds, and planes of existence? If so, he or she can use the mudra as a physicist might draw lines between various universes. Each mudra forms a different shape, and therefore accesses energies for a different cause. What might we spin into—or out of—existence with this intentional use of spin?

NUMEROLOGY: QUALITIES OF HARMONY

The most learned of the ancients believed that numbers presented the fundamental principle of the universe, providing the only true explanation of the enigmas of reality. Today many scientists are drawing upon the workings of mathematics, frequency, geometry, and other numerically based approaches to explain healing, create new therapeutic modalities, and solve the puzzles of medicine.

This concept is part of an esoteric and mystical lore called *numerology*, which is the study of numbers for practical application. Cultures across time and space have reduced reality to numerical equations. Even today, practitioners derive numerical formulas using birth dates, astrological figures, the letters in names, and other ideas to explain personality, life lessons, soul purpose, health problems and solutions, and relationship and partnership potential, as well as to forecast future events.

Numbers are the basis of ancient Sumerian thinking, as well as healing modalities among many Hindu, Vedic, Egyptian, Tibetan, Mayan, Siberian, Chinese, Jewish Kabbalah, Christian, and crosscultural sects. Certain Quabalists, for example, analyzed Ezekiel, Enoch, and IV Ezra (the fourth book of Ezra, part of the Apocrypha), to speculate on the hidden meanings of numbers and letters.[63] In Hindu scripture, numbers are often correlated to astrological bodies and their supposed traits.

Ayurveda, the East Indian medical system, often relies upon a person's number, often determined by one's birthdate and a formula based on name, to diagnose illness and present solutions, which might include fasting or the ingestion or topical use of vibrational medicines, such as powdered gemstones, which are used for electrochemical healing. Fasting days are often based on numerology, as are the choices of gemstones.[64]

Pythagoras is considered the historic father of numerology for the Western world, although he learned the mysteries from other ancient traditions. (See Chapter 26, "Sacred Geometry: Fields of Life.") He believed that the universe was orderly and ever-evolving, subject to progressive cycles measured with the numbers one through nine. Pythagorus differentiated between the *values* of the figures and the *numbers themselves*. Zero was not considered a number and therefore had no numerological value, and was not even introduced into the Western hemisphere until a few hundred years ago. In the East, however, zero, sometimes called Sunya (*shoonya*) or the void, has been known since the "dawn of civilization." As such, it is the cornerstone of Buddhism.

This discussion of the meanings of the numbers is drawn from Egyptian, Chaldean, and Pythagorean philosophy.[65]

HELPFUL AND HARMFUL NUMERICAL SYMBOLS

Numbers can be perceived psychically in various parts of the energy field and chakras. When intuitively seen as whole or normal in appearance, the field or chakra is probably healthy. When they look altered in shape or form, the energy body could be sustaining problems. A practitioner then energetically or intuitively transforms the misshapen number into its appropriate shape to provide healing.

Some healing systems have linked various diseases or problems with numbers that can superimpose healing. A process called *Energy Healing and Wellness of Numbers*, for example, prescribes specific numbers for different issues. One creates a statement using the healing number and visualizes a particular symbol to perform healing.[66]

The following chart outlines the positive influences of numbers one through twelve, as well as the negative impacts when these numbers appear "altered" in a field or chakra—that is, broken or misshapen, indicating a problem.

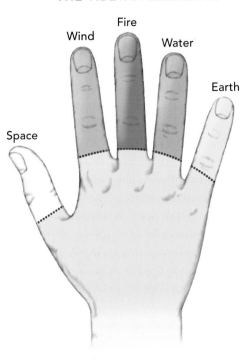

FIGURE 6.17

THE FIVE FINGERS AND THE TIBETAN ELEMENTS

Wind
Fire
Water
Earth
Space

FIGURE 6.18

HELPFUL AND HARMFUL NUMERICAL SYMBOLS

Number	Positive Influences	Negative Influences
1	Beginnings. Represents the Highest Form, the Creator.	Prevents a conclusion.
2	Pairing and duality. Reflects that everything in the universe is made of dualities, which are the same.	Forces unhealthy liaisons, keeps victims feeling powerless.
3	The number of creation, which lies between and emanates from a beginning and an ending.	Causes chaos.
4	Foundation and stability. The number of complete balance.	Imprisons or causes craziness.
5	Direction setting. Space for making decisions. Represents the human figure and ability to go in any direction at will.	Creates trickery or delusion.
6	Choices. The presence of light and dark, good and evil, and gifts of love, offered through free will.	Causes confusion and disorder, convincing the victim to choose evil; the number of the lie.
7	Spiritual principles. The Divine. The number of love and action that produces grace. Key number of the third dimension.	Establishes doubt about the Creator's very existence.
8	Infinity. Recurring patterns and karma. Recycling of patterns. Knowledge.	Stifles learning and recycles harmful patterns.
9	Change. Elimination of what was. Ending of cycles of the eight. The highest single-digit number, it can erase evil.	Instills terror and fear about change; keeps victims stuck in their patterns.
10	New life. Release of the old and acceptance of the new. The number of physical matter. Can help create the heavenly on earth.	Prevents new beginnings.
11	Acceptance of what has been and will be. Release of personal mythology. Opening to divine powers.	Obliterates self-esteem and seeks to convince victims to sacrifice their humanity.
12	Mastery over human drama. Mystery of the human as divine.	Disavows forgiveness and casts shadows over goodness.

POLARITY THERAPY[67]

Polarity therapy is a touch-based therapeutic process that balances the flow of energy inside the human body. Based on the assumption that energy fields and currents exist within the self and nature, it presents principles and tools to release energy blocks.

Polarity therapists believe that blockages manifest first in the subtle realms and then in physical reality. Releasing these blocks returns a person to his or her natural state. This healing is accomplished through working with the human energy field and electromagnetic patterns that are mental, emotional, and physical.

Polarity Therapy outlines three types of energy fields in the human body:

- Long line currents, which run north to south.
- Transverse currents, which travel east to west.
- Spiral currents, which emanate from the navel and expand outward.

Like the Ayurvedic tradition, this system also works with five chakras and three main principles of healing. It also draws upon the traditional Chinese models of expansion/contraction or yin/yang.

QIGONG: MOVING WITH THE MERIDIANS

Qigong, also spelled Chi Kung, Qi Gong, Chi Gung, or Quigong, accesses the subtle energies in your body for physical, emotional, and mental well-being. *Chi* means "life energy" and *gong*, "benefits from persistent efforts." These two terms aptly apply to the practice and art of Qigong, which accomplishes change through a series of exercises that move the chi throughout the body. While it is physical in nature, its focus is often mental: the exercises help you move your mind through the body's blocks and stagnation.

Qigong has been shown to positively enhance nervous system activity and reduce stress hormone levels. A Swedish study showed that Qigong helped women in their forties who had challenging computer-based jobs to slow their heart rate and blood pressure during the day.[68] A study at the Hong Kong Polytechnic University revealed that Qigong might be more effective at easing depression than drugs. Participants reported a 70 percent drop in depression symptoms after two months of practice. It has also been shown to boost immunity, deepen sleep, and ease headaches.[69]

Another fascinating study was reported in the *American Journal of Chinese Medicine* in 1991. Using infrared detectors, researchers measured the output from the palms of advanced Qigong practitioners. They concluded that at least a part of the emitted energy, or chi, was in the infrared band of the electromagnetic spectrum. They also detected measurable and positive changes on human fibroblasts (connective-tissue cells) in reaction to this energy. The emanating energy increased DNA and protein synthesis and cell growth in all human cells.[70]

This energy was more specifically measured in a study led by Dr. Akira Seto, who found an extremely large magnetic field (a thousandth of a gauss) emanating from the palms of three individuals emitting chi. This is a thousand times stronger than the naturally occurring human biomagnetic field (a millionth of a gauss). The emitted chi created significant changes in infrasound, electromagnetism, static electricity, infrared radiation, gamma rays, particle and wave flows, organic ion flows, and light.[71]

Qigong arose about four thousand years ago in China. It is currently a national Chinese phenomenon: at least sixty million people in China alone practice the art.[72] It is now practiced around the world. It employs the meridians, chakras, and auric fields. It also relies upon many elements of traditional Chinese medicine. For example, some Qigong practices follow the cycle of chi in their recommendations of certain exercises. It is similar to both Tai Chi and yoga, except that Tai Chi primarily involves identifying the chi within one's own body, and yoga concentrates on holding poses. In comparison, Qigong involves mentally generating and directing chi through movements that often imitate the natural motions of animals, such as the crane, deer, or monkey. These exercises are accompanied by breathing techniques.

There are two basic types of Qigong:

Wai Dan (also called Wei Dan): Wai Dan is considered yang, or male, because it involves physical exercise to create yang chi. Beginners often start with Wai Dan because it quickly stimulates the flow of chi. There are two kinds of Wai Dan practices.

- Still Wai Dan (also called Zhan Zhuang) focuses on bettering physical health. It involves freezing in particular positions while relaxing the muscles.
- Moving Wai Dan involves tensing and relaxing different muscle groups while shifting position.

Nei Dan: Nei Dan is more yin because it uses mental exercises to form yin chi. Participants often combine mental concentration and activity, imagery, and breathing techniques to circulate chi to the bodily channels and organs.

There are several styles of Qigong. Some employ the practices of Taoism or Buddhism to produce spiritual effects, while others are strictly physical in nature. In general, these are the basic styles:

Mental Qigong: Focuses on managing and directing the mind to reduce stress. As it is estimated that 80 percent of all diseases are stress-related, mind control can certainly make a difference in one's physical health.[73] Mental Qigong requires regulation of the mind and emotion, and also helps practitioners gain better control of their minds and feelings.

Medical Qigong: Used for both self-healing and healing others, medical Qigong has been fruitfully employed for arthritis, asthma, anxiety, neck pain, postpartum depression, stress, bowel complaints, and other maladies.[74]

Martial Qigong: The key focus is learning how to fight and defend oneself.

Spiritual Qigong: Aims at controlling emotions and increasing spirituality. This has been a favored process for the Taoist monks of China for centuries; they also use it for developing psychic ability.

RADIONICS: HEALING THROUGH THE FIELD

Radionics is a method of diagnostic assistance that reacts to the energy field outside of the body. As a healing practice, it is firmly grounded in the belief that every living organism has its own electromagnetic field and is also bathed in the earth's field. Also, each organ, disease, and remedy oscillates on its own specific vibrations, which can be assessed as numerical values. These values are expressed either as "rates" or as a geometric pattern. By recognizing these values, often intuitively, a practitioner can assess a problem and create a remedy, which can be sent long distance as a vibration.

Arthur Abrams developed radionics in the early 1900s. He found that the human nervous system, under certain conditions, will react to the energy field of something outside the body. By observing these reactions in the body, he not only diagnosed disease, but used this technique to indicate a treatment.[75]

Science is now suggesting that we are all connected through higher dimensions of the universe. Most scientists suggest the existence of ten dimensions—the same number as taught in the Kabbalah. Radionic treatment works through all the dimensions, asserting that change occurs first interdimensionally, and second in the physical body. Healing can only occur if someone is made well in all the dimensions, not just a single one.[76]

Practitioners of radionics use tools such as a pendulum or L-rod to amplify the body's signals in a form of radiesthesia. Many such devices and procedures are quite complex and reveal a great deal of detail about a patient.

Typically, a radionic assessment will involve evaluation of a patient's spiritual character, personality, and inherited and genetic disposition, as well as environmental influences and physical symptoms.

RADIESTHESIA

Radiesthesia is the principle behind dowsing: the use of pendulums, divining rods, or other means to track and evaluate electromagnetic fields in the body or the earth. Dowsing involves sensing changes in the dowsing instrument and one's own intuitive self to obtain information, receive answers to questions, diagnose health conditions in self or others, and discover what lies under land—such as in dowsing for water or determining origins of geopathic stress. Dowsing is also used to determine the extent of a subject's field.

The use of dowsing stretches back through history; Queen Cleopatra, for instance, was known to employ dowsers to obtain information, and some experts believe that dowsing goes back seven thousand years.

The fundamental belief behind radiesthesia is that everything emits energy or radiation. A pendulum serves as a medium connecting the dowser and an energetic source, such as land, or the dowser and another person's unconscious. The pendulum or rod receives information from the field emitted by people or places, which the dowser then interprets.

Besides a pendulum, dowsers often use Y-shaped rods made of hazelnut, beech, alder, or copper. An interesting aspect of preparing a dowsing tool for use is that the practitioner uses verbal instruction to "tell" it which direction indicates a "yes" or a "no."

REFLEXOLOGY AND ACUPUNCTURE:
WORKING WITH THE BODY THROUGH ITS PARTS

Reflexology is a time-honored method of healing that has been clinically substantiated. It involves using acupuncture needling, acupressure, colorpuncture, or electroacupuncture, among other methods, on specific points and zones on the feet, hands, scalp, or ears, to influence the organs, glands, and systems of the body, as well as diagnosis and treatment of the teeth.

Reflexology has descended from early Chinese, Japanese, Russian, East Indian, and Egyptian cultures and is based on the idea that zones of energy run throughout the body and can most easily be accessed through the feet, hands, and scalp.[77] In 1917, Dr. William Fitzgerald, a physician, divided the body into ten longitudinal zones running from the head to the toes. These formed the foundation of zone-based reflexology. In addition, he theorized three latitudinal cross-zones.

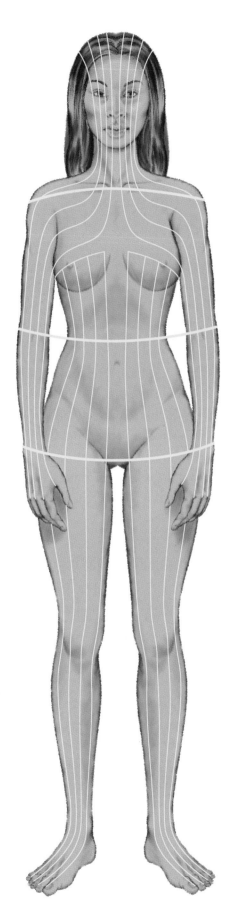

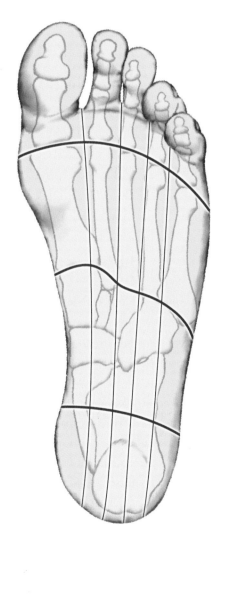

FIGURE 6.19

LATITUDINAL CROSS-ZONES

Reflexology is a healing method based on the idea that zones of energy run through the body. This is a picture of the main zones.

Working through the skin has a basis in early research by British neurologist Sir Henry Head, who lived in the early 1900s. He outlined skin zones (or head zones) that represent specific organs. An organ-based illness can cause the associated skin zone to react by becoming more sensitive or painful. By working on the skin site, you can alleviate the illness.

The skin is replete with blood vessels and nerves. They connect to the muscles and organs and to all parts of the body. If you work on the right area of the body, you can therefore assist its related areas.

Foot Reflexology and Acupuncture

In the 1930s, a physiotherapist named Eunice Ingham concluded that the feet were the most sensitive access points to the meridians. Her "genesis system" is the most widely accepted and is used around the world with only minor alterations.[78]

Hand Reflexology and Acupuncture

Our hands are unique tools, providing us with the ability to grasp, work, and manipulate objects. They are also highly sensitive organs with thousands of capillaries and nerve endings that enable us to sense and touch our world.

Hand reflexology involves working with the hand zones and analyzing the basic condition of the hands. Well-cared-for hands hint at the ability for self-care. Rough, callused hands reveal a hardworking character. Bitten nails shout "nervousness." In some ways, a hand reflexologist is a "hand therapist."[79]

Head Reflexology and Acupuncture

Head reflexology has evolved from scalp acupuncture and is considered an effective way to treat pain as well as functional disturbances, especially those that are stress-related or involve nervous system disorders.[80] Head reflexology can involve the use of needling and massage.

AURICULAR THERAPY WITH LIGHT

THE RUSSIANS WERE the first to experiment with using lasers on ear acupuncture points. They affirmed that the points on the earlobes correlated to bodily organs and discovered how to evaluate the organs' metabolic processes by measuring the electrical resistance at these points.[81] They primarily measured the galvanic skin response (GSR) or electrical resistance on the skin. A reading below normal on an ear point would indicate a problem with the related meridian. After several minutes of light-emitting diode (LED) stimulation on the ear point, the skin resistance readings would return to more normal levels.

Dr. Toshikatsu Yamamoto, who went to medical school in Japan, Germany, and the United States, developed the best-known contemporary version of scalp acupuncture, which is the basis for head massage. He systematically uncovered the scalp's energy points and found that they formed a microsystem—a sort of independent body. Yamamoto named the head zones in an alphabetical fashion. Figure 6.24 illustrates the different zones.

Auricular Reflexology and Acupuncture

Ear massage and acupuncture are primary treatment sites in various Eastern—and now Western—practices. The process was discussed in the classic Chinese textbook the *Huang Di Nei Jing*, and was used by followers of the Greek physician Hippocrates around 400 BC. The Chinese outlined twenty therapeutic points on the auricle during the Tang dynasty, between AD 618 and 907.

We owe our modern system to French physician Paul Nogier, who in the 1950s observed small burn zones in specific areas of the ear on patients who had seen a folk healer for back pain, one of the ailments most typically treated by auricular therapy. Nogier experimented to discover a reflex map of the ear, comparing it with an upside-down embryo. His system has become the most accepted in recent times. It is frequently used for chronic pain, dyslexia, and a variety of addictions.[82]

REIKI: CHANNELING UNIVERSAL LIFE ENERGY[83]

Reiki is an energy practice involving the channeling and delivery of universal life energy, an animate energy found everywhere within and around us. The term *reiki* literally means "spiritually guided life energy."

There are many forms and founders of Reiki. One of the main originators is Dr. Mikao Usui, who developed the practice in the beginning of the twentieth century in Japan. Other key leaders include Dr. Hayashi and Mrs. Hawayo Takata. Currently, Reiki training involves passing three or four stages of teaching. Accredited Reiki masters are now often employed as energy therapists in hospitals and clinics in the West.

The Reiki system draws on chakra knowledge as well as specific symbols. A practitioner is initiated into the use of these symbols, which are considered sacred: the keys that open the doors to the higher mind, triggering an intention or belief that brings about specific results. By using these symbols in a process called *attunement*, a Reiki master can perform hands-on or distant healing.

FIGURE 6.20
THE THREE MOST IMPORTANT REIKI SYMBOLS[84]

The Power Symbol (Choku Rei) boosts the Reiki energy and can be used for protection.

The Mental/ Emotional Symbol (Sei He Ki) integrates the brain and the body and helps release the mental and emotional causes of a problem.

The Distance Symbol (Hon Sha Ze Sho Nen) sends energies over a distance.

FIGURE 6.21
FOOT REFLEXOLOGY: TOP AND BOTTOM OF FOOT

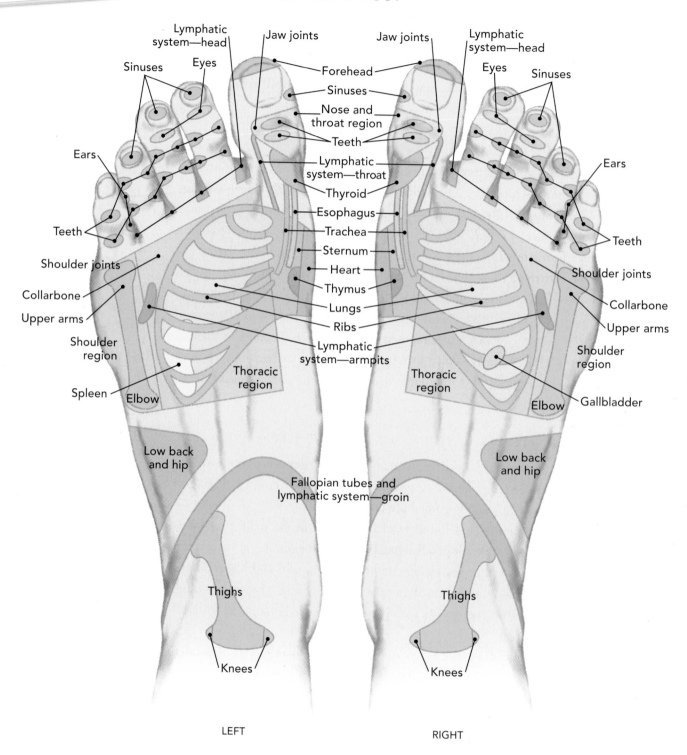

Lymphatic system—head
Eyes
Sinuses
Jaw joints
Jaw joints
Lymphatic system—head
Eyes
Sinuses
Forehead
Sinuses
Nose and throat region
Teeth
Ears
Lymphatic system—throat
Thyroid
Ears
Esophagus
Teeth
Trachea
Teeth
Sternum
Shoulder joints
Heart
Shoulder joints
Collarbone
Thymus
Collarbone
Upper arms
Lungs
Upper arms
Ribs
Shoulder region
Lymphatic system—armpits
Shoulder region
Spleen
Elbow
Thoracic region
Thoracic region
Elbow
Gallbladder
Low back and hip
Low back and hip
Fallopian tubes and lymphatic system—groin
Thighs
Thighs
Knees
Knees

LEFT

RIGHT

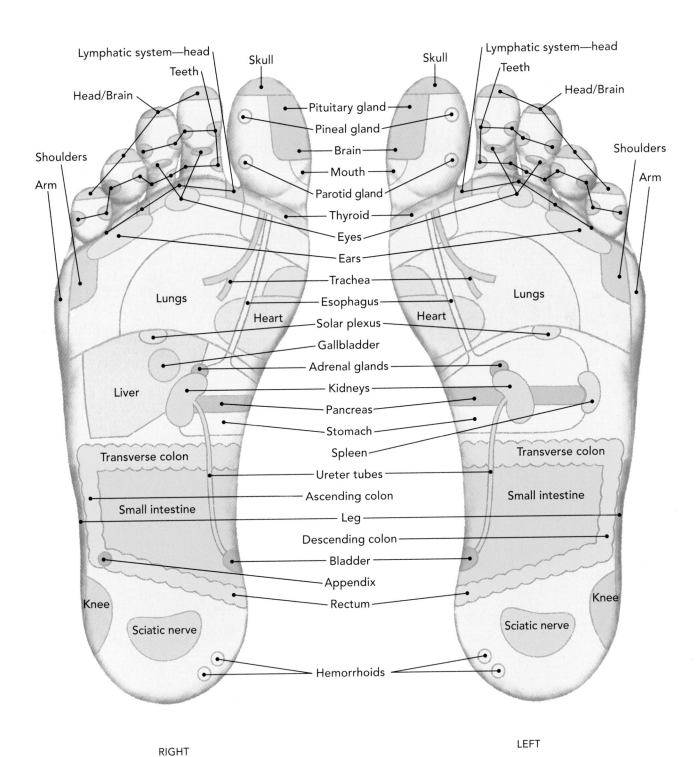

Lymphatic system—head
Teeth
Head/Brain
Shoulders
Arm
Skull
Pituitary gland
Pineal gland
Brain
Mouth
Parotid gland
Thyroid
Eyes
Ears
Trachea
Lungs
Heart
Esophagus
Solar plexus
Heart
Gallbladder
Adrenal glands
Liver
Kidneys
Pancreas
Stomach
Spleen
Transverse colon
Ureter tubes
Ascending colon
Small intestine
Leg
Descending colon
Bladder
Appendix
Knee
Rectum
Sciatic nerve
Hemorrhoids

Skull
Lymphatic system—head
Teeth
Head/Brain
Shoulders
Arm
Lungs
Transverse colon
Small intestine
Knee
Sciatic nerve

RIGHT

LEFT

FIGURE 6.22

FOOT REFLEXOLOGY: INNER AND OUTER FOOT

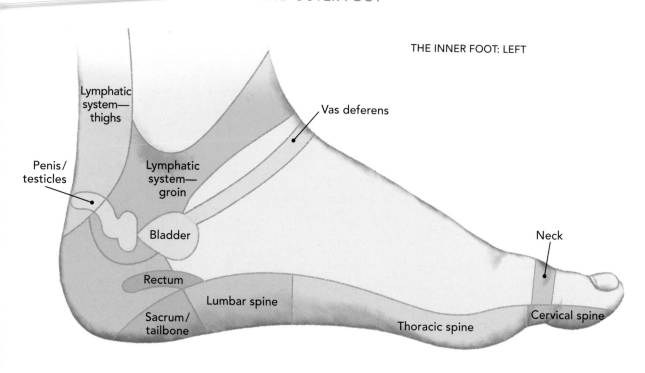

THE INNER FOOT: LEFT

Lymphatic system—thighs

Vas deferens

Penis/testicles

Lymphatic system—groin

Bladder

Neck

Rectum

Lumbar spine

Sacrum/tailbone

Thoracic spine

Cervical spine

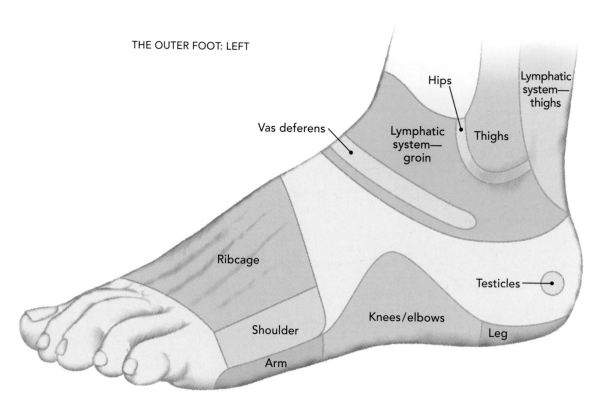

THE OUTER FOOT: LEFT

Hips

Lymphatic system—thighs

Vas deferens

Lymphatic system—groin

Thighs

Ribcage

Testicles

Knees/elbows

Shoulder

Leg

Arm

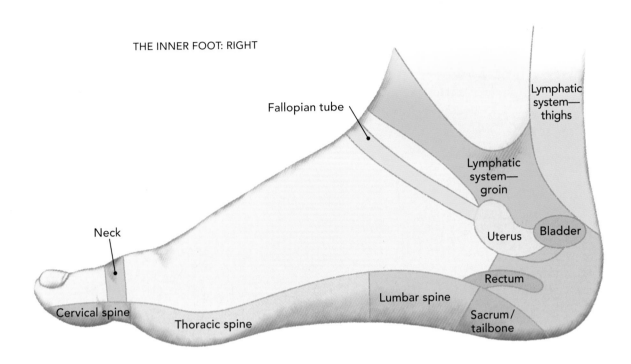

THE INNER FOOT: RIGHT

Fallopian tube

Lymphatic system— thighs

Lymphatic system— groin

Neck

Uterus

Bladder

Rectum

Cervical spine

Thoracic spine

Lumbar spine

Sacrum/ tailbone

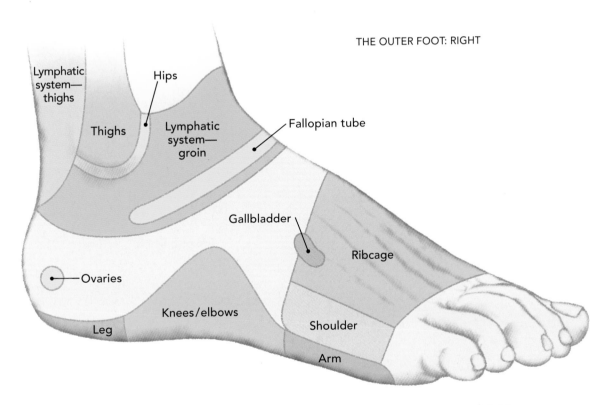

THE OUTER FOOT: RIGHT

Lymphatic system— thighs

Hips

Thighs

Lymphatic system— groin

Fallopian tube

Gallbladder

Ribcage

Ovaries

Knees/elbows

Leg

Shoulder

Arm

FIGURE 6.23

HAND REFLEXOLOGY

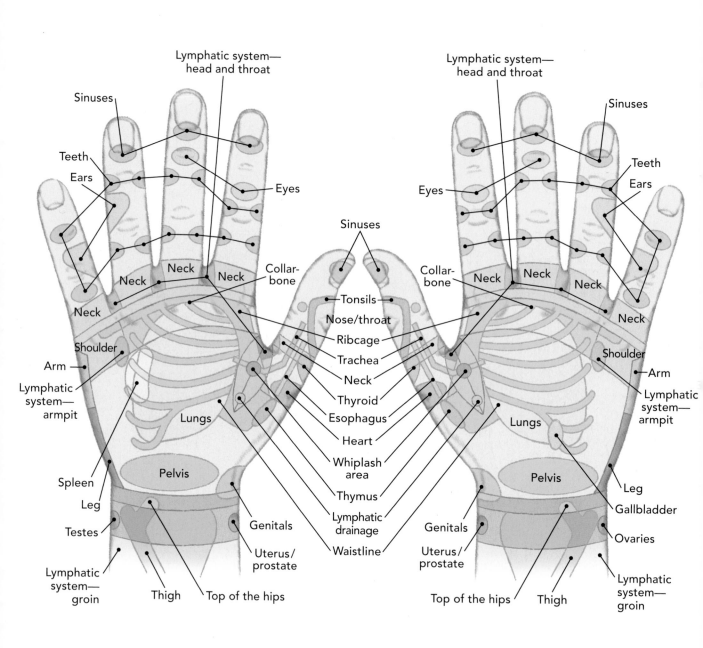

LEFT

RIGHT

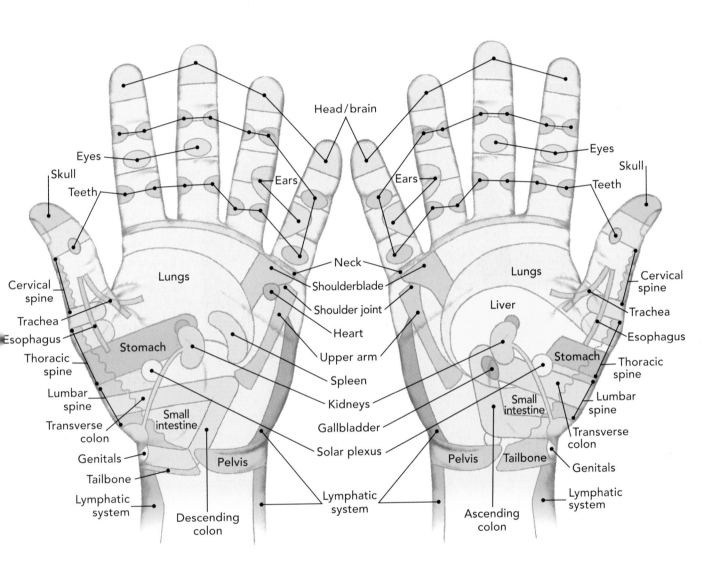

Head/brain

Eyes

Skull

Teeth

Ears

Ears

Eyes

Skull

Teeth

Neck

Shoulderblade

Shoulder joint

Lungs

Lungs

Cervical
spine

Trachea

Esophagus

Thoracic
spine

Lumbar
spine

Transverse
colon

Genitals

Tailbone

Lymphatic
system

Stomach

Small
intestine

Descending
colon

Heart

Upper arm

Spleen

Kidneys

Gallbladder

Solar plexus

Pelvis

Lymphatic
system

Liver

Stomach

Small
intestine

Cervical
spine

Trachea

Esophagus

Thoracic
spine

Lumbar
spine

Transverse
colon

Genitals

Lymphatic
system

Pelvis

Tailbone

Ascending
colon

LEFT

RIGHT

FIGURE 6.24

HEAD REFLEXOLOGY

A zones: Head and cervical vertebrae

B zones: Cervical vertebrae, neck, and shoulders

C zones: Shoulders, upper and lower arms, and hands

D zones: Lumbar spine, pelvis, and lower body

D points: Each represents one of the vertebrae of the lumbar spine

E zones: Ribcage, thoracic spine, and stomach

F zones: Sciatic nerve

G points: Knee joint

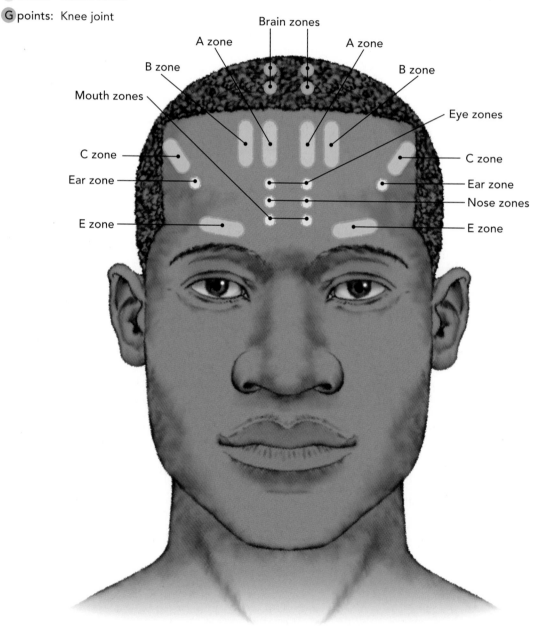

Brain zones

A zone

A zone

B zone

B zone

Mouth zones

Eye zones

C zone

C zone

Ear zone

Ear zone

Nose zones

E zone

E zone

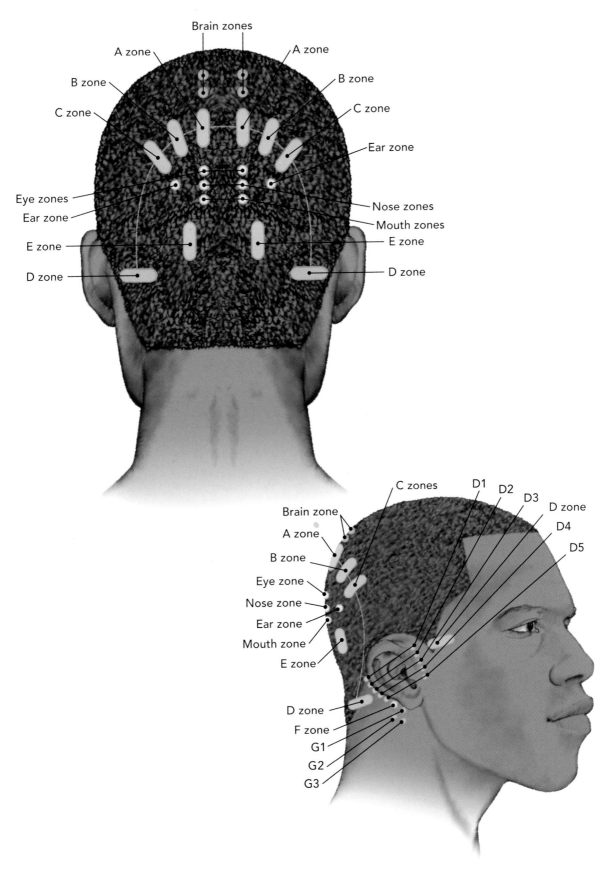

FIGURE 6.25

AURICULAR REFLEXOLOGY

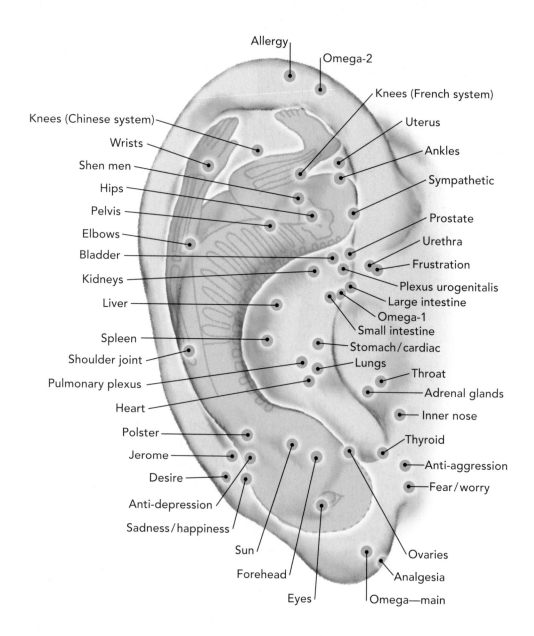

Raise your hand. Though inaudible to your everyday senses, the invisible energy of this movement sounds a note.[85] Certain notes or tones can be harmful. Very low infrasonic frequencies can collapse internal organs; ultrasonic energy can decalcify and soften bones.[86] But sound can also heal. In the 1970s, researcher Fabien Maman sounded a tuning fork on a cancer cell. The cell dissolved.[87]

Sound healing employs sound to create balance and healing. As an energy medicine, it is a vibrational therapy that impacts all levels of the human self—as well as all living organisms. Since water conducts sound four times faster than air, it can be a useful entrainment (joining of vibrations) tool—especially for our bodies, which are 70 percent water. Sound delivers healing vibrations faster than many other methods. It is frequently employed in chakra and auric field therapy, but has also been used by allopathic practitioners for autism, insomnia, and other conditions, and is now introduced in varieties of acupuncture.

This is the science behind sound therapy: constructed of electrons, protons, neutrons, and subatomic particles, each atom is surrounded by electrons that move at over six hundred miles per second. Motion creates frequency, which creates vibration, which in turn generates sound (whether audible or not). Vibration is one-half of our energy quotient, and therefore it is information. However, as we saw in "Cymatics: Seeing Sound, The Fields of Life" on page 141 and "Geometry and Sound in Healing" on page 363, sound information forms patterns out of matter. Therefore, it must contain the information needed to form these patterns.

Sound moves in waves, and in turn creates fields. Particular sounds are passed into, out of, and through the body through molecules, which act as transfer points for information. A molecule can literally take on the vibration of an initial pulse and pass this vibration on to its neighbors, which is why sound can shape and change the body and its fields. Water molecules, formed from crystals, will actually shape and reshape according to the vibration of a sound or the information coded into it—for better or worse. As we saw in the section "Magnetic Field Interactions with Water: Formations of Geometry" in Part III, negative thoughts form ugly and harmful shapes, and positive thoughts, beautiful and sustaining ones.

One of the most important issues in relation to sound is that of *resonance*, which occurs when one object, vibrating at its own unique frequency, begins to vibrate at the same frequency as another object. When multiple systems vibrate or resonate together, the result is called *entrainment*. When the body entrains to positive thoughts, such as faith, hope, and love, studies show that overall health improves. When the body resonates to negative thoughts, parts of the system might either entrain to this negativity (and result in dis-ease or "lack of ease"), or enter discord, which also creates a lack of ease. (See Index for *heart, entrainment,* and a related term, *coherency*.)

Not every object can entrain to a presenting vibration. If a tuning fork is attuned at 100 Hz, an ordinary table fork will create a resonance with it. Strike a 440 Hz tuning fork, however, and the 100 Hz tuning fork will not respond. It will not even glance at the nearby tuning fork. Tissue, wood, and bone—all sorts of matter will resonate if struck by a vibration within its *frequency range.*

This is important information for healers. Every single person generates his or her own *personal harmonic,* or a vibratory range that is particular to the self. Living beings will "pick up" and respond to the people, ideas, or even medicines that vibrate within their personal range, and resist the ones that do not. If a stronger vibration "overrules" our personal one, such as a pathogen or a negative opinion from someone else, disease can set in.

A *sympathetic vibration* is one that suits the living being that is in its range. Its effect is not produced by intensity—such as loudness—but by *pitch.* The inaudible humming of a fluorescent light or the thought of a person sitting nearby—or even a thousand miles away, but connected through the quantum field—can disturb a living being's vibratory rates and therefore, individual energetic fields. This is part of the reason that artificial electromagnetic fields and other forms of geopathic stress are so dangerous. The bombarding energies actually create dissonance within living beings.

Appropriate music or sounds can help restore the natural vibrations of a living being and therefore health, as long as these vibrations resonate with the natural vibration of that being. Classical music that beats at sixty to ninety beats a minute, for instance, calms the heart and, through entrainment, soothes the entire body. Information on sound in healing is featured in every section in this book.

There are dozens of energetically based sound therapies. This list by Jonathan Goldman, a respected sound therapist and author, outlines a few of them:[88]

- Music in imagery
- Music therapy
- Cymatic therapy
- Tapes with specifically designed frequencies
- The Electronic Ear (special music filtered through headphones to treat a variety of conditions)
- Toning and overtoning
- Harmonic resonance

- Bioacoustics (missing frequencies of a client's voice are found and played back via synthesized sounds)
- Hemi-Sync (balances the hemispheres of the brain and induces altered states)
- Mantric chanting
- Tuning forks (applied directly or indirectly to the physical body)
- Vibro-Acoustic beds, chairs, etc. (specially designed equipment projects music into a client's body)

Everything in the world functions at an optimal frequency or has its own sound—even a virus. When a person is operating at optimal health, his or her "tones" are attuned with each other and aligned with the external world. Any stress-related condition—an emotion, negative belief or event, or pathogen—can be labeled as an "invading sound" or frequency that can disrupt the body's natural frequencies or vibrations. If the body or those parts of the body (including the energetic structures) are unable to attune the "out-of-tune" frequency to its personal frequency, the invading frequency "takes over" and eventually causes disease.

Sound therapists work in a number of ways, but ultimately must diagnose or determine the invading frequency. They must then determine which frequencies will eliminate the invading force, strengthen the person's natural frequencies, or compel the two forces (the invading and the individual's frequencies) to work together in a healthy way.

Besides paying attention to pitch or harmonics, a sound therapist also addresses tempo or rhythm, which is measured in beats per minute (bpm). Generally, a tempo of 40 to 60 bpm is calming, while a tempo of 80 to 120 bpm is stimulating.[89]

One of the most important ways music and sounds affect the body is by altering brain waves. The brain has four basic waves, as discussed in Chapter 7: beta (14 Hz and above; normal waking state), alpha (8–13 Hz; dreaming and light meditation), theta (4–7 Hz; inward focus and transitions), and delta (.5–3 Hz; deep sleep).

The brain is particularly responsive to certain sounds, depending on pitch and tempo, among other factors. Different frequencies of sound entrain the brain to different brain waves. For instance, a drumbeat, frequently used by shamans during healing, typically operates at 240 to 270 bpm and shifts brain waves from beta to theta.[90] In the early 1970s, Gerald Oster discovered a binaural beat or rhythm. When a different frequency of sound is played in each ear through stereo headphones, such as 100 Hz and 109 Hz, the brain perceives a 9 Hz frequency, which provides pain relief, stress reduction, and visioning, among other benefits.[91]

Sound is frequently conjoined with chakra work to produce beneficial results. Here are two theories about sound and chakras.

Tonal Chakra Work: The Twelve-Chakra System[92]

Each musical note holds a vibration and creates unique results. There are many theories that fix certain tones to specific chakras. These vary from culture to culture, as different cultures accentuate different chakras. As well, each culture works with its own scales—chromatic, tonal, atonal, octave-based, fifth-based, and so on.

According to the twelve-chakra system, the human body is attuned to the note A. Each chakra has an inner and outer wheel. The inner wheel reflects one's spiritual self while the outer wheel reveals the personality. An A note will attune the inner wheel of each chakra to each of the others, naturally balancing the system. This shift in the inner wheel will also create balance in the outer wheel. The outer wheel of each chakra, on the other hand, has its own unique tone. Another approach to attuning the chakras is to work with this outer wheel and attune it to its own note, thus balancing the system from the outside in. Tones can both heal and harm. Off-tones—tones that don't match the frequency of your body, a particular chakra, or physical organ—create dissonance/disease. Beneficial tones blend with your core harmonic and keep you strong. Tones can be used both in diagnosis and to enable healing.

Here are the meanings of the basic tonal vibrations used in the West, which are based on the octave.

FIGURE 6.26
WHOLE NOTE FUNCTIONS

Note	Governs	Function
A	Spirit	Attunes human to divine nature, the human self to the spiritual self
B	Mind	Attunes the lower and middle mind to the higher mind
C	Feelings	Attunes human feelings to spiritual feelings
D	Body	Attunes the physical body, condition, and material needs to the spiritual body, gifts, and manifesting abilities
E	Love	Attunes whatever is out of love to unconditional divine love
F	Miracles	Attunes any aspect of one's being to the spiritual forces needed at that time, breaking through duality into the miraculous
G	Grace	Delivers grace, which is divine love and divine power, to the situation at hand

Sharps and Flats

Sharps and Flats

Sharps bring spiritual reality into material reality. An F-sharp, for instance, activates that part of your internal spirit that links you with the force you require at the time. Flats allow release. A G-flat, for instance, which is the same as an F-sharp, pushes out any negative or evil forces preventing your spiritual destiny. The difference between working with a sharp and a flat is intention. If you desire to get rid of something, think flat; to attract something, think sharp.

Core Tones

Many esoteric groups work with a C-based system of musical scales. In the twelve-chakra system, this is the theory that is most accepted among contemporary healing practitioners. The system, which initiates with C, describes the physical body and its chakric health. A second twelve-chakra theory begins with A, and relates to the subtle energy systems and alchemy.

FIGURE 6.27
CORE TONES AND THE CHAKRAS

Chakra	Color	Meaning of Color	Esoteric Theory Tone	Twelve-Chakra Theory Tone
First	Red	Passion	C	A
Second	Orange	Feelings, creativity	D	B
Third	Yellow	Wisdom, power	E	C#
Fourth	Green	Healing	F	D
Fifth	Blue	Communication, guidance	G	E
Sixth	Purple	Vision	A	F#
Seventh	White	Spirituality	B	G#
Eighth	Black	Karma/effects from the past	C	A
Ninth	Gold	Soul purpose and unity with others	D	B
Tenth	Earth tones	Relationship to environment	E	C
Eleventh	Pink	Transmutation	F	D
Twelfth	Clear	Link to the Divine	G	E

Sonic Waves and Meditation: The Kundalini Healing Process

The spinal cord is a sounding board, and the vertebrae (with the chakras) resonate according to internal and external melody, harmony, and modulation.[93] The brain, the other main part of the central nervous system, is highly reactive to sound waves as well, especially as part of it actually functions sonically.

Itzhak Bentov, a long-time meditator and researcher, discovered that heart and brain activities alter significantly during deep meditation. Through tracking this finding, Bentov created a theory he calls the *physio-kundalini* model, which embraces many aspects of energy theory.[94] To paraphrase Dr. Richard Gerber's explanation of Bentov's work, the heart stimulates sonic vibrations within the deep recesses of the brain, which create mechanical and electrical responses in the nervous tissue. An oscillatory cycle starts within the sensory cortex, which sends waves of electrical firing from the toes upward through the body. In meditators, this cycle affects the right hemisphere more than the left, beginning in the left side of the body. Along with another researcher, Dr. Lee Sanella, Bentov linked these symptoms to the rising of the kundalini. In deep meditators, this cycle repeats over and over, repeatedly clearing chakra blockages and therefore life issues. As the current strengthens, pleasure centers are stimulated and brain waves become increasingly fixed at the higher levels.[95]

SOUND AND COLOR

In his book *Mind, Body, and Electromagnetism*, John Evans has created a chart of corresponding sounds and colors, including their correspondence to yin and yang on a continuum. In this system, D is the strongest yang note and A-flat is the most intense yin tone. The B represents the transition between yin and yang and the F, still a yang note, begins to transition to yin. The associated colors follow the same line of reasoning. Evans points out that the Chinese concept of yin and yang is exactly opposite that proposed by this chart. Evans reasons that his system mirrors the Western rather than Eastern mind.[96] I have added the chakras that usually relate to each color.

FIGURE 6.28
SOUND AND COLOR

Note	Audio (Hz)	Light (10^{12} Hz)	Color	Chakra	Yin/Yang
F	683	751	Purple	Sixth	
E	645	709	Violet	Sixth	
E-flat	609	669	Indigo	Fifth and sixth	
D	575	632	Blue	Fifth	Yang
D-flat	542	596	Blue-green	Fourth and fifth	
C	512	563	Green	Fourth	
B	483	531	Yellow-green	Third and fourth	

FIGURE 6.28
SOUND AND COLOR

Note	Audio (Hz)	Light (10^{12} Hz)	Color	Chakra	Yin/Yang
B-flat	456	502	Yellow	Third	
A	431	473	Orange	Second	
A-flat	406	447	Orange-red	First and second	Yin
G	384	422	Red	First	
G-flat	362	398	Ruby-red	First	

TRADITIONAL CHINESE DIAGNOSIS

There are four methods, called *szu-chen*, that are used in traditional Chinese medicine to make a correct diagnosis and choose a beneficial treatment. They are: inspection, auscultation/olfaction, inquiry, and palpation.

Each of these methods garners information about the five phases, related organ systems, and the additional processes outlined in the five-phase theory. For example, a practitioner might assess for zang and fu, chi, fluids, or blood, or causative issues such as wind-heat, cold-evil, or warm-wind. Did the problem originate internally—such as through an emotion—or externally, such as through an invading pathogen? Is the problem caused by excess or deficiency? To arrive at these answers, the practitioner follows the four methods to find a logical solution, examining everything from meridian-related factors to lifestyle issues such as eating, sleeping, work, and exercise, as well as energy level, emotional satisfaction, sexual activity, and mental acuity. Every piece of information is sewn into a whole picture, so the practitioner can determine a *pattern of disharmony*, or *bian zheng*.

There are many complexities, and knowing these methods enables a practitioner to determine not only the correct treatment method, but also the right times to deliver the healing. A system is at its most receptive when it is at its peak cycling. Chi passes through the body every twenty-four hours, and each organ is center stage for two hours. Ideally, you want to work on that organ during its primary stage. As well, every meridian has its polar meridian, or exact opposite. These directly balance and affect one another, indicating a secondary treatment site and process. (See "The Cycles of Chi: The Body Clock" on page 228.)

A practitioner might also identify a person based on his or her constitution. There are five basic constitutional types, and each is to be treated a different way. (See "Five Basic Constitutions" on page 408.)

FOUR MAIN METHODS

Following are descriptions of the four main methods of traditional Chinese diagnosis.

Inspection

This involves a visual analysis of a patient's spiritual self and physical body. The visual assessment provides practical clues. Wan and pale skin, for instance, can indicate a yin or fu syndrome. A hot and flushed complexion points to an entirely different set of issues and can help the practitioner home in on the problem. Some practitioners consider facial issues to determine a patient's basic constitution before beginning further diagnosis. Practitioners also understand that general appearance, dress, voice, and eyes reveal a person's spirit. A positive spirit is key to a positive prognosis.

FIVE BASIC CONSTITUTIONS

THERE ARE FIVE basic types of constitutions according to traditional Chinese medicine. Defining someone's constitution is one of the basic protocols for diagnosing and treating symptoms. The type determines the elements, foods, exercise, and meridian points to use.[97]

FIGURE 6.29
THE FIVE BASIC CONSTITUTIONS

Basic Type and Description	Clinical Signs
Dark and obstructive type (energy congestion and blood coagulation)	Darkened skin, lips, and surrounding layers of the eyes; congested chest; swollen abdomen; deep, retarded, and relaxed pulse; purple-black coloration to tongue
Water and sputum type (damp sputum type)	Overweight; swollen stomach; sweet taste in mouth; heavy feeling in body; loose stools; thirst with no desire to drink; sliding pulse; greasy coating on the tongue
Dry and hot type (yin-deficient)	Underweight; dry mouth and throat; constipation; internal heat; discharge of short streams of yellowish urine; digestive disorders; love of cold drink; ringing in ears; deafness; digestive disorders; thirst; insomnia; wiry and rapid pulse; red color of tongue with little or no coating
Cold and slow type (yang-deficient)	Overweight; poor complexion; fear of cold; pale lips; cold limbs; excessive perspiration; loose stools; frequent urination with discharge of long streams of whitish urine; hair loss; ringing in ears; deafness; love of hot drink; deep and weak pulse; light color of tongue with tooth marks on it; tender tongue
Fatigue and deficient type (energy and blood deficiencies)	Pale complexion; shortness of breath; fatigue; dizziness; palpitations; forgetfulness; prolapsed anus and uterus; excessive perspiration; scanty menstrual flow; numb hands; weak and fine pulse; light color of tongue

Aromatherapy: Use of aromas or scents based on the theory that each different scent operates at a unique frequency. Specific aromas affect the body in different ways, creating calm, healing, energizing, or other effects.

Bau-biologie: This practice involves the effect of buildings and materials on health. Bau-biologie supports buildings that benefit inhabitants' health of spirit, mind, and body and have a low impact on the environment. Toward this end, it advocates buildings made of natural and renewable resources; decreased exposure to pollutants, chemicals, and mold; proper thermal and moisture conditions; and minimal exposure to natural and artificial electromagnetic fields and radiation.

Be Set Free Fast (BSFF): Focused energy therapy for eliminating negative emotional roots and self-limiting belief systems embedded in the subconscious mind.

Bio Energetic Synchronization Technique (B.E.S.T.): A holistic treatment that works with all systems of the body, including the subtle. Practitioners (usually chiropractors) test for electromagnetic imbalances using their hands. These irregularities might be mechanical, but also emotional, mental, or spiritual. Health is returned through pulsing techniques.

Bioenvironmental medicine: Changing the internal environment of the body—through, for example, probiotics, which are foods or supplements containing beneficial bacteria or yeasts—to alter the entire system.

Biofeedback: Use of high-technology devices to read the brain waves, respiration, skin temperature, blood pressure, pulse, muscle activity, and sweat to measure stress and response to mind-body techniques.

Biogeometry: Biogeometry involves design principles that use sacred geometry, sound, and color for healing and to establish healthy environments. Founded by Egyptian architect and scientist Dr. Ibrahim Karim after more than thirty years of research, the system is based on a unique energy found in the energetic centers of all living beings. It employs proprietary shapes to alter the energy in food, water, the environment, and the body for increased health and wellness.[106]

Biomechanical model: Achieving change by working with the mechanics of the body.

Biomedical model: Concentrates solely on biological factors (excluding psychological or social) to understand an illness.

Biopsychosocial model: Health and healing that result from the interactions of biological, psychological, and social factors.

Bodywork: Use of massage to achieve healing.

Bowen method: Gentle touches on key points to stimulate energy flow through the fascia, assisting the body in healing itself.

Breath work: Breathing practices that result in healing.

Chiropractic: Chiropractors manipulate with their hands, and sometimes instruments, to treat mechanical disorders in the spine so as to affect the musculoskeletal and nervous system and improve health. The basic theory is that subluxations create disorders, and the appropriate spinal adjustments can heal them.

Craniosacral therapy: Involves the manipulation of the skull bones and sacrum to alleviate pain, boost the immune system, and correct disorders, attuning the body to a rhythm initiated in the uterus after the dural tube closes. This rhythm flows at six to twelve times a minute.

Electro-biologie: This involves the effect of electromagnetic energies from electrical systems. It advocates the reduction of all negative electromagnetic radiations, such as those from power lines, cell phones, and computers. (A subdivision of bau-biologie.)

Electromagnetic therapy: Manipulation of the electrical, magnetic, or combined fields in the body.

Energy medicine: Use of physical or subtle energetic treatment to alter energetic properties of, in, or around the body to affect change.

Energy therapies: Manipulation of energy bodies, channels, and fields for change.

Essential oils: Various oils, each of which operates at a specific vibratory level, can be used topically or in aromatherapy to elicit a specific response.

Eye movement desensitization and reprocessing (EMDR): EMDR uses a variety of techniques, including eye movement therapies, to examine and release issues from the past.

Family constellation work: Developed by Bert Hellinger, family constellation work asserts that families create unseen forces that entangle generation after generation in negative patterns. These crossgenerational patterns must be healed if one is to achieve the independence necessary to live as his or her true self.

The Feldenkrais method: A series of movements that help people reengage their natural abilities to move, think, and feel.

Feng shui: Works with the effect of the landscape and our surrounding environments, including form, history, shape, color, placement, and orientation. This Chinese-based process includes components of weather, astronomy, and geomagnetism and has a positive effect on wealth, health, and relationships. Foundational theories include chi, or a universal energy; polarity, or yin and yang opposites; the involvement of magnetic north and a Luopan compass; and the employment of the *Bagua*, or eight symbols that are based on the four cardinal directions.

Flower essence healing: Flower essences are specially created liquid tinctures containing flower and plant material. These work vibrationally to help balance emotions and therefore alleviate physical and mental conditions. Flower essence therapy is accredited to Dr. Edward Bach, who began this work in the early 1900s. Bach Flower Remedies continue to be popular, although there are now many other lines of tinctures.

Gemstone therapy: Gems have been used medicinally for thousands of years. Crystals and other stones each represent a unique molecular structure, through which a practitioner can program or channel intentionalized energy for healing or to obtain information. Gemstone healing is often used in conjunction with the chakras or to create specific effects in the auric or other biofields.

Geobiology: Concerns the effects of different types of natural and artificial radiations.

Hakomi: Combines Western psychology, systems theory, and body-centered techniques with mindfulness and nonviolence.

Healing dimensions (holographic memory resolution): Resolving trauma in body, mind, and spirit.

Healing touch: A well-documented hands-on healing method that uses the chakras and auric fields, as well as specific techniques, to assist with healing.

Heller work: Restores the body's natural balance by connecting movement and body alignment.

Herbalism: Use of herbs in their natural or prepared state to perform healing.

Holographic repatterning: Founded in holographic theory, invites positive change where we experience limitation. (Now called *resonance repatterning*.)

Holotropic breathwork: Use of breathing techniques to work the "hologram" of mind, body, and soul for clearing issues across time.

Hyaluronic acid: The FDA has approved injections of hyaluronic acid for the treatment of knee osteoarthritis. Some practitioners are considering administering the injections at the acupoints. Supplements are being touted as the "Fountain of Youth."

Hypnotherapy: Release of a symptom, disease, or addiction by helping a client achieve an altered state of consciousness in order to access various levels of the mind.

Iridology: Analysis of the iris of the eye to determine health.

Jin Shin Jyutsu: An ancient Japanese technique for energy healing, involving deep breathing and placement of hands on the body. The latter process is called safety energy locks.

Johrei: A Japanese-based hands-on healing approach involving spiritual healing.

Katsugen undo: Use of specific movements to release conscious control over the body and so let it heal itself.

Macrobiotics: Macrobiotics is a dietary approach to health that emerged in the time of Hippocrates. It relies on whole grains and unprocessed food and employs Eastern concepts like yin and yang and cooking according to the time of year.

Massage therapy: Manipulation of muscles, skin, and soft tissue to help repair the body and increase stimulation. There are at least seventy-five "brands" of massage, according to complementary medicine researchers.

Matrix energetics: Healing energy work done through quantum healing frequencies.

Matrix repatterning: Draws upon a scientifically proven model of organic structure—the *tensegrity matrix*—which explains many of the observed phenomena related to complex movement, structural integrity, and tissue reaction to trauma. Reorganizes the matrix and releases forces to bring balance to body, mind, and emotions.

Matrix work: Transpersonal energy psychotherapy that treats difficult issues.

Meditation: Achieving a state of mental calm through suspending thoughts or through focused concentration. Has been found to reduce stress, elevate mood, and alter bodily stress patterns.

Myofascial release: Hands-on technique with sustained pressure to eliminate myofascial restrictions.

Naturopathic medicine: Also called naturopathy, a medical practice that bolsters the body's innate abilities to recover from illness and injury. It combines practices drawn from several modalities, including Ayurvedic medicine and holistic medicine, to offer herbal therapies, hydrotherapy, acupuncture, emotional counseling, manual therapy, environmental therapy, aromatherapy, and the use of tinctures and holistic medicines to encourage health and wellness.

Neurolinguistic programming (NLP): Accesses the brain and neural networks to exchange a life-enhancing program for a destructive one.

Osteopathy: Treatment of the musculoskeletal system by doctors who often combine traditional medical training with knowledge of somatic problems.

Panchakarma: The purification system used in Ayurveda.

Pilates: Stretching and movements to align the body and strengthen its core, using mindfulness techniques.

Pranic healing: Involves circulating prana through the chakra system and then out through the hands and chakras. Cleanses and energizes the patient's etheric body.

Quantum-touch: A hands-on healing system that accesses chi to assist oneself and others in healing physical and emotional issues.

Rolfing: Restructuring of the body through deep massage and manipulation of the fascia; often involves release of body-mind issues.

Seichim: Use of a "parent energy" delivered through hands-on healing. Some believe it originated in Egypt.

Seitai: Traditional Japanese method of manipulative therapy combining acupuncture theory and bone setting.

Shamanism: Shamans are priest-healers who perform healing or divination on various planes of existence.

Sonopuncture: Use of sound signals on acupoints.

Specific human energy network (SHEN): A healing-touch treatment that combines healing touch and polarity therapy. The system alleviates emotional stress through the bioenergetic fields.

Spiritual healing: Reliance on an outer or "higher power" as a source of healing energy.

Tai Chi Chuan (usually called Tai Chi): One of the most popular forms, a "soft" or noncombat martial art that promotes health and a long life. Practitioners employ a variety of stances and movements that stimulate the chi.

These postures are based on the meridians and serve as both exercise and a therapeutic healing process. Tai Chi is considered an "internal martial art," done solo for the purpose of improving one's own internal self, physically and spiritually.

Tapas acupressure technique (TAT): Drawing on traditional Chinese medicine theory, allows information and energy to be processed by the body-mind system.

Thought energy synchronization therapies: Uses the body's magnetic polarity and meridians through which the subtle bioenergy flows to interact with our thoughts and associated emotions.

Touch and breathe (TAB) or Thought Field Therapy (TFT): While touching an acupoint, the patient takes a full breath cycle. This system led to the emotional freedom technique.

Trigger point therapy: Compression of hyperirritable spots in the skeletal muscles, which are associated with nodules that cause pain.

Tui na (pronounced twee-na): This is a massage process that relies on the acupuncture points. It literally means "push-pull," as it involves pushing and pulling chi from and around the body. Practitioners rely on a variety of hand techniques and passive and active stretching to correct the musculoskeletal system, fix aberrant neuromuscular patterns, and strip biochemical irritants from the body.

Vibrational medicine: Treatments based on the premise that human bodies are made up of interconnecting fields of energy. Disease occurs when one or more of these fields are imbalanced. Rebalancing these energies will establish wellness.

Visualization: Use of internal visualization to reduce stress symptoms or connect to particular energies.

Yoga: Use of a combination of breathing exercises, postures, and meditation to balance the mind, soul, and body. There are many kinds of yoga; most work with the chakras.

The Yuen method: Energetic healing technique that combines traditional Chinese energy medicine and Western concepts. It presents the body as a computer and pain as a sign of imbalance. Various techniques enable a practitioner to track the imbalance to its root cause—including chemical, energetic, or emotional—and a time frame of inception.

Zero balancing: Zero balancing is a hands-on bodywork system that aligns the energy body with the physical structure. It employs a specific form of touch known as *interface*, which helps to connect these two bodies.

CONCLUSION

We've examined energy maps of the body from around the world, and from ancient times to the present. We've explored sacred traditions from India, medicine from the Orient, fields beyond the electromagnetic spectrum, and concepts that are still "cooking" in contemporary physics laboratories. We've examined vast planetary forces and the microscopic activities of subatomic particles. We've looked at the reality of energy—the subtle energies that underlie everything in the universe.

The subtle energies that compose the concrete world also create the human body. Organized into three main systems—fields, channels, and bodies—the subtle actually instructs physical matter in how to operate. One could say that we are subtle beings dwelling in the physical universe, rather than the other way around.

Knowledge of these subtle energy structures is vital to the practicing healer. By understanding the forces at work inside and outside of the body, the dedicated healer can best diagnose and resolve illnesses and problems. The subtle sensitive can determine the most effective treatment and work holistically—with all, instead of only some, of the body's systems. And he or she can draw on an ever-developing body of tools that can augment both Eastern and Western treatments.

Some of these tools are legendary, passed down by our ancestors. Healers through the ages have perceived subtle energies intuitively and proven their existence through application. These energies have been encoded in systems as wide-ranging as auric field healing, meridian therapies, and chakra balancing. Modern healers have much to gain by reviewing and adopting relevant practices. They worked yesterday, whether measured or not; they will work today.

To these ancient methods we add contemporary research and healing treatments. In this book we have studied the science and applications of dozens of current energetic modalities. We've explored the use of medical devices, light-based therapies, supplemental care, and more. All of these treatments, now scientifically verified, are based on energetic theories. At one point we couldn't measure radio waves, electromagnetic radiation, or X-rays, but these once-subtle energies are now front and center in contemporary health care settings.

A great healer, however—one who dares to expand his or her reach for better effect—would do well to move beyond the techniques and ideas that have recently been verified and embrace the subtle methods that have yet to be proved in a lab, contingent on following an ethical code such as that offered in this book.

The invisible energy fields of the earth *do* affect our health and welfare. We *do* have an auric field; photographs are revealing these colorful coronas. Altering this invisible field shifts our visible self. The meridians *do* traverse through our connective tissue. Researchers in white coats have demonstrated this statement through valid experimentation. Still other scientists have presented intriguing evidence of the chakras and nadis—enough verification to leave us begging for more research and analysis. I hope that the information in this book will lead to further investigation by readers—as well as within the scientific community.

The real purpose of this book, however, has been to expand the boundaries of health care for everyone affected by or involved in the profession—practitioners, students, teachers, and patients and their loved ones. Could knowledge of tongue diagnosis, shiatsu points, hands-on healing, or color therapy one day save your own or another's life? Could understanding of the subtle reality underneath the physical universe perhaps create an even better reality for us all?

Subtle does not mean "weak." Logic tells us that if the subtle underlies reality, we can reshape reality by working with subtle energies. And even though we are thousands of years into the process of studying and applying subtle energy knowledge, we are yet at the frontier—the place of jumping off. Will we embrace the ancient knowledge and science's newfound ideas—or retreat to the safety of ignorance? Will we stop asking only, "What do we know?"and ask also, "What do we still not know?" Through open-minded study and practice, each of us has the opportunity to further the understanding of the subtle principles underlying illness and health. And each of us can contribute to the body of knowledge that will lead to the subtle body healing techniques of the future.

NOTES

PART I

1. George Vithoulkas, *The Science of Homeopathy* (New York: Grove Weidenfeld, 1980), xii–xiii.
2. Paul Pearsall, *The Heart's Code* (New York: Broadway, 1988), 13.
3. Seth Lloyd, *Programming the Universe* (New York: Vintage, 2006), 69.
4. www.iht.com/articles/1995/05/16/booktue.t.php.
5. www.trepan.com/introduction.html.
6. http://utut.essortment.com/whatisthehist_rgic.htm.
7. James L. Oschman, "Science and the Human Energy Field," interview by William Lee Rand in *Reiki News Magazine* 1, no. 3, Winter 2002, available online at www.reiki.org.
8. Ibid.
9. Ibid.
10. Míceál Ledwith and Klaus Heinemann, *The Orb Project* (New York: Atria, 2007), xix.
11. W. A. Tiller, W. E. Dibble, Jr., and M. J. Kohane, *Conscious Acts of Creation* (Walnut Creek, CA: Pavior Publishing, 2001).
12. W. A. Tiller, W. E. Dibble, Jr., and J. G. Fandel, *Some Science Adventures with Real Magic* (Walnut Creek, CA: Pavior Publishing, 2005).
13. Ledwith and Heinemann, *The Orb Project*, xx.
14. Barbara Ann Brennan, *Hands of Light* (New York: Bantam, 1993), 49.
15. Richard Gerber, *Vibrational Medicine* (Santa Fe: Bear & Co., 1988), 125–126.
16. Lawrence Bendit and Phoebe Bendit, *The Etheric Body of Man* (Wheaton, IL: Theosophical Publishing House, 1977), 22.
17. www.le.ac.uk/se/centres/sci/selfstudy/particle01.html.
18. www.biomindsuperpowers.com; www.tillerfoundation.com/energyfields.html; William Tiller, "Subtle Energies," *Science & Medicine* 6 (May/June 1999); William A. Tiller, *Science and Human Transformation: Subtle Energies, Intentionality, and Consciousness* (Walnut Creek, CA: Pavior Publishing, 1997).
19. James Oschman, "What is Healing Energy? Part 3: Silent Pulses," *Journal of Bodywork and Movement Therapies* 1, no. 3 (April 1997): 184.
20. Chris Quigg, "The Coming Revolution in Particle Physics," *Scientific American*, February 2008, p. 46–53.
21. Lloyd, *Programming the Universe*, 111–112.
22. Ledwith and Heinemann, *The Orb Project*, 47.
23. Lloyd, *Programming the Universe*, 72.
24. Ibid., 66–67.
25. Kenneth Ford, *The Quantum World* (Cambridge, MA: Harvard University Press, 2004), 34.
26. Lloyd, *Programming the Universe*, 112.
27. http://en.wikipedia.org/wiki/Hippocratic_Oath.
28. Daniel J. Benor, "Intuitive Assessments: An Overview," *Personal Spirituality Workbook*. www.WholisticHealingResearch.com.
29. Rollin McCraty, Mike Atkinson, and Raymond Trevor Bradley, "Electrophysiological Evidence of Intuition: Part I. The Surprising Role of the Heart," *The Journal of Alternative and Complementary Medicine* 10, no. 1 (2004): 133.
30. Herbert Benson with Marg Stark, *Timeless Healing* (New York: Scribner, 1996), 63.
31. www.medicalnewstoday.com/articles/84726.php.

32. J. A. Turner, et al., "The Importance of Placebo Effects in Pain Treatment and Research," *JAMA* 271 (1994): 1609–1614.

33. Tamar Hardenberg, "The Healing Power of Placebos," www.fda.gov/fdac/features/2000/100_heal.html. FDA consumer magazine, January–February 2000.

34. www.washingtonpost.com/ac2/wp-dyn/A2709-2002Apr29.

35. Ibid.

36. R. W. Levenson and A. M. Ruef, "Physiological Aspects of Emotional Knowledge and Rapport," in *Empathetic Accuracy*, ed. W. Ickes (New York: Guilford, 1997) 44–116.

37. Pearsall, *The Heart's Code*, 55.

38. Rollin McCraty, *The Energetic Heart* (Boulder Creek, CA: HeartMath Institute Research Center, 2003), 1. (E-book: Publication No. 02-035, 2003: 8–10; www.heartmath.org.)

39. Ibid., 1–5.

40. Ibid.

41. Ibid., 5.

42. Hoyt L. Edge, et al., *Foundations of Parapsychology: Exploring the Boundaries of Human Capability* (Boston: Routledge and Kegan Paul, 1986); Carroll B. Nash, *Parapsychology: The Science of Psiology* (Springfield, IL: Charles C. Thomas, 1986); J. B. Rhine, *Extrasensory Perception* (Boston: Branden, 1964); Louisa E. Rhine, *ESP in Life and Lab: Tracing Hidden Channels* (New York: Macmillan, 1967); Louisa E. Rhine, *Hidden Channels of the Mind* (New York: Morrow, 1961).

43. D. J. Benor, "Scientific Validation of a Healing Revolution," *Healing Research 1, Spiritual Healing (Professional Supplement)* (Southfield, MI: Vision Publications, 2001), www.WholisticHealingResearch.com.

44. David Eisenberg, et al., "Inability of an 'Energy Transfer Diagnostician' to Distinguish Between Fertile and Infertile Women," *Medscape General Medicine* 3 (2001), www.medscape.com/viewarticle/406093.

PART II

Information on anatomy, as well as on metabolism and the senses, is sourced from the following four books:
James Bevan, *A Pictorial Handbook of Anatomy and Physiology* (New York: Barnes & Noble Books, 1996).
Paul Hougham, *Atlas of Mind, Body and Spirit* (New York: Gaia, 2006).
Emmet B. Keefe, Introduction to *Know Your Body: The Atlas of Anatomy* (Berkeley, CA: Ulysses Press, 1999).
Kurt Albertine and David Tracy, eds., *Anatomica's Body Atlas* (San Diego, CA: Laurel Glen Publishing, 2002).

1. www.pubmedcentral.nih.gov/articlerender.fcgi?artid=1634887; http://diabetes.diabetesjournals.org/cgi/content/full/53/suppl_1/S96; www.angelfire.com/pe/MitochondriaEve.

2. G. J. Siegel, B. W. Agranoff, S. K. Fisher, R. W. Albers, and M. D. Uhler, *Basic Neurochemistry*, 6th ed. (Philadelphia: Lipincott Williams & Wilkins, 1999); www.iupac.org/publications/pac/2004/pdf/7602x0295.pdf.

3. www.medcareservice.com/MICROCURRENT-THERAPY-Article.cfm.

4. www.sciencemaster.com/jump/life/dna.php.

5. J. W. Kimball, "Sexual Reproduction in Humans: Copulation and Fertilization," Kimball's Biology Pages (based on *Biology*, 6th ed., 1996), quoted in http://en.wikipedia.org/wiki/Mitochondrion.

6. Richard Dawkins, *The Ancestor's Tale: A Pilgrimage to the Dawn of Life* (Boston: Houghton Mifflin, 2004).

7. R. L. Cann, M. Stoneking, and A. C. Wilson, "Mitochondrial DNA and Human Evolution," *Nature* 325 (1987), 31–36; Bryan Sykes, *The Seven Daughters of Eve: The Science That Reveals Our Genetic Ancestry* (New York: W. W. Norton, 2001).

8. http://dailynews.yahoo.com/headlines/sc/story.html?s=v/nm/19990421/sc/health_autoimmune_1.html; J. Lee Nelson, "Your Cells Are My Cells," *Scientific American*, February 2008, 73–79.

9. www.washingtonpost.com/wp-dyn/content/article/2007/01/22/AR2007012200942.html.

10. Ethan Watters, "DNA is Not Your Destiny," *Discover*, November 2006, 32–37, 75.

11. www.discovermagazine.com/2006/nov/ cover/article_view?b_start:int=2&-C= - 42k -.

12. Ibid.

13. Lynne McTaggart, *The Field* (New York: Harper Perennial, 2003), 44.

14. Ibid., 43–55.

15. Jacob Liberman, *Light: Medicine of the Future* (Santa Fe, NM: Bear & Co., 1991), 110.

16. David A. Jernigan and Samantha Joseph, "Illuminated Physiology and Medical Uses of Light," *Subtle Energies & Energy Medicine* 16, no. 3 (2005): 251–269.

17. www.cell.com; www.cell.com/content/article/abstract?uid=PIIS0092867407007015, N.K. Lee, H. Sowa, E. Hinoi, et al., "Endocrine regulation of energy metabolism by the skeleton," *Cell* 130, no. 3 (Aug 10, 2007): 456–469.

18. www.rolf.org; www.shands.org/health/imagepages/19089.htm.

19. Jernigan and Joseph, "Illuminated Physiology and Medical Uses of Light," 252–253.

20. Ibid., 255.

21. Dawson Church, *The Genie in Your Genes* (Santa Rosa, CA: Elite Books, 2007), 137–138.

22. Arden Wilken and Jack Wilken, "Our Sonic Pathways," *Subtle Energies & Energy Medicine* 16, no. 3 (2007): 271–282.

23. http://en.wikipedia.org/wiki/Brain; Anne D. Novitt-Moreno, *How Your Brain Works* (Emeryville, CA: Ziff-Davis Press, 1995).

24. Robert O. Becker, "Modern Bioelectromagnetics & Functions of the Central Nervous System," *Subtle Energies & Energy Medicine* 3, no. 1 (1992): 53–72.

25. Daniel G. Amen, *Change Your Brain, Change Your Life* (New York: Three Rivers Press, 1998).

26. Ibid., 37–38.

27. Candace Pert, *Molecules of Emotion: the Science Behind Mind–Body Medicine* (New York: Scribner, 1997).

28. Ibid., 23.

29. Ibid., 24–25.

30. http://64.233.167.104/search?q=cache:lTt8NZxlWAQJ:www.intermountainhealthcare.org/xp/public/documents/pcmc/eeg.pdf+how+an+EEG+works&hl=en&ct=clnk&cd=2&gl=us.

31. Amen, *Change Your Brain, Change Your Life*, 143; Rosemary Ellen Guiley, *Harper's Encyclopedia of Mystical and Paranormal Experience* (Edison, NJ: Castle Books, 1991), 58.

32. www.monroeinstitute.com/content.php?content_id=27; Marcia Jedd, "Where Do You Want to Go Today?" Interview with Skip Atwater of the Monroe Institute, *Fate Magazine*, July 1998, 36.

33. www.emotionalintelligence.co.uk/ezine/downloads/23_Book.pdf.

34. http://wongkiewkit.com/forum/attachment.php?attachmentid=596&d=1107898946; http://en.wikipedia.org/wiki/David_Cohen_(physicist).

35. Ibid.

36. www.affs.org/html/biomagnetism.html; Bethany Lindsay, "The Compasses of Birds," *The Science Creative Quarterly* 2 (September–November 2006), www.scq.ubc.ca/?p=173, reprinted from Issue 1 (June 6, 2005); www.item-bioenergy.com.

37. Guiley, *Harper's Encyclopedia of Mystical and Paranormal*, 58.

38. Hougham, *Atlas of Mind, Body and Spirit*, 30; Amen, *Change Your Brain, Change Your Life*, 143.

39. Guiley, *Harper's Encyclopedia of Mystical and Paranormal*, 48–49.

40. "Alleviating Diabetes Complications," M, U of Michigan Alumni newsletter, Fall 2007, 5; www.warmfeetkit.com/gpage3.html.

41. www.item-bioenergy.com.

42. I. Haimov and P. Lavie, "Melatonin—A Soporific Hormone," *Current Directions in Psychological Science* 5 (1996): 106–111.

43. Cyndi Dale, *Advanced Chakra Healing: Energy Mapping on the Four Pathways* (Berkeley, CA: Crossing, 2005), 4, 139, 272.

44. www.acutcmdetox.com/tryptophan2.html; http://en.wikipedia.org/wiki/Tryptophan.

45. http://lila.info/document_view.phtml?document_id=21, referencing various works, including S. M. Roney-Dougal, "Recent Findings Relating to the Possible Role of the Pineal Gland in Affecting Psychic Abilities," *The Journal of the Society for Psychical Research* 56 (1989): 313–328.

46. Ibid., referencing J. C. Callaway, "A Proposed Mechanism for the Visions of Dream Sleep," *Medical Hypotheses* 26 (1988): 119–124.

47. Ibid.

48. http://www.rickstrassman.com/dmt/chaptersummaries.html.

49. Cyndi Dale, *Advanced Chakra Healing: Heart Disease* (Berkeley, CA: Crossing, 2007), 6–7.

50. Stephen Harrod Buhner, *The Secret Teachings of Plants* (Rochester, VT: Bear & Co., 2004), 82.

51. Ibid, 79.

52. Ibid, 103.

53. Ibid, 103–115.

54. Ibid, 61.

55. Ibid, 83.

56. Puran Bair, "Visible Light Radiated from the Heart with Heart Rhythm Meditation," *Subtle Energies & Energy Medicine* 16, no. 3 (2005): 211–223.

57. http://en.wikipedia.org/wiki/Metabolism; http://www.kidshealth.org/parent/general/body_basics/metabolism.html; http://www.vivo.colostate.edu/hbooks/pathphys/endocrine/bodyweight/leptin.html; http://www.onsiteworkshops.com/manage/pdf1140126696.pdf.

58. www.merck.com/mmhe/sec09/ch118/ch118a.html; http://en.wikipedia.org/wiki/Digestion.

59. www.merck.com/mmhe/sec09/ch118/ch118a.html; Novitt-Moreno, *How Your Brain Works*; http://psychologytoday.com/articles/pto-19990501-000013.html; Michael Gershon, *The Second Brain* (New York: HarperCollins, 1999).

60. psychologytoday.com/articles/pto-19990501-000013.html.

61. http://en.wikipedia.org/wiki/Excretory_system.

62. http://en.wikipedia.org/wiki/Male_genital_organs; www.kidshealth.org/parent/general/body_basics/female_reproductive_system.html.

63. http://preventdisease.com/healthtools/articles/bmr.html; http://preventdisease.com/healthtools/articles/bmr.html.

64. www.trueorigin.org/atp.asp.

65. http://en.wikipedia.org/wiki/Taste.

1. www.spaceandmotion.com/Physics-Quantum-Theory-Mechanics.htm; http://au.geocities.com/psyberplasm/ch6.html.
2. http://imagine.gsfc.nasa.gov/docs/science/know_l1/emspectrum.html; J. D. Berman and S. E. Straus, "Implementing a Research Agenda for Complementary and Alternative Medicine," *Annual Review of Medicine* 55 (2004): 239–254.
3. www.teachersdomain.org/resources/lsps07/sci/phys/energy/waves/index.html.
4. Lloyd, *Programming the Universe*; Ford, *The Quantum World*.
5. Curt Suplee, "The Speed of Light Is Exceeded in Lab: Scientists Accelerate a Pulse of Light," *Washington Post*, July 20, 2000, A01; L. J. Wang, A. Kuzmich, and A. Dogariu, "Gain-assisted Superluminal Light Propagation," *Nature*, July 20, 2000.
6. Ford, *The Quantum World*, 242.
7. Larry Dossey, MD, *Alternative Therapies in Health and Medicine* 8, no. 2 (2002): 12–16, 103–110; www.noetic.org/research/dh/articles/HowHealingHappens.pdf.
8. Vestergaard Lene Hau, "Frozen Light," *Scientific American*, May 2003, 44–51.
9. McTaggart, *The Field*.
10. http://hyperphysics.phy-astr.gsu.edu/hbase/ems3.html; www.magnetotherapy.de/Schumann-waves.152.0.html.
11. www.magnetotherapy.de/Bioenergetically-active-signals.153.0.html.
12. Michael Isaacson and Scott Klimek, "The Science of Sound," lecture notes, Normandale College, Bloomington, MN, spring 2007.
13. Konstantin Meyl, trans. Ben Jansen, "Scalar Waves: Theory and Experiments 1," *Journal of Scientific Exploration* 15, no. 2 (2001): 199–205.
14. Paul Devereux, *Places of Power* (London: Blandford Press, 1990); John B. Carlson, "Lodestone Compass: Chinese or Olmec Primacy?" *Science*, September 5, 1975, 753–760.
15. Judy Jacka, *The Vivaxis Connection: Healing Through Earth Energies* (Charlottesville, VA: Hampton Roads, 2000), 197.
16. Ibid., 198.
17. http://users.pandora.be/wouterhagens/biogeometry/grids_uk.htm.
18. Jacka, *The Vivaxis Connection*.
19. Ibid., 6.
20. Steven Ross, ed., "Magnetic Effects on Living Organisms," *World Research News*, 2nd Quarter 2007.
21. www.wrf.org/alternative-therapies/magnetic-effects-on-living-organisms.php.
22. Georges Lakhovsky, *The Secret of Life* (London: True Health Publishing, 1963).
23. George W. Crile, *A Bipolar Theory of Living Processes* (New York: Macmillan, 1926).
24. George W. Crile, "A Bipolar Theory of the Nature of Cancer," *Annals of Surgery* LXXX, no. 3 (September 1924): 289–297.
25. Thomas Colson, *Molecular Radiations* (San Francisco: Electronic Medical Foundation, 1953), 140–141.
26. R. E. Seidel and M. Elizabeth Winter, "The New Microscopes," *Journal of Franklin Institute* 237, no. 2 (February 1944): 103–130.
27. Jesse Ross, "Results, Theories, and Concepts Concerning the Beneficial Effects of Pulsed High Peak Power Electromagnetic Energy (Diapulse Therapy) in Accelerating the Inflammatory Process and Wound Healing" (paper presented at the Bioelectromagnetics Society, 3rd Annual Conference, Washington DC, August 9–12, 1981); Dr. Euclid-Smith, "Report on 63 Case Histories," available from World Research Foundation.
28. Steven Ross, "The Waves that Heal: Georges Lakhovsky's Multiple Wave Oscillator," *World Research News*, 2nd Quarter 1996: 1.
29. Ibid., 5.
30. Steven Ross, approved in e-mail to the author, March 4, 2008.
31. Harold Saxton Burr, "Excerpt from Blueprint for Immortality," reprinted as "The Electrical Patterns of Life: The World of Harold Saxton Burr," *World Research News*, 2nd Quarter 1997: 2, 5.
32. Ibid.
33. Albert Roy Davis and Walter C. Rawls, Jr., *Magnetism and Its Effects on the Living System* (Hicksville, NY: Exposition Press, 1974); Albert Roy Davis and Walter C. Rawls, Jr., *The Magnetic Effect* (Kansas City: Acre, 1975).
34. Ross, "The Electrical Patterns of Life," 1–2.
35. http://en.wikipedia.org/wiki/L-field.
36. Edward Russell, *Design for Destiny* (London: Neville Spearman Ltd., 1971), 58.
37. Peter Watson, *Twins: An Uncanny Relationship?* (New York: Viking, 1981); Guy Lyon Playfair, *Twin Telepathy: The Psychic Connection* (New York: Vega, 2003).
38. Rollin McCraty, Mike Atkinson, and Raymond Trevor Bradley, "Electrophysiological Evidence of Intuition: Part 2. A System-Wide Process?" *Journal of Alternative and Complementary Medicine* 10, no. 2 (2004): 325–336.
39. Russell, *Design for Destiny*, 59.
40. Ibid., 60.

41. Ibid., 61–62.

42. Ibid., 62.

43. E. Cayce and L. Cayce, *The Outer Limits of Edgar Cayce's Power* (New York: Harper and Row, 1971); W. A. McGarey, *The Edgar Cayce Remedies* (New York: Bantam, 1983).

44. C. N. Shealy and T. M. Srinivasan, eds., *Clairvoyant Diagnosis: Energy Medicine Around the World* (Phoenix, AZ: Gabriel Press, 1988).

45. http://www.pubmedcentral.nih.gov/articlerender.fcgi?artid=1361216.

46. W. A. Tiller, W. E. Dibble Jr., R. Nunley, et al., "Toward General Experimentation and Discovery in Conditioned Laboratory Spaces: Part I. Experimental pH Change Findings at Some Remote Sites," *Journal of Alternative and Complementary Medicine* 10, no. 1 (2004): 145–157.

47. James Oschman, *Energy Medicine* (New York: Churchill Livingstone, 2000), 60.

48. Russell, *Design for Destiny*, 70.

49. www.mercola.com/2000/aug/13/geopathic_stress.htm.

50. www.healthastro.com/geopathic_stress.html.

51. Anders Albohm, Elisabeth Cardis, Adele Green, Martha Linet, David Savitz, and Anthony Swerdlow, "Review of the Epidemiologic Literature on EMF and Health," *Environmental Health Perspectives* 109, no. S6 (December 2001): 9; Tore Tynes, L. Klaeboe, and T. Haldorsen, "Residential and Occupational Exposure to 50 Hz Magnetic Fields and Malignant Melanoma: A Population Based Study," *Occupational and Environmental Medicine* 60, no. 5 (May, 2003): 343–347; N. Wertheimer and E. Leeper, "Electrical Wiring Configurations and Childhood Cancer," *American Journal of Epidemiology* 109 (1979): 273–284; Anders Albohm, "Neurodegenerative Diseases, Suicide and Depressive Symptoms in Relation to EMF," *Bioelectromagnetics* 5: S132–143; J. Hansen, "Increased Breast Cancer Risk Among Women Who Work Predominantly at Night," *Epidemiology* 12, no. 1 (January 2001): 74-77; Y. N. Cao, Y. Zhang, and Y. Liu, "Effects of Exposure to Extremely Low Frequency Electromagnetic Fields on Reproduction of Female Mice and Development of Offspring," *Zhonghua Lao Dong Wei Sheng Zhi Ye Bing Za Zhi* 24, no. 8 (August 2006): 468–470.

52. Richard Gerber, *A Practical Guide to Vibrational Medicine* (New York: HarperCollins, 2000), 282.

53. www.darvill.clara.net/emag/emagradio.htm.

54. www.mercola.com/forms/ferrite_beads.htm.

55. http://sprott.physics.wisc.edu/demobook/chapter6.htm.

56. http://hyperphysics.phy-astr.gsu.edu/hbase/ems3.html.

57. www.darvill.clara.net/emag/emaggamma.htm.

58. http://tuxmobil.org/Infrared-HOWTO/infrared-howto-a-eye-safety.html; www.ryuarm.com/infrared.htm.

59. www.mercola.com/article/microwave/hazards2.htm.

60. http://hyperphysics.phy-astr.gsu.edu/hbase/ems3.html.

61. www.springerlink.com/index/Q192636T8232T247.pdf; Gerber, *Practical Guide to Vibrational Medicine*, 274.

62. www.magnetotherapy.de/Bioenergetically-active-signals.153.0.html; www.magnetotherapy.de/Schumann-waves.152.0.html.

63. www.healthastro.com/geopathic_stress.html.

64. Jacka, *The Vivaxis Connection*, 197.

65. http://users.pandora.be/wouterhagens/biogeometry/grids_uk.html.

66. www.in2it.ca.

67. www.healthastro.com/geopathic_stress.html.

68. http://users.pandora.be/wouterhagens/biogeometry/grids_uk.html; www.healthastro.com/geopathic_stress.html.

69. "The Scientific Basis for Magnet Therapy—Analytical Research Report," Innovation Technologies and Energy Medicine, www.item-bioenergy.com; www.shokos.com/science.htm; www.consumerhealth.org/articles/display.cfm?id=19990303184500.

70. Gerber, *Practical Guide to Vibrational Medicine*, 279.

71. Ibid.

72. Ibid., 279–280.

73. Ibid., 128.

74. Ibid., 280–288.

75. Ibid., 267–68.

76. G. M. Lee, Michael Yost, R. R. Neutra, L. Hristova, and R. A. Hiatt, "A Nested Case-Control Study of Residential and Personal Magnetic Field Measures and Miscarriages," *Epidemiology* 13, no. 1 (January 2002): 21–31; De-Kun Li, Roxana Odouli, S. Wi, T. Janevic, I. Golditch, T. D. Bracken, R. Senior, R. Rankin, and R. Iriye, "A Population-Based Prospective Cohort Study of Personal Exposure to Magnetic Fields During Pregnancy and the Risk of Miscarriage," *Epidemiology* 13, no. 1 (January 2002): 9–20; Maria Feychting, Anders Ahlbom, F. Jonsson, and N. L. Pederson, "Occupational Magnetic Field Exposure and Neurodegenerative Disease," *Epidemiology* 14, no. 4 (July 2003): 413–419; Niklas Hakansson, P. Gustavsson, Birgitte Floderus, and Christof Johanen, "Neurodegenerative Diseases in Welders and Other Workers Exposed to High Levels of Magnetic Fields," *Epidemiology* 14, no. 4 (July 2003): 420–426; Tore Tynes, L. Klaeboe, and T. Haldorsen, "Residential and Occupational Exposure to 50 Hz Magnetic Fields and Malignant Melanoma: A Population Based Study," *Occupational and Environmental Medicine* 60, no. 5 (May 2003): 343–347.

77. Robert O. Becker, "Modern Bioelectromagnetics and Functions of the Central Nervous System," *Subtle Energies* 3, no.1: 6.

78. Gerber, *Practical Guide to Vibrational Medicine*, 276.

79. Ibid., 62.

80. Ibid., 63.

81. Davis and Rawls, *Magnetism and Its Effects on the Living System*; A. Trappier, et al., "Evolving Perspectives on the Exposure Risks from Magnetic Fields," *Journal of the National Medical Association* 82, no. 9 (September 1990): 621–624; Davis and Rawls, *The Magnetic Effect*; www.magnetlabs.com/articles/journalbioelectroinst.doc; www.magnetage.com/Davis_Labs_History.html.

82. www.magnetage.com/Davis_Labs_History.html.

83. Gerber, *Practical Guide to Vibrational Medicine*, 275.

84. E. Keller, "Effects of Therapeutic Touch on Tension Headache Pain," *Nursing Research* 35 (1986): 101–105; D. P. Wirth, "The Effect of Non-Contact Therapeutic Touch on the Healing Rate of Full Thickness Dermal Wounds," *Subtle Energies* 1 (1990): 1–20; G. Rein and R. McCraty, "Structural Changes in Water and DNA Associated with New 'Physiologically' Measurable States," *Journal of Scientific Exploration* 8 (1994): 438–439; Jeanette Kissinger and Lori Kaczmarek, "Healing Touch and Fertility: A Case Report," *Journal of Perinatal Education* 15, no. 2: 13–20.

85. Daniel J. Benor, "Distant Healing, Personal Spirituality Workbook," *Subtle Energies* 11, no. 3 (2000): 249–264; www.WholisticHealingResearch.com.

86. www.healingtouchinternational.org.

87. R. C. Byrd, "Positive Therapeutic Effects of Intercessory Prayer in a Coronary Care Unit Population," *Southern Medical Journal* 81, no. 7 (1988): 826–829; www.healingtouchinternational.org/ index. php?option=com_content&task=view&id=83.

88. Oschman, *Energy Medicine*.

89. L. Russek and G. Schwartz, "Energy Cardiology: A Dynamical Energy Systems Approach for Integrating Conventional and Alternative Medicine," *Journal of Mind–Body Health* 12, no. 4 (1996): 4–24.

90. Daniel J. Benor, "Spiritual Healing as the Energy Side of Einstein's Equation," www.WholisticHealingResearch.com.

91. B. F. Sisken and J. Walder, "Therapeutic Aspects of Electromagnetic Fields for Soft Tissue Healing," in *Electromagnetic Fields: Biological Interactions and Mechanisms*, ed. M. Blank (Washington, DC: American Chemical Society, 1995), 277–285.

92. J. Zimmerman, "Laying-on-of-Hands Healing and Therapeutic Touch: A Testable Theory," *BEMI Currents, Journal of the BioElectromagnetics Institute* 2 (1990): 8–17.

93. M. S. Benford, "Radiogenic Metabolism: An Alternative Cellular Energy Source," *Medical Hypotheses* 56, no. 1 (2001): 33–39.

94. B. Haisch and A. Rueda, "A Quantum Broom Sweeps Clean," *Mercury* 25, no. 2 (March/April 1996): 2–15.

95. V. Panov, V. Kichigin, G. Khaldeev, et al., "Torsion Fields and Experiments," *Journal of New Energy* 2 (1997): 29–39.

96. Ledwith and Heinemann, *The Orb Project*, 54–55.

97. www.byregion.net/articles-healers/Sound_DNA.html.

98. www.sciencedaily.com/releases/1998/09/980904035915.htm.

99. www.chiro.org/ChiroZine/ABSTRACTS/Cervical_Spine_Geometry.shtml.

100. www.healingsounds.com.

101. Mark Alpert, "The Triangular Universe," *Scientific American*, February 2007, 24.

102. John Evans, *Mind, Body and Electromagnetism* (Dorset, UK: Element, 1986), 134. http://www.luisprada.com/Protected/the_planetary_grids.htm; http://www.aniwilliams.com/geometry_music_healing.htm; http://www.odisease.com/oplatinicsolid_rest.html.

103. www.sacredsites.com/europe/ireland/tower_of_cashel.html.

104. www.luisprada.com/Protected/the_planetary_grids.html; www.aniwilliams.com/geometry_music_healing.html.

105. www.odisease.com/oplatonicsolid_rest.html.

106. P. S. Callahan, "The Mysterious Round Towers of Ireland: Low Energy Radio in Nature," *The Explorer's Journal* (Summer 1993): 84–91.

107. Harvey Lisle, *The Enlivened Rock Powders* (Shelby, NC: Acres, 1994).

108. Steve Gamble, "Healing Energy and Water," www.hado.net.

109. Ralph Suddath, "Messages from Water: Water's Remarkable Expressions," www.hado.net.

110. Ibid.

111. www.frankperry.co.uk/Cymatics.htm; www.physics.odu.edu/~hyde/Teaching/Chladni_Plates.html.

112. Ibid.

113. www.redicecreations.com/specialreports/2006/01jan/solfeggio.html.

114. Ibid.

115. Ibid.

116. www.tomatis.com/English/Articles/how_we_listen.html.

117. www.tomatis.com/English/Articles/add_adhd.html.

118. www.byregion.net/articles-healers/Sound_DNA.html.

119. Ibid.

120. Ibid.
121. Michael Shermer, "Rupert's Resonance," *Scientific American*, November 2005, 19; Rupert Sheldrake, *A New Science of Life* (Rochester, VT: Park Street, 1995).
122. Brennan, *Hands of Light*, 49.
123. Bendit and Bendit, *The Etheric Body of Man*, 22.
124. Gerber, *Practical Guide to Vibrational Medicine*, 125–126.
125. www.bearcy.com/handsoflight5.html.
126. John White and Stanley Krippner, *Future Science* (New York: Anchor, 1977).
127. http://en.wikipedia.org/wiki/Jan_Baptist_van_Helmont; www.theosociety.org/pasadena/fund/fund-10.htm.
128. http://gvanv.com/compass/arch/v1402/albanese.html.
129. http://en.wikipedia.org/wiki/Odic_force; www.bearcy.com/handsoflight5.html.
130. Walter J. Kilner, *The Human Aura* (New York: University Books, 1965).
131. Wilhelm Reich, *The Discovery of the Orgone, Vol. 1, The Function of the Orgasm*, trans. Theodore P. Wolfe (New York: Orgone Institute Press, 1942), 2nd ed. (New York: Farrar, Straus and Giroux, 1961); Wilhelm Reich, *The Cancer Biopathy* (New York: Farrar, Straus and Giroux, 1973).
132. P. D. and L. J. Bendit, *Man Incarnate* (London: Theosophical Publishing House, 1957).
133. Dora Kunz and Erik Peper, "Fields and Their Clinical Implications," *The American Theosophist* (December 1982): 395.
134. www.bearcy.com/handsoflight5.html; http://biorespect.com/lesnews.asp?ID=5&NEWSID=119.
135. www.mietekwirkus.com/testimonials_friedman.html.
136. Valerie V. Hunt, Wayne W. Massey, Robert Weinberg, Rosalyn Bruyere, and Pierre M. Hahn, "A Study of Structural Integration from Neuromuscular, Energy Field, and Emotional Approaches" (1977), sponsored by the Rolf Institute of Structural Integration; www.rolf.com.au/downloads/ucla.pdf.
137. Oschman, *Energy Medicine*.
138. Ibid., 30.
139. Ibid., 34.
140. Brennan, *Hands of Light*, 34.
141. Evans, *Mind, Body and Electromagnetism*, 22.
142. Ibid., 47-54.
143. Ibid.
144. http://homepage.ntlworld.com/homeopathy_advice/Theory/Intermediate/miasm.html.
145. Gerber, *Practical Guide to Vibrational Medicine*, 146.
146. Jon Whale, "Core Energy Surgery for the Electromagnetic Body," www.positivehealth.com/article-list.ph"p?subjectid=95.
147. Dale, *Advanced Chakra Healing*, 131–132.
148. www.sevenraystoday.com/sowhatarethesevenrays.htm.
149. www.assemblagepointcentre.com; Jon Whale, "Core Energy, Case Studies," www.positivehealth.com/article-list.ph"p?subjectid=95.
150. Samuel Hahnemann, *Organon*, 5th ed. (R.C. Tandon: B. Jain Publishers Pvt. Ltd., 2002).

PART IV

1. Imre Galambos, "The Origins of Chinese Medicine: The Early Development of Medical Literature in China," at www.zhenjiu.de/Literature/Fachartikel/englisch/origins-of.htm; www.logoi.com/notes/chinese_medicine.html; Manfred Pokert, *The Theoretical Foundations of Chinese Medicine: Systems of Correspondence* (Cambridge, MA: MIT Press, 1974); Nathan Sivin, "Huangdi Neijing," in *Early Chinese Texts: A Bibliographical Guide*, ed. Michael Loewe (Berkeley, CA: IEAS, 1993).
2. www.logoi.com/notes/chinese_medicine.html.
3. www.herbalhealing.co.uk/Acupuncture_Introduction.htm; http://en.wikipedia.org/wiki/History_of_science_and_technology_in_China.
4. www.compassionateacupuncture.com/How%20Acupuncture%20Works.htm; www.peacefulmind.com/articlesa.htm.
5. Beverly Rubik, "Can Western Science Provide a Foundation for Acupuncture?" *Alternative Therapies* 1, no. 4 (September 1995): 41-47. www.emofree.com/Research/meridianexistence.htm.
6. www.compassionateacupuncture.com; www.peacefulmind.com.
7. Pokert, *Theoretical Foundations of Chinese Medicine*; www.acupuncture.com/education/tcmbasics/mienshiang.htm; http://biologie.wewi.eldoc.ub.rug.nl/FILES/root/publ/2006/acupunctuur/rap69acupunctuur.pdf; www.compassionateacupuncture.com/How%20Acupuncture%20Works.htm; www.emofree.com/Research/meridianexistence.htm; Ted Kaptuchuk, *The Web That Has No Weaver* (New York: Congdon and Weed, 1983); Henry C. Lu, *Traditional Chinese Medicine* (Laguna Beach, CA: Basic Health Publications, 2005); Giovanni Maciocia, *The Foundations of Chinese Medicine: A Comprehensive Text for Acupuncturists and Herbalists*, 2nd ed. (New York: Churchill Livingstone, 2005); Giovanni Maciocia, *The Practice of Chinese Medicine*, 1st ed. (New York: Churchill Livingstone, 1997); www.acupuncture.com; www.acupuncture.com/education/theory/acuintro.htm; http://nccam.nih.gov/health/acupuncture/; www.informit.com/articles/article.aspx?p=174361.

8. http://tcm.health-info.org/WHO-treatment-list.htm; http://en.wikipedia.org/wiki/Meridian_(Chinese_medicine).

9. L. V. Carnie, *Chi Gung* (St. Paul, MN: Llewellyn, 1997); Waysun Liao, *The Essence of T'ai Chi* (Boston: Shambhala, 1995).

10. www.informit.com/articles/article.aspx?p=174361.

11. www.matzkefamily.net/doug/papers/tucson2b.html.

12. http://paraphysics-research-institute.org/Contents/Articles/Physics%20and%20the%20Paranormal.htm.

13. Ruth Kidson, *Acupuncture for Everyone* (Rochester, VT: Healing Arts, 2000), 34.

14. Ibid.; www.compassionateacupuncture.com/How%20Acupuncture%20Works.htm.

15. www.peacefulmind.com/articlesa.htm.

16. Gary Taubes, "The Electric Man," *Discover*, April 1986, 24–37.

17. Björn Nordenström, *Biologically Closed Electric Circuits: Clinical, Experimental and Theoretical Evidence for an Additional Circulatory System* (Stockholm: Nordic Medical Publications, 1983).

18. Ibid., 26.

19. www.ursus.se/ursus/publications.shtml.

20. Ibid.

21. Robert O. Becker, *Cross Currents* (New York: Penguin, 1990), 159.

22. Ibid., 159–160.

23. Ibid., 153–154.

24. Rubik, "Can Western Science Provide a Foundation for Acupuncture?"

25. www.peacefulmind.com/articlesa.htm.

26. M. M. Giraud-Guille, "Twisted Plywood Architecture of Collagen Fibrils in Human Compact Bone Osteons," *Calcified Tissue International* 42 (1988): 167–180.

27. Tiller, *Science and Human Transformation*, 117–119.

28. Ibid., 120.

29. www.tillerfoundation.com/science.html.

30. www.astronutrition.com; www.healthguidance.org/entry/3441/1/Hyaluronic-Acid-The-Fountain-of-Youth.html.

31. P. H. Weigel, G. M. Fuller, and R. D. LeBoeuf, "A Model for the Role of Hyaluronic Acid and Fibrin in the Early Events During the Inflammatory Response and Wound Healing," *Journal of Theoretical Biology* 119, no.2 (1986): 219–234.

32. www.naturalworldhealing.com/body-energy-imaging-proposal.htm.

33. www.energymed.org/hbank/handouts/harold_burr_biofields.htm.

34. www.harmonics.com.au/acuenergetics.shtml.

35. www.bibliotecapleyades.net/ciencia/ciencia_humanmultidimensionaanatomy.htm.

36. http://links.jstor.org/sici?sici=0305-7410(196507%2F09)23%3C28%3ACTMAPV%3E2.0.CO%3B2-9; S. Rose-Neil, "The Work of Professor Kim Bonghan," *The Acupuncturist* 1, no. 15 (1967): 15-19; W. Tiller, "Some Energy Observations of Man and Nature," *The Kirlian Aura* (Garden City, NY: Doubleday, 1974), 123–145; www.okmedi.net/English/ebody01/meridians01.asp; www.okchart.com/English/ebody02/ehistory02a.asp; wwwsoc.nii.ac.jp/islis/en/journalE/abst231E.htm.

37. www.biomeridian.com/virtual-medicine.htm.

38. www.miridiatech.com/acugraph/originandhistory.htm; www.sanavida.info/acupuncture-q-and-a.html.

39. Z.-X. Zhu, "Research Advances in the Electrical Specificity of Meridians and Acupuncture Points," *American Journal of Acupuncture* 9 (1981): 203-216.

40. www.medicalacupuncture.com/aama_marf/journal/vol13_1/article7.html.

41. http://sci.tech-archive.net/Archive/sci.physics/2005-02/4794.html; http://marquis.rebsart.com/dif.html; I. F. Dumitrescu, "Contribution to the Electro-Physiology of the Active Points," International Acupuncture Conference, Bucharest, Romania, 1977, quoted in "Research Advances in the Electrical Specificity of Meridians and Acupuncture Points," *American Journal of Acupuncture* 9, no. 3 (1981): 9.

42. M. Mussat, trans. E. Serejski, *Acupuncture Networks* 2 (1997).

43. http://biologie.wewi.eldoc.ub.rug.nl/FILES/root/publ/2006/acupunctuur/rap69acupunctuur.pdf; Jia-Xu Chen and Sheng-Xing Ma, *The Journal of Alternative and Complementary Medicine* 11, no. 3 (2005): 423–431.

44. P. de Vernejoul, et al., "Etude Des Meridiens D'Acupuncture par les Traceurs Radioactifs," *Bulletin of the Academy of National Medicine* (Paris) 169 (October 1985): 1071–1075.

45. Jean-Claude Darras, Pierre de Vernejoul, and Pierre Albarède, "A Study on the Migration of Radioactive Tracers after Injection at Acupoints," *American Journal of Acupuncture* 20, no. 3 (1992): 245–246; Fred Gallo, "Evidencing the Existence of Energy Meridians," www.emofree.com/Research/meridianexistence.htm.

46. Darras, de Vernejoul, and Albarède, "A Study on the Migration of Radioactive Tracers after Injection at Acupoints."

47. Ibid.; Gallo, "Evidencing the Existence of Energy Meridians."

48. Rubik, "Can Western Science Provide a Foundation for Acupuncture?"

49. Ibid.; www.peacefulmind.com/articlesa.htm.

50. Hiroshi Motoyama with Rande Brown, *Science and the Evolution of Consciousness* (Brookline, MA: Autumn, 1978): 112–113, 145–147.

51. Yoshio Nagahama and Masaaki Maruyama, *Studies on Keiraku* (Tokyo: Kyorinshoin Co. Ltd., 1950), quoted in Motoyama, *Science and the Evolution of Consciousness*, 112–113.

52. www.drdanazappala.com/Colorlight.asp; www.acupuncturetoday.com/archives2003/jul/07starwynn.html; www.holisticonline.com/LightTherapy/light_conductor.htm.

53. Hiroshi Motoyama, Gaetan Chevalier, Osamu Ichikawa, and Hideki Baba, "Similarities and Dissimiliarities of Meridian Functions Between Genders," *Subtle Energies & Energy Medicine* 14, no. 3 (2003): 201–219.

54. David Olszewski and Brian Breiling, "Getting into Light: The Use of Phototherapy in Everyday Life," in *Light Years Ahead*, ed. Brian Breiling (Berkeley, CA: Celestial Arts, 1996), 286.

55. www.yinyanghouse.com/acupuncturepoints/locations_theory_and_clinical_applications.

56. www.worldtaa.org/acupuncture/meridians-acupuncture.html.

57. www.chinesemedicinesampler.com/acupuncture.html.

58. www.acupuncture.com.au/education/acupoints/category-antique.html; www.findmyhealer.co.uk/acupuncture.html; http://en.wikipedia.org/wiki/Acupuncture_point; www.yinyanghouse.com/acupuncturepoints/point_categories.

59. George T. Lewith, Peter J. White, and Jeremie Pariente, "Investigating Acupuncture Using Brain Imaging Techniques: The Current State of Play," http://ecam.oxfordjournals.org/cgi/content/full/2/3/315.

60. www.chinesemedicinesampler.com/acupuncture.html.

61. Maciocia, *The Foundations of Chinese Medicine*; Maciocia, *The Practice of Chinese Medicine*.

62. Lu, *Traditional Chinese Medicine*; http://deepesthealth.com/2007/chinese-medicine-and-the-emotions-what-does-the-neijing-say; Karol K. Truman, *Feelings Buried Alive Never Die* (Brigham City, UT: Brigham Distributing, 1991).

63. www.periodensystem.ch/Tmax_english.html; http://tuberose.com/meridians.html.

64. William Tiller, *Science and Human Transformation* (Walnut Creek, CA: Pavior Publishing, 1997), 121.

65. Ibid.

66. Evans, *Mind, Body and Electromagnetism*, 43.

67. Motoyama with Brown, *Science and the Evolution of Consciousness*, 81–85.

68. Ibid., 81–86.

69. www.windemereschoolofmassage.com/meridian/LightBody/villoldo2.asp.

70. Alberto Villoldo, *Shaman, Healer, Sage* (New York: Harmony, 2000).

71. Hernan Garcia, A. Sierra, H. Balam, and J. Conant, *Wind in the Blood: Mayan Healing & Chinese Medicine* (Taos, NM: Redwing Books, 1999).

PART V

1. Dennis William Hauck, *The Emerald Tablet* (New York: Penguin, 1999), 51.

2. N. N. Bhattacharyya, *History of the Tantric Religion*, 2nd rev. ed. (New Delhi: Manohar, 1999), 385–386.

3. Arthur Avalon, *The Serpent Power* (New York: Dover, 1974), 1–18.

4. Brennan, *Hands of Light*, 54.

5. Katrina Raphaell, *The Crystalline Transmission* (Santa Fe, NM: Aurora Press, 1990), 19–38.

6. Caroline Shola Arewa, *Opening to Spirit* (New York: Thorsons/HarperCollins, 1998), 51.

7. Ibid., 54.

8. Martin Bernal, *Black Athena* (New York: Vintage, 1987).

9. Arewa, *Opening to Spirit*, 51–53.

10. Ibid., 57.

11. Muata Ashby, *Egyptian Yoga Volume I: The Philosophy of Enlightenment*, 2nd ed. (U.S.A., Sema Institute/C.M. Book Publisher, 2005); Muata Ashby, *The Black African Egyptians* (U.S.A., Sema Institute/C.M. Book Publisher, 2007).

12. Avalon, *The Serpent Power*, 2.

13. C. W. Leadbeater, *The Chakras* (Wheaton, IL: Quest Books, 1927).

14. Anodea Judith, *Eastern Body Western Mind: Psychology and the Chakra System as a Path to the Self* (Berkeley, CA: Celestial Arts, 1996).

15. Avalon, *The Serpent Power*, 36.

16. Naomi Ozaniec, *Chakras for Beginners* (Pomfret, VT: Trafalgar Square, 1995); www.geocities.com/octanolboy/bpweb/Chpt6.htm; www.universal-mind.org/Chakra_pages/ProofOfExistence.htm; www.bioenergyfields.org.

17. www.emaxhealth.com/26/1115.html.

18. Valerie Hunt, Wayne W. Massey, Robert Weinberg, Rosalyn Bruyere, and Pierre M. Hahn, "A Study of Structural Integration from Neuromuscular, Energy Field, and Emotional Approaches" (Abstract, 1977, www.somatics.de/HuntStudy.html).

19. Shafica Karagulla, *The Chakras and Human Energy Fields* (Wheaton, IL: Quest, 1989).

20. www.geocities.com/octanolboy/bpweb/Chpt6.htm.

21. www.bibliotecapleyades.net/ciencia/ciencia_humanmultidimensionaanatomy.htm.

22. www.geocities.com/octanolboy/bpweb/Chpt6.htm; www.bibliotecapleyades.net/ciencia/ciencia_human-multidimensionaanatomy.htm.

23. Motoyama with Brown, *Science and the Evolution of Consciousness*, 86.

24. Harish Johari, *Chakras: Energy Centers of Transformation* (Rochester, VT: Destiny, 2000).

25. Arthur Avalon, *Mahanirvana Tantra* (Lodi, CA: Auromere, 1985).

26. Avalon, *The Serpent Power*, 261.
27. Jean Varenne, *Yoga and the Hindu Tradition* (Chicago: University of Chicago Press, 1976), 159.
28. www.beezone.com/DevatmaShakti/Chapter7.html.
29. www.wholebeingexplorations.com/matrix/SpSt/nadis.htm.
30. Don Glassey, "Life Energy and Healing: The Nerve, Meridian and Chakra Systems and the CSF Connection," www.ofspirit.com/donglassey1.htm.
31. Johari, *Chakras*, 29–30.
32. Ibid., 29–41; Varenne, *Yoga and the Hindu Tradition*.
33. Tommaso Palamidessi, *The Caduceus of Hermes* ed. Archeosofica (1969); retrieved from http://en.wikipedia.org/wiki/Nadi_(yoga).
34. Varenne, *Yoga and the Hindu Tradition*, 161–162.
35. www.sunandmoonstudio.com/YogaArticle/InvisibleAnatomy.shtml; Johari, *Chakras*, 16–17.
36. Varenne, *Yoga and the Hindu Tradition*, 158.
37. Ibid., 156–158.
38. Tenzin Wangyal Rinpoche, *Healing with Form, Energy, and Light* (Ithaca, NY: Snow Lion, 2002).
39. Ibid., xix-xxi.
40. Tenzin Wangyal Rinpoche, *Tibetan Sound Healing* (Boulder, CO: Sounds True, 2006).
41. www.tantra.com/tantra/what_is_tantra/a_definition_of_tantra.html.
42. Gyalwa Changchub and Namkhai Nyingpo, trans. Padmalcara Translation Group, *Lady of the Lotus-Born* (Boston: Shambhala, 2002).
43. Hunbatz Men, *Secrets of Mayan Science/Religion* (Santa Fe, NM: Bear & Co., 1990), 58.
44. Ibid.
45. Ibid., 111.
46. Dhyani Ywahoo, *Voices of Our Ancestors* (Boston, MA: Shambhala, 1987).
47. Ibid., 90.
48. Ibid., 29.
49. Ibid., 273–277.
50. Ibid., 19.
51. Ibid., 100–103.
52. Villoldo, *Shaman, Healer, Sage*, 106.
53. Ibid., 76.
54. Zachary Lansdowne, *The Revelation of Saint John* (York Beach, ME: Red Wheel/Weiser, 2006).
55. Ibid., 68.
56. Kerry Wisner, *Song of Hathor: Ancient Egyptian Ritual for Today* (Nashua, NH: Hwt-Hrw Publications, 2002); www.hwt-hrw.com/Bodies.php; www.spiritmythos.org/TM/9energybodies.html; www.theafrican.com/Magazine/Cosmo.htm; Ra Un Nefer Amen, *Metu Neter, Vol. 1: The Great Oracle of Tehuti, and the Egyptian System of Spiritual Cultivation* (Brooklyn, NY: Khamit Media Tran Visions, Inc., 1990); Ra Un Nefer Amen, *Tree of Life Meditation System (T.O.L.M)* (Brooklyn, NY: Khamit Publications, 1996); Charles S. Finch, III, *The Star of Deep Beginnings: The Genesis of African Science and Technology* (Decatur, GA: Khenti, 1998); A. David and Paul Rosalie, *The Ancient Egyptians* (London: Routledge & Kegan Paul, 1982); Dimitri Meeks and Christine Favard-Meeks, *Daily Life of the Egyptian Gods* (Ithaca, NY: Cornell University Press, 1996); http://findarticles.com/p/articles/mi_qa3822/is_200410/ai_n14681734/pg_14.
57. www.theafrican.com/Magazine/Cosmo.htm; www.wisdomworld.org/additional/ancientlandmarks/AncientWisdomInAfrica1.html.
58. Ra Un Nefer Amen, *Tree of Life Meditation System*.
59. Joseph W. Bastien, *Mountain of the Condor* (Long Grove, IL: Waveland Press, 1985), 8–9.
60. Cyndi Dale, *Advanced Chakra Healing* (Berkeley, CA: Crossing, 2005); Cyndi Dale, *New Chakra Healing* (Woodbury, MN: Llewellyn, 1996).
61. Shyam Sunda Goswamik, *Layayoga* (Rochester, VT: Inner Traditions, 1999), 160–164.
62. Johari, *Chakras*, 141–143.
63. Varenne, *Yoga and the Hindu Tradition*, 170.
64. David Furlong, *Working with Earth Energies* (London: Piatkus, 2003).
65. Raphaell, *The Crystalline Transmission*, 19.
66. Georgia Lambert Randall, "The Etheric Body" (lecture notes, 1983); Georgia Lambert Randall, *Esoteric Anatomy* (Tape series, Wrekin Trust UK, 1991), quoted in Arewa, *Opening to Spirit*, 5.
67. Diane Stein, *Women's Psychic Lives* (St. Paul, MN: Llewellyn, 1988), 26.
68. Dale, *Advanced Chakra Healing*.
69. www.getprolo.com/connective_tissue2.htm.
70. Dale, *Advanced Chakra Healing*.
71. Cyndi Dale, *Illuminating the Afterlife* (Louisville, CO: Sounds True, 2008).
72. Dale, *Advanced Chakra Healing*, 53–57.
73. Cyndi Dale, *Zap, You're a Teen!*, e-book (Minneapolis, MN: Life Systems Services Corp., 2005), www.cyndidale.com; Cyndi Dale, *The Spirit's Diet*, e-book (Minneapolis, MN: Life Systems Services Corp., 2005), www.cyndidale.com; Cyndi Dale, *Attracting Your Perfect Body Through the Chakras* (Berkeley, CA: Crossing, 2006).
74. www.americansportsdata.com/obesityresearch.asp.

75. Ted Andrews, *Simplified Magick* (St. Paul, MN: Llewellyn, 1989); Will Parfitt, *Elements of the Qabalah* (New York: Element, 1991); Gershon Winkler, *Magic of the Ordinary* (Berkeley, CA: North Atlantic, 2003); Rabbi Laibl Wolf, *Practical Kabbalah* (New York: Three Rivers, 1999).
76. Parfitt, *Elements of the Qabalah.*

PART VI

1. www.centerforaltmed.com/?page_id=5.
2. H. L. Fields and J. C. Liebeskind, eds., *Pharmacological Approaches to the Treatment of Chronic Pain: New Concepts and Critical Issues—Progress in Pain Research and Management*, Vol. 1 (Seattle: IASP Press, 1994); D. L. Gebhart, G. Hammond, and T. S. Jensen, *Proceedings of the 7th World Congress on Pain—Progress in Pain Research and Management*, Vol. 2 (Seattle, WA: IASP Press, 1994); J. S. Han, *The Neurochemical Basis of Pain Relief by Acupuncture*, Vol. 2 (Hubei, China: Hubei Science and Technology Press, 1998), quoted in www.chiro.org/acupuncture/ABSTRACTS/Beyond_endorphins.shtml.
3. Subhuti Dharmananda, "Electro-Acupuncture," www.itmonline.org/arts/electro.htm.
4. www.answers.com/topic/electroacupuncture.
5. www.chiro.org/acc/What_is_Ryodoraku.shtml.
6. Julia J. Tsuei, "Scientific Evidence in Support of Acupuncture and Meridian Theory: I. Introduction," www.healthy.net/scr/article.asp?Id=1087, originally published in *IEEE, Engineering in Medicine and Biology* 15, no. 3 (May/June 1996).
7. www.naokikubota.com.
8. www.spiritofmaat.com/archive/mar1/aurasoma.html.
9. Kubota chart p 336.
10. http://veda.harekrsna.cz/encyclopedia/ayurvedantacakras.htm; Alan Keith Tillotson, *The One Earth Herbal Sourcebook: Everything You Need to Know About Chinese, Western, and Ayurvedic Herbal Treatments* (New York: Kensington, 2001).
11. Steven Ross, ed., "Dr. Giuseppe Calligaris: The Television Powers of Man," *World Research News*, 1st Quarter 2005: 1.
12. Ibid.
13. Ibid., 4.
14. Hubert M. Schweizer, "Calligaris," lecture presented at the University of York, September 3, 1987, distributed by World Research Foundation.
15. Ibid., 11.
16. Ibid.
17. Dale, *Advanced Chakra Healing*, 63–66.
18. Liz Simpson, *The Book of Chakra Healing* (New York: Sterling, 1999).
19. Dale, *Advanced Chakra Healing.*
20. www.wrf.org/men-women-medicine/spectrochrome-dinshah-ghadiali.php.
21. M. Terman and J. S. Terman, "Light Therapy for Seasonal and Nonseasonal Depression: Efficacy, Protocol, Safety, and Side Effects," *CNS Spectrums* 10 (2005): 647–663; Bruce Bowser, "Mood Brighteners: Light Therapy Gets Nod as Depression Buster," *Science News* 167, no. 1 (April 23, 2005): 399.
22. http://en.wikipedia.org/wiki/Light_therapy.
23. Jacob Liberman, *Light: Medicine of the Future* (Santa Fe, NM: Bear & Co., 1991), 9.
24. Ibid.
25. Reed Karaim, "Light That Can Cure You," Special Health Report: Caring for Aging Parents, Health, *USA Weekend*, February 4, 2007.
26. Liberman, *Light: Medicine of the Future*, 27–34.
27. Ibid.
28. McTaggart, *The Field*, 44–51; H. E. Puthoff, "Zero-Point Energy: An Introduction," *Fusion Facts* 3, no. 3 (1991): 1.
29. Steven Vazquez, "Brief Strobic Phototherapy: Synthesis of the Future," in *Light Years Ahead*, 79.
30. Ibid., 97.
31. Ibid., 85.
32. Ibid., 79, 85.
33. Dale, *Advanced Chakra Healing*, 190–193.
34. Akhila Dass and Manohar Croke, "Colorpuncture and Esogetic Healing: The Use of Colored Light in Acupuncture," in *Light Years Ahead*, 233–257.
35. Olszewski and Breiling, "Getting Into Light," 237–238.
36. www.emofree.com.
37. Ibid.
38. Dale, *Advanced Chakra Healing*, 190–193.
39. Ibid., 193–94.
40. Tiller, *Science and Human Transformation*, 255. His footnote is G. Vithoulkas, *The Science of Homeopathy* (New York: Grove, 1980).
41. Gerber, *A Practical Guide to Vibrational Medicine*, 121.

42. Tiller, *Science and Human Transformation*, 255. His footnote is M. Rae, "Potency Simulation by Magnetically Energised Patterns (An Alternate Method of Preparing Homeopathic Remedies)," *British Radionic Quarterly* 19, no.2 (March 1973): 32–40.

43. www.masaru-emoto.net.

44. www.appliedkinesiology.com; www.kinesiology.net/ak.asp; www.healthy-holistic-living.com/electrodermal-testing.html; www.drciprian.com; www.touch4health.com.

45. James Tyler Kent, *Repertory of the Homeopathic Materia Medica and a Word Index*, 6th ed. (New Delhi: B. Jain Publishers, 2004).

46. D. Cohen, Y. Palti, B. N. Cuffin, and S. J. Schmid, "Magnetic Fields Produced by Steady Currents in the Body," *Proceedings of the National Academy of Science* 77 (1980): 1447–1451.

47. C. Shang, M. Lou, and S. Wan, "Bioelectrochemical Oscillations," *Science Monthly* 22 [Chinese] (1991): 74–80.

48. R. O. Becker and A. A. Marino, *Electromagnetism and Life* (Albany: State Univ. of New York, 1982).

49. www.magnetlabs.com/articles/journalbioelectroinst.doc.

50. M. Tany, S. Sawatsugawa, and Y. Manaka, "Acupuncture Analgesia and its Application in Dental Practices," *American Journal of Acupuncture* 2 (1974): 287–295. http://pt.wkhealth.com/pt/re/ajhp/fulltext.00043627-200506150-00011.htm.

51. www.item-bioenergy.com/infocenter/ScientificBasisMagnetTherapy.pdf.

52. Kiyoshi Ikenaga, *Tsubo Shiatsu* (Vancouver, BC, Canada: Japan Shiatsu, Inc., 2003), 39.

53. Ibid.

54. Ibid., 31.

55. Ibid., 34.

56. Ibid., 35–36.

57. Asokananda (Harald Brust) and Chow Kam Thye in *The Art of Traditional Thai Massage Energy Line Chart*, ed. Richard Bentley (Bangkok: Nai Suk's Editions Co. Ltd., 1995).

58. Chart from Ralph Wilson (www.NaturalWorldHealing.com), who added associated emotions based on work of Dietrich Klinghardt, MD (www.Klinghardt.org and www.NeuralTherapy.com); Louisa Williams, www.RadicalMedicine.com.

59. www.cancertutor.org/Other/Breast_Cancer.html; http://pressreleasesonline.biz/pr/Cancer_Care_Expert_Says_Root_Canals_Should_Be_Illegal.

60. Irini Rockwell, "The Five Buddha Families," *Shambhala Sun*, November 2002.

61. http://members.tripod.com/~Neurotopia/Zen/Mudra.

62. www.buddhapia.com/tibet/mudras.html.

63. Faith Javane and Dusty Bunker, *Numerology and the Divine Triangle* (West Chester, PA: Whitford, 1979), 2.

64. Harish Johari, *Numerology with Tantra, Ayurveda, and Astrology* (Rochester, VT: Destiny, 1990), 14–15.

65. Dale, *Advanced Chakra Healing*, 195–196.

66. www.numericwellness.com.

67. www.polaritytherapy.org/page.asp?PageID=2; www.polaritytherapy.org.

68. www.prevention.digitaltoday.in/fitness-features/the-energy-workout-114.html.

69. Natalie Gingerich, "The Energy Workout," *Prevention Magazine*, December 2007, 152–155.

70. C. H. Chien, J. J. Tsuei, S. C. Lee, et al., "Effects of Emitted Bio-Energy on Biochemical Functions of Cells," *American Journal of Chinese Medicine* 19, no.3–4 (1991): 285–292.

71. A. Seto, C. Kusaka, S. Nakazato, et al., "Detection of Extraordinary Large Bio-Magnetic Field Strength from Human Hand During External Qi Emission," *Acupuncture & Electro-Therapeutics Research, the International Journal* 17 (1992): 75–94.

72. L. V. Carnie, *Chi Gung* (St. Paul, MN: Llewellyn, 1997), 5.

73. Ibid., 51.

74. David W. Sollars, *The Complete Idiot's Guide to Acupuncture & Acupressure* (New York: Penguin, 2000), 64–65, 78–79, 119, 163–164, 190, 203, 205–206, 210.

75. Nick Franks, "Reflections on the Ether and some Notes on the Convergence between Homeopathy and Radionics," www.Radionic.co.uk/articles.

76. Linda Fellows, "Opening Up the Black Box," *International Journal of Alternative and Complementary Medicine* 15, no. 8, 9–13 (1997): 3, www.Radionic.co.uk/articles; Tony Scofield, "The Radionic Principle: Mind over Matter," *Radionic Journal* 52, no. 1 (2007): 5–16 and 52, no. 2 (2007): 7–12, www.Radionic.co.uk/articles.

77. Sollars, *The Complete Idiot's Guide to Acupuncture & Acupressure*, 24.

78. Olszewski and Breiling, "Getting into Light," 291.

79. Ibid., 290.

80. Bernard C. Kolster and Astrid Waskowiak, *The Reflexology Atlas* (Rochester, VT: Healing Arts, 2005), 134.

81. Olszewski and Breiling, "Getting into Light," 288.

82. Olszewski and Breiling, "Getting into Light," 288.

83. www.reiki.nu.

84. www.reiki.nu.

85. Itzhak Bentov, *Stalking the Wild Pendulum* (Rochester, VT: Destiny, 1977), 9.

86. Evans, *Mind, Body and Electromagnetism*, 98.

87. www.aniwilliams.com/geometry_music_healing.htm.

88. www.healingsounds.com.

89. www.chronogram.com/issue/2005/08/wholeliving.

90. Ibid.

91. Ibid.

92. Dale, *Advanced Chakra Healing*, 198–202.

93. Evans, *Mind, Body and Electromagnetism*, 87–97.

94. I. Bentov, "Micromotion of the Body as a Factor in the Development of the Nervous System," in *Kundalini:Psychosis or Transcendence?* ed. Lee Sanella (San Francisco: H.S. Dakin, 1976), 72–92.

95. Gerber, *Vibrational Medicine*, 401–408.

96. Evans, *Mind, Body and Electromagnetism*, 96.

97. Lu, *Traditional Chinese Medicine*, 74.

98. www.itmonline.org/arts/pulse.htm; http://sacredlotus.com/diagnosis/index.cfm; http://www.giovanni-maciocia.com/articles/flu.html.

99. Subhuti Dharmananda, "The Significance of Traditional Pulse Diagnosis in the Modern Practice of Chinese Medicine," www.itmonline.org/arts/pulse.htm; Xie Zhufan, "Selected Terms in Traditional Chinese Medicine and Their Interpretations (VIII)," *Chinese Journal of Integrated Traditional and Western Medicine* 5, no. 3 (1999): 227–229.

100. Xie, "Selected Terms in Traditional Chinese Medicine and Their Interpretations (VIII)," 227–229.

101. Tiller, *Science and Human Transformation*, 163–166.

102. J. N. Kenyon, *Auricular Medicine: The Auricular Cardiac Reflex, Modern Techniques of Acupuncture*, Vol. 2 (New York: Thorsons, 1983), 82, 191.

103. Cathy Wong, "Tongue Diagnosis," http://altmedicine.about.com/b/2005/09/20/tongue-diagnosis.htm; Ni Daoshing, "Why Do You Keep On Asking Me to Stick My Tongue Out?" www.acupuncture.com; Xie Zhufan and Huang Xi, eds., *Dictionary of Traditional Chinese Medicine* (Hong Kong: Commercial Press, 1984); Robert Flaws, "Introduction to Chinese Pulse Diagnosis," in Flaws, *The Secret of Chinese Pulse Diagnosis* (Boulder, CO: Blue Poppy Press, 1995); www.healthy.net/scr/article.asp?id=1957.

104. J. H. Navach, *The Vascular Autonomic System, Physics and Physiology* (Lyon, France: The VIII Germano-Latino Congress on Auricular Medicine, 1981), www.drfeely.com/doctors/acu_ear_bib_2_5.htm.

105. www.amcollege.edu/blog/massage/amma-massage.htm.

106. www.biogeometry.org.

BIBLIOGRAPHY

PART I

www.amsa.org/ICAM/C6.doc.

www.answers.com/topic/electricity.

www.arthistory.sbc.edu/sacredplaces/sacredgeo.html.

Barnes, Frank S., and Ben Greenebaum, eds. *Bioengineering and Biophysical Aspects of Electromagnetic Fields*, 3rd ed. New York: Taylor & Francis, 2007.

Becker, Robert O. *Cross Currents*. New York: Penguin, 1990.

Bendit, Lawrence, and Phoebe Bendit. *The Etheric Body of Man*. Wheaton, IL: Theosophical Publishing House, 1977.

Bengtsson, I., and K. Zyczkowski. *Geometry of Quantum States: An Introduction to Quantum Entanglement*. New York: Cambridge University Press, 2006.

Benor, Daniel J., "Intuitive Assessments: An Overview." *Personal Spirituality Workbook*. www.WholisticHealingResearch.com.

———. "Scientific Validation of a Healing Revolution," Healing Research, Vol. 1, *Spiritual Healing* (Professional Supplement 2001). Southfield, MI: Vision Publications. www.WholisticHealingResearch.com.

Benson, Herbert, and Marg Stark. *Timeless Healing: The Power and Biology of Belief*. New York: Scribner, 1996.

www.beyondtheordinary.net/NC-bellstheorem.html.

www.biomindsuperpowers.com.

www.bioprodownloads.com/pdf/Beverly_Rubik.pdf.

Brennan, Barbara Ann. *Hands of Light*. New York: Bantam, 1993.

www.cern.ch/livefromcern/antimatter.

Church, Dawson. *The Genie in Your Genes*. Santa Rosa, CA: Elite Books, 2007.

www.colorado.edu/physics/2000/quantumzone/photoelectric2.html.

www.eas.asu.edu/~holbert/wise/electromagnetism.htm.

Edge, Hoyt L., et al. *Foundations of Parapsychology: Exploring the Boundaries of Human Capability*. Boston: Routledge and Kegan Paul, 1986.

Eisenberg, David, et al. "Inability of an 'Energy Transfer Diagnostician' to Distinguish Between Fertile and Infertile Women." *Medscape General Medicine* 3, no.1 (2001).

www.emc.maricopa.edu/faculty/farabee/BIOBK/BioBookEner1.html. www.enchantedlearning.com/math/geometry/solids.

www.esalenctr.org/display/confpage.cfm?confid=8&pageid=69&pgtype=1.

Evans, John. *Mind, Body and Electromagnetism*. Dorset, UK: Element Books, 1986.

www.fda.gov/fdac/features/2000/100_heal.html.

Fetrow, C.W., and Juan R. Avila. *Complementary & Alternative Medicines*. Springhouse, PA: Springhouse, 2001.

Ford, Kenneth W. *The Quantum World*. Cambridge, MA: Harvard University Press, 2004.

www.ftexploring.com/energy/definition.html.

www.geocities.com/r_ayana/Time.html.

Gerber, Richard. *Vibrational Medicine*. Santa Fe, NM: Bear & Co., 1988.

www.halexandria.org/dward154.htm.

Hemenway, Priya. *Divine Proportion*. New York: Sterling, 2005.

www.hpwt.de/Quantene.htm.

www.iht.com/articles/1995/05/16/booktue.t.php.

www.imagery4relaxation.com/articles-benson.htm.

http://imagine.gsfc.nasa.gov/docs/science/know_l1/emspectrum.html.

Johnson, Steven. *Mind Wide Open*. New York: Scribner, 2004.

www.jracademy.com/~jtucek/science/what.html.

www.lbl.gov/abc/Antimatter.html.

www.le.ac.uk/se/centres/sci/selfstudy/particle01.html.

Ledwith, Míceál, and Klaus Heinemann. *The Orb Project*. New York: Atria, 2007.

Levenson, R.W., and A.M. Ruef. "Physiological Aspects of Emotional Knowledge and Rapport," in W. Ickes, ed., *Empathetic Accuracy*. New York: Guilford, 1997.

http://library.thinkquest.org/3487/qp.html.

Lloyd, Seth. *Programming the Universe*. New York: Vintage, 2006.

www.mariner.connectfree.co.uk/html/electromagnetism.html.

McCraty, Rollin, *The Energetic Heart*. Boulder Creek, CA: HeartMath Institute Research Center, 2003. E-book: Publication No. 02-035, 2003, 8–10. www.heartmath.org.

McCraty, Rollin, Mike Atkinson, and Raymond Trevor Bradley. "Electrophysiological Evidence of Intuition: Part I. The Surprising Role of the Heart." *The Journal of Alternative and Complementary Medicine* 10, no. 1 (2004): 133.

www.medicalnewstoday.com/articles/84726.php.

Nash, Carroll B. *Parapsychology: The Science of Psiology*. Springfield, IL: Charles C. Thomas, 1986.

www.ndt-ed.org/EducationResources/HighSchool/Electricity/hs_elec_index.htm.

www.need.org/needpdf/infobook_activities/ElemInfo/ElecE.pdf.

http://www.nidsci.org/articles/morse.php.

http://www.nidsci.org/pdf/puthoff.pdf.

Oschman, James L. *Energy Medicine*. New York: Churchill Livingstone, 2000.

———. "Science and the Human Energy Field." Interview by William Lee Rand in *Reiki News Magazine* 1 no. 3 (Winter 2002). www.reiki.org.

———. "What is Healing Energy? Part 3: Silent Pulses." *Journal of Bodywork and Movement Therapies* 1, no. 3 (April 1997): 184.

Pearsall, Paul. *The Heart's Code*. New York: Broadway, 1988.

www.physicalgeography.net/fundamentals/6e.html.

Poole, William, with the Institute of Noetic Sciences. *The Heart of Healing*. Atlanta: Turner Publishing, 1993.

Quigg, Chris. "The Coming Revolution in Particle Physics." *Scientific American*, February 2008, 46–53.

Rein, G., and R. McCraty. "Structural Changes in Water and DNA Associated with New Physiologically Measurable States." *Journal of Scientific Exploration* 8, no. 3 (1994): 438–439.

Rhine, J. B. *Extrasensory Perception*. Boston: Branden, 1964.

Rhine, Louisa E. *ESP in Life and Lab: Tracing Hidden Channels*. New York: Macmillan, 1967.

———. *Hidden Channels of the Mind*. New York: Morrow, 1961.

Roychoudhuri, C., and R. Rajarshi. "The Nature of Light: What is a Photon?" *Optics and Photonics News* 14 (November 2003): S1.

http://science.howstuffworks.com/electricity.htm.

http://scienceworld.wolfram.com/physics/Photon.html.

www.3quarks.com/GIF-Animations/PlatonicSolids.

Tiller, W. A. and M. J. Kohane. *Conscious Acts of Creation*. Walnut Creek, CA: Pavior Publishing, 2001.

Tiller, W. A., W. E. Dibble, Jr., and J. G. Fandel. *Some Science Adventures with Real Magic*. Walnut Creek, CA: Pavior Publishing, 2005.

Tiller, William A. "Radionics, Radiesthesia and Physics." Paper presented at the Academy of Parapsychology and Medicine Symposium on "The Varieties of Healing Experience," Los Altos, CA, October 30, 1971.

———. *Science and Human Transformation: Subtle Energies, Intentionality, and Consciousness*. Walnut Creek, CA: Pavior Publishing, 1997.

———. "Subtle Energies." *Science & Medicine* 6, no. 3 (May/June 1999).

www.tillerfoundation.com/energyfields.html.

www.trepan.com/introduction.html.

Turner, J. A., et al. "The Importance of Placebo Effects in Pain Treatment and Research," *Journal of the American Medical Association* 271 (1994): 1609–1614.

http://twm.co.nz/McTag_field.htm.

http://utut.essortment.com/whatisthehist_rgic.htm.

Vithoulkas, George. *The Science of Homeopathy*. New York: Grove Weidenfeld, 1980.

www.washingtonpost.com/ac2/wp-dyn/A2709-2002Apr29.

http://en.wikipedia.org/wiki/Hippocratic_Oath.

http://en.wikipedia.org/wiki/Sacred_geometry.

Wurtman, Richard J., Michael J. Baum, and John T. Potts, Jr., eds. *The Medical and Biological Effects of Light, Annals of the New York Academy of Science*, Vol. 453. New York: The New York Academy of Sciences, 1985.

Yam, Philip. "Exploiting Zero-Point Energy." *Scientific American*, December 1997, 82–85.

http://zebu.uoregon.edu/~soper/Light/photons.html.

PART II

www.abanet.org/soloseznet/threads/0508/myback.html.

www.acutcmdetox.com/tryptophan2.html.

www.affs.org/html/biomagnetism.html.

Albertine, Kurt, and David Tracy, eds. *Anatomica's Body Atlas*. San Diego, CA: Laurel Glen Publishing, 2002.

"Alleviating Diabetes Complications," *M*, U of Michigan Alumni newsletter, Fall 2007, 5.

Amen, Daniel G. *Change Your Brain, Change Your Life*. New York: Three Rivers, 1998.

www.angelfire.com/pe/MitochondriaEve.

Bair, Puran. "Visible Light Radiated from the Heart with Heart Rhythm Meditation." *Subtle Energies & Energy Medicine* 16, no. 3 (2005): 211–223.

Becker, Robert O. "Modern Bioelectromagnetics and Functions of the Central Nervous System." *Subtle Energies & Energy Medicine* 3, no. 1 (1992): 53–72.

Bevan, James. *A Pictorial Handbook of Anatomy and Physiology*. New York: Barnes & Noble Books, 1996.

Brown, Tina. *The Diana Chronicles*. New York: Doubleday, 2007.

Callaway, J. C. "A Proposed Mechanism for the Visions of Dream Sleep." *Medical Hypotheses* 26 (1988): 119–124.

Cann, R. L., M. Stoneking, and A. C. Wilson. "Mitochondrial DNA and Human Evolution." *Nature* 325 (1987): 31–36.

www.cell.com.

www.cell.com/content/article/abstract?uid=PIIS0092867407007015.

Champeau, Rachel. "UCLA Seeks Adults with Asthma for Study Testing Device to Alleviate Symptoms." www.newsroom.ucla.edu/portal/ucla/UCLA-Seeks-Adults-With-Asthma-for-7265.aspx?RelNum=7265.

Church, Dawson. *The Genie in Your Genes*. Santa Rosa, CA: Elite Books, 2007.

Colthurst, J., and P. Giddings. "A Retrospective Case Note Review of the Fenzian Electrostimulation System: A Novel Non-invasive, Non-pharmacological Treatment." *The Pain Clinic* 19, no. 1 (2007): 7–14.

http://dailynews.yahoo.com/headlines/sc/story.html?s=v/nm/19990421/sc/health_autoimmune_1.html.

Dale, Cyndi. *Advanced Chakra Healing: Energy Mapping on the Four Pathways*. Berkeley, CA: Crossing Press, 2005.

———. *Advanced Chakra Healing: Heart Disease*. Berkeley, CA: Crossing Press, 2007.

Dawkins, Richard. *The Ancestor's Tale: A Pilgrimage to the Dawn of Life*. Boston: Houghton Mifflin, 2004.

http://diabetes.diabetesjournals.org/cgi/content/full/53/suppl_1/S96.

www.emotionalintelligence.co.uk/ezine/downloads/23_Book.pdf.

www.fenzian.co.uk/#.

Gershon, Michael. *The Second Brain*. New York: HarperCollins, 1999.

Guiley, Rosemary Ellen. *Harper's Encyclopedia of Mystical and Paranormal Experience*. Edison, NJ: Castle Books, 1991.

Haimov, I., and P. Lavie. "Melatonin—A Soporific Hormone." *Current Directions in Psychological Science* 5, (1996): 106–111.

Horrigan, Bonie, and Candace Pert. "Neuropeptides, AIDS and the Science of Mind-Body Healing." *Alternative Therapies* 1, no. 3 (July 1995): 70-76.

Hougham, Paul. *Atlas of Mind, Body and Spirit*. New York: Gaia, 2006.

http://64.233.167.104/search?q=cache:lTt8NZxlWAQJ:intermountainhealthcare.org/xp/public/documents/pcmc/eeg.pdf+how+an+EEG+works&hl=en&ct=clnk&cd=2&gl=us.

www.item-bioenergy.com.

www.iupac.org/publications/pac/2004/pdf/7602x0295.pdf.

Jedd, Marcia. "Where Do You Want to Go Today?" Interview with Skip Atwater of the Monroe Institute, *Fate Magazine*, July 1998, 36.

Jernigan, David A., and Samantha Joseph. "Illuminated Physiology and Medical Uses of Light." *Subtle Energies & Energy Medicine* 16, no. 3, 251–269.

Keefe, Emmet B., MD. *Know Your Body: The Atlas of Anatomy*. Berkeley, CA: Ulysses, 1999.

www.kidshealth.org/parent/general/body_basics/female_reproductive_system.html. www.kidshealth.org/parent/general/body_basics/metabolism.html.

Kimball, J. W. "Sexual Reproduction in Humans: Copulation and Fertilization." Kimball's Biology Pages (based on *Biology*. 6th ed., 1996). http://en.wikipedia.org/wiki/Mitochondrion.

Liberman, Jacob. *Light: Medicine of the Future*. Santa Fe, NM: Bear & Co., 1991.

http://lila.info/document_view.phtml?document_id=21.

Lindsay, Bethany. "The Compasses of Birds." *Science Creative Quarterly* 2 (September–November 2006). www.scq.ubc.ca/?p=173. Reprinted from Issue 1, June 6, 2005.

http://en.wikipedia.org/wiki/Male_genital_organs.

McTaggart, Lynne. *The Field*. New York: Harper Perennial, 2003.

www.med.nyu.edu/people/sarnoj01.html.

www.medcareservice.com/MICROCURRENT-THERAPY-Article.cfm.

www.merck.com/mmhe/sec09/ch118/ch118a.html.

http://en.wikipedia.org/wiki/Metabolism.

www.monroeinstitute.com/content.php?content_id=27.

Nelson, J. Lee. "Your Cells Are My Cells." *Scientific American*, February 2008, 73–79.

Novitt-Moreno, Anne D. *How Your Brain Works.* Emeryville, CA: Ziff-Davis, 1995.

http://psychologytoday.com/articles/pto-19990501-000013.html.

www.onsiteworkshops.com/manage/pdf1140126696.pdf.

Pert, Candace. *Molecules of Emotion: The Science Behind Mind–Body Medicine.* New York: Scribner, 1997.

http://preventdisease.com/healthtools/articles/bmr.html.

www.pubmedcentral.nih.gov/articlerender.fcgi?artid=1634887.

www.rickstrassman.com/dmt/chaptersummaries.html.

www.rolf.org.

Roney-Dougal, S. M. "Recent Findings Relating to the Possible Role of the Pineal Gland in Affecting Psychic Abilities." *Journal of the Society for Psychical Research* 56 (1989): 313–328.

www.sciencemaster.com/jump/life/dna.php.

www.shands.org/health/imagepages/19089.htm.

Siegel, G. J., B. W. Agranoff, S. K. Fisher, R. W. Albers, and M. D. Uhler. *Basic Neurochemistry,* 6th ed. Philadelphia: Lippincott Williams & Wilkins, 1999.

http://sleepdisorders.about.com/od/nightmares/a/netabollic.htm?p=1.

www.sovereign-publications.com/fenzian.htm.

Sykes, Bryan. *The Seven Daughters of Eve: The Science That Reveals Our Genetic Ancestry.* New York: Norton, 2001.

Tiller, William A., R. McCraty, and M. Atkinson. "Cardiac Coherence: A New Noninvasive Measure of Autonomic Nervous System Order." *Alternative Therapies* 2, no. 52 (1996): 52–63.

www.trueorigin.org/atp.asp.

http://video.google.com/videoplay?docid=-6660313127569317147.

www.vivo.colostate.edu/hbooks/pathphys/endocrine/bodyweight/leptin.html.

www.warmfeetkit.com/gpage3.html.

www.washingtonpost.com/wp-dyn/content/article/2007/01/22/AR2007012200942.html.

Watters, Ethan. "DNA is Not Your Destiny." *Discover,* November 2006, 32–37, 75.

http://en.wikipedia.org/wiki/Brain.

http://en.wikipedia.org/wiki/David_Cohen_(physicist).

http://en.wikipedia.org/wiki/Digestion.

http://en.wikipedia.org/wiki/Excretory_system.

http://en.wikipedia.org/wiki/Taste.

http://en.wikipedia.org/wiki/Tryptophan.

Wilken, Arden, and Jack Wilken. "Our Sonic Pathways." *Subtle Energies & Energy Medicine* 16, no. 3 (2007): 271–282.

http://wongkiewkit.com/forum/attachment.php?attachmentid=596&d=1107898946.

PART III

Albohm, Anders. "Neurodegenerative Diseases, Suicide and Depressive Symptoms in Relation to EMF." *Bioelectromagnetics* 5 (2001): S132–143.

Albohm, Anders, Elisabeth Cardis, Adele Green, Martha Linet, David Savitz, and Anthony Swerdlow. "Review of the Epidemiologic Literature on EMF and Health." *Environmental Health Perspectives* 109, no. S6, (December 2001): 9.

Alpert, Mark. "The Triangular Universe." *Scientific American,* February 2007, 24.

www.assemblagepointcentre.com.

Atiyah, Michael, and Paul Sutcliffe. "Polyhedra in Physics, Chemistry and Geometry." *Milan Journal of Mathematics* 71 (2003): 33–58.

www.bearcy.com/handsoflight5.html.

Becker, Robert O. "Modern Bioelectromagnetics and Functions of the Central Nervous System." *Subtle Energies* 3, no. 1 (1992): 6.

Bendit, Lawrence, and Phoebe Bendit. *The Etheric Body of Man.* Wheaton, IL: Theosophical Publishing House, 1977.

Bendit, P. D. and L. J. Bendit. *Man Incarnate.* London: Theosophical Publishing House, 1957.

Benford, M. S. "Radiogenic Metabolism: An Alternative Cellular Energy Source." *Medical Hypotheses* 56, no. 1 (2001): 33–39.

Benor, Daniel J. "Distant Healing, Personal Spirituality Workbook." *Subtle Energies* 11, no. 3 (2000): 249–264. www.WholisticHealingResearch.com.

———. "Spiritual Healing as the Energy Side of Einstein's Equation." www.WholisticHealingResearch.com.

Berman, J. D. and S. E. Straus. "Implementing a Research Agenda for Complementary and Alternative Medicine." *Annual Review of Medicine* 55 (2004): 239–254.

www.Biogeometry.org.

http://biorespect.com/lesnews.asp?ID=5&NEWSID=119.

Blumenfeld, Larry. Ed. and comp. *Voices of Forgotten Worlds, Traditional Music of Indigenous People.* New York, Ellipsis Arts, 1993.

Brennan, Barbara Ann. *Hands of Light.* New York: Bantam, 1993.

Burr, Harold Saxton. "Excerpt from Blueprint for Immortality." Reprinted as "The Electrical Patterns of Life: The World of Harold Saxton Burr" in *World Research News*, 2nd Quarter 1997, 2, 5.

Byrd, R. C. "Positive Therapeutic Effects of Intercessory Prayer in a Coronary Care Unit Population." *Southern Medical Journal* 81, no. 7 (1988): 826–829.

www.byregion.net/articles-healers/Sound_DNA.html.

Callahan, P. S. "The Mysterious Round Towers of Ireland: Low Energy Radio in Nature." *The Explorer's Journal*, Summer 1993, 84–91.

Cao, Y. N., Y. Zhang, and Y. Liu. "Effects of Exposure to Extremely Low Frequency Electromagnetic Fields on Reproduction of Female Mice and Development of Offsprings." *Zhonghua Lao Dong Wei Sheng Zhi Ye Bing Za Zhi* 24, no.8 (August 2006): 468–470.

Carlson, John B. "Lodestone Compass: Chinese or Olmec Primacy?" *Science*, September 5, 1975, 753–760.

Cayce, E., and L. Cayce. *The Outer Limits of Edgar Cayce's Power.* New York: Harper and Row, 1971.

www.chiro.org/ChiroZine/abstracts/Cervical_Spine_Geometry.shtml.

Colson, Thomas. *Molecular Radiations.* San Francisco: Electronic Medical Foundation, 1953.

Coxeter, H. S. M. *Regular Polytopes*, 3rd ed. New York: Dover, 1973.

Crile, George W. *A Bipolar Theory of Living Processes.* New York: Macmillan, 1926.

————. "A Bipolar Theory of the Nature of Cancer." *Annals of Surgery* LXXX, no. 3 (September 1924): 289–297.

www.darvill.clara.net/emag/emaggamma.htm.

www.darvill.clara.net/emag/emagradio.htm.

David, Albert Roy, and Walter C. Rawls, Jr. *The Magnetic Effect.* Hicksville, NY: Exposition Press, 1975.

————. *Magnetism and Its Effects on the Living System.* Hicksville, NY: Exposition Press, 1974.

Devereux, Paul. *Places of Power.* London: Blandford Press, 1990.

Dossey, Larry. *Alternative Therapies in Health and Medicine* 8, no. 2 (2002): 12–16, 103–110; www.noetic.org/research/dh/articles/HowHealingHappens.pdf.

"Energy Medicine, An Overview." NCCAM Publication No. D235, updated March 2007. www.nccam.nih.gov.

Evans, John. *Mind, Body and Electromagnetism.* Dorset, UK: Element, 1986.

Euclid-Smith, Dr. "Report on 63 Case Histories." Available from World Research Foundation, 41 Bell Rock Plaza, Sedona, AZ 86351.

Fellows, Linda. "Opening Up the Black Box." *International Journal of Alternative and Complementary Medicine* 15, no. 8 (1997): 3, 9–13. www.Radionic.co.uk/articles.

Feychting, Maria, Anders Ahlbom, F. Jonsson, and N. L Pederson. "Occupational Magnetic Field Exposure and Neurodegenerative Disease." *Epidemiology* 14, no. 4 (July 2003): 413–419.

Ford, Kenneth. *The Quantum World.* Cambridge, MA: Harvard University Press, 2004.

www.frankperry.co.uk/Cymatics.htm.

Franks, Nick. "Reflections on the Ether and Some Notes on the Convergence Between Homeopathy and Radionics." www.Radionic.co.uk/articles.

Gamble, Steve. "Healing Energy and Water." www.hado.net.

Gerber, Richard. *A Practical Guide to Vibrational Medicine.* New York: HarperCollins, 2000.

http://gvanv.com/compass/arch/v1402/albanese.html.

Hahnemann, Samuel. *Organon*, 5th ed. RK, Tandon: B. Jain Publisher Pvt Ltd. (2002). www.homeopathyhome.com.

Haisch, B. and A. Rueda. "A Quantum Broom Sweeps Clean." *Mercury* 25, no. 2 (March/April 1996): 2–15.

Hakansson, Niklas, P. Gustavsson, Birgitte Floderus, and Christof Johanen. "Neurodegenerative Diseases in Welders and Other Workers Exposed to High Levels of Magnetic Fields." *Epidemiology* 14, no. 4 (July 2003): 420–426.

Hansen, J. "Increased Breast Cancer Risk Among Women Who Work Predominantly at Night," *Epidemiology* 12, no. 1 (January 2001): 74–77.

www.healthastro.com/geopathic_stress.html.

http://healthcare.zdnet.com/?p=430.

www.healthy.net/scr/article.asp?Id=2408.

Heath, Thomas L. *The Thirteen Books of Euclid's Elements, Books 10–13.* 2nd unabr. ed. New York: Dover, 1956.

http://homepage.ntlworld.com/homeopathy_advice/Theory/Intermediate/miasm.html.

Hunt, Valerie V., Wayne W. Massey, Robert Weinberg, Rosalyn Bruyere, and M. Pierre Hahn. "A Study of Structural Integration from Neuromuscular, Energy Field, and Emotional Approaches." 1977. Sponsored by the Rolf Institute of Structural Integration. www.rolf.com.au/downloads/ucla.pdf.

http://hyperphysics.phy-astr.gsu.edu/hbase/ems3.html.

http://imagine.gsfc.nasa.gov/docs/science/know_l1/emspectrum.html.

www.in2it.ca.

Isaacson, Michael, and Scott Klimek. "The Science of Sound." Lecture notes, Normandale College, Bloomington, MN, Spring 2007.

Jacka, Judy. *The Vivaxis Connection: Healing Through Earth Energies.* Charlottesville, VA: Hampton Roads, 2000.

Keller, E. "Effects of Therapeutic Touch on Tension Headache Pain." *Nursing Research* 35 (1986): 101–105.

Kilner, Walter J. *The Human Aura.* New York: University Books, 1965.

Kissinger, Jeanette, and Lori Kaczmarek. "Healing Touch and Fertility: A Case Report." *Journal of Perinatal Education* 15, no. 2 (May 2006): 13–20.

Kunz, Dora, and Erik Peper. "Fields and Their Clinical Implications." *The American Theosophist*, December 1982, 395.

Lahovsky, Georges. *The Secret of Life*. London, UK: True Health Publishing, 1963.

Lawlor, Robert. *Sacred Geometry*. New York: Thames & Hudson, 1982.

Ledwith, Míceál, and Klaus Heinemann. *The Orb Project*. New York: Atria, 2007.

Lee, G. M., Michael Yost, R. R. Neutra, L. Hristova, and R. A. Hiatt. "A Nested Case-Control Study of Residential and Personal Magnetic Field Measures and Miscarriages." *Epidemiology* 13, no.1 (January 2002): 21–31.

Li, De-Kun, Roxana Odouli, S. Wi, T. Janevic, I. Golditch, T. D. Bracken, R. Senior, R. Rankin, and R. Iriye. "A Population-Based Prospective Cohort Study of Personal Exposure to Magnetic Fields During Pregnancy and the Risk of Miscarriage." *Epidemiology* 13, no.1 (January 2002): 9–20.

www.lind.com/quantum/Energetic%20Healing.htm.

Lippard, Lucy R. *Overlay: Contemporary Art and the Art of Prehistory*. New York: Pantheon, 1983.

Lisle, Harvey. *The Enlivened Rock Powders*. Shelby, NC: Acres, 1994.

Lloyd, Seth. *Programming the Universe*. New York: Vintage, 2007.

Logani, M. K., A. Bhanushali, A. Anga, et al. "Combined Millimeter Wave and Cyclophosphamide Therapy of an Experimental Murine Melanoma." *Bioelectromagnetics* 25, no.7 (2004): 516.

www.magnetage.com/Davis_Labs_History.html.

www.magnetic-therapy-today.com/reference.html.

http://www.magnetlabs.com/articles/journalbioelectroinst.doc.

www.magnetotherapy.de/Bioenergetically-active-signals.153.0.html.

www.magnetotherapy.de/Schumann-waves.152.0.html.

Martiny, K., C. Simonsen, M. Lunde, et al. "Decreasing TSH Levels in Patients With Seasonal Affective Disorder (Sad) Responding to 1 Week of Bright Light Therapy." *Journal of Affective Disorders* 79, no. 1-3 (2004): 253–257.

McCraty, Rollin, Mike Atkinson, Raymond Trevor Bradley. "Electrophysiological Evidence of Intuition: Part 2. A System-Wide Process?" *Journal of Alternative and Complementary Medicine*, 10, no. 2 (2004): 133–143.

McGarey, W. A. *The Edgar Cayce Remedies*. New York: Bantam, 1983.

McTaggart, Lynne. *The Field*. New York: Harper Perennial, 2003.

www.mercola.com/article/microwave/hazards2.htm.

www.mercola.com/forms/ferrite_beads.htm.

www.mercola.com/2000/aug/13/geopathic_stress.htm.

Meyl, Konstantin, trans. Ben Jansen. "Scalar Waves: Theory and Experiments." *Journal of Scientific Exploration* 15, no. 2 (2001): 199–205.

www.mietekwirkus.com/testimonials_friedman.html.

Mison, K. "Statistical Processing of Diagnostics Done by Subjects and by Physician." Proceedings of the 6th International Conference on Psychotronics Research (1968), 137–138.

Morris, C. E. and T. C. Skalak. "Effects of Static Magnetic Fields on Microvascular Tone in Vivo." Abstract presented at Experimental Biology Meeting, San Diego, CA, April 2003.

Narby, Jeremy. *The Cosmic Serpent: DNA and the Origins of Knowledge*. New York: Tarcher, 1999.

nccam.nih.gov/health/backgrounds/energymed.htm.

Oschman, James. *Energy Medicine*. New York: Churchill Livingstone, 2000.

Panov, V., V. Kichigin, G. Khaldeev, et al. "Torsion Fields and Experiments." *Journal of New Energy* 2 (1997): 29–39.

www.phoenixregenetics.org.

www.physics.odu.edu/~hyde/Teaching/Chladni_Plates.html.

Playfair, Guy Lyon. *Twin Telepathy: The Psychic Connection*. New York: Vega, 2003.

Reddy, G. K. "Photobiological Basis and Clinical Role of Low-Intensity Lasers in Biology and Medicine." *Journal of Clinical Laser Medicine & Surgery* 22, no.2 (2004): 141–150.

www.redicecreations.com/specialreports/2006/01jan/solfeggio.html.

Reich, Wilhelm. *The Cancer Biopathy*. New York: Farrar, Straus and Giroux, 1973.

———. *The Discovery of the Orgone, Vol. 1, The Function of the Orgasm*. Trans. Theodore P. Wolfe. New York: Orgone Institute Press, 1942; 2nd ed. New York: Farrar, Straus and Giroux, 1961.

Rein, G, and R. McCraty. "Structural Changes in Water and DNA Associated with New 'Physiologically' Measurable States." *Journal of Scientific Exploration* 8 (1994): 438–439.

Rojavin, M. A., A. Cowan, A. Radzievsky, et al. "Antipuritic Effect of Millimeter Waves in Ice: Evidence for Opioid Involvement." *Life Sciences* 63, no. 18 (1998): L251–L257.

Rojavin, M. A. and M. C. Ziskin. "Medical Application of Millimetre Waves." *QJM: Monthly Journal of the Association of Physicians* 91, no.1 (1998): 57–66.

Ross, Jesse. "Results, Theories, and Concepts Concerning the Beneficial Effects of Pulsed High Peak Power Electromagnetic Energy (Diapulse Therapy) in Accelerating the Inflammatory Process and Wound Healing." presented at the Bioelectromagnetics Society 3rd Annual Conference, Washington DC, August 9–12, 1981.

Ross, Stephen, ed. "Dr. Giuseppe Calligaris: The Television Powers of Man." *World Research News*, 1st Quarter 2005, 2, 5.

———. "The Electrical Patterns of Life: The World of Harold Saxton Burr." *World Research News*, 2nd Quarter 1997, 2, 5.

———. "Magnetic Effects on Living Organisms." *World Research News*, 2nd Quarter 2007, 1, 4.

———. "The Waves that Heal; Georges Lakhovsky's Multiple Wave Oscillator," *World Research News*, 2nd Quarter 1996, 1, 5.

Russek, L., and G. Schwartz. "Energy Cardiology: A Dynamical Energy Systems Approach for Integrating Conventional and Alternative Medicine." *The Journal of Mind–Body Health* 12, no. 4 (1996): 4–24.

Russell, Edward. *Design for Destiny*. London: Neville Spearman Ltd., 1971.

www.sacredsites.com/europe/ireland/tower_of_cashel.html.

Schneider, Michael S. *A Beginner's Guide to Constructing the Universe: Mathematical Archetypes of Nature, Art, and Science*. New York: Harper, 1995.

Schweizer, Hubert M. Lecture available from World Research Foundation, 41 Bell Rock Plaza, Sedona, AZ, 86351.

www.sciencedaily.com/releases/1998/09/980904035915.htm.

"The Scientific Basis for Magnet Therapy." Innovation Technologies and Energy Medicine. www.item-bioenergy.com.

Scofield, Tony. "The Radionic Principle: Mind over Matter." *Radionic Journal* 52, no. 1 (2007): 5–16 and 52 no. 2 (2007): 7–12. www.Radionic.co.uk/articles.

Seidel, R. E., and M. Elizabeth Winter. "The New Microscopes." *Journal of Franklin Institute* 237, no. 2 (February 1944): 103-130.

www.sevenraystoday.com/sowhatarethesevenrays.htm.

Shealy, C. N. *Clairvoyant Diagnosis, Energy Medicine Around the World.*, ed. T. M. Srinivasan. Phoenix, AZ: Gabriel Press, 1988.

Sheldrake, Rupert. *A New Science of Life*. Rochester, VT: Park Street Press, 1995.

Shermer, Michael. "Rupert's Resonance." *Scientific American*, November 2005, 19.

Sisken, B. F., and J. Walder. "Therapeutic Aspects of Electromagnetic Fields for Soft Tissue Healing." In *Electromagnetic Fields: Biological Interactions and Mechanisms*, ed. M. Blank. Washington, DC: American Chemical Society, 1995.

www.spiritofmaat.com/archive/aug1/consciouswater.html.

www.springerlink.com/index/Q192636T8232T247.pdf.

http://sprott.physics.wisc.edu/demobook/chapter6.htm.

Suddath, Ralph. "Messages from Water: Water's Remarkable Expressions." www.hado.net.

Suplee, Curt. "The Speed of Light is Exceeded in Lab: Scientists Accelerate a Pulse of Light." *Washington Post*, July 20, 2000.

Szabo, I., M. R. Manning, A. A. Radzievsky, et al. "Low Power Millimeter Wave Irradiation Exerts No Harmful Effect on Human Keratinocytes In Vitro." *Bioelectromagnetics* 24, no. 3 (2003): 165–173.

Tansley, David V. *Chakras-Rays and Radionics*. Saffron Walden, UK: C. W. Daniel Co., 1985.

www.theosociety.org/pasadena/fund/fund-10.htm.

Tiller, W. A., W. E. Dibble, Jr., R. Nunley, et al. "Toward General Experimentation and Discovery in Conditioned Laboratory Spaces: Part I. Experimental pH Change Findings at Some Remote Sites." *Journal of Alternative and Complementary Medicine* 10, no. 1 (2004): 145–157.

Trappier, A., et al. "Evolving Perspectives on the Exposure Risks from Magnetic Fields." *Journal of the National Medical Association* 82, no. 9 (September 1990): 621–624.

http://tuxmobil.org/Infrared-HOWTO/infrared-howto-a-eye-safety.html.

Tynes, Tore, L. Klaeboe, and T. Haldorsen. "Residential and Occupational Exposure to 50 Hz Magnetic Fields and Malignant Melanoma: A Population Based Study." *Occupational and Environmental Medicine* 60, no. 5 (May 2003): 343–347.

http://users.pandora.be/wouterhagens/biogeometry/grids_uk.htm.

Vallbona, C., and T. Richards. "Evolution of Magnetic Therapy from Alternative to Traditional Medicine." *Phys-Med-Rehabil-Clin-N-Am* 10, no. 3 (August 1999): 729–754.

Vestergaard, Lene Hau. "Frozen Light." *Scientific American*, May 2003, 44–51.

Vincent, S. and J. H. Thompson. "The Effects of Music Upon the Human Blood Pressure," *Lancet* 213, no. 5506 (1929): 534–538.

www.vogelcrystals.net/legacy_of_marcel_vogel.htm.

Wang, L. J., A. Kuzmich, and A. Dogariu. "Gain-assisted Superluminal Light Propagation." *Nature* 406, no. 6793 (July 20, 2000): 277-279.

Watson, Peter. *Twins: An Uncanny Relationship?* New York: Viking, 1981.

Wertheimer, N. and E. Leeper. "Electrical Wiring Configurations and Childhood Cancer." *American Journal of Epidemiology* 109 (1979): 273–284.

Weyl, Hermann. *Symmetry*. Princeton, NJ: Princeton University Press, 1952.

Whale, Jon. "Core Energy, Case Studies" www.positivehealth.com/article-list.ph"p?subjectid=95.

———. "Core Energy Surgery for the Electromagnetic Body." www.positivehealth.com/article-list.ph"p?subjectid=95.

White, John, and Stanley Krippner. *Future Science*. Garden City, NY: Anchor, 1977.

http://en.wikipedia.org/wiki/Jan_Baptist_van_Helmont.

http://en.wikipedia.org/wiki/L-field.

http://en.wikipedia.org/wiki/Odic_force.

Wirth, D. P. "The Effect of Non-Contact Therapeutic Touch on the Healing Rate of Full Thickness Dermal Wounds." *Subtle Energies* 1 (1990): 1–20.

www.world-mysteries.com/sci_cymatics.htm.

Zimmerman, J. "Laying-On-Of-Hands Healing and Therapeutic Touch: A Testable Theory." *BEMI Currents, Journal of the BioElectromagnetics Institute* 2 (1990): 8–17.

PART IV

www.acumedico.com/meridians.htm.

www.acupuncturetoday.com/archives2003/jul/07starwynn.html.

www.astronutrition.com.

Becker, Robert O. *Cross Currents*. New York: Penguin, 1990.

Bensky, D., and R. Barolet. *Chinese Herbal Medicine: Formulas & Strategies*. Seattle, WA: Eastland Press, 1990.

Bensky, D., and A. Gamble. *Chinese Herbal Medicine: Materia Medica*. rev. ed. Seattle, WA: Eastland Press, 1993.

www.bibliotecapleyades.net/ciencia/ciencia_humanmultidimensionaanatomy.htm.

http://biologie.wewi.eldoc.ub.rug.nl/FILES/root/publ/2006/acupunctuur/rap69acupunctuur.pdf.

www.biomeridian.com/virtual-medicine.htm.

Chen, Jia-xu, and Ma Sheng-xing. *Journal of Alternative and Complementary Medicine* 11, no. 3 (2005): 423–431.

Cheng, X., ed. *Chinese Acupuncture and Moxibustion*. "New Essentials" rev. ed. Beijing: Foreign Languages Press, 1999.

www.colorpuncture.com.

www.compassionateacupuncture.com/How%20Acupuncture%20Works.htm.

Darras, Jean-Claude, Pierre de Vernejoul, and Pierre Albarède. "A Study on the Migration of Radioactive Tracers after Injection at Acupoints." *American Journal of Acupuncture* 20, no. 3 (1992): 245–246.

De Vernejoul, Pierre, et al. "Etude Des Meridiens d'Acupuncture par les Traceurs Radioactifs." *Bulletin of the Academy of National Medicine* (Paris) 169 (22 October 1985): 1071–1075.

http://deepesthealth.com/2007/chinese-medicine-and-the-emotions-what-does-the-neijing-say.

Deng, T., ed. *Practical Diagnosis in Traditional Chinese Medicine*. New York: Churchill Livingstone, 1999.

www.drdanazappala.com/Colorlight.asp.

Dumitrescu, I. F. "Contribution to the Electro-Physiology of the Active Points," International Acupuncture Conference, Bucharest, Romania, 1977. Quoted in "Research Advances in the Electrical Specificity of Meridians and Acupuncture Points." *American Journal of Acupuncture* 9, no. 3 (1981): 203.

www.emofree.com/Research/meridianexistence.htm.

www.energymed.org/hbank/handouts/harold_burr_biofields.htm.

Evans, John. *Mind, Body and Electromagnetism*. Dorset, UK: Element, 1986.

Galambos, Imre. "The Origins of Chinese Medicine: The Early Development of Medical Literature in China." www.zhenjiu.de/Literature/Fachartikel/englisch/origins-of.htm.

Gallo, Fred. "Evidencing the Existence of Energy Meridians." www.emofree.com/Research/meridianexistence.htm.

Garcia, Hernan, A. Sierra, H. Balam, and J. Conant. *Wind in the Blood: Mayan Healing & Chinese Medicine*. Taos, NM: Redwing Books, 1999.

Giraud-Guille, M. M. "Twisted Plywood Architecture of Collagen Fibrils in Human Compact Bone Osteons." *Calcified Tissue International* 42 (1988): 167–180.

www.harmonics.com.au/aequotes.shtml.

www.healthguidance.org/entry/3441/1/Hyaluronic-Acid-The-Fountain-of-Youth.html.

Hecker, H.-U., A. Steveling, E. Peuker, J. Kastner, and K. Liebchen. *Color Atlas of Acupuncture*. Stuttgart, Germany: Georg Thieme, 2001.

www.holisticonline.com/Light_Therapy/light_conductor.htm.

Hsu, Hong-yen, and W. G. Peacher, eds. *Shang Han Lun: The Great Classic of Chinese Medicine*. Long Beach, CA: Oriental Healing Arts Institute, 1981.

Ionescu-Tirgoviste, Pruna. "The Acupoint Potential, Electroreception and Bio-Electrical Homeostasis of the Human Body." *American Journal of Acupuncture* 18, no. 1 (1990): 18.

www.itmonline.org/arts/electro.htm.

Kaptuchuk, Ted. *The Web That Has No Weaver*. New York: Congdon and Weed, 1983.

Kidson, Ruth. *Acupuncture for Everyone*. Rochester, VT: Healing Arts Press, 2000.

Liao, Waysun. *The Essence of T'ai Chi*. Boston: Shambhala, 1995.

http://lib.bioinfo.pl/auth:Wieser,HG.

http://links.jstor.org/sici?sici=0305-7410(196507%2F09)23%3C28%3ACTMAPV%3E2.0.CO%3B2-9.

Maciocia, Giovanni. *The Foundations of Chinese Medicine: A Comprehensive Text for Acupuncturists and Herbalists*. 2nd ed. New York: Churchill Livingstone, 2005.

———. *The Practice of Chinese Medicine*. 1st ed. New York: Churchill Livingstone, 1997.

Mäkelä, Reijo, and Anu Mäkelä. "Laser Acupuncture." www.earthpulse.com/src/subcategory.asp?catid=7&subcatid=2.

Mandel, Peter. *Esogetics: The Sense and Nonsense of Sickness and Pain*. Hasselbrun, Germany: Energetik Verlag, 1993.

http://marquis.rebsart.com/dif.html.

www.matzkefamily.net/doug/papers/tucson2b.html.

www.medicalacupuncture.com/aama_marf/journal/vol13_1/article7.html.

www.miridiatech.com/acugraph/originandhistory.htm.

Motoyama, Hiroshi with Rande Brown. *Science and the Evolution of Consciousness.* Brookline, MA: Autumn Press, 1978.

Motoyama, Hiroshi, Gaetan Chevalier, Osamu Ichikawa, and Hideki Baba. "Similarities and Dissimiliarities of Meridian Functions Between Genders." *Subtle Energies & Energy Medicine* 14, no. 3 (2003): 201–219.

Mussat, M. trans. E. Serejski. *Acupuncture Networks* 2 (1997).

Nagahama, Yoshio, and Masaaki Maruyama. *Studies on Keiraku.* Tokyo: Kyorinshoin Co., Ltd (1950).

www.naturalworldhealing.com.

www.naturalworldhealing.com/body-energy-imaging-proposal.htm.

Ni, M., and C. McNease. *The Tao of Nutrition.* Exp. ed. Los Angeles: SevenStar Communications Group, 1987.

Nordenström, Björn. *Biologically Closed Electric Circuits: Clinical, Experimental and Theoretical Evidence for an Additional Circulatory System.* Stockholm, Sweden: Nordic Medical Publications, 1983.

———. "An Electrophysiological View of Acupuncture: Role of Capacitive and Closed Circuit Currents and Their Clinical Effects in the Treatment of Cancer and Chronic Pain." *American Journal of Acupuncture* 17 (1989): 105–117.

———. *Acupuncture: A Comprehensive Text.* Seattle, WA: Eastland Press, 2003.

O'Connor, J., and D. Bensky, trans. and eds. *Standard Meridian Points of Acupuncture.* Bejing: Foreign Languages Press, 2000.

www.okmedi.net/English/ebody01/meridians01.asp.

Oschman, James L. "What Is 'Healing Energy'? The Scientific Basis of Energy Medicine." *Journal of Bodywork and Movement Therapies* (Series of articles October 1996–January 1998): Parts 1–6.

http://paraphysics-research-institute.org/Contents/Articles/Physics%20and%20the%20Paranormal.htm.

www.peacefulmind.com/articlesa.htm.

Pokert, Manfred. *The Theoretical Foundations of Chinese Medicine: Systems of Correspondence.* Cambridge, MA: MIT Press, 1974.

Rae, M. "Potency Simulation by Magnetically Energised Patterns (An Alternate Method of Preparing Homeopathic Remedies)." *British Radionic Quarterly* 19 (March 1973): 32–40.

Reichstein, Gail. *Chinese Medicine in Everyday Life.* New York: Kodansha, 1998.

Rose-Neil, S. "The Work of Professor Kim Bonghan" *Acupuncturist* 1 (1967): 5–19.

Rothfeld, Glenn S., and Suzanne Levert. *The Acupuncture Response.* New York: Contemporary, 2002.

Rubik, Beverly. "Can Western Science Provide a Foundation for Acupuncture?" *Alternative Therapies* 1, no. 4 (September 1995): 41–47.

www.sanavida.info/acupuncture-q-and-a.html.

http://sci.tech-archive.net/Archive/sci.physics/2005-02/4794.html.

Shang, C. "Bioelectrochemical Oscillations in Signal Transduction and Acupuncture—An Emerging Paradigm." *American Journal of Chinese Medicine* 21 (1993): 91–101.

———. "Singular Point, Organizing Center and Acupuncture Point." *American Journal of Chinese Medicine* 17 (1989): 119–127.

Shanghai College of Traditional Chinese Medicine. *Acupuncture: A Comprehensive Text.* Seattle, WA: Eastland Press, 1981.

Sivin, Nathan. "Huangdi neijing." In *Early Chinese Texts: A Bibliographical Guide*, ed. Michael Loewe. Berkeley: IEAS, 1993.

Taubes, Gary. "The Electric Man." *Discover*, April 1986, 24–37.

www.tillerfoundation.com/science.html.

Truman, Karol K. *Feelings Buried Alive Never Die.* Brigham City, UT: Brigham Distributing, 1991.

www.ursus.se/ursus/publications.shtml.

Villoldo, Alberto. *Shaman, Healer, Sage.* New York: Harmony, 2000.

Vithoulkas, G. *The Science of Homeopathy.* New York: Grove, 1980.

Weigel, P. H., G. M. Fuller, and R. D. LeBoeuf. "A Model for the Role of Hyaluronic Acid and Fibrin in the Early Events During the Inflammatory Response and Wound Healing." *Journal of Theoretical Biology* 119, no. 2 (March 21, 1986): 219–234.

www.windemereschoolofmassage.com/meridian/LightBody/villold02.asp.

www.wipo.int/pctdb/en/wo.jsp?wo=1997017020& IA=WO1997017020&DISPLAY=DESC-33k.

http://pt.wkhealth.com/pt/re/ajhp/fulltext.00043627-200506150-00011.htm.

http://wongkiewkit.com/forum/attachment.php?attachmentid=596&d=110789894

Yang Shou-zhong, trans. *The Pulse Classic.* Boulder, CO: Blue Poppy Press, 1997.

Yo-Cheng, Zhou. "Innovations. An Advanced Clinical Trail with Laser Acupuncture Anesthesia for Minor Operations in the Oro-Maxilofacial Region." Originally published in *Lasers in Surgery and Medicine* 4, no. 3: 297–303. http://doi.wiley.com/10.1002/lsm.1900040311.

Zhu, Z. X. "Research Advances in the Electrical Specificity of Meridians and Acupuncture Points." *American Journal of Acupuncture* 9 (1981): 203–216.

PART V

Aczel, Amir D. *The Mystery of the Aleph.* New York: Pocket Books, 2000.

Amen, Ra Un Nefer. *Metu Neter, Vol. 1: The Great Oracle of Tehuti, and the Egyptian System of Spiritual Cultivation.* Brooklyn, NY: Khamit Media Tran Visions, Inc., 1990.

———. *Tree of Life Meditation System (T.O.L.M).* Brooklyn, NY: Khamit Publications, 1996.

www.americansportsdata.com/obesityresearch.asp.

Andrews, Ted. *Simplified Magick.* St. Paul, MN: Llewellyn, 1989.

Arewa, Caroline Shola. *Opening to Spirit.* New York: Thorsons/HarperCollins, 1998.

———. *Way of Chakras.* London: Thorsons, 2001.

Ashby, Muata. *The Black African Egyptians.* Sema Institute/C.M. Book Publishing, 2007.

———. *Egyptian Yoga Volume I: The Philosophy of Enlightenment.* 2nd ed. Sema Institute/C.M. Book Publishing, 2005.

Avalon, Arthur. *The Serpent Power.* New York: Dover, 1974.

Awschalam, David D., Ryan Epstein, and Ronald Hanson. "The Diamond Age of Spintronics." *Scientific American*, October 2007, 84–91.

Bastien, Joseph W. *Mountain of the Condor.* Long Grove, IL: Waveland Press, 1985.

www.beezone.com/DevatmaShakti/Chapter7.html.

Bernal, Martin. *Black Athena.* New York: Vintage, 1987.

Bhattacharyya, N. N. *History of the Tantric Religion.* 2nd rev. ed. New Delhi: Manohar, 1999.

www.bibliotecapleyades.net/ciencia/ciencia_humanmultidimensionaanatomy.htm.

www.bioenergyfields.org.

Brennan, Barbara Ann. *Hands of Light.* New York: Bantam, 1987.

Bruyere, Rosalyn. *Wheels of Light.* Sierra Madre, CA: Bon Productions, 1989.

www.buddhapia.com/tibet/mudras.html.

Bynum, Edward Bruce. *The African Unconscious.* New York: Teacher's College Press, 1999.

Dale, Cyndi. *Advanced Chakra Healing.* Berkeley, CA: Crossing, 2005.

———. *Illuminating the Afterlife.* Boulder, CO: Sounds True, 2008.

———. *New Chakra Healing.* Woodbury, MN: Llewellyn, 1996.

David, Rosalie. *The Ancient Egyptians.* London: Routledge & Kegan Paul, 1982.

www.emaxhealth.com/26/1115.html.

Finch, Charles S., III. *The Star of Deep Beginnings: The Genesis of African Science and Technology.* Decatur, GA: Khenti, 1998.

http://findarticles.com/p/articles/mi_qa3822/is_200410/ai_n14681734/pg_14.

Furlong, David. *Working with Earth Energies.* London: Piatkus, 2003.

www.geocities.com/octanolboy/bpweb/Chpt06.htm.

www.getprolo.com/connective_tissue2.htm.

Glassey, Don. "Life Energy and Healing: The Nerve, Meridian and Chakra Systems and the CSF Connection." www.ofspirit.com/donglassey1.htm.

Goswami, Shyam Sundar. *Layayoga.* Rochester, VT: Inner Traditions, 1999.

Hauck, Dennis William. *The Emerald Tablet.* New York: Penguin, 1999.

Hunt, Valerie, Wayne W. Massey, Robert Weinberg, Rosalyn Bruyere, and Pierre M. Hahn. "A Study of Structural Integration from Neuromuscular, Energy Field, and Emotional Approaches." Abstract. 1977. www.somatics.de/HuntStudy.html.

Johari, Harish. *Chakras: Energy Centers of Transformation.* Rochester, VT: Destiny, 2000.

The Chakras and Human Energy Fields. Wheaton, IL: Quest, 1989.

Judith, Anodea. *Eastern Body Western Mind: Psychology and the Chakra System as a Path to the Self.* Berkeley, CA: Celestial Arts, 1996.

Kelly, Robin. *The Human Antenna.* Santa Rosa, CA: Energy Psychology Press, 2006.

Lansdowne, Zachary. *The Revelation of Saint John.* York Beach, ME: Red Wheel/Weiser, 2006.

Leadbeater, C.W. *The Chakras.* Wheaton, IL: Quest, 1927.

Meeks, Dimitri, and Christine Favard-Meeks. *Daily Life of the Egyptian Gods.* Ithaca, NY: Cornell University Press, 1996.

http://members.tripod.com/~Neurotopia/Zen/Mudra.

Men, Hunbatz. *Secrets of Mayan Science/Religion.* Santa Fe, NM: Bear & Co., 1990.

Motoyama, Hiroshi, with Rande Brown. *Science and the Evolution of Consciousness.* Brookline, MA: Autumn Press, 1978.

Ozaniec, Naomi. *Chakras for Beginners.* Pomfret, VT: Trafalgar Square, 1995.

Palamidessi, Tommaso. *The Caduceus of Hermes.* Archeosofica ed. 1969. http://en.wikipedia.org/wiki/Nadi_(yoga).

Parfitt, Will. *Elements of the Qabalah.* New York: Element, 1991.

———. *Esoteric Anatomy.* Tape series, 1991. Wrekin Trust, UK. Quoted in Arewa, *Opening to Spirit.*

Randall, Georgia Lambert. "The Etheric Body." Lecture notes, 1983.

Raphaell, Katrina. *The Crystalline Transmission.* Santa Fe, NM: Aurora, 1990.

Schultz, Mona Lisa. *Awakening Intuition.* New York: Harmony, 1998.

Simpson, Liz. *The Book of Chakra Healing.* New York: Sterling, 1999.

www.spiritmythos.org/TM/9energybodies.html.

Stein, Diane. *Women's Psychic Lives.* St. Paul, MN: Llewellyn, 1988.

www.sunandmoonstudio.com/YogaArticle/InvisibleAnatomy.shtml.

Tenzin, Wangyal. *Healing with Form, Energy, and Light.* Ithaca, NY: Snow Lion Publications, 2002.

www.theafrican.com/Magazine/Cosmo.htm.

www.universal-mind.org/Chakra_pages/ProofOfExistence.htm.

Varenne, Jean. *Yoga and the Hindu Tradition.* Chicago: University of Chicago Press, 1976.

Villoldo, Alberto. *Shaman, Healer, Sage.* New York: Harmony, 2000.

www.wholebeingexplorations.com/matrix/SpSt/nadis.htm.

Winkler, Gershon. *Magic of the Ordinary.* Berkeley, CA: North Atlantic, 2003.

www.wisdomworld.org/additional/ancientlandmarks/AncientWisdomInAfrica1.html.

Wisner, Kerry. *Song of Hathor: Ancient Egyptian Ritual for Today.* Nashua, NH: Hwt-Hrw Publications, 2002. www.hwt-hrw.com/Bodies.php.

Wolf, Rabbi Laibl. *Practical Kabbalah.* New York: Three Rivers, 1999.

Ywahoo, Dhyani. *Voices of Our Ancestors.* Boston: Shambhala, 1987.

PART VI

www.acupuncture.com.

www.acupuncture.com/education/tcmbasics/mienshiang.htm.

www.acupuncture.com/education/theory/acuintro.htm.

www.acupuncture.com.au/education/acupoints/category-antique.html.

www.aetw.org/jsp_katsugen_undo.htm.

www.ahealingtouch.com/html/cam_practices.html.

www.amcollege.edu/blog/massage/amma-massage.htm.

www.angelfire.com/mb/manifestnow/seichimovr.html.

www.aniwilliams.com/geometry_music_healing.htm.

www.annals.org/cgi/content/abstract/135/3/196?ck=nck.

www.answers.com/topic/electroacupuncture.

www.anthroposophy.org.

www.appliedkinesiology.com.

www.aromaweb.com/articles/wharoma.asp.

Asokananda (Harald Brust), Chow Kam Thye. *The Art of Traditional Thai Massage Energy Line Chart.* Ed. Richard Bentley. Bangkok, Thailand: Nai Suk's Editions Co. Ltd., 1995.

www.associatedcontent.com/theme/165/holistic_healing_practices.html.

www.awakening-healing.com/Seichim.htm.

www.ayurveda.com/panchakarma/index.html.

www.ayurveda.com/panchakarma/pk_intro.pdf.

www.bachcentre.com.

Becker, R. O., and A. A. Marino. *Electromagnetism and Life.* Albany: State University of New York, 1982.

Bentov, I. "Micromotion of the Body as a Factor in the Development of the Nervous System." In *Kundalini: Psychosis or Transcendence?* Ed. L. Sanella. San Francisco: H. S. Dakin Co., 1976.

Bentov, Itzhak. *Stalking the Wild Pendulum.* Rochester, VT: Destiny, 1977.

www.biologicalmedicine.info.

www.bowenmethodcenter.com.

Bowser, Bruce. "Mood Brighteners: Light Therapy Gets Nod as Depression Buster." *Science News,* April 23, 2005, 399.

www.cam.hi-ho.ne.jp/h_sakamoto/thought/medicine.htm.

Campbell, Don. *The Mozart Effect.* New York, William Morrow and Co., 1997.

www.cancertutor.org/Other/Breast_Cancer.html.

Carnie, L. V. *Chi Gung.* St. Paul, MN: Llewellyn Publications, 1997.

www.centerforaltmed.com/?page_id=5.

Chien, C. H., J. J. Tsuei, S. C. Lee, et al. "Effects of Emitted Bio-Energy on Biochemical Functions of Cells," *American Journal of Chinese Medicine* 19, no.3–4 (1991): 285–292.

www.chinesemedicinesampler.com/acupuncture.html.

www.chiro.org/acc/What_is_Ryodoraku.shtml.

www.chirobase.org/06DD/best.html.

www.chronogram.com/issue/2005/08/wholeliving.

Clark, Linda. *The Ancient Art of Color Therapy.* Old Greenwich, CT: Devin-Adair, 1975.

Cohen, D., Y. Palti, B. N. Cuffin, and S. J. Schmid. "Magnetic Fields Produced by Steady Currents in the Body." *Proceedings of the National Academy of Science* 77 (1980): 1447–1451.

Dale, Cyndi. *Advanced Chakra Healing: Energy Mapping on the Four Pathways.* Berkeley, CA: Crossing, 2005.

Dass, Akhila, and Maohar Croke. "Colorpuncture and Esogetic Healing: The Use of Colored Light in Acupuncture." In *Light Years Ahead,* ed. Brian Breiling. Berkeley, CA: Celestial Arts, 1996.

Dharmananda, Subhuti. "Electro-Acupuncture." www.itmonline.org/arts/electro.htm.

———. "The Significance of Traditional Pulse Diagnosis in the Modern Practice of Chinese Medicine," http://www.itmonline.org/arts/pulse.htm.

www.drciprian.com.

www.emdr.com.

www.emdr.com/briefdes.htm.

www.emofree.com.

Evans, John. *Mind, Body and Electromagnetism.* Dorset, UK: Element, 1986.

www.feldenkrais.com.

http://fengshui.about.com/od/thebasics/qt/fengshui.htm.

Fields, H. L., and J. C. Liebeskind, eds. *Pharmacological Approaches to the Treatment of Chronic Pain: New Concepts and Critical Issues — Progress in Pain Research and Management.* Vol. 1. Seattle: IASP Press, 1994.

www.findmyhealer.co.uk/acupuncture.html.

Flaws, Robert. *The Secret of Chinese Pulse Diagnosis.* Boulder, CO: Blue Poppy Press, 1995.

Gebhart, D. L., G. Hammond, and T. S. Jensen. *Proceedings of the 7th World Congress on Pain — Progress in Pain Research and Management.* Vol. 2. Seattle, WA: IASP Press, 1994.

Gerber, Richard. *Vibrational Medicine.* Santa Fe, NM: Bear & Co., 1988.

Ghadiali, Dinshah P. *Spectro-Chrome Metry Encyclopedia.* 3 vols. Malaga, N.J.: Spectro-Chrome Institute, 1933.

Gingerich, Natalie. "The Energy Workout." *Prevention Magazine,* December 2007, 152–155.

www.giovanni-maciocia.com/articles/flu.html.

Goldman, Jonathan. "The Sound of Healing: An Introduction with Jonathan Goldman"; "New Frontiers in Sound Healing"; Overview, Sound Healing"; "Science of Harmonics"; "Sound Healing." www.healingsounds.com.

www.hakomi.com.

Han, J. S. *The Neurochemical Basis of Pain Relief by Acupuncture.* Vol. 2. Hubei, China: Hubei Science and Technology Press, 1998. Quoted in www.chiro.org/acupuncture/ABSTRACTS/Beyond_endorphins.shtml.

www.healingsounds.com.

www.healingtouch.net.

www.healthy-holistic-living.com/electrodermal-testing.html.

www.healthy.net/scr/article.asp?id=1957.

www.heartlandhealing.com/pages/archive/bach_flower_remedies/index.html.

Heline, Corine. *Healing and Regeneration Through Color.* Santa Barbara, CA: J. F. Rowney Press, 1943.

www.hellerwork.com.

www.hellingerpa.com.

www.hellingerpa.com/constellation.shtml.

www.holisticwebworks.com.

www.holotropic.com.

Hunt, Roland. *The Seven Keys to Colour Healing.* Ashington, UK: C. W. Daniel, 1954.

Ikenaga, Kiyoshi. *Tsubo Shiatsu.* Vancouver, Canada: Japan Shiatsu, 2003.

www.informit.com/articles/article.aspx?p=174361.

www.iridology.com.

www.item-bioenergy.com/infocenter/ScientificBasisMagnetTherapy.pdf.

www.itmonline.org/arts/pulse.htm.

Javane, Faith, and Dusty Bunker. *Numerology and the Divine Triangle.* West Chester, PA: Whitford, 1979.

www.jinshininstitute.com.

Johari, Harish. *Numerology with Tantra, Ayurveda, and Astrology.* Rochester, VT: Destiny, 1990.

www.johrei-institute.org.

Karaim, Reed. "Light That Can Cure You." Special Health Report: Caring for Aging Parents. *USA Weekend,* February 4, 2007.

Kent, James Tyler. *Repertory of the Homeopathic Materia Medica and a Word Index.* 6th edition. New Delhi, India: B. Jain Publishers, 2004.

Kenyon, J. N. *Auricular Medicine: The Auricular Cardiac Reflex, Modern Techniques of Acupuncture.* Vol. 2. New York: Thorsons, 1983.

www.kinesiology.net/ak.asp.

Kolster, Bernard C., and Astrid Waskowiak. *The Reflexology Atlas.* Rochester, VT: Healing Arts, 2005.

Lewith, George T., Peter J. White, and Jeremie Pariente. "Investigating Acupuncture Using Brain Imaging Techniques: The Current State of Play." http://ecam.oxfordjournals.org/cgi/content/full/2/3/315.

Liberman, Jacob. *Light: Medicine of the Future.* Santa Fe, NM: Bear & Co., 1991.

www.lightparty.com/Health/Radionics.html.

www.logoi.com/notes/chinese_medicine.html.

Lu, Henry C. *Traditional Chinese Medicine.* Laguna Beach, CA: Basic Health Publications, 2005.

www.macrobiotics.org.

www.magnetlabs.com/articles/journalbioelectroinst.doc.

www.matrixenergetics.com.

www.matrixrepatterning.com.

McTaggart, Lynne. *The Field.* New York: Harper Perennial, 2002.

www.mienshang.com.

www.morter.com.

www.myofascialrelease.com.

www.naturalchoice.net/glossary.htm.

www.naokikubota.com.

http://nas.com/~richf/hakomi.htm.

Navach, J. H. "The Vascular Autonomic System, Physics and Physiology." Lyon, France: The VIII Germano-Latino Congress on Auricular Medicine, 1981, as found in www.drfeely.com/doctors/acu_ear_bib_2_5.htm.

www.nccam.nih.gov.

http://nccam.nih.gov/health/whatiscam.

Ni, Daoshing, "Why Do You Keep On Asking Me to Stick My Tongue Out?" www.acupuncture.com.

www.nlm.nih.gov/medlineplus/chiropractic.html.

www.nlpinfo.com.

www.northshorewellness.com/HMR-Definition.htm

Olszewski, David, and Brian Breiling. "Getting Into Light: The Use of Phototherapy in Everyday Life." Brian Breiling, ed. *Light Years Ahead*. Berkeley, CA: Celestial Arts, 1996.

www.osteohome.com.

www.periodensystem.ch/tmax_english.html.

www.pilates.com/BBAPP/V/about/pilates-benefits.html.

http://www.polaritytherapy.org.

www.pranichealing.com.

http://pressreleasesonline.biz/pr/Cancer_Care_Expert_Says_Root_Canals_Should_Be_Illegal.

www.prolotherapy.org.

Puthoff, H. E. "Zero-Point Energy: An Introduction." *Fusion Facts* 3, no. 3 (1991): 1.

www.quantumtouch.com.

www.radionics.com/company/info.

www.radionics.org.

www.reiki.nu.

www.repatterning.org.

www.repatterning.org/resonanceexplained.htm.

Reuben, Amber. *Color Therapy*. New York: ASI, 1980.

www.rolf.org/about/index.htm.

www.sacredlotus.com/diagnosis/index.cfm.

www.seemorgmatrix.org.

www.seishindo.org/practices/katsugen_undo.html.

Seto, A., C. Kusaka, S. Nakazato, et al. "Detection of Extraordinary Large Bio-Magnetic Field Strength from Human Hand During External Qi Emission." *Acupuncture & Electro-Therapeutics Research, The International Journal* 17 (1992): 75–94.

Shang, C., M. Lou, and S. Wan. "Bioelectrochemical Oscillations." *Science Monthly* [Chinese] 22 (1991): 74–80.

Sollars, David W. *The Complete Idiot's Guide to Acupuncture & Acupressure*. New York: Penguin, 2000.

www.spiritofmaat.com/archive/mar1/aurasoma.html.

Tany, M., S. Sawatsugawa, and Y. Manaka. "Acupuncture Analgesia and its Application in Dental Practices." *American Journal of Acupuncture* 2 (1974): 287–295.

www.tcmch.edu/id36.html.

http://tcm.health-info.org/tuina/tcm-tuina-massage.htm.

Terman, M. "Light Therapy for Seasonal and Nonseasonal Depression: Efficacy, Protocol, Safety, and Side Effects." *CNS Spectrums*. 10 (2005): 647–663.

www.thehealingspectrum.com/healing.html.

http://www.tftworldwide.com/tab.html.

Tiller, Wiliam. "Some Energy Observations of Man and Nature." In *The Kirlian Aura*. Garden City, NY: Anchor Press/Doubleday, 1974.

Tiller, William A. *Science and Human Transformation: Subtle Energies, Intentionality, and Consciousness*. Walnut Creek, CA: Pavior Publishing, 1997.

Tillotson, Alan Keith. *The One Earth Herbal Sourcebook: Everything You Need to Know About Chinese, Western, and Ayurvedic Herbal Treatments*. New York: Kensington, 2001.

www.touch4health.com.

www.tptherapy.com.

Tsuei, Julia J. "Scientific Evidence in Support of Acupuncture and Meridian Theory: I. Introduction." www.healthy.net/scr/article.asp?Id=1087. Originally published in *IEEE, Engineering in Medicine and Biology* 15, no. 3 (May/June 1996).

Vazquez, Steven. "Brief Strobic Phototherapy: Synthesis of the Future." In Brian Breiling, ed. *Light Years Ahead*, Berkeley, CA: Celestial Arts, 1996.

http://veda.harekrsna.cz/encyclopedia/ayurvedantacakras.htm.

www.webmd.com/kidney-stones/extracorporeal-shock-wave-lithotripsy-eswl-for-kidney-stones.

http://en.wikipedia.org/wiki/acupuncture_point.

http://en.wikipedia.org/wiki/Chiropractic.

http://en.wikipedia.org/wiki/Feng_Shui.

http://en.wikipedia.org/wiki/Glossary_of_alternative_medicine.

http://en.wikipedia.org/wiki/Hypnotherapy.

http://en.wikipedia.org/wiki/Light_therapy.

http://en.wikipedia.org/wiki/meridian_(chinese_medicine).

http://en.wikipedia.org/wiki/National_Center_for_Complementary_and_Alternative_Medicine.

http://en.wikipedia.org/wiki/Naturopathic_medicine.

http://en.wikipedia.org/wiki/Osteopathy.

http://en.wikipedia.org/wiki/Seitai.

http://pt.wkhealth.com/pt/re/ajhp/fulltext.00043627-200506150-00011.htm.

Wong, Cathy. "Tongue Diagnosis." http://altmedicine.about.com/b/2005/09/20/tongue-diagnosis.htm.

Wurtman, Richard J., Michael J. Baum, John T. Potts, Jr., eds. *The Medical and Biological Effects of Light.* New York: New York Academy of Sciences, 1985.

Xie, Zhufan. "Selected Terms in Traditional Chinese Medicine and Their Interpretations (VIII)." *Chinese Journal of Integrated Traditional and Western Medicine* 5, no. 3 (1999): 227–229.

Xie, Zhufan, and Huang Xi, eds. *Dictionary of Traditional Chinese Medicine.* Hong Kong: Commercial Press, 1984.

www.yuenmethod.com/about.asp.

www.zerobalancing.com/aboutzb.shtml.

ILLUSTRATION CREDITS

All illustrations by Richard Wehrman in consultation with Cyndi Dale, unless otherwise noted.

PART II: HUMAN ANATOMY

2.1 **A Human Cell.** Illustration from Shutterstock, by Sebastian Kaulitzki
2.2 **DNA Nebula.** Photograph courtesy of NASA/JPL-Caltech/UCLA. Illustration from Shutterstock, by James Steidl
2.3 **Fascial Cells.** Photograph courtesy of Drs. Bing Gan and Jeff Howard, Hand and Upper Limb Center, Lawson Health Research Institute, London, Ontario.
2.4 **Pituitary Gland.** Illustration from Shutterstock, by Sebastian Kaulitzki, adapted by Karen Polaski
2.5 **The Electromagnetic Field of the Heart.** Illustration from Shutterstock, by Sebastian Kaulitzki, adapted by Karen Polaski
2.6 **"Killer" Cells Attacking a Virus.** Illustration from Shutterstock, by Sebastian Kaulitzki

PART III: ENERGY FIELDS

3.3 **The Schumann Resonance.** Adapted from König, H.L Bioinformation – Electrophysical Aspects. In *Electromagnetic Bioinformation*, Popp, F.A., Becker,G., König, H.L.Peschka,W.,(eds.) Urban und Schwarzenberg p. 25, 1979
3.4 **Global Ley Lines.** Illustration by Karen Polaski
3.7 **Sine Wave.** Illustration from Shutterstock, by Bernd Jurgens
3.8 **Sphere.** Illustration from Shutterstock, by Kheng Guan Toh
3.9 **Fibonacci Sequence.** Illustration from Shutterstock, by Viktoriya
3.10 **Torus.** Illustration from Shutterstock, by Tatiana53
3.11 **The Golden Section.** Illustration by Karen Polaski
3.12 **The Merkaba.** Illustration by Karen Polaski
3.13 **Metatron's Cube.** Illustration by Karen Polaski
3.14 **Flower of Life.** Illustration from Shutterstock, by Marcus Tuerner
3.15 **Pentachoron.** Illustration by Karen Polaski
3.16 **The Underlying Geometry of the Chakras.** Illustration by Karen Polaski, adapted from John Evans, *Mind, Body and Electromagnetism* (Dorset, UK: Element, 1986)
3.17 **The Platonic Solids.** Illustration by Karen Polaski
3.18 **Cymaglyph of the Human Voice.** © 2008 Sonic Age Ltd., www.sonic-age.com
3.19 **Cymaglyph of the Rings of Uranus.** © 2008 Sonic Age Ltd., www.sonic-age.com

PART IV: CHANNELS OF ENERGY: CHANNELS OF LIGHT

Page 165 **Yin-Yang.** Illustration from Shutterstock, by Joanne van Hoof
4.2–4.18 All meridian illustrations by Richard Wehrman, adapted from H.U. Hecker; A. Steveling; E. Peuker; J. Kastner; K. Liebchen; *Color Atlas of Acupuncture* (New York: Thieme, 2001), p. 2–102; Arthur Annis D.C., www.AcupunctureCharts.com, Anatomical Illustrations by Sharon Ellis M.A., CMI; Graphics by Lauren Keswick M.S., www.medicalartstudio.com; and www.yinyanghouse.com

PART V: ENERGY BODIES: CHAKRAS AND OTHER "LIGHT SWITCHES"

PART VI: ENERGY PRACTICES

6.14 **Thai Energy System.** Illustration by Richard Wehrman. Adapted from Asokananda (Harald Brust) and Chow Kam Thye in *The Art of Traditional Thai Massage Energy Line Chart*, Richard Bentley, ed. (Bangkok: Nai Suk's Editions Co. Ltd., 1995)

6.19–6.24 **Reflexology illustrations by Richard Wehrman.** Data from Ontario College of Reflexology hand and foot charts, © 1999 Donald A. Bisson.; Richard Feely, *Yamamoto New Scalp Acupuncture: Principles and Practice* (New York, NY: Thieme Medical Publishers Inc., 2006); Kolster and Waskowiak, *The Reflexology Atlas* (Rochester, VT: Healing Arts, 2005) p. 244-251; Olszewski and Breiling, "Getting Into Light" in *Light Years Ahead,* p. 290-291

bulbourethral glands, 77
bundle of His, 68
Burr, Harold Saxton, 115–116, 125, 174

C
Cabal, 354
caduceus, **278**
Caitanya Mahuprabhu, 319
calcite, **347**, **348**
calcitonin, 72
calcium ions, magnetic fields and, 128
Callahan, Philip, 138–140
Calligaris, Giuseppe, 3, 341
Calligaris System, 341–342, **341**
cancer
    electricity and, 171
    electromagnetic radiation and, 112
    magnets/magnetic fields and, 128, 129, 171,
      370
    as miasm, 153
    sound and, 401
    teeth and, 380
    X-rays and, 121
cardiac muscle, 49
cardinal points, 210
carnelian, **347**
cartilage, bone formation from, 47
Cashel, Ireland, 138–140
catabolism, 81
causal body
    in Hindu system, 268, 282, **283**, 286
    in twelve-chakra system, 317
causal dynamical triangulation (CDT), 137
causal field, 147
causay, 298
cavities, in acupuncture, acupressure, and
    Qigong, 168
Cayce, Edgar, 117
CDT (causal dynamical triangulation), 137
cekes, 230
celestial field, 147
celestine, **348**
cell-mediated immune system, 84–85
cell phones, 121
cells, 37–40
    electromagnetic, 38–39
    growth of, 8
    human cell, **39**
    metabolism, 38
    microcurrents in, 39–40
    mother cells, 42
    substructures in, 37
cellular radiation, 111–112

central nervous system (CNS), 53–54
cerebellum, 55
cerebral cortex, 55–56
cerebrum, 55
cervix, 79
chacla, 292
chakra healing, 6, 404–405,
chakras, 7, 10, 235–240, 245–272. *see also* chakras,
    specific
    addictions and, 320, **320–321**
    anatomy of, **236**
    around the world, 251–321
    aura/auric field and, 151, 153
    chakra-based psychic gifts, 30, **30–32**
    Chinese model, 237
    color spectrum of, 246, **247**, 248–249
    colors in healing and, 354–359, **358**
    definitions of, 236–237, 239
    development and age, 257, 310–311
    diagnosis with, 249
    Egyptian and African systems, 302–303,
      303
    elements and, **259**
    endocrine system and, **248**, 249, 307–310,
      308–309
    energy egg and, 306, **308–309**, 316
    energy fields and, 95
    evaluation of: shape, spin, and speed, 342–345
    five additional, 238–239
    gemstones and, 346, **346–349**, 417
    geometry of, **138**
    Himalaya Bonpo model, 287–291, **288–289**
    Hindu model, 237, 242, 251–269, **258–259**
    chakra types (personality), 269–272
    history of knowledge on, 239–240
    Incan Energy Model, 296–301, **297–299**
    interfaces with other systems, 233
    Jewish Kabbalah/sephiroth and, **326–327**
    kundalini energy and, 10, 242
    light energy and, 230, 246, **247**, 355
    lotus and, **259**
    masculine and feminine qualities, 354–355
    Mayan energy system and, 292
    measurements of, 249
    nadis and, 233, 242, 250, 251
    numbers of, variations in, 236
    overview of, 236–237
    pendulum for evaluation of, 345
    personality types, 269–272
    pineal gland and, 61
    scientific principles and, 245–250
    scientific research on, 247–250
    secondary, 229–230

ABOUT THE AUTHOR

CYNDI DALE is recognized worldwide as an authority on subtle-energy anatomy. She is the author of several books on energy healing, including *New Chakra Healing*, which has been published in more than ten languages, and six other bestselling books on the topic, including *Advanced Chakra Healing* and *Illuminating the Afterlife*. Through her company, Life Systems Services, she provides intuitive assessments and life-issues healing for thousands of clients a year, seeking always to uplift and inspire others to their true purpose and personalities. Her enthusiasm and care ignite all who attend her workshops, training sessions, and college classes, which are offered around the world.

Cyndi has created several DVD and CD trainings, including *Advanced Chakra Wisdom*, *Illuminating the Afterlife*, and *Healing Across Space and Time: Guided Journeys to Your Past, Present, and Parallel Lives*, produced by Sounds True; and *Healing Across Time*, coproduced by Sounds True and One Spirit. Cyndi has studied crosscultural healing and energy systems and led instructional classes in countries including Peru, Costa Rica, Venezuela, Japan, Belize, Mexico, Morocco, Russia, and across Europe, as well as among the Lakota and the Hawaiian kahunas. She currently lives in Minneapolis, Minnesota, with her two sons and five pets (at last count). More information about Cyndi's classes and products is available at www.cyndidale.com.

ABOUT THE ILLUSTRATOR

RICHARD WEHRMAN is an independent graphic designer, illustrator, and poet whose award-winning art has been exhibited at the Society of Illustrators Gallery in New York, the Rochester Institute of Technology, the UNESCO International Poster Show, and the St. Louis Art Museum. His work has been recognized by the Society of Illustrators, *PRINT*, *Communication Arts Illustration Annuals*, *Graphis Annuals*, the New York Art Directors Club, and the American Advertising Federation. He has also received a gold medal from the National Society of Illustrators. Richard studied for fifteen years with Roshi Philip Kapleau and Toni Packer at the Rochester Zen Center, and with Dale Goldstein of the Heartwork process. Richard currently serves on the Board of Directors of the Heartwork Institute, Inc., and lives and works in East Bloomfield, New York. To learn more about Richard's work, please visit www.richardwehrman.com.

SOUNDS TRUE was founded in 1985, with a clear vision: to disseminate spiritual wisdom. Located in Boulder, Colorado, Sounds True publishes teaching programs that are designed to educate, uplift, and inspire. We work with many of the leading spiritual teachers, thinkers, healers, and visionary artists of our time.

To receive a free catalog of tools and teachings for personal and spiritual transformation, please visit www.soundstrue.com, call toll free at 800-333-9185, or write to us at the address below.

SOUNDS TRUE
PO Box 8010
Boulder CO 80306

THE
SUBTLE BODY

Books

Illuminating the Afterlife: Your Soul's Journey Through the Beyond
New Chakra Healing
Advanced Chakra Healing: The Four Pathways
Advanced Chakra Healing: Cancer
Advanced Chakra Healing: Heart Disease
Attracting Prosperity Through the Chakras
Attracting Your Perfect Body Through the Chakras
The Littlest Christmas Star

Audio Programs

Advanced Chakra Wisdom
Healing Across Space and Time: Guided Journeys to Your Past, Future, and Parallel Lives
Illuminating the Afterlife
Healing Across Time: Guided Journeys to Your Past and Future

THE
SUBTLE BODY

An Encyclopedia of Your Energetic Anatomy

....

CYNDI DALE

SOUNDS TRUE
Boulder, Colorado

Sounds True, Inc.
Boulder CO 80306

Cover and book design by Karen Polaski
Illustrated by Richard Wehrman

Printed in Korea

Library of Congress Cataloging-in-Publication Data

Dale, Cyndi.
  The subtle body : an encyclopedia of your energetic anatomy / Cyndi Dale.
      p. cm.
  Includes bibliographical references.
  ISBN 978-1-59179-671-8 (pbk.)
  1. Energy medicine. 2. Healing. 3. Chakras—Health aspects.
I. Title.
  RZ421.D35 2009
  615.5'3—dc22

                                    2008031838

10 9 8